M

Annette Jahnel

My Year of Beds

BookClub
ROTARY CLUB OF EVANSTON LIGHTHOUSE

Presented in Honor of

ANNETTE JAHNEL

29 July 2014

Rotary Club
of Evanston Lighthouse

My Year of Beds

COVER DESIGN   Robert Fahrbach

ALL PHOTOGRAPHS   Annette Jahnel

Now that we have the legal formalities out of the way, it must be said that copyright law is a strange thing. It is the attempt by lawyers to control what can only be controlled by the self-control of each individual. If you do decide to reproduce this book, what can I do? Nothing. I probably would not even know about it. However, we all want to change the world for the better, and this can only be achieved through each of our commitments to self-control. Not committing the heinous crimes is easy; it is resisting petty crime that defines us as civilized human beings.

While every effort has been made to ensure that the information contained in this book is meticulously researched, the book was written in context of 2006–2007 and what was true then might not be true now. The book is an opinion piece and is not intended as a reference. The opinions expressed in this publication are those of the author and do not reflect or represent the opinions of the publisher.

First edition   2011 AJ Publishers

ISBN   978-0-620-49532-5

Background, sources and the business of names

The road trip that this book describes took place from April 2006 to April 2007. While the world has changed tremendously since then, any comments or observations that might seem prophetic were not added as knowledgeable afterthoughts, but were formed as a result of my observations at the time. During my travels, I kept detailed notes that form the basis of this narrative. I also took tens of thousands of photographs, which aided in my descriptions of places and people. As the book was written in isolated places, far from libraries, the historical details, facts and figures were sourced from the Internet. Wikipedia was a great help, and so were the official websites of the towns and countries mentioned in this book.

To change, or not to change, the names of the characters in the book? In the beginning, I attempted to send out e-mails to all the people in the book to get permissions from them, but discovered that if I were to wait for replies, this book would never see the light of day. Therefore, I made an executive decision to keep the names where I do not think I insulted or defamed anyone in my descriptions of them. Where I was less than flattering, the names have been changed or replaced by descriptions, as in 'the short fat man', and so on. In doing so, I hope to keep off everybody's toes.

Content

Maps

Photographs

Interactive book

'My Year of Beds' is an interactive book.

To allow you to explore the world from your computer, the location of each bed was recorded with a GPS reading, photographed, and put onto Google Earth. The bed numbers in the book coincide with the numbers on My Year of Beds, Google Earth file

You can access the file by entering my website

www.ajahnel.com

Click to/

Writing /

My Year of Beds/

Google Earth interactive file.

By clicking on the bed number in the list on the left of your page, you will be transported to the approximate location of my bed for the night.

Audio Book

'My Year of Beds' is available as an audio book from www.ajahnel.com.

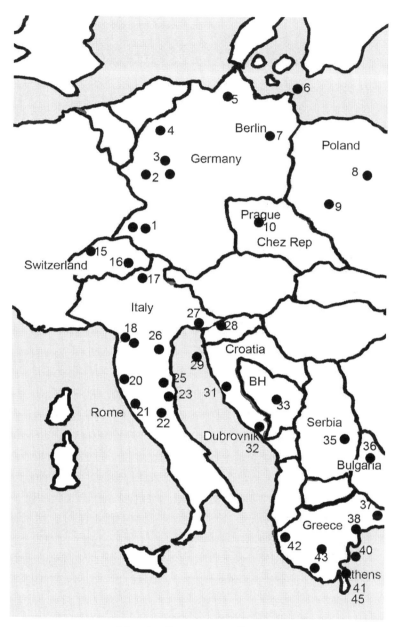

Map 1: Germany to Greece

Map 2: Greece to Russia

The eagle dropped like a stone from the sky, hissed past the windscreen, and vanished into a pothole. The Wish Mobile, noticing that my interest has shifted, misses the narrow ridges of tar I had been aiming for, slips off the road and, as the shocks bottom out, bucks like a rodeo horse, thereby regaining my full attention. I hit the gas, yank the steering left, we spin up the side of the pothole and, shrouded in a great cloud of dust, come to a halt, straddling a pothole disguised as a plunge pool.

Muttering furiously to myself I stumble about on the potholed, cracked and heaving thing called a road in these parts, to try and find a spot of tar big enough to lie down on. Sticking my head under the Wish Mobile I survey the damage.

'Mm, no leaking, can't see any new dents.'

Sounds like I have some idea of what I am doing when it comes to cars, doesn't it? Haven't the faintest; as long as nothing is dripping or swinging about, I'm happy.

Letting my head loll back into the sandy side of the pothole that is doing double duty as a mechanic's pit, my eyes slowly focus on each wheel in turn. Taking in the narrow ridges of crumbling tar and sand they are balancing on, a little warning bell tinkles in the back of my head.

'If any one of those little ridges of tar gives way, you are going to lose your head faster than you can say Marie Antoinette – the car's fine – I'm out of here.'

Dusting off the talcum powder sand, I survey the bleak empty scene. Above me, the huge vault of sky, void of clouds, fades dull blue into the horizon that vanishes dry, dusty and beige, relentlessly beige in every direction. My view is momentarily obscured as the silence shifts aside for a rustle of wings. The eagle settles on the other side of the road, observing me with cruel eyes.

'Oh, what are you staring at? I'm not lunch.'

With a smirk, the eagle looks down his beak at me.

'But you could be.'

In all fairness, this business, of my standing alone in some dusty hellhole conversing with an eagle, requires some background information. Eighteen countries and six time zones ago, my life was perfectly normal by Western standards. According to the rules laid out by society, I was doing well. I had the house, the cars, the successful career, the interesting friends, the happy divorce, and have seen perfection in my wonderful daughter. I was more or less sure I knew everything about life, love, and the world at large, and had my set opinions on these matters, which I trotted out with cheerful confidence to everyone who cared to listen.

But, hidden behind the locked doors of social convention, the cold wind of boredom, doubt and slow stagnation blew in the secret corridors of my mind. Was this it? What else was there to do? I could continue to acquire stuff, perhaps buy a new car each year or perhaps get a bigger house. Or, I could work on my shoe collection. In the 3 am hour of cold self-analysis I realized my life had slowly and without great fanfare turned into a traffic roundabout. If only I had hit the proverbial crossroads, then my choices would have been fairly simple: left, right, forward, and for the truly desperate moments, back. But life is never that simple. Round I went past endless off-ramps that beckoned to new adventure or greater challenge. But because it was convenient, comfortable and familiar, I chose to continue going round and round, until finally I was so good at going in circles I could do it at top speed, with my eyes closed and while talking on the phone.

Then out of the brilliant blue sky, a thunderbolt came to shock me out of my middle-aged stupor. It was a delicious Sunday afternoon, friends lazing on the terrace after a long lunch, the contents of empty wine bottles fuelling the conversation, when I stepped into the kitchen just as the radio whispered a name; a fatal river-rafting accident. My oldest friend died without warning that bright Sunday afternoon. She lived life at top speed, always saying she was afraid she might miss something. Perhaps she knew, life is only now; there is no tomorrow. As I watched the white lilies and roses slowly float out into the Atlantic, to join her ashes that were scattered there, I knew in my life the time had come to do a little attic cleaning. Time to step away from generic media-induced thought, and out of a cotton wool-wrapped zone of discontent. I needed to reinvent myself. I needed to look at things from a new perspective and to do that I needed distance.

A perfect excuse to flee to Germany.

Another Sunday, another lunch, another collection of empty bottles – I sound like a complete alcoholic – Annette and I sat looking deep into the echoing birch forest surrounding her tiny wooden house in Bavaria. The conversation had disintegrated into that middle-aged mantra: no fun no sex no love just work and money, what kind of life is that? After a long silence, she declared she would take up mountaineering. I informed the forest in front of me that I would drive to China. Annette pulled back from her mountain fantasy long enough to announce.

'You can't do that.'

'Why not?'

'Because there are all those countries in between.'

I considered for a moment.

'Which countries?'

'How should I know?'

She handed me a bottle.

'Have another beer.'

Hoping – I suppose – that with the addition of enough alcohol I would soon forget this latest harebrained scheme.

But, while staring at the stars through the airplane window during my flight back to Cape Town, while painting yet another oversized cream kitchen, while cooking yet another evening meal, and while fighting with the garden – I really don't like gardening; it's like setting up a private war zone with nature – thoughts of China stuck in my head with the tenacity of a blob of black paint on a white wool carpet.

Tentatively I started exploring the web. I discovered Google Earth, and then I discovered Kazakhstan. Kazakhstan looked big, very big, and empty. Was there even a road from north to south? I flew in as close as Google would let me. The straight line cutting through the endless white and eerie green landscape seemed road enough. I scoured the bookstores for maps. However, when you live in Cape Town – the self-proclaimed most beautiful spot on the face of the earth – the need for maps of other places is not high on bookstores' lists of priorities.

'Where is Kazakhstan?'

Shopkeepers asked with perplexed expressions.

'Between the Caspian sea and China.'

Was my, by now, rather lofty reply. For someone who two months ago didn't know that Kazakhstan existed, I was certainly lording it up with my newly found knowledge.

My evenings were spent in a frenzy of surfing. Driving through China had been done before. Not often, and even more rarely by an individual driving her own car. The obstacles were high, but the more I surfed, the more real this little fantasy became.

'I dare say I am really going to do this.'

I thought one night in the middle of a surfing supertube. Just then, the computer screen did that lovely little trick where it flashes out and then sucks back into its own little black hole, 'blip' gone, finished. No amount of thumping, screaming or tearing my hair out would bring it back to life.

The computer guy shook his head in sympathy, but he could not hide the dollar signs glinting in his eyes.

'The hard drive is gone.'

'The hard drive is gone? Where has it gone? It cannot be gone for goodness sake!'

'You have a back-up, don't you?'

He said, trying to sound sincere. I looked at him fiercely.

'Of course not! I am not that kind of person! Oh what the heck what do I care, I am driving to China.'

He took a moment to process this fairly random piece of information.

'Oh cool.'

Quick recovery, I was impressed.

Yeah, damn right it's cool, but not easy, or cheap.

Incredible though how once a decision is made, the jigsaw pieces fall into place.

Indecision, the silent death of dreams.

I would drive to China alone, in my own car. That way I would be free from schedules and completely independent. I wanted to see what the 'real' world looked like, how others lived outside the glossy travel brochures. Living in a major tourist destination I was well aware that the tourist perception of a place bears no relation to the lives of the inhabitants thereof. I would try to break through that barrier. I wanted to drive off the beaten track, away from the government-prescribed tourist sights. I wanted to explore the back streets, the road less travelled. I wanted simply to experience whatever I came across and find interest and beauty in that.

The cost was easily dealt with – property prices in Cape Town had soared in the last few years – so by selling the house I made myself a rand millionaire and then some. Quite enough money to pay off the debts, drive to China, and have a little safety net for my return.

Time to tackle the Chinese bureaucracy.

The young woman behind the counter looked at me blankly. I tried again, speaking slowly, clearly and a little louder.

> 'I am planning to drive from Munich to Shanghai and was wondering if you could tell me what the entry requirements for China are?'

The words still stuck to my tongue, even though I had said them aloud to friends and family quite a few times by then; often having to repeat them several times before my friends grasped the full meaning of this short sentence. The reaction of the young Chinese woman behind the consulate counter was therefore not totally unexpected. Finally realizing that she was out of her depth, she called for reinforcements.

A highly groomed man with slick black hair took the trouble to step out from behind the counter to lead me to the very impressive 3D map of China, plastered against the wall. In slow measured tones – so I was sure to understand his every word – he started to explain how very large and very dangerous China was.

By now, I had become accustomed to people thinking that I had also just heard of my plan to drive to China and had given it the exact two seconds of thought that they had. So I took a deep breath, counted backwards from ten, and listened politely, as I was hoping to extract some information from him that up to now had proven elusive. The Internet had information about the entry and exit requirements of all the countries on my route, but getting a private car into and driving it through China? This bit of information had so far eluded me. The man – now joined by the young woman, who nodded vigorously every time he mentioned the word 'dangerous' – was hopefully going to fill in the gaps. No such luck.

He concluded his impromptu geography lesson with a firm brook-no-argument.

> 'It cannot be done.'

And so it began.

> 'It cannot be done.'

> 'That is impossible.'

A compulsion to assail me with travel horror stories overcame all who heard of my plan – stories of friends of friends, who on their travels were raped, maimed, pillaged, strung out to dry never to be seen again. My car would be stolen, my possessions forcibly taken from me. E-mails started to arrive, which stated in reasonable tones and well-thought-out logic, endless reasons that positive failure in my endeavour was the only result to expect. Insurance and indeed travel companies responded to my requests with:

'We have no protocol for that request.'

'I am sorry but that is outside our field of expertise.'

Or worst of all.

'You want to do what?

Before bursting into incredulous laughter and simply putting down the phone.

Preparations
Bed 1

Replacing the dead receiver, I watch the snow falling silently around the little wooden hut in the Bavarian forest, which has become my operations HQ, before looking at the dining-room table where the growing piles of forms and papers that require filling in, copying, signing and sending off – with vast amounts of accompanying money – cover every square centimeter.

> 'The actual driving is going to be a piece of pie compared to hacking through the endless red tape that getting to Shanghai entails.'

I mutter to the deer eating the birdseed on the terrace.

After phoning the Chinese embassy several times and braving the endless queues at the Russian embassy I decide – for the sake of my sanity – to hand over my Russian, Kazakh, Uzbek and Chinese visa requirements to the professionals, along with another hefty fee. The Russia specialist is all business,

> 'Yes, of course, madam, the Russian visa will take three weeks; the Uzbek and Kazakh visas can take up to three months.'

> 'Three months!'

I stare at the little woman in front of me.

> 'I don't have three months. I am leaving in three weeks.'

She shrugs her shoulders.

What to do? Let's see what the Chinese specialists have to say.

> *'Guten Morgen, Ich moechte mit eigenem Auto von Muenchen nach Shanghai fahren.'*

> *'Das geht nicht!'* Comes the instant reply.

What is it with people? How come the first reaction to a new idea is always that it is impossible? Not, let me think about that for a moment; always an instant knee-jerk reaction. 'It cannot be done. I haven't thought about it. I have no intention of thinking about it, but that is my final word on the subject, good day.'

Annette and the Wish Mobile
Munich Germany, April 2006

Had I not done my homework, I might actually have believed the silly girl, but I had, and I knew it could be done; it just wasn't going to be easy.

'May I speak with your manager, please?'

A well-fed German gentleman – smug in his imagined self-sufficiency – comes down the stairs.

'Good morning, I believe you would like to drive to Shanghai in your own car. I am afraid it cannot be done.'

I am inclined this morning to disagree, and point out that it has been done, only once or twice, but it has been done, and therefore it can be done.

He starts rattling off that I will need a Chinese driver's license, special visas, my car will need Chinese number plates, and I will need to employ a guide for the duration of my stay in China. I am six steps ahead of him on this and confidently tell him that I know. This brings about an amazing change of face.

'Well, in that case I am sure we can arrange something.'

At this point I should have been little less smug at my own victory and a bit more attentive of the € signs flashing in his eyes. He starts telling me that he has in fact arranged such a trip before (huh?) and giving advice on the route I should take and on and on. I have other ideas – I always do.

I want to travel via Volgograd (Stalingrad). This will force me to then travel the entire length of Kazakhstan, as I also want to make a quick detour into Uzbekistan. By the time I hit China I think I will be heartily sick of deserts, so want to enter China through Korgass, not via the Turugat Pass.

'Yes, but the market at Kashi is famous.'

For a minute I am tempted, but then reason steps in; people shop everywhere on the planet, and I think markets will be a fairly common occurrence on my travels. Then a little memory from all my surfing pops into my head. Some blogger's opinion of the Kashi market was that this is a market for package-deal tourists – that did it. I stick to my guns and insist that they arrange the route via Korgass. The travel agent and I agree that by the end of this week they will send me a list of all the Chinese requirements. I am totally chuffed with the morning's work.

Only one more thing to sort out: how to keep my passport and get it visa stamped at the same time? I discover with the application of money, anything is possible, and in special circumstances, a second passport can be obtained. My circumstances are deemed special enough, and now and with my second passport traveling from embassy to embassy to get all the required visas, I am left only with the far more interesting job of finding the vehicle that will transport me across the Eurasian continent.

With the help of a friend, I finally settle on buying a glorified silver delivery van, equipped with all the bells and whistles, but it is within the budget, and in the long run I will be grateful for the added comfort. When choosing the car, the colour was very important, right up there with the suspension and diesel consumption, as, to add some small meaning to my journey, I have conceived of an artwork which I have dubbed, 'One planet One people.' This art project will depend on the participation of men, above the age of thirty-five, wherever in the world I might find them. They will be requested to write a wish for the world on my car, which I have officially named 'The Wish Mobile.' Why only men above the age of 35? Because cars on the whole are still a male thing. Don't get me wrong, I love my car, not for the car itself, but for what it can do for me, like drive me to China. Men love their cars because they are cars, and an extension of their manliness, and other such silly stuff. But more importantly I have singled out this group of humans as, despite all the advances made by women, men are still in the driving seat of the planet and it seems to me the planet is spinning out of control, so I am curious to know what the brains behind the wheel will come up with.

Unfortunately, before I can drive the car, I must run the German bureaucratic gauntlet. The Germans have red tape down to a fine art. They can weave it, wrap it, knit it, crotchet it and tie it into a thousand different knots, but I have mentally prepared myself for this. Bureaucracy is what it is, and no amount of ranting will change that. Once the Wish Mobile and I are legally on the road, it is time to turn the delivery van into a makeshift camper.

To inform myself about any equipment I might need, I acquire a catalogue from the biggest overland expedition supplier in Germany. This doorstop of a book is now on the table in the place of the endless documents. The trip when looked at in its entirety is huge, but I will only be travelling on average 350 km per day. Will I really need an axe, a tire pump, sand ladders or a flashlight? Do I need a satellite phone, in case of emergencies? Whom would I phone? Good grief, this is enough to scare the wanderlust right out of me.

Is driving in strange territory really so perilous that I might need flares or a bowie knife? I don't think so. I am consumed by guilt and contrition when swatting a cockroach; I will not be stabbing anything. Although a friend did insist that I take a can of pepper spray (totally illegal in many countries and if I am found out, it could cause me more trouble that it might save me from). As for the GPS, toys for boys as far as I can tell, and an enormous amount of work is involved in mapping routes, I decide to buy a compass and paper maps instead. I take a moment to reflect and then toss the catalogue into the recycle bin.

I have no intention of going off-road. My opinion of four-wheel-drive vehicles is fairly low, and I feel that if you cannot get there by normal road, get a horse or walk. I am not a great camping fan, and the mini-camper is for emergencies only. My camper is fitted with the bare essentials: a very small pot, a little gas burner, a car kettle, an air mattress with pump and a mosquito net. For eating on the road, I have a sharp knife, a twin set of silver flatware and a multiple opener. Two thermo mugs, two metal plates and two highly ornate silver shot glasses. I am equipped with several different sized plastic containers with snug-fitting lids. I have two jerry cans, one for water, one for fuel, a set of spanners, which I don't know how to use, and Olga, a collapsible army spade.

To document my journey and for entertainment I have my camera, my laptop, iPod, various battery-charging devices and a nifty little portable printer. I have five prepared canvasses, my paint and brushes, and my yoga mat. For those iffy beds that I am sure to encounter, I have my own bedding and plastic slipslops for moldy showers and bathrooms. In addition to the standard jeans and t-shirt daywear, I have a shimmering red cocktail dress and a pair of sparkly heels. With that, I feel I am fully equipped for a trip to China.

Having come this far – and as we still have a very long road to travel together – I think a brief visual introduction will not be out of place here. One of those – she was a tall elegant blonde with a sway in her walk that made hot men shiver – descriptions à la Mills & Boon. Unfortunately that is not quite the right image. I am tall, but a brunette, I am middle aged, as in I have lived as many years as I can reasonably still expect to live. I have green eyes that do flash when my irritation levels get out of hand, and I am about to discover that I am a latent racist. Now that is more information than a Mills & Boon novel would ever give you about the heroine, which is exactly why you should never believe anything you read in a Mills & Boon novel.

Speyer Cathedral, Speyer Germany

Germany

I am organised! The next three weeks of my life are planned down to the last detail. The hotels are booked, family and friends alerted to my exact time of arrival. The Wish Mobile is spotless; all cupboards are neatly packed, all t-shirts precision folded and colour coded. My route is mapped out, the 350 km I intend to travel per day calculated to the nearest meter. My driving skills on the right-hand side of the road have advanced to the point where my right hand is fully versed with the changing of gears, and my left hand no longer grabs at the door handle every time I put my foot on the clutch. I remember to look more often into the left-hand rearview mirror than the right and, most importantly, I now automatically look right then left then right. Getting that little detail wrong can kill you. I am – I think – ready to leave. But as with most things too much anticipated, the great moment is, well, just a little disappointing. The band didn't arrive, the mayor couldn't make it, and the international media had better things to do. Even the weather on this bleak day leaves much to be desired.

On that low note, I set off into the land of my birth and immediately get held up by roadworks. Sitting here with nothing to occupy my mind, a little thought pops unbidden into my head.

'Hmm, look at that, the men digging the ditch are all white.'

Come again? I turn the thought over in my head while staring at the group of men going about their business. But no matter how I look at it, this picture seems to me just a little off. In South Africa, skin colour still distinguishes you; white men don't dig ditches, and so I discover – to my horror – that I am a racist.

As the traffic starts moving slowly through the quaint Bavarian landscape I have plenty of time to consider this rather disturbing discovery. Then the road plunges into a tiny copse of winter-bare trees, rattles over a wooden bridge, and climbs up a hill, where my first glimpse of the gleaming white Alps, pasted against the now brilliant blue sky, jolts me out of my orgy of self-castigation. I have a strong urge to keep heading south, to drive over those massifs, but must contain myself. The first country to be explored is Germany, and for the next few weeks I will be turning my back on the Alps.

The whimsically named Romantic Road takes me through fairytale hamlets and tiny farmlands. Tall rectangular farmhouses, bottom half wood, top half whitewashed plaster, with red terracotta roof tiles and windows framed by faded green shutters, stand tight against the road. Behind them the barns, grey with age, shelter goats, while the carthorses stand in meadows that with this morning's rain have become shallow lakes. The dry stone walls spout temporary waterfalls, turning the roads into rivers. The Wish Mobile leaves a cockscomb spray, its undercarriage now as spotless as the rest of the car.

My arrival at the pilgrimage church of Wies, the 'Wieskirche', coincides precisely with the arrival of a convoy of tour busses, a United Nations of tourists stream, chattering incessantly, up the snowy lane. The restaurant is fortunately open, so while the tourist masses go to church I appease my stomach. 'Leberkaes' is on the menu, which literally translated means liver cheese. Not a very appetising name, but as my stated aim is to experience different cultures I take the plunge. 'Leberkaes' turns out to be very similar to German sausage meat presented in the shape and size of an average loaf of government bread. A thick slice is cut and fried, then served with a fried egg, refried potatoes and good German mustard. The normal accompaniment to this greasy protein glut is beer, but, as I am driving, I opt for an Apfelschorle, apple juice with sparkling water.

Sated, and tourist busses departed, I stroll over to view what is considered the best example of Rococo architecture in the world. From the outside, the church looks enormous. Once inside, it seems much smaller, perhaps an illusion created by the overwhelming amount of decoration. It is a great pink and blue space filled with swirls and curls in marble and gold. Heavenly scenes in bright pastel shades, each framed by its own elaborate confection of stucco and gold, float up the walls to the triumphant ceiling, where women, cast in the buxom German ideal, lounge fully clothed on fluffy clouds. This, combined with soaring marble altars and intricately carved window frames, creates a setting in which naive country folk must once truly have believed they were at the portals of heaven.

Heading now for Oberammergau, where the castle Neu Schwanstein of King Ludwig II stands, I try to apply my road trip rule one: seek the road less travelled. I seek and I seek and I seek. An hour later, I realise that in Germany there is no road less travelled. The country roads are a navigational nightmare. Mapping a detailed course before you leave is essential, but not foolproof. You must expect your chosen road to be closed for whatever reason and then expect endless detours. In villages a speed limit of 30 km/h must be observed and, as the villages follow every 5 km or so, this makes for very slow going.

'Find most convenient highway'

becomes my road trip rule for Germany.

Roaring along the uninterrupted stretch of tar, my thoughts return to my newly discovered character flaw, drawn there like a tongue to a broken tooth. My only defence for my subtle, latent form of racism is that I grew up as a stranger in a stranger land. Arriving as a small Aryan immigrant to South Africa in the sixties was to arrive in a land where apartheid had done its work. I lived, played and went to school in an all-white world. Until one cold winter morning, next to a lamppost in the frozen veldt, a small black boy lay with frost in his curly black hair and tiny icicles on his eyelashes; he was barefoot; his trousers too short; he had frozen to death. I was seven when their world, the world of the non-whites, suddenly entered into mine. A big white man covered the boy with a piece of dirty cardboard and told me not to look, to go to school. But you cannot unlook, that which is seen, remains seen. And then I suddenly saw them, they were the ones that walked and worked at the roadside, and it remains the same. Despite twelve years of one man, one vote, twelve years of promises, this morning was the first time in my life that I saw a white man digging a ditch on the roadside. Through apartheid I am a racist: not by choice or belief in my superiority, but purely by social conditioning. This seems like a very good place to start reinventing myself.

The rain on the windscreen pulls my attention back to the road. In the distance icy clouds press down on Neu Schwanstein, which is apparently beautifully situated on an enormous rock and usually presents the ultimate romantic vista. Not today. Today it is freezing, raining and foggy; the castle is barely to be seen. But, as this is the castle that inspired Disney's 'Cinderella' fairytale castle, arriving by horse-drawn carriage is a must. As the horses heave my lazy bones up that hill, their exertions bring on a worrying case of flatulence, to which I am fully exposed. So I discover there is only one thing to recommend this mode of transportation, and that is that you don't have to walk by yourself. As for romantic – forget it – I will walk down.

Viewing Neu Schwanstein is tourism in high gear: the entrance is packed with a multitude of nations, all clutching their electronically activated tickets, intently watching the large clock overhead. The electronic gates will only admit them at the time stated on the ticket; entering too early or too late is not possible; German efficiency at its uncompromising best. At the exact time stated on my ticket, I am admitted into Neu Schwanstein along with the others that make up my group. One little lady gets it wrong, the machine spits her ticket back at her, and the grey steel gate remains firmly shut. As her group vanishes into the fog, she squeals in panic, and only after close scrutiny of her ticket is she admitted, all the while groveling her thanks. This is meant to be fun? With the tour guide keeping a careful eye on the groups ahead and behind us, we get whipped through the fantastic interiors in half an hour. Tour done. I vaguely remember lavishly decorated rooms in jewel colours, but otherwise nothing. A huge amount of effort for very little reward.

Beds 12 and 2

In a sodden grey traffic jam I find my way to the Bodensee. I had hoped to make it as far as the Black Forest, but the day is nearly done. As I drive along the shoreline, the clouds break to admit angelic fingers of light that catch playfully at the swans floating on the steel grey water. In the tiny village of Sippelingen a happy sign flaps in the breeze *'Zimmer frei'*. This will be bed for the night. A well-rounded granny in starched white apron with lace all along the edges opens the door, a ferocious German shepherd dog at her side. The double room is a German Gemütlichkeit of floral, frill and flowery water colors in shades of pale green and pink and, at 20€ inclusive of breakfast, a bargain.

Setting out to explore the tiny village of wood-frame houses and impeccable minute gardens, I get summoned from a dark doorway.

'Komm rein, komm rein.'

Beckons a gnarled old man in blue overalls He flashes me a smile of alarmingly yellow teeth. Not at all reassured, I hesitate at the doorway to his pungent lair. Then, taking a last breath of clean mountain air, step over the threshold into the dark underground world of the German garagista.

The air is liberally laced with alcohol. The ceiling low in this labyrinth of cellars, where walls seem to have been knocked down at random to make more room as the success of his venture grew, the house above is supported now only by a few strategically placed pillars. In the gloom, huge plastic vats filled with a brown, unpleasant-looking liquid fill the dark corners. Clambering over boxes that spill labels and bottles, and around a tumble of distilling equipment, he shows me his pride and joy with a triumphant flourish. A copper distilling kettle, two heads taller than he, gleams smugly in the corner, knowing full well, that without it, this enterprise could not be. Absentmindedly stroking the smooth amber surface, he explains in serious tones how regulated the life of a German garagista is. He is only allowed to distil so many litres per year and his brew gets checked and evaluated at every stage to ensure that he does not sully the reputation of the German schnapps industry.

Shelves line every available wall, where bottles in fancy shapes and multitude sizes are filled with brilliant liquid that concentrates then shatters the light from the bare bulb. Each bottle is neatly labeled; Birne, Pflaume, Kirsch ... He slams down a schnapps glass, whips out flavor one and pours a convex tot.

'Moechten Sie kosten?'

I protest.

'Nein nein!'

He waves his hand in dismissal.

'Trink, trink.'

Birne (pear) is very good, the liquid brilliantly clear, the flavor clean, yet full-summer ripe with a beguiling lingering perfume that teases the nose. Scarcely have I appreciated the quality of his art when the next glass is slammed down; Pflaume (plum), oh well, in for a penny in for a round, lots of rounds. Once again the liquor is a triumph of the fruit distiller's art; clear plumy flavors mix gallantly with the sharp bite of alcohol.

Detecting a warm glow in the pit of my stomach. I compliment him on his product and, selecting two small bottles, try to leave. But he knows his business; Kirsch is next, then Himbeergeist, ghost of the raspberry, always my favourite. By now I feel a distinct buzz and, with the lack of actual oxygen in that cosy cellar, I must make a concerted effort to pull myself toward myself. Thanking him profusely, I try to gather up my collection of bottles, which seems to grow each time I look at the table.

Suddenly inspiration hits to take photographs. Too late, too late, not a sharp shot among them. Note to self: photo shots first, alcohol shots second. I make to leave, but he is just as good at selling his brew as he is at making it. He slams down another glass and pours a dark amber tot.

'A medicinal herb for your digestion perhaps?'

Digestion? Food? Good idea! I grab my bottles and flee into the crisp evening air.

Sunshine! I stand with my eyes closed facing the sun until the icy wind sends me indoors to get properly dressed. Heading north into the Black Forest, the narrow country road winds past spring green meadows, over brooks and through tiny hamlets where no paint peels, no leaf litters the cobbled streets, and the sun casts curly shadows from shop signs onto perfect pastel pink walls. On the spur of the moment, I guide the Wish Mobile off the tar onto a narrow track deep into the dark forest. My silent footsteps vanish in the soft moss that carpets the forest floor, each footstep releasing the scent of pine needles, a sharp note against the deep primal smell of the damp earth. A ray of sun skims through the dark trees, highlighting tiny spring leaves that throw a veil of green lace over bare brown branches. Along high mountain ridges and past deep forested ravines I make my way to Gimeldingen in the Palisades, where almond trees in pink blossom splendor line the narrow road and the distant view across the valley vanishes in a golden haze.

My hosts for the evening, Ina and Peter, have taken up the challenge to cook me something traditional. They are preparing an ancient dish made internationally famous by Helmut Kohl, who served it to all visiting dignitaries, including Maggie Thatcher. She apparently politely pushed it about her plate, but not into her mouth. The dish in question? Saumagen or sow's belly. Fortunately, visions of haggis are quickly dispersed by assurances that the meat is lean pork fillet, and what appear to be large pieces of fat are in fact potatoes. Who thinks up these things? What inspired some medieval chef to decide that the only way forward in German culinary development would be to take the stomach lining of a pig, stuff it with a variety of vegetables and meat, boil it and serve it up for dinner? And why is it still being done? When cooked, the monster meatball is sliced, fried and served with sauerkraut, bratkartoffeln and fresh thyme. Accompanied by an excellent Rhein Riesling, the wine of the region, it is surprisingly good – old Maggie missed out.

Over dinner, a heated discussion ensues as to the best cultural sight to take me to. In the end, the Imperial Cathedral of Speyer, built *circa* 1030, wins the vote. The red sandstone building is considered the best example of the Romanesque architectural style in existence. There is a polar difference in style from the churches of Bavaria. Gone are the garish colors, the carved marble, the gold leaf and cherubs. Instead the church is a subtle mix of stone shades, intricate stone carving and an atmosphere of quiet restraint that is totally missing in the Rococo style.

Our wanderings take us to the village of Diedesheim, where I discover that my fellow countrymen have a window decoration 'makke'. The curtains come in every style of frill and lace; things on strings and doodads on sticks totally clutter the small view the tiny windows presents. To obliterate the view completely, window boxes are vibrant with flowery cheer. The need for bright colors I am beginning to understand, but while my appreciation of the smallest amount of sun is growing in leaps and bounds, I have not quite reached the desperation for spring of the locals. The Mediterranean microclimate for which the area is famous, allowing not just grapes, but also almonds and figs to be cultivated here, is not at all apparent today. An icy breeze snipes at every exposed bit of skin, yet the locals eat ice-cream; great big dollops of the frozen stuff are being consumed all around. Hot chocolate, now that would make sense.

Before I head north, I invite Peter to add his wish to the 'One planet One people' project. He agrees hesitantly and finds a very unobtrusive spot to write 'Tolerance'. It seems to take some measure of will for men to scrawl all over the shiny new surface of my car with a permanent marker.

'Das macht man doch nicht!'

Visions of plummeting resale values tear through their minds. In the modern world, only things have value, thoughts don't, and yet, every thing springs from a thought. No thought, no thing.

Beds 3 and 13

Alexandra is arriving early this evening to join me on the first of the three legs of my journey she will share with me, so I must make haste to Frankfurt. Fortunately, my route is on the A5 where making haste is the only way to go. This is an autobahn where the Germans do Formula 1 time-trials. I am in the slow lane travelling between 120 and 140 km/h, but this is reduced to granny speed by drivers in shiny sports cars who, two lanes to my left, attempt to break the sound barrier.

The curls and frills of southern Germany are quickly replaced by glass and steel towers that reflect the cold blue sky. Driving into Frankfurt am Main, Germany's financial heart, I make my way by precise written instructions to a narrow side street in the centre of the city. In a street with neat pavements and three-storey buildings, pale yellow in the bright sunshine, Klaus is waiting. Carefully groomed and exuding the satisfaction of a life well lived, he represents that generation of Germans on which Germany's reputation for hard work and attention to detail is based. We shake hands; he urges me inside. The elegant apartment is a subtle palette of yellows and creams, and smells faintly of the fresh lilies on the table. In a house of strangers I am surrounded by a careful politeness.

'A cup of tea?'

'Why, thank you, that would be delightful'.

Over tea, made from a blend of expensive leaves, timed to brew exactly for three minutes, Ula and Klaus have a small discussion on which coats to wear. Is it warm enough yet for summer weight or shall they play it safe with the winter coats? Summer coats it is, and we step out into the fading spring day.

After a U-bahn trip under the unseen city, we emerge in the old centre, at a catholic convent, which glows warm with the candle offerings of the rushing commuters. They pause for brief prayer, a gentle bow of the head, a longing look at the Madonna, then an automatic crossing of the chest, before they blend once again into the masses. To give me an overview of Frankfurt, Ula and Klaus take me to the top of the Commerz Bank, currently the tallest building in the European Union. From this high vantage point the city of Frankfurt spreads flat into the distance, and the sky is as crisscrossed with jet streams as a shunting yard with tracks. The airplanes circle above Europe's busiest airport, then, in a stepped queue, line up to land. The margin for error in this overcrowded airspace is frighteningly small. Here Alexandra will land, but only at midnight, her flight delayed by five hours.

With our original dinner plans disrupted by the tardy flight, we stroll over the River Main into a neighborhood of small boutiques and cider taverns that specialize in Frankfurter fare, in a quest to find dinner and to kill time. The interiors of age-stained murals of old Germany contrast with the modern clientele, who play musical chairs at the long communal tables, where seating companions constantly swap and change. This is not the place for intimate dinners, but Klaus has a fine time with the opening line.

'Meet Annette; she is driving to China.'

'Why?'

Is the pragmatic German reply.

'Because growing up in South Africa cultivated a healthy mistrust in me of the media. I want to get an overview, see the big picture, not just the luxuriously edited one you get by hopping from airport to airport. I want to make up my own mind about what's going on out there, about what's important, and I want to do it with first-hand information.'

My little soliloquy results in a small debate around the table while I consider whether to eat the house specialty of *Handkaese mit Musik*. It is a pungent, translucent, hand-formed orb of cheese that is served with raw onions and dark rye bread; the music you supply and it comes later. The meal is an olfactory assault that is best washed down with apple wine, which soon enhances the conversation and we break into unforced laughter. In companionable silence we ride the streetcar home, past shop windows where beautifully lit luxury goods glow enticingly in the dark. At the stroke of midnight, happy birthday to me, and the best birthday present arrives as my child, my person, my Alexandra strolls through the arrivals gate.

After a breakfast of bread and cold meats – Germans eat a stupendous amount of bread; they even call mealtimes *Brotzeit* (bread time) – we wish our new friends farewell and hit the highway. But not for long as we are making a brief pit stop to visit friends in Buedingen, which is a small town with a long and living history. A town where every building fits and a town of which Einstein said; 'Here the Middle Ages shows off its most beautiful side.' It is a small town with a big castle, in which the lord of the manor still lives, and can trace his family tree to the 12th century. This is small potatoes compared with the old church, which dates precisely from 1047; this can be determined by its still original wooden beams. That the church and town have weathered the centuries unscathed is a miracle that Heiner explains was made possible by poverty.

Buedingen was always a small insignificant town that quietly grew through the centuries. It never had anything worthwhile plundering, and even the bombers of the Second World War had more interesting targets to keep them busy. Today – in the unpredictable way of economics – the long lack of money has made Buedingen very wealthy. Our walk takes us past beautifully preserved houses, over arched bridges where ducks come to shore, past a small fresh-produce market, and ends at an ice-cream store where we pick up a few flavors for dessert. Back at the house, Irene is just preparing the bright green sauce that will accompany our lunch. *Gruene Sosse*, the specialty of Frankfurt, is a blend of seven spring herbs: borage, sorrel, cress, chervil, chives, parsley and salad burnet. These are chopped together with hardboiled eggs, and lashings of crème fraiche, and the resulting tart, fragrant deep green sauce is served with new potatoes and boiled beef.

After lunch we head north towards Essen. I hand Alexandra the map and the address where we want to go. She knows her way around a map, having been the navigator on many a road trip since learning to read. With the nonchalance of experience, she opens the map and promptly bursts into nervous giggles.

'Have you seen this?' she asks.

'Why do you think I gave it to you?'

Like spaghetti on a plate, the map is a chaotic tangle of roads, a telling testament to the high-density living in the Ruhrgebied. Alexandra settles down to untangle the mess of roads in front of her, while I concentrate on negotiating the Autobahn. The German driver is an impatient, aggressive beast, but a very correct one. So while everything moves at subsonic speed, everyone is fortunately behaving impeccably. Cars immediately move out of the fast lane after overtaking, no overtaking on the right, the trucks adhere strictly to the lane advisors, and the lack of toll roads make for very speedy and safe driving. With Alexandra's impeccable navigating, we reach Essen, the city of my birth, in no time.

Beds 4 and 6

I have no memories of Essen. When I was a wee toddler we immigrated to South Africa, where my parents started a new life. As a young child, with no memory of my German culture or history and no desire to be part of the apartheid culture of South Africa, I became part of an increasing global population that is culturally rootless. This part of my journey is partly to introduce Alexandra to her German heritage, and to see how I fit into the German culture. To help in this quest, old family friends Alfred and Margaret have arranged a visit to the apartment of my birth; this is somewhat closer to the truth than I had expected to get.

Now, standing in a grey drizzle in front of the rather sad buildings, memories of a distant childhood ambush me: older boys dug an enormous hole in the sand pit, which does not seem to have moved. I was terrified that I might fall in. In the winter I remember slip-skating in the ice tracks left by the cars driving in the snow. I see my three-year-old self sitting in a snug restaurant, peering through dark wood-framed windows, frosted outside by snow and steamed up inside by my own breath. Through the misty glass, I watch the snow-covered street outside that glows with the warm light of candles in paper lanterns that all the children carry on long sticks to celebrate St Martin's day.

In those long-forgotten days Essen suffered under the black pollution cloud of the coalmines and heavy industry that had been the driving force of the Ruhr since the 1400s, culminating in the arms production of the Second World War and the rebuilding of Germany after that. We stroll along the elevated steel walkways of the industrial site 'Der Zollverein' that is today a UNESCO World Heritage Site. At the height of production, twelve mineshafts fed this Dante's inferno, which with its massive scale dwarfed the men who worked here. This evokes images of dark winter mornings, with coal-dust-laden fog swirling around the miners' lamps as they make their way to the shafts that will take them down to the coalface, from which they will emerge at the end of their shift, as black as the coal itself. Today the coalmines, miners and the black pollution cloud are long forgotten. 'Der Zollverein' is the centre of Essen's cultural and art scene and the Ruhrgebied now boasts the highest living standard in Germany.

Our route north takes us through Bremen, Hamburg, Luebeck and Rostock, the great Hanseatic cities of the High Middle Ages. Here we discover the German Wurststube and that we have a farmhand's appetite for wurst. 'One City, One Wurst' becomes our credo. Bratwurst, Weisswurst, Bokwurst, Wurst with Bratkartofflen, Wurst with Pommes rot weiss and the great German favorite, Currywurst. To work off the Wurst calories we visit old churches and climb the bell towers.

In these far northern cities, the wealthy merchants of old felt the urge to display their wealth in their buildings. They had only one niggling problem, no building material, as up in the lowlands of the north there was no stone with which to build. Not deterred, the ever-inventive Germans put the readily available red clay to task and perfected the making of red bricks. They developed this process to the point where delicate filigreed arches and fluted pillars became as detailed as any carved stone or marble. This gave rise to the Red Brick

Gothic architectural style in the 12th century. The Marienkirche of Stralsund is a beautiful example of this building style, and also gives us a bird's-eye view from the top of the 104 m bell tower.

Below us, Stralsund displays its dominant colour, brick red, in full: red rooftops, red walls, red facades, and not so long ago even the streets were paved with red bricks that arched like a well-fried bratwurst. From here, we also have a good view of our goal for the day, the island of Ruegen, which is separated from the German mainland by a narrow strait of water, Strelasund. The bridge, which currently forms part of the only road on and off the Island of Ruegen, must be one of the island's best fishing spots as, while the fisherman stand shoulder to shoulder peering into the water far below, bumper-to-bumper cars stream by behind them. Fishing from this bridge is a highly skilled endeavor as lines, lovingly loaded with sinker, hook and bait, are swung with military precision between the cars. Mainly the fishermen seem to miss the cars, but the occasional hit could result in a most unpleasant confrontation; the Germans are very particular about their cars.

Today the herring are running and the fisherfolk are having the time of their lives as they bait up again and again. Fishing rods dip and weave through the air as yet another slice of silver is hauled out of the jade green water. In the rapidly filling buckets the iridescent silver fish, with pleading eyes and gasping mouths, seem somewhat less happy with the situation. The fisherfolk toss more and more living fish into the buckets, which quickly become mass graves. Interesting how we treat animals. The ones we think are most like us, we value most. The ones we think are cute and cuddly must be protected. The ones that obey us we consider our best friends. But the ones that live in foreign environments, the ones we cannot own, understand or control, we reduce to merchandise. But then again, why not, we treat people the same way.

Running the gauntlet of hook, line and sinker, we make it across the bridge with no hits, and arrive on Ruegen as the late afternoon sun sinks low over the flat green land that presents no barrier to the lengthening shadows. After finding a room for the night in the tiny hamlet of Moisselbritz, we immediately set out for a walk in the dramatic light that paints the scenery bright gold and green against a deep purple sky. Leaving the green meadows behind we enter a domain where the boundaries of water and soil are blurred under a dense bed of reed, a gentle sag underfoot warns us that dry land was some way back and we now venture where only ducks dare go. Picking our way closer to the mirror blue sea, we find the remains of a swan. It reminds us of the media circus that played out here not two weeks before. Some swans died on the island and it was confirmed that the cause was bird flu. A hysterical wave of fear was whipped up by the media, whose continued existence depends on making sure that we are always afraid. This fear resulted in all eggs being boiled blue, chickens being reclassified as life threatening, and a slew of Easter weekend cancellations, which is probably the reason we managed to find a room here at such short notice.

On Easter Sunday a cold wet wind blows us into the cozy restaurant where all guests are treated to hard-boiled, brightly colored Easter eggs for breakfast. Here in the far north people have a thing about Easter eggs. The bare branches of fruit trees are gaily festooned with colorful plastic eggs. In gardens, long strings of hand-painted Easter eggs are draped over plants and garden features. However, Ruegen's most famous feature is the Koenigstuhl: high chalk cliffs that plunge into the Baltic Sea.

The cliffs are reached through the ancient beech forest at Jasmund National Park. In the cold drizzle the forest is reduced to a grey graphic of tall upright trunks, where the echoes of children's cries bounce hollow across the black water of the small lake in front of us. Visions of Iron Age people, fur-clad hunters and women drawing water from the lake, freezing winters and smoking fires spring to mind. At an offering stone streaked with artificial blood, Alexandra sticks her neck out; it fits the hollow in the great stone perfectly; she does not stay there long.

Finally the forest gives way to the Baltic Sea, where the white chalk cliffs crumble slowly into the ocean, turning the water a milky green. In a clearing a small caravan is doing brisk trade selling coffee and, of course, Wurst, but also Pfannekuchen und Apfelmuss. What this translates to is super-size waffles with applesauce, a messy but delicious meal. Energized we make our way to the beach. It is grey, forlorn and littered with storm debris, which consists mainly of a very small cousin of the kelp we are accustomed to in Cape Town. But diving here would be across a kelp meadow rather than in a kelp forest. The little waves struggle under the weight of the little kelp and it is just a little cold, a little smelly and a little disappointing, and we leave.

Bed 7

With the memory of a huge German breakfast of home-baked bread rolls, a variety of cheeses, cold meats and delicious homemade jams still lingering on our taste buds we set off south; today's destination Berlin. The road is arrow straight and only the slick white wind turbines add any height to the flat green fields.

Both sides of my family come from that far north-eastern part of Germany that has been Poland, Germany, Poland, depending on the direction of the political winds of the day. At the close of the Second World War, when the Russians came to avenge Stalingrad and when the new borders of Germany, Poland and the Czech Rep were drawn, millions of people were deported or fled in fear of their lives, taking only what they could carry. My father's family were railed in cattle trucks to the north-west of Germany, while my maternal grandmother fled south, on foot, through the frozen forests, six small children in tow. Alexandra and I loosely trace her route to Berlin and now find ourselves at the entrance of the apartment building where members of my family have lived since before the Second World War. If our family were to have a family seat, I guess this would be it.

'Die Sonne scheint. Jooha! Wir machen eine Bootsfahrt.'

Doris declares with her usual exuberance.

Eberhard, attending carefully to his first pipe of the day, looks out of the window, and agrees that it is a good day for a boat trip.

Doris leaps into action: phoning for timetables and inviting further family members to join us. Within the hour we are all gathered at the River Spree to board the pleasure cruiser that will ferry us under the multitude bridges of Berlin. There are more bridges in Berlin than in Venice. Our little party settles itself on the outer deck. Doris leans back, eyes closed, to enjoy the full pleasure of the sun's warmth on her face.

As we float by endless buildings, Berlin slides into focus. After the solid dose of ancient towns with quaint cobbled streets and redbrick structures, I am at a loss as what to make of this architectural hodge-podge. Gleaming high-rises compete with aged green copper towers. Giant modern sculptures dwarf old heroes on stone horseback. Shiny chrome reflects ancient brick. A stone sculpture rescued from the rubble of war is given pride of place on a clean glass facade. The old, the new; shiny and matt; neutral stone and bright plastic shades all cluster together to make for an architectural smorgasbord. Bizarre is the knowledge that buildings that look hundreds of years old were in fact only built in the mid 20th century, a reminder that at the close of the Second World War, Berlin was reduced to rubble by the Russians avenging the destruction of Stalingrad.

This memory is kept alive by the blackened ruin of the Church of Remembrance, which stands at the hub of Berlin's foremost shopping street, Kurfurstendamm, where we dodge ladies with poodles, girls with piercings, men with Mohicans, slick suits and vagabond hippies. By the time we have finished shopping, we are convinced that Berlin is a very cool place, but are not sure the locals feel the same about us. The keep right, pass left rule – that is in force even on the sidewalks – brands us as outsiders. Accustomed to doing things the opposite way around, we are constantly involved in the face-to-face, left-right jive of the undecided pedestrian. The locals roll their eyes in exasperation. Then at the traffic lights, we don't give the pedestrian light a second glance; jay walking is the way to go in South Africa. The German drivers are not happy about this, but come to a complete halt to allow us to complete our lawless behavior. This is a bit embarrassing. Just keep moving; we come from Africa; we know how to dodge speeding cars.

But no, here we are expected to wait for the *Ampelmaennchen* – the little green walking man on the pedestrian traffic lights that has become a cult figure in Berlin – just like everybody else. The herd makes the rules in Germany and a very well behaved if somewhat impatient herd it is. I still need to acquire a few things for the car before heading to Poland, and must travel to the opposite side of Berlin. The busses and U-bahns all play along, and we disembark and board at our connecting points without a moment's delay. Public transport German style is convenience epitomized. Even the bus stops have digital signboards that announce the ETA of any given bus, and yet the Germans still look despairingly at their watches if they have to wait for more than a minute.

On our last day in Berlin, we decide to devote the day to culture and history. Top of my list is the 'Memorial to Murdered Jews'. Having seen the busloads of tourists flowing through the site at midday I think an early morning visit would be best. Alexandra, knowing a small adventure is in the offing, is game right away. Eberhard hums and haws – these are not morning people – but decides to come along anyway. Doris begs off, happy in the knowledge that she will have the apartment to herself for a few hours.

The 6h00 alarm sees us commuting with the working masses, and we reach the memorial just as the first rays of sun skim across the flat grey stone. The sculpture, as large as a football field, stretches grey and square into the distance like a sleeping skyscraper. The 'Memorial to Murdered Jews', I like the name: it is hard, harsh, and allows no hiding behind euphemisms. It is a name that announces recognition of fault and admission of guilt with a clarity that no spin doctor can dull.

Slowly approaching the stone blocks that are no higher than our ankles, we are soon separated. The stones are monotonous in their similarity yet, disturbingly, they lean in slight and haphazard direction. The morning sun creates Esheresque play with perspective, black against grey, but finds no blemish on the smooth surfaces. My solitary musing is slowly pierced by dark shadows, making me aware that the grey stone no longer just stretches off into every direction, but unnoticed has risen high above my head, black against the sky, obscuring the sun. The path undulates unevenly, adding to the sense of queer unease. The view through the rows of blocks brings no relief, as the deep depression in which the stones stand abruptly ends the narrowing perspective in yet more slightly askew blocks. Emerging at different points of the grey maze, we look back over the unassuming stretch of flat stone that once again lies at our feet, and have all come to understand that evil grows without fanfare and soon engulfs the unwary.

Our ramblings take us to the Brandenburg Gate, where the giant cranes bear testament to the game of catch-up still being played out in the eastern parts of Berlin. I suddenly remember the rattle of carriage doors at a midnight border crossing into Eastern Germany, dogs searching the undercarriage of the train, while armed men scrutinized our passports. Even as a teenager this did not strike me as a happy adventure. That was a long time ago, when the only way to enter East Berlin was with a government tour bus after long searches with mirrors and dogs. Then, we stood on a western lookout tower, staring at the death strip, bare of tar or concrete, laced with barbed wire and dotted with eastern watchtowers where not tourists, but armed soldiers with orders to shoot looked back at us.

The death strip has completely vanished, and only a few ragged pieces of the wall still stand. Today the wall needs protection by steel mesh against souvenir seekers. Only small round stones still mark the wall's path through the city. At Potsdamer Plazt, the steel and glass towers offset a few choice, brightly graffitied pieces of 'the wall'. Graffiti, the rebellious child of art and self-expression, has here been tamed and put on display as a symbol of the 'freedom' of the human spirit that will endure in spite of all odds, while elsewhere on Berlin's grey concrete walls the silent battle between bureaucrats and the human spirit rages on.

Haunted Castle Hotel, Southern Poland

Poland

Beds 8 and 9

Leaving Berlin early to avoid the commuter traffic, Alexandra, not quite awake, gets into a small disagreement with the road map. We zip up and down unexpected off-ramps before finally getting the Wish Mobile facing east. Before long, we are at the Polish border, and have to show our passports for only the most cursory of glances. The shift from West to East is immediately apparent. The road surface deteriorates to an unsynchronized yet interesting rhythm of bumps and jolts. This is soon interposed with a ripple of cobble and then a long slide of clean new cement. We dodge and dive, rumble and roll over this highway variety show.

After almost 100 kilometers of unbroken forest we reach Wroclaw and without mishap make it into the old town, which is teeming with potential long-distance runners. Our visit has coincided with the Wroclaw marathon. I haven't made an advance reservation, and the harried man at tourist information assures me that every hotel within running distance is booked solid. We decide to press on in the direction of Opole.

In a cold blue dusk we reach the rather forlorn town of Brzeg. Here we locate three churches, three weddings and one agriculture show, where I attempt to ask about a hotel.

'Hello, could you tell me where I might find a hotel?'

Blank shrug.

Hmm … I try again.

'Koennten Sie mir zu einem Hotel hinweisen?'

The young lady looks me over, raises an eyebrow, then rattles off in a language, which I, by supreme powers of deduction, identify as Polish. My turn to shrug blankly as my brain slams shut, and refuses to come up with a sensible plan on how to proceed. I have language tapes for France, Italy, Greece, Russia and China, but suddenly realize that there is a vast swathe of Central and Eastern Europe for which I don't even have maps – a rather unfortunate oversight that leaves us with only one course of action.

We randomly zigzag through the grey, tatty streets until we stumble on a hotel with yet another wedding in full swing. The hotel is not the kind we would normally consider, but after three further expeditions into the outer reaches of Brzeg we come up empty handed, and are faced with the choice of sleeping in the car or the iffy hotel. Alexandra has visions of us spending the night in the car and feels this could be a fun adventure. Having full knowledge of the size of the in-car bed, I am quite sure it will just be downright uncomfortable. Hotel it is. Unfortunately, Poland does not have laws against smoking indoors – the room is an ashtray – flinging open the room windows we set off to explore the immediate vicinity while allowing the room to breathe.

In a derelict park a group plays bongos, people cycle, children swing, and garbage lies peacefully in the undergrowth. A family friend recently said that people the world over are litterbugs; the difference is the amount they are prepared to spend to clean up after themselves.

We wander through the almost deserted streets of Brzeg, where the buildings are grey, square and losing their plaster, the sidewalks are uneven and the gutters overflowing with litter. Not exactly a scenic walk, but zlotys are required and Alexandra remembers seeing a cash machine around here during our search for a hotel. Locating the money machine next to a dirty little supermarket, we try to work out the conversion from zloty to euro to rand. Getting it totally wrong we draw way too much money, zloty all over the place. What the heck, now we have enough to pay for the room in cash. On the intersection of a busy road we chose a table at a pizzeria with a good view of the bustle around us. The waiter waits expectantly while we wrestle with the menu. We are defeated and have to resort to pointing at the plates of food that look most appealing at the other tables. The language thing, which was a vague consideration before, is coming into focus pretty quickly.

Back in our room we realize that the smell of stale nicotine will not be removed by simply opening the window; the hotel would have to be burnt to the ground to fully sanitize it. Opening the window also has the unfortunate result of exposing us to the full volume of the wedding below. Currently the chicken dance is blaring. Even here, this seems to be a wedding standard. To drown out the wedding we turn on Polish TV and, what do you know, American reruns in Polish. We sleep fitfully in our smelly little room, and after a halfhearted breakfast we leave, never to return again. Brzeg is really not a town that anyone needs to put on their to-do list

It is Sunday and in Poland the streets are empty, while the churches are filled to capacity, and the air rolls with the sound of sung mass. Our aim today is to find the birthplace of my father, which will require some nifty navigation from Alexandra.

She starts reeling off directions.

> 'We must head towards Skorogoszcz; turn right towards Dabrowa and left at Michlowec; then we pass through Tulowice, Sowin and Wierzbie; and Bob's your uncle,we should be in Korfantow.'

She lost me at Skorwhatsitsname. I give her a baleful stare.

> 'Are we being clever this morning? Here's the deal; you say left, I turn left, you say right, I turn right. Right?'

> 'Right.'

Sticking to this master plan, we end up in a tiny village by a railway siding where both the railway and the road end in a forest. It is not Korfantow.

> We stare ahead at the forest, at each other, at the old man watching us from the railway guardhouse. I think to ask him for direction but … no … probably not.

> Alexandra, let's try that again. Aha, we should have turned at Niemodlin, not Michlowec. An understandable mistake; all Polish names look the same, don't they?

> Without further mishap we arrive at Korfantow where the church is bigger than the village and which is where all the villagers currently are. The exterior of the church is familiar; a sketch of it hangs in my parents' dining room; and it is my father's only memento of his hometown and youth. Curious to see the interior, I peek around the door, but receive such disapproving stares from the worshippers that I decide we best go for a walk in the village. It brings no reward. I don't know what I was expecting to find, someone who remembers my ancestors? Korfantow is an obscure little village where the streets are deserted, the shops shuttered, the architecture bland and grey and, well, yes, been there, done that, and off we go.

> Our road takes us through a succession of small grey towns with unpronounceable names. The most interesting and colorful things are the graveyards, which are overflowing with flowers, as are the roadside shrines, where great bouquets of plastic and real flowers crowd around statues of Jesus hanging on the cross. Thoughtfully looking at a particularly brutal rendition of the crucifixion, Alexandra asks,

'Why did they decide to use this image to represent the Christian religion? It is just so horrible and violent.'

Staring at the bloody, emaciated Jesus hanging from the cross by brutal nails I have no reply, and decide that some things you have to work out for yourself.

While we negotiate our way along narrow tree-lined roads, where the first spring shoots give the brown fields a green shimmer, the roadworks throw up an interesting contradiction in this once Communist, but always Catholic country. Men are hard at work building roads, even on a Sunday.

Alexandra, who has been scrutinizing the map with great care, announces

'I think we should spend the night in Miedzygorze.'

'Miewhat?'

No, actually it's easier to stick with the plan. I drive, she navigates, and so we make our way to Bystrzyca Klodzka from where the road quickly moves us skywards to the tiny village of Miedzygorze, which is smaller than its name and that by a wide margin. Miedzygorze is a holiday destination in the ski area of Poland. Here we have a choice of accommodation in huge villas that are a mix of carved wood, rusting tin and pale stone, set against the wooded slopes from which snowmelt waterfalls tumble.

The sight of snow has Alexandra champing at the bit to get out and at it. Snow is a bit of a novelty for us southern types, so we immediately set out on a walk up the mountain, where the snowdrifts still lie thick on the foresters' track. Here Alexandra learns a thing or two about snow: it is cold; it melts; and canvas sneakers are not good snowshoes. Frozen toes soon force the decision to turn back, but not before we see a most bizarre sight.

Picking our way through the slushy snowdrifts, a stone suddenly hops out of our way. This is reason for closer inspection, and no less bizarre than hopping stones is the discovery that these mobile stones are in fact mating frogs. Hundreds and hundreds of frogs all with one thing on their mind. This is apparently normal behavior for cold weather frogs. To them snowmelt means just one thing, sex. With the rising temperatures they literally defrost and as soon as they can move, hop-skip-skedaddle to the nearest mating pond, which in this case is a muddy patch of road, and turn it into a huge orgy of froggy sex:

twosomes, threesomes, foursomes, anything goes in the ski resorts of Poland.

Further down the mountain, fate plays into our hands. We meet up with a group of overlanders giving their four- wheel-drives a wash in the river, an action that involves driving their cars into the rapids, making a u-turn and driving back out again. YeeHa, mucho macho. They are speaking English, time to make some new friends. By now I have learnt that the sentence, Hi! I am from Cape Town driving overland to Shanghai, is a sure attention-getter and in this case it wins us an invitation to join the group of Belgians for dinner. Over a dinner of Barszcz and Bigos – a beetroot soup followed by a meaty stew – the Polish tour leader, Andrzej, a short powerfully built man with a grey American-style crew cut and nasal twang to match, tells us that he will be leading an overland tour through Kazakhstan. We immediately have much in common, so he offers to guide us to various spots the following day before our departure to the Czech Rep. Excellent, here is a man who is going to show us parts of Poland we would never find by ourselves.

After breakfast, we meet up with Andrzej and his enormous bullmastiff. Our private tour starts with a visit to the 27-m high 'Wolves Fall' just below the restaurant. Then in convoy we travel the tiny back roads, over bridges, along streams, and up the road of a thousand bends to a high lookout point onto the ski slopes of Poland. Our route then takes us through tiny villages along winding back roads to the grey town of Stronie Śląskie, which is the hometown of one of Poland's many crystal factories. The showroom is all glitterball sparkle, but I am far more interested in walking in the morning market that is taking place across the river on a patch of open mud. Here the sparkling world of luxury goods is replaced by 'made in China' plastic in all flavors, from toys, to plates, to hair curlers and roller-neck pullovers. People stop and chat and rummage and sigh. Andrzej thinks this is a complete waste of time, pointedly looking at his watch, time to move along.

Through pale green forests to a sleeping beauty castle, its ancient red bricks half hidden by the forest that is slowly reclaiming its ground. Half in ruins, half renovated, the sweeping crumbling staircases lead to high-walled courtyards. Ruined Rapunzel towers soar above the trees, but to our extreme disappointment the owner is not home and, as the castle is guarded by forty rather unsociable dogs, we dare not enter. Andrzej, who has spent a night in this alternative hotel, declares it to be drafty, cold and haunted. He claims to have seen a ghost himself: a haunted hotel for hair-raising honeymoons.

In a tiny restaurant, which on our own we would never have recognized as such, we drink hot black tea out of glasses with no handles; a very delicate operation. When I mention that we have never seen graveyards with quite so many flowers in them, Andrzej explains that in Poland, Easter is the most important religious celebration, when all the family gather, and attending to the family graves forms part of the Easter ritual. This is why all the graveyards are overflowing with flowers. The conversation moves to the image Poland has in Germany, when I relate the horror stories I had heard about Poland. Germany and Poland have had neighbour issues since the forced removals after the war, and even today many German friends are quite convinced that travelling in Poland would be a dangerous affair. Andrzej is visibly angered by this, but also philosophical.

People are always scared of the unknown.

Therefore, it follows that by the end of this trip I will be either terrified or fearless.

We thank our host. He writes his wish on the Wish Mobile.

'May the sun shine for everyone.'

Then with a gallant bow and a kiss on the hand wishes me well.

'Perhaps we will meet in Kazakhstan?'

What are the chances?

Czech Republic
Beds 10 and 11

At Kudowa Zdroj we cross the border into the Czech Republic. The E 67 to Prague is just a narrow country road and the traffic is bumper-to-bumper trucks; it takes us hours to travel the 150 km to our destination. The rural landscape is an endless succession of small brown fields, flat under the heavy grey sky. For entertainment we take to counting the roadkill, and discover that the fox is the most inexperienced of road users. Just outside Prague a field is swarming with rabbits: two choices, either one very unhappy vegetable farmer or the rabbits are his livestock.

At our hotel we are given the keys to our room with the instruction that we are on the top floor and have to climb a flight of stairs to get to it. The instruction rings warning bells, as this establishment is three times the price of any other place we have stayed at. I had made a prior booking based on the totally over-the-top Rococo-style rooms on show on their website, thinking that it would be appropriate accommodation in this beautiful city. Taking the keys we drag our luggage through the fire door, up a flight of concrete stairs to arrive at a garret shoved under a steeply slanting ceiling, no bathroom and two tiny narrow cot beds. Instructing Alexandra not to make herself at home, I make my way back to the reception, trying to keep as calm as possible. Scarcely have I begun to complain about the room than the receptionist whips out another key to a room on the second floor?

Our new room is a vast improvement on the first, but pretty ordinary and still not worth half the money we are paying for it. It seems the fancy room they had used to advertise the hotel on the Internet is one of a kind, which is always fully booked, and the garret room is palmed off to anybody who does not complain. Dishonesty is one of humanity's deepest flaws; nothing good can come of it.

I make my way down to reception again. The poor woman is pink with embarrassment. She apologizes and refers me to the owner who may or may not be in the following day. There is nothing to be done; they have my deposit; it is getting dark; and we are not about to go gallivanting all over a strange city to try to find better accommodation. So we kick the disgusting carpets under the bed and go out to dinner

Prague, Czech Rep

To get to the historic centre of Prague we must board the metro. Nothing new or exciting there, but this metro deserves a special mention. The metro tunnels run deep under the city. This is normal in ancient cities with hidden artifacts and deep rivers to consider. But in Prague the space for metro stations seems to be at a premium. This scarcity has resulted in an escalator that gives pause for thought. It plunges down into the depths of the earth in one uninterrupted flow, at a vertigo-inducing angle. The sheer height of the beast would be manageable, were it not for its impossible speed. Sparing a pitying thought for little old ladies and mothers with babies, Alexandra and I leap onto the flashing stairs with force of will. We are carried down to the bowels of the earth with a chill wind blowing through our hair.

In the underground station we try to work out the ticket system and finally find an automaton – with a twist – it only takes exact change in a limited type of coin. How much more inconvenient can they make this? Fortunately the teeming masses are mainly tourists who, all having had their own problems with these narrow-minded machines, quickly come to our aid with pockets of change. The train itself is purely functional. Narrow hard benches run the length of it, leaving most of the train over to standing room. It is jam-packed with people hanging onto the frayed overhead straps, while desperately trying to hear the station announcements in Czech, English and German. But trying to decipher the station names announced over the shaky PA and over the hubbub of the packed train is almost impossible, so we take to counting stations, and manage to emerge into the fading day just one station shy of our intended destination.

Prague at night is a romantic place. The Vlatava River drifts by, a velvet midnight blue, reflecting the golden streetlamps and beautifully lit buildings that glow gently against the translucent pink and blue dusk. As we have no map, and have no idea where we are, we keep our wanderings to a minimum, but by a stroke of good fortune, we have landed in an area well stocked with restaurants. The warm glow from the old wooden windows of the Colonial Restaurant invites us inside. The ambience is dark wood, offset by raw concrete walls and white linen tablecloths. After a long indulgent dinner, we are somewhat appeased and make our way back to the hotel via the escalator funfair ride.

The following morning we are treated to that most horrific of hotel breakfasts: the semi-set table with the ready poured orange juice and the yoghurt and bread standing waiting on the table. We just know that these articles are trotted in and out of the kitchen until one of the guests finally plucks up the courage to eat them. Gross. Also, I am still on the warpath about the room, but the owner is not to be found during our entire stay. Despite many changes of staff no one is prepared to own up to being the manager or owner. The buck here was removed from play once they had their grubby hands on my deposit.

With map in hand and equipped with a metro day pass we escape from the hotel and venture into the old town of Prague. Emerging at Mustek station at Vaclavske Namesti, we bump against the modern concept of tourism for the first time. All around huge groups of tourists, decked out in various shades of cap, dutifully trot after tour guides, who, equipped with fake red roses and mini microphones, tell them in which direction to look, at which time, and for how long, all the while chattering away in one of a multitude of languages. We walk up the street while the entire world tourist population seems to be walking down. This is no fun, so because we have a day ticket for the public transport, we hop aboard the nearest tram and let it take us where it will.

The old city fades quickly into a memory as the real Prague of grotty graffitied buildings, beggars on street corners, dirt and grime begins to unfold. The city slickers and tourists on the tram are replaced by the working classes. Gaunt and careworn faces speak of long hours of work, too little money, and even less fun. The old grey faces are occasionally interspersed by the youth of the city that smoke and lounge and grope and swap saliva. They really have a thing for OTT public displays of affection. But affection seems too tame a word. Free sexual expression would be closer to the truth; it's like they have just heard of the sexual revolution.

As we move further and further from the tourist centre of Prague, the neighborhood gets poorer and poorer. The buildings are grey and functional, like giant chests of drawers where people are stored after a day of labor. But the drawers are too small, and the clothing spills over the edges, and flaps sadly in the breeze. Alexandra and I look at each other silently; we are getting just a little concerned about where this tram will take us, then finally, everybody out, as we reach the end of the line. The end station is a grim concrete block, brightened by anarchic graffiti and colorful litter. Having had the foresight to check the tram number that we arrived on, we hop on board the next tram No 3 that comes along and experience the reversal of fortunes again.

Now accustomed to the make-out sessions going on all around, our attention is drawn to the hair color of the citizens of Prague. Pink, orange, purple, red, they like their hair multicolored and nothing subtle about those shades. But the prize for most outrageous hairdo goes to a very elegantly attired elderly lady, who seems to be balancing a strawberry vanilla soft-serve ice-cream on her head. She sports a bouffant sweep of snow-white hair with a swirl of bright pink running through it. Is it a wig? Surely. Imagine trying to do that hair every morning. Just trying to sort the pink hair from the white hair must take hours and then to get the whole lot to remain so perfectly in place for the day … the tram passes her by and we arrive back in the pretty part of Prague.

Here we toss the map and simply do the anywhere-the-wind-blows thing. As we have no particular schedule, getting lost is not really possible, and with the hordes of tourists, we just need to go with the flow and are sure to arrive somewhere famous. But more often, we arrive at some gorgeous alley that has been invaded by souvenir shops that all sell the same schlock, kitsch junk, at extraordinary prices. Prague does not strike me as a city beloved by its people, but rather as a giant tourist discount supermarket, a golden goose that is being exploited shamelessly.

After a long hot day of people dodging, Alexandra and I make our way back to the hotel. We have tickets to the Prague State Opera and we need to smarten up. We go the whole hog, the make-up, the hair, the shoes, the dress, the jewelry and, as reward for our efforts, the driver leaps out of his very smart black Mercedes and whips open the car doors in most gallant fashion, then delivers us to the imposing steps of the Opera House in grand style. Where he leaps out to open those doors again and promises to be waiting right here when the last curtain falls. Now that's more like it.

The opera house is a neo-Rococo extravagance in gilt and burgundy. In my burgundy red dress, I am well disguised. In a sumptuous reception room we smile and nod at fellow opera buffs, sip champagne, and nibble at delicate treats before taking our seats, which are interestingly placed just under the roof. Always on the look out for the silver lining, I am rather pleased at the new perspective on those ornate gilded ceilings you normally see only from ground level. The opera on offer is a very minimalist version of Rossini's *The Barber of Seville*. This is disappointing, as to me the whole point of opera is that it should be a sumptuous indulgence of sight and sound. The modern take, justified, I am sure, purely by shrinking budgets, is like expecting a rich cream sauce and receiving instead a watery gruel. I barely manage to stay awake. Our driver arrives on cue, whips open those doors again, and we are whisked back to our horrible hotel.

Before we leave Prague, we are determined to see it without the tourist hoards and the impossibly awful souvenirs hanging out of every shop. The only way to achieve this is in the early morning when we find ourselves in a city inhabited only by locals. There is frantic maintenance going on all around. People are painting and sweeping and replacing bulbs. But mercifully the tat shops are firmly closed behind beautifully carved wooden doors with huge silver and brass handles. The low morning light streams through the narrow alleys, turning yesterday's chaos into a wonderland of golden carved stone. We have the old town square to ourselves and gaze at the astrological clock as long as we please, and with the rising sun, we walk in perfect solitude over the Karluv Most (Charles Bridge). During the day the artists, the souvenir vendors and the tour groups turn this narrow space into a New York sidewalk at peak hour. Now, as we stand quietly looking over the river, the only other people to be seen are the fisherman rowing to shore. As we climb up the uneven stone stairs to Prague Castle, a panoramic view over Prague unfolds; a soft haze of morning mist scatters the morning light veiling the city in gold. With this romantic last impression fixed in our memories, we leave Prague behind and head once more for Germany.

By the day's end we are back in the small hut in the Bavarian forest. I look back at the month and decide that this is not the way I want to travel. The constant deadlines and the hunting for addresses remind me far too much of an everyday workday. Time to change the travel mode from tourism to traveler, time to slow down just a little, and to let each day unfold as it will.

With Alexandra now on her way back to South Africa, I am itching to leave on what I consider my journey proper, but must attend to the last few things on my administration to-do list. The first thing I discover is that in spite of my having provided them with all the papers they requested over a month ago, the Chinese travel agent has done nothing to further organize my trip through China. Sitting in their small office in the centre of Munich, I cannot believe my ears. The little assistant flaps a schedule in front of my face.

'But we have worked out a schedule.'

A cursory glance reveals that it is a standard package-deal bus tour through China that anyone with a computer could download in two seconds, my requests to stay in local hotels and out-of-the-way places totally ignored. I am having serious doubts about these people, but at this late hour I am stuck with them. Other than postponing my departure – which is not really possible as the Russian travel agent is as efficient as this bunch are incompetent – my visa for Russia has been obtained and my passport is already on its way to the Kazakhstan embassy. As a stopgap measure I get a six-month Chinese tourist visa. If push comes to shove, at least I will be granted entry into China, if not the car. In order to complete the transaction I give them my credit card details – BIG mistake – but that story comes later.

On my last night in Germany, I reflect that a shared language or knowing how to celebrate a German Christmas does not grant entry into a culture. Culture is a sum of our memories, springing from a shared history. It is passed along through education, reading and learning. Culture is enlarged and improved by the arts and kept alive by living it. Under these conditions, I have as little claim to the German culture as to the South African one. This is a touch depressing until I decide that if I am to have no country's culture, I shall be totally hippy about it and become an earthling, a global citizen, picking and choosing the best from all the cultures I come across.

Ladies urinal, Winterthur

Switzerland

Beds 15 and 16

A very genteel discussion ripples around the slick glass and chrome table. Heiner leans forward, the sun making a halo of his silver hair; he believes that the only place to overnight is Poschiavo. Markus, thoughtfully untying his bright pink and purple bowtie, agrees, but feels that owing to the storm that is threatening the high passes of the Alps, I should delay my departure for a day. Ragi, ever quietly in charge, declares that I should stay another night, and Heiner should work out the most scenic and accessible route through the Alps. That decided, Markus recharges our glasses with a fine white wine – whose quality, character and suitability for drinking in the afternoon had been decided on earlier – and the conversation shifts to this afternoon's stroll about the Swiss town of Winterthur.

Winterthur was built on the ruins of a Roman settlement called Vitudurum. These ruins keep popping up at the most inconvenient times and places. Our first stop is a building site where Heiner is the architect. It has come to a complete halt as a few ancient pottery shards were discovered here and now the whole area must first undergo extensive excavation before the building of modern houses can continue.

In the old town we make our way along cobbled streets where stone fountains bubble crystal-clear water over discarded beer bottles. I am somewhat shocked at this. Isn't Switzerland meant to be obsessively neat? A hotel façade covered in graffiti puts another dent in my image of the neat Swiss. It seems that with globalization and the massive movement of people from country to country, all the pigeon-holes we have put nations in must be discarded.

On the terrace of a high-street hotel, we are enjoying the crisp air and bright sunshine when Markus casually mentions that should we want to use the toilet, this would be a good time, as there would be little opportunity later on. While this strikes me as a rather odd comment, I know by now that these quietly eccentric people weigh and consider every possibility. I therefore dutifully trot off to the ladies, where I am confronted with a toilet such as I have never seen before. I have been warned about the dreaded hole in the floor and the decreasing level of sanitation to expect as I travel east, but the last thing I expected in super-clean Switzerland was to be confronted by a toilet that would cause me concern.

In front of me, mounted on a black mosaic tile-clad wall, at just below crotch height, is a long funnel-shaped piece of white porcelain with curves on either side that I assume are to accommodate my legs. What I cannot work out is, which way do I approach the thing. Do I stand facing the wall like a man and try to aim. But unless I take my jeans off altogether, I cannot get a wide enough spread of leg, so I turn around to do the time-honored public toilet hover, but the thing is too high and the opening very small. This is ridiculous. It had to have been designed by a man. Deciding not to risk a soggy accident, I pull up my jeans and open every other door in the room until, to my relief, I find a good old toilet where, while doing the hover, I consider that the hole in the floor would probably put a lot less strain on the thighs and the brain. Back in the sunshine my new friends are looking at me with grins of anticipation; I have been the butt of a gentle joke. They too have no idea how to use the ladies' urinal.

My hosts are strangely mysterious about our next stop. We walk through the ruins of a castle. The stone walls are softened by pillows of moss from which wild fern gardens grow. Steep steps lead past walls of rock, slippery green and brown. The air is dancing with fine mist that sparkles in the late afternoon sun. A low growl that fills the narrow space seems to be coming from the rock itself. We step out of the rock tunnel and are suddenly within centimeters of a roaring wall of water that is tearing at the teeth of the rock with a ferocity that whips the water to white froth, shooting spray high in the air. The swirling wind is laden with icy droplets, allowing small rainbows to spring to life. The dazzling colors vanish as the sparkling droplets fall and soon cover us with tiny points of light. While this might sound romantic, the reality is wet and freezing. We pick our way down moss-covered stone steps into the sun and closer and closer to the water until we are standing on a platform not two meters above and built directly in the flow of the ill-tempered river.

At 23 m the Rhinefall is not high, but for so much water to be interrupted in its path to the ocean by a few impertinent rocks results in a watery temper tantrum that shakes the concrete platform. The water is moving at such a pace that looking down into the seething mass brings on a rail grabbing case of vertigo; to fall in would be instant death.

The sun rises behind a cloud of fine mist, but the weather forecast is a happy one and so, armed with Heiner's route instructions, I wish my new friends farewell. My visit in Winterthur was just as I imagined my stays with members of the international friendship organization –

Women Welcome Women World Wide or 5W for short – would be. It was warm, welcoming, and gave me instant access to the daily lives of the locals, exactly what I had hoped to achieve on this journey. Before I drive off, direction Alps, Markus wants to add his wish to the 'One planet One people' project, but is disappointed to find tolerance has already been written.

'It's not a competition for originality. If every man on the planet writes "Tolerance" that too will be fine.'

Say I, and tolerance appears for the second time, and this is good.

As the morning mist fades, the Alps come into view for the first time in weeks. Excitement wells up in my stomach and a silly grin attaches itself to my face. So looking like a close cousin of the Cheshire cat, I wind my way into the land of Heidi, where, in the green valleys, churches with wedding-cake spires preside over their congregations of steep-roofed houses. As I follow the steep switchback road, the green and yellow meadows are soon left far below, replaced by dense stands of dark pines that dwindle until there are only the rocks, the snow and the sky. At the highest point of the Julier Pass, I park the Wish Mobile next to a small stream and walk into the thin air. The cold chews at my ears as I turn in slow circles, taking in the distant peaks all round. In this white, brown and blue world high in the Alps, where the only sound is of the snowmelt rushing down the boulder-covered slopes, the realization – Freedom – shoots through my body like an electric current. Adventure! I spin around and fling my arms wide to embrace the moment, I feel as high as a kite ... and so I am, higher than I have ever been with my feet still firmly attached to the ground.

As I drive deeper into the mountains, the walls of snow rise steadily on both sides of the road, obscuring all but the blue sky above. Driving through this narrow pale blue canyon cut off from the world, my thoughts wander. Then the sun slants through an opening, and the canyon erupts in glaring white light. Blinded I narrowly avoid a collision with snow – nothing else to hit really – this is a little wake-up call. Daydreaming and driving are not a good combination. The road bends down toward Italy, leaving the snow behind. It leads through St Moritz, where the lake lies still and clear, a perfect reflection of the mountains that surround it. In the distance an elderly couple strolls slowly along the shore. Stooping, he skims a pebble, breaking the perfect reflection into a thousand bright lines. After driving through a brief springtime I arrive in Poschiavo, where the world has already warmed to summer, the trees are in full leaf, and the air thick and fragrant.

Poschiavo is, as Heiner promised, a little postcard of Italy in Switzerland. In a pale pink hotel with white lacy detail around the doors and windows, I freshen up, then amble across the cobbled village square as the sun skims the mountain peaks and slants through the pale yellow, blue and pink buildings, spotlighting a small group of tables and chairs. Across the way are a group of Italian mamas, of the svelte designer version, where every item of clothing has been considered and carefully assessed before being deemed worthy of adorning the fair lady. In comparison, I look a bit of a frump. I will have to up my standards.

The styling ladies make their way to the sunshine tables with their designer bambini in tow. The young mothers with glossy dark hair and deep brown eyes coo over their offspring, who consume chocolate ice-cream with no regard for the designer labels they are wearing. Golden bangles flash in the sun as manicured hands dab ineffectually at the chocolate-covered babes. I chuckle into my tea; children will behave like children, no matter how expensively you dress them.

When only the highest snow-covered peaks are still luminous pink against the deep blue sky, I set off in the darkening streets to find dinner. A small window spills warm light onto the cobbles. Through the doorway I see a table of locals in the middle of a raucous game of cards. I step inside, silence falls, am I interrupting a private party? But no, they were just taking a moment to look me over and deciding I look harmless break into a chorus of hearty,

'Buonasera avanti!... avanti!'

I am ushered to a table where no menu is required, as all the locals start advising me in fast and furious Italian what I should eat. As I break into uncomprehending laughter, the Mama in charge decides I will eat whatever she brings me. A small selection of antipasti, some breadsticks, a few bites of cheese and olives are accompanied by a red house wine.

The locals chat to me in broken English.

'Where are you from?'

'Cape Town, South Africa.'

Knowing nods all around the table buy time as their minds spin around the globe to try to locate Cape Town.

They try an easier question.

'Where are you going?'

'Shanghai.'

'Scusi.'

'I am driving to Shanghai.'

'Shanghai?'

'Yes, Shanghai, China.'

'Mama mia.'

This earns me my first Limón cello of the evening, presented in a glass that has its own built-in flashing light. Where do people find these things? And why do we feel they enhance our lives? I consider the energy spent in making the glass, the batteries that will soon run dry, the distinct possibility that the whole contraption will break within days. All this excess just so I can have a cheap thrill. I don't know, I think the sincerely given Limón cello would have tasted just as good in an ordinary old-fashioned glass. The pasta arrives – drawing my focus from the glass that is still creating its own very tiny disco atmosphere – the pasta is simply dressed with walnut sauce and is delicious. As I eat, the locals return to their card game. Then Mama tries to convince me to continue to eat my way through the customary six courses of an Italian dinner, without success. I am going to have to work on my appetite. But before I leave, she insists that I have another Limón cello and the entire restaurant joins in a toast to my safe journey and good health.

Villa Reale , Italy

Italy

Bed 17

My slow descent from the Italian Alps takes me to where the mountains bathe their feet in the water of Lake Como. My intention is to drive its full lazy length from Gera Lario to Como on the west leg and Lecco on the east. From the deep blue water rise conifer-covered hills, which reveal glimpses of red terracotta rooftops that hint at magnificent mansions. Imagining the fabulous lifestyle of the inhabitants of a gracious stucco villa where a yacht is slowly moving to anchor, I am not as alert as I should be, when an Italian police woman leaps into the road wielding a small lollipop sign in front of her, like some Dracula-slaying priest.

> 'Woman! You have far more faith in that thing than I would give it credit for.'

Skillfully I avoid killing the silly woman who, noticing my foreign number plates, waves me on with a flicking of the fingers before vanishing once again into the shrubbery at the side of the road.

Headlights: the Italians insist that your headlights are on during the day, and will risk life and limb to ensure that you comply. Italian drivers also have an extreme take on tailgating. They drive right up your butt; when you go fast to shake them, they go fast. When you go slow to try to get them to pass, they go slow – intercar intercourse – it is as if they are egging you on to break the speed limit for them. The only way to rid yourself of the hangers-on is to pull over and force them to drive past.

In the late afternoon, I arrive in the tiny village of Pusiano, overlooking Lago Pusiano, which lies between the two legs of Lake Como. Here it is time to test my first bit of Italian; I have been rehearsing in the car all the way around Lake Como and now it is time to perform.

> 'Bwon-jor-no.'

> 'A-vay-tay oo-na –ka-may-ra payr sta-not-tay?'

The clerk promptly assaults me with a barrage of Italian.

Whoa, an unforeseen problem. I know exactly what I am saying, but what he is saying? I have no idea. I try to stem the flow with a series of *Non ho capitos*. It takes several tries before he realizes that I understand no word. We stare at each other, stalemate. I can see the wheels turning as he thinks his way out of this situation.

'*Scuzi.*'

He vanishes for a moment. On his return he is carrying his car key.

Gesticulating, he indicates for me to follow him as he leaves his business to lead me along winding village roads, past a dairy, into a forest and up a tiny private road to a villa high on the hill overlooking the lake. He negotiates my stay, and with a grin hops in his car and drives off. I stand looking after him, somewhat dumbstruck at his gallantry. In the beautiful villa I am the only guest, and now sip Campari while the light fades and the clang clang of the local church bell tolls the dinner hour. On the distant shore the stone houses glow orange in the setting sun and water birds fly to their nests in the reeds.

My goal for tomorrow will be Bellagio. Bellagio is the Italian's Italy, the Italy of everybody's imagination – a place where red geraniums cascade over wrought-iron balustrades, and ochre plaster peels delicately off rough stonewalls. Narrow stone steps, promising hidden delights, lead steeply down to the lake, where the main shopping road is the place to strut your stuff. Dressed in elegant white linen, the Italians make their way from their soft-top sports cars to their favorite cafés, where with kisses on cheeks they settle down to coffee, pointedly ignoring the tourists that swarm around them. The tourists are easy to recognize. Glaringly dressed for comfort, they look as if they have come to do the gardening. I have by now discovered that by putting some effort into my dress, I get a far better reception from the locals, but unfortunately the camera, which is slowly being grafted to my hand, and of course the little language issue brand me as a tourist as well.

I take lunch at a small table on the water's edge. Over a crisp garden salad and crusty bread I settle into relaxed contemplation of the water, sky, mountains and the enormous villas that with their pillars, arches and elegant conifers preside graciously over their surroundings. One day, when I am filthy rich, I will buy a villa here.

Leaving Bellagio I wind my way along the lake to Como. On the way I pass a small village that has grown up right next to a high horsetail waterfall, where a group of young men sip cocktails on a balcony that teeters on the edge of the cliff, while an old woman sits reading in her small garden, oblivious to the water crashing down in front of her house. The water plunges under the road and plummets into the lake 50 meters below, where another magnificent villa, with two yachts in the harbor, gives lessons in grandiose lifestyle.

The road narrows and is soon hemmed in by houses that cling to the cliff, both left and right. The houses with their rough stonewalls crowd out the curbs and pavements, until the road becomes so narrow that traffic lights make an alternate one-way of it. This system is not really observed by the locals, so where the road makes a blind corner around a house, a great blowing of the car horn is required to warn the oncoming traffic that you are coming, but not stopping; that would be totally un-Italian. So everybody is blowing their horn and dodging wildly to avoid numerous head-on collisions, before quickly correcting their direction to avoid either driving into a house, or over the cliff, and all this is happening at a speed more appropriate for the autostrada.

With frazzled nerves I reach Como in time to join the locals for a late afternoon stroll along the promenade as the sun vanishes behind the crest of a hill and the city of Como fades into a blue and white mist. Steps lead down and into the water where candy-stripe wooden poles act as anchor points for non-existent boats. The stone arches that support the promenade are softened by cascades of delicate flowers that anchor themselves in the nooks and cracks of the rock. Aiming my camera to capture the contrast between hard grey stone and soft white flowers, a man, watching me intently, comes into focus in the viewfinder.

With a small rush of adrenaline, I realize that the man watching me from above has been following me since I started my stroll along the lake, and now the promenade is empty of people. Typical, just when one could use a little moral support, there is suddenly no one to be found. The gaze of the man from above is becoming a touch unnerving, but I have always believed that attack is the best line of defense, so give him a cool appraising stare, to let him know he has been seen, assessed and found wanting. Then I turn away deliberately in what I hope is a highly disdainful fashion. He continues to stare. This calls for more physical action. Climbing the stairs I walk past and beat him about the head with my camera – actually no, I merely zap him with a look of pure venom, then nose in the air stride away. He does not follow: either my look worked or I was mistaken and just put another brick of misunderstanding onto the wall between men and women.

But now I discover I am confronted with a more serious problem. I have forgotten where I parked the car. Forgetting where you parked your car in a parking lot at the local supermarket can be solved eventually, or as a last measure you could call a friend. Forgetting where I parked my car in a huge unknown city, of which I have no map, and even if I had a map, I have no idea what the road was called where I left the car, and of course I have a little issue with the language, so calling anyone for help is all but impossible. Turning in confused circles as the blue shadows deepen to black and the last commuters hurry to board the bus boats that will take them to their homes, I force myself to stand very quietly in the empting plaza and allow my panic to fade with the light. The Wish Mobile cannot be too far away. Mentally I evoke my random path through Como, turning the corners in my mind until I lift my head and walk purposefully directly to where the Wish Mobile waits. With relief, I sink into the driver's seat. Where I park the car is really something I will need to pay more attention to in the future.

The next morning's breakfast is an in-car affair while overlooking the view from the Capella Alpi, high in the mountains outside Bergamo. As the bell tolls seven, villagers walk by, staring at me with silent suspicion. As I watch them vanish into the dark of the church, I realize that with freedom comes loss. For the next year I will always be a stranger and my lack of language will create barriers that I will have to overcome purely with behavior. This is a challenge that will force me to step out of a comfort zone that is not just physical, but deeply personal. Being an observer will not be good enough anymore. I will need to allow myself to be fully absorbed in the company of those whom I meet. I am not sure that this is what I signed up for.

But there is no time to dwell on this problem, as on this glorious sun-drenched day, the whole of the west of Italy seems to be moving east, to Venice on the Autostrada 4. I don't get far before I am brought to a grinding halt by the unfamiliar obstacle of the Italian toll plaza. What is the system here? I search frantically for a little symbol with a man in a hat holding some cash, but nothing, just lots and lots of Italian, and various signs and symbols that are completely meaningless to me. Not understanding why the cars do not slow down as they pass through the gates – are they all equipped with electronic chips – I park on a small island in the roar of traffic to give myself a moment. Which gate should I approach? I consider simply driving up to the nearest gate to see what will happen, but the image of me getting stuck is similar to those rocks at the Rhinefall, instant furious pandemonium, as the Italians are not shy to vent their spleen. Standing in the stink and noise of the highway, I feel like a complete twit, and then a voice in deeply accented English throws me a lifeline.

'Wha-te arre you do-ing?'

'I have no idea.'

'Hav-e you brok-en down?'

Does this question cover nervous breakdown? Probably not.

'I don't know how these tollgates work and am terrified to cause a major traffic jam if I get it wrong.'

The cute Italian in the car rolls his eyes to confirm what I am feeling: what kind of idiot is this woman?

'You jus-te drri-ve thrrough any gate, excep-te de Telepass, grab-be de ticket the machi-ne spit at you and whe-ne you get off de highway, den-e you pay.'

Everything is simple when you know how.

Using my newly found knowledge, I confidently drive up to the first tollgate when exiting the highway at Cremona. And, you guessed it, got it wrong. Of all the gates I could choose, I chose the one that only accepts Italian credit cards and, as expected, within seconds the traffic behind me builds up to a frothing hooting mass. Then the man in the hat, whom I have been hunting for, suddenly appears in very unfriendly fashion at my window. As I roll it down, he greets me with a blast of irritated Italian.

'Pardon, non comprehendo.'

Is my meek response.

He looks at me in disgust, storms off and, pushing a hidden button, opens the gate. Waving me through with a flick of his hand, he releases every irritation he has ever had to endure in that one small gesture. But it doesn't take me long to work out that I have just saved myself about 7€, and a fiendishly clever plan starts to hatch in my head – which I attempt to put into practice at the very next tollgate. But the Italians were not born yesterday. The next autostrada off-ramp is one step ahead of my devious money-saving plan and has a lane especially reserved for tourists. It says so in several languages; drat, foiled again.

Bed 18

In Cremona, all plans to see specific things are chucked out when I realise that if I am going to be set in my aims and desires, I could end up spending my whole trip being lost and confused, with all my attention focused on a map. If, however, wherever I am is the right place to be, I can spend my entire trip being in the moment, as opposed to waiting for the moment to happen. So I don't find the Stradivari Museum, assuming there is one, but Antonio Stradivari – of violin-building fame – is Cremona's most famous son, so I guess it must be here somewhere. I don't find the nougat for which Cremona is famous, but I do find myself flat on my face in the middle of the road, the result of too much looking up and about, and not enough paying attention to the pavement. So there I am, sprawled on the not-too-clean pavement of Cremona, just taking a moment to gather enough strength to spring up, dust myself off, pretend that it never happened, and get on with my life. But the Italians are faster than me, and leap to my aid with such loud expressions of regret and extravagant attempts to help me up that my private little 'flat on my face moment' becomes a very public spectacle. If this were the movies, some handsome and of course rich Italian man would insist that I sit down and have a coffee to recover; we would chat, fall in love, and live happily ever after. But in the real world I am just embarrassed and a touch irritated; okay already, move along, I am fine, there is nothing to see here.

But there is something to see as I have accidentally found the Torrazzo, the bell tower of the Duomo di Cremona. It is the symbol of Cremona, the tallest pre-modern tower in Italy and the second highest brick tower in the world; so not a terribly difficult thing to find really. Getting to the top of the 112.7 m Torrazzo tower involves climbing 338 marble steps, 70 spiral stone steps, 86 wooden steps and then 59 steps up a free-standing spiral staircase, which is not recommended for those suffering from vertigo. Finally I reach the top, heart rate up, muscles aching and heaving breath: a good workout with spectacular reward.

From above, the city is a sea of terracotta, a sharp contrast against the verdigris of the pointed church steeples. The city streets extend like the spokes of a wheel from the cathedral, and my vantage point allows me voyeuristic glimpses into lush private gardens that are hidden at ground level. Far below, the locals are gathering in the church square. At small café tables they enjoy their mid morning coffee in the sun. Those without tables lounge on the pink and grey marble steps or lean against the grey stone pillars of the main facade of the Duomo di Cremona. When I get back on ground floor, I amble back to the car via the flower market, using the turn-by-turn directions I had noted in a small pad; losing the car is not something I want to do again.

Back on the road, I change my route on the spur of the moment. I want to see the sea, so instead of heading to Bologna, I get on the A15 and head for the Mediterranean and Carrara instead. The autostrada carries me in gentle curves over high bridges and through deep mountain valleys. Slowly the broad leaf trees of the north that reach up to the sun, their brilliant green leaves greedy for every bit of light, are replaced by the somber green shrubs and hard spiky leaves of the south, where the vegetation recoils from the heat, growing low and dark against the ground. My excitement at reaching the Mediterranean is dealt a blow as I stop at Marina di Carrara, which, with its unappealing brown sand, complete with all the tatty beachfront trimmings and sad off-season hotels, is just depressing. The Mediterranean will have to wait.

Turning away from the sea to look at the mountains I believe for a moment that they are covered in snow; then the dazzling reality of the Carrara marble so beloved by Michelangelo hits home. The Apuan Alps of Carrara are solid marble where, over the centuries, man has made perfect cliffs that bounce the pale light like giant reflectors into the valley and around the small city of Carrara. Carrara floats in a hazy cloud of sparkling dust. The world here seems slightly out of focus and the colors just a little less brilliant than the surrounding areas. Following a switchback road I reach a high 'Cave', where the soft stone is cut deep out of the mountain, creating cathedral caves with soaring walls of fine white marble. The sun breaks through the clouds and sends me scrambling for sunglasses to watch as cranes swing giant blocks of marble across the face of the cliffs. Getting the giant marble blocks cut and transported down the narrow and treacherous mountain road must still be a logistical nightmare; in the days of Michelangelo, the work with handsaws, wooden wedges, log rollers and ox wagons must have been life threatening.

In Carrara I start to wonder about how the value of a thing is defined. These mountains are the birthplace of David, and provided Michelangelo with his favorite sculpting material, but in Carrara it is the only stone available and has been used to serve the most mundane purpose. It forms the roadside curbs and lines the walls of the public toilets. The steps leading to the stone-cutters' houses are Carrara marble, while everywhere else in the world it is highly prized and can only be obtained at huge cost. A pink blush creeps over the marble cliffs, warning me that night is coming and, as I can find no accommodation in Carrara and the concept of sleeping in the Wish Mobile is still a bit out there, I consult my map, then hot-foot it to Lucca, which is the next big centre down the drag.

Lucca is one of Italy's great cities, once rivaling Florence for wealth and general magnificence. Today it retains its historical beauty behind a fully intact wall from the Renaissance era that shields the ancient city from the modern world. The arched gates lead into a city of narrow alleys, tiny shops and restaurants. As Lucca has a reputation for serving the best food in Tuscany, I stop off in a small and intimate restaurant – couples occupy most of the tables – possibly not the best choice for a single woman. Not wanting to seem nosy by staring at the diners all around me, I stare out of the window and conclude that eating alone in a restaurant is not really the problem. The problem is waiting for a menu, waiting for service, waiting for food, waiting for plates to be cleared, waiting for the bill and finally waiting for the money to be collected. These are all spaces in time designed to be filled with conversation. Alone, staring out of the window onto the street, I merely wait and watch the road outside, where a river of tourists flows around deeply stooped beggar women hidden in black rags; their small plastic cups remain forever empty. The throng steps lightly past a man on his knees with his head touching the pavement, his empty cap laid out beside him, while the tourists spend and spend on meaningless knickknacks that will soon gather dust on some forgotten shelf.

The following morning visitors stream through every gate, renting bicycles and buying maps. The flood of people fills the narrow streets, creating a relentless current in which individual choice is lost. To avoid the clamor, I explore the back roads of Lucca, which are silent, empty and cool in the morning shadows. I am soon lost in a maze of alleys with high walls, weathered doors and shutters in fading shades of blue and green, which hint at lives that are hidden from prying tourist eyes. Around an ochre corner a man approaches with a bouquet of red roses in his bicycle basket. A heavy wooden door opens, a young girl with a basket overflowing with white daises and carnations appears; the shaft of sunlight from the briefly glimpsed garden behind her draws a golden halo through her hair and flowers. For a moment, she glows against the dark stone wall, then the door closes, and she steps into the everyday – where there are family groups everywhere, mothers and fathers with children in tow, eating ice-cream, sitting in street cafés. The atmosphere is so warm and inviting I want to be a part of it, and take a seat at a small table where I trot out my normal,

'Do you speak English?'

The waitress looks at me in delighted surprise.

'You're from South Africa.'

And so is she – got married to the man who will be cooking my lunch. She is so sorry, would love to chat, but she has lots to do; they are fully booked as it is Mother's Day. What a pity, I was just beginning to believe the massed flowers, the sense of family and happy serenity were everyday occurrences among the Lucchesi.

Beds 19 and 20

This corner of Italy is the home of several of the great cities of the Renaissance, and as Sienna, Florence and Pisa are all a short drive from Lucca, I decide to stay awhile and find a room in an old country house in the tiny village of St Genese. Here red poppies line the country lanes and the farmers drive their tractors to work while, under a pergola in the garden, my toes curling in the soft green grass, I enjoy possibly the unhealthiest breakfast in the world. The Tuscan breakfast is a medley of sweet tarts, biscotti, sweet croissants with sweet jam, and yet another sweet cake, all of which are washed down with strong coffee – allowing you to fly on caffeine and sugar high for about an hour then, before you crash, more coffee is required.

Sugar fuelled, I feel the sudden urge to be the domestic goddess of all I possess, which thankfully is not much. I hang my washing in the field below the stone house where red poppies, darting swallows, emerald green lizards and white petals floating in the breeze conspire to make even doing the laundry seem romantic. In between doing the domestic goddess thing, I paint in the garden and wander down the neighborhood road that winds through intensely farmed fields of olives, peas, beans, corn and pumpkin, and yet there is still room for wild flowers in clashing shades of purple, red and yellow.

A day of silence and domestic ritual has revived me for the sightseeing marathon I now embark on. Starting with a quick trip to the Villa Reale, the once-home of Napoleon's sister Elisa Bonaparte Baciocchi, who, when Napoleon took control of the city-state of Lucca, was put in charge as 'Queen of Etruria', much to the amusement of the established royals. The estate is still in private hands and only the gardens are open to the public. Being the only person here –which in Italy is a miracle that can only be achieved by having one's own transport and traveling on the spur of the moment – the guide considers it too much effort to do the guided tour and sends me inside to wander as I please. This is a brilliant bit of good fortune that sees me poking my nose in where guided tours never go.

The gardens are impressive, but what really gets my imagination going is the deserted and falling into ruins villa on the property. In the inner square of the ruin, heavy stone planters are still tended by the gardeners; they stand in manicured green contrast to the peeling ochre walls. Old rooms are decorated with abandoned urns and wheelbarrows. Windows, cracked and cobwebbed, allow the soft evening light into the ancient kitchen, making mystery of the old coal stove. Up silent marble stairs I reach two very large locked doors. Peering through the keyhole brings no reward; broken pillars end under a phantom floor, its existence now only confirmed by the tracings on the wall and mysterious bricked-up openings that in a time of faded history led somewhere. The crumbling ruin puts me in melancholy frame of mind. The invisible remains of life once lived here create silvery cobwebs in the air that send cold shivers down my spine.

Honeysuckle sweetens the evening air as I stroll along the formal footpaths of the water garden that is fed by ornate fountains. The water flows in strictly ordered canals, past moss-covered pedestals on which stand marble urns so large that they could house full-grown trees. In the gathering dusk I reach Pan's grotto where, surrounded by nightmarish fish and monstrous creatures emerging out of underworld slime, being all alone no longer seems such a good idea. But the gardens are huge and I am right at the bottom end. A brisk, slightly edgy walk takes me past a lake, a giant topiary garden, a small forest, a massive waterfall fountain and an intricate flower carpet, to the Villa Reale. The shuttered house stands as a monument to the lives of the very wealthy, where grand houses stand waiting in constant readiness for owners that might never return. In the service buildings behind the main house, dusty windows reveal an enormous children's playroom, a world of villas and gardens in child-size miniature. Old-fashioned pink roses perfume the air, but the silent melancholy remains. It is time to leave, and a good thing too. The gatekeeper was about to come and look for me; he is not happy; his supper must be getting cold. Locking the gate in a huff, he speeds off in his rust-streaked white Fiat.

In the heat of the next day I visit Pisa, where the famous tower and surrounding buildings are huge and decorated like wedding cakes. The tower leans and it leans a lot; it is rather a good testament to the cement and building craft of the day, if not to their choice of location. The buildings are impressive, but it is the visiting masses that are the true attraction. They are pushing and heaving at midair, photographers directing a little left, a little right. A whole lawn full of superheroes:

apparently you have not done Pisa, unless you have a photograph in your album of you holding up the tower. Florence is an hour away by autostrada and this is my next goal.

Leaving the Wish Mobile on the outskirts of the old town I make my way through inner-city suburbs to the historic centre; my quest is to find David. Armed once again with only a shred of a map, I find myself in a narrow side street, where a man with an ugly dog steps out of a beautiful doorway. A woman with skinny trousers and 10-cm black patent leather stilettos cycles by. A section of wall has become an impromptu neighborhood notice board, where things and services are for sale, wanted and to rent. As I close in on the historic centre, I pass tiny cafés that have hit on an ingenious way to enlarge their floor space. During the day they set up a small platform in the parking space in front of their shops. Within minutes a piece of tarmac is transformed into a wood-floor terrace with tables, chairs, bright umbrellas, and even the obligatory flowerboxes overflowing with fake geraniums. The transformation is impressive, as is the sudden shift from Florence local neighborhood to tourist central.

By turning a corner the quiet side street is replaced by the heated bustle of hawkers' stalls, selling everything from the leatherwear for which Florence is famous to African curios and the pirated brand-name sunglasses that no such market can be without. Tourists throng in standard tourist garb: sleeveless tight-fitting t-shirts, in pastel shades that show every wrinkle and roll to full effect, combined with ill-fitting khaki shorts for the women; striped golf shirts straining over well-padded stomachs and khaki shorts, held up by sheer mystery, for the men. What we all have in common are good comfortable walking shoes, in glaring contrast to the locals, who wear only the latest in footwear fashion, comfort be damned.

My mission to find David continues; I find several churches, a post office, which I put to good use, a couple of lesser sculptures, and then I stumble upon the Duomo of Florence. The Santa Maria del Fiore is intricately clad in black and white marble, but the queue to go into this fourth largest church in Europe has proportions more impressive than the church. It snakes around the huge piazza, where on the steps and dirty pavements exhausted tourists – the envy of all their friends back home – sit and lie in the sun, waiting their turn to see the beauty within. Not me. I will come back in the cold heart of winter and perhaps manage to see the attractions of Florence without the distraction of the queue.

My quest to find David is thwarted again as I find instead the River Arno and the Ponte Veccio, a very old bridge upon whose spine the butchers of Florence once traded. At some point the Medici decided that the butchers were too smelly and they got booted out in favor of the goldsmiths. Today these craftsmen have also vanished, and all that remains are tiny jewelers' stores whose glittering merchandise competes for the tourists' attention with the gelaterias, who display their mouthwatering wares in huge whipped piles of decadent delight. Choosing which of the flavors I will try absorbs my full attention for long delicious minutes. Shall I attempt to be healthy and go for the fruity flavors or just let it all hang out and go for creamy … creamy.

Gelato in hand I cross the Arno River to reach the royal rooms of the Medici in the Palazzo Pitti. But although Catherine de' Medici was rumored to be a great fan of gelato, and it appeared regularly as dessert at the royal banquets, gelatos are not allowed inside today. My delicious hazelnut and chocolate confection is far too good to discard. The royal rooms will have to wait, while I do the acceptable tourist thing, sit myself on the nearest marble step, and enjoy the cool creamy delight before entering the palace, which is itself a decadent confection of gold and pomp, hand-painted tiles, trompe l'oeil and ceilings rampant with angels and chariots. Walls are covered top to bottom with paintings, by every Italian master in memory, with a couple of Spanish and Dutch chaps thrown in just to round out the selection.

Getting through the Palazzo takes hours, and now the sun is starting to dip really low. I must make a concerted and focused effort to find the David fellow, how hard can it be? He hasn't moved in centuries. Actually he has. The real David has been living in the Academy of Fine Arts in Florence for a couple of hundred years, but the copy should still be in the original spot. To speed things along a bit I hatch a brilliant plan, which involves following the first tour group that crosses my path. They lead me down an unlikely-looking ally, past some famous old olive tree then, by sheer fluke, I am face to pedestal with the man/boy himself. He looks like a bit of a wuss; I much prefer the arrogant stare and manly figure of Neptune to his right. But whatever your taste in male physique, the determination, patience and vision of the old masters to carve these colossi out of huge blocks of brittle stone is awe inspiring. When returning to my car I discover that Florence has beauty in the most mundane places, even the street lampposts are a somewhat obscene delight. This is sure evidence of what art-loving patrons with pots of money can achieve.

Leaving Lucca for Orbetello, on the Mediterranean coast, my route will take me through Sienna. But first a quick stop to try out my changing tent. I have totally underdressed and am freezing. At the first *statione servicio* I unfurl the tent and proceed to get changed in the middle of the parking lot. Using the lady's rest rooms would be easier, but this method adds a nice little surreal note to my day and now, properly dressed, Sienna, which some claim to be the most beautiful city in the world

I get to Sienna far too early; the city is only just wiping the sleep from its eyes; and all major attractions will only be opening their doors at 10h30. I don't feel like waiting for opening time and the accompanying masses, so I wander about the empty streets, dodging the street-sweeping trucks and watching the tradesmen set out their wares. Purple eggplants against a red stone wall and a twig of red cherries dropped under a stone eagle fountain make good photographs. But who ever said Sienna is the most beautiful city in the world must have been a paid travel writer. It is not bad; maybe it is just not at its best first thing in the morning.

In Orbetello I will be visiting Carla from 5W, who read about my trip and invited me to stay for the weekend. She is keen to know all about my journey, and I am looking forward to being in company again. She is tall and elegant with a fiery temperament. She introduces herself with a thousand questions and immediately analyses the wishes on my car. Psychotherapist by profession she, by some strange psychic coincidence, homes in on the wish of another psychotherapist. Very odd that.

> *'When you come to a new place, observe, learn, participate; don't dominate.'*

This she proceeds to interpret in all sorts of ways that I had not even considered. Apparently this is not so much a wish for the world, but a comment on my character. I consider this possibility, but then decide to stick with the original plan: I will not judge what men write. I will merely provide the vehicle on which to write.

Carla lives a gracious life in a villa high on the hill, overlooking the deep blue water of the Mediterranean. We sip a cup of tea on the terrace, where I learn that she was once married to a prince. But she warns me that all Italian men are so spoilt by their mothers that they never really grow up, and are always tied to their mothers' apron strings. Also, that their reputation for being good lovers is a bit of yes and a bit of no. They are apparently very good at the initial romance, the flowers and the love songs, but once the conquest has been made, they have no idea what to do next. I file this nugget of information away in case I should ever be wooed by an Italian.

Going to explore Carla's world of sun, sea and brown-black beaches, I follow a footpath to a restaurant, which has rented the beach between it and the sea. Here the sand is impeccably clean and swept to billiard-table perfection.

A reed fence demarcates the restaurant's property, and once that boundary has been breached, the shock of the mountains of litter on the beach gets me to thinking about the ways of man. Why is it that we have the incredible urge to sully all that is beautiful? Or perhaps it is just sheer laziness that prevents us from taking the containers that are full when we arrive back home when they are empty. They are lighter, squashable, put-in-a-bagable; what can be so hard about cleaning up after ourselves?

But walking along the water's edge and seeing the garbage bobbing about in the sea and the sheer scale of the litter problem here makes me suspect that this little cove has an unfortunate current configuration. This ensures that all the garbage that is deposited in the streets, then swept into the storm water drains of the surrounding towns, eventually lands on this beach. This forms a tiny part of a global problem that is mainly invisible. There are hidden islands of garbage in the Pacific. One of these has the highly descriptive name of the Great Pacific Garbage Patch, and it is bigger than Texas. This litter never vanishes. In time the plastic breaks down into smaller and smaller particles until it eventually forms part of the food chain. The consequence is that when you throw down your piece of litter in the street, that litter will eventually end up back on your plate.

Over our last breakfast together Carla expresses the wish that I find love. This is a statement so personal and out of context of the conversation that I am taken aback – what unconscious signals am I sending out – but I am also deeply touched by her honesty. She warns me that it is no life without love. Humans need to love and be loved, and should never stop striving for love. I carefully wrap that bit of wisdom in a to-go bag so I can chew it over on the way to Rome.

Bed 21

In Italy they say, all roads lead to Rome and privately all non-Roman Italians say all Romans are mad. And there seems to be truth in this. The Romans pride themselves on their expert driving abilities, but whether simply doing as you please and hoping that nobody else minds is good driving, I am not about to judge. As I enter the city, all street markings are abandoned and it is only the signage on a variety of poles that tries desperately to control the traffic flow. But as the signs are highly prized by graffiti artists and often vandalized, they can be mainly ignored for their original purpose. Traffic lights, when they are to be found, are merely suggestions not to be taken seriously. If you are in a side street and want to get into the main traffic flow, slowly, slowly edge forward until it is no longer possible for the oncoming traffic to go around you. This is the moment for decisive action; now is the time for speed; nothing to it. If, however, you expect somebody to actually, willingly, give way for you or expect a break in the traffic flow, you are going nowhere.

The same goes for the pedestrian traffic. You have the right of way at a pedestrian crossing, but nobody is going to give it to you; you have to take it. But you cannot grab that right, you will die. It is once again a matter of gently, gently stepping into the traffic flow, with your eyes firmly and sternly fixed on the oncoming vehicles, paying extra attention to the mopeds; they really don't like slowing down, let alone stopping for pedestrians. Now that you have started moving, do not hesitate; slowly and with determination move forward and, like Moses parting the sea, you will get across unscathed. And like Moses you will be leading a whole slew of pedestrians used to more disciplined driving conditions through the tempest and they will be grateful. How a Swiss tourist ever comes out of Rome alive is a mystery. In Switzerland the pedestrians abuse the right of way with aggressive arrogance, so that huge traffic jams build up because the pedestrians simply walk into the road, without so much as a glance at the oncoming traffic, completely confident that the cars will stop – not just slow down, but come to a complete and absolute halt, as the pedestrians dribble across the road. Swiss pedestrians and Roman drivers, now that must be an interesting mix.

An early morning bus ride deposits me in the centre of Rome. It is a place of giants wrestling with serpents that writhe between their legs, and naked goddesses leap out of fountains on the bare backs of wild white horses. Priests in black tunics stare in befuddled confusion at ticket-vending machines that vend no tickets. Nuns drink pure water from dirty fountains while plainclothes policemen play cat and mouse with illegal vendors. Rome is a place where gentle aging has become just plain filthy and the sewers heave and burp under the flood of humanity. Mom and Pop Tourist, who have been saving for years to live out the Italian dream, now stand for hours in the sweltering heat, without bench or shade or indication of the length of queue they are in, to see fleeting glimpses of long imagined sights. They buy massively overpriced lunches from the street vendors, which they eat like beggars, sitting on filthy sidewalks, where they share the crumbs of their takeout lunch with the fat grey pigeons that waddle from group to group like officious ticket collectors. The wail of ambulances is constantly in the background as another grey-haired tourist succumbs to dehydration or heatstroke. Exhausted tourists and don't-care Romans face off over extravagant entry fees. The Romance of Italy is not to be found on a package tour bus.

Watching the hundreds of tourist groups, bound in brief brotherhood by a particular color of hat or scarf, standing in a queue that snakes the perimeter of St Peters Square, I realize that today to be alone in the Sistine Chapel or St Peters would be to be the Pope. I decide to keep my old memories: of being able to walk about the Sistine Chapel at will, even climbing the hundreds of stairs to the levels just under the famous ceiling – memories of walking quite alone between the giant pillars of St Peters, and the cool silence of the basilica that, when disturbed by a whispered prayer, reverberated slightly like the shimmering reflection of a pond stroked by a breeze. In my memory the Pieta is unprotected and lit only by a high window. I remember gazing in confusion at the sculpture; it seemed to me impossible that it was knocked out of stone with a hammer and a chisel. I reached out to gently touch the hem of her skirt, fully convinced it might be soft. The realization that a human created this filled me with awe and confirmed to me what art is and why we need it. It is to know you belong to a species that can create such superlative beauty, which inspires us all to do better. But the Pieta was created in a time when artists could say with confidence;

'It matters not how long it takes, but that it is beautiful.'

Today whether it is beautiful is a question too quaint to contemplate. Time is the thing. And time is money, so the crowds shuffle slowly in and out of these famous places, never once allowed the sheer luxury of silent solitary contemplation of the beauty surrounding them.

Leaving the tour groups to their misery, I duck into a back street and come across a church wholesaler, where I discover that it costs a lot to furnish a Catholic church. The chalice, the cheapest one I saw, 550€; a Jesus figure on a cross anything up to 2500€, depending on size; Madonna figure, around 700€; candles 6€ per kilo. No wonder churches have changed to electric candles. In tiny streets local craftsmen labor to sew the perfect shirt or re-gild yet other 400-year-old putti. A carpenter puts the final polish on gleaming dark wood chairs and, balancing high on a scaffold, a lone artisan repairs ancient stucco leaves that have fallen from the high church towers. The Pantheon requests silence in every language, but the masses babble and the children scream. Leaving the noise, I find an empty cathedral with unadvertised works of the Renaissance masters. Here I stare as long as I please at beautiful ceilings and get nose to toe with a lesser known Michelangelo sculpture; tree-climbing toes those.

At lunch I stop in a restaurant and pay an extravagant price in exchange for a limp salad, a glass of water, and a place to sit out of the sun and, most importantly, for the use of a toilet. The life of a tourist is never knowing when you will find the next toilet. Replenished and relieved, I wander to the Trevi Fountain, where I think I finally grasp the meaning behind mass tourism. It is the pursuit of photographic trophies of oneself in front of famous and preferably far-off sights that you can show the less fortunate back home. But at the Trevi Fountain the tourist crush in the small piazza is such that people must climb lampposts and the steps of the buildings opposite just to get a glimpse of the famous horses. To actually be close enough to throw a coin into the fountain is like getting front-row tickets to a Robbie Williams concert and to achieve a photograph of just you and the fountain would be the equivalent of a back-stage pass.

By late afternoon I arrive at the Colosseum, where my imagination fills the crumbling seats with 50 000 toga-ed Romans. In my mind's eye, the wooden boards that cover the gladiators' cells and animal cages below slowly turn red as wild animals and gladiators fight desperately to a bloody savage death. The air, filled with the smell of perfumed oils, sweat and blood, reverberates as thousands roar and howl their approval. I yank my mind back into the present, and wonder whether we have changed much since then. Death and carnage still fascinate; only today we get our violence fix properly sanitized and plastic-wrapped in cinemas and on television.

On the Colosseum Square, to sounds of a huge American brass band, complete with gladiator helmets and flag swirling dancing girls, a bent old lady trundles a baby carriage towards me. From behind pieces of ancient Rome appear, like magic, dozens of cats. The old lady reveals that her baby carriage contains only cat food, and the cats, knowing this, gather in anticipation. I watch the ritual and wonder at the need for old women to feed cats and old men to feed pigeons. These creatures don't really need human help, but I think the humans need to feed the creatures in order to feel that they are doing something of value. Perhaps the worst part of being old is the feeling of uselessness in a world obsessed by youth. I believe this is one of the prime reasons humanity doesn't move out of its endless destructive cycle. As soon as humans have obtained a modicum of wisdom, they are deemed old and therefore useless, and the world turns its ear to some new wunderkind, who spouts the same gumpf that we've all heard before, only in different slang. As the sun sets, the lady trundles off and the cats vanish into the city to move onto the main course of rats and sleeping pigeons.

Beds 22 and 23

Leaving Rome behind, I set off into the highlands of the Appennino Abruzese. A little winding road, hemmed in by dry stone walls and poppies, takes me up a hill where the view of Tivoli across the valley becomes the background to my lunch of cheese, bread, peaches and water. A vagabond traveler with a rucksack on his back draws my attention from the waterfall view. He strolls up to the church across the road, knocks firmly on the massive wooden doors, and after a brief wait, a blue-frocked man of the church appears. A few words are exchanged, and five minutes later the man in the frock presents the scruffy fellow with a delicious-looking lunch of bread, soup, salad and a bottle of water. Scruffy man shares the wall at polite distance; together and yet apart we eat our lunch in silent contemplation of Tivoli and its giant waterfall.

The old road to L'Aquila winds up, down, around and sometimes through the Appennino. The falling petals of the wild chestnuts hover, torn between the pull of gravity and the push of tarmac thermals, until the turbulence of my slipstream sends them spiraling down the mountainside. On the high plateau of Avezzano, Italy has kicked off its fashionable, painful, high heels and has put on comfortable slippers. The squabble of space has been left behind on the Roman plains. Here the houses spread out ranch-style; small agricultural fields blend into huge fields of wild flowers, where white sheepdogs tend their woolly charges free of human intervention.

This is Italy's big-sky country where the high snow-covered peaks march far into the distance. I play with the idea of sleeping in the

Wish Mobile, and even choose a spot with a far-away view, but the cooling afternoon warns me that my car will be a fridge before long and I am still not quite ready for camping. In a small village I try my slightly improved Italian on an old man smoking his pipe on a flower-laden balcony.

'*Scuzi.*'

'*Buonasera.*'

'*Dov e l'albergo piu vicino?*'

He looks at me, waiting. I attempt this small request again, trying to put a bit more Italian swing into it.

'*Do ve l'albergo pee yoo ve chee no?*'

This time round he understands, but then bombards me with Italian words, so many words, which ones are important, which ones can I ignore? He stops talking for a moment and looks at me expectantly. I have no idea how to respond, so shrug my shoulders and smile ruefully. I am beginning to believe that understanding a language is far more difficult than speaking it. Unable to break through the language barrier I accept there will be no small Italian village hotel and home cooking for me this evening, and find a hotel in the student town of L'Aquila. Here I eat a midnight pizza on the square in the company of Italy's youth that drink red wine and flirt to the rhythm of Italian pop music.

Descending from the Gran Sasso d'Italia, the fields of flowers change from white to yellow and finally, down at sea level, fields of brilliant red poppies strike a strangely disturbing note among the fields of patchwork green. My sightseeing stop for today is Loreto, which prides itself on having the next most impressive basilica to St Peters in the Vatican. The mood is somber in this pilgrimage church. Visitors wait patiently in queues to confess to grey-bearded priests in brown frocks that sit in pools of warm light in gleaming dark wood confessionals. A small chapel with a dizzying array of angels, putti, figures of saints and sinners, all woven together in a cool marble silence, is dwarfed by the soaring vaulted ceiling of the basilica. A queue files slowly through the chapel door. I join in and discover that this is not just a chapel, but the resting place of the 'holy house', the actual house of the Virgin Mary that was airlifted here from Nazareth by a host of indecisive angels. Apparently the holy house was first landed in Croatia, then in Recanti, before it ended up here, and then the ornate marble screen and basilica were built around it.

Because of all this flying about, Our Lady of Loreto was appropriately named patron saint of pilots. Back in the basilica, a priest caught in a ray of light prays fervently. A young nun curtseys and crosses herself before crossing the floor. A small child is lifted by his father to put a coin into an offer stand; his reward, a light bulb flickers to life, I wonder how much 'on' time his coin bought him. Looking at images of Mary, Jesus and various saints that I recognize from the church wholesaler in Rome, I wonder whether anyone can set up shop to make and sell these images or are they copyrighted and need a papal blessing to turn them from banal merchandise into holy images worthy of the bowed heads and prayers of the faithful.

Beds 24 and 25

Loreto is in the Italian province of Acona, where rolling green hills are dotted and lined with olive trees and grapevines, and the Italians are very thorough when signposting the villages. For the next week, I will be staying in Cupra Montana and am looking forward to sitting still and seeing nothing new. But first I have to find the place. This is a touch complicated as at every one of the hundreds of traffic circles, huge signs list every village within a day's drive in every direction. To try and find the next village I am looking for requires me to drive around the circles several times, speed-reading as I go, and I still end up getting lost.

For directions, I stop at a monastery, but stepping through the arched doors I am confronted by a scene straight out of an Italian lifestyle advert. The monastery now houses a restaurant, and the enclosed courtyard glows golden in the reflected light of the pale stone walls. A long table dressed in white linen stands under the dappled shade of the trees. In generous chairs sits the chef and proprietor, surrounded by his staff and the crumbs of their lunch; the head waiter has just brought him his cognac and coffee. He glances at

me from under heavy brows as he sips his coffee, his handsome face framed by well-maintained five o'clock shadow. Leaning back to savor his cognac he slowly looks me over ,and I notice he is a large man, but where other men of his girth might evoke the reaction, get thee to a gymnasium, he somehow manages to be very appealing, in much the same way as some big women are voluptuous and others simply fat.

I attempt my Italian again; he gives me about thirty seconds of airtime, smiles, shakes his head, and sends for his phone; calls my hostess; gets directions, then leaves his coffee and cognac to escort me to my goal. Generosity of spirit or perhaps he felt he would get back to his cognac faster this way? No chance, together with my new hostess and the translation on the back of the Wish Mobile I convince him to add to the 'One planet One people' artwork. He dutifully writes a wish, wishes me well and kisses me soundly on both cheeks, hmm … cute. But I have so many administrative things to do that any thoughts of a brief Italian romance immediately get pushed aside.

Months earlier Annette and I had arranged to meet up in Italy. At the time I thought it would be fun. Now I discover that I have moved further into my silence than I had realized, and have no real inclination to talk about life back in Munich, or to answer any questions about my plans. My mind is open, looking forward and my internal compass faces due east. I leave my friends to their sightseeing as I make calls, e-mail, make reservations and shout at my tardy Chinese travel agents who have still not even presented me with an acceptable schedule, let alone a price. Then my portable phone rings and a male voice introduces himself.

'I am calling from the Kazakhstan embassy.'

A small thrill runs through me, the Kazakhstan embassy.

'Yes?'

'We are finalizing your visa and need to be sure you do not require a re-entry visa.'

'No, I will be traveling through China to Shanghai.'

is my nonchalant reply.

'Very well then, goodbye.'

I sit grinning to myself like some demented cartoon character when slowly the shouting match I have just had with the Chinese travel agent creeps back into my mind. An unpleasant image of myself stuck in some no-man's-land, with no entry visa into China and no re-entry into Kazakhstan, wipes the grin off my face.

Thoughts like these are not something that day-to-day life can prepare you for.

For a brief moment I consider flying back to Germany to give the Chinese travel agents a face-to-face wake-up call, but decide that it would be more practical to get a friend to step into the fray for me. Hopefully his acid sarcasm will cut through their lethargy.

Days later I finally make it to the beach in Rimini, the great Italian tourist centre on the shores of the Adriatic, where I bed down close to the action, which in Rimini is the beachfront. The beachfront strip is shoulder-to-shoulder boutiques and shoe stores. If a shoe exists on the planet, you will find it here. There are cowboy boots for cowboys, for drag queens and roller derby queens. There are boots Queen and Kiss members would be proud to wear. There are shoes from 10-cm-high Perspex platforms, killer red stilettos, diamante encrusted sneakers to pure leather health shoes. If you need a shoe, get yourself to Rimini. But if a beach is what you are wanting, I suggest you look elsewhere. Rimini does not have a beach, it has a very large sandpit where the sand is swept and cleaned hourly, and no sea creature has lived in centuries. I am quite sure that if a crab so much as waved a timid claw here, they would fumigate the place. The sandpit is parceled off into 2 m^2 plots that are rented out for the day and the whole area is swamped with plastic of every colour and description: plastic toys and playpens for the bambini, plastic recliners and umbrellas for mama and papa, and plastic paddleboats for the teenies to amuse themselves with in the pond they call the Adriatic. Used to the crashing waves and wild empty beaches of Africa, I am not impressed, and head for Padua in bumper-to-bumper traffic.

On the way I stop off for lunch in Forli, where I have been invited by 5W Maria. In a town with modest houses I follow my instructions to a parking lot from where Maria will lead me to her small-holding where they grow cherries, apricots, peaches, figs and a colorful assortment of vegetables. To break the ice, Maria hands me a huge bowl and sends me outside to harvest dessert. With birds, insects and a warm breeze floating about, we pick luscious sun-hot cherries, while Maria and Monika interrogate me about my travels and South Africa. Through the sweet-sour tang of cherry juice I answer all the usual questions – is it safe, how bad is the crime, are lions still walking freely in the streets? – they didn't really, but I wish someone would ask the lion question. I think it is just an urban myth that people actually still believe this of Africa. Lions are far too scarce and valuable to be allowed to walk free among humans, and it is not considered safe, for the lions that is.

After a lunch of simple pasta dressed with garlic fried in olive oil and accompanied by a crisp green salad from the garden, Monika serves dried figs so delicious that I insist on getting the recipe, which is disarmingly simply. The ripe figs are tailed to ensure they stand upright, then given a deep cross cut on the top, arranged on a baking tray, then generously sprinkled with brown sugar, placed in a low 180 C oven for 20 minutes, and then left in the oven to cool and dry overnight. After this treatment the figs can be frozen for use during the winter months. These figs are served with sharp pale cheese and round off the simple but satisfying meal with aplomb. Sated, we women lounge in the sun, while Papa goes back to picking boxes and boxes of cherries. The conversation floats slowly from corrupt politicians to high taxes, from low wages to ever-increasing living costs. Our worries and woes are the same everywhere, it seems.

Bidding 5W Maria and Monika farewell I once again plunge into the traffic chaos with a huge box of cherries for 5W Mary as a gift from one 5W member to another. 5W Carla has recommended me to her friend 5W Mary; the 5W network is really working to my advantage in Italy.

Beds 26 and 27

5W Mary lives in Padua, which is only an hour away from Venice, but is another city that until a few days ago I never knew existed. As Venice is so close, we toy with the idea of visiting, but it is high season and Venice in high season is for crowd lovers only. Armed with Mary's inside knowledge, we head instead for Chioggia, a little fishing village on the lagoon, complete with canals and boats, but far off the tourist beat. We arrive in time for the market that lines the banks of the canal with peaches and apricots, huge hams and bigger cheeses. In Chioggia, Mary teaches me to walk the Italian walk. A slow saunter, as if time means nothing, and nothing can touch you. Slowly we saunter up the canal over an arched bridge, past a coffee shop, decide to have some, and saunter back, we sit, we sip and we smile discreetly at the Italian men, who pause briefly in their sauntering and return the favor by looking us over and nodding their heads in approval. *La dolce vita*, but if you are a rampant feminist, maybe this is not the place for you.

Back in Padua we saunter to St Anthony's Cathedral. St Anthony of Padua is the accredited saint for finding things and also Mary's patron saint, so we have many reasons to visit. St Anthony's tomb is resplendent in gold and fresh flowers, and while a group in the pews rehearse this Sunday's sung mass, a priest in a brown robe shuffles about on top of the holy tomb, refilling the oil candles, watering the flowers and giving things a bit of a dusting. But in the cathedral they not only have St Anthony's tomb, but also his tongue; black and wrinkly it is on display in a gilded cage, bizarre. And why? Because when his body was exhumed, about 336 years after his death, it had biodegraded, as is to be expected, but his tongue was miraculously mummified. This phenomenon was attributed to the perfection of his preaching, hence the gilded cage for the golden tongue. The viewing of the tongue allows some really close up viewing of some pretty nifty marble sculpting. The detail is incredible, down to the wrinkles on the toes. What is disturbing is that none of the people depicted have detailed eyes, just blank vacant orbs. If a toe wrinkle was no problem, what was the problem with eyes?

On the journey between Padua and Trieste the road winds between the Kras Plateau and the Adriatic, whose waters are such a spectacular shade of blue that the nobles of old considered very carefully where to build their villas, in order to take the best advantage of the blue view. In the distance the city of Trieste shines white in the midday sun. It is one of the world's crossroad cities; it straddles cultures and marks the end of the European Union for a while. Beyond Trieste are countries that are completely unfamiliar to me. But I feel a serious case of sightseeing fatigue coming on and, as my journey is still a mere babe, I will need to pace myself to prevent complete information overload.

In Trieste I make my first attempt at staying in a hostel. This is brought about by the shock of finally getting a price for my month in China. The Chinese travel agents are completely insane! But at this stage there is not much I can do about it; perhaps this was their devious strategy all along. So now that China is about to eat up a huge chunk of my budget, I need to economize. While walking to the hostel from the multistory parking lot, where the Wish Mobile will rest for the next few days, I pass rows and rows of red lanterns that hang from age-grey stone windows. Red lanterns … they seem vaguely familiar … and then I realize these are Chinese lanterns. My hostel is right next to the Chinatown or -street of Trieste. My excitement rises a notch.

Unfortunately the dark stairwell and depressing reception of the hostel wind down my level of joy somewhat. At least I have a private room, but I am not sure about the bedding, so bring mine in from the Wish Mobile. The bathroom-sharing thing is a bit more difficult to get around and I think I will go dirty before using the shower. It is not that bad, and it is probably clean, but I am still a bit of a priss. I will have to get over that pretty soon. Most depressing is that, with the parking fee, which is extra, the room ends up costing more than a comfortable bed & breakfast. But, for the first time I meet other travelers, with mixed results.

In the dark hostel corridor I bump into Shui from China. I consider this a brilliant opportunity to get some inside skinny on my ultimate destination, so I promptly invite her to join me for a saunter – Italian style – around Trieste. She steps into the street, and I immediately regret my decision. I'm a style snob after all, I'm afraid. In her haste to join me, she completely forgot to finish her toilette. She combs her wet, stringy hair while walking down the street. The wet strands make transparent stains on her saggy white t-shirt, which collapses in exhaustion over a tartan micro-mini, from which protrude pasty, fat-kneed, dumpy legs that sink into ankle socks and battered white high-heel shoes.

I give myself a mental whack over the head for my ungracious thoughts, and attempt to make small talk, when I discover she is loud, very loud. Like Minnie Mouse on steroids, she shrieks with glee, and jumps up and down with excitement at my every suggestion – the mini bounces alarmingly – I am agog and in mortal fear for her dignity, so I immediately stop making suggestions and opt for the safer route of asking:

'What do you like doing?'

'Rather ask what I don't like,' she replies.

Okay – 'What don't you like?'

'I don't like boring things.'

Give me a break!

Tottering about on the cobbled stones with those heels, she loses the war, falls, skins her knees and bleeds all over the place. She then makes a beeline for the harbor, where she baths her knees in the rather dicey water. By now the snob in me is making a serious play for attention. She wants to been seen at a chic little Italian bar. I don't want to be seen at all. Finally I sit her down; at least the legs, which have been receiving disbelieving stares, are out of sight. I order a small glass of white wine, while she orders a large chocolate ice-cream, which she proceeds to eat with her mouth open, so that I may share, visually, every spoonful. I need to leave, now, so I plead work and head off for the hostel. She probably considers me most boring. But frankly, I don't give a damn.

Early the next morning I meet Irving from Chicago in a Laundromat. Oh, the glamour of it all. We chat as our washing goes through its cycle. While I fold my intimate wear in full view and presence of a totally strange man, I realise that I am becoming a hardened traveler who pooh-poohs at such niceties as privacy. As Irving seems a good companion, I enquire about his plans for the day. He suggests we should meet up for lunch, and then he leaves. Ouch, got the American let's-do-lunch-sometime brush-off.

But it is all for the best, as I have so many last minute administrative tasks to do that I am fully occupied until late afternoon, when I finally consider myself as prepared for what tomorrow will bring as I can possibly be. There is a thunderstorm brewing, and it promises for interesting lighting conditions, so I set off into the darkening city. In the harbor I watch a man carefully putting the finishing touches to a paint job on his yacht. He is not much of a sailor or his barometer is on the blink. Just as he steps back to admire his handiwork, the first raindrops fall, he shakes his fist and yells at the sky; a classic case of shouting at thunder.

A solid sheet of rain moves across the harbor, pushing wind and rainbows ahead of it. The squall passes as quickly as it came, but the rainbows remain. The direction of the light and the position of the clouds tell me that there will be rainbows over the Piazza Unita d'Italia. To me, photography is not a creative experience, rather one of hunting down your quarry. You recognize the signs in the sky; you memorize the locations of possible photographs; and you hope you are there to capture it when it all comes together. So like the average bushman I settle into a slow jog to hunt my prey. Sounds great, doesn't it. Fact is, I never jog, so I am huffing and wheezing, while the camera bag bangs against my flabby hips. I keep stepping into puddles, and the Italians, who only saunter, look at me as if I have completely lost it and the style snob in me goes into embarrassed hiding. But I make it in time to catch the rainbow over the piazza, and the camera devours yet another image. How frightfully dramatic. After this massive exertion on my part, I treat myself to a sundowner at one of the numerous cafés and on my last night in Italy I drink my very small, very expensive beer and photograph very small and very expensive dogs.

Slovenia

Bed 28

Before leaving Italy I treat myself to a last gelato and, Straciatelli in hand, go and collect the Wish Mobile. After settling into the driver's seat – home, sweet home – the Wish Mobile and I head off to Slovenia.

By crossing the border into Slovenia I am entering a territory about whose history and culture I know nothing. My first discovery is that this is cave country. There are approximately 7 000 caves of note in the classical Karst region of Slovenia. My introduction to these is the UNESCO world heritage site Skocjanske jame; in this cave is the largest known underground canyon in the world. The walk to the cave is through waving grassland that stands tall and fearless of the farmers plough. Butterflies flit from our advancing legs. After the intensive farming of Italy, this is a happy change.

The guide is very matter of fact, leading us into the cave at a clipping pace. We have three kilometers to cover in 1½ hours. So we whip through the 'Labyrinth', passing stalactites and mites – all worth a second look – but we have no time to tarry, we have a cave to get through. We speed-stare and marvel at the sheer scale of the Orjaki, giant stalagmites that rise up to 15 meters, before they vanish behind us in the darkness. Does our guide have a pressing date?

But then we step into Tiha jama, a great hall with a vast domed ceiling, festooned with thousands of white stalactites that reach down to their partner-mites, which soar high into the great space, but they don't touch – yet – perhaps next millennia. The silence in the cave is warm and total; the guide's explanations form small talk bubbles above her head, before *pop* they vanish. She stops talking, and the silence grows until it reaches deep into my mind, pushing all thoughts away. Wrapped in private cloaks of awe, we move deeper into the cave; a faint rumble makes a small hole in the silence. The guide slows as she picks her way down a slippery stair hacked out of the rock; the ceiling of the cave slowly vanishes into a grey yellow gloom. She flicks a hidden switch, and in the distant dark tiny lights now string along the canyon wall, showing us our path forward. Slowly the rumble grows and we see the river; far below it roars white and green through the abyss. Our path leads over a 20-meter gorge by a narrow swing bridge. This is an involuntary grin moment when I expect to see Gandalf fight off the Borlock, before they plummet into the depths. As we pass, the guide turns off the lights behind us; the nightmare black that engulfs the huge chamber makes me wonder again at the sanity of cave explorers.

Emerging into the light 143 m below our starting point, where the disappearing river, the Reka, reappears as a fierce water chute that shapes the rocks around it into smooth bowls, all my plans of visiting Ljubljana get washed out. I want more caves. I think I have seen enough old buildings for a while.

Finding a guesthouse in Postojna is no problem. Dropping in at the bar downstairs where the locals gather, I announce my arrival with a friendly grin and *dober dan*. My shaky pronunciation of hello in Slovenian gives me away, but I quickly discover that all the people in the bar speak a smattering of either German or English, and that asking for the best local beer is a very effective ice breaker. The whole bar joins in animated discussion, trying to convince me to try their particular favorite. As no consensus can be reached, the barmaid hands me the beer in the green bottle, a Zlatorog, a long tom costs 1.2€; a mere 200 ml in Italy cost more than twice that. This, combined with the extremely reasonable price for the room, allows my budget to ease its belt and heave a sigh of relief.

While exploring this unknown world, I sense that I have acquired a new confidence and self-assurance that puts a bounce in my step; I have broken in my travel boots. Strolling through the neat streets with flower-filled window boxes I stop in at the first restaurant I find. Now, instead of staring vacantly out of the window while waiting for the usual restaurant ritual to wind its course, I use the time to nod at the people at the neighboring tables and for chatting to the waiter, who assures me that the biggest and best cave to visit is Postojnska jama. It is a cave so big you travel to its centre by train. The total length is 20 km underground: the longest cave in Europe. Before the waiter has finished his descriptions, the decision is made, tomorrow's schedule is set.

The alarm rings in the new day but, to my surprise, my eyes do not fly open and I do not see the light. I try again, with conscious effort, but my eyes steadfastly refuse to open and the world remains dark. In a small panic I grab the water glass and pour the remaining contents onto my face. Then I try slapping myself about to get the blood flowing. This has the desired effect of opening my eyes, but now, staring at my swollen face in the mirror, I conclude that my system has finally given up on the struggle against the wheat and cheese diet that it has been subjected to for the last month. Last night's four seasons pizza, which ended up being a four cheeses pizza, put the last nail in the coffin.

Today hiding behind sunglasses and sightseeing in a dark cave are my only beauty solutions.

Over breakfast the hotel owner comes over to let me know he is ready to write on the Wish Mobile. He has been consulting with his daughter and they have decided,

'Stop *vojna*'

will be their wish for the world, and considering the history of these parts – which have for centuries been the rope in the tug of war between east and west – stop war is fair comment.

At Postojnska jama dozens of tour busses stand in convoy and my enthusiasm wanes, but there are no queues. Where are all the people vanishing to? At the subterranean station the answer soon appears in the form of a yellow tunnel train that arrives with the precision of an early morning commuter train. We are carried into the cave at bone-chilling speed; the thin wind makes my eyes stream. In the gloom we duck as we plunge into narrow tunnels where the speeding train twists and turns, dodging stalactites and mites large enough to support the Colosseum. When we reach the inner cave station, we get sorted into languages. Slovenian, English, German and French are all well supported. Italians nil. This has me wishing I could speak Italian; it would make this an exclusive tour. Officials keep a close watch that no photographs are taken, but the Germans snap away regardless; their logic seems to be that it's not a rule we made, so it cannot possibly be important.

In a cavern – that could house many of the cathedrals I have seen in the last months – the hundreds of visitors are slowly swallowed by the vast space. By devious and strategic maneuvering I install myself between the German group ahead and the French group behind, and so manage to hear, on occasion, the caves growing drip by drip.

My wish for the world: shut up already. How is it possible for two old bats to carry on a conversation about Fifi back home throughout a tour of the most incredible cave they are likely to see in their lives? If they are not interested, why did they not just stay at home? Both the German and the French groups are in a roaring hurry to get back into the sunlight. The Germans' speed is great. At least they have left me behind. It's the French I wish to ask whether they don't like what they are seeing, and can they not find one marvelous thing to stop them in their tracks. And shut up already!

Then the Germans vanish around a distance corner and the French have finally found something worth their attention. For a few minutes I walk alone, aware that 90 meters above me the grasses wave in the sunshine and butterflies flit from flower to flower as people walk to the cave entrance; our world is floating on a very thin crust. The path winds through a forest of dripstone pillars that are softy rounded like massive wax drippings; they glow soft blush, pale gold or, most treasured, pure white limestone. By some fluke of acoustics, the silence in this part of the cave is broken only by the drip of time as Mother Nature sculpts whimsical forms through the ages. A drop falls, plop, onto the crown of my head. All my attention focuses on the cold drop of limestone. Am I now a fraction of a mm taller? If a stalagmite grows only 1mm in 10 years, how many drips does it take to make it grow 15 meters tall? Or how many drips fall in 500 000 years. I start calculating, but my math does not stretch that far; it amounts to lots of drops of time and every one counts.

The path leads out of the limestone forest past a field of massive stalactites that lie shattered on the cave floor, new forms growing slowly around them. Touching the fallen stalactites I reach through time and touch the age of the dinosaurs. For millennia this beautiful space was sculpted in a dark timeless silence broken only by echoing drops. I realize with some sadness that my curiosity is aiding in the inevitable destruction of this beauty. With my need for light, fresh air and with every breath I expel I subtly alter this fragile environment. My unthinking touch has left an acid imprint on the porous stone. Every footstep and every shout send tiny vibrations into a space that has for an eon been absolutely still ... do we really have the right to see it all? But the chattering French are approaching, and in the distance the Germans start whistling, and the moment goes the way of the dinosaurs.

Croatia

Beds 29, 30 and 31

Struggling to wake up, I wonder if my clock is right.

What time is it?

The clock says it is twenty past seven, but is that really the time?

I should ask somebody, but I can barely even say hello.

What day is it?

I don't know, does it matter?

Well maybe, I need to go and buy some food if it's Sunday I can't, I don't think it's Sunday, Sunday? No, its Saturday. Saturday is fine. I must get up then.

Looking in the mirror and the strange room reflected behind me, I turn to look at the small lake across the daisy-covered meadow.

Where am I exactly? Ko Ko kosomething ... what time is it?

The days of the week have long been melting into one another, but up to now I have had a fairly good grip on the hours of the day. I have been traveling east for a while though; have I crossed a time line? Do they bother with such things here or is it still the same time as in Munich? The irrational need to know the time hurries me to the breakfast room; their clocks and mine are in agreement. This bit of knowledge is strangely reassuring; relaxed I settle down to a huge English-style breakfast; nothing like a greasy protein glut to start the day.

Destination today the island of Krk; halfway there I cross a border, and again the disorientation that stems from a complete lack of daily routine hits me. What country am I in? I know where I am heading, but what my actual geographical /political position is I couldn't say. The disjointed thoughts disturb my sightseeing so much I stop and dig out the map of Europe and with some difficulty, as I am still not clear on where I started this morning, retrace my route. With the discovery that I am now in Croatia, I make a mental note to stop at the nearest automatic bank teller as I will need new currency. The map also shows me that hundreds of small islands string along the coast of the mainland. Putting the Wish Mobile onto a ferry seems like a brilliant plan. With that settled, I once again sink into silent contemplation of the scenery flying past the Wish Mobile windows.

Rab, Croatia

Krk, on the island of Krk, is reached via a huge sweeping bridge. Here in the marriage between sky, stone and sea there is an innocence of excess that allows beauty in even the simplest thing. The gleaming pale stone roads – where fishermen's boats, peeling years of paint, rest in the shade of church towers that are topped by copper domes green with age – are quiet and empty. The buildings of pale pink stone are flooded by a clear clean light that is barred from disturbing the siesta of those inside by shutters in faded blues and greens. The quiet of the siesta hour tells me that I must leave, as the ferry to the island of Rab departs only twice a day, space is limited, and the only way to reserve a place is to be sure that your car is on one of the parking spaces at the ferry port. I leave Krk in a roaring hurry, which is soon slowed by cloud castles that hang motionless in a deep blue sky. They slow my hurry to a halt, to let the herb-scented breeze stroke my face while I climb a white stone hill dotted with small green shrubs, to find a view of the Adriatic, which is smooth swimming pool blue. Later I pass a young man walking purposefully on the side of the road, should I give him a lift? The thought of having a stranger in the car disturbing my silence decides me against it.

Hours later he arrives just in time to board the ferry. My guilt at denying him a lift drives me to approach him to apologize. He is Paul from Germany, and he would not have accepted my offer of a ride anyway. Tall and blonde, he looks at me with steady blue eyes as he speaks in the slow hesitant tones of one who has not spoken a full sentence for some time. As he weighs and tests each word, I watch the prow of the boat push swirling indigo and silver ripples aside. They blend back into the smooth surface of the water that reflects barren stone islands. Paul is a young student using his gap year to walk to the Holy Land and has been on the road for five weeks. By walking about 30 km a day, he hopes to arrive at the Wailing Wall in August. It makes my journey seem frivolous by comparison. I have always envied people who know exactly what their goals and purpose are. I seem to be the eternal student, curious about everything and sure about nothing. We discuss accommodation, and he mentions that he has been staying in monasteries. I also want to stay in a monastery, but somehow I don't think arriving in a natty new car that is slowly being covered in wishes is convincing pilgrimage disguise.

As the island of Rab appears on the horizon, the storm that has been following the ferry is about to catch us. For brief moments the stone islands change from white to deep gold against the purple clouds, the sea is glossy smooth, and fisherfolk draw in their nets to hurry home. We reach Rab with the storm, and the young pilgrim sets off in the thundering rain. It is no use offering him a ride, he has penance to pay. So I yell good luck through the downpour, and set off to find a room for the night. The clouds move on, and a golden full moon rises over the island Rab.

Early morning on the road to the ferry at Msjek, I again meet with the young man who is walking to Jerusalem. I take his photograph against his will; he thinks I want the image for myself. But while he continues his trek, I turn the Wish Mobile into an impromptu print-while-you-wait photo shop. It takes a while to catch up with him again, and I start wondering if he has leapt into the bushes to avoid me, but discover that he just walks really fast. At this rate he will reach the Wailing Wall by end July. When I hand over the freshly printed postcard of him walking, just ten minutes before, he is so surprised that a small breeze is able to snatch the print away. I drive off chuckling, while he chases the wind to retrieve this unexpected gift.

Back on the mainland of Croatia, my route south is on the R8, the coastal road, which hugs the outline of the continent. In places it plunges down to sea level, so I am eye to eye with the fishing boats; in others it soars high, giving a bird's eye view of the stone islands that lie just off shore. As it is Sunday, the road is empty and the tiny nameless villages silent in the hot sunlight that bounces shadowless off white stonewalls. Wooden fishing boats hang motionless on the glass clear water. A dog barks, a too thin cat darts across the road, somewhere someone is frying garlic. Music and laughter float over a tiny harbor, and looking back, I see a small balcony with chairs and tables set out. Here I eat a lunch of fresh fish, green salad and cheese from the island of Pag, which is a local delicacy. The cheese is pale yellow with no discerning aroma, it has a slightly sharp flavor, but is somewhat lacking in salt for my taste. Then while slowly sipping a chilled white wine, I allow the lazy Sunday afternoon to wash over me.

The following morning, my intended trip to China wins me an invitation to breakfast. We meet at a table overlooking the placid waters of the Adriatic that reflect the morning pink mountains on the far side of the bay. Guesthouse owners Miho and his wife Nada are curious to know about my journey, and I am curious to know about them.

All their adult lives they worked as guest workers in Germany, always not quite citizens, always a little bit outside society, and now finally, they are retiring in their homeland. Talking to them, I remember the constant discussions in Germany about the guest worker 'problem', and how people arrived, when all the Germans really wanted was cheap labor. With the morning sun warming my back, looking over the beautiful view it occurs to me that no one would want to live their life as a lower-class citizen in a cold grey city of central Europe, leaving their friends, family, language and social status behind, if they had a choice. Miho writes his wish for the world on my car.

Stop war – there is only one God.

With the pen still in his hand he stares thoughtfully over the water and after a silent moment he turns and taking both my hands in his, he sends me on my way with a deeply felt blessing. May Allah be with you.

But it soon becomes apparent that the god of all things traffic is on holiday. With the start of the working week, the commuter traffic combines with the roadworks to create massive tailbacks, and the driving conditions change from a gentle cruise to rip-your-hair-out. For relief from the traffic, I make a detour through Split, but find only the part of town that is all business, huge flat buildings, light industry and the harbor for the main ferry lines. I can find no reason for stopping, and so I make my way back into the traffic jam that is Route 8 this morning, where my irritation grows and grows until it spills over onto everything I see and do. My visits to Omnis and Makarska are a failure. My heart is not in it. Finally, after 9 hours and 300 km I arrive in Dubrovnik, with the setting sun.

Bed 32

All entrances to George Bernard Shaw's idea of an earthly paradise are dramatic. Mine takes me over the Ombla River by way of the 481-m long Dr Franjo Tudjmann Bridge, named after the first president of Croatia. I have been instructed to wait here by Danka, the owner of the hostel in which I will be staying, so she can lead me to her hostel home, which is high on the mountain, overlooking the harbor of Gruz and the suburb of Lapad opposite. Far below, a yacht, under full white sail, skims across the deep blue water, the sun warms my back, and I feel the stress of the day falling away.

To break the ice – the hostel is her home after all – Danka invites me for a sundowner on the balcony. While we watch the fishing boats drag tails of orange sunlight behind them as they slowly make their way home between the golden islands, Danka listens to my past month's travels and my future plans with some concern. She decides that this is far too much alone time for one person, and immediately takes me under her wing, insisting that I enjoy meals with her and her daughter.

My introduction to the Croatian kitchen is with crisp fried chicken and salad, fresh from Danka's garden. She cuts me a slice of baked cheese pie as we chat about life in Dubrovnik. While telling me how the bus-boats work and where to board, she throws together a huge cherry strudel, which is a delicious combination of sour cherries and vanilla-sweetened fresh cheese, held together by a light crisp pastry. Her mother-in-law, who lives in the apartment below, is responsible for the vegetable garden, and daily brings in salads and marrows; the marrows are cooked and served like mash potatoes. As a light snack, Danka fries up some garlic mushrooms, which she serves with a dry crumbly cheese, a cross between Feta and Parmesan. The Croatian diet contains a huge amount of cheese. But this is not the store-bought plastic processed stuff. The Croatians are cheese connoisseurs. When discussing the cheese to use in her dishes, Danka describes the best village and person to buy from, and specifies the time of year you should order your cheese to get the best flavor – July-August if you were wondering, as then the grasses are at their best. To be quite sure that the cheese is just right for the dish she is preparing, she specifies the mix ratio of cow, goat and sheep's milk.

On my first walks to the walled city of Dubrovnik, I never get further than the Internet café on the main street, where I spend hours attending to the administrative duties that pile up between stops. I surf for hostels in Sarajevo, check on the Uzbekistan visa progress, try to finalize car insurances for non-EU countries, pay the bills back home, and finally check on the progress with the Chinese travel agent. I still have no schedule or any news on papers for the car, and am really getting concerned that my journey will come to an abrupt halt on the Kazakh–China border. In answer to my queries, the fat man complains that I have not paid them any money yet. Flabbergasted I enquire what I should be paying them for, for giving me a quote that took three months to produce and still no usable schedule. I demand to see something on paper that will prove that they are indeed progressing with the required paperwork for the car. This demand results in the confession that they have still not sent the application to China, and I must now please pay for express delivery, otherwise there will be insufficient time for the Chinese bureaucracy to grind through its motions. I nearly have a heart attack, right there in the middle of the

Internet café. But I bite my tongue and try to be as pleasant as possible, as this fat, smug individual has me over a barrel.

To take my mind off the China problem, I finally treat myself to my first visit to the old town of Dubrovnik, two days after my arrival here. Heeding Danka's suggestion that I get there before the cruise liners disgorge their passengers, I arrive along with the fresh produce bound for the morning market. My first impression of the walled city is a grey stone arch, framing a steep flight of shadowy stairs that lead under shop signs and dripping washing into the golden morning light that flows through the narrow cobbled streets and floods the main piazza. The marble flagstones gleam from the polishing feet of hundreds of years. The streets are empty, but the sky is wheeling with swallows that duck and chatter through arches and over statues. Their restless movements give an air of disquiet and foreboding to this ancient city, which reflects its mixed history in rich architecture that takes inspiration from the Byzantine, Venetian, Ottoman and Austro-Hungarian empires.

Men trundle their wares in pushcarts to small squares, where wooden trestle tables are set up against backdrops of Gothic palaces and Rococo churches. Slowly the fresh produce adds splashes of color to the scene: purple onions, rosy peaches, apricots and deep red cherries. Old ladies cover tables with handmade lace, while old men pin down the delicate stuff with pots of wild rose honey. Early morning conversations take place under bright umbrellas. For breakfast, I select a rosy peach, a string of figs, each fruit separated from its neighbor by a bay leaf, and two apricots.

While sucking gently at the sugary soft peach, I watch as a fisherman – his face and hands are leather tan from long days in the sun, and his eyes the same color as his silver hair – instructs his assistants. Scrutinizing the fisherman, I decide that the Croatians are a very handsome bunch, tall, regal and well proportioned with clear grey eyes. The women have elegant features, no button noses here, and the men have proud handsome heads with strong jaw lines. My assessment of the fisherman is interrupted by his assistants moving off, carrying the huge basket of fish between them. I follow them surreptitiously as they walk rapidly through the narrow streets delivering the fish that will soon appear on restaurant menus as the catch of the day. The fishermen lose me in the labyrinth of tiny alleys, and I find myself fighting against a tide of tourists. The city fills with people, so I climb the hundreds of stairs back 'home'. On the way, I pass several old men and women standing in the road holding small handwritten signs, 'Rooms to let,

Zimmer frei'. Behind the beautiful walls poverty lurks. Looking at the old folk trying to make a small living out of the tourist attraction they live in, I wonder whether one moves into places like the walled city of Dubrovnik or must one be born there.

In the hot afternoon Danka takes me swimming at her favorite spot. Our path to the diving rock leads past a ruin of a villa with a private jetty and beach. Off-hand Danka mentions it used to belong to an Austrian, but after it got bombed out in the war, he never returned, so it is slowly being reclaimed by nature. I step inside to investigate further, but the ruins of war are not mysterious or romantic, merely sad. Finding a spot on the rocks, we watch the huge cruise liners, small motor boats and boat-busses come and go in the Bay of Dubrovnik. There is so much boat traffic here that Miss Priss comes out in full force; swimming in this water must be like rolling around half-naked on a highway. I lose any desire to swim, but the locals don't share my apprehension and float about in the water, while big ships float through their local swimming hole.

As the day cools, we prepare for church because Danka and Maria wish to attend the feast of St Anthony, and as I have already made acquaintance with St Anthony in Padua, it seems appropriate I tag along. It is tradition to walk to this church festival barefoot, but, as the church is half an hour's downhill walk on a tar road, we walk, but decide to break with tradition on the barefoot issue. The church must once have been romantically positioned on the banks of the Omla River, but the riverbank has become a busy road that traps the small building between it and the cliff-face behind. The church can accommodate only twenty people, so the bulk of the congregation stand under the trees in the tiny churchyard and spill out onto the road. This is an act of faith in itself, as there are no pavements and the cars are in a hurry to get to tonight's other important event, the Soccer World Cup.

The service goes as Catholic services do, and I sing along to 'When the saints go marching in'. I am rather pleased that I know the words, although I am the only person singing in English. While we are singing, children wriggle through adult legs to place their candles on the tablet of stone set into the cliff. They are more enraptured by the hundreds of tiny flames and malleable wax than the service. Owing to the small size of the chapel, the priest brings communion out to the people; under the trees in the fading day, in a bread and fishes scene, he offers the blood and body of Christ to the faithful. Finally, the priest blesses the community, and says a brief prayer for the Croatian soccer team, to general soft laughter. Their opening match in the World Cup is against Brazil; Croatia will need all the help it can get.

In the early morning I step out onto the balcony; the water far below is the colour of the summer sky. Breathing the crisp clear air, I make the decision.

'Island hopping! This is a perfect day for island hopping.'

Descending the 500 steps to the harbor, I purchase a day ticket, and find the small open-sided boat that will be my means of transportation for the day. These small boats are the public transport of the islanders and, like a normal bus, adhere to strict timetables. A day ticket will take me to each of the three inhabited islands of the Elafiti group. We set off in the cool morning air that smells of salt and sunshine.

The first stop is the tiny harbor of Kolocep. I disembark with two locals, who make their way swiftly up stone stairs in the assured way of those who have a fixed destination. Having no destination, I turn slowly to take in the small harbor with its mussel-encrusted jetty, barely higher than the clear jade sea. The island rises steeply from the shingle beach; there are steps left and right. I opt to go right, through dense foliage where white dog roses drape elegantly over bright orange pomegranate flowers. Slowly the small patches of agricultural land on either side of the path rise, supported by dry stonewalls, until the grass and burnt orange poppies are at eye level and my shadow scares lizards from their sunbathing. A cluster of trees casts a welcome shade. While I enjoy the cool relief, I notice that they are cherry trees dripping with fruit. Breakfast! A handful goes into my hat, then in perfect solitude I make my way up the hill, spitting cherry pips with gay abandon.

A graveyard on top of the hill is watched over by a tiny pink stucco church. In the growing heat, I spend a moment sharing the view of the surrounding blue sea and distant islands with the dead. The lane goes straight ahead and straight up; if there is no turn up that next rise, I am going back. Then providence steps in. Over the next rise, the main harbor of Kolocep comes into view. By the water's edge, under a shady awning, I sip a cup of rosehip tea, while I wait for my boat to come in.

At the island of Lopud yachts cluster in the tiny harbor, and sun-worshippers fill the white sandy beaches. As sun tanning is not my thing, I look around for other distractions. A sign catches my eye: 'St John's Church'. Oh good, I haven't seen a church in ages, I'll do that. The signs point up stone roads, up stone steps, and up and up. Hitching my skirt to immodest heights and converting my sunhat to a fan, I sweat my way up that mountain in the blazing sun. There had better be a good reason for this suffering. On the top of the mountain there is a 1 500-year-old ruin, a view, and best of all a breeze. Sitting in the roofless church under the shade of an ancient pine, skirt about my hips, I complete my sweat cycle. I am not very chaste and reverent about it, but hell's teeth be dammed, they could warn a person that these ancient churches were built in difficult-to-reach places, so the act of getting there would be a form of penance. Penance paid, I make my way back down that mountain, and off to the island of Sipan.

Here I take lunch at a linen-covered table at the water's edge. An item on the small menu intrigues: cheese from olive oil. While I know nothing about cheese making, I am interested to know how it is possible to produce cheese from oil. My expert interrogation of the waitress informs me that the cheese is not made from, but preserved in olive oil. A firm hard cheese made from a mix of goat's and cow's milk is cut into bite-sized blocks, and then covered in olive oil, sealed, and in a dark cellar allowed to cure for 40 days. This results in a cheese with a pale orange mold and a very pungent, but not unpleasant flavor, which goes well with a crisp white wine.

While I try this new dish, I eavesdrop on a conversation between two New York businessmen and their skipper. All the men seem to be around thirty years old, but the businessmen had hired the skipper and his boat as private guide and transport for the day. To make small talk over lunch, the businessmen enquire after the skipper's lifestyle. He proudly tells them that he lives with his parents, knows all his family, and sees them all the time. His life is upwardly mobile, but he is taking his whole family with him. The businessmen are at first quite obviously amused at the skipper's quaint need to drag the masses along, but the quiet conviction of the skipper slowly makes them realise that it is not what you have, but being satisfied with what you have that is missing in the American 'never enough' concept of success.

After lunch, I contemplate whether to attempt the hour-long walk, through valleys where olives, figs, pomegranates and almonds grow, to the ruins of the summer residence of the Bishop of Ragusa, built around 1600. The midday sun forces me to dismiss this idea as folly and I stroll instead through the tiny village of Sipan ska Luka, where young girls sit in narrow streets shaded by closely pressed stone houses, at small tables displaying shells and other flotsam for sale. On the jetty colorful fishing nets lie in untidy piles, while the secret of the brilliant water of the Adriatic is revealed. All along the Croatian coast, fresh water springs erupt in the sea, making shimmering swirls as the fresh and salt water mingle to the clearest jade and cerulean blue.

'Sitting on the dock of the bay, I watch the clouds float away, wasting time'. I have an hour-long wait before my bus-boat will arrive. So I spend the time feeling envious of the local children who leap and play in water so clear that every pebble on the harbor floor is visible. So what?, you might say. But minutes later the children hoot and scramble for the dockside ladder as a massive cruise ship comes and parks in their pool, so deep is the water here. My boat comes in, but just before it can leave, a private yacht attempts to park at the jetty. With the giant cruise ship on one side and the half a dozen bus-boats filled with tourists and locals on the other, the elderly skipper has a huge audience to witness his expert steering as he crashes the front of the yacht into the concrete jetty. I cringe in sympathetic embarrassment as he yells at his poor wife, who tries to pull the yacht straight by the mooring line, but she would need to be superwoman to manage. Flustered, he fires the engines, spins the wheel, overshoots the mark and the side of the yacht grinds along the concrete. While the tourists on the bus-boats try to decide whether this is comic or tragic, the local skippers and their crew leap to the rescue without so much as a sly grin. Quickly they have the matter in hand, with such diplomacy that the elderly sailor comes away with his dignity more or less intact.

As I am the only one going to my local end station, I have the bus-boat all to myself. So I sit on the prow and pretend I am rich and famous, while the skipper gets in on the act and races the other boats home. At the harbor, he helps me from my perch with a small bow and raffish grin, and I step onto dry land with film star attitude. Hey, it costs nothing to let the imagination run wild.

With the fading of the day, I am to meet Danka in the church of St Blasius, who is the patron saint of Dubrovnik. The church is standing room full, and small children dressed in immaculate white wait impatiently for the mass to run its course. Listening to the sung mass, I realize that the only time I have visited churches in Croatia is to attend a church service. Religion here is a private affair, and churches are still there for the use of worshippers, not to make money from tourists. Not being the least bit religious, I feel a bit phony and sneak out into the Dubrovnik night.

The fresh produce has given way to restaurant tables and chairs as every candlelit alley and every firelit square try to outdo each other for romantic setting. The streets reflect the firelight, and are so clean and beautiful that elegantly dressed tourists take off their shoes to feel the gleaming marble with their bare feet. There are ongoing music concerts in several venues. The music escapes the confines of the beautiful buildings and floods into the alleys, where old men sit in doorways and on fountain walls, eyes closed, listening to the muffled sound. Soon it is drowned by the sound of singing as the congregation spills out of St Blasius. The cardinal in front, under gilded canopy, followed by men in white, then the male choir, then the little boys in lace, then more men in white, then little girls in white, nuns in white, nuns in black, and, at the end, the congregation, in whatever they feel shows them to best advantage. And so, arranged according to their station, they move through the streets, bestowing blessings on every church. As they walk off their song fades slowly, its place filled by the muffled sounds of a string quartet.

Enough sun and sea, it is time for an inland excursion. Over breakfast, Danka is a font of bright ideas, and sends me off to Konavle on the River Ljuta. The winding mountain road takes me into a valley, where I cross the Ljuta River. On a small wooden platform, shaded with reeds, stands a family table in the middle of the river. Here children dip sticks into the flow, while adults gaze at the surrounding mountains during the lull of conversation. My destination is the watermills, which are core to this natural heritage site. The moss fronds covering the steps of the wheels tell of many years of turning. The river is liquid crystal, and seems to come from everywhere. Parts of the road bubble clear cool water; the water flows over stone walls and tumbles down the mountain; then it is tamed for a brief moment and directed by stone channels to flow through the restaurant and the fish holding tanks, whose inmates will soon be lunch. This is freshwater fish at its freshest.

The water is so inviting I must control a very strong urge to rip my clothes off and leap in, but when I do put in a hand, I discover that the water is freezing. Further up the mountain I spy a tiny path through the thicket. Over smooth stones I make my way into the cool green forest. The familiar smell of figs fills the air. The trees are heavy with fruit. I test a likely-looking specimen; a dry white interior is my reward; it is too early. Like your average Pocahontas I clamber barefoot over round white boulders, trying to find that swimming hole that I know is around here somewhere. And there it is. Lit by dappled sun, glass-clear water rolls in a white stone basin, moss and ferns softening the rocks. One problem, it is ten meters down some pretty slippery and very large boulders. Sense prevails and I content myself with lunch overlooking the pool. But the mosquitoes are faster than I am, and before long, I am lunch. I'm out of here and out of Dubrovnik; it is time to move along.

Bosnia Herzegovina

Beds 33 and 34

Leaving the Adriatic behind, I head inland into Bosnia Herzegovina, then out of Bosnia Herzegovina, then back into Bosnia Herzegovina. The world is a bit of a political jigsaw puzzle here. The road leads through a huge fertile valley, little California they call it, where trees are dotted pink with peaches and in hothouses tomato vines sag under their fruit. The road leads out of the valley into an alpine scene with – to my eyes – the unusual addition of mosques and minarets. The East has moved onto centre stage here, the Christians replaced by the people of Islam. A brown road sign indicates a sight worth seeing. A church, yippee! Being a good little tourist, up I go to view my first tourist attraction in Bosnia Herzegovina.

A man with a fez squats on the wall chatting to an unseen someone below.

'May I enter?' I ask, ever so politely.

'Yes.' Says he, shaking his head.

Confused by this contradiction I ask again.

'Yes, please enter.' He says shaking his head.

Is the man unsure or not in a position to say either yes or no, but too polite to say so. I stare at him, not too sure what to do next, when it hits me, I am in Turkish cultural – well, sort of – territory where nodding the head means no, and shaking means yes, and with that I set foot in my first mosque, but forget to take off my shoes. His slight wince says it all; I am stepping all over his culture with my blundering ignorance. To minimize the damage, I remain rooted to the spot, letting my gaze wander over the light-filled space with its carpet-covered floor, intricate geometric shapes decorating the walls and the delicate pointed arches of the doorways, and I realize I am entering a country where I have more to learn than just a new language.

Reaching Sarajevo in the late afternoon, my first impressions are woeful. The place is grim, grey, hazy, hot and morosely humid. While following my instructions to wait for my hostel host at the Holiday Inn parking lot, the thought pops into my head that the hotel has some historical importance. Why would a Holiday Inn have any importance at all, especially one that seems to be made of bright yellow plastic?

Before I can solve this riddle, the hostel owner arrives and leads me to the hostel, which is in a building that has not yet recovered from the war. It sits in a park that is litter strewn and inhabited by aimless men with beers in hand. I am not happy, and am beginning to see the 'leading to hostel service' not as a polite gesture, but one that ensures that you will not run away in horror on seeing the accommodation on offer.

On check-in, the usual questions;

'Where are you from?'

'South Africa.'

'South Africa! I think perhaps South Africa is all right to live in, but then it is with the disadvantage of living with blacks. To live anywhere else in Africa must be terrible.'

The small, weasel-faced man seems quite sure that his opinion is universally accepted. His presumption leaves me speechless.

'Have you visited Africa?' is all I can think of to say.

He declares that he gained his detailed and authoritative knowledge on local Bosnia-Herzegovina television and, based on that, has laid down judgment on the entire African continent.

Thinking back over the past few months, I realize that we are all guilty of the same thing. The world has become so indoctrinated by the media, and especially that great mind controller, television, that we take every word broadcast as gospel, and are quite happy to base our opinions on the snippets of news the TV feeds us. The only difference is the frame of reference. With the information glut of the information age, there are now opinions floated in the media to support any prejudice, as long as it brings a profit. Yet the media is quite indignant if its right to freedom of speech is ever questioned. Although freedom of speech is commendable when one is trying to expose the truth, it becomes a poisoned chalice when politicians, shareholders and advertisers decide what the truth should be exactly.

As I watch as this ignorant fool going through the motions of registering me in his sorry little hostel, finding new accommodation moves to the top of my to-do list.

My search leads direction old town. A burnt-out helicopter lies rusting in the grounds of an old mansion. The facades of the buildings on both banks of the Miljacka River all bear the rat-tat-tat scars of gunfire. I can imagine the noise and dust of battle. Where is the blood, pops into my head? Twit, it was more than ten years ago. But the wounds of the buildings are so fresh it could have been yesterday. There are still imprints of tank treads in the buckled pavement, and bombs make strange interior decorators; crumpled roofs lie in buildings, displaying their rusting sides through shattered plaster and broken windows. Graffiti and billboards grow like ivy on these ruined buildings. A kitten mews plaintively from the bombed-out rubble of an old cinema, where I see a woman drawing water from a public tap; she is followed by a toddler in bright red dress; they live somewhere in this broken building.

The destruction of war lingers long after the media-men have moved on to uncovering the truth in the next breaking story. Breaking – is good news, broken – is news, but fixing is no news. In Sarajevo the fixing still goes on every day. Builders high on scaffolding watch me as I slowly photograph my way up the street. They are bemused at my choice of subject matter, as if they cannot imagine what could be interesting about the bombed-out buildings. I feel a bit embarrassed as if I have been caught picking at a scab that has formed over things the people here would rather forget. But they shout their hellos and mock-pose. We share a laugh, before they turn back to the work of restoring the city.

When cutting across a side street, I first notice the brass plaques on the walls, inscribed with rows and rows of names, all with the same death dates, 1992, 1993, 1994. Is this a memorial for a battle fought right here? Did these names belong to men who fell dead where I am now standing? Why don't I know these things? What was I doing in 1992, 1993, 1994? The early nineties were the once upon a time days, when there was no satellite television, no Internet, and certainly no 'YouTube'. We relied completely on the local broadcasters to inform us about the outside world. South Africa was in turmoil; the last riots were being played out; Nelson Mandela had been freed; and we were preparing for our first fully democratic election. Our news reports had quite enough to fill them. The horror of Sarajevo was a brief headline, not really important, not part of South Africa's reality.

But the bright yellow Holiday Inn was newsworthy enough, and these plaques trigger the memory of news clips from the siege of Sarajevo. The Holiday Inn was then considered the 14th most dangerous place on earth, and the road in front of it gave birth to a new English phrase 'sniper alley'. Now I realize that I am standing in one of the notorious sniper alleys where the citizens of Sarajevo risked their lives each time they had to cross this road. The bullet-riddled buildings take on a much more sinister and real meaning. Another memorial plaque catches my eye just before I step into the Ferhadija, the main shopping street of Sarajevo, where all the international brands are on glittering display, and the street is a flood of tourists and locals. Here I spot several more plaques, but they have become part of the architecture, as the people in the street much prefer to consider their next material acquisition.

Stepping over an invisible boundary, I enter the Turkish Quarter. The modern glass-fronted shops are replaced by hundreds of tiny stalls that spill copper and carpets onto the pale cobbled streets. On a street corner, brooms and buckets stand next to a small fountain where the tourists fill their water bottles, and the locals draw water for the coffee that is carried from shop to shop on small trays. In the deepening dusk, the graceful arches and domes of the Gazi Husrev Beg Mosque form a quiet centerpiece to the teeming streets that surround it. The spot lit minaret is a glowing needle against the indigo sky. At the mosque, men take off their shoes and wash their feet before entering to pray. Beautiful Bosniak women with porcelain skin, their hair in high buns, hidden from view by tightly wound scarves, drift by in serene elegance. The sky deepens to black, and the streets lose their luster as the shops close for the night, hiding their wares behind heavy wooden shutters.

I trawl from bed and breakfast to guesthouse to hotel. The Sarajevos are friendly, but apologetic; not to book in advance during the summer season is a bit of a gamble. But they try their best to help; one owner makes a few calls on my behalf. After a bit of Bosnian chit-chat on the phone, he gives me a small hand-drawn map and a name with an exotic ring. Zlatan, a guesthouse owner, has a room available.

Zlatan is a perfect textbook example of tall, dark and handsome, with the added attraction of being wise. On hearing that I am from South Africa, his response is, that must be such a cool place to live. When he hears of his fellow Sarajevo's take on living with the people of Africa, his hair literally stands on end. He apologizes profusely, and assures me that this is the exception, and offers to escort me to the parking garage where the Wish Mobile will live for the next few days. We fall into easy conversation. He was twelve when the shells and bullets started blazing down from the mountains. Zlatan's father reassured his family, saying that those were their troops, and could not possibly be shooting at them. He believed it must be a military exercise; it didn't take them long to find out how wrong he was.

When a bomb dropped on their family home, they took refuge in the parking garage that the Wish Mobile is now staying in. Looking at the grey cold space, I visualize hundreds of terrified and confused families huddling together, trying to make sense of a senseless situation. Zlatan is very matter of fact when he mentions that they were lucky to be in this particular parking garage, as they had access to water. People sheltering in other garages had to venture out to find water, and then were shot by the snipers, who made daily sport of killing Sarajevos.

Zlatan carries none of the shame and guilt of the war that I have noticed in the older generations. The war was something that happened to him; then he was sent to Norway as a refugee; and as a result, he speaks fluent Norwegian. The remainder of his family fled to various parts of the world to earn money, which they sent back to the family patriarch, who used it to rebuild their lives. The bombed-out family home is now a 12-bedroom guesthouse, where I am happy to take up residence in a small attic room with a view over the minarets of the Turkish quarter.

The first call to prayer drifts into my room at 04h40. While the light outside is perfect for photography, I only got to sleep at 01h00 and opt for more sleep. Later, yet still very early, I climb up a hill that yesterday an elegant Sarajevo woman with glass green eyes suggested. 'To get the view for a beautiful picture.' Sarajevo lies in a valley of the Dinaric Alps, surrounded by steep green meadows and pine-covered hills. The houses are robust and square, with red terracotta roof tiles. In the distant valley the glass buildings of the central business district rise out of the haze. As the city slowly wakes and people make their way to work, I turn a full circle to take in the view of the surrounding suburbs, where the white obelisks of the dead are everywhere to be seen. In huge memorial parks, rose bushes grow between the tightly packed white marble headstones. The early morning light skims across the smooth stone surfaces, but finds no blemish. There is nothing to distract the eye from the cold brutality of the block; a memorial for murdered Moslems – 1992 – 1993 – 1994 – 1992 – 1993 –1994 – the death dates are repeated over and over. The boundary between civilization and barbarism is a delicate thing; some don't even notice when they have breached it.

In my absence, the Turkish quarter has transformed itself from shuttered empty streets to an Ali Baba cave of copper kettles, trays, silk scarves and carpets, all displayed for the tourist's pleasure. From the terrace of a small café, I watch the locals going through their early morning rituals over a breakfast of a fizzy lemon drink and a burek, a strange coiled pastry filled with spicy meat. The shop owners fuss over their wares while the coffee waiters rush in and out of the myriad little stores, delivering tiny cups of coffee with tall glasses of water. They carry these on large trays balanced on one hand stretched high above their heads, while they duck and dodge through the crowded streets, never spilling a drop. Men sit outside their tiny shops sipping coffee and smoking the first or fourth dark brown cigarette of the day, while young mothers tend their babies. In the Turkish quarter everything happens on the street – not surprisingly, some shops are no bigger than a small closet.

Across the road of my guesthouse, the heat of the morning has convinced a fat man with pale skin to remove his shirt. Sitting on a typist chair that has lost its back, and looks soon to lose the battle of supporting the pale fat man, he holds court in front of his shop, which stocks what look like gutters and roofing material. People pass, some with a greeting, some stop for a brief exchange, some sit and chat for a while.

Setting off to explore Sarajevo, I find myself in a small shopping street in the more modern part of town. Here the traffic chokes the three-lane streets, while the sidewalks are washed by the shopkeepers. Small fountains are everywhere, and on every patch of open ground Muslim headstones with turban tops stand askew in the grass. Are there really corpses under the grass? The disturbing thought brings me to a halt in front of a shop window, where my focus moves through my reflection and onto a freshly skinned sheep, its head intact with milky blue bulbous eyeball and teeth bared in a ghastly grimace. Shuddering involuntarily, I quicken my step to the open-sided market where I can view the far more comforting displays of fresh fruit and vegetables. As a good city girl, I am used to seeing my meat prettily cut into rosy slices, topped by a sprig of parsley and hygienically plastic wrapped for my shopping comfort, and graves are usually in neat rows situated way out of town.

In the late afternoon I make my way back to the Turkish quarter, where the fat, now sun-roasted red man has been joined by an accordion-playing friend. The melancholy sounds of Bosnian folksongs fill the small alley, and as the fat man sings in despair-drenched voice, he slowly acquires an audience that pay him in beer.

At the guesthouse, Halla, an unreal redhead from Norway, introduces herself and suggests we have dinner together. She wants a salad, but I am following Zlatan's recommendation and am on the search for chivapcici. He directs us to a small corner restaurant where we sit at a pavement table lit by the overhead street light. Halla sticks to her salad plan, and I go all out for the chivapcici. The dish consists of flat squares of highly spiced, garlicky minced lamb placed inside chewy flat bread that has been fried in the mince fat. This is accompanied by chopped raw onion and whole fresh chilies, and to wash it down, a glass of natural yoghurt. A Sarajevo specialty that comes with heartburn guaranteed. Back at the guesthouse the fat man and his friend are still singing, and have acquired a whole collection of empty beer bottles.

Halla has the room opposite mine on the top floor of the guesthouse, and as we are the only two up here, I take the opportunity to leave my door open and throw open the windows to allow a much-needed cool breeze to blow through my little kingdom. Working at my computer, I sense someone behind me. Halla has slipped into something more comfortable, and leans against my doorpost in what must surely be a seductive manner; for someone even just slightly more interested than me, an unspoken question hangs in the air.

Ah no, I duck the silent question with feigned innocence.

'I was just cooling the room, is the draft disturbing you?'

Enough said. She gives me a slow grin, turns and leaves.

My destination today is Serbia, as far as I can get. While Zlatan collects the car, I slowly sip a cup of mint tea. The night manager, who has been watching me, rattles off something, rushes out and returns moments later with an enormous chocolate bun for my breakfast. With this, he settles down for a chat, but he speaks only Bosnian, and is convinced that if he keeps speaking, I will eventually understand. I suppose so, but as I am leaving in a few minutes, I don't really have the time it will take. This has been a common trait among people. They talk at me; talking and repeating and louder and louder, unable to comprehend that what to them is perfectly clear, is to me a complete mystery. Then out of the blue he starts reciting German nursery rhymes. For the fun of it, I join in, and while the Turkish quarter lies sleeping, we share a laugh at the silly common ground we have found in the words of a few children's rhymes. When Zlatan returns, I discover that all the man was trying to tell me is that today is the first day of summer, and it's hot enough to prove it. Before I drive off Zlatan writes his wish on my car.

'Kad su srca VELIKA * suijet je mali, sretan * i SIGURAN.'

Just outside Sarajevo, a small disagreement between the map and myself sees me on a dirt road that is slightly narrower than I feel totally comfortable with, but as my compass assures me I am heading east, I stick with it. The road follows the contours of the cliff in minutest detail on the right, and on the left the Wish Mobile sends small stones plummeting down a ravine, through which a river whitewaters its way to the sea. Before I have time to adjust to the hair-raising driving conditions, I enter a tunnel – wah – daylight is instantly pitch black, and before my eyes have time to adjust – whoop – I explode back into the light. Feeling the same slight disorientation of inadvertently skipping a page in a book, I slam on anchors to try and get a grip on what just happened. The tunnel, as is the road, is fully organic: no tar, no concrete, no reflectors, no ventilation and no lights. The only thing plastic is the solar-powered traffic light, which allows you to enter this tiny bit of hell. I drive on slowly, hoping that this was the one and only tunnel of its kind.

But around a sharp bend a small solar light blinks red, commanding me to stop in front of another black hole through the cliff. While waiting, I realize my jaw is tightly clenched, I really don't want to go in there, but the light changes and grants me access to this little piece of purgatory. In the tunnel the dark is complete, the headlights meaningless with nothing to reflect off, and the barely visible raw rock oppressively close. Blue carbon-soaked air hangs like a deadly fog in the curves of the tunnel that allow no air or light to enter. On and on, the dark presses closer and closer, finally out into the light. But hardly out than back in, hell is not hot and fiery, it is totally dark and damp. My eyes strain to see, and my nerves grate as my hands cling to the steering wheel.

Dark thoughts start growing in my mind; there is not one person on the planet who knows where I am right now. If the Wish Mobile and I plummeted into the ravine we would vanish from sight ... I start to wonder how long it would take for someone to raise the alarm at my absence ... but just before my thoughts become totally morose, a happy surprise.

In the middle of the tunnel there is a cleft in the rock through which pours welcome daylight. A Kodak moment, I park the Wish Mobile in the stream of light and hop out to take a photograph. The tunnel is silent, dank and cold; the air smells evil. Shuddering, I walk into the dark to get enough distance to photograph the Wish Mobile in these strange surroundings. Then the sound of an engine jolts me into the realization that the solar-powered lights allowing traffic into the tunnels do not make allowances for people to go for walks while they are in there. I make a hasty retreat to the comfort of the Wish Mobile, and am relieved to see truck lights approaching from the rear. Reversing out of this tunnel is not something I want to even think about.

At the tunnel exit I let the Panda ice-cream truck pass, and happily trundle along in its wake. It seems to have done this before, and I am well pleased to have the face of the fat ice-cream-munching panda grinning at me from the truck. Organic tunnel follows organic tunnel, some short, some endless. But by now there is a car behind me, and I am quite at peace with the world. At a red light, a young man leaps out of the Panda ice-cream truck, whips open the fridge door, and out of the billowing fog conjures up an ice-cream for each of us. As he hands me my ice-cream, he introduces himself as Mohammed, and puts out his hand. This is a bit forward, thinks I, but respond quite naturally with a handshake. In the truck his companion emits a burst of rough laughter. I contemplate this while munching at the ice-cream; something is not quite halal here. Then I recall my previous dealing with persons of the Islam faith; touching between strangers of the opposite sex is not done. So it occurs to me that this was a young man's 'dare' to touch the wild Western woman. At the crossroads, where organic road meets tar, Mohammed once again hops out of the Panda truck, and approaching the Wish Mobile, he again wants to shake my hand. But I am onto him, and look him straight in the eye with raised eyebrow and wicked grin. He glows red and bows off, totally flustered. Do not underestimate the strange Western women, young man. We are a different breed from what you are used to.

Turkish Quarter Sarajevo
Bosnia Herzegovina

Serbia

Bed 35

At Donje Vardist I cross the border into Serbia and all hell breaks loose.

With the border crossing the trucks have been condensed into a long single file. The main artery road has shrunk to a narrow strip of tar that is overwhelmed by trucks and cars in various stages of fall-apart. All of these are steered by the most uncouth drivers I have yet come across. Overtaking in Serbia is a team sport; here there is no polite waiting in line for your turn to overtake. When a gap comes, everybody moves en masse into the left-hand lane, and with loud hooting and wildly flashing lights, all try to overtake the truck at the same time. Only when the oncoming cars are so close that head-on collisions are imminent, do the hooting mass realise that, alas, they are not going to make it past this time and then – all together now – they move back into the right-hand lane, without even a cursory glance to see if perhaps there is a car next to them.

It takes me two rounds of this to adjust to current driving conditions. When the next gap appears, I quietly and calmly simply start overtaking, regardless of whether the overtaking lane is occupied. The hog next to me is so busy with the hooting and the flashing of lights it takes him a moment to realize he is slowly being pushed off the road. When he does, he has about six generations of kittens, but he slows down and lets me in; I get my gap and overtake the truck. But there is always another truck, and my life is worth more than some uncouth driver's bad habits. I slow down and enjoy the view while the Serbs rage and hoot around me like soccer hooligans on the rampage. Soon they vanish out of sight.

The road leads through rolling farmland and small villages with surprisingly large houses. Everyone everywhere is making hay; it seems to be a national obsession. Bare-backed men scythe the grass, while women cart it to tiny tractors, donkey carts and wheelbarrows, which, when dwarfed by their enormous loads, transport it to the villages where the grass is flung onto untidy teepees made out of stout sticks around a central pole. The grass catches on the irregular points, and slowly develops into the termite hill haystack you have all seen in your nursery rhyme books.

Some people laboring in their vegetable fields catch my eye. I stop in front of a ramshackle small-holding where geese hiss and a very small dog barks at my impudence. I pooh pooh them away as I walk back to photograph the rural scene. The locals are a friendly lot; they wave and smile as we tip hats in greeting. A goatherd ties his adoring goats to a piece of shade, while the remaining peasants settle down for early tea, their backs resting comfortably against a haystack.

When I return to my car, the owner of the small-holding is waiting for me. Have I parked illegally? It seems highly unlikely. But all she wants is to invite me in for coffee. As I enter the gate to her property, the small dog ducks under the waist-high corn, glaring at me in mute rage; the invitation does not meet with his approval. With gestures and smiles I introduce myself to Zoritsa, who busies herself with making the coffee. She draws water from a makeshift tap that pokes through the corrugated iron wall and hangs loosely over the basin. The wastewater splashes onto the ground one floor below. The ducks seem to rather like this surprise shower. The front porch is also the dining room, where we will take our coffee, but first Zoritsa shows me her little house with some pride. It is basic in the extreme. Just inside the cracked and sagging front door stands a chair dressed in a dirty knitted coverlet, against a wall decorated with shiny blue foil. To the right there are cooking facilities, a table with a hotplate, a pot and a small stack of crockery. This is a kitchen for one; the space is so small that I cannot enter and stand halfway in the front door. As she opens her bedroom door I must move outside to allow her room to do so. The bedroom has one bed, with white sheets that dazzle in their grubby surroundings, and on a round table in the middle of the room stands a huge ghetto-blaster blaring away in Serbian. I don't dare ask where the toilet might be. I am guessing long drop way out the back somewhere, but I don't really need to know.

Over a thick, blindingly strong coffee we settle on the front porch for a chat. She brings out some photographs of people at a wedding, which she spreads in front of me on the brightly colored oilcloth. With much gesticulating I understand that these are her sons, this, her husband, and I recognize the dark-haired olive-skinned and well-groomed lady in the photograph as the woman sitting in front of me. But I cannot put the two together. The people in the pictures look fairly well off, they are wearing expensive-looking clothes, and the table is cluttered with glasses, bottles and the remains of a large meal. Today Zoritsa is dressed in peasant clothes; we drink our coffee out of chipped cups that have me mentally rummaging through my medical aid kit for cold sore cream; her house and surroundings give dirt-poor full meaning. She notices my puzzlement and with hands and feet explains that she has another house in a town somewhere; this is just the workhouse for the growing season.

Using my pictionary dictionary she indicates that they grow grapes, cabbage, onions, corn, peppers and chilies that all go to market, and if I understand her correctly, the peasants I photographed earlier are her seasonal hired help. This explains the huge stacks of wooden pallets that all but hide the house from the road. Getting into the swing of this impromptu show-and-tell, Zoritsa invites me on a tour of her domestic stock. Hens with chicks, ducks with ducklings, geese with goslings all flock around our feet and a fat bad-tempered turkey lurks all alone on one side. Under a massive hayloft, several ordinary wooden house doors are firmly closed. Her little dog attacks the top door with unbridled ferocity. The smell tells me what lives here, a sow of massive proportions. Behind another door live a white nanny goat and her kid. Downstairs a grey donkey and a brown cow share quarters. A boarding house for animals, do they ever go outside?

We chat away, she in Serbian, me in English. It is a very interesting conversation where neither understands a word the other is saying, but we pretend that we do, and so the conversation goes swimmingly. As I leave, Zoritsa gives me her phone number and indicates I should call her at any time. I look at the number and wonder just how that would work. While we can see each other, we make happy monkey faces and kindly noises, we gesticulate and point at pictures, and so a small connection is made. How we are to communicate on the telephone is beyond me. But this is not a question that can be discussed by facial expression alone, so I thank her kindly, smile widely, and then Zoritsa and I part on the best of terms.

With the traffic pandemonium and unexpected socializing, the sun is setting long before I have reached the Bulgarian border. I have no great desire to hunt for accommodation in the dark, so trawl up and down the grey inner city streets of Nis to try and find a bed. Nis is an ugly form-meets-function grey city, with perhaps only the river to recommend it, but the two riverfront hotels are fully booked, a further two hotels are closed for renovations, another hotel is closed due to strike action, and the last hotel I find is just closed. The sun is setting fast and soon this will not be fun anymore. I find a highway leading out of Nis – who would have thought it possible – and the E80 is a three-lane highway in excellent condition. Traveling north to south in Serbia seems to be no problem; traveling west to east, that takes a little longer.

The dusk slowly turns purple and I feel a slight pang of concern, I need a place to stay. Taking the first available off-ramp I stumble on a little spa town, Niska Banja, where I spy the sign I have been waiting for, 'Sobe, Zimmer, Rooms'. Here I rent a quite adequate room for 10€, but I have to share a bathroom with the group of paragliders who are occupying all the other rooms. With my small experience of sharing bathrooms with strangers I have learnt that using it first is best, so I get in early, while they are still sharing flight stories of the day.

In the early morning, I take a little stroll about the spa town of Niska Banja, before heading towards Bulgaria. Ornate stone balustrades and complex water fountains tell of a time when this must have been a well-off town. The sanatorium is still open, but the surrounding parkland is shabby and falling into disrepair. Litter clogs the empty and cracked fountains; the grass is too long; and the benches have been reduced to metal skeletons as the wood has rotted away. There is a battalion of caretakers and cleaners that lean on their broomsticks, chatting and smoking, until they see my camera, and when I point it at them, they leap into action and start sweeping madly. In front of the hotel, which in reduced circumstances has become a boarding house, aimless men stand about, some already drinking their first beer of the day.

I am quite ready to leave Serbia behind me. But as I reach the Bulgarian border a queue of trucks blocks the way forward. For the next five kilometers I play hopscotch with the trucks, constantly ducking into the small gaps left between the parked trucks, to let the oncoming ones past. The chap in the car behind me just cannot get his timing right, and with each oncoming truck has to reverse to the nearest gap. A prime example of two steps forward, three steps back.

Judging by the chairs, tables, and games of chess the truck drivers have set out, the border crossing into Bulgaria will be tedious. The cars are a bit better off than the trucks, but the crossing is the slowest so far. For the first time, I have to wait in a queue. The passport control is thorough, and the customs officials have a good look inside my car and ask if I have anything to declare. Having no idea what I am meant to declare, I shrug stupidly; it works and they move on to carefully inspecting my green card car insurance. After asking if my trip is for business or private reasons, my passport receives its first stamp. I am rather pleased at this. I have been through seven countries and the passport is still in its virginal state; now it looks at least a little used.

But before being allowed onto Bulgarian soil, the Wish Mobile must be disinfected; 2€ allows me to drive through a shallow ditch filled with some liquid; after which I pay 4€ for road toll; and with a little blue sticker on my window proclaiming to the world that I have paid my dues, I am allowed to enter Bulgaria.

Sophia shop, Bulgaria

Bulgaria

Bed 36

Today in the European Union the concept of a border is all but lost, but here this man-made boundary is all powerful. Crossing it turns the money in my wallet into worthless paper. The language of the Serbs is reduced to strange sounds, and the driving style changes – snap – just like that.

In Bulgaria, overtaking cars goes more or less back to normal, other than the use of the hooter, which is still considered to be of utmost importance. This leads me to think that Bulgarians don't use their rearview mirrors much, and the hooter is there to warn other drivers that you are coming. Just as I start considering the wisdom of adopting this particular driving tactic, I get pulled over by a dark-blue uniform with mirror shades, who is wielding a radar speed gun. I was going at 70 km/h; we are in the middle of nowhere; what's the problem here. But he informs me that we are in a 50 km/h zone; the speed limits in Bulgaria are as slow as their economy. He demands to see my car papers and driver's license and then he gets quizzy.

'Where are you going?'

I am sure he was not thinking any further than the next Bulgarian border post but I am the smart Alec today and reply,

'I am driving to Shanghai.'

This makes no impression, so I broaden the scope of my destination.

'Shanghai China?'

He raises both eyebrows right over the top of his shades and after a moment of silence sends me on my way with a

'Jus drrrive slooowly' warning.

If I am to stick to Bulgarian speed limits, I will need the next five years to get to China.

But I soon reach Sofia, for which I am fully prepared. I have done my research, listed my sightseeing schedule, mapped my course through the city and booked a place to stay.

Yeah right!

I hit the city, oops, big place, biggest since Rome, 12th most populous city in the Europe, and I have no map, no place to stay, no idea why I am here and, worst of all, I really should have paid more attention in Bulgarian reading class.

When I started on this journey, I felt that I would gain something, but up to now I have slowly lost all the guidelines that one doesn't even notice in life. The first thing that went was the blindfolded drive to work. At the beginning of this journey I would leap into the Wish Mobile and drive off, only to have to stop at the next convenient spot as I remembered that I actually had no idea where I was going. I have, by now, acquired the habit of first spending a few minutes mapping my course before turning on the ignition.

The next thing that I lost was the ability to understand everything that was being said. Since leaving Germany every new hello has required thought and research. Understanding the written word went next, but, as I could still read and look up words in my dictionary, this was merely inconvenient. It also showed me how much of the information we absorb daily is completely unnecessary. I haven't read a newspaper, book or magazine in months. I don't understand the advertising billboards, radio or television programs and I don't feel in the least deprived. Here I feel I am making some gains, as my mind is no longer constantly processing useless information; it is coming up with thoughts and opinions all of its own.

The loss of familiar brand names has made buying food a time-consuming mental challenge. Then at the shop pay points I smile blankly at the cashiers, who rattle off in incomprehensible language the amount owing. As till displays always seem to face away from the client, I constantly find myself peering over the cashier's shoulder to try and see what my goods have cost me. I sense the people in the queues behind me mentally tapping their feet, while I try to get the correct amount together by inspecting each note and coin in ever-changing currency.

But now, staring at the street names, I realize I have lost the use of one of my most important skills, the ability to read. The Cyrillic script is completely meaningless, and for first time in my life I have a small inkling of what it must feel like to be illiterate. My chest closes in frustration.

The roadsigns have been in Bulgarian Cyrillic ever since I crossed the border. But I felt that in a big centre, the capital of the country, the signs would surely be bilingual. No chance, all Cyrillic. But to make matters worse, pictograms, the savior of many a stranger in a new city, are completely missing. My navigation system falls to pieces. Driving aimlessly down a central city street, I stop at a huge intersection with tramlines and roads crisscrossing in all directions. At a complete loss on how to proceed I adopt the Zen 'follow the car in front of you' method of navigating – thinking that, as the car in front of me is a German make, it must be reliable.

The light changes, the car drives off, and makes a sharp, almost u-turn to the left. I follow and together we drive into a tunnel. It doesn't take me long to realize I am driving on rail tracks and there are only two cars down here, the white Golf and the Wish Mobile. The Golf zips up a side tunnel that does not look like it was built for cars. Are we in a subway tunnel? In a complete panic I bounce across the tracks, turn a sharp left, abandon the road/tracks altogether and vault the Wish Mobile over a subway station platform, just before it gets too high to navigate. The commuters standing on the platform stare at me in amazement. Zooming up a tunnel with daylight at the end, I hope and pray it ends on a street. In the sunshine a quick left and I am once again on a road. Finding a parking, I replay the last few minutes. Was I on a road or actually driving down a subway tunnel? I have no idea. When my adrenaline subsides to normal levels, I spot just what I need, across the road, an Internet café.

The interior of the café is dark blue and stale, the silhouettes of young men and schoolboys are etched against their computer screens, where they kill, maim and destroy their virtual enemies. My enemy is once again the specter of sleeping in the Wish Mobile. I will have to cross that particular mental hurdle soon, as the business of finding a bed each night is fast becoming tedious, although I am getting very good at it. The biggest challenge today is getting Google to speak to me in English. After that has been achieved, I quickly find the local tourist site and a few hostel booking sites. With hostel addresses in hand I set out to find a map of the city.

Bookstore, map, one problem, the map is in the Latin alphabet, the street names are in Cyrillic. Which brilliant brain thought this out? Using a Latin alphabet map in a country that does not use that particular writing style is about as effective as finding your way by reading tea leaves. I cannot make the actual streets and those on the map fit together. The pedestrians whom I ask for help look at the map in blank confusion. They have no idea, have never seen a map before, let alone one in English. My frustration plus the heat and humidity put me into a foul mood. I start snapping at all and sundry until I realize that this is no way to befriend the locals; it is hardly their problem that I don't read Cyrillic. In Bulgaria, Cyrillic is the written language of choice. Adapt or get lost is pretty much the situation I find myself in.

Time out.

Back in the Wish Mobile I find my Russian phrase book. It has the Cyrillic alphabet translated from English. With this, I try my hand at some Cyrillic writing. The results are not perfect, but at least I have something that can be related to the streets signs. An hour after arriving in Sofia, not bad, methinks, I find the first hostel.

'Do you have a room?'

The receptionist nods her head.

'Excellent. May I see it?'

The receptionist nods her head.

I wait expectantly, nothing, I try again.

'May I see the room?'

The receptionist nods her head.

Today perhaps? Then a guest ambles by.

'They nod for no in Bulgaria and shake their heads for yes.'

Now I cannot even rely on gestures to communicate. My situation is getting fairly desperate.

But the management, reluctant to let a paying customer get away, sends me to some other rooms they rent out. I walk there; it's less complicated; and gives me the opportunity to look at where I am. Sofia looks in worse shape than Sarajevo, and it doesn't have a recent war to blame. The streets are bleak and devoid of plants; the most colorful thing is the graffiti that covers every surface. The pavements are cracked and uneven; litter is everywhere. The buildings are dull grey with years of dirt and neglect. Flaking paint and peeling plaster, which in Italy looked delicately aged, here is overwhelmingly depressing. Electrical cables of every type hang from drainpipes and balconies like nightmare ivy. Next to the building to which I have been directed, two oriental tourists, nattily dressed in spotless little tourist suits, stare in disbelief at the boarded-up 'hotel' into which they must have booked through the Internet.

I know as soon as I have pushed open the front door to my building that I will not be staying here, but climb the six flights of stairs to the top floor just to make sure. Piles of discarded furniture are crammed into the corners and fill the landings. The building smells of damp and decay. My key does not fit any of the doors. Not really interested anyway, I make my way back to the first hostel via the other hostels on my list. All are by some good fortune in the same area. I look at several rooms in varying degrees of disgusting, for rent at prices that have me suppressing scornful snorts of laughter. Sofia does not seem to have any sort of regulation for hostels. Most of the places look as if the owners have taken their tiny apartments, subdivided the rooms to the size of a bunk bed, and then stuffed triple-decker beds into the narrow spaces – with the result that up to twelve strangers could share one shabby bathroom.

Giving up on the hostel idea, I stop in at a likely-looking travel agent. The owner is rather cute – pity about the pageboy hair style; it is just sad – but he does live up to the Prince Valiant image, and soon arranges a home-stay for me in the city centre. Back in the car I take a moment to work out my route to the accommodation with the help of my map. It doesn't look too difficult: straight ahead, third right and then the second road left should get me to my destination. Unfortunately my information deficient map does not just have a language barrier, it also fails to indicate the multitude of one-way streets in Sophia.

My plan falls to pieces within seconds. I am just about to drive straight out of Sofia and try my luck elsewhere, when I spot my goal on the other side of the street. I make a quick right, find a parking, and am immediately accosted by a blue uniform. He starts giving me a stern talking to in Bulgarian. I have no clue what I have done wrong or what he wants, so I allow him to get it all off his chest before telling him that I don't understand. He glares at me.

'Passport!'

Okay, that I did understand. He inspects my passport and when he is convinced that I am probably being quite honest when I say I don't understand a word he is saying, he softens a bit.

'Where you go?'

I figure that this is not the time to be clever, so whip out the address that I am hunting for. Recognizing the address, he becomes quite the gentleman, picks up my bag, and leads me to my destination, where he warns me to drive carefully before wishing me a cheery goodbye, as I enter the building that will be my home for the next two days.

The building is a brutalist architectural horror. Perhaps that is why the peeling paint and plaster look so terrible in Sofia – the architecture is so ugly that nothing could redeem it. Up three flights of stairs, the door is opened by the smallest little old lady I have ever seen. I look down onto the top of her head, where the grey re-growth creates a small yarmulke in her bright red hair. In spite of the heat, she is wearing a hand-knitted pink jersey, a dark sensible skirt, thick stockings and slippers. She is a curious old thing, and asks endless questions in broken English while she shows me to my room. The apartment is not a pretty sight; a bright yellow painted passage remains in constant darkness to save electricity. The bathroom is in shiny pink with blue sanitary ware, which, on cursory inspection, is not clean. My room is airless and stale. I immediately throw open the balcony doors that look down onto an inner courtyard. Above the bed hangs an image of the Madonna, who looks down at me pityingly as I sniff delicately at the pillow – No – and at the towels – No. While I wanted to see how people around the world live, and I am certainly doing just that, one has to maintain certain standards, so back to the car to get my bedding. Bed recovered and armed with my own towel, the question is, do I or don't I shower? The day has been hot and sticky and with all the walking about trying to find a room, I think had better risk it or I will start attracting flies.

In the bathroom I look the amenities over carefully. By keeping my rubber slops on I should be okay, except for that shower curtain. I hate shower curtains; they are the possibly the most disgusting invention ever. The bottom of the curtain is always suspect with that grey moldy discoloration that just tells me that things are not as hygienic as they could be. The worst part of the shower curtain experience comes just when I am at my most vulnerable. Standing naked in the shower, covered in soap, the curtain comes to life. Helped by some highly complex physical phenomenon that has to do with the hot air inside and the cold air outside, high and low pressure systems or just plain physical attraction, the shower curtain inexorably starts sucking inward. I don't want to touch any part of it with any part of me, but the slimy thing is about to cling to my whole body, so I desperately poke at it with my fingertips, withdrawing quickly just before the curtain closes in around my hand. I discover that the only way to kill it is by turning off the water. I shudder as the shower curtain slowly dies, hanging limply in all its slimy glory. But as I am still covered in soap, I have no choice but to turn on the water again. Using the shower head as a water gun, I fight off the advances of the curtain that come at me from all sides. While the curtain hangs back in brief retreat, I hose myself down. The battle rages until I am more or less clean. All the while around my feet grimy water dams up in mockery of my rubber slops. I will not be showering here again, I would rather stink.

The room is not the kind I want to linger in, so I step out to find supper, but find instead that I am not in the best part of town. Young people hang out on the street, and everybody is eating swarmas. Swarmas and pizza are the street food in Sofia: you can buy your giant slice of pizza from street vendors, and then you stand on the filthy pavement, preferably right next to an open garbage can, and shove that thing down your throat. I have no intention of joining the pizza-guzzling masses, but I don't have the energy to find and sit in a restaurant, so I stop in a local supermarket, thinking to get some basic supplies. But now the inability to read, plus the absence of known brand names puts me in a position where I don't know if I am buying yogurt or lard. This is too much for my brain. Back in the street I get a take-out swarma and return to eat it in my smelly little room, and then I sleep like a rock, with the balcony door wide open.

The next morning I am woken by car alarms. I had quite forgotten about car alarms. In South Africa they are background noise – like the Chinese cricket – you worry when they are not going off. In Europe they have not been much in evidence. In Sofia they suddenly make a comeback as the car alarm equivalent of the nightingale. The alarms don't just go wheehdah weehdah, they go through the whole car alarm repertoire of the world; starting with a police siren, then a fire alarm, moving onto an ambulance siren, and ending with a cacophony of squawks and wails.

Wide awake now and refreshed after a surprisingly good night's rest, I set out with determination to see the beauty in this city. A feature of Sofia is its many parks, and one of the biggest, Borissova Garden, is just around the corner. The little old lady has recommended I go to see it. But even this early in the morning the light is washed to dingy grey by the blanket of humidity that is caught by the surrounding mountains and sags over the city. Good light makes all the difference, so I am hard pressed to find anything I want to photograph.

In the children's play park, cute stone statues of squirrels and other cuddly animals have been given a macabre twist with graffiti blood dripping from their eyes. Modern sculptures that seem to be constructed from sewage pipes are also covered in violent graffiti. Even the huge statues honoring war and collectivism have not been spared. In this garden, the flower beds have been converted to dog toilets, the fountains are cracked and empty, and steps collapse under the weight of skate board ramps, all of which are decorated by Sofia's highly productive graffiti artists. The hot sticky wind blows dirt and litter around my legs; I am obviously at the wrong end of the park.

Crossing Vassil Levski and Tsar Osvoboditel roads, I notice an interesting feature about the traffic lights. When the light changes to green, numbers immediately start counting down from 24, so you have precisely 24 seconds to cross the road, and you have no excuse for getting stuck in the middle when the light changes. This would bring into play another interesting feature of Sofia. There are watchtowers at every intersection in which sits a blue uniform ready to pounce on any wrongdoer. I have never seen so many police officers in one city. The people are under constant guard. No wonder the city is covered in graffiti; it is the people's silent protest against the leash that controls them.

However, I believe police officers are there to serve the public, and as I am now totally lost, I put the dark-blue uniforms to good use. A bundle of them are enjoying morning coffee when I present the map and ask,

'Where am I?'

They crowd around the map, pointing to the route and the streets, and then they start again, then turning the map, start again, then another man comes and starts pointing to the route again. I get the picture! Thank you. And then they start again and then I catch myself. Stop with the nodding already. It takes some discipline to say yes, I understand, thank you, while vigorously shaking my head from side to side – much like that child's game of patting yourself on the head while rubbing your stomach.

With my route instructions drilled into my head, I find my way to the St Alexander Nevski Memorial Church with no further problem. It is the biggest Orthodox Church on the Balkan Peninsula. It has 12 domes, and materials from three continents were used in its construction. It has the biggest chandeliers, the longest this and the widest that, but here, bigger is definitely not better. The church looks to have been built by a committee that could not come to any agreement on style, so they just threw everything at it. The church squats like an over-attended dowager, primped, preened and bejeweled with overblown makeup and silly curls, which all come together in a clunking big building that does nothing for me. The interior is painted in dark and gloomy colors. The guide books mention fabulous murals, but perhaps these are in need of some cleaning and restoration. The famous chandeliers are certainly big, but the lights are off, so they are not terribly impressive. I much prefer the Russian church of St Nikolai the Miracle Maker, a green and white confection trimmed with golden lace and bulbous towers. Unfortunately St Sofia, the church that gave Sofia its current name, is closed. But next to it is the tomb of the Unknown Soldier, with an eternal flame in attendance. In Sofia, they have lit a flame that will burn for all eternity. Wow, that's some forward planning. Still contemplating this bit of grandiose thinking, I wander past a fresh produce market just in time to see a dog lift its leg and urinate all over a bag of green beans.

Then by a fortunate twist of fate, I find myself back at my building just as the clouds that have been pressing down on the city all morning surrender their fight against the load of water they are holding. With a clap of thunder that makes the windows rattle, the skies open and drop a comic book-load of water on the city. This is not rain; this is a sky-wide waterfall. The windows in my building all leak, so the water starts flooding down the stairwell, creating interior waterfalls to rival those pouring from the heavens. My room remains dry, but the courtyard downstairs rapidly turns into a small dam. Soon the water starts to flood into the offices below. Young men leap about daintily in the grimy water to try to stem the flood, but cannot find a way to let the water out of the courtyard, other than straight through their offices. Throughout the city, the storm water drains are taken completely by surprise, the roads turn into rivers within minutes; and then the rivers burst their curbside banks and flood filthy water into every basement store in town.

A peculiar feature of Sofia is the basement store. With a window at pavement height and the outside walls displaying the merchandise for sale in narrow glass display cabinets, small basement shops and bars trade on every street. To be served, you must crouch right down onto your haunches. Quite an art for the ladies in miniskirts as the person serving you would be just at crotch height. These stores must be great for voyeurs and cheap to run, but they are at a distinct disadvantage in a flood. Finally the rain lets up and in the delicate afterglow I set out once again, determined to find something to photograph. The fire brigade pumping basements dry holds my attention for a while. Then I discover that the place where it all happens in the centre of Sofia is along the tramline.

Here are the pedestrian zones with the fancy international labels, the coffee shops, the computer stores, and a multitude of Internet cafés. I have noticed that the poorer the population, the more frequent the Internet café. In rich countries, everybody has their private connections, but in places like Sofia the Internet café is doing a roaring trade. In the space of a few meters I find a computer store where getting connected is free; a few doors down is an all-night Internet spot; and every coffee shop seems to provide Internet access. As I need to do some banking, I decide to make use of the free Internet. Free only for those who read and write Bulgarian, the keyboard symbols are Cyrillic, and even setting the screen to English is not helpful, as the keys are not in the same position as on an English keyboard. Foxed! I have been denied access to the Internet by a keyboard.

To console myself, I have a cup of tea at a sidewalk café and watch the crowds go about their business. A book market is slowly peeling layers of dripping plastic from its wares. Young men and women are preoccupied with their portable phones. Old women sit on street corners trying to earn a small income by assembling tiny daisy posies, which they offer to every passer-by. Old men sit on the street benches, their heads in their hands. Ripped billboards and posters, advertising events long past, hang in shreds from walls, poles and doorways. Beggars amble past, their sodden possessions in leaking bags.

In Sofia there is a listless resignation, a feeling of surrender to the inevitable fate. It's in the dirty grey streets, in the peeling paint and falling plaster. It's in the tired faces and the lack of ownership and pride that allows beautiful parks and buildings to sink slowly into decay. Perhaps people who live under constant control lose their imagination and ambition. They simply don't see the need to do anything, because it is all controlled for them. People do best when there is a challenge, when they have to think. Or then again, perhaps I have just landed on the wrong side of town. Either way, I cannot get to grips with this place and, come morning, I am happy to leave.

Not so easy. The map – I really should have thrown it out, but seem to enjoy the subtle torture it provides – does not indicate through roads out of Sofia unless the end destination happens to be in Bulgaria. In fact, neither do the road signs. The Bulgarians are not interested. As far as they are concerned, the world stops on the Bulgarian border. It takes me hours and one nervous breakdown to finally find the E70 direction Greece. To celebrate, I stop at a most unlikely-looking restaurant that has a table and two chairs set out right on the curb of the busy route between Sofia and Thessalonica. In the noise, diesel fumes and swirling tail-wind dust of the trucks that roar by, I eat a hamburger and drink a coke. My stopping at this restaurant is inexplicable; the hamburger I can sort of justify; but the can of coke? This tells me that life as I know it is starting to slip away from me. I need to regroup.

But first I have to cross the giant obstacle that is the Bulgarian Greek border. The trucks once again form queues that stretch for kilometers. Is this really the most cost-effective way to get goods across the European continent? But today the border crossing for cars also takes hours on the Bulgarian side. On the Greek side, in a queue made a of a rag-tag assortment of cars from the former Eastern European countries, the cars from the EU distinguish themselves with their shiny paintwork and modern trim. This helps the Greek border officials sort the EU members from the non-EU members. We get escorted out of the endless queue and waved across the border with only the briefest glimpse at our passports. I had better appreciate the VIP treatment, as once out of Greece the EU will be a thing of the past, and I will be just another shmo.

Delphi , Greece

Greece

Bed 37

I have not had a private bathroom for a month. I have slept in rooms that I would normally not set foot in. I have experienced new things every minute of every day, and it's been fun or at least educational, but now there is only one thing on my mind, only one thing I want to see, only one thing I want to experience: a decent shower. Zeus and his band of merry men seem to be in agreement, and with the gods on my side, I find the perfect room in the first hotel I come across in Sidrokastro, the first town after the Bulgarian/Greek border. The hotel has just opened; everything is brand new; and the staff are champing at the bit to ensure the service is top class, oh joy. My private bathroom is fitted with a giant glass shower cubicle, and there is not a speck of mold to be seen, hallelujah. There is no smell of stale smoke, no suspect odors of a hundred unwashed bodies, and on the floor, no carpet that makes me wish I could float. There is a limitless wireless connection in my room and safe parking for the Wish Mobile. Heaven, I'm in heaven … and then Zeus brings me back to earth.

'Woman you need a shower.'

Half an hour later I step out of the bathroom in a billow of sweet smells, pink as a piglet, and steamed to perfection. After a few minutes spent at the mirror, I carefully select my blue jeans and white t-shirt, before taking a sundowner on the broad terrace overlooking the sparkling swimming pool. Sinking into an oversized lounger, I contemplate the view of Sidrokastro twinkling in the distance, while the staff hop about bringing snacks and drinks. I think I can stand this for at least a weekend. Then the manager comes over to apologize on behalf of his friends; they are so sorry they are not speaking to me; it's not that they don't want to, but they can unfortunately not speak English or German. If all Greeks are this considerate, July will be a very happy month.

Christos, tall, dark with a carefully maintained five o' clock stubble that frames a sensual mouth and elegant nose and underlines golden lion eyes, is the son in this family-run hotel. He has been reading the Wish Mobile and curiosity lures him over for a chat.

'Why are you letting people write on your car?'

'Because it is an art work, but you are not old enough to participate.'

He raises an eyebrow; men of a certain age don't like to be told they are too young. The pretty decorator, who is adding the last touches to the elegant lounge, giggles into her floral arrangement.

'Where are you heading?'

'Shanghai, China.'

This has the expected response. His eyes widen, and soon all the staff, management and friends gather around my chair. I feel like a bit of a twit as the perfectly groomed young Greeks look me over carefully as if to memorize exactly what a person who drives to China looks like. To move the conversation along a bit, and to get my barely adequate grooming out of the spotlight, I ask what there is to see and do in Sidrokastro. Christos immediately offers his services as a tour guide, and is not swayed in his resolve on learning that I want to be out and about at 6 am, for the light, you understand.

The next morning I am quite happy to forget the light and the sightseeing, and stay all day in my big, fat, comfortable king-size bed, which is dressed in snow-white sheets so crisp they rustle. But, before dawn Christos – fired up by his heroic mission – sends room service with a cup of tea. Bye bye, delicious bed, but not farewell, we will meet again tonight, bliss.

Christos takes me way off the beaten track to a secret waterfall by way of a tiny road that is tightly edged by river and cliff. As I negotiate the tight bends, I silently curse at the fact that I am going to have to reverse halfway down the mountain to get out of here. But Christos is being the hero, and I am being nonchalant – I am driving to China after all, I sniff at roads such as these – so into the wilderness we go, with no regard to how in the blue blazes I am going to get back out. But when I start having difficulty distinguishing the road we are on from a footpath I have to ask;

'Do you normally drive here?'

'Oh no, we park on the main road and walk up.'

Fabulous. And with that the Wish Mobile stops and we walk –deep into the green shadow of the valley where the white water of the falls comes to rest in dark mirror ponds and ancient pines bend down to their brilliant reflections. Settling under a tree, Christos mentions that in a cave higher up the cliff there are excavations in progress. My curiosity forces me to scramble up some hefty grey rocks until I overlook the excavation site. This can be exciting only for those who know what they are looking for. Square bits of soil chopped out of the cave floor, crisscrossed with string strung from needle to nail, probably trace the history of some fantastic cave culture, but I just don't see it.

By ignoring Christos, who is waving his arms about in a charming but useless fashion, I manage to reverse down the mountain without mishap. Next on our sightseeing list is an old castle on the top of a hill. From here, a rolling green and gold patchwork of olive trees and wheat fields stretches into the distance. On the only other hilltop, the multiple cupolas of a Greek Orthodox Church dazzle white against the purple clouds. It's all very pretty, but I confess to Christos that really, all I want to do is go back to my room, sit in my bed, and take shameless advantage of the wireless Internet connection. I can tell he cannot quite understand this. Tourists and sightseeing are synonymous, and I want to spend my day in a hotel room?

Yes, please. The Chinese travel agent in Munich has not contacted me since Dubrovnik. It's only been two weeks, but two weeks, five countries, four currency changes and seven different beds equal a lifetime, and I have lost all faith in the pompous Bavarians, and am getting myself into a complete flap about getting the Wish Mobile into China. To convince myself I am doing something useful, I start surfing all over the world to try and find alternative ways of getting into China. It is a lost cause, I know. The Internet is good for a lot of things, but when you are not moving with the masses, it does not have a lot to offer. In total I can find two references of people who have driven through China, independently, with their own cars, and they were both affiliated to some or other charity. It seems that I am way out on a limb here. Finally my numb bum forces me to admit defeat. I shut down the computer and decide that I will give this matter my full attention in Mesapotamos.

Beds 38 and 39

Now it is time to slowly make my way down to Athens. Very slowly. Greece is tiny and I have a whole week to cover a few hundred kilometers. But there is much to see in this land of myth and mountain. My goal for the day is Litochoro at the foot of Mount Olympus. Giving the pollution of Thessalonica a wide berth and swapping the A1 highway for a narrow country road, I start following some fairly suspect-looking road signs that point to Mount Olympus. The signs are not up to the normal tourist sign standard, but, hey, this is the Greek hinterland; perhaps this is how things are done here.

The road leads through head-high cornfields, silent dusty villages, past colorful churches, and through olive groves. By now I am quite aware that the roadsigns are leading me to an obscure back route to Mount Olympus, but curiosity drives me on and up, at a very steep angle. The road quickly leaves the olive groves far behind, then it leaves the tar behind, then the safety barriers, and finally any sense that this might be a road for normal cars. This is confirmed in an impossibly steep hairpin bend, where the Wish Mobile meets its match. The wheels spin on huge chunks of loose gravel and for one brief moment we are stationary, then the gravel starts moving down the mountain, Wish Mobile and all. A shock of adrenalin shoots through my heart.

With no power, no traction, and no safety barriers, this road trip could end in freefall and soon. I force the brake pedal right into the chassis, I yank up the handbrake, but learn the hard way that when the wheels are not what is moving the car, these actions are pretty useless. I try to power out of the situation, rev the engine, pop the clutch, but succeed only in flooding the car with a vile smelling smoke. In a moment of desperate brilliance I yank the steering to the left and drive the butt of the Wish Mobile into the side of the mountain. The gravel avalanche slips gracefully over the edge of the cliff, leaving behind a delicate plume of dust that is swept away by the breeze.

Stepping out of the car might not be the best plan at this point so I let down all the windows and have a good look at the ground around me. It is all loose gravel, but my wild swing of the steering has placed the car into the classic second position of a three-point turn, right in the bend of the hairpin bend that got us into this position in the first place. If I swing the wheel hard right, the road should be wide enough to turn around in. I turn the steering wheel as hard as I can and then put my full weight behind it. The wheels creak as they give me just a little more movement. Gently I ease the clutch, willing the Wish Mobile to turn. The gravel starts moving again, but before it can sweep us along, the wheels find grip, and we shoot from our position. I steer left, brake, we skid, I hit the gas, turn left, and just before driving over the cliff, I find a more or less level place to stop and regroup. On wobbly legs I stroll to the cliff to have a little look over the edge … those olive trees look very small.

Just then a posse of four-wheel-drive vehicles come up the road. As they drive past they stare at the Wish Mobile in amazement. It seems the signs I was following forgot to mention that this is an advanced 4x4 route, not a scenic outing for some insane woman in a glorified delivery van. The Wish Mobile is quick to agree with the opinion written all over the faces of the 4x4 drivers, and starts blinking a huffy little red light at me – stop immediately – service – stop immediately – service. Unfortunately stopping halfway up the rear end of Mount Olympus is not going to get us a service. I wonder if phoning the German Automobile Association will get me a tow-in service in Greece. I try to phone, but there is no reception in Zeus's backyard and so there is nothing to be done but to nurse the Wish Mobile down the mountain, and creep along the highway, all the while patting its dashboard gently for moral support. We reach a service station before long, but it is siesta time, so I pull into the shade, let down the front seat and have a little siesta of my own.

By the time the service manager gets back to work the Wish Mobile has calmed down, and has forgotten its little hissy fit. But I let the man look the engine over just to be sure. It seems I overheated the clutch. You don't say. Not a problem, just have it properly looked at during your next service. Service the car, there's a thought, and one more thing to do before I leave the European Union.

Approaching the earthly seat of the gods from the main entrance is a much more sedate affair. The road climbs into the deep valley that shields Olympus from undeserving eyes. It winds past the Platform of the Muses, but ends at the entrance of the Olympus National park soon after. To sit with the gods, you have to work hard. The only way to the top is by foot and that is good. Not all things should be revealed to the lazy, which, I am afraid, includes me. I never did understand the 'because it's there' mindset. But, 'I climbed Mount Olympus to sit with the gods' has a certain ring to it, and the thought of hurling thunderbolts to earth moves me to climb a few of the thousands of meters to Zeus. Then I see the hardier and better prepared return from their hike. Ah-ha, you need a rucksack, sturdy climbing shoes, water bottles, hats, sticks and you must book a bed in the mountain hut at Spilios Agapitos, situated at 2 817 m; the hike can take nine hours. As this is obviously not a spur of the moment activity, I content myself with photographing the mountain horses.

These are hippy horses: they have rings on their fingers and bells on their toes. Or at least they would have if they did have – fingers and toes that is – but they do have bells round their throats and beads around their heads with funky medallions that hang at jaunty angles under their forelocks. These are not just frivolous decoration, but have the serious task of protecting the horses from the evil eye. The hippy image is complete with brightly colored saddle blankets and exotic saddles that are highly complex constructions of carved wood and padded leather, which are held on the horse's back with wide leather straps around the horse's rump and chest. The eccentric-looking horses also like drinking their water directly from the drinking fountain by putting the whole drinking spout in their mouths. Fellow mountaineers, be warned. That drinking spout comes straight from a horse's mouth.

Descending the slopes of Mount Olympus, I find a room in Litochero. An ice-cream sundae of a village that has been discovered by the rich city folk and tourists, it has an over-sanitized – modern pretending to be old – feel about it. The town square is decorated by a fountain that is a slush puppy machine on acid. It squirts funnels, fountains and spires of water in pastel shades of pink, orange, green and purple, and is very festive and fun to look at while drinking a little glass of ouzo.

Feeling a little festive myself while getting dressed this evening – after today's narrow escape and all – I slipped into a sleeveless, form-fitting little black dress. But now, on the town square, which seems to be frequented only by Greek men, the ouzo, the dress, and the fact that I am alone is attracting frank stares that make me feel decidedly uncomfortable. The ouzo doesn't seem such a good idea anymore; I lose my appetite and make my way back to my hotel room. While walking under stone arches and through tiny cobbled streets, where newly renovated holiday homes stand next to fall apart ruins, in which feral cats are wailing and sparring, I come to the conclusion that Western city-style women's lib has not yet reached all parts of the Western world, let alone the world at large. I shall have to pay more attention to the dress of the local women in future.

Beds 40 and 41

As I head south, it gets so hot that the only sensible thing to do is to find a spot by the Aegean Sea. But I have my doubts about the pollution levels in these very confined, highly used waters. So I inspect the map to find a spot that faces out to broad water. The island of Evvia has the broadest stretch of water to be found in these parts, and becomes my destination for the day. One ferry crossing and a picnic lunch of roast chicken and salad later, I am on the road driving along the east coast of Evvia. The road winds through screeching olives groves – the mating call of the cicada requires some getting used to – plunges down to the deep blue sea, then works its way back up the bottle-green mountains. It is here that I come to the conclusion that the driving habits of a country, good or bad, rest squarely on the shoulders of the road planners and designers. The Greeks, despite their reputation, drive no better or worse than any other nation I have come across – excepting perhaps the Serbians and the Transkei minibus taxi drivers; those two fall into a singular category. The problem in Greece is the endless mountain passes that have no legal overtaking zone, be it an occasional double lane, a short straight stretch or even the occasional relief from the over-taking-forbidden road markings. After several tedious kilometers behind a bus, even the most law-abiding driver is going to take the first feasible-looking gap. And of course, if you drive the road daily, those gaps become more and more daring, and then comes the reputation of dangerous drivers. Not so; dangerous road planning.

By midday I have found the hamlet of Psaropuoli, a long stretch of beach, and my bed for the next two nights, and immediately retire to my siesta. In the Greek summer, a siesta is not the silly indulgence of the siesta further north, but a survival tactic. The midday heat is deadly, and the only thing to do is to lie very still on a pure cotton sheet, preferably a white one, in a suitably air-conditioned room and wait it out.

In the manageable heat of the early evening the reflection-still Aegean matches seamlessly the pale blue sky. The water is clear and bath warm, but a dive to the bottom brings an equal dive in temperature. Back on the surface, I swim with slow breaststroke, pushing my reflection ahead of me, while the setting sun paints gold a boat that floats past between sky and sea. I feel very small and alone in this flat round empty blue expanse. In shallower water, an old couple bob about, their silver hair still dry. I can hear their murmured conversation as it floats across the water. Little discussions about this and that, nothing important, just sounds humans make to stay in touch.

There is a table and chair under a pergola on the edge of the sea, where the guesthouse owner brings me a Mythos – the local beer – in a frosty glass. I feel a little 'Shirley Valentine' moment coming on, but I don't feel daft. In the last months I have had the time to learn that only when doing nothing becomes doing something, can you fully relax into the moment. In this moment there is much to experience. As the fishing boats return to shore, their lights make swirling golden patterns on the silver blue water. Night fishermen set up their folding chairs on the beach and hang small lanterns from sticks that they plant in the sand. From this small spot lit stage they cast their lines, which pull delicate threads of sunlight across the deep orange sky. In the distance a storm brews, and a sudden chill sends me indoors. As I work at my computer, my quiet musings are disrupted when downstairs the guesthouse erupts into full-blown family spat. Glasses are flung, doors are slammed, was that a slap? Where have I landed? Cars roar off with a spray of gravel, then quiet returns to the guest house, while lightning shows the horizon, and the sky grumbles.

Watching the dawn from behind heavy white lace curtains, I succumb to a sudden urge. Quite alone, I wade into the pale pink sea; the sun is a ball of fire attached to the world with a horizon-to-shore tail of red. A small pink wave flows around me as I swim due east down the red watery road. If I continue in this precise direction for long enough I will reach China – the land of the rising sun – or is the land of the rising sun Japan? In trying to find the answer to this question I stop swimming and my feet sink slowly into the cold depths. The shore is a distant smudge, the endless sea curves over the horizon, the silence pushes at my ears. I feel panic rising as I look down into the black water under the shimmering red surface. Too deep, too big, too empty! Gripped by an attack of agoraphobia, I forget all about the sedate breaststroke and windmill my way back to land, where my pounding heart is soon pushed to the background as my skin starts burning. Red itching welts start to form all over my body. Back in my room, the mirror reveals that I am fast beginning to look like a mutant measles victim. The shower to the rescue, and after a liberal application of fresh water, soap and lashings of antihistamine cream, my skin calms. What is lurking in the water this morning? No more swimming in the Aegean for me.

Finally the time has come to make my way to Athens. I will be staying with Viviane, a member of the Women Welcome Women World Wide organization. Viviane and Dimitri live high in the mountains of the Athens northern suburbs. The house is shaded by giant trees, and looks very inviting, but entry is not allowed. A pack of very nervous dogs bark hysterically, baring their fangs and mock-charging the gate. I get the message; strangers are not welcome, but I come by invitation. The dogs are less than impressed. At last, Viviane, looking majestic with her hair in a high towel turban and purple gown, steps out to call them to order. She is a one-woman rescue station as the Greek concept of animal rights is very basic, if not non-existent. In Greece there are mangy dogs and feral cats everywhere and, as it is breeding season, there is also the delightful sight of kitten-roadkill all over the place. And unfortunately, the pathetic sound of dogs yelping in pain is a common occurrence; one must assume therefore that beating one's dog is the accepted mode of canine discipline in Greece. Viviane, in response, has adopted several street dogs, but their sad experiences with humans have made them highly nervous, scared of strangers and therefore unpredictable. I wait on the safe side of the garden fence while she brings them to order.

Dogs contained, Viviane and I meet face to face. She is an old hand at welcoming strangers into her house. So she sweeps up the staircase to the top floor of her very modern home, where the guest wing will be my private domain for the next three nights. She then excuses herself as she has to finish her bath, which I interrupted. Later we meet again in the brightly colored kitchen ,where I come to the conclusion that, when you are a complete stranger briefly visiting the house of complete strangers, the only way to behave is to pretend that you are not a stranger at all, but a seldom-seen friend. We will only be together for a very short time and we may never meet again, so there is no time to waste on silly chit-chat and over-exaggerated politeness. That is not to say that you should immediately hand over your dirty washing to be laundered or open the fridge door and start rummaging around for a beer, but maintaining a Victorian stiff upper lip is simply a waste of time. So I pretend we have all met before, and fall right in with the things that I need to do.

And what I need to do is to work out how to get to Turkey from Athens. All my surfing has come to nothing, and I am hoping with the help of insider knowledge and more precisely, someone who can surf the Greek websites, I will have more luck. Dimitri starts surfing straight away, but even on Greek websites there is no answer to be found. There are several ongoing disagreements between the Greeks and the Turks, one of which is the dispute over their territorial waters. Perhaps because of this, a direct ferry to Turkey doesn't exist, and booking a ferry online is not possible, as the Greek and Turkish ferries lines don't communicate. I also need new car insurance as the EU green card is not valid in Turkey. After much surfing it comes to light that there are two ways of doing this online; the cost would be about 180€. For the three days I will be in Turkey, insanity. My other option is to try my luck at the Turkish border post. I will try my luck.

After a dinner of little Greek delicacies washed down by retsina, I go to bed early and as excited as a child on Christmas Eve. Alexandra arrives at 6 am, and I must leave for the airport at dawn. After months of being a stranger, I will be with my child, with someone I love, someone who loves me, someone with whom I can have little discussions about this and that. Nothing important, just sounds humans make to stay in touch.

By the time Alexandra and I arrive back in Athens, the heat has already decided Viviane and Dimitri that we will spend the day at the beach. We all pile into Dimitri's car and drive along the world's first marathon route to the town of Marathon. Dimitri tells the tale of the heroic battle in 490 BCE, when the Athenians defeated the Persians on the beach of Marathon. This resulted in a legendary run by a messenger from Marathon to the Acropolis to bring word of the victory over the Persians. Apparently, after the messenger handed over his message he fell down dead. This legend was used to fire the imagination of the world in the first modern Olympics in Athens in 1896, and started the tradition of the marathon. But the death at the end was considered unnecessarily dramatic, so seconds and water stations were introduced to prevent any more such incidents. While the legend of the messenger is but myth, the truth is the victory of the Athenians over the Persians was the beginning of the Golden Age of Classical Greece and a pivotal moment in the history of Western civilization.

This is heady stuff to think about while lazing on a crowded beach. Alexandra finds it all too much and has a little nap on a lounger in the shade of a reed-covered umbrella. Later we stroll along the narrow beach where music blares from small beachfront cafés; people play bat and ball, drink cocktails and eat ice-cream. To escape the heat, we bob about in the slop slop waves, while the songs of the Beach Boys bounce across the water; it all adds up to quite the 60s beach party atmosphere.

Bed 42

For the next month we will be staying in the holiday cottage of a friend in Mesapotamos, a tiny village situated on the north- west coast of Greece, and in the centre of the dead zone of Greek antiquity. Here flows the Acheron, the mythological boundary between this world and the underworld, over which Charon the ferryman escorted the souls of the dead to Hades. According to Homer, here is where Odysseus made offerings to Tiresias the Seer to try to find his way home. Mesapotamos also lies in the shadow of the temple of Persephone, Queen of the Underworld, and the Necromantic Oracle of the Acheron, where high priests through dubious means claimed to communicate with the dead.

To get there, we must head back west on the A1. The road wiggles its way around the Amvrtikos lagoon, past idyllic beaches to Mesapotamos, a tiny unassuming village built on a hill of history. This area was already inhabited in the 14th century BCE, and all this time the turquoise waters of the Acheron have been flowing from the highlands of Ioannina through the Fanari plain to the bay of Ammoudia. In rocky mountainous Greece, the Fanari plain with its ample water is valuable agricultural land and is farmed intensively. There is currently an abundance of tomatoes, cucumbers, eggplants, and marrows with huge yellow flowers, peppers, watermelons, honey melons and peaches. As our neighbors in Mesapotamos get over their initial shyness, we find our fridge overflowing with the vegetables they grow in their gardens. Here, eating in season is as natural as the sunrise.

For swimming, the locals recommend Alonaki beach, a secluded bay surrounded by high cliffs that are covered with gnarled and ancient pines. The beach is soft golden sand, and at the entrance to the bay squats a huge rock that looks like a camel swimming back to Egypt, through water that is warm, clear and still as a pond. Our own favorite beach is scenically somewhat lacking, but perfect for swimming. At Kanali beach, the sea ends on a steep shelf of tiny pebbles, and the water goes from shallow to deep in a single step. This has the happy effect of sitting at the edge of a swimming pool with waves breaking over you. The waves push us about on the smooth pebbles like pieces of driftwood; all-over exfoliation was never this much fun. We don our goggles, and find that we have little fishy friends that follow on our heels like well-trained dogs. As we disturb the pebble bed, we kick up little fishy delicacies that our scaly companions hurry to snap up. Floating upside down under the water surface of the water, we watch as the sea shakes out its liquid silver mirror, the sand and pebbles are juxtaposed onto pale blue sky for an instant, and then tossed into a frothy mix as the waves shatter on the shore.

We fall into a daily routine of early morning and late afternoons on the beach. While Alexandra rolls about in the surf like a demented seal, I lie in the shade of a tatty blue and white beach umbrella, trying to get my head around the Russian alphabet and language. As soon as I leave Turkey I will be in ex-Soviet states and Russia proper, where Cyrillic is sure to be the written language. My experience in Bulgaria has taught me that I will have to navigate with a Cyrillic map until I reach Kazakhstan, maybe even through Kazakhstan and Uzbekistan. So besides trying to be polite to the locals by using at least a few Greek words, I am trying to get my tongue around Russian.

But when I start confusing my barely there Greek with even more shaky Russian and start greeting startled Greeks with *dobrei sehn* instead of *kali mera,* when my *parakalo* become *paschauwesta,* and I swap *ne* the Greek yes for *nieht,* the Russian no, I realize something has to give, and it is the Greek. All the Greeks we have met so far speak either German or English and all the roadsigns are bilingual, so the nice Greeks lose out, no more Greek lessons. Learning two writing styles and two tongue-twisting languages at once is just too much for my brain.

There is just one little thorn on this rose, the noise. In a little Greek village, way out in the country, inhabited by very few people, noise is not something one would even consider. But here the people subscribe firmly to the view that unless the music is ear splittingly loud, they are not having a good time. It is three in the morning; the music from a dinner-dance joint across the valley is playing to an audience of twenty at noise levels that could fill a rock stadium. The sound echoes and bounces off the houses and the distant mountains. Every now and then the lead singer lets out a yelp of excitement, Woopah! At his noisy prowess, I flitch involuntarily.

At 6 am, sudden silence, but not for long, soon the roosters will crow, trucks will rumble by, generators will start, scooters will hoot, and dogs will bark. This has got to be the noisiest spot on the planet. Adding to this symphony of noise is an interesting feature of rural shopping, the portable shop. Vans filled to overflowing with a variety of goods from fruit and vegetables to plumbing supplies trawl the little villages, hawking their wares. As advertisement, they all employ their own public announcement systems, set to full volume. Here the van drivers play out their disc jockey fantasies as between the endless lists of produce, they play their current favorite Greek top of the pops, and so no sliver of silence is able to penetrate this rural fortress of noise. But there is always a remedy: industrial strength earplugs as recommended by the local pharmacist; she uses them herself.

Part of my daily routine is to drive to the nearby town of Kanalaki, where during the heat of the day I spend hours on the Internet trying to ensure that my travels will run more or less to plan. Here I discover that, although I still have received nothing further from them than a schedule outline and a quote, the Chinese travel agents have helped themselves to a very large chunk of my funds. An enquiry results in the rather sniffy reply that, yes, actually they had tried to withdraw the full amount owing, but my bank only allowed half. I am flabbergasted, at both the fact that the travel agent seems to think it is entitled to my funds without permission from me, and that the bank gave them any money at all. How did they manage that, anyway? Then I remember the credit card details I gave them for the 50 € Chinese visa. Fraudsters, swindlers, call the police! But after I calm down, I come to the conclusion that now that the travel agent has taken my money – illegally at that – I have legal recourse if they don't come up with the goods, so relent and allow them to keep the 50% payment they have helped themselves to. But I inform them and my bank that no further payment will be allowed until I and the Wish Mobile are safely in China, and could I please have some sort of proof that they have in fact done something to achieve this goal.

A week later a detailed schedule arrives in my inbox. I immediately notice a tiny problem. Entry into China, 12 September – that cannot be – I check my Kazakh visa, exit Kazakhstan, 9 September. So for three days I will have to perform a magical disappearing act. I have always been a great believer in German excellence and attention to detail, but this travel agent is really letting the team down.

More e-mails.

Dear Chinese travel agent, please note that the entry date into China is incorrect.

Chinese travel agent:

Sorry we cannot do anything about this; please change your Kazakh visa.

Astounding.

Russian travel agent:

Yes, certainly, this can be done, but it will take time and cost another 50€.

Dear Chinese travel agent, please ensure that you pay the Russian travel agent the required money so that they can correct your mistake.

Chinese travel agent:

Sorry, we take no responsibility for any mistakes we make.

How very European of them. I might still end up stranded in the no-man's-land between Kazakhstan and China. The Chinese travel agents then enquire whether I require their help in shipping the car back to Europe.

NOT.

But the issue must be addressed somehow. Although shipping the car back to Europe just doesn't sound quite right – something sort of tail between the legs about it – how difficult can it be to get the car into America?

So, just as I decide to be positive about getting the car into China, I add to my worries the problem of getting the car into America. It seems I am just not happy unless I am tearing my hair out about something. After sending off letters to everybody whom I think might be able to help, I receive almost an equal number back telling me that to bring a car into America is impossible. Why don't I just sell the car and buy a new one in America? What they don't understand is that the Wish Mobile is not just a car; it is my travel companion, which is slowly becoming a deeply meaningful piece of global art, and very soon I suspect it will be my house. Besides, trying to sell a German-registered French car in China is probably ten times more difficult than getting it into America.

Finally, my dear Dad remembers that he knows someone who is in the shipping business, and that someone has business colleges in the shipping business in Shanghai. Two e-mails later I am in contact with Andy. He is very skeptical about the whole affair, but reading between the lines, I can tell he is also intrigued and, better yet, has a sense of humor. I see a very distinct light at the end of the eastern tunnel. Now to address the darkness of the western one. One good thing about dealing with America is that absolutely everything can be found on the Internet. I don't think there are any holes in the information blanket that covers the USA. A few well-phrased enquiries soon have me in touch with David. He sends me the list of required documents for the temporary import of a car. Not a problem, I have them all at hand and what do you know – we are all going to America – for three months the Wish Mobile has free rein in the US of A.

I am becoming quite the international jetsetter. Well not quite the jetsetter, rather a car setter or delivery van setter. Point is, I am fast learning how to get around the world. According to the Chinese travel agents – can I believe one thing they tell me – I may drive my car in China up until 12 October. Then it will go into Andy's storage while I explore southern China by train. Then, when I am ready, the car will be popped into a container. While it floats across the ocean, I will visit Japan and arrive in America just in time to pick it up from the harbor.

With my travel plans more or less in hand, I can relax, and as a change from all the salt water, we drive to the town of Gliki to explore the Narrows of the Acheron. The path to the river leads through a holm oak forest, where the great oaks were afflicted by a fungal attack that has caused strange faces to appear in the twisted trucks and branches, like the spirits of the dead that are rumoured to be trapped in the lake beyond the rocks. It is not hard to believe that a hidden lake is contained in these white calcareous cliffs. The Acheron River wells liquid crystal out of rock basins, it flows from under the roots of the gnarled trees, and reflects the grass and flowers in moving mirrors that turn to water under our feet. Massive smooth white rocks rise in gentle curves out of the water. From up high, tiny waterspouts tinkle to the river below and waterfalls magically pour out of the cracks in the rocks.

We step into the liquid jade; the cold contracts and twists our nerve endings, sending shooting pains up our legs; but soon the beauty of our surroundings pushes the cold into the background. The river rushes over round white pebbles that are swept into an underwater walkway by the flow. It leads us through clear shallows that wind around pools of pale morning sky. Wild figs penetrate the crevices of the rocks, and make bonsai of themselves, while delicate maidenhair ferns trail green lace in the water. We round a corner and see the reason that people are all striding upstream in only their bathers. The rocks close in, and the river deepens to late afternoon blue. The cold and the current make heroes of them all, as one by one they steel themselves and in slow-motion breaststroke make it to the other side. We, laden with clothes and camera, are denied the sights that await them around the bend, so we turn back. We are starving, anyway, and my skin is so cold I get the most incredible itch attack as I slowly defrost.

As the month winds to a close, we visit Preveza, and while the Wish Mobile gets a full inspection and service, we dawdle about the town. In a narrow alley between white-washed buildings we find a small coffee shop, and quite unexpectedly start our day with ice-cream and chocolate cake. We drift about town trying on leather sandals and linen trousers. In a church, old ladies dressed in black stand in line to kiss each silver-framed icon in turn; I hope those icons get disinfected regularly. They light thin beeswax tapers that soon bend and bow to the intense heat of the day. As a fire precaution, to prevent the droopy candles from annihilating the church, water is poured into the bottom of the candle altars. As the last old lady shuffles out of the church, I climb up the creaking wooden stairs to the upper level to get a better view of the beautiful wall paintings; the brilliant deeply saturated colors of Greek religious art are here matured and mellowed by age. In silence I look down over the now empty church to Alexandra, a spinning dervish in a shaft of sunlight, her white skirt floating in full circle around her.

At lunchtime we find a restaurant with an exotic menu. On offer are roast lamp, lamp in tomato sauce and scorching salad. But we are finally ready to eat octopus. Alexandra, an experienced sushi eater, chews about on a morsel of octopus for a while, then declares it a dubious

'Not bad.'

My turn. The piece of meat in my mouth is sort of bouncy, like a tooth trampoline. I chew manfully, thoughtfully; it tastes smoky, and slightly fishy; but then images of octopus finding their way through mazes and gliding through tiny openings slide into my mind. As I chew, I remember that this animal is really intelligent, it can solve problems, it has a memory and it doesn't taste good, and the texture is gross. Why am I eating it? Why does anyone eat octopus? There is nothing about this meat that entices me to say: 'Please, sir, may I have some more.' Then I remember the huge eyes of the octopus; that when you look into them, you just know that the creature is checking you out, weighing you up, and, frankly, I would rather be eating cat. I push the plate of octopus towards Alexandra;

'You can have it all.'

She looks at me in horror. Now that's what fake politeness gets you, a plate of bouncy octopus flesh. Giggling we push the offending meal aside, and concentrate on enjoying the baked eggplants, mushrooms and cheese.

As we saunter down the promenade on the seaside, where yachts from around the world bob in the placid water, the cafés opposite the yachts beckon with comfortable chairs in the latest designs. The Greeks love their cafés, and the cafés show their appreciation by being as trendy, stylish and elegant as their clientele requires. For the pleasure of sitting in these designer havens, the Greeks pay budget-busting prices for long glasses of iced coffee, which are nursed through at least five cigarettes, while the problems of the world are aired, solutions discussed, and a final agreement is reached.

'What can we do?'

'Nothing.'

With the mechanical parts of the Wish Mobile now in tiptop shape, I apply myself to getting the interior up to speed. After being on the road for four months I should have a slightly better idea of what I will need to get me to China. Rephrase: from now on I am not just driving to China, I am driving around the world. Sounds great. Starting in the front, I work through the Wish Mobile in methodical fashion. I find five pairs of sunglasses? I find the steering wheel clamp, which I bought because I was scared the Polish would immediately steal my car, what a ninny. I find tissues, sun block and garbage bags, which are all very important items that may remain. With the interior of the car cleaned and ordered, I decide it is high time to give the bed a test run. This evening I will sleep in the Wish Mobile.

It takes me a while to work out what needs to move where, so I can fold out the bed support and inflate the mattress. The pump is a beast; it howls the air into the mattress; the mattress grows much quicker and bigger than expected; it starts folding double by pushing against the car roof and forcing its way out of the side door, sweeping everything out of its path. Take two: first place mattress in the approximate final position, remove all objects that may damage the mattress or vice versa, only then proceed to inflate mattress. Once the mattress is nice and firm, I start rummaging about for the bedding. Note to self: prepare bedding first. Of course, a sleeping bag would have been more practical, but I don't like sleeping bags, so I have my duvet, my sheets and my pillows; snow white and covered in lace. Who was that person who thought that this would be a good idea? Finally the bed is made, and I must admit it looks very comfy, and sort of sexy, in a camping in a delivery van kind of way. A sleeping bag would never have achieved this particular look. Then with the addition of my custom-made white mosquito net, I have my very own boudoir on wheels. I put down all the blinds, and instantly the interior is cozy and dark …and hot. Sleeping late or during the day will not be on the agenda.

To run a proper camping test, I set up my tiny gas burner, my little pot and boil up some rice for dinner, using water from the water canister. Alexandra is watching all this with great amusement.

I try my rice; very good, says I.

She raises a skeptical eyebrow.

Yes, all right, it tastes like rice boiled in plastic water. It needs salt, a touch of roasted cayenne, some onions, possibly a splash of grappa and a few olives. The one thing I think I will continue to miss is a kitchen.

On the last day in Mesapotamos we finally get to the 2 500-year-old ruin of the Necromantic Oracle. Priests of this order welcomed those who wished to commune with their ancestors with a diet of lupine beans that induced the right mindset to see the dead. The guests were bathed, led through dark candlelit passages to altars where they paid for the services of the oracle with offerings. Then, lightened of their material load and floating in a cloud of lupine bean-induced hallucinations, they were led through a labyrinth and down steep dark stairs into an arched underground chamber. In this room, the dead were called up with trickery and cunning by priests, creating suitable noises and shadows, while hiding in passages that ran through the three-meter thick walls. The guests were then sworn to secrecy under pain of death, and sent home out the back door. So the myth was maintained, and the priests lived very well indeed off the souls of the dead and the gullibility of the living.

Beds 43, 44 and 45

With the little cottage spick and span we turn off the electricity and gas, lock the door and head east again, Delphi is our destination for the day. But before we get there, a little navigational meltdown see us driving through narrow gorges, and then across flat mirror-smooth lagoons, where grey castles seem to float in the water. Then by crossing a modern lock bridge where luxury yachts wait for access to open sea we arrive, quite unexpectedly, on the island of Lefkada. On the banks of the shallow lagoon, fishermen in saggy underpants repair ramshackle fishing boats, while chic tourists sit in the shade of white canvas umbrellas sipping coffee.

The houses of Lefkada are a mix of plastered stone and corrugated iron, in a sweetshop riot of pastel. At the end of the long pier, where tourist cafés jostle for space, an old villa stands forgotten. It is a beautifully proportioned successful mix of Doric pillars, pale yellow stone and peeling painted wood, offset by tatty blue shutters. Its wrought-iron gates and balconies are slowly turning to rust. Once someone worked hard for this house, poring their time, energy, money and love into it. Where are those people now, why did they not sell the house when they no longer wanted it? Houses like these are silent mysteries. Why is something that was once so important now left to slowly weather its value away?

Leaving Lefkada behind, we make an effort to head in the right direction. Our route takes us around the Corinthian Sea, where the road is caught between high red cliffs and deep blue water. We reach Delphi just before dark.

It is rumoured that Zeus once summoned two eagles from the ends of the earth for a rendezvous at Delphi, which he then declared to be the navel/centre of the world. So if you ever want to do some global navel gazing, be advised that the navel of the world clings to the southern face of the Parnas Mountains, approximately 550 m above sea level. Being the centre of the world, Delphi soon became a platform for cultural and physical competitions, where the best of the antique world fought it out for honor and to win a laurel leaf or two. I wonder if we would have any sports heroes at all today if we paid them in laurel leaves. Soccer would definitely be a thing of the past.

The modern town of Delphi is higher up the mountain, hanging onto the edge of a deep gorge for dear life. Restaurants and hotels on the gorge side of the street offer startling views across and straight down the mountain. Be warned, though, that the view doubles your room price. Strange concept that: premium prices for a hotel room with a view, considering that most of the time when you are in your hotel room you are sleeping, with the curtains firmly closed. Incredible what some people will pay for. We stay on the opposite side of the street and pay half the price for a room that is twice as nice.

In the midsummer heat of Greece, sightseeing after 10 am is madness, so we are up with the sun and immediately head for the ancient city of Delphi. The temples, gymnasiums, treasuries and baths that once admitted only the nobles now admit anyone who can pay the entrance fee. Wild flowers adorn ancient altars, and the treasury contains only weeds. I see in my mind's eye the proud Greeks of old, promenading along boulevards, admiring the view and each other, while sipping retsina in stone cafés. It would have been inconceivable to them that all their splendor and wealth would be reduced to ruins, to a barely remembered brief amusement for tourists who are always clamoring for some new delight. We sweat our way around the stony site. The pillars that remain of the temple of Apollo strike a chord; they stand proud and huge against the stone mountain from which they were hewn. But the heat defeats us and driving to Athens in air-conditioned comfort seems the best idea of the day.

In Athens we will be staying with Julian, a friend from art school days. Alexandra is very curious to meet this friend from my distant past. To prime her, I remember stories of Julian 'happenings'.

Like when we decided to christen the new university campus with pots of powder paint and toilet paper streamers, and how a lighting fast thunder storm sent us running for shelter in the giant, still-to-be-installed wastewater pipes, which we turned into huge chimneys as we smoked our beedies, while the rain drew a curtain around us. Then with the return of the sun we emerged into a world where the building sand ran multicolor waterfalls into puddles of color that rivaled the rainbow sky. Julian also taught us scream therapy; immediately Alexandra wants to learn scream therapy too. All I can remember is that you just let go of your inhibitions and scream your little heart out. We give it a try, and it is surprisingly difficult; at first we can manage only little squeaks. But with a bit of practice we are soon having competitions to see who can scream the longest, loudest, highest, lowest and fall about laughing at the ridiculousness of it all. And the scream therapy works. By the time we hit the Athens traffic we are totally relaxed.

I have been warned countless times about the traffic in Athens. Yeah, yeah. No matter how busy, a road can hold only so many cars. The drivers might be impatient, but in the end there is not one, or perhaps only very few drivers, who really want to drive into you and destroy your car as well as their own. We negotiate the Athens traffic without a problem or a single hooter blast, and arrive, still relaxed, at Julian's apartment, which is in a suburb by the sea.

Over a dinner of wild rice, tofu, crunchy green salad, cooked beans, pickled beetroot and fresh fruit salad, Julian and I twitter our way through the missing years.

The early evening is still warm enough to entice us to the beach for a swim. The 'beach' is a rocky ledge, from where we dive straight into the ink-blue depths. The cliff creates an underwater amphitheater, from where fish watch us turn slow somersaults in the clear water. Armed with goggles and flippers, we break our chains to the land for brief moments as we push our limits and race out to the boat-channel buoys, where the water turns blue black and the buoy anchor chain lends perspective as it vanishes in the inky depths. Feeling out of our depth, we decide to swim back to land and off to the Plaka for a drink, via the Pnyka Hill.

While Mount Olympus was the earthly seat of the gods; Pnyka Hill is far more important to humans, as it was the seat of the Greek philosophers and the birthplace of democracy. But over the centuries the rock of democracy has been worn to treacherous smoothness by countless feet. When we arrive in the dark moment between dusk and moonrise, we must pick our way through hundreds of moongazers with utmost care, before finding a spot to sit just as the moon rises over Athens. When the moon is overhead, Julian guides us down past the Wind Temple to the restaurant district of the Plaka. Here we discover we are hungry again and have a second supper – Greek-style – at 11h30 at night.

The Greeks party hard and sleep late. Recently the Greek government, realizing that this was not good for the economy, tried to correct the partying habits of its citizens. The attempt ended in revolt, so the Greeks party on and, while the rest of Europe is up and about, Athens slumbers safely in the bosom of the EU. Alexandra and I are on the move long before the commuter traffic has properly started. The Athens public transport is very efficient, air-conditioned, clean and not expensive. This is thanks to the 2004 Olympics, as in pre-Olympic days apparently it was complete shambles. After rumbling about for a while, the system spits us out at Syntagma Square, where two most unfortunate fellows must, by government decree, guard the Houses of Parliament with a rather silly walk, great big pom-poms on their shoes, and massively frilled skirts. But other than the pom-pom men and the delivery men, who leave bags of onions, potatoes and vegetables on the steps of closed restaurants, the Ermou, a pedestrian shopping street appropriately named after the god of merchants, is empty. There is more action in the Plaka, where behind piles of nuts and fruit hawkers sleep off the excesses of the night, while shopkeepers, already shirtless in the fast growing heat, set out their wares: baskets, shirts, gladiator helmets, blue glass talismans to ward off the evil eye, and slippers with pom-poms, in anticipation of the tourists that will soon fill the narrow streets.

At the Acropolis we dodge the huge tour groups that gather around their guides and climb the many marble stairs up to the web of scaffolding that currently surrounds the giant pillars of the Ur-Parthenon, which were erected to commemorate the Athenian victory over the Persians at Marathon. Stepping into the inner courtyard, sunglasses are immediately required; it is a vast shimmering white-hot space created by the sun bouncing off the white marble temples and the holy rock. Far below the city is still visible, but slowly city noises and pollution fill the air. By midday Athens will be hidden behind a veil of yellow smog. The Acropolis is a giant marble jigsaw puzzle that an army of craftsmen are trying to put together again. While the Parthenon is hugely impressive in the clinical way one is impressed by a modern skyscraper – an impression that is reinforced by the cranes and scaffolding, which give it the look of a modern building site – I must confess that I have not got to grips with the Greek aesthetic. It is all so considered; even the highly stylized paintings of the icons and church decorations are somehow passionless.

Dutifully we drag ourselves around the Acropolis, like old warriors going into final battle against the heat. It is relentless and soon whittles our needs and desires down to just one thing, air-conditioning. A trip to the Archaeological Museum will provide just that, and so much more. The museum is enormous and filled with statues of people who lived thousands of years ago and they looked just like us, just bigger, or perhaps the Greeks of old just liked doing things on a grand scale. Before long, we realize that to try to give each piece our full attention would take weeks, which is far too long to wait for lunch. We have been doing the tourist thing for hours, it is hard work and we are hungry, and I still have a few important things to do, such as book a ferry to Turkey.

With the help of Julian's friends I have found a travel agent who knows the way around this problem. The only way to get the car from Greece to Turkey by sea is in two steps: first, a ferry to the island of Chios; then a Turkish ferry from Chios to Cesme. A direct ferry doesn't exist. Also I cannot book the Turkish Ferry from Greece. I have to do it directly at the Turkish ferry office in Chios, and hope there is a place   available.

But time is flying, and Alexandra leaves tonight, so with my ferry ticket to Chios in hand, we rush back to the air-conditioned comfort of Julian's apartment. While Alexandra pushes her possessions into her bag, Julian and I go into when-we mode; we are both the product of the apartheid-style Afrikaans school. Those schools treated history as a propaganda lesson, and believed that to spare the rod was to spoil the child. Alexandra, whose school career is light years removed, shakes her head and makes disbelieving noises as we walk down a memory lane that is lined with beatings and barely contained sadism, set in an environment of brain washing that passed as schooling in those days. Julian and I forge a bound of old warriors; we survived the system. During this orgy of story swapping, we all forget the time and are late, not very, but enough to make the Athens midnight traffic jams seem much worse than they are.

At the airport, the usual hectic rush whips my child away. I am beginning not to like airports much, horrible impersonal places that reduce everyone to terrorists and cater to great silver machines that swallow up those you love and whoosh them away. To be cool, you pretend you don't mind, but you do and you worry ... until the dearly departed send word that they have arrived safely on the other side and then life can go on.

Julian writes on the Wish Mobile and with a bear hug we part; he to his yoga lesson, and I plunge into the Athens traffic direction Piraeus. It is all very well signposted, so without any illegal maneuvering, I am soon in the queue to drive abroad the fast ferry to Chios. Taking a seat at table at the back of the boat, I haul out a book and read until we dock in Chios six hours later. In the busy little harbor the tourists stream onto waiting busses that will take them to the more scenic spots of the island, while I trawl the harbor for ferries to Turkey. A small boat with a bright red flag adorned with white crescent moon and star attracts my attention. The ferry can take only five cars across. I buy the last ticket. We leave at 5h30 am tomorrow; I had better get some shuteye then.

But although night has caught up with me, I have no bed. I had forgotten about this daily logistical problem during this last month with Alexandra. It has been a month of small adventures, but also of routine and sleeping in the same bed for more than just a night or two. I realize we need routine; like sleep, it allows our minds to do the filing and sorting. It gives our bodies the time to regenerate. The routine in life is the time when we get out of the river and allow the flow to pass us by, while we catch our breath and regain our body temperature, before once again diving in and swimming either upstream, or downstream, depending on our nature. I have no choice now but to dive right back in and start trawling the harbor for a hotel.

Map 3: Turkey to Kazakhstan

Map 4: Kazakhstan to China

Yeni Mosque Istanbul , Turkey

Turkey

Bed 46

Dragging my bag up the dimly lit stair of the seedy hotel and slamming the door behind me, I run my eyes over the crummy room, where the narrow bed, plastic dressing table and dirty white walls are laid bare under the glaring ceiling light. Shrugging my bag onto the bed, I take heart in the fact that it is just one night, and I have more pressing things to think about. Rummaging about in my bag I find the syringe, hold it up to the light, and give it a quick tap like I have seen it done on TV, then I try to insert the needle into my arm. But skin is resilient and rubbery, and the injection needle is not going in as easily as I thought it would. Feeling a touch queasy, I try again, this time going for the quick jab rather than the slow push. Stealing myself, I jab at my upper arm, the needle pierces my skin, and plunges deep into my muscle. Wincing, I empty the contents of the syringe into my body, then withdraw the needle with a tiny twist of my stomach and a whole lot of blood and, with that, finally complete my course of vaccination against hepatitis B that I had started some months ago in South Africa.

Early morning, the small ferry is being loaded by expert arm-wavers; not a centimeter of space can be wasted if we are all to fit. Cars reverse, forward, reverse, forward, until they are packed so tight it is a miracle the last driver can manage to get out of his car at all. The trip is a quick skip skip skip across the Aegean, and ends with an equal amount of forward, reverse, forward, reverse, that got the cars into their positions, to get them out.

In Cesme, my unease about my reception in Turkey vanishes as a customs man slowly trawls the queue and, spotting me, walks over to enquire in perfect and polite German how he can be of assistance. I get ushered past the queues of men, out of the blazing sun and into the air-conditioning. When he discovers that I have no car insurance, he apologises so profusely for the delay I might have to endure that I am almost convinced that my lack of insurance is his fault. He calls for chai, and while I sip the refreshing cup of tea, phone calls are made, couriers arrive, chairs are gallantly given up, pulled out pushed in, papers are stamped, friendly smiles are flashed about, and within half an hour I have my necessary insurance, costing only 20€, compared with the 180 quoted on the Internet.

Refreshed, relaxed and feeling like a retuning pasha, I set out into the land of the Turks, with not a care in the world, straight onto a road that puts the roads of Greece to shame. It is well maintained and wide, with ample opportunity to overtake. The driving in response to this is perfectly civilized, no dangerous overtaking maneuvers, and no bullying. I think my theory that there are not dangerous drivers, but dangerous roads, is proven here.

As I have become quite the connoisseur of roadside rest stops, I pull in at the first Turkish one I come across. Expecting the dreaded hole in the ground, I am astounded to find high-tech self-cleaning toilets that compete with those on the German autobahns. The restaurant has a large selection of fresh and crispy salads, and also local delicacies such as pickled beans and stuffed eggplants. At the meat counter, the cuts are on display in a butcher's fridge, and are prepared to your specification by the very helpful staff. No fast-food slap-dash here. In five minutes about ten misconceptions have been corrected. So far, travelling Turkey is not what I expected at all.

Heading north, the surrounding scenery is hilly and dry; the lack of trees is disturbing, as are the high-rise buildings: like giant multi-colored candy sticks they are stuck neatly on the top of every hilltop, marring the horizon forever. While the Turks seem to have a way with buildings, they are not so very good at choosing the position for them. I pass Izmir, Manisa and Akhisar without mishap or aggravation and am decidedly bored by the time I get to Balikesir, so decide to see what the hinterland of Turkey looks like. My map indicates a scenic route ,starting at Mustafakemalpasa. What a name. It is longer than the main road, where I spy an Internet café. I don't really have any pressing business online, but the Internet has become my only connection to the outside world, and I need my daily fix. It also provides me with a little glimpse into the life of others. Here the Internet café is bare bones, where computers from last decade stand on small school desks. Young men – always young men – are playing war games. Some things are the same wherever you go. Why do men need to kill stuff, even virtual stuff? Huge question, and no e-mail.

At the end of the main road, I turn right, as indicated by my map, but here the map and the reality come to blows. After several misguided forays into the surrounding countryside, I return to town and start hunting for the bus station; in the course of my travels I have worked out that the best people to ask for directions are bus and taxi drivers. At the station I scatter chickens and goats as I stroll to the nearest bus. Peering inside, I find the other side of Turkey, the one I was expecting. A young boy squatting on a crate stares at me; his eyes are the color of the sea on a still evening when, just after sunset, the water turns a silver grey turquoise that seems to be lit from beneath. The boy's face is finely chiselled with high cheekbones and dark golden brown skin, suffused with a delicate rosy blush, which is probably brought about by my intent stare. As he moves uncomfortably, the chickens in the crate shake their feathers, while the shrouded women that sit all around him stare back at me, a silent sea of shimmering turquoise eyes.

I show them my map, pointing at the direction I want to go, with, hopefully, a suitably perplexed and questioning look on my face. They stare silently. Then I remember that questioning the driver, not the passengers, is the way to find your way, and turning away from the bus find a huge group of curious bus and taxi drivers watching me. I question one driver after another, and by patching all the bits of information together, am once again on my way. The road winds up and up through struggling sunflower fields, where rusting roadsigns point to villages called Killik and Kabulbaba. The land is irrigated by baby aqueducts that run all along the roadside. On a high back road I drive through Turkish marble country. The road leads over square-cut dusty marble mountaintops, where great blocks of marble lie discarded on the roadside. In the valley far below, patchwork farmlands vanish into a lakeside forest. From this high vantage point, it looks so idyllic I figure it must be a tourist area, where accommodation is sure to be found.

Inspecting my map, I learn that I am looking at Golyazi, a small island village in Lake Ulubat Golu. The village is reached via olive groves and a narrow bridge, under which a shepherd watches his sheep as the sun sets slowly over the lake. In the shadow of a disproportionately large mosque sit the men of the village, watching soccer on the collective television. I park the Wish Mobile, walk over, and standing in front of the mass of seated men, it hits me: I am wearing a vest very similar to the ones they have on. To them it must seem as if I am standing about in only my underwear. I am really going to have to apply my mind to my dress code. The men stare silently; all this silent staring is getting a bit disconcerting. I ask the hotel question, in English, does anyone understand a word I am saying? All the men nod; it takes me a moment to remember that they mean no. But just to be sure I drive through the higgledy streets, and soon realize that the poverty here would make a hotel seem like a Black Forest cream cake at a pauper's tea.

But as the village throws up Kodak moments at every turn, I decide I will camp in the Wish Mobile for the first time, to be close at hand for an early morning photo session. But where exactly do I camp? Not in the main road. I leave the village behind, looking left and right into the trees. Shall I stop here or here or perhaps there? I dither about, but the light is going fast, and if I don't decide on a camping spot soon, I will have to set up camp in the dark. I turn left onto the very next dirt road, and bounce deep into an olive grove. When I feel fairly sure I am secluded from all eyes, I set up camp. Swiftly, and with the spare movements of the slightly guilty – what do I know, I have never done this before, is it even legal to camp in someone's olive grove – I run through the steps I practiced in Mesapotamos. In about half an hour I have a bed, tuna and rice for dinner and a hot cup of tea. I download the day's photographs, take a GPS reading, close the doors , let down the blinds, and have a wonderful night's sleep. When the sound of birdsong wakes me, I cautiously lift the blind to spy out my surroundings, hoping not to encounter some over-zealous olive farmer. But all is clear so I step into nature, and allow the cool morning to wake me properly. But the sun is rising fast, and the light I was anticipating is already waiting in the wings. Breaking camp in five minutes, I make my way back to Golyazi.

In Europe this would be a booming tourist trap with motor boats, water-skis and children paddling about in the shallows. Here is just an impoverished village in the middle of a lake. The only movement is of cats testing the rotting remains of a fish on the shore and water birds that balance on their reflections. The buildings are in deep shades of orange, ocher and red, and the window shutters brilliant green and blue. Grape vines grow over makeshift trellises, and storks nest on the chimney pots. The huge mosque glows deep yellow against the pale morning sky, while in the foreground women cloaked in black bring faded carpets from their homes to air them over the dry stone walls lining the lake.

Fishermen row back to shore in small wooden boats; the cats wait in anticipation. A small breeze lifts the smell of the lake and delivers it to my nose: the bitter, putrid smell of an open sewer. The harsh reality of the poverty of these people is hiding behind the romance of the ramshackle houses, the tumble of pink roses over ancient walls, the carpets, and the women in black. The lake that surrounds them feeds them, but is also the depository of their seepage and waste water; a deadly food chain.

Hypocrite that I am, I don't find the scene quite so picturesque anymore, and now also see the garbage piling in the alleys between the houses. I see the patches on the trousers of the men and the isolation of the women, who sit on the curbs, sorting stones from lentils, while gossiping about their neighbors. As I walk past, silence descends. With my fitted jeans and t-shirt, my camera and car, I represent a foreign world. I smile in greeting, they all grin back, and I immediately have uncharitable thoughts. But I cannot help noticing their teeth. Poor people have incredibly bad teeth. I imagine that when you are worried about where your next meal is coming from, you are not so concerned about how you are going to eat it. The thought that a set of shiny white gnashers might be a status symbol that will set you apart from your peers is as foreign to them as sprouting wings.

Bed 47

By midday I have reached the Sea of Marmara, where the borders between towns and cities are blurred by patchwork houses. This eastern part of Istanbul is densely packed with five-storey buildings that are polka dot with satellite dishes. Shoehorned between the buildings are little shacks and tumbledown houses that crowd the sides of the ten-lane highway. The trucks claw their way up the steep hill, while cars clamor for the front line, and I calmly thread my way through all of this, while consulting my map. If you do a thing long enough and often enough, you start getting pretty blasé, and I am developing some very exotic driving habits – like holding the map on the steering wheel while driving and consulting it every now and again to ensure I am heading in the right direction, which hopefully will never include the back of a truck.

The traffic is massive, but actually terribly well behaved; I get hooted at once or twice, but only to remind me to pull up my jaw, stop sightseeing, stop consulting the map, and continue driving. Taking the off-ramp onto the highway that leads to the enormous Brogaz Bridge over the Bosphorus, deep blue far below, I am back in Europe, and in front of me stretches the business end of Istanbul. The skyline confirms my view that the Turks know a thing or two about building. The skyscrapers are sculpture-elegant as they reflect the sky into which they rise. This is a green city where beautiful parks and tree-lined streets provide ample shade from the blazing heat. But the difference between Golyazi and Istanbul can be measured in centuries.

I skirt along the edge of the modern city, cross the Galata Bridge, and follow Kennedy Street to my turn into Istanbul's historic quarter. I have booked a room in a bed and breakfast, just down the road from the Haghia Sophia. The owner, Hafiza, and I have been having friendly Internet communications, and at the last moment she asked if I would mind changing rooms, as she had a little problem with one of her clients. Ever friendly and accommodating, I agreed, but now discover that my new room is not cozy as promised. It is a closet, no, not a closet; it is an error of judgment. They thought they had room for another room; they were wrong. This is not a room; this is a monument to greed. Then I see the room I had booked. Why was I moved? Why did I agree and then see her?

Some women scare the living daylights out of me. She is huge, broad shouldered with cropped bleached blonde hair and strong make-up, a multi-colored bohemian-style scarf draped casually over one shoulder, under which hides a heavy bag with strap securely across her chest, emphasizing melon breasts. Three-quarter khaki trousers cover ample hips and on her feet, socks and trekking sandals. She is a female cast from the Valkyrie mould. I feel quite the little mouse and, hey, I have never been called petite. I can just imagine what the tiny Hafiza must have felt when this woman saw the room I must now be content with, and with an emphatic

'Das geht ja garnich!'

demanded different accommodation.

I almost forgive Hafiza, almost, but not quite, from now on, no more Mr Nice Guy.

When the day has cooled to the point where air and skin are in perfect harmony, I step out into the street. The air ripples around my arms and legs as I stroll through the royal gardens, where the locals and the visitors are set apart by their stride. Locals look neither left nor right as they walk with purposeful step towards their goal, while visitors amble here and there, looking at this, pointing at that, thinking of sundowners.

Leaving my sightseeing too late, the Topkapi Palace and Harem are closed for the day, but Haghia Sophia waits. Commissioned by Emperor Justinian in 532, she remained the most important church in Christendom for nearly 1 000 years and thereafter, with the arrival of the Turks, was declared a mosque. Since 1934, she has been a museum, where Christian and Moslem symbols live in happy harmony. Her age is revealed in the worn slope of her pale marble steps, her spiritual history acknowledged by the silent awe of her visitors. Heads are raised to the great ochre arches above, and bowed to the distant pale grey marble floor below. The evening sun slants through the western windows, sending brilliant shafts of light through the cool dark interior. The light flows around green marble pillars and skims lacy stone balustrades; it bounces off the golden mosaics, leaving flecks of light on the gleaming floors before catching in the glass of the oil lamps, which hang like bells from curved metal chandeliers. Dusk slowly creeps into the great corridors, and people vanish through marble arches and copper-clad doors until it is just me, Haghia Sophia and the guards, who, although it is minutes past closing time, remain at respectful distance to allow me the rare pleasure of having this space to myself. I find the centre of the great dome that was said to 'change the history of architecture', and in the ringing silence stare up into the vast space. Time resides there. With a little nod the nearest guard lets me know that my time has come, they would like to go home now, would I mind?

Across Sultanahmet Square, at the Blue Mosque, life is still moving apace. Salep vendors – men in traditional Turkish outfits who carry huge silver pots of tea on their backs – dispense steaming cups of tea with a slight bow. Others sell flutes, spin taffy lollies or tell your fortune with a psychic rabbit. Hawkers sell boiled corn on the cob, and salesmen roam the square, balancing giant trays of crisp sesame rings on their heads.

'Where are you from?'

The question is obviously addressed at me. I look around and am face to face with a beautiful young man with dark hair, square jaw, piercing eyes and sensuous mouth, set in a pale complexion.

'I just want to talk a minute.'

The pretty boy falls into step beside me. What does he want? He is not a beggar; he is far too groomed for that.

'Can I show you around?'

As I climb the steps to the Blue Mosque, I try to work out what I am dealing with. Is this a hustler, a thief or just a friendly local trying to make a visitor feel welcome? I am reluctant to get rude and huffy until I am sure it is appropriate. I don't have a handbag filled with valuables flapping about, so am not concerned about being robbed, but do I really want this man to be quite so close? Looking back over the crowds in front of the Blue Mosque, I notice that there are pretty boys everywhere. Where are you from? Do you need a guide? The questions are asked over and over. The penny drops; these pretty boys are working boys. It seems they have found that a certain group of women, middle aged and traveling alone, are fair game for a bit of tour guiding, company and dinner. The pretty boys would probably sell their souls along with all the accompanying flesh if the price were right. I am not interested; pretty poor boys, I am sure, make pretty poor company. I politely dismiss my hanger on.

As I step into the Blue Mosque, Miss Priss comes out to play. Along with hundreds of other visitors I have left my shoes at the entrance as instructed, and due to my lack of head covering was supplied with a blue head cloth at the door. The day has been long and hot, and the result of all the freshly exposed feet in an enclosed space is an overwhelming smell of schtenk foot. My toes curl at the thought of walking on the carpet; I reluctantly put the cloth on my head, the thing stinks, and visions of head lice flash brilliant blue in my brain. My abrupt u-turn catches the visitor behind me by surprise. With a small collision and mumbled I beg your pardon, I rip the cloth off my head, and flee the smelly space. Tomorrow I shall be better prepared.

Up with the sun again. Soon I will collapse with exhaustion, but not now. Now there are things to do, places to see. Istanbul would take a lifetime to explore, but I only have today, and decide to concentrate on the bazaars. But to be ready for any mosque I might pass, I consciously commit the fashion faux pas of all time. Then again to commit a fashion faux pas is a contradiction in terms. The entire concept of fashion is a faux pas that depends on its constant renewal by coming up with more and more outlandish ways of dress. So who knows, what is faux pas today might be the height of fashion tomorrow and vice versa. But while it is possible that the sock and sandal combo might one day become high fashion, it will never have style. But the sock and sandal combo is the most practical way to minimize the inconvenience of constantly having to take your shoes off before entering buildings and to maintain some level of personal hygiene. I do, however, attempt to disguise the style stumble with black socks, black sandals and long wide black trousers and then, by slapping a broad-brimmed hat on my head, am prepared for any mosque I might decide to visit.

After a typical Turkish breakfast of tomatoes, cucumbers, mild goat's milk cheese, olives, crusty bread, yoghurt, honey, melon and tea, I make my way to the Kalpali Carsi, where I step into the world of Ali

Baba. The bazaars are a twinkling, glowing, sparkly, shoppers' dream-nightmare. Exotic merchandise is stacked, layered, hung, piled in tiny stores, and spills into the labyrinth of narrow covered streets, where hundreds of lights and lanterns tax the electrical cables that snake around ancient pillars and cluster in corners like giant spiders' webs. Shoemakers and carpet repairers, framed by beautiful blue and white tiles, sit on low wooden stools; they chat and laugh, while their hands fly through the familiar routine. Men wash mops and feet at marble fountains that form the central hubs to yet more treasure cave streets.

Salesmen tease and entice; they offer tea and a seat to rest my feet. In a happy mood I play the game; I tease and flirt my way from cashmere scarf to 'ancient' pot, from piles of spice to sticky sweet Turkish delight, where the vendor surprises me, by knowing all about AmaBokkeBokke and the 2010 World Cup in South Africa. He stares deep into my eyes, and informs me in sultry tones how beautiful they are, then suggests we meet later. I think not, and move along to the next vendor who assures me that his Turkish Viagra – five times a night – really works, would I like a demonstration? Whoa, time out, these lads are really up and ready for it. To escape the salesmen, I find a traditional teagarden, where men sit on low carpet-covered divans, sucking water pipes, sipping chai and discussing the world's problems under leafy awnings, where white doves flutter from branch to branch. A charming fellow from the carpet store in the small enclosed garden sits down next to me to help me decipher my map. No off-color propositions from him, though, thank goodness; it is all getting just a tad tiresome.

Leaving the Kalpali Carsi by the Mahmutpasa gate, I enter a shopping district that is aimed at the locals. Here tiny shops sell chains and ropes; fabric stores are floor to ceiling texture and color; and men walk by bent double under the weight of giant boxes containing televisions that are strapped to their backs with thick ropes. Broom sellers vanish behind the sticks and bristle of their trade. This is a city of brooms; everybody is sweeping; clean is king here. I have see parents admonishing their children for littering. I have seen people bend down and pick up litter to place it in the bin. This puts the Turks right up there in my estimation; they are a totally fastidious bunch.

Women with their hair covered under bright scarves riffle through piles of sneakers. No sale is made without a fight: prices are asked, refused, fingers wagged, jokes cracked, until finally a deal is made to everyone's satisfaction. Kittens tumble over multicolored plastic beads, and men with barrows trundle fresh fruit to the Misir

Carsisi. Here the flirting game continues, but with the added advantage that a smile wins me free samples of olives, nuts, fruit and cheese; soon I have had lunch, all paid for with a smile. Walking out of the huge gates facing the sea, I step into a flurry flight of feathery chaos, as the resident pigeons of the Yeni Mosque dutifully fly across to yet another plate of seeds that an expectant child holds for them. The pigeons are so fat and full it is just greed that drives them to waddle through the motions.

While I am standing on the small dividing wall in the middle of the road, to try and fit the Yeni Mosque and surroundings into one photograph, a young man watches me so intently that his car dies for lack of attention. I laugh, and he leaves his car right there, in the middle of the traffic, to come over and proposition me. Being friendly is obviously a sign that you want a man and you want him now, right there in the middle of the four-lane traffic jam. Is this how the men of the east believe one approaches the wanton Western woman? I imagine that by looking at American television, one can quickly come to the conclusion that all moral and sexual boundaries were burnt along with the bra; but no, not really, that would just be a little East/West misconception.

In the courtyard of the Yeni Mosque the faithful prepare for prayer by washing their feet, hands and heads. They should make the tourists do that as well; it would keep the smelly feet stink down. But armed with my socks and hat I am ready to finally visit my first mosque properly. The atmosphere inside is calm and quiet. yet filled with sound. An old man has a nap stretched out full length on the carpet. A baby enjoys a marathon crawl session; the baby's mother is unconcerned as for many meters in every direction there is nothing but intricately patterned carpet. Men stop to tickle the baby's feet before joining the other men for prayer. Patterns climb the walls, curve around the arches, fill out the domes, until no space is distinguished or defined, no part more important than any other. Unlike the imagery of the Christian churches, here there is nothing to focus your gaze – except perhaps the giant wheels of light that are suspended in the centre of the high space by long chains. Behind the light someone recites the Koran in melodic singsong. A man silhouetted in a window niche kneels facing Mecca and with metronome regularity he touches his head to the floor. I am reminded of little old ladies dressed in black ,sitting in church pews, rocking backwards and forwards as they recite their Hail Mary, all the while counting on their rosaries. All religion is centered on private meditation and public rituals. Traditions, rituals, religion are those things that define a country and its history, and as such, should be respected, even if they are not understood.

Sightseeing done, I am back on my quest for stuff. Maps of Romania and the Ukraine are on the agenda, so I make my way across the Galata Bridge to the more western part of Istanbul. This end of Istanbul is completely different from the old town, no head coverings here. People throng the wide boulevard that is lined with Western brand names, but still the Turkish habit of putting things in districts is evident. In the food district Greek-style coffee shops do roaring trade. Street cafes prepare mussels, fry calamari, boil corn, build swarmas, and sell sesame rings. In the music district, things are distinctly bohemian and slightly down at heel, with shabby buskers on every corner. In the bookshop district there are hundreds of bookshops, big and small. I systematically visit every store, but find no maps other than for Istanbul. In frustration I mutter aloud to no one in particular:

'Does no one ever leave Istanbul?'

From behind a screen of smoke a hot-potato English voice informs me

'Not if they can help it.'

A small face with white beard and round spectacles appears out of the smoke, just long enough to give me a cheeky grin before vanishing once again, much like the Cheshire cat.

Across the Galata Bridge, the clustered mosques glow in the evening light. The dozens of fishermen on the bridge are more interested in watching their fishing lines. I peek into their buckets, nothing but tiddlers. It is not really surprising; fishing here would be similar to going hunting on a highway, a complete waste of time. From morning to night, ferries roar from shore to shore, creating a sea of chaos as the waves meet and break in all directions; any fish that swims here is certifiably insane. On the café terrace under the bridge, ladies with oversized sunglasses sip chai from the comfort of bright orange and lime beanbags, while the working masses stream through sunlight tunnels, and dissipate into the old town, where the locals and the visitors are set apart by their stride. The locals are focused on home, while the visitors dawdle here and there, pointing at this, looking at that, thinking of sundowners.

I make my way back to my corrupt little room, pack my bags, then climb the steep stairs to the roof terrace. While I watch the sun set over the Marmara Sea, I sip a cold beer and wonder if perhaps I should have employed the company of a pretty boy after all.

Galati, Romania

Bulgaria, Romania, Moldova

Bed 48

Today my race around the Black Sea starts. I now have dates on which visas begin and end, and must get my timing right to be at the Chinese border on 12 September. But I still don't have car papers or a guide for China, so who knows, perhaps I shall have to be airlifted out of the no-man's-land between Kazakhstan and China after all.

The master plan for the next two days, however, is to cross from Turkey into Bulgaria, drive right through Bulgaria without stopping, cross into Romania, and find a place to stay for the night. Then tomorrow I will drive straight through Romania and into the Ukraine, where I will be meeting Olena in Nikolaijev.

This plan needs modification as soon as I turn on the ignition of the Wish Mobile. The normally placid dashboard has mysteriously turned into a raging disco inferno. Every single little light is flashing its urgent warning at me. Either I have an electrical fault or the car can be scrapped right here. Hafiza's father is on the phone right away. He warns the local service station that I am coming, scribbles a map and within minutes the Wish Mobile is in car hospital. Here a crew of incredibly polite mechanics intently watch my hands-and-feet explanation of my problem. They nod their heads, then phone a friend who speaks English – I was never much good at charades – so I go through the whole thing again, this time using only my tongue. When they fully understand my problem, the mechanics go on a seek-and-find mission in the Wish Mobile, while I sip tea and leaf through Turkish motor magazines.

An hour and a half later they discover that I, when shoving my computer bag under the passenger seat, had dislodged a slew of wires. They politely request that I stop doing this, as it could cause enormous problems in the future. Publicly I agree, but privately I know that I will just be a bit more careful with my shoving in future. Despite all this effort, there is no charge, but the manager wants to add his wish to the 'One planet One people' project. My artwork is showing unexpected advantages.

After a short and uneventful trip, I arrive at the Turkish-Bulgarian border post, which is set in a little forest. My delight at discovering there is no queue, and my hopes of making up lost time are short-lived. The computers are down, and no crossing into Bulgaria will be possible until they are up and running again. My master plan is obviously a bit of wishful thinking, but there is no point in ripping my hair out, so I park in a patch of shade, sit back and practice my Russian.

Once the queue of vehicles loses its tail deep in the forest, and is well stocked with tour busses, the Turkish border opens for business. The people – who have been crowding the doors – storm the counters, all desperate to be first. I suppose the five minutes they might save will come handy at some later point in their lives. But I know that with a private car I will have the added pleasure of standing in two further queues to get the obligatory five stamps that make a Turkish border crossing.

In the no-man's-land between borders we wait, and wait; now there is no forward, no back, only wait. Getting in and out of Bulgaria is a time-consuming affair. As the Bulgarian border post comes into view, I see the reason for the delay. There are serious-looking men in black swat team outfits searching every car very thoroughly. Cars coming from Turkey must arouse deep suspicion among the Bulgarians. I make peace with the fact that this border crossing could set a time record, and will turn my master plan into a piece of fiction.

The customs officers look at me carefully as I drive up to the next available search station. My German number plates win me brownie points, but the writing all over the Wish Mobile puts me very deep into hippy territory. When I get out, the black-clad men summon a strapping lass to deal with me. My heart sinks, no chance of chit-chatting my way out of this one; the only thing to do is to follow the example of the guy in the next search station. He is talking into his shiny phone, seemingly oblivious of the treatment that his very fancy black four-wheel-drive with tinted windows is getting from the swat team. One man starts pulling off plastic coverings in the rear of the car; he then uses special tongs to separate the window fleece, where he checks with tiny torches. Another chap rolls under the car, where he taps various cavities with a little hammer. I expect at any minute for him to haul out a stethoscope. These guys mean business. But the owner of the car hides any anger, frustration or other emotion behind mirror shades. This is the way to go it seems.

So I fling open all the Wish Mobile doors, and stand back to let the lady do her worst. She spies the Bulgarian road tax sticker, inspects the date, and with that her suspicion turns to curiosity, saved by a sticker. Then she starts opening a few zips and drawers, pokes about a bit, and concludes her search by asking if I am carrying narcotics. Bizarre. Yes, officer, if you look in the left door cavity, you will find six kilograms of Turkey's finest. What possible answer does she expect other than no?

But I am obviously an innocent-looking sort and am sent on my way with insider tips on the most scenic route to Burgas, while the man with the shiny phone and mirror shades must now watch as the swat team slowly take apart the interior of his car. Thinking to expand my collection of wishes, I offer my permanent black marker around, but the men are far too busy searching cars to be writing on them. The whole crossing takes more than four hours, so much for sleeping in Romania. I will book into the first hotel I find.

Over a high hilly meadow I catch my first glimpse of the Black Sea, 12 km outside Burgas, a harbor town and a holiday resort. This is the Riviera of Bulgaria, and it is not pretty: huge brutalist Soviet buildings with paint peeling and bits falling off surround tourists, who run about with bikinis, Speedos, bleached hair, and bad taste hanging out all over the place.

I make an unplanned right turn, and happen to find a holiday complex of the package-deal variety. The reception staff are not used to dealing with walk-ins, and my request for a room results in a large receptionist convention. Eventually they sell me the 'last' suite of rooms: two bedrooms, three bathrooms and a massive lounge. My Turkish room could fit in here a hundredfold, and the price is just twice as much, but with three meals included. How the value of a hotel room is defined continues to be a complete mystery.

This resort is family-holiday heaven, and is clamorous with English people coming and going by the busload. Music is blaring by the swimming pool, where preteens are taught dance moves by a rah-rah girl. In the pool teenagers flirt, while mom and dad lounge at the water's edge sipping cocktails, before getting ready for the massive 'eat as much as you can' buffet dinner that covers every possible food style and taste. After feeding, the adults retire to the small theater, where a loud cabaret is on, while unguarded children scream and run, playing catch in the dark. The cool boys play billiards and computer games; behind them a padded door opens to release blaring dance music.

I have never enjoyed the noisy smoke-and-mirrors nightlife world of endless alcohol and false expectations, and now, after months of almost solitude and silence, the idea of making conversation in a smoky room over loud music is repulsive. I escape to the dark expanse of the Black Sea, and while walking along the scalloped edges of the moonlit wave-slicks that darken the fine white sand, I take stock of where I am. This sudden and unexpected confrontation with the English language, people and customs familiar to me has pulled into sharp focus how we are conditioned to judge people by their looks, mannerisms, language or accent; how we make snap decisions about others based on the cut of their trouser or style of their shoe. First impressions count is our credo, perhaps, but only a small amount.

With the loss of language, reading ability and cultural knowledge, I have also lost the ability to judge people on these outward things, and I have started to notice subtle differences in my behavior as I adjust to this new way of living. The total media blackout that lack of understanding brings has started a growing silence and complete calm in the centre of my mind, allowing me to process information differently, independently, and at my own pace. The silence in my mind is also allowing my other senses to grow stronger. I have started seeing more, hearing more, or rather listening between the words. I am noticing not just the body language, hand movements, intonation, but also the subtle emotional temperature of others. It is as if my intense concentration on trying to understand the people I meet is beginning to open doors to primal senses that are drowned out by the noise of everyday. Even my sense of smell is growing more acute. In a big city, this is not necessarily an advantage. But these unexpected developments make me very happy with my choice to travel alone. When traveling in a team we look inward, towards the people we know, and we talk, talk, talk, often for no good reason.

But despite the daily changes of behavior, bed and country, I have fallen into a routine. Back in my enormous suite of rooms I go through my familiar evening ritual of downloading my photographs and transcribing the commentary from my Dictaphone. I summarize the day's events and post them to my blog. Finally I take a GPS reading and photograph my bed. This routine is a full stop to the day; the memories and impressions safely filed away, and with my mind now clear, I am ready for bed and what tomorrow will bring.

Today my aim is to be in the Ukraine by evening. I am up with the sun and the first to sample the breakfast buffet, and then I hit the E87 north. It is about 300 km to the Bulgarian-Romanian border and another 200 to the Ukrainian border. Even with border delays I should reach my goal long before dark. The road makes its way through cornfields and then back to the sea, where vines, thriving in the moist heat, which makes the air so thick you don't breathe it, you chew it, cover the trees, climb the buildings, and try to take over the cranes that line the sky around the port city of Varna. Here dingy buildings from the Soviet age stand like rotten teeth between modern supermarkets and new European-style high-rises.

A sign points to Thracian ruins. The Thracians were an ancient Indo-European people, whose kingdom, Thrace, stretched across the modern Bulgaria, Greece and Turkey.

My favorite Thracian is Democritus, a philosopher who was actively thinking years before Plato. From his name you might think he dreamt up the democratic political system, but no. Around 400 BCE, this man floated the theory that all matter is made up of small indivisible particles that he called atoms. But unfortunately he could not afford a good public-relations officer, and this left his theories moldering under piles of parchment. Meanwhile, the scientific theories of Plato (who disliked Democritus so much he wanted all his books burnt) and Aristotle – the philosophical superstars of their day – sent the world of science on a merry goose chase involving four elements, heavenly spheres, celestial symphonies and a mysterious substance called ether. It took scientists more than 2 000 years to finally get back to the atom theory.

The moral of this little story is that the famous guy is not always right, and all knowledge is based only on the information we have at hand. Tomorrow everything we believe to be the truth, the whole truth, and nothing but the truth could be mere mist before the sun. In this complicated, over-informed world of ours, it is becoming more, not less difficult to know what the truth is. When delving for the truth, all sides must be considered, but when the sides become too many to fathom, we choose to simplify our lives and believe whatever is presented as most easily digested fact. This does not make what we believe true; it merely makes it convenient.

Some free-standing houses in a neighborhood overlooking the sea pull me out of my introspection, and I slam on anchors to take photographs. Camera in front of face, I wonder why, why did I think this was worth stopping for? It is a rather surprising reaction to a perfectly normal and not terribly well-to-do suburb. But the last time I saw free-standing houses in a city was in Dubrovnik. Since then dwellings in cities have been either tightly packed, fall-apart semi-detached houses, or more often huge, grey concrete blocks in neglected disrepair, where the only color was the washing hanging from every balcony and the litter floating in the breeze. In comparison these houses are very upmarket. Opposite the houses there is a yacht club; this must be where the money of Bulgaria comes to party. And yes, there it is, a party beach and a dolphinarium: a place where creatures of immeasurable intellect are forced to do stupid tricks to entertain humans.

Soon I reach the border where bored Bulgarians wave me through and the Romanians are quite relaxed. This time the official business is dealt with in minutes. The border crossing brings about an immediate change in the look of things. The houses are finished, freshly painted and clean. The public spaces are neat; flowerbeds are tended and trim; the trees are pruned and painted with white socks to keep the insects off. From the signs in front of the restaurants advertising roast lamb with mint sauce, I am guessing that this part of Romania is a tourist destination favored by the English − who don't seem to pack their inhibitions when going on holiday. There is no beach or swimming facility in sight, but women in horrible bikinis are strolling about in the middle of the road, quite forgetting that it is an international thoroughfare. Actually, the bikinis are fine; the contents are the horrible bit, and all that in full public view. Have you no shame, women? Miss Priss again, I'm afraid.

The speeding fines must be very high in Romania. Romanians drive very slowly and the 'keep right, pass left' rule does not seem to apply here. Romanians like to drive more or less in the middle of the road, and when they get into a town, they really slam on anchors. To try to speed things along a bit, I apply the driving tricks that I learned in Italy, and tailgate the guy in the flashy car in front of me. He goes fast, I go fast; he goes slow, I go slow. He doesn't like it, and as punishment for being a roadhog I miss my turnoff and end up driving through, instead of around Constanta.

But in Constanta the truth about Romanian driving is revealed; they drive so slowly because they just don't know how to drive. It is as if they are not all there at all, like they are hoping someone else will make the decision to overtake, to turn left, or right. The inner city roads have no lane indicators, so people drive all over the place. Some drivers feel there are three lanes; some believe there are two; and some believe we can all squeeze together and make a fourth lane. So we weave drunkenly through town, sometimes cutting left, sometimes right, sometimes dodging drivers who have taken time out from the stress of it all, and have turned the unmarked tar into a parking lot. But I soon learn who rules the road: the drivers in the Trabants; they have nothing to lose and drive like lunatics. On Romanian roads everything goes but remember, the Trabant goes first.

After Constanta the road goes inland, and the planet folds open huge cornfields that are followed by sunflowers and vineyards. Monster machines work the fields, which stretch to the tiny trees on the horizon. The harvested fields are burnt, and then the ashes ploughed under. Crows lift and fall behind the plough, feasting on barbequed snakes, moles, and mice. On the long straight roads a speed limit countdown starts kilometers before the occasional curve, until finally, one is expected to creep around the corner at 20 km/h. A dull orange Trabant, towing a tiny trailer carrying three huge cows – cow sardines – is keeping strictly to the speed limits, as are the other road users, who are transported mainly by horse-drawn cart. One horse power is the norm in Eastern Romania, and often it is one-donkey power, so the 20 km/h ruling is not so outlandish after all.

The carved and brightly colored carts present great photo opportunities. The cart drivers think this is fun and stop in the middle of the road to pose nicely for their pictures. We exchange a few words of greeting and some pleasantries about the sparkling weather, both parties simply choosing to ignore the fact that we actually don't understand a word the other is saying. The peasants point at the line of deep purple on the horizon – storm coming – we nod in agreement, and then wave each other goodbye like old friends.

For two days I have been following the E87, and all this time something has been bothering me about this bit of road. According to my map, when the road reaches the Danube delta it just dies, and then starts again on the Ukrainian side. My brain refuses to believe that an international road can simply stop, bam, right there. I convince myself that there must be a tunnel, a bridge, a ferry, something; the road cannot be a dead-end. But when I reach Tulcea, the horrible truth is revealed: it is a dead-end. Tulcea is the end of the line. At the Tulcea Hotel I go into mime mode to try to discover from the receptionist, who is protected from her guests by a metal cage, how I can get to the Ukraine. From her shrugging and negative expression I gather that there is no way this can be achieved. But I persist, and with an impressive combination of hand movements, facial expressions, and pointing at the map, I ask her, if she were to go to the Ukraine, how would she do it? She looks at me in horror, and makes it quite clear that they would have to drag her kicking and screaming across the border.

This woman lives in the land of Transylvania and Dracula fame; one of her forefathers could have been Vlad the Impaler; and she is scared of the Ukrainians? Should I be worried? Then I remember my own good advice: when asking directions, ask a taxi driver, one of whom is conveniently lounging just outside the hotel doors. According to him, the only way forward is to drive to Galati, then cross the border at Reni. I check my map; a detour of about three hours, but it looks feasible.

As I wind my way along the Danube delta at the end of the European road, it is shocking to see how small the spread of the wealth of Europe is. These far-eastern parts of Romania could be somewhere in Africa. Reed-roofed huts plastered in mud stand in hand-to-mouth plots of land, half in and half out of the water. Chickens scratch around the feet of women in faded aprons who gossip by the village well, while a young boy rolls water home in a rusty barrel on a handmade cart, and I get held up in peak-hour traffic, involving two bicycles, a horse-drawn cart, a herd of swine, a gaggle of geese and me. The sky quickly darkens over the sunflowers; the wind roars through the small village ,where it picks up the road and blows it over the fence, behind which a mother in lime green and daughter in pink glow against the dusty dark. The street flies off over the sunflowers, and paints a black bruise against the sky.

In the downpour I make it to a more familiar traffic jam of trucks and cars that queue across a bridge and through a small copse of trees. Under the bridge, ducks float on the slimy water, while the rain paints the world grey, and we wait. The trees prevent me from seeing the cause of the traffic jam; the rain prevents me from going to find out. Slowly it dawns on me. It's a ferry! Damn! I am having a bit of a problem reading my map today; there it is clear as day, ferry, and I have no Romanian money. Euros would normally work, but I have no small change, so try to buy my ferry crossing with a 50€ note. The cashier takes one look at it, and then simply ignores me. I could rot right there in front of her; she is not getting involved. Now what? Then a knight in bright red t-shirt steps up to the plate, and enquires in perfect English what my problem might be. In a jiffy he pays my ferry fee and I am once again in business. The kindness of a stranger saves the day. He joins his family on the ferry, and vanishes across the Danube, never to be seen again.

In Galati I find my way to the customs office, where a group of ladies – who express great concern at my driving all alone into the Ukraine – find maps and schedules. They make phone calls and finally come to the conclusion that the road to Reni goes through Moldova for a few kilometers and, as I don't have a visa for Moldova, it is not possible for me to cross into Ukraine from Galati either. I must drive a further 60 km to a hamlet called Oancea, and there cross the Prutul River into Moldova at Cahul, where they have a 24-hour consulate and a visa can be obtained. But not tonight. It is getting dark, it is Saturday, and I am going to see what the folk of Galati get up to on a Saturday.

Bed 49

My first impression of Galati is that the Danube is a very big slab of water, which is not blue at all, but rather sludgy grey. Galati has a small measure of fame in the literary world: Bram Stoker had Count Dracula disembark here during his escape to Transylvania. A tree-lined boulevard connects the river to the town. and under every tree there is a dog lying in a dog-shaped hole. These animals live here permanently, and have been here for a while. The promenade on the Danube is lined with riverboat restaurants, reached by shaky gangplanks decorated with bright flowers. Plastic tables and chairs line the landside of the boulevard, where Galatians drink beer and gypsies sell balloons.

At a riverside restaurant I try to keep things simple and order pizza. Pizza is pizza anywhere in the world and I am starting to see it as comfort food. While eating, I watch the gypsies plying their trade. They have a very interesting sales technique. As they pass the restaurant tables, they slam down their merchandise: small plastic gee-gaws whose only purpose is to make money flow, and to pollute the planet. These items are left on the tables, until one of the patrons picks one up for a closer look; then the gypsies pounce, and proceed to try to close the sale. People with children have a hard time of it as the children believe the objects were given to them and cannot understand why they must now give them back.

Finishing my pizza, I call for the bill, it amounts to 23 000.00 leu! I am horrified. With all the changes of money I have been going through, I no longer have a firm grasp on the value of it, and have fallen into the habit of always taking the middle amount of money on offer when drawing money at the automatic teller. So I have on me 100 new leu, but one pizza is 23 000.00 leu! The waiter sees my distress, and tries to explain the Romanian old leu/new leu monetary system in broken English and fast-flowing Romanian. I am now a world expert in this matter. Suffice it to say, I have no idea how much the pizza cost. He takes my money; brings me change. Is the change correct? I have no idea. I tip him anyway, possibly extravagantly or possibly not. I have no idea. Time for bed, not knowing anything about anything is exhausting, and sleep is one thing I still fully understand.

On a sunny Sunday morning I try to get rid of the last new leu before leaving Romania, but the chap at the duty-free office refuses his country's own currency, demanding that I pay in euro. As my only reason for shopping here is to get rid of the new leu, I refuse and leave with the knowledge that as soon as I step into Moldova, the money in my wallet will turn into paper, and for this paper, people in Romania work their fingers to the bone.

Crossing from Romania into Moldova is no problem, one quick stamp, and off I go. In Moldova things become a little surreal, as life turns into a Kafka play. The crossing starts with a woman in military uniform opening a large gate and directing the Wish Mobile through a quick sprinkle of disinfectant. As a germ-killer this treatment is totally ineffectual, but as they will charge me for it later, some show has to be made. She then walkie-talkies my arrival to the main buildings, which I can see about twenty meters ahead. I can also see that there are no other cars or travelers at the border post, and that my welcoming party of three people in blue uniform and three in green is ready and waiting. They can surely see me too, but a long conversation on the walkie-talkie is required before I am allowed to move forward. At the customs house, a lady in green takes my passport, inspects it carefully, discusses it at length with her comrades, and then explains to me that I don't have a visa. I bite my tongue and await further instructions, which soon follow.

I must leave my car here, and walk to the consulate to get a transit visa. Perhaps they are afraid that I might make a wild dash for the Ukrainian border. I have visions of the Wish Mobile bouncing through the sunflowers with the border guards on bicycles in hot pursuit. This thought amuses me while I sit on a hard chair in a dull green office, waiting for the customs official to work her way through her red tape. My name is filled into a ledger, and I am given an invoice of 30 USD for a 48-hour transit visa. Then I am sent back to green lady one, who now retains my passport along with the car. In exchange I am given a document, which I am to present to an old gentleman in a small office. He has some work to do that involves making a great display of opening several large dusty ledgers. Huffing and puffing, he writes my details down in one ledger after another, adds another stamp to my document and 3€ to the bill. He sends me to the police to register the car, more big ledgers, more stamps, and 5€ to the bill. I then go to another office where, thinking that this is where I should pay, I put a 50€ note on the counter. The man whips the note away with such speed that I smell rat, and demand the money back. He reluctantly returns it with my document, which he has adorned with more stamps and directs me to the bank. In Moldova a large part of the population live off less than 2USD per day. The 50€ note I was flapping about so carelessly could represent someone's monthly income here. At the bank, a clerk fills in another ledger, adds more stamps to my document, which is starting to look like a very interesting piece of modern art, before I hand over my cash to yet another lady, who is protected from me by heavy metal bars. Account paid, I return to my car via all the officials I had visited before, each one confirming the transaction with more stamps, until finally, green lady one checks the whole lot and seals it with a last stamp, and with that returns my passport.

As I am about to leave, one man asks:

'Will you be returning through Moldova?'

'No, I am driving to China.'

He stares, a glimmer of understanding, then his brain slams shut.

'Yes, but will you be returning through Moldova, as your visa is only valid for one transit and if you return you would need another transit visa?'

In the tiny town of Cahul about 25 people wake up every morning, put on their smart uniforms, and report to work at the Romanian – Moldovan border in the middle of the sunflower fields, fully convinced that they are doing something useful and valuable. I hope they never see the futility of it all.

Crossing the Prutul River, I enter Cahul, where the arts and crafts movement moves in real time. While the people here also live in mud-plastered houses, the plaster is carved and sculpted in floral designs, and the wooden eaves, window frames and shutters are decorated with wood carvings. Two colors are used to decorate the houses: mid green and cyan. Bicycles replace the horse-drawn carts, and donkeys graze in the shadow of a small white church. The air smells of sun-baked grass and dust.

I start photographing the gazebos that protect the water wells, which stand at regular intervals along the dusty road. Water well 217, built *circa* 1983, is a particularly fine example. The wood-slat walls are painted bright blue, yellow and green, and its octagonal steeply sloping roof is decorated with metal flowers, herald angels on every corner and stamped metal filigree that reminds me of St Nikolai in Sofia. The interior is minimalist and functional, with a beautifully turned wooden spindle, from which dangles a large tin bucket. The mirror of water lies far below, and shows an unexpected reflection. Looking up, I am impressed to find the roof decorated with naive biblical scenes: the holy family, a shepherd, some crusaders on horseback, several swans and St George slaying the dragon all form part of this rural chapel to water.

In my absence, the Wish Mobile has drawn attention to itself; geese and young men on bicycles have come to look it over. They call friends on portable phones, and one man tries out his English.

'Where you go?'

'Shanghai, China.'

He smiles uncertainly.

'Why writing …'

He indicates with a squiggly hand movement.

I try to explain, but fall victim to our missing language bridges.

This is a day of border crossings, and soon I reach the Moldova–Ukraine border. Getting out of Moldova is simply a matter of handing over my stamp-laden document, which I had really hoped to keep as a souvenir, but it seems it has some very important file to fill. On the Ukraine side of the border post I sense that here all procedures are adapted to suit whatever officer or traveler happens to be at the border post. Six slovenly customs officials descend on the Wish Mobile. I am not happy, but allow them to open and shut various boxes and drawers. When one man demands to know how much money I have, I figure we are now in ad-lib territory. I have never had to answer this question before, and decide it is none of their business, and that being honest could be dangerous.

'I use a credit card.'

That's the end of that discussion.

'Do you have any drugs?'

'No.'

'Guns?'

'No.'

These must rate as the stupidest questions in any language. If I am carrying contraband, surely they must realize that I would try to keep it as secret from them as possible. I am not sure that these chaps grasp the point of their employ, but am relieved that they are far too lazy to do any searching, and are far more interested in writing on the Wish Mobile. They all want to sign their names, but when I make it clear that they actually have to think up some wish for the world, it all becomes too much and they walk away, muttering that I must now proceed to the environmental protection office.

The environmental protection office is itself a danger to the environment. It is dingy grey and reeking of stale cigarette smoke; a rust-streaked fridge leans against the yellow nicotine stained wall. The dull light struggling through a filthy window slides over the greasy hair of a small thin man sitting behind a grimy table. He indicates that I should sit on the battered chair opposite him. I indicate that I would rather not, but he is insistent and refuses to conduct any business with me while I remain standing. Perching like a prim schoolmarm on the very edge of the chair I enquire why I am in his office. When he discovers I do not speak Russian he bellows 'EnglES' with a strong emphasis on both Es. From the back room I hear the creaking of a metal spring bed. A slovenly oaf of a man, shirt unbuttoned and vest hanging out, walks over and leans on the table, his oily face far too close to mine for comfort. I can see the dirt on his unshaven face; I can smell his sour skin and fetid breath. How to move out of smelling distance without insulting the man? I have a cough attack; he backs off an inch, and then stuns me with a smile of gold and black. Why not just make all your teeth gold, mate? What are you hanging onto those last few black ones for.

But I soon realize he is saving up for them and here's his little scheme; the cost to disinfect the car at the Ukrainian border is 10€ – ten euro to drive through a pit of chemicals is outrageous. Irritated I slap a 50€ note on the table. They stare at it in astonishment. They don't have change. If they are charging everybody 10€ to disinfect their cars, surely they would have plenty of 10€ notes in change. But no. So the man with the teeth escorts me to the currency exchange office; they don't have sufficient money to change 50€ either. By now I know I am being scammed, and can barely contain my fury. The man with the teeth keeps shouting at me as if I am deaf. I tell him in fast-flowing English that he is a thief and a liar. This makes me feel much better ,as I know I am in no danger of this man understanding. He has no more than six words of English that he uses in any given situation, as it gives him a one-up on his comrades. The money man and I come to a compromise: he gives me as many Euros as he can manage and fills up the rest with Gruebna. I will need some Ukrainian money, anyway, so other than probably getting the worst possible exchange rate, no real loss.

But now that I am onto their scheme, I take a leaf out of the Moldovan book, and demand an invoice with a stamp before I hand over my money – total confusion and much rushing about to find an invoice book. Then I demand to see the disinfectant facilities. With all my border crossings, I have seen plenty, and know what to look for. There is nothing here that looks anything like a disinfection centre. In response to my demand, the thin man hauls out a portable insecticide pump, and squirts a couple of drops of chemical onto the hubcaps of the Wish Mobile wheels. So that's where the germs are, never mind the tire-tread and the undercarriage. No, in his great experience, the bulk of 'foot and mouth' disease and 'swine flu' germs are carried on the vehicles' hubcaps.

I drive into the Ukraine muttering furiously to myself.

Ukraine

Beds 50 and 51

Hardly am I in the Ukraine than the road skims through a tiny slice of Moldova again. The Ukraine customs man checks my passport and waves me through. In the heat and dust a young Moldovan solider, with gun slung over his shoulder, scribbles my car registration and passport number on a small scrap of paper and hands it to me. Okay, whatever. After ten minutes in a stop-start traffic jam I am once again at a Moldovan border where I hand over my little scrap of paper to another gun-toting solider. He inspects the tiny document with great care. With their highly complex border procedures, one would think that the Moldovans have a problem with people from all around the world flooding their country in hope of a better life. I don't think so. The border guards probably make small paper bonfires at night to hide the shameful evidence of their futile existence, before the next day creating yet more little piles of meaningless paper.

The stop-start traffic jam continues across no-man's-land to the Ukrainian border, where all the cars get waved across after just a brief inspection. But in me they see profit. I may not enter the Ukraine again until they have inspected my car documents. The soldier flips through them, then, documents in hand, marches off. This is not good; I park as quickly as possible, and after making sure that all valuables are more or less out of sight, follow my documents to an office in a shipping container. A heavy man behind a blue cloud of smoke informs me that I cannot enter the Ukraine without buying personal insurance for a minimum of 10€. The first Ukrainian border post has obviously not yet twigged onto this little money-making scheme, as they probably would have used it on me. I therefore know that this is just self-enrichment, and politely but firmly decline the insurance. He insists, while waving the car documents at me in implied threat. No insurance, no documents.

Shaking with rage and having the most uncharitable thoughts about the Ukrainians in general, I excuse myself, return to the Wish Mobile, find my most impressive-looking insurance paper, bring it back to the man, and shove it under his nose. The document is in German and in the Latin alphabet, so he cannot make out one word, but in trying to decipher the insurance paper he makes the mistake of putting down the car documents. This is the moment of truth. I pick up the car

Informal market, Nikoliaev Ukraine

documents, retrieve my insurance paper, and wish him a good day. He stares in disbelief as I walk – fairly quickly – back to the Wish Mobile.

But what are they going to do, shoot me? They could. There are lots of guns about.

Not one kilometer further, I get pulled over at a police roadblock. Have they been warned to look out for me? Are they going to arrest me? A jolt of apprehension makes my hands clammy and my throat contract. I sense that in the Ukraine one could easily vanish. But the officer only wants to see my car papers and license, and I am so slow on the uptake I actually hand them over: idiot, idiot, idiot. The papers get dragged to the standard container office, where I must again dutifully follow. The container is inhabited by the familiar stink and another greasy man. The greasy slob paws through my papers with hands that make me want to hurl just by looking at them. Do I have a disinfectant spray ... I mentally rummage through the car. I don't think so, but acquiring some has now reached top spot on my shopping list. He waves his hand at a chair; to refuse is pointless; I sit down and stare at him.

He wants something from me.

I want nothing from him, except my papers back.

He speaks only Russian.

I speak no Russian; silence descends.

Surrounded by the smell of unwashed body I watch in disgusted fascination as a bead of sweat rolls slowly down his temple, making a detour around a ripe pimple. The grease on his forehead reflects the light from the dirty window. Flies crawl over his hand and my documents. That's it! No one is touching those papers again, except me. Finally he realizes the situation is beyond him, so he returns the papers, which I bury deep in the Wish Mobile. I find the color photocopies, made for just such occasions, put them in the cubby-hole, and they have served me very well at countless roadblocks.

My muttering, moaning and groaning at the injustice of it all distracts me from the road, and I end up on the totally wrong end of Odessa. The famous steps and sights are nowhere to be found, but I have found the beach, where ramshackle cars and small square busses crowd the streets and parking lots. Semi-dressed locals are licking ice-cream and eying the opposite sex, as they stroll up and down on a beachfront that has the feel of a deserted building site about it. All enthusiasm for sightseeing vanishes, and I press on to Nikolaijev, where Olena from 5W waits. I am a couple of days late, but she knows how things work around here, so is quite relaxed about the whole affair.

Driving through the streets of Nikolaijev, I am reminded of the less savory neighborhoods of Hillbrow in Johannesburg. I am quite sure that the Wish Mobile would not last the night on the street, so I am relieved that there is secure parking behind a heavy gate in the courtyard of Olena's apartment building.

The apartment building is a prime example of the brutalist square blocks in the same shade of neglected grey that house the masses in every once-was-communist country. We climb narrow concrete stairs to her front door, which is a thick steel security door that would not be out of place on a bank vault. I don't think that even in Hillbrow they have these. Olena lectures English literature at the University of Nikolaijev, which is not a very highly valued occupation, judging from my surroundings. The minute bathroom cannot be entered if the front door is open, and the kitchen is a space for one. I sleep in the narrow all-purpose living room and cannot help comparing this to the living standards of my teacher friends in the West. Olena tells of a time when she had to hold down three jobs, so that at the end of the month she was more or less sure she would receive at least one salary.

This sorry tale of dishonesty and corruption is apparent everywhere in Nikolaijev. Olena plays tour guide, and walks me along broken pavements and weed-fringed paths to the 'dry fountain', a zany sixties construction of cascading ponds with metal daisy fountains and enamel black seals, but no water. To save money it gets used only on special occasions, and judging by the weeds growing in every pond, special occasions don't come around much in Nikolaijev. In the central business district the wide tree-lined boulevard gives an initial impression of improvement, but soon it is apparent that the buildings and public spaces all suffer from the same lack of upkeep as elsewhere. Corruption has cracked the pavements and allowed weeds to grow in unkempt parks. The buildings are peeling and losing their plaster, and rusting balconies make me fear for the safety of the tenants and the pedestrians below. Here the poverty is as ingrained as coal in a miner's hands. Beaten and cowed people walk with mouths draw down in dissatisfaction.

All except the youth. They have adopted American-style clothing, and the girls have taken the packaged pop diva slut-style of dressing to heart and let it all hang out, although the guys, who are wearing so many clothes they look like walking wash-baskets, are not even looking. With so much female flesh on display, I guess they have become blind to it. Rap music blares from music stores, and the Internet cafés are the gathering spots of the hip and happening, where some new pop diva grinds her glittering hips on an overhead television. Pity really that these are the best role models for capitalism that the West has been able to provide.

Across a very wide and empty street there is a recently built Russian Orthodox Church with gleaming golden domes and gold leaf interior. It stands out from the grey surroundings like the first freshly shorn sheep in the flock. This church was built on the same site where the old one was imploded one dark night in Soviet times. In the evening, when the people went to bed, there was a church. The next morning, when they got back, it was flat. How's that!

In the late afternoon we reach the Yuz Bug River and a restaurant complex designed and decorated by someone never trained or given the opportunity to appreciate beauty. The complex has a cheap fairground feel, with the same unloved air that hangs over everything here. The restaurant overlooks the yacht marina, where people swim in the garbage-laden water. A fat lady sitting on the pier makes me wish I was less inhibited about sticking my camera into people's faces, but to me it's like littering – just not done. But to ask permission is to lose the moment. The fat lady is taut, round, pink and white, with huge comic-book boobs, four tummy rolls and bowling-pin legs. Her pink polka-dot bikini – which strains to maintain the lady's dignity – deserves a medal for perseverance and service above and beyond the call of duty. The perfect fat lady is topped off by bouncy golden curls and a huge straw hat adorned with flouncy pink roses. In all the drab greyness surrounding her, she is like an Italian gelateria. Pure delight.

Less delightful, the service at the yacht marina restaurant. 'Yacht marina' makes the place sound so fancy, but we are sitting at a bare wooden table on hard benches, all of which are bolted to the floor. The railing keeping us from the river is made of the kind of metal that makes your hands stink when you touch it. The restaurant service is so bad that I am sure they are purposefully ignoring us. When I walk up to the management to enquire what the problem might be, I am not sure who is more horrified at this, the management or Olena. After eventually placing an order, the food takes another lifetime to appear. Finally it is set before us: is it an old horse or goat? I would normally send this type of food straight back to the kitchen, but by now I am so embarrassed on my hostess's behalf that I manfully chew my way through some of it. Olena starts giggling. I am not sure if she is embarrassed or simply giggling for the fun of it all. Then it occurs to me: this is the sort of place where the staff would quite happily spit in your food. I stop eating and send the food back. The waiter is surly to the point where an expletive is appropriate. He just really couldn't give a shit. I should have just given Olena the money, and enjoyed another delicious supper of pink borscht, hand-made pilmeni with sour cream, and pink quince juice, prepared by her mother.

Early morning I head direction Russia, I am happy to move on. I cannot say that I like this part of the world. On the outskirts of Nikolaijev I pass an informal roadside market. Huge trucks carry mountains of pale yellow honey melons. Bottle-green watermelons, cut in half to display their bright pink interiors, attract bees and buyers. A small yellow Trabant is hidden behind piles of yellow peppers. From the boot the owner transfers armloads of deep purple aubergines into the bags of waiting customers. Boxes of bright red plum tomatoes are stacked next to bags of short fat cucumbers. The fresh produce on offer is the best I have seen in months. How is it possible that a country so richly endowed by nature, so centrally located and with sea access to huge markets for its produce, can be in such dire straits? But the mere fact that this impromptu produce market takes place here is the answer: the corruption that has filtered into every part of Ukrainian life ensures that the farmers live poorly off the richness of the land. Their best option is to bring their huge truckloads of produce to this roadside market, where they can set a fair price, rather than use any middlemen or government-controlled market.

The frustration of the people shows in their driving, and the brute aggression on display is shocking. The concentration that driving here requires is all-consuming and exhausting. This is not helped by the road surface, which swaps and changes between normal tar and concrete blocks that with time have shifted and create the effect of driving on a railway track. Then there are potholes, open manhole covers, and leftover cobblestone sections in the middle of the tar that are all obstacles on the worst roads with the worst drivers that I have come across on my journey.

To add to the mayhem, the roads are too narrow for the volume of traffic. This brings out a super-exotic driving style, where the overtaking maneuvers spell quite clearly that the drivers couldn't care whether they kill you or themselves. The culprits here are not the people in fall-apart Trabants, but those in black Mercedes Benz with black-tinted windows. The invisible drivers of these luxury cars, whose invisible money-making business dealing sets them apart from their impoverished countrymen, believe they own the road, overtaking with such narrow margins that the on-coming traffic swerves onto the dirt shoulder of the road. They overtake trucks on the left and via the dirt shoulder on the right, often two cars at the same time, both trying to get to the other side of the truck first. When the constant overtaking becomes too tedious, the black Mercedes simply drive on the wrong side of the road, with no regard for the oncoming traffic.

My sixth sense and the scattering evasive action of all the other road users tells me that this game of chicken is deadly serious, and I give them as much space as they need to vent their fury and spleen at the world and its ways. Despite my attempts at remaining Zen and calm, the driving style rubs off, and by the time I reach the Ukrainian–Russian border, I have added some tricks to my driving repertoire that would get me arrested anywhere else in the world.

A small twist of apprehension turns my stomach as I approach the border. Borders are still the only things that cause me real concern on this trip. Our species loves borders. From our youth we are programmed to use them to define value by what is mine and what is yours: from the space squabbles on the back seat of the car to the careful division of a chocolate bar. We draw imaginary lines across the earth, turning friend to foe. We plant flags to declare ownership over things that cannot be owned, and then will fight to the death to defend what we falsely we believe is ours. In our minds and hearts we put walls and boundaries around everything: between work and play, between love and friendship, between people of color, creed and religion and all we achieve are fear and mistrust. Divide, conquer and control is the goal of every border.

Borders are often far-flung, isolated places where I am forced to stop and allow bored ill-paid men with guns to play out their power games, and every Ukrainian border control adds a new rule to this unpleasant game. The passport control man wants to see my Russian visa, but he seems unable to read either Russian or Latin script. He reads and rereads and checks his computer, flips through my passport again and again, until I finally ask what the problem might be. He commands me to sit and wait in my car. But I am done with being ordered to sit and wait by incompetent men with more power than their intellect can cope with, and reply that as he has my very important documents, I shall stay right here and keep an eye on them. He slows down to sloth pace, while he tries to work out just how he can scam the obligatory 10€ out of me.

I simply stare the impenetrable thousand-mile stare of the Xhosa. When you know you can do nothing, understand nothing, do not have the language to defend your rights, it is best to become the rock, and just let life wash over you like a wave, and once the wave is past, you can move on. Finally he realizes he can find no fault; there is nothing to be done but stamp the passport.

But before I can leave, the customs guys insist on searching the Wish Mobile.

I am leaving your country. What the heck do you have here that anyone would possibly want to smuggle out? Carrots?

They demand to know how much money I have. As I am leaving their country, this is really none of their business. Fortunately the credit card answer stops this line of questioning. They find my tripod ,and demand to know if I am a professional photographer, and then want to confiscate my camera and my collection of CDs, along with all my photographs.

Then a man with a gun leans into the Wish Mobile and picks up the CD holder, at which point I flip out completely, and in acid tones tell him to take his cotton-picking paws off my possessions. He understands the tone, if not the language. Walking around the car, slamming doors as I go, I inform them that their rights ended when the passport stamp fell, and that I was now leaving their god-forsaken country, whether they like it or not. Slamming the final door I drive off, men with guns staring after me. This is happing far too often for comfort.

Please, please to all ten thousand gods out there, don't let there be a problem with my Russian visa. Coming back this way again could be very unpleasant after that little scene.

Russia

Bed 52

The Russian border post is like a military compound where cars are let in one by one. My turn comes, a steel gate swings shut behind me, and I am in Russian territory. The magic trick of the borderline still amazes me. It's like doing a jump through space-time. The Ukraine could be on another planet. Officials in crisp uniforms work together towards a single goal. The customs men search the car with lighting efficiency. I sense order and method, and am quite relaxed about the whole thing; they are just doing their job after all. My passport is scanned, taxes paid, and car insurance finalized, all with a click of a mouse. Printers spew out documents in duplicate, and my border crossing is filed away in two neat dossiers, one for me and one for them. I am informed that I must guard mine with my life, as I will need it to exit Russia.

Yes, sir!

I had Olena translate the 'One planet One people' project into Russian, and now, with the translation stuck to the back window of the Wish Mobile, new interest is aroused in the project. The chief customs official writes,

'May all men be human.'

Then another steel gate opens, and I am released into greater Russia.

The roads are wide with such niceties as crash barriers around dangerous curves and tarred emergency shoulders. Just as I am thinking that were this in the Ukraine, they would certainly turn it into a third lane, a little Trabant zooms by, doing just that. But the Ukraine has reached top spot for bad driving. In comparison Russian drivers are pussycats, but then there are so many policemen on the road it is not surprising that everybody is fairly well behaved. There is a police roadblock at the entrance to every town, and I get stopped at every one, and at every one the conversation is the same;

'Dobri sehn.'

'Dobri sehn.'

Then the policeman rattles off something. The words *Ya gachu* and *paschaweste* come up at regular intervals. I now know he wants something, please, but I cannot work out what. I try the

'ya nee gevarou pa ruskia'

Plotting the route to Kazakhstan , Volgograd Russia

route, which results in another flood of Russian that now includes words such as *nieht ya gachu* and *spasebe*. People just don't believe you, when you tell them that you don't speak their language, while speaking their language, so I try

'*Ya nee poni maiyo.*'

This is the magic bullet; the police officers stop talking and start gesticulating that they want to see my papers. At each roadblock I whittle down the conversation, until at the day's end I have it down to a concise.

'*Dobri sehn.*'

'*Ya nee poni maiyo ruskia*'

Then hand them my stack of photocopies and wait for them to work it out. Usually it takes about a minute for the police officers to realize that they cannot read the words and, as I have told them that I don't understand a word, there is no way forward except to check that my photograph is in fact me, and wave me on with a friendly

'*Desvedanye.*'

What these constant roadblocks do illustrate quite clearly is how little traffic there is on the roads. Try this in any Western country and you would have a massive traffic pile-up at the entrance to every town.

While my spoken Russian is limited to these few phrases, reading the Cyrillic alphabet has become a non-event. I no longer even notice that I am reading something that only a month ago would have been illegible. I don't understand the meaning, but I do recognize the words or at least I think I do.

As the sun starts setting, I am in the vicinity of Rostov na Don, where the traffic is appalling. Trucks and cars spew poison smoke that gives my tired brain a thudding headache. I need time out. But the traffic load pulls me along, and I find myself heading towards Mockba. I hunt frantically on the map to see whether I want to head towards Mockba, but Mockba is not to be found. Mockba, Mockba, where the heck is Mockba? It is not anywhere near Rostov na Don, which is the biggest city around here, so why are all the signs pointing toward Mockba. My compass is telling me I am heading north, not east, and therefore Mockba is probably not where I want to be going, but I cannot find it anywhere on the map to confirm this. Driving past another sign pointing to Mockba, the penny drops, I have been reading the Russian word as in English; in Russian it says Moskwa, which is what the Russians call Moscow. And no, I don't want to go to Moskwa.

An emergency turn to the right finds me on a dirt road, and within minutes a veil of green has drawn in front of the hot dry rumble of traffic, and I am cool and alone in a silent forest, which on the spur of the moment becomes tonight's camping spot.

While setting out my little gas burner on the forest floor, and busying myself with rustling up some dinner, I get to wondering about Mockba, and why the rest of us don't call Moscow Moskwa. It is rather arrogant of nations to simply change the names of foreign countries and cities to suit themselves. Not just that, but it is very confusing as well. Did you know that the Germans still insist on calling Beijing Peking? Even their maps have still got Peking on them. The Chinese changed the official Latin spelling of their capital city to Beijing in 1949. Surely it is a matter of respect to do so as well. Also, why does the whole world insist on calling Muenchen Munich? Is the one so much more difficult to grasp than the other? Language courses always have a section in them where you must learn the names of countries in the new language. As if learning a new language isn't complicated enough, without having to relearn all the country and city names as well. A name is a name. It would make life a lot easier if we could all just agree on at least that small detail. World peace, man, I don't know; it seems a long way off when we cannot even get each other's names right.

Over a forest birdsong breakfast of two peaches from the Ukraine, almonds from Istanbul, and Earl Grey tea from Greece, I plan my route. After days of traveling on international artery roads, and dealing with the bizarre driving habits of six nations, I feel I am in need of a little driving downtime, and head off onto a road with no name. In Southern Russia the road less traveled is not difficult to find. The world turns yellow, as I drive through endless fields of sunflowers. If I were ever to become a farmer, I would farm sunflowers for the sheer delight of the late summer blaze of color. The disadvantage of driving through the sunflowers is the great nectar-filled bugs that thunk against the windscreen. The clear sprays of sticky body juices soon trap tiny dust particles, leaving the Wish Mobile looking as if it has freckles. With the addition of some water and a quick sweep of the windscreen wipers, I coat the windscreen with a thick sugary, protein-based varnish that forces me to stop in a small village for an emergency cleaning session.

Here I photograph a bright red Russian Orthodox church, topped with golden domes and a round white bell tower, its bright blue bulbous dome decorated with a sprinkling of golden stars. All around are small wooden houses, brightened by carved window shutters painted cyan and white. When I stop at a pedestrian crossing to let an old babushka with bright apron and floral headscarf across, she just stands there and looks at me as if I am completely demented. Even after I indicate that she has the right of way, she remains rooted to the spot. People here do not cross the road unless there are absolutely no cars to be seen.

Hours later I realize my map has a macabre sense of humor; it says Volgodansk is a place worth visiting for the scenery. I don't know. Perhaps if you live on the steppes, and have never seen anything else but flat fields, like those people who are paddling about in the water and sunbathing on the beach, where the bright sun umbrellas add the only color. If with my camera I focused in just on the beach, water and sun umbrellas, I could turn this into a little holiday resort. The reality is that Volgodansk is an industrial town, set next to a dam. The beach is leftover building sand, and the road into town runs on the dam wall above the bathers, and just a few meters from the sluice gates, which tower high above the cars. Volgodansk has a warehouse feel about it, where huge slabs of glaring white concrete make up the public spaces. The main street is four lanes wide, and carries hardly any traffic. When I get into a tangle with my preschool Russian reading abilities, I find myself smack in the industrial zone, where colossal chimneys are in fierce competition to see which can spew out the most black smoke and poison into the foul-smelling air. Enough industrial sightseeing, it is time to head toward Volgograd.

As I make my way through the boundless flat lands that are the great steppes of Russia, small birds in huge flocks fly in swirling panic in front of the Wish Mobile, which leaves a long tail of dust hanging in the hot air. The shadows of solitary clouds float like ghost ships on the pale grass seas and vanish into islands of dark trees. After chasing the horizon hour after hour, I push my mind out to measure the size of space – I drift past the moon, do backstroke through the rings of Saturn while looking at the earth vanishing bright blue behind the sun. But my mind is like an obstinate balloon, I stretch and stretch, then as I float past Pluto, I lose concentration and, phrrrt, my mind shrinks back down to the endless steppes – where the electrical poles still draw a line of perspective over the horizon that remains far, hour after hour. The horizon is only stationary for those who never move.

Somewhere past Tormosin I discover that I am heading for a dead end. At the tail end of the Cim l'Anskoje dam in the tiny village of Niz Cir, the road vanishes into the water, and the map cannot help me any further. I need some inside information. With a *'Dobri sehn'* I call over a strawberry blond youth who has the physical build of someone who labors daily for a living.

'Munija nushna Volgograd.'

He jabbers away while he jabs at my map with a stubby finger that is innocent of manicure or indeed any form of nail clipping device other than the ripping action of his teeth. By ignoring his words and watching his finger carefully, I more or less get the direction I should travel.

Bed 53

Following the M21, I arrive at the skinny city on the River Volga in the late afternoon. It's been a while since I have had access to a shower and I think a hotel would be in order. My first stop is the 'InTourist Hotel', a huge imperialist edifice. The foyer is decorated with monstrous crystal chandeliers, oversized gilded mirrors and tiny couches that are all designed to make the inmates feel a sense of prestige and power. This is obviously not the place for me, but as I am here.

'Dobri sehn, Ya ghatseelebe komnete?'

The man at reception looks down his nose at me, then informs me in plummy English that,

'Well, actually, we are fully booked, you...

The word comes out like an insult.

... should try the Volgograd Hotel.'

I guess I should have showered before I attempted to get a room here.

The Volgograd Hotel is a true Soviet relict. They should apply for UNESCO World Heritage Status. The reception is inhabited by three men and two women in what looks like full military dress uniform. They refuse to even talk to me until I have presented my passport and all other supporting documents. When they are happy that I am legal, they start entering my name into the register. But wait a minute, how much is the room and what does it look like, is what I want to know. Up several flights of dingy stairs a floor manageress, of a stature you don't want to mess with, is waiting. She leads me through a labyrinth of musty passages, decorated in a color that in someone's imagination must have appeared gold, but is really just a strange green beige. We step past discarded, stained mattresses and an assortment of furniture stacked into forgotten corners. She opens a heavy dark door to a room that has not been redecorated since Stalin rode triumphant through the streets of the rebuilt 'Stalingrad'. The room reeks of stale smoke, images of a decadent Marlene Dietrich, lounging on the red chaise lounge, springs to mind. The bed, dressed in wine-red velvet with golden tassels, starts telling me of its long history and the many bodies that have lain in its hollow curves and, no thank you. Hotels can be truly disgusting places. I want my little camper. Who would have thought?

The problem is the sun is starting to set, and I cannot find my way out of the city. Camping in nature has a 'king of the wild frontier' feel about it, but camping in a city is just a homeless person sleeping in a car, and simply not acceptable. After ending up in several unsavory-looking neighborhoods, my situation is not looking good. But really, it is probably just the spoilt Western Miss Priss in me that thinks these places are unsavory; here they possibly represent solid middle class. When the sun tucks away its last rays, and the streets lights are rare pools of comfort, I slide into a bit of a panic as the homeless person sleeping in the car thing becomes more and more of a reality. Then my basic Russian reading skills allow me to recognize a rOCTNHNUa sign. Hotel or homeless, I find myself between a rock and a hard place; I will just take a peek at the hotel.

The hotel foyer is shiny green enamel paint, bare linoleum floor and hard benches. The reception desk is a small school desk, behind which stands a motherly Russian. She looks at me in bemusement. Late night walk-ins are not their bread-and-butter trade. She is not too sure about me, and I am not too sure about the hotel. Yes, no, do I stay or do I go? And then a whole squadron of young children storm in. This makes me see the hotel in a completely new light. It is a sort of holiday resort, summer camp situation for children. I guess then I am the suspect ingredient in this little stew. But the motherly type relents, checks my passport, and gives me a price for the room, which is so cheap I feel the need to ensure that I will not be sharing a dorm with thirty giggling girls.

The room is manageable, private, with bathroom en suite, but I am not totally convinced by the silver satin curtains, and the plumbing is just weird. The ancient pipes, thick with paint, make no effort to conceal themselves behind tiles or plaster; they snake up the walls along the shower and behind the toilet. I discover later that there is method in this. The hot water pipes have several functions, including the obvious one. They also act as clothing dryer, heated towel rail, and heating for the room, which in the winter must be a very good idea. In the summer it turns the room and bathroom into a furnace. But at 17€ the room is incredibly cheap, and gives me a brilliant view over the Volga. For the rest, I keep my plastic slops on while showering, and am very careful not to let any bit of me touch the shower curtain. I also employ my own bedding. All of these precautions are probably once again due to my inner spoilt Western Miss Priss.

The rising full moon sends a silver path across the Volga, allowing me to see its full width. The river is a massive obstacle, and I try to visualize stealthy late-night crossings in those dread war days when the river formed the border between the invading Germans on the west bank and the defending Russians on the east, who fought for this city in one of history's most barbaric and bloody battles. My reason for driving the 'long way round' is that I am particularly interested to see how the two cities, Stalingrad (Volgograd) and Berlin, which were so destructively linked in the closing chapters of the Second World War, have rebuilt themselves.

Mamayev Hill is where the Russians finally won the guerilla war that raged for months in the bombed-out streets of Stalingrad. Here there is now a memorial to this pivotal victory over the Germans. On the crest of the hill stands a colossal avenging woman, urging her invisible followers to battle. With her fierce stride, flowing windswept garments, and sword arm held high, 'The Motherland Calls' is the antithesis of the 'Statue of Liberty', but strangely, she represents liberty as well. I, like all the other visitors, am drawn toward this terrible figure. Up wide stairs, where Russian flag sellers are doing a brisk trade, I am confronted with the Russian embodiment of the terminator. A massive statue of a powerfully muscled man holding a machine gun portrays pure undiluted aggression. The stairs continue steeply upwards, bordered on both sides by huge representations of a war-ravaged city, from which emerge desperate, violent soldiers. Sounds of war propaganda, the whine of bomber planes, the whistle and detonation of bombs, of men shouting and of fiercely patriotic singing fill the space between the walls. I am becoming decidedly uncomfortable. By a long reflecting pool, gigantic granite war heroes carry fallen comrades. Under the massive figures, living soldiers fill spent bullet cartridges with the soil of Mamayev Hill.

An immense statue of a grieving mother cradling a dead soldier is surrounded by a lake of water, symbolic, I am sure, of her tears. This is a favorite tourist photo-trophy spot, where pretty young Russian women and their soldier boyfriends pose for pictures. The path leads into a round hall, the soaring space filled with an 'Ave Maria'-type sound track that creates an overwrought emotional atmosphere. Visitors have their photographs taken in front of a giant hand, which holds the mother of all eternal flames. An eternal flame seems to be an obligatory ingredient in war memorials. I wonder if anyone gives serious thought to the length of eternity, and the sheer logistical impossibility of keeping that flame burning for all eternity. But of course it is just a symbol, which, like all the other oversized symbols here, represents the unfathomable depth of the human ego.

The war lives on without apology or contrition in this scary monument. I can imagine how small children are told again and again of this great victory; how national pride is still built up around this tragic event. I stupidly start wondering what these people would do if they discovered that I was a German, the enemy. Idiotic as this thought might be, I feel very out of place and no longer need to visit the ferocious woman on the hill. The Second World War lives on here as Volgograd clings to its past. Berlin won in the end as it embraced the future.

Just a little further, in the shadow of Mamayev Hill, locals shop at a fresh-produce market. The space is ramshackle, dusty and unconsciously eco-friendly. Nothing here is refrigerated or pre-packed, and no packaging is supplied. Buyers come equipped with their own jars, bottle and bags. They have them filled with honey, which is scooped from milk urns with giant ladles, and sunflower oil is decanted into pre-used bottles. Butter is cut from giant blocks that fill large cardboard boxes and eggs that are sorted according to color, size and yolk quantity are piled into delicate pyramids. Besides the normal display of fresh fruit and vegetables, there is the odd – to my mind – display of rotten apples and overripe bananas that are also for sale.

There is no shortage of anything, except possibly Western-style hygiene. Flies that are a small nuisance generally become a swarm over the fish sellers, where crowds pick through the selection of dried fish, before waiting patiently for their choices to be weighed. In the fresh-meat hall, a man with an evil-looking axe chops a sheep into saleable chunks. The axe falls as it will on the carcass. Over time, the enormous tree stump that acts as a chopping block has built up a thick mud of blood and cardboard, which his violent chopping sends into a bloody spray pattern on the floor and counters around him. Standing well back, I watch as he flings the chunks of meat to the sales ladies, who carelessly display them on open counters, which are covered in more blood-soaked cardboard. Here the meat is fondled, touched and turned by saleswomen and clientele alike. 'Move on already!', yells my stomach to my macabrely fascinated brain.

In the city centre, enormous imperialistic-style buildings have been dubbed 'Stalinist' by the Russians. The pavements, roads and open spaces are far bigger than is entirely necessary, reducing the people to ants. We all walk endless steps for no good reason. It is quite exhausting, but confirms that Volgograd is a one-hit wonder. The city was rebuilt in a moment of glorious victory; Soviet pride is evident in every oversized building and super-sized street. In the centre of town, things are fairly well maintained, but just a few hundred meters away, fountains that peel paint are set in vast squares of cracked and weed-veined concrete, in front of buildings flaking with the same decay and neglect that seems to inflict all Soviet buildings.

In a newer part of town, in a cold empty mall, I find what I have been looking for through 14 countries – a map book that has detailed roadmaps of Russia, Uzbekistan, Kazakhstan, Tajikistan and every other -stan around these parts. It even has roadmaps of Iran, should I feel inclined to travel there. In my hotel room I devour the Cyrillic map book as if it were the most thrilling suspense novel. It even indicates fuel stations, which is very important, considering they are separated by desert distances of up to 250 km. I am so happy with my book that I take it along to read on the beach by the river, where I have spotted hordes of locals taking the water and sun, and I am going to join them.

But Miss Priss pulls up her nose. I am going to have to put a hit out on her, but then again, perhaps she has a point. The beach is strewn with litter, which the locals do not seem to notice as they laze about, exposing acres of pale flesh. Here the Western obsession with skinny is nowhere to be seen: men, women and children are all very well fed. I guess that to go hungry for the fun of it is a pastime that only those who have never felt the bite of real hunger are naive enough to indulge in. In the water, children leap about, but keep a wary eye on strange floating objects that remind me that the water of the Volga has come a very long way. With the help of man-made waterways, the river stretches from the Baltic to the Caspian Sea, and along the way it has been severely abused by humans. The dangerously high chemical content of the water presents a growing ecological problem, of which the locals seem blissfully unaware. Miss Priss, however, withdraws permission for me to take off even my shoes. So I photograph round Russian women in small bikinis and rounder Russian men in Speedos instead.

Bed 54

Unpack, pack, unpack, pack, unpack, pack, a rhythm and system: toiletry bag from behind the door; slipslops from the floor; check the heater for the loofah (forgot two of those already); bend the head to check under bed. Computer cords and cables, GPS and mouse. Camera charged, but don't forget the multi plug, clothes all packed, zip the bag. Camera bag on the left shoulder, computer bag on back, canvas bag in the left hand, which leaves the right hand free to deal with doors and keys, and so I take leave of yet another bed.

Today I have the bedroll, which means a second trip upstairs, but soon everything is stashed exactly in its Wish Mobile place. Before I drive off, a bit of spring cleaning is required, as today the Wish Mobile and I will be entertaining guests. I am meeting with Tatyana and her daughter Olga, Russian members of the Women Welcome Women Worldwide organization. Getting hold of someone in Russia has been a test of resolve, and I am particularly keen to meet them, as I am sure that with their help I will be experiencing a totally different side of Volgograd. We meet in front of the InTourist Hotel. Mother and daughter are both blue-eyed honey blondes, with wide cheekbones and beautiful translucent skin. Tatyana speaks no English, but with Olga acting as interpreter we are soon on the excellent footing that mutual curiosity brings. They have a plan of action: first stop is the home of Tatyana's cousin, an ex-KGB agent.

A drive over bumpy dirt roads into an outlying suburb brings us to the driveway of one of the small wooden houses I had seen all around the outskirts of Volgograd. We enter the house through the back garden, where piles of wood lie between the fruit trees. A ginger cat lazes on a windowsill, framed by lacy shutters that are losing their pale green paint. Stepping into the house, I am again struck by the impossibly high standard of living the West accepts as normal. In the course of my journey I have slowly had to adjust my concept of middle-class living standards. What people of the developed West simply take for granted is becoming a greater and greater luxury as I move further east. This Russian middle-class house is modest in the extreme. The modesty defined not necessarily by its size but by its finishes and filling. The entrance hall is a narrow wood-paneled space that leads to two bedrooms to the right and a linoleum-floored and pale green kitchen to the left with a small lounge straight ahead.

As we sit down on a variety of mismatched sofas and chairs, I notice that the ceiling sags, and the walls are in need of damp-proofing.

I make a quick trip to the bathroom, more out of curiosity than need. The room is minute and totally functional, with the plumbing once again on full display. The indulgence of the long lazy bubble bath is not something one would expect to do here.

Back in the lounge, tea is served, Russian style. In a china teapot a very strong tea is brewed, a small amount of which is poured into small bowls, which are then topped up with hot water to everyone's individual taste. I like this way of making tea, as it allows the full flavor to develop, but everyone can have the tea as strong or as weak as they choose. Accompanying the tea are tiny individual pots of honey, which we eat instead of cake with teaspoons in tiny mouthfuls. The honey is supplied by the ex-KGB uncle, who now spends his days tending his beehives and fishing in Kazakhstan.

Tatyana's plan is becoming clearer.

We pile into two cars and head for our next stop, which is the local spring discovered by the Germans who settled here in response to an invitation from Catherine the Great in 1763. The invitation was partly to develop the region, but also to provide a buffer zone between the Russians and the Mongol hordes to the east. The settlers became a minority group in Russia, known as the Volga Germans, who in a moment of startling originality called the spring Schoenbrunn. In honor of my distant German links to this place all my bottles are filled with water straight from the earth. Our third stop is also a watery, but a salty one. In the middle of a suburban neighborhood there is a natural mineral spring. It has formed a salty pond, in which the locals swim, and rub the slimy black mud on their aching limbs, in the belief that the mud is healing. My hosts thought that perhaps I would enjoy a swim. I politely refuse, saying I don't have a bathing suit, but actually Miss Priss prefers her swimming pools sparkling clear. Next on our to-do list is the riverside home of another family member, also ex-KGB and also a regular visitor to Kazakhstan.

So I discover that one person's end of the earth is another's favorite fishing hole; it just depends on your point of view. While the two ex-KGB agents dressed only in Speedos, with huge bellies hanging out – there must be a law against this somewhere or, if not, there should be – pore over my map book. I focus my eyes firmly on the women, who are rustling up lunch with fresh ingredients plucked straight from the garden. Watermelon, grapes and a huge mixed salad are accompanied by a strong garlic sausage and pilmeni: tiny ravioli-type things shaped like old-fashioned sailors' hats and filled with meat, which when served with sour cream are delicious.

While we eat, questions are fired backward and forward. Olga has put her brain into top gear to keep the translations flowing. People with language skills have a huge advantage over those without. Olga is the only person at the table who knows exactly what is going on at all times.

I am interested in all the dried fish I have been seeing. The fish, in all sizes, hang from strings at the roadside. It can be selected from huge boxes in the fresh-produce markets and is vacuum packed like any other savory snack in the supermarket. Do they soak it or use it as flavoring? Actually no; they eat it as a snack, just like that. I wrinkle my nose, but then remember the biltong from South Africa. I explain that we cut raw beef into strips, spice it, air-dry it and eat it as a snack, just like that, and it is their turn to wrinkle their noses.

The men have come to a decision, and after much intelligent-sounding Russian – it really is a very intelligent-sounding language – I am told that the consensus is that the roads in Kazakhstan are shaky at best, and although there is a road crossing into Kazakhstan at Astrakhan, neither man is sure of its condition or how far it will take me in Kazakhstan. It would be wisest to stick to the main artery road, and cross into Kazakhstan at Oralsk. This means driving an extra 1 200 km north, all the way to Camara, before heading south into Kazakhstan. But what the heck, when one is driving around the world, what are a few thousand kilometers, after all. The men write a global wish for world peace from Stalingrad on the Wish Mobile, then we part company with hugs and kisses and a great outpouring of mutual regard.

Tatyana and Olga are supplying me with my bed for the night. They live about an hour out of the centre, but still in Volgograd; it really is a very long and skinny city. Here we stroll down a neighborly boulevard alongside young parents pushing their offspring in brightly colored carts; boys on bicycles play at fully functional fountains; and grey-haired couples sit on park benches, while teenagers strut their stuff. On each side of the sunny flower-fringed boulevard Soviet apartment blocks stretch monotonously into the distance, custom-built to house and depress people.

I discover that I will not be staying with Tatyana after all, and that our final stop for the day is my 'hotel' for the night. Tatyana is the headmistress of a very large school, and I shall be sleeping in her office. She cannot offer to accommodate me at home, as she and Olga share a space of only 18 m^2. Olga states most pointedly that intellectuals have prestige, but no money in this society. Prestige is all good and well, but it does not put the potatoes on the table, and a society that does not honor and reward its teachers is on a slippery slope to oblivion.

At the school I am introduced to the caretaker. It will just be him and me in the school tonight. As Tatyana leads me to her office, I wonder if she is aware of just how weird this is. She spends most of her life in this place, and to her it must seem like home; to me it is an empty echoing school. In her office, she has constructed a bed for me out of school benches. I realize to my embarrassment that my simple request to meet her has put her under enormous strain, and that Tatyana must have worried about and given tremendous thought to the problem of how she could accommodate me. I wonder why she didn't mention the lack of living space before; I could have happily stayed in my summer-camp hotel for another night. But the effort has been made, the office looks comfortable enough, and as I proposed to set aside all comfort zones and prejudices when I embarked on this journey, I resolve to learn something new in this school as well. I learn that school benches do not make comfortable beds: strange, then, how so many school children can sleep their school days away on them.

Beds 55 and 56

On the P228 I head north, past rolling grassland, hour after hour, my silent meditation interrupted only by the police roadblocks, *dobri sehn, ya nee poni mayo, ruskia* papers and *desvedanye*. My head starts amusing itself by solving math problems: 128 x 345, 100 x 345 = 34 500, 20 x 345 = 6 900 8 x 345 = 2 760, 34 500 + 6 900 = 41 400 + 2 760 = 44 160. After several calculations, one truck accident, and subsequent detour through virgin grasslands, I arrive in Saratov, where hectares of dead factories, their skeletons falling into slow decay, and grey buildings convince me that I want to camp tonight. For a dedicated non-camper I am really getting into this camping thing. Half an hour north of Saratov I spy a steep dirt road going up a deserted-looking hill that overlooks a field of sunflowers. That looks like home for the night. The Wish Mobile just manages to heave itself over the crest of the hill as the sun sets low on the horizon, and I sniff a hint of autumn in the air. My high country road takes me into fields of pale apple-green grasses that make a delicate background for tiny purple flowers, which attract tiny purple butterflies that float across the green field like periwinkles on the wing. With a small copse of trees at my back and a view of the distant Volga over the sunflowers, I set up camp for the evening with not a care in the world.

Then it starts raining in the middle of the night and, as the drops thunder down on the metal roof, my mind starts thinking about the steep dirt road that led me here. As the rain gets heavier, and the sound becomes deafening, I imagine huge dongas and mudslides. Then I see the Wish Mobile rolling down the track and landing wheels up in a haystack. As the rain continues to beat down, I play out this fantasy until I am in the grip of a full-blown panic attack. In the chill grey morning, I reach for the long sleeves and jerseys for the first time in months, and walk to the downhill that has kept me awake half the night. It is steep, but hardly life threatening. It is a flaw of the human mind that it is never happy unless it has something to worry about, as only then does it believe it is actually thinking.

It rains hour after hour, and slowly the Wish Mobile and all its wishes vanish under a layer of mud thrown up from the horrible roads by trucks with no mudguards. The driving conditions are vile, and any excuse to stop is welcome. In a nameless town in a street through which the traffic roars like a river in a canyon, I walk from house to house documenting the fine detail and subtle use of color on houses. Here the wooden houses are far more beautiful than those I had admired in Volgograd. Layers and layers of wood, carved in delicate patterns and extravagant detail, give the effect of wooden lace around the windows. The shutters of each house are finished in slightly different designs and color; faded steel blue combines gently with soft ochre; storm-ocean green is set off by white wooden lace. These houses are the only example of traditional craft and individual expression I have seen in Russia so far, and are a crumbling reminder of the Russian aesthetic before the communist system all but annihilated independent thought and deed.

The air is sour with the smell of gas and carbon; each breath pounds another nail into my aching head. In every village gas pipes make arches over the roads, run across the rooftops, and cut across the landscape. There was no thought given to their design. Like the plumbing in Russian bathrooms, their design is pure function and they are incredibly ugly. I pity those whose lot it is to breathe this air all day, every day. I can fortunately get into the Wish Mobile and leave it all behind.

Teatime comes, and I take a left turn off the main road to find a place for a picnic. But here nature seems to be on a little acid trip; the trees on the roadside are doing things no tree was ever meant to do. It is as if the cellulose in the tree fiber is slowly melting. The trees bend in strange directions, until the bend is too great, the trunks simply snap in two, and the splintered remains point skywards, as the broken tops slowly turn brown in the green grass. I stop to investigate. The sour smell of gas hangs thick in the air. Next to the trees on both sides of the road rusting gas pipes run half hidden through the grass and wild flowers. Could this be the cause of the softening trees? The smell of gas chases me back into the Wish Mobile, where I discover that a swarm of bright red ladybugs have taken the opportunity to seek refuge. The dashboard is covered with tiny red polka dots with polka dots. I transport them safely away from the stinky gas pipes and, in a yellow field of sunflowers, set them free.

Hours later, highway off-ramps and on-ramps lead me into the centre of Camara, which has a real Wild West boomtown feel about it. It is big, brash, and light years away from the fall-apart Russia I have seen so far. The first hotel in Camara is a truck stop. As I have slept in bed & breakfasts, hostels, hotels, with friends, family and strangers, in a school and in the Wish Mobile, but never in a truck stop, I decide to have a look. At the reception on the third floor – Russian hotel receptions are often on the third floor or else a hotel will just be one floor of a building – I am confronted with a whole display of men's toiletries, and every sex magazine available on the planet, accompanied by an assortment of products to aid in that department. I think perhaps I am the wrong kind of single lady for this place.

My next stop is Geo Tours to ask about a hotel. The Internet cafés are of no use to me, as I cannot surf in Cyrillic, let alone work the Cyrillic keyboards. Here the boss-lady, Ludmilla, for reasons I don't understand, decides to take me under her wing, and walks her fancy leather heels through building sites and from hotel to hotel to try to help me. I have yet to meet a Russian that wasn't nice, from the border guards to the police officers, the ex-KGB agents, and now this totally strange lady, who has taken an hour out of her day to help me for no good reason. Perhaps Russians really do believe in the whole share-and-share-alike thing, which is possibly why they were conned into communism. They probably thought that it sounded like a very good way of all being happy together – too bad, really, that due to corruption in the seat of government, things didn't turn out that way.

Then with Russia's entry into the glitzy world of capitalism, this corruption was simply legitimized. The Russian change from communism to capitalism was not due to ideological reasons, but because a couple of corrupt big cheeses close to the throne said to each other: Do you know how much money we can make by privatizing Russia's state-owned assets? And, to the standing ovation of Western capitalists, they did just that, and so a couple of 'businessmen' got rich beyond belief within moments, and the normal people struggle as before, and by looking at the huge gap in wealth that has arisen here, just as in other newly capitalized countries, the really poor struggle more than before.

Sure, the shops are full of produce now, but only a small percentage of Russians can afford to shop in the Western-style supermarkets where European brand names appear on the shelves, although I am grateful for the opportunity the modern supermarket, stocked with familiar brands, presents, as I need to stock up on a few basics and some much-needed toiletries. Trying to work out what is shampoo and what is conditioner is a bit of a business, but at least with familiar brands and a familiar product layout I know I am buying a hair product, and not bubble bath or moisturizer. The dairy fridge is still a blank zone, though. I would really like some yogurt, but after accidentally buying sour cream, buttermilk and other sour milk products on previous occasions, I have more or less given up on dairy. The problem is with the packaging: everything is in blue and white with a cow on it – not terribly helpful if you are illiterate. I also buy a torch and a small folding chair, as these items have shown themselves to be missing in my small camping experiences. As a safety precaution, I decide to fill both of my jerry cans, one with water and one with fuel, for the first time. The distances in Kazakhstan look huge, and the roads do not have a very good reputation. The hotel selected for me by Ludmilla has all the mod cons with wi-fi on tap, so I take the opportunity of getting my computer in order. I haven't had an Internet connection for a while, and I am concerned that I still have no further news about my entry into China. Tomorrow I enter Kazakhstan, so this is really cutting things very fine.

Karakum Desert : Kazakhstan

Kazakhstan North

Bed 57

'Dobri sehn .Ya gahstu Kazakhstan?'

'Da pri-ahmo thpi-route.'

That cannot be. Soon after, I stop again to ask a man walking his dog on the roadside.

'Get-si-e Kazakhstan?'

'Pri-ahmo.'

My compass disagrees. Where is the problem here? Dear Russians, where are your route markers? They would make my life so much easier. After half an hour of driving through unspectacular grassland, shrubby greyish plants and rolling hills, I stop again to ask a man selling honey by the roadside.

'Dobri sehn Kazakhstan pri-ahmo?'

'Da.'

Everybody agrees, this is the right road, and Kazakhstan is straight ahead – everybody except my compass and me. I have never been here, yet disagree with their local knowledge, based on the information received by my little compass. Technology rules okay? How idiotic is this? But my trusty compass has not let me down before, and it insists that I am heading in the wrong direction. This gives me something to worry about again, happy little brain. Finally, 100 km outside Camara a route marker – thank you, the Russians. How hard was that? The M32 is right where I want to be. Time to check the compass. I give it a sound rap on the dashboard, and what you know, the needle swings south, and I can stop thinking about anything until I reach the Kazak border in the middle of fields of wheat that stretch to the horizon.

The entry into Kazakhstan is a simple enough affair. The officials are young, enthusiastic and speak a smattering of English. They want to know what exactly I am up to.

'Where are you going, Mongolia?'

'No, I am driving to Shanghai.'

'China?'

'Yes.'

'In this car?'

'Yes.'

I am getting a touch worried about where this line of questioning is heading.

'Are you part of a rally?'

'No.'

'You are alone?'

No, I have six asylum seekers hiding in the cubby hole. Haven't we covered this?

'Yes, I am alone.'

They seem quite used to groups of gung-ho men, in cars usually covered in garish sponsors' stickers, heading off to Outer Mongolia. But a woman alone – in a glorified delivery van covered in wishes – heading for China, is not something they have had to deal with before.

They very carefully check my Chinese visa. I don't let on that I don't actually have car papers to enter China; some things are best not revealed at a border post. They double-check my details and car registration, making sure that the information is entered perfectly into the computer. I get the distinct feeling that they are covering all their bases, in case my entry into China does not take place smoothly, or at all. The whole procedure from Russia to Kazakhstan takes about three hours. By the time I reach Oral, the sun is sinking low.

Oral is a town on a crossroads to nowhere, set in a vast dry steppe, pale grey in the dull light. The roads are wide, grey and empty, the blocks of flats grim clones of the buildings that have been housing the masses in every ex- and Soviet country I have travelled through. The Soviets certainly did things by strict formula. Pity they didn't test the formula first. I don't want to stay here. Sleeping in the Wish Mobile seems like a far-happier choice. The sun is just touching the horizon, when I decide that my best camping option will be in the windbreak of a dusty field. There is nowhere else to shelter in this flat featureless land. Bumping across the furrows, I reverse the Wish Mobile between some thorn trees, and within minutes I have set up camp, rustled up some wild rice from Turkey into which I mix tuna from Russia – only to discover that it is spectacularly disgusting – but now it is mixed in with the rice, and if I don't want to go to bed hungry, I am bound to eat it. With a splash of Greek olive oil and a squirt of Croatian lemon juice it becomes edible, just.

Over a cup of chamomile tea I watch the last light fade from the sky. Closing the blinds, I sleep. When the sun rises, I wake; what could be more natural than that.

Bed 58

With no appointments, no television programs, no bus or train schedules to control my day, clock time has lost all meaning for me. Also by crossing a border the time leaps backward or forward, depending to which city the country orients itself. In Russia it was to Moskwa; here it is to Astana. At the border, time moved forward about two or three hours, so yesterday's border crossing actually cost me six hours in modern measured time. But time zones are merely a measuring stick, and mean nothing in a timeless world. A thousand years ago Avicenna said that, 'If nothing moved, there would be no time.' But movement does not create time; time was created to measure movement. There is no time, it does not pass, the changes we see are life passing, defined by chemical changes moving through their endlessly repeated cycles. In modern society we have confused the issues, shifted the values, and time, like money, is no longer just a measurement; they have both become values to be measured themselves. In the modern world, time measures money, while money measures time, and value is nowhere to be found.

But there is no more wholesome and optimistic time of the day than the sunrise. In this flat dry world, with no humid atmosphere and no haze of pollution, the sun rises naked, white gold from a horizon of deep crimson into a sky of clean cerulean blue. The air is still, cool, and smells faintly bitter of the dusty earth, blended with the sour herbal scent of the small thorn trees and a sweet smoky note from my cup of breakfast tea. The world here is silent, until I listen. Then small rustlings in the grasses tell of night creatures returning home, tiny brown birds flit and tweet between the thorn branches. The low clung clung of cow bells fills my small camp; the morning sun draws golden haloes around a herd of cows that are urged across the road by a boy on bicycle. My camping spot will soon be somebody's pasture; time to move on.

My goal for the next two days is Aktobe. At only 474 km this is not very ambitious, but I have been having nightmares about this part of the trip. The Kazakh reputation for bad roads is widespread in this part of the world. But the day starts on excellent roads, and I am somewhat apologetic to the Kazakhs for my doubts. The semi-desert scrub recedes into the pale morning glow; there is nothing but endless open flat land that flies by unnoticed until I am jolted back into reality by a detour, which runs directly through the desert, parallel to the main road. Trucks have worn the dirt track into two canyons, creating a centre ridge so high it hits the bottom of the car. To avoid base damage, I try driving on the ridges, but the sand is so unstable the Wish Mobile keeps sliding back into the trenches.

Thinking that a side road looks more user-friendly, I make a snap decision, and with a quick right, whoop, am immediately stuck chassis-deep in liquid fine sand. It slides into my shoes, and hangs like a low mist in the still air. Olga gets a promotion from latrine service to heroine duty, but she is not a very big spade, so no matter how fast I dig, the sand flows back to fill whatever clearance I manage to create. To try to speed things up, I recklessly start flinging the sand in every direction, but as it flies through the air, it catches in the smallest breeze, and flies straight back at me. It sticks to my sweaty skin, and soon I am covered in a fine layer of Kazakhstan. And then …trataratata … across the desert sands a truck roars to my rescue, but I have chosen my spot so well that the truck also gets stuck. Fortunately the driver is experienced in matters sandpit, and does not let such a small thing faze him. Turning the truck wheels at a right angle to the chassis, he revs the engine to a howl, pops the clutch, and gets as close to putting a truck into a wheelie as I think is physically possible. The truck lurches forward, plowing the offending sand out of the way. Should I try that? Perhaps not. The truck driver ropes me in, and, with an almighty belching of smoke and roaring of engine, hauls the Wish Mobile out of its trap.

Meekly I fall into the queue of cars and creep along the prescribed detour. But even at 20 km/h, having a car in front of you makes driving impossible, as the fine sand creates a dense impenetrable cloud of dust. Parking in the shade of an electrical pole, I brew a cuppa to allow the traffic jam to pass me by, and for my nerves to settle. In the distance, a whirlwind towers the desert sands into the sky. As it floats across the small patches of grassland, the whirlwind vanishes into a barely seen ripple, gaining physical form again as it charges across the dusty road.

After tea, the road is empty, but now the wind lifts the talcum powder sand, creating little eddies and whirlwinds that obscure and reveal the road in a moving veil of sand. As the detour becomes more and more like virgin desert, I reach far into my memory for whatever sand-driving skills I can dredge up. I do remember that getting into second gear is best, and to maintain a steady momentum. The latter is a bit difficult, as the road is not just a thick bed of sand; every now and then it falls away into a pothole so large that there is no choice, but to drive through it. Speeding up is necessary to gain momentum to get back out, but then the sand suddenly reveals rock-hard ridges in the pothole, and I am forced to slam on brakes to avoid axle damage, only to be immediately confronted by a steep slope from which sand runs like water, and traction is minimal. After five torturous hours, a final bump turns the sand into smooth new tar. Soon the day's hardships are forgotten, and despite the road I make it to Aktobe in one day. The Paris-Dakar? Bring it on.

Aktobe is a frontier town, surrounded by nothing in the middle of nowhere, with very few people elsewhere on the planet actually knowing that it even exists. The economy of the area is based on its mineral wealth: chromium, nickel and copper are mined here, and they are obviously selling their resources well. All around, wooden houses are being built on small desert ranches. There is lots of space for everybody in this big flat place. The CBD of Aktobe is reached via a four-lane highway, lined by shiny glass high-rises. Just past a pink casino hotel I spy a huge bazaar that sells just about everything. This is sort of collectivist capitalism, where tiny individual stores huddle together under one roof, selling everything from fruit and cosmetics to small electronic goods. After cobbling together dinner and a few snacks for the road, I discover a man waiting by the Wish Mobile. His *ya gachu* combined with a squiggly hand movement tells me that he wants to write on it. This is a first. Before I have always had to invite men to write a wish. The first representative from Kazakhstan to write on the car writes his wish in beautiful flowing script, using up the entire passenger door for his offering. No concern about writing on cars in Kazakhstan or perhaps the sheer scale of the space they live in makes them expansive in all things.

Deep in the remains of a cotton-field disaster zone with my pickle and my carbanossi for dinner, I watch the sun set over the grasses, upon which balance my socks and underwear to dry. I have for some days now been the proud owner of an automatic washing machine. One of my large plastic containers with snug-fitting lid gets a splash of water, a dash of soap, a smooth round stone, after which the dirty socks and such like are added, and then, with the lid firmly in place, the whole lot bounces about all day at the back end of the Wish Mobile. At night, after a quick rinse, voila, perfectly clean socks.

Bed 59

Early morning, the world is flat and getting drier, but the road is in very good shape; hopefully it will remain that way. It takes me past Khromtau, which has perhaps the largest deposit of high-grade chromium ore in the world, and is busy, busy, busy. Tractors and busses zoom about their business past mineshafts, mine dumps, square mining houses and tightly packed electrical poles that stretch four rows deep into the dusty heat. On the roadside, small scraggly trees are heavy with ravens. They fall, black confetti onto the tar … the reason for their gathering a desert hare hit-and-run victim, now breakfast for the birds. Soon Khromtau vanishes over the horizon behind me, and the horizon in front remains always far.

A little pheasant-type bird scuttles across the road, and it gets me to thinking about the roadkill, the size of the country, the length of the road, and the six cars on it. What are the odds of an animal being hit? It is just so infinitesimally small, but there they are, roadkill jackals and hares. Perhaps the hares like the night-time heat of the road; then the jackals chase the blood of freshly squashed hare; and the ravens breakfast on both. They peck out the eyes of the hare first, then they pull out the entrails by the anus. More information than you need perhaps, but in the desert there are no rules of polite society to stop the mind from drifting into strange neighborhoods.

Then a road sign shows bumpy road ahead. Nooo, it was too good to last. But I have very clear ideas on any experience, be it good or bad: at least learn something from it. My driving experience from yesterday has taught me a few things about reading the road conditions ahead. When the road gets bad, there are little detour bulges on either side of the tar. When the road gets worse, the detour plunges into the desert. When the desert detours get really bad, you can see the deltas that are created by previous desperate drivers from kilometers away. Finally the deltas simply collapse, and then you have a selection of sandpits to choose from – at which point I create a new road through the desert, and apologise profusely to the fragile ecosystem.

That was yesterday's lesson. Today I am learning that Kazakhstan not only has bad roads, it has them in several categories. While yesterday I learned a few short sharp lessons in driving on sand, today I am dealing with a road that looks like a truck-load of tar was dumped on a bed of loose sand and gravel and left for the passing cars to flatten out however they saw fit. Having a slightly warped sense of humour, I think this is funny and imagine that I am actually in training for the Paris- Dakar. Then, driving past a series of speed limit signs that warn me to slow down to 60, 50, 40 makes me realise that the Kazakh sense of humour is more bent than my own. These signs are not based on any reality: anyone driving faster than 10km/h on this road is insane.

After hours of struggling with the tar I come to the conclusion that sand is actually easier to drive on and less damaging to the Wish Mobile, so slide off the tar onto the sand, but the Kazakh road always has another trick up its sleeve. A perfectly drivable track branches in two, then three, then four, five, six different tracks ,all leading helter-skelter through the desert. Choices, choices, which one is best? I try left, but the sand flows away from the car wheels, causing unnecessary spin; then I try right, speeding up to keep on top of the sand when WHAP WHAP, the dreaded bounce. In the bleak midday light, the white sand absorbs all shadows, making the ridges and holes invisible. Slow down, slow down; but then the Wish Mobile sinks into the soft sand; speed up, speed up. Both front wheels hit an invisible ridge at the same time and WHAP WHAP WHAP. I am gripping the steering wheel so hard my hands are starting to cramp. Like a late-night drunk, I start driving in wide s-curves. This way I can keep some speed, and avoid hitting the ridges straight on. It seems to be working. My concentration is so focussed on the road surface that I don't even think to look left or right when the sand track crosses the tar road, and I nearly collide with an orange Trabant.

We are both so surprised to see someone else on this hellish road that we promptly stop and approach each other like long-lost friends. He is an old man with silver eyes, narrow face with high cheekbones, and skin the color of golden bread. On his head he wears a colorful but faded fez, decorated with gold thread. He takes my hand in both of his, holding them for the length of our conversation. This simple contact reminds me of Africa, where handholding during conversation is common, and reinforces the bond of communication. His hands are leather hard, dry and cool like the trunk of a tree in the midday sun. He looks exhausted, and tells me he left Aral at eight; it has taken all this time to travel this far. That means at least another six hours of torture for me. He tells me that he has been driving on the tar road and indicates that this road is okay and that I should drive on it. Insanity, the road is not okay, not even close, but it is obviously better than what he must have driven on before. I am not looking forward that. With rueful smiles we part, each to tackle the stretch of road the other has just passed, each knowing that the other is in for a hell of time.

In what language did we just have that conversation? I try to remember. Was it English? Perhaps I was speaking English and he was speaking Russian or Kazakh or perhaps I threw in some Russian and he had a few English words. Strange and exhilarating is the fact that the language made no difference; I understood him. I have become so uninhibited in my thinking that I fully understood a man who might have been speaking Kazakh or Russian.

To cheer me up even more, the main road does become more or less acceptable, and in the distance there are no bulges and tracks in the desert. Perhaps my fellow traveler was right. I start praying to Mary, Peter and Joseph, send entreaties to Zeus, Mercury and Mars, and to the great god Og. Please, please just let the road stay like this. Driving at 40 km/h is fine; I'm happy, no complaints from me. In the far distance I see an at least four-lane-wide stretch of tar and becoming positively squirrelly with joy – until, in the shimmering mirage of the late afternoon heat, I start recognizing the signs, the bulging detour, the tracks in the desert sand, and I know; it is not over.

My maps and reality have had their occasional disagreements, but the Russian map book is displaying a level of deceitful sadism that is scary. How can they put this down as a road, and not just any road, the main national road? This is not a road; this is a wrecking alley. In front of me lie the mangled remains of something that once must have been a highway, but now looks to be the gruesome aftermath of a war between tar and truck, sun and sand. It seems as if a very area-specific earthquake has inflicted injury on this jumble of tortured, carbuncled tar. In places it is as if a truck skidded broadside, taking the tar surface with it, creating thigh-high tar waves, their frozen sides torn by weeds, allowing desert sand to flow in wind-ruffled rivers to the bottom of the neighboring potholes.

Bursting into slightly hysterical laughter I stop to try to find a route that will be least damaging for the Wish Mobile. On the side of the road there is the same swirling delta of tracks in the fragile sand that earlier I thought was the worst possible road; now I would like nothing better than to get down there. But this rotting corpse of a highway is laid out on a high dyke with steep sides of loose grey rocks. Driving down that would mean an instant full stop to this little jaunt around the world. Slowly and at snail's pace I nurse the Wish Mobile around the bumps, waves and potholes. Each meter forward is a test of balance, logistical planning, and sheer dumb luck; one misstep left or right would mean disaster.

Here my road trip rule three – never go back – is cast in tortured tar. Reversing here would be impossible, and then as an eagle dives in front of the car, I lose concentration for a moment. The front wheels miss the narrow ridges of tar I was aiming for, the shocks bottom out, and while the Wish Mobile bucks like a rodeo horse, I try frantically try to power out of this hellhole. The wheels spin up the side of the pothole, and precariously balancing on slivers of tar, the car comes to a shuddering halt. Using the pothole I have come to rest over as a convenience, I poke my head under the car to survey the damage. As I slowly focus on each wheel in turn, taking in the narrow ridges of crumbling tar and sand they are balancing on, a little warning bell tinkles in the back of my head.

> 'If any one of those little ridges of tar gives way, you are going to lose your head faster than you can say Marie Antoinette – the car's fine – I'm out of here.'

Dusting off the sand I survey the bleak empty scene. Above me the huge vault of sky, void of clouds, fades dull blue into the horizon, which vanishes dry, dusty and beige, relentlessly beige … in every direction. To the north a black stallion gallops across the sand; his herd follows at more sedate pace. On the western horizon a cowboy urges his cattle home; they kick up a dust storm that the heat spirals into the sky. My view is obscured as the silence shifts aside for a rustle of wings. The huge eagle settles on the other side of the road. I am not impressed.

> 'Oh, what are you staring at? I'm not lunch.'

With a smirk, the eagle looks down his beak at me.

> 'But you could be.'

And you could make an excellent photograph.

I slowly reach for the camera on the car seat behind me, but the bird is not interested and levitates without any visible effort from the roadside to the only bush within a 500 km radius. With only his head peeping out to keep an eye on me, the ferocious bird of prey actually manages to look cute. Picking my way slowly around the potholes I try to find a position for a shot, but with a crack of wing and branch, the eagle lifts out of the bush and spirals to a pinprick in the sky.

Enough messing with the wildlife, the sun is sinking and unless I want to camp in the middle of this 'road' I have got to find a way out of this fix. Climbing onto the Wish Mobile roof to get an overview of my situation, the distance reveals an actual off-ramp, fantastic, but it is on the other side of the road. This is somewhat less fantastic. Crossing the road here is a test of courage or foolishness, and requires a complete survey of the route, a distance of perhaps 200 meters as the eagle flies, but by way of the pothole and standing tar wave, a much longer and time-consuming journey.

Once back on the desert floor I instantly get involved with six sand traps. Using this morning's whap whap experience, I approach the sand gently, gently, too gently, damn, stuck. No chance of a truck roaring to my rescue this time. There is nothing to be done, but haul out trusty old Olga, and start digging. It doesn't look too bad, but the wind sends the sand flying about me, no matter how I try to avoid it. Giving the Wish Mobile a little test rev shows me that digging will not free the car; traction is needed. Applying my mind to the problem over a lukewarm fruit juice, I conclude that I need four flat objects of most resistance. While small desert midges use my arms as a cocktail lounge, I stare thoughtfully into the Wish Mobile. Then it comes to me. I put the yoga mat under the wheel most in need of traction and the three little cupboard lids under the remaining wheels, and I am free within seconds. Forget sand ladders and all that heavy stuff, yoga mats are the answer. But it's been 12 gruelling hours in which I have travelled scarcely 350 km. Time to find a place to camp and basta.

Within sight of the main road, in the middle of a holey city of desert voles, I set up camp, strip down to my birthday suit, and give myself a sponge bath. The fine sand has worked its way into places where no sand has gone before, and it must out, and if any roving Kazakh happens to catch a glimpse of my great white nakedness, so be it.

Naked and alone in the vast silent space, I become aware of the spin of the earth as the enormous orange sun slides behind the curved horizon of pale ochre sand. Stars start pinpointing the deep blue sky above, and with the slow realization that I am spinning backwards, I turn to face the rising tide of the Milky Way – a dazzling stream of light swept together by currents of dark matter that recede into ancient time. The still unfamiliar stars of the northern hemisphere are lost in the blizzard of light – our little galaxy one of millions, our sun a grain of sand. In star shadow the universe draws me in; my mind drops its defences, and travels through dark spaces that are filled with mystery and wonder. Our planet is not a watch tower; the Milky Way is not passing me by; I am part of the vast expanse of space; I am a piece of dark matter, I am the sea of possibilities. I am totally alone, totally at peace, totally happy; a current of deep content flows around me. Staring at the brilliant star-filled sky above me, I think that perhaps our minds are not like obstinate balloons, but like the night sky. The minds of most are like the night sky as seen from a city. The minds of some are like the night sky as seen from the country. And only a lucky few have a mind as clear as the night sky as seen from the middle of the desert, where its full beauty and possibility can first be guessed at.

A dashing shadow on the desert floor draws my attention to the night critters that are out to play. Time for bed. Snug in my little silver and lace bedroom, my thoughts float back to a time when lying in my car in the middle of the Karakum desert of Kazakhstan would have been unthinkable. There was a time, only about two years ago, when I couldn't have found Kazakhstan on a map.

Beds 60 and 61

With the return of the sun, my mind must return to the problem in hand. While majestic eagles turn lowly signposts into seats of power as they scan the flat land for breakfast with cruel eyes, I, with apprehensive eye, scan the land for an alternative to 'the road'. There is a track running diagonally across the desert, which should cut about 5 km off my need to drive 'the road'. But in the end there is no avoiding it. I must climb back on that horse. After an hour of bump and grind a policeman stops me. By now I have started to see them as a valuable source of information – if you can't beat 'em, use 'em – and before he can say or do anything, I regale him with questions in impossible Russian. What's the story with this road? How long will this continue? In trying to answer he quite forgets his official business of looking at my papers, which he cannot read anyway, and informs me that the road will soon be normal all the way to Shymkent. HALLELUJAH. And so it was. Well, sort of. The road 100 km from Aral looks like granny's patchwork quilt, but at least I am going 80 km an hour.

Aral is a small dusty town in the middle of the Karkum Desert, whose only reason for being here is fish. Aral is or, more correctly, was a port, or maybe it is still a port, as the port is still here. The sea is missing. The environmental and economic devastation of Aral is the direct result of long years of human abuse of the ecosystem around the Aral Sea – abuse that culminated in the Soviet 'Virgin Lands' project in the 1950s. This was the Soviets' grandiose plan to green the desert by planting fields of wheat and cotton. The fields were to be irrigated by diverting the Amu Darya and Syr Darya rivers, rivers whose waters, according to the Soviets, were just going to waste into the Aral Sea. The Soviet collective farmers put the sand to the plow; they planted and sowed and irrigated and irrigated and irrigated; and at some point, they took just a touch too much water and, unknowingly, tipped the balance of the ecosystem of the region, which started the shrinking of the Aral Sea.

By the time anyone noticed the problem, the Aral Sea was already dying, and then there was nothing to be done to stop it. The sea continues to shrink, and the sandstorms that now plague the region blow polluted sand far around the planet, degrading agricultural land and water wherever it lands. The Aral Sea disaster is proof that human activity can change the climate, yet, as global climatic change is still too large and vague for us to measure, we continue to believe we are too small to each make a difference.

Today the only indication that there is still a body of water somewhere out there – beyond the white chemical-encrusted sand and shimmering lake mirage on the horizon – is the occasional seagull that scavenges in the marketplace, where things hang off strings at throttling height, and the awnings make me stoop low.

The produce for sale is ample and varied, considering the very isolated position of Aral and the state of the road to the north. With the help of my pictionary I stock up on freshly baked crusty bread, short stubby desert cucumbers, and sweet deep red tomatoes; then I try for cheese, but the Kazakhs can make nothing of the illustration of a yellow wedge with holes in it. I try the picture of the cow, then the picture of a glass of milk; this is more successful, and sees me at the end of a dusty alley in a hot dark shed where I find the dairy department. Here the Western wedge meets the Kazakh curdle, and our differences are written in cheese: the white curdles that they scoop out of an unsavory-looking barrel do not appeal. Next on the shopping list is water; no bottled Evian here, but a man with a rolling rusty barrel walks by, indicating the direction from where fresh water might be acquired. In a muddy puddle between some shanty houses stands a hand-operated pump. I soon have the situation under control, and fill up all my containers with perfectly clear looking water; it tastes just fine; and I shall soon see the effect it has on my bowel.

Finally and most importantly.

Muhnia nushna dizel.

But the Aral diesel pump is dry, and there is no way of knowing when new supplies will arrive. This is a small problem, as I was counting on filling up here, and my fuel is running dangerously low. The map indicates that there should be a pump about 100 km down the road; this will be touch and go. At a very sedate pace, I follow a tiny ribbon of wrinkled grey tar, which makes it way past yellow sand, tufts of grass, camels, and silence. The camels are unaccustomed to sharing the road with cars, so a sharp warning from the Wish Mobile scares a baby camel into a pale white flight. He charges across the road, while his elders look on in cud-chewing amusement. The wind picks up dust-devils, and sends them dancing across the plains, then it changes its mind, and sweeps away the dancing devils with a huge wave of sand. The wave hits the Wish Mobile side on, and bullies us into a fuelling station of the bare-bones primitive kind.

The diesel pump is off to one side, standing in a swamp of diesel-soaked mud. In Kazakhstan you calculate the amount of fuel you need in advance, and then the service manager dials in the requested amount of fuel at the control point in the office. From there he opens the valve, and the fuel gushes out until the liters you had decided on earlier have been dispensed; you get it wrong, and the fuel goes all over the ground. The man in charge and I discuss, by using the dust on my car as blackboard, that 35 liters should do the trick.

We quickly discover that as the fuel nozzle is made for trucks, it is a bit large for the Wish Mobile, but the fuel guy is not deterred. He grunts as he shoves and pushes, until he has jammed the nozzle in good and tight. He then walks back to his office where he hits the switch. Watching this primitive situation I know there is something not quite right about the picture, and am about to take a photograph when the mistake in the image becomes perfectly clear.

The pipe is such a snug fit that, as the fuel shoots in, the air in the tank cannot escape. The pressure builds inside the tank until the fuel starts shooting out backward. When the nozzle starts shifting, I foresee disaster, and while yelling *neht neht* over the roaring wind and whine of the fuel pump, I try to hold the nozzle firm, a desperate and futile action. My puny strength is no match for the basic laws of physics. With a loud bang the nozzles explodes out of the tank, flies backwards, shooting liters of diesel into the sky and up my nose, into my mouth, in my eyes and all over the camera. The chap in the office, finally noticing the fountain of diesel, turns off the pump and comes running, to be greeted by a spewing fuming cursing diesel-soaked wild woman. I demand to use the *dusch* and, no, of course I do not expect him to have a shower in this godforsaken outback, but it is the only Russian word that springs to mind that describes that I need to wash and I need to do it now.

Ripping open the Wish Mobile, I haul out fresh clothes, soap and a towel, and storm to the office where I demand the use of their ablution facilities. The small huddle of people look up from whatever they are eating and stare, dumbstruck, at the ranting diesel-covered insane woman in the doorway. Finally one man twigs that, yes, actually, the lady might want to wash the diesel off herself. But unfortunately, as he shows me, their water supply comes from a 20-gallon metal milk drum, with a soup ladle as dispenser.

My fury knows no bounds as I storm back to the Wish Mobile, where, right there, next to the stinking diesel pump, I unfurl my changing booth. By now the wind is howling across the desert, picking up tons of sand, and flinging it against the tent with a fury to match my own. Stark naked, I fight off the tent, while the automatic washing machine does double duty as a bathtub, and yesterday's t-shirt becomes my pre-soaped wash cloth. On a bench, in the wind-shade of the office, sits a group of Kazakhs – transfixed – they cannot believe their eyes. I am sure there is a tote going on the odds of the tent being whipped away by the wind to expose my diesel-soaked butt to the world. What they don't know is that I am organized; this tent is going nowhere without my say so. Washed and scrubbed, I emerge more or less clean and ready for battle. But of course with no common ground in the language department, what am I to do? I am not about to beat the guy up, although the thought is incredibly satisfying. He says he dispensed 19 liters of fuel, and there no use arguing that most of it went all over me, and had he been paying attention, this would not have happened. His grasp of basics physics is probably such that he believes that I am actually insane, and my diesel shower was self-inflicted. This suspicion is confirmed when he grabs my money, and starts shooing me away like I am a rabid dog.

Now there is only one thing on my to-do list: a hot shower. The next town is Kyzl'orda where I don't expect a decent hotel room, but hope there is just a hotel with a hot shower. Approaching the town, things get greener and greener, until the road is on a dyke of sorts. On both sides of the road cows stand belly deep in water, grazing on floating water plants. But the town, caught in the middle of the dust storm, is bleak grey and gritty. The truck ahead of me sheds its load of garbage into the roaring gale with every bump and rut it hits on; yet another fine example of Kazakh roads. The hotel I find is not yet finished, charges a fortune, makes lots of promises, but fulfils none. But at least I manage to have that shower, after which my attention focuses on my camera. I clean it as best I can, but it continues to smell of diesel, and I am sure than very soon it will start breaking down, and this is a very bad thing.

Shymkent is my goal for today; the road is a ruler-straight pencil line through the beige, and vanishes in a mirage lake on the horizon. I stop often for no other reason than to experience the immense size of the planet. On my left, some faint purple mountains ruffle the earth's curve, and distant rows of electrical poles hint at a human habitat hidden somewhere in the flat tufty sand-land that is a palette of grey against grey against brown against beige. The stark grandeur of the landscape puts all my woes into perspective, and soon a smile that starts in my chi, my deep centre, finds its way back onto my face.

In each tiny town surrounded by bleak barren nothing, there is a police road block, where stopping me is the highlight of their day, week, month, year. By now I feel am doing my bit for society; at least they have something different to talk about over dinner tonight. We make friendly small talk while they pretend to read my official papers. They walk around the Wish Mobile, nodding wisely, but no policeman wants to write a wish; perhaps it is against regulations.

Seventy kilometers north of Shymkent I stop in one of the villages of the dead that lie on the outskirts of every village of the living. The houses of Kazakhstan's living citizens appear to be built according to a government-approved blueprint, which states that every house shall be a single-storey, square grey construction, built of sun-baked adobe bricks, with a tin roof, four windows, two doors, and the only paint color that shall be used is cyan. When the good folk of Kazakhstan lay their dead to rest, they let out all their building creativity. The tombs are decorated with scalloped arches, resting on ornate pillars, in front of mud-plastered walls, which are carved with swirling floral patterns, and decorated with pieces of mirror and colored glass that are pushed into the mud cement to create sparkly flowers, diamonds, moons and stars. Many tombs are two or three sections high, climbing from a square base to a second octagonal section, and then a steeple or bread-oven-shaped dome, and every tomb is topped by a metal crescent moon or star. The tombs stand clustered together in haphazard fashion; some are well tended, but many are slowly being reclaimed by the desert.

Twenty kilometers north of Shymkent the land is being farmed again with huge plows and tractors, and there are trees. I haven't seen a tree in days. Trees are valuable here, and each trunk is protected from the onslaught of insects by a white painted sock. The traffic is increasing, and the drivers dodge wildly for the smallest bump in the road. They should try driving to the north of their country to get some perspective. In Shymkent ,the first hotel I see is the huge Shymkent Hotel; it has four stars, so a bit out of the budget, but I feel I deserve some pampering after the last week, and the price is surprisingly good – so good that I smell rat and ask to see the room. Someone has definitely been awarding themselves stars in this establishment, but the price to room ratio is fine, and so it will be home for the weekend.

Early Saturday evening I walk out into Shymkent. The city is Asian in the small tightly packed shops and bright neon lights; Russian in the writing; and touches of Islam show in the architecture, parks and water features. It feels as if I have been out of touch with the world for months, so I rent a taxi to take me to the nearest Internet café. It is in a street of tiny, tightly packed shops, where neon lights flash and advertise their little store with frantic 'offs' and 'ons'. The Internet café is in a shop behind a shop, and requires a squeeze down a narrow corridor painted bright green and yellow. The place is packed, and seems more like an entertainment centre than an Internet café. In the glow of computer screens, the racial mix of Kazakhstan reveals itself: Asian faces, Arabic faces, round Mongolian features, and the finely chiseled faces of the northern Kazakh. There are heavy-jawed Russians and the Russian-Asian mix, which is not a very successful blend of strawberry blond with tiny slit eyes. Young men are busy with the usual kill, maim, destroy the virtual enemy thing; there is group Skyping going on; and young girls watch soppy movies that they are probably not allowed to watch at home.

And there is no mail for me. I stare sadly at my empty mailbox; nobody loves me; everybody hates me. After eating a half-hearted dinner of worms, while watching small children in floating bumper cars bounce about the rectangular pond in front of the hotel, I return to my room, where the flashing neon lights color the white walls from blue to green to flashing red and orange. In the mirror I watch my face change from blue to green to flashing red and orange, and my alienation comes full circle. I understand nothing, can speak to no one, I have to deal with the seventh monetary system, and am sleeping in the sixteenth bed in 20 days. The emotional rollercoaster of the last few weeks overwhelms me, and hot tears flow unchecked down my cheeks.

I am a small raft alone in a stormy ocean, the waves just keep breaking over me, and I wish they would stop, but they are relentless.

Time to regroup: I impose a ban on sightseeing and any new experiences. Shymkent will remain unexplored. After a weekend of sleeping, foraging for food, blogging and beating the overly enthusiastic Shymkentians off the Wish Mobile, the 'One planet One people' project has take wings down here. Everybody wants to sign their names, but nobody wants to think; no thinking, no writing is my creed. By Monday I feel ready to face the world again, and to match my mood, the Wish Mobile needs some sprucing up.

At the carwash, all the men – car owners and car washers alike – gather around and I sense again something that I started noticing a while ago – the looks of longing, of take me with you, take me away from it all. Men, it seems, also long for rescue, and I must represent the female version of the knight in shining armor or shiny silver Wish Mobile, as the case may be. I think men, sometime in the distant past – round about the time that they decided that all gods should be male – set a standard for themselves which was never achievable, and which they are finding harder and harder to maintain. The macho concept of man must be the boss, breadwinner and master of all he beholds is really about silly expectations that men impose on themselves.

Unfortunately the world is reaping the bitter fruit of this self-imposed superiority and invincibility in which boys don't cry, and any sign of weakness or emotion must be denied and hidden. When men explode with the frustration and tension of it all, they strike out like children placed in a position beyond their abilities to cope with, resorting to that primal thing that they believe defines them as male. However, when last did a man really need to venture forth to slay a beast for dinner or rescue a fair damsel from a dragon? More and more, the male need to show physical strength is corrupted, and the world continues to be defined by violence of every shade, nuance and hue. Yet I think that most men want to be rescued and taken away from it all, just as much as any sappy girly girl you ever could meet.

But I am not in the rescuing business, and tell them to stop gawking at the car, and get on with washing it – cow.

It seems I have not yet regained my full good humor, and this will not do. I make a concerted effort to pull myself toward myself. The thing is, the Wish Mobile is now covered in good wishes for the world, which inspire people to leave little good luck letters under the windscreen wipers. Now that the Wish Mobile has been labelled a wise and friendly car, and with everybody staring, waving and making peace signs at it, I cannot very well sit here scowling like a sour old dragon. I have got to smile and wave, and generally behave myself in a world peace kind of way. So I force a smile on my face, and very soon I am quite a happy person again. It is incredible how simply smiling, even if at first you don't mean it or want to, soon turns into a real smile.

Like everything else in life, being happy, is a choice you make.

Uzbekistan

Bed 62

An elaborate marble arch framing a huge gate gives access to the land of the Uzbeks. This most extravagant border post sets a standard of grandeur that is belied by the chaos that pours through it: rusty cars, skinny cows, bleating goats, sweaty pedestrians, persistent moneychangers and more so beggars. Taxis drivers shout for customers and hawkers jingle their wares. The dust and heat mix with the smell of sweat and goats to a pungent stew. I get harangued and harried and sent from counter to counter, but by now I have regained my balance and push the chaos aside, until a man simply walks to the front of the queue and demands to be served. The first time this happens I am dumbfounded; the second time I get all English about it. The local ladies might have to put up with this male-dominated queue jumping, but I don't.

With a tap on the shoulder I gain his attention.

'Excuse me, but there is a queue here.'

He gives me an enquiring look, but doesn't move.

'Sir, by rule of the queue it is now my turn to be served.'

With an imperial wave of the hand and meaningful glance to the back of the queue, I indicate that he should move out of my way.

In a state of shock the man falls back, and I claim my right to service. I can sense, if not see the hidden smiles of the women around me.

Border crossings are such a drag. Hundreds of women, bent under huge cloth bundles, cross freely between the countries, yet I get the whole nine yards. A thousand forms need to be filled in, and the Wish Mobile is thoroughly searched then finally the usual questions.

'Are you carrying any drugs?'

'No.'

'Weapons?'

'No.'

'How much money do you have?'

'Credit card.'

'Are you married?'

'What?'

Samarqand: Uzbekistan

That's a new one, and what business is this of his?

But in this part of the world, marriage still seems to be the single most important event in the life of a woman and a man; as in conservative societies, getting married equates with getting some. So the girl gets to put on the billowing white princess dress, and the guy gets to take it off, and both are so excited at these diametrically opposed events that masses of money is spent on celebrating their two separate moments of glory. The marriage carriage is a very important public part of the celebration. It is of the white sedan variety; how big and what make depend on the wealth of the girl's parents and their need to show off. Stretch limousines squeeze out of dusty side streets, bedecked with the obligatory vehicle decoration, which consists of some form of corsage on the car roof, such as a Barbie-type doll mounted in a golden glitter heart, or simply a large golden crown, tastefully set in a bed of plastic roses. All this flimflam goes, hooters blaring, through the town to the chosen registrar's office, and not just any registrar's office. There seems to be a certain ranking that makes some offices so popular that they are booked out months, if not years in advance. As the location of registrar is of utmost importance in the wedding planning, weddings take place any day of the week at any time of day.

On the outskirts of Tashkent, I spy a wedding cavalcade in my rearview mirror. I know by now to treat them the same way as one would an ambulance in the West, so pull over to allow a wedding vehicle so bedecked with fake flowers it could easily join the Mardi Gras to pass me. The length and breadth of the car is obscured by 'LOVE', written in bright red roses, and as the car roars by, it occurs to me.

Love? What do you know?

The writing in Uzbekistan is in the Latin alphabet. Now I have Uzbek-speaking streets signs, written in Latin, but my map is Russian, and is written in Cyrillic. Bulgaria in reverse, back to Zen and the art of navigating.

My first call of action is to get some Cym, as money is called in Uzbekistan, but at the money exchange the ladies don't want to change my 100€ note. I cannot understand why, and persist until the lady makes her point quite clear by stacking bricks and bricks of notes on the counter. As she slowly vanishes from view I finally get the picture. In this office they only have two hundred Cym notes available and at the current exchange rate of 1€–1 554.00 Cym, the 100€ amounts to 155 400.00 Cym and a huge stack of 200 Cym notes. This is not practical. At my hotel I have more luck and get three quite manageable wads of 5 000 Cym notes. The Uzbeks are very good at counting money; their fingers are a blur as they count their way through the fat wads of cash every transaction amounts to. In the beginning I attempt to check my change after each transaction, but, you know, life is too short.

Tashkent is a modern city, rebuilt after the 1966 earthquake according to the Soviet dream-city blueprint. Tashkent has no space limit, so the Soviets were able to indulge their love of massive public squares and wide roads. In places the city has roads ten lanes wide; the tar to car ratio here would be any European's dream come true. But the Uzbeks find the wide empty roads confusing, so in order to orient themselves, the Tashkent drivers use the white lines not as lane dividers, but as an aiming aid. By driving Scalextric fashion with the white line in the centre of the car, they all manage to stay in nice straight lines. Crossing the road here is such a time-consuming affair I just walk on the islands between the lanes – where to add a rural note there is a cow tethered to a tree in the park-like boulevards that separate the lanes of the monster road.

To speed things along a bit more, I find a taxi to take me to the government buildings of Tashkent. At my destination I hand the man a 5000 Cym note and wait for my change.

He looks at me wondering why I am not getting out of the taxi. With hands and feet I demand my change, which according to me should be 4 500 Cym. He responds with a vehement. *Neht neht* five five and throws his five fingers in the air in front of me.

Da and I gave you five …

Then my brain catches up with the country I am in. I realize that I am paying in Uzbek Cym, not Kazakh Tenge, and the fare of 'five', as quoted by the driver, would be five thousand Cym, not five hundred Tenge. I stoop and grovel my apologies, mentioning Tenge and Cym, and my poor brain, and it is all just too much for me – an odd place to look for sympathy and understanding. His face tells me that, really, he just wants me to get out of his taxi so he can get on with his life.

The government house is a very impressive building that is fronted by a standing wave fountain, 50 m long and 5 m high, which sheds diamond drops of water into a long rectangular pool, where old men wearing doppilar – the traditional Uzbek square skullcap – are sweeping with twig brooms, while children splash about in the shallow water. Thinking that the little girls in bright swimsuits make a good contrast to the imposing fountains and bombastic government building on the little rise, I whip out my camera, but before I can bring it to eyelevel, three uniforms jump at me from all sides. No photo! Such neurosis. There are children playing in the fountains, old folk taking the sun, and a satellite high above filming our current confrontation and sending it straight back to the computers of whoever might be interested. Get with the program already.

This neighborhood is the part of Tashkent that foreign government officials get to see. Here the city is like an enormous park, with forests of baby trees, shaded walkways and fountains of every description. Traditional jets shoot white geysers of water high into the air; giant Middle Eastern filigree crowns are stacked into multistoried waterfalls and modern water sculptures that bounce sausages of water from pond to pond. They all catch the late afternoon sun, casting diamonds and rainbows around the children of Tashkent, who make the most of all these rather fun swimming holes. Swimming is the only sensible thing to do in the mid summer heat, and from restaurant piers locals dive into the bright green water of the Chirchik River. A young man, high on love, life, and perhaps vodka, lies with his head in the lap of his beloved, a blowsy Russian bottle blonde. Forgetting himself, he tries to undress her right there and then on the banks of the River Chirchik, but she is having none of it, and swats him about the head.

Trying to avoid having to cross the enormous road again, I walk into what I think is a subway, where I discover that Tashkent has a metro, the only one in central Asia. The interior is a cool grey space with star-shaped marble pillars supporting domed ceilings, above a floor of gleaming marble, and there is not a speck of dirt or advertising billboard in sight. To document this auspicious occasion, I photograph the metro station, and magically a military uniform materialises out of the shadows. No photo. Too late, mate; the deed is done. Before he can say another word, I step into a cyan train, and it carries me off into the wild blue yonder.

Quite relaxed, I ride along until I am cool and rested, then choosing an arbitrary station, emerge back into the light, right at a fun-fare – where I find the Tashkentians, who are all having lots of fun, swinging, bouncing, spinning, eating, drinking and laughing. In Tashkent the mix of nations is very apparent: a family walk by: dad is of Far East extraction; mom is a local tribe. The children have the father in them with button noses, almond eyes, golden skin and thick black hair, while mom supplies the cheekbones. They split a group of Russians: the heavy-jawed pale pink faces are unmistakable between the golden tan, high cheekbones of central Asia.

When darkness falls, I discover that impromptu Metro rides are all good and well, but they do tend to throw out the internal mapping system. But I have not come this far and learned nothing about finding the Wish Mobile. I have with me my hotel card and, as in this part of the world you negotiate your taxi fare before you start your journey, it takes only a short taxi ride before I am reunited with my stuff.

Bed 63

Up with the sunrise, I am on the road in the cool of day. The road to Samarqand runs back through time. Tashkent is an oasis of modern flash in this dusty desert country. Village follows village without pause or punctuation; the mud-houses are the same same same: rectangular, made of mud bricks, plastered with mud, topped with grey corrugated iron roofs, and surrounded by blue metal fences. The streets are lined with trees that are so densely planted that they grow into very tall and skinny hedges. Everywhere, women, in long garishly tie-dyed shapeless dresses, are occupied with the painting of the trees. This is a mammoth 'Alice in Wonderland' task, but it is all quite neighborly. The women chat and laugh, as they paint a white sock onto every tree. In the dusty fields, farmers are bent double in the blazing sun, plowing with handheld hoes, while on the roadside a young cowhand and his bull get into a little scrap; the boy prudently puts a freshly painted tree between himself and the belligerent animal.

Somewhere between here and there, the road suddenly widens into a huge concrete rugby field. Unconcerned – I have seen some strange roads by now – I continue driving straight ahead, until I discover that I am head to head with the oncoming traffic. I have no way forward. Where is my road? Making a pit stop on the edge of the concrete, I try to work out what is going on, when a tap at the window disturbs my map consultation. A very round little old lady, dressed in purple with gold thread and with not tooth in her mouth, takes the opportunity to demand a lift. It seems churlish to refuse, so she gets in with glee, wedging a huge cloth-covered bowl between her stomach and the dashboard. She is amazed how cool the car is, the music, the comfort, she strokes the seat, the dashboard; and the Wish Mobile wriggles with pleasure.

She indicates that the road we should take is way on the other side of the concrete field. It seems that in constructing the road, the road surveyors made a little mistake, and the two roads did not quite match up, so they just filled in the blanks with a field of concrete. On reaching this I should have immediately made a u-turn right, which would have led me by snaking round about onto my side of the road. She points out the route, and then continues to babble non-stop. I nod and smile, hopefully at the appropriate moments. Finally she calls her stop and offers to pay for the ride. Refusing to take no for an answer, she starts to open her enameled bowl. Curious, I let her fiddle her way through one knotted cloth after another. Getting them all undone, she presents me with baked goods that look like samoosas, but are soft like buns. As she gets out, she rewards me with an enormous toothless grin. Behind her, small children have run out of the house, and then come to a sudden stop at a safe distance. Granny will have lots to tell them.

The soft samoosas fill the car with the smell of faintly rancid cooking oil and onions. Breaking one open reveals crispy stodge around stodgy stodge, flavored by onions cooked in slightly rancid oil. What a waste of the old lady's food, but it has got to go. I know, I know, snob, spoilt brat and all that, but taking good care of one's bowel movement is vital to comfortable road tripping. I would rather eat the crisp red apples that are currently for sale at the roadside.

Alongside a gravel river lined with the pink and white cosmos, two grown men astride a very small donkey herd their goats to the water. I bounce past on a road in desperate need of repairs, and arrive in the 'Shining Star of the Orient' via the backdoor.

Although Samarqand was founded in 700 BCE by the Persians, the magnificent city that we see today was inspired by the vision of a lame Mogul king, Amir Temur, who claimed to be a descendant of Genghis Kahn. In the 14th century he ruled a kingdom that stretched from Siberia to Afghanistan. Amir Temur was an enthusiastic scholar, and a man of great wisdom and foresight. He dreamed a dream of a city so beautiful that the whole world would be in awe. To achieve this, he gathered from his great kingdom all the most talented architects and artisans to build the 'Shining Star of the Orient'. The talented men labored long and hard to create the magnificence that was Samarqand.

In his palace is inscribed: 'If you doubt our might, look at our buildings.'

Samarqand conjures up images of hot winds fanning the burning sands, of turbaned nomads, tents, camels, horses, fire and smoke; of women in brilliantly colored clothing who serve piles of roast lamb with chickpeas and couscous tinted golden with delicate strands of saffron, stuffed eggplants, tomatoes and peppers to men leaning on richly decorated pillows, the smoke of the men's narghiles mingling with the smell of cloves and ginger. Samarqand conjures up images of plump peaches, dried apricots with almonds, and honey-sweetened lips as batchas – the dancing boys – sway in sensuous rhythm to drums beating in the hot Persian nights.

And the reality? It is all there, in pieces.

Amir Temur's remains now lie in a mausoleum that encompasses the extravagance of his dreams. At Gu-e-Amir, where several generations of the Temurid dynasty are buried, Uzbek women in brilliant red, green and yellow dresses walk under a peaked arch that reduces them to doll size. The walls of the arch are covered in intricate organic patterns, picked out with delicate mosaic in cyan, indigo, white and ochre. The arch frames the mausoleum, which is a simple building with extravagant detail. Its dome is decorated with tapering ceramic ribs covered with small mosaic tiles set in tight geometric designs. The minarets on either side are covered in bands of tiles, forming a monumental Kufic inscription, which repeats over and over, 'God is eternal'. The interior walls of the mausoleum are covered in small tiles that plait together to create complex geometric forms, which contain more complex geometric forms, with gold leaf picking out the relief of smaller complex geometric forms. The dome is built like a honeycomb made by bees with a preference for rounded shell shapes, each small shape a dazzling decadence of indigo, cyan and gold: the colors of wisdom, paradise and wealth. In the centre of the high dome a crystal chandelier floats in the dazzling golden reflections of its own creation.

Aktur, my guide, relates an event, which happened in 1941 when nosy scientists wanted to clarify a few important historical points, such as was Timur really lame. Three wise old men felt that this was a fairly lame excuse to open the grave, and prophesied that if the scientists were to open the sarcophagus, the spirit of war would be released. The scientists dismissed the old men as crackpots – not an unusual reaction from scientists – and continued with their very important research, discovering that Timur was indeed lame. I am so glad they cleared that up. Then the remains of Timur were placed back in the sarcophagus, but it was too late, two days later the Second World War – according to Russian history books – began. In Uzbekistan many folk believe it is all because of the opening of Timur's grave.

Aktur relates this with the earnestness of a teacher to his first pupil, and then he abruptly interrupts his history lesson to ask whether I am married. Aktur is about 13 years old, why would he care, but from the Uzbek point of view this is one of life's most important questions. It crops up in every conversation. In the West we ask, How are you? In Africa they ask, Where are you from? Here they ask, Are you married? Before he has a chance to propose, I take my leave, and make my way back to my bed.

In Samarqand I have hit the jackpot with my choice of accommodation. In the Malika, the room to cost ratio is so outrageously good, I wish I could pack the whole place into the Wish Mobile, and not have to worry about a bed for the rest of the trip. After a delightful night's rest in an enormous suite decorated with locally carved woodwork, I amble down to the courtyard, and to the sound of birdsong and the gentle splashing of fountains, I slip onto a sura.

The sura is the traditional seating arrangement in Uzbekistan, which consists of a low wooden platform, beautifully carved and covered with brilliantly colored and patterned carpets and pillows. To sit on a sura, you take off your shoes, climb onto the carpeted platform and use the cushions to make yourself comfortable. In the centre of the platform is a low table, onto which the staff pile my breakfast of fruit, yoghurt, filled pancakes, both sweet and savory, flapjacks with delicious quince mousse, omelettes and endless chai. Lean-lying against the pillows, surrounded by the sound of water and birdsong, the dusty desert outside world slips from my reality. This is a table to solve the world's problems at. Not now, though. I have things to do, places to see, and stepping into the street, reality returns.

Water flows along the side of the dirt pavement, which a small girl directs to the trees with a primitive hoe that is taller than she. In a side street, a young girl has set up a cool-drink stall. On a small metal trolley several colors of flavor are displayed in long glass tubes. She injects a small amount of color into a plastic cup, and tops it up with fizzy water from a siphon. Giving it to me, she refuses payment. She's sort of missing the point there, so I pay her anyway. I'm not sure how much, just a casual note from my giant wad of Cym. Having such a huge bundle of money makes me feel quite wealthy, sort of like winning at monopoly.

The early morning market is a battlefield of sights, sounds and scents. from the brown on brown of the potato sellers to the brilliant greens of the salad ladies. The saffron sellers sidle up like stolen-watch merchants and I wonder if what they are selling is indeed saffron. Dried-fruit sellers pile their produce high, and entice sales with tasty offers of pistachios and apricots. In the grain and pulse department, the neutral tones of rice and chickpeas are offset by the brilliant dresses of the women, who methodically sift tiny stones from huge bags of lentils. Spice dealers crush their merchandise, freeing the delicious aromas into the mouth-watering air. Bakers balance their delicate wares in great golden mounds. Fresh nan – in the clumsy shape of a child's pottery plate with a thick round ridge that dips into a shallow basin centre – was packed too soon, and now lies sweating in its plastic confines. The butcher waves a lazy hand at the flies that settle on the carcass hanging in his stall, while giant sausages gleam in fear of the knife grinders, whose wheels turn endlessly, sharpening the blades that customers bring. The kettle-fixer welds and patches ancient pots and pans, and sloe-eyed children beg to be photographed, delighting in their own digital images.

In the shadow of a giant mosque, a group of teenage boys admire the bicycle of a friend. A bicycle is a luxury in this donkey-powered world, and this bike has been sooped up with bright shiny blue decorations plaited through the spokes; it has a sound system attached to the back carrier; and six headlamps, all of which are powered by an assortment of batteries that create a decorative effect along the front fork. The boys look about sixteen, and are totally absorbed in the abilities of this home-made Heath Robinson device. In consumer-driven societies this would be considered totally naïve. Children in 'developed countries' have been taught by television and advertising that if it is not factory made, bought in a fancy shop, and carrying an international brand name, it simply isn't good enough; homemade just doesn't cut it.

In downtown Samarqand women and girls in ankle-length colorful floral dresses shield their fair skins from the sun with bright purple umbrellas; suntans are not a status symbol here. Young men in jeans and Western t-shirts slouch about, and then the snarfing starts. A loud sniffing and guttural hawking results in a spit-splat expectoration onto the most convenient pavement. Noticing the pavement for the first time, I have one of those moments of enlightenment that one can really do without. The pavements are covered in the yellow oyster-like contents of the nation's sinuses, which to me seems somehow worse than dog pooh. This has to be the vilest and most disgusting habit known to man. Unfortunately, now that I have become aware of this habit, it becomes like a dripping tap in the dark of night, louder and louder, until I stop looking at the pavement, and shove my fingers in my ears at first sound of a deep throat gurgle.

Away from this local bustle, I find tourist central at the Registan Ensemble: an enormous complex of mosques, madrasas and minarets set around an imposing central square. At the entrance I pay my 7 000 Cym and an extra 2 000 Cym because I want to take photographs. This is an interesting system, which makes me feel obliged to snap away with vigor. A guard slides up to me, and asks in sotto tone if I want to climb the minaret. I consider this for a minute and decide why not; for 2 000 Cym I get to look behind the scenes.

The Registan Ensemble is a bit like a film set. The part on public display is an impressive assortment of pillars, minarets domes and arches, all covered in a blizzard of tiny blue, ochre, white and black tiles, arranged in a visual maze of geometric shapes. The space where I now find myself is a wall-fall of crumbling mud bricks, half stairs and missing floors. The guide allows me to ascend the stairs first, but the steps are muscle-aching steep, and each step is so high that any elegant finishing school technique of floating up and down stairs floats right out of the window. With no handrail to help me climb, my legs have to heave me up, step by step, causing me to bend forward with the effort. On the narrow winding stair I am painfully aware that the guard's face is far too close to my sticking-out butt. This simply will not do. I indicate that he should go first. This way I can keep my dignity, and take rest stops, while pretending to take photographs of my surroundings.

The guard starts his way up the tiny spiral of the minaret, where I follow at respectable distance. This works very well, until we get to the top. Here there is only space for one on the minaret platform, and the staircase is so narrow I have to squeeze past the guard with almost full body contact, so that my nose hits the peak of his blue pillbox hat. This is far closer to a totally strange man than I need to get. I have visions of *A passage to India*, but not being a silly old duck, I look him straight in the eye, and covey a silent yet clear message. Any funny business from your side, mate, and you are mince.

From the top of the minaret, the full panorama of modern Samarqand spreads into the dusty white heat. Massive mosques, topped by cyan ceramic domes, draw my focus; they are surrounded by small adobe houses with tin roofs and blue metal gates, each property edged by small round trees. Far below is the inner courtyard of the Registan Ensemble. The place is big and beautiful, but lacking in soul and history. It feels like a themed shopping complex, where the prince's chamber now sells carpets, and in the king's room silk is for sale. I am impressed, but not overwhelmed.

On the recommendation of Ulugbek, the owner of the Malika, I eat dinner at a local restaurant, where women sway to the beat of tambourines and flip-fold their hands through the air to the sound of high wailing song. An underage boy is the only male on the dance floor, and all the women dance with and around him. The waiter presents me with a huge menu and I try to look intelligent, while browsing through the food on offer, but, really, I have no idea what I am ordering, so opt for a shashlik of some sort. The plate of food arrives, and I am surprised to find my shashlik is a wad of minced meat that has been hand-pressed onto a stick, and then grilled, an unusual and very unappetizing-looking hamburger patty. This is not helped by the fact that it is raw, but the waiter, having served the food, feels his work is done, and ignores my delicate attempts at drawing his attention. An elegantly dressed young man at the neighboring table comes over to see if he can help. When he discovers that I speak English, he takes the opportunity to show off in front of his friends. He summons the waiter, send the offending meal back to the kitchen to be properly cooked, and then introduces himself as Vladimir – at which point I burst out laughing. Clapping my hand in front of my mouth I apologize for my rudeness, but cannot suppress my giggles.

Vladimir is one of those irrepressible individuals who exude good humor, charm and energy, and instead of taking offense at my rudeness, he agrees ruefully that, yes, indeed it is very funny. You see, Vladimir is a moon-faced, olive-skinned Korean, a more unlikely looking Vladimir you could not hope to meet. He explains to me that his mother has an inexplicable love for all things Russian. Vladimir sits back, carefully adjusting the fold of his shirt cuffs, then lights up a slender cigarette. Through a thin stream of smoke he starts to interrogate me. Once he has it quite clear in his head what it is that I am up to, he declares that he will come along. He has always wanted to see China and America, and life in Samarqand can be a bit tedious for an elegant young Korean named Vladimir. I convince him that life with me would be one of constant disappointment for him, so as we part he presents me with his keyring, a small plastic cube that holds a glitter swirl world of a Samarqand mosque, so that I will never forget him.

Bed 65

Up at 04h30, today's destination Bukhara. Although it is only 290 km away, the Malika staff assure me it will take at least 4 hours to get there, and as I only have a one-night stop in Bukhara, I want to leave as early as possible. This is no problem for the staff at the Malika Hotel, who serve me the standard enormous breakfast long before daylight. The sun is just rising as I set out, but already the early morning traffic jams of donkey carts that are on their way to market make getting out of Samarqand slow going. The tiny knock-kneed donkeys drag enormous loads of fresh produce, piled high in patched-together wooden carts. At first I was all animal rights huffy about the treatment of the donkeys. But after my visits to the market, I realised that the boy who is pulling the donkey forward will soon be the beast of burden, as he will single-handedly have to unload and carry his produce to his stall in the vast market.

Leaving the extravagance of Samarqand behind, the roads lead through vineyards, where small platforms built on long stilts tower over the vines. On each platform sits a woman; her job is to create noise to prevent the birds from settling on the fruit. As I drive by, they shout and wave, I hoot my hellos, but as Bukhara is set in far drier climes than Samarqand, the vineyards soon turn to low scrubland and dust.

I enter Bukhara at the modern end, where the wide road is lined with glass-fronted buildings, but my hotel is in the old town, where everything is the color of sand. On foot, I set out to explore this UNESCO World Heritage Site, which in its golden years was the intellectual centre of the world. Under the cool arches of a converted madrasa, weavers turn skeins of brilliant silk into long scarves in the traditional brilliant yellow, red and green bleeding diamond shapes of Uzbekistan. A doll-faced girl embroiders intricate patterns of gold on a deep blue background. In the jewelry market a metal chaser practices his age-old craft. While his friends chat and joke around him, he slowly tap tap, tap taps his way round the edge of a brass platter, and using only his imagination, a small hammer and tiny metal punch, he embosses an elaborate organic pattern in the smooth metal. In his workshop rows and rows of punches, tongs, hammers and pliers hang under a small brick smelting oven. On display are deadly looking sabers and more comforting metal tea urns and water pitchers. Then I am accosted by carpet, carpetbag, fez and embroidered cloth sales people. I don't really want to be dragging things around with me, so duck into an ally to escape their insistent cries.

The alleys that branch and fork into crisscross chaos are potholed and veined with wastewater, which sinks slowly into the desert sand. High mud and straw walls protect the privacy of the houses and courtyards, which are entered through beautifully carved doors, whose heavy wood has faded to the color of sand under ancient coats of blue paint that are threadbare and transparent with wear. An open door gives a tantalizing glimpse into a courtyard, where a sura is shaded by vines that are heavy with tiny, deep purple desert grapes. I try one. It is so sweet it makes my nose twitch.

The roads are without system, and soon I have no idea where I am. In order to have some purpose and goal, I follow the sound of a drumming tambourine. Turning sand-colored corner after sand-colored corner, I stumble on a wedding, where the clapping drumming women are dressed in overwhelming pattern: pink spot over purple swirl over green stripe with rainbow flowers and gaudy check over riotous paisley. The longing for bright colors in this dull dusty land is as strong as the European's longing for sun after a long hard winter. Accompanied by the beat of tambourine, the blaze of color vanishes around a sand-colored corner.

A small boy calls hello, hello, photo, photo. His older brother, standing rigid straight, pulls his younger brother to order. I wait while they pose themselves most suitably for their image to be captured. Two small boys amble by; they are more relaxed about their photo shoot, and hang on each other's necks, waving peace signs at the camera. Around a corner, I meet the local baker. He agrees to be photographed, but must first rearrange his only product, the flat breads that are for sale from small trolleys all around the neighborhood. The bread gets baked in a brick oven fuelled by gas, which arrives in his shop from the pipes that run all along the mud walls, resting on concrete poles just above head height. Once he has arranged his bread to his satisfaction, he flashes me a smile, gold teeth agleam. Have I mentioned the gold teeth? They are all the rage down here; everybody has at least one.

Just as I start worrying about ever finding my way out of this maze, the sound of a string instrument, accompanied by singing, lures me around sand-colored corners. In a leafy park, an outdoor restaurant is serving lunch to the locals, while a threesome serenades them with high wailing song. All around, clusters of men discuss the day, the gold thread in their doppilar catching the shafts of sun filtering through the trees. A gaggle of girls distracts me; they are digging for clams in the cracked mud of a dry well. A little girl with short-cropped dark hair, impish grin and creamy skin runs over to show off her find; the clams are bigger than her hands; do they eat them? In the knot of a small tangle of lanes, a woman sells watermelons and warm coke from a market barrow. Under a tree outside their yard, on a spread of bright carpets and cloths, a family has gathered for tea, bread and dried fruit. At their centre sits the family matriarch. Dressed in a rainbow of colors, she is a human flowerbed in the beige surroundings. She agrees to be photographed; her eyes, deeply desert-lined, stare proudly into the lens; they tell of a life of hard work and dignity.

Then just as easily as I lost my way, I find it again, and emerge from the maze, right next to my hotel. As the desert wind has now reached tumble-dryer status, I feel a bit of air-conditioning is in order until the day cools to a manageable temperature. In the velvet warmth of the late afternoon, I set out again.

Under the Kalyan Minaret – also known as the tower of death, as for centuries criminals were thrown from its 45,5 m height; a spectacular but messy way of ridding yourself of your criminals – I photograph a young girl in bright red walking by; she is a tiny dot of red in a sea of sand.

'Hello.'

I turn to see a tall sweaty individual approaching me. He is trying to sell me or tell me something.

'You like food, I have restaurant in house.'

I rather like the idea of getting behind one of those ornate doors, but a meal on a first date is too much commitment, so I play it safe, and agree to a cup of tea. He leads me here, there and everywhere, and I start wondering at the wisdom of following a complete stranger deep into the maze that is the local neighborhood of Bukhara. But this man exudes no threat, only a total exhaustion with life and living. His house is at the end of a narrow alley; only the width of his courtyard door separates the two rows of houses.

The courtyard is bare concrete, shaded by one scraggy olive tree, under which his wife squats while preparing cucumbers to be pickled for winter. He leads me into his makeshift restaurant, which is the front room of his tiny house. Here we sit on the carpeted floor while he busies himself with the tea. Tea in Uzbekistan is an art form: the habit borrowed from the Turks and Chinese: but the art added by the superlative craftsmanship of the Uzbeks. Small tea shops sell secret blends of herb and spices, dried fruit, blossoms and, on occasion, even an actual tealeaf enters the mix. In the heat there is nothing more refreshing.

His daughters waft in and out of the room, neither interested nor disinterested in me, I am a merely a necessary intrusion in their lives. While Fardin fusses over the tea, we make stilted small talk. He is Tajik; his wife is Uzbek. He travels to Moscow in the winter to work as a laborer on building sites. She cooks for a stall that she runs in town. Fardin complains about the corruption in the land; power and corruption go hand in hand. I mention that I had hoped to buy a carpet. He offers to take me to a dealer.

Before we leave, I ask what I owe him for the tea. He says, whatever I wish to pay. Clever lad. Tea in Bukhara costs a few euro cents, but tea in Europe costs a few Euros. It is far better business for him to let his customers pay what they are accustomed to paying at home. As the poorer you are, the cheaper you see things, because you relate the value to your own income, so for him to charge 2,50€ for a cup of tea, which is probably more than he gets for an hour's back breaking labor, is impossible. The reverse is also true; the richer you are, the more expensive you want things to be, so the price sets you apart from the masses. This fluid capitalism is practiced by everybody here. Nothing has a fixed price; they assess you by your clothing and manner; and when you select an item, it is miraculously always the oldest and most expensive; the last item made by his dying mother, and other such rot. For someone who does not like shopping, this is pure torture. When trying to buy an ice-cream the stall-keeper first has a long discussion with his son on how much to charge me. I tell him to keep his wares – life is too short to haggle over the price of an ice-cream.

But I would not be surprised if this fluidity has not made it into the thinking of famous Western luxury brands, like the 'rip-off bags' for sale at street markets, which are indistinguishable from the real thing. This rip-off market could be controlled by the famous brands themselves if they decided to move into the penny business. Why sell one bag at 28 000€ or 100 bags at 2 800€ when you can sell millions at 28€. As long as the famous brand mock-fights against the rip-off bags, the rich can continue to believe that they are the only ones with the real McCoy. Those who buy the rip-off know that it is a rip-off, but it is indistinguishable from the real thing, so what's the diffs'. It is still a sort of status symbol that indicates that you know what good taste is; a debatable point. And all the while the famous brand pays pennies to cheap labor to produce all the bags, and rakes in the bucks from all sides. So the value of the bag is determined not by the bag, but by the size of the wallet of the person buying the bag; as is the cup of tea, normal price for me, but for him unbelievable.

Leading me to the carpet seller, Fardin navigates the twisting lanes with the assurance of a born-and-bred local. Another labyrinth crossed, we enter the carpet dealer's yard. From the street, the door is indistinguishable from all the others, but stepping over the threshold, I step into a world of fountains, manicured trees, graceful arches and delicate mosaics. I am ushered into the front room, where the walls are a jigsaw of tiny shelves, filled with an Aladdin's cave of clutter. The dealer makes his appearance; he is a toad of a man, to whom I take an immediate dislike, and want to leave immediately. But he is a carpet salesman, and doesn't let a customer go without a fight.

He starts opening carpets.

'This is a very beautiful carpet.'

He says flinging open a shrill green and white carpet with bright pink flowers. Is the man blind, or perhaps blinded by his garish carpets?

'I don't like it; may I see something else.'

He rolls open a deep blue and red offering, thick woolly and modern. This is not quite what I had in mind.

'I was hoping for something not quite so modern.'

He comes back to the shrill green carpet, which I must admit does shout for attention.

'This is a very beautiful carpet.'

'But I don't like it.'

'But see the flowers.'

Yes, the flowers. That could be the thing I like least, just after the green, which is starting to jump around in front of my eyes. Perhaps he feels the same way, which is why he is so desperate to get rid of the thing. He just won't let it go.

'You make me an offer.'

Why would I start to bargain for something that makes me ill just looking at it?

'I don't like that carpet.'

'But it is a very beautiful carpet.'

Irritated, I say my prettiest thank-you and walk out of the door. Carpet salesmen are hard to shake; rudeness is sometimes the only answer.

As the day fades, I reach the Lab-i-Hauz where I slide into a sura next to the muddy pond, which becomes mysterious and romantic as the fairy lights go on. These ponds were once the only water source in Bukhara, but were notorious for spreading disease, so all but this one have been filled in. The pond is surrounded by restaurants and sura, where locals and tourists gather for dinner, while boys jump into the slimy water from iron camel sculptures and white ducks float over the green and blue reflected lights.

The restaurant menu is short and to the point. Pilaf, polo, polao or, as it is known in Uzbekistan, plov can be had in several flavors. Plov has been on restaurant menus since Greece, and has always something to do with steamed rice. In Bukhara plov is made by simmering rice in a stew of vegetables and meat, usually mutton, but here the choices have been broadened to include beef and chicken, until all the liquid is absorbed into the rice. The resulting meal is a fragrant pile of rice, dotted with meat and carrots, spiced with cumin, coriander and garlic.

While I eat, I think about the two men I met this afternoon. Their financial status is worlds apart, but they both live and are bound by the social rules of the makhalla in which they live. This is a system within the Islam faith, which was created by the people for the people, a system that even the Soviets couldn't fault. Within a makhalla – a neighborhood traditionally defined by the reach of the mu'adhdhin's voice when calling to prayer – there is a strong sense of community, order, and a tradition of mutual help and education. This system provides a safety net for the old and infirm, and allows children to play in the streets without fear of their neighbors. While in Uzbekistan the traditional walled courtyards hide the difference in wealth, in the Muslim community of Cape Town, this same strong attachment to neighborhood and mosque is easy to see in streets where mansions, hovels and middle-class three-bedroom houses all share the same streetlights. So the money circulates in the neighborhood and everybody benefits a little from the rich man's success. Compared to the separatist thinking of the rich in their gated communities, protected by barbed wire and guns, as seen in Johannesburg's leafy suburbs, I think the makhalla is the better idea.

By now, the dreamy skyline of ancient Bukhara is deep gold against the indigo sky, a faded memory of wealth and wisdom. Time for bed; tomorrow I head back towards Kazakhstan; and my Uzbek visa will allow me just enough time to get there.

Stuck in the Karakum Desert: Kazakhstan

Kazakhstan South

Bed 69

At the Uzbek–Kazakh border I am greeted like a long-lost cousin, and now that everybody has had time to think about their wish for the world, the border folk quite forget to ask to usual questions as they queue up to write on the Wish Mobile.

Мир у Мир, Мир у Мир, Мир у Мир, [mirou mir]

is repeated again and again; world peace is wanted by just about everybody, and the way to achieve this is simply to make peace more profitable than war. Whoever manages that gets first prize and a 50% discount on his next organic duck.

Reaching Shymkent at lunchtime, I follow my nose through a huge market to a restaurant in a yurt. The yurt is like a small white circus tent with bright red decorations. Folding tables are covered with plastic, and the bench seating allows for plenty of customers. On the menu are shashlik, fresh nan, a small selection of soft drinks and tea. Shashlik is a mutton kebab, made by marinating small pieces of meat overnight in a mix of garlic, spices and pomegranate juice. The meat, interspersed with chunks of fresh sheep's tail fat, is threaded onto thin metal skewers, then roasted over open coals on a shashlik grill.

The shashlik grill is a design in which form meets function in perfect harmony. A long metal box, which is just wide enough for the meat skewers to rest on either edge, is placed on a metal stand. A large stump of wood is lit, and when it starts forming coal, the whole stump is placed in one end of the narrow box. Coals are scraped from the stump, and pushed under the grilling shashlik whenever more heat is needed. The shashlik chef adds raw shashlik to the hottest end of the grill, and with a twist of his wrist grabs a dozen skewers at once and flip-turns them with brief pauses, until they reach the cool end of the grill, at which point they get flipped onto a plate. The grill is usually situated at the entrance to a restaurant, with a strategically placed fan wafting the delicious smell of roasting meat and spices far and wide, thereby attracting more and more customers. The shashlik meat is tender and spicy, the freshly roasted fat as good as English crackling, and the nan light, open-textured and chewy. The fragrant tea comes in a bottomless cup, and my lunch costs the grand sum of 1€. Refreshed, I head out, destination Almaty via Taraz.

Taraz is a city with a 2 000-year history, which has laid claim to introducing paper to the West through the capture of Chinese papermakers during the Battle of Talas. But with the dwindling importance of the silk route, Taraz fell into decline, only making a comeback with the arrival of the Russians in 1864, and experienced a population boom in the 1930s, when millions of Volga Germans, along with many other minority groups that no longer suited the Soviet master plan, were driven into internal exile.

Today Taraz is a grey Soviet-style city, where during the day the streets are drab and dull. But at night the brightly colored lights strung from pillar to pole, from building to tree, create a festive fun-fare atmosphere. From my hotel room window, I watch a wedding group with no money walk to the registrar's office opposite my hotel. In the sparkle lights the bride's meringue princess dress magically changes from strawberry to lime to blueberry to vanilla and back again. The group is overtaken by a wedding party with money; they blare by in a garishly decorated white stretch limousine. Yet, both parties stand before the same official, say the same vows, and the 'happy ever after' is assured for neither. After the brief ceremony, the wedding party with no money makes its way across the square to the town photographers – their open-air photographic studios are inhabited by a variety of giant cartoon characters – here the bride and groom snuggle up to Shrek to immortalize this happiest day of their lives.

The next morning the sun rises in my face as I head due east into a world where the heat has sucked every juicy drop from the dry yellow grass. A flock of sheep trample low clouds of golden dust into the still air. In the far southern distance, pale lavender mountains buckle the horizon. Small grey towns, that even the morning sun cannot paint beautiful, dot the road at 100 km intervals. In a dusty village street each paw drop of a little dog leaves a puff cloud of dust; it shimmers gold for a small second; then settles back into anonymity. Ravens circle and land, circle and land, in an eerie dance with the seldom cars and the roadkill. A golden fowl breaks cover, and nearly dies under my wheels, but a quick dodge keeps it off the raven roadkill menu of the day. Roadkill in Kazakhstan includes people. I have counted four dead so far. The car wrecks are placed on small mounds of sand on the side of the road, which turn into public sculptures to death. When the road turns north, trains approach a distant bridge from east and west. I race the trains, and we all arrive at the bridge precisely on time. For long seconds, the bridge conjures a horizon-to-horizon train; it shrinks then grows again, horizon-to-horizon train. The clack-clack, clack-clack a jagged edge in the silence.

As Almaty nears, the road starts dressing itself for the occasion. Almaty is the biggest city in Kazakhstan after all. First, a central line appears, then shoulder lines, then barriers around dangerous curves, reflectors flash in the sun; and finally, cars appear, first ramshackle Soviet leftovers, then busses and finally pearl pink Mercedes Benz. Just as I believe that all is civilized and positively first world, the image explodes in the face of a man on his great brown stallion galloping down the highway. A white Mercedes of the overbearingly large variety slides into the lane next to me. Hooting, the driver draws my attention.

Pull over, points he.

Pull over, me? Why? shrug I.

Pull over, points he with a squiggly finger.

By now we have slowed to unacceptable speed, the cars behind us start voicing their concern, so I pull over. The man wants to know what I am doing, and why my car has got writing on it. At times like these, a common language would be good; without it, we are reduced to silly smiles and half-understood gestures. But we finally get it together, and in the emergency lane on the highway into Almaty, the Wish Mobile gets another wish,

muphy mup

We shake hands, bow slightly in farewell, and I ease back into the high-speed traffic jam with a smile at the guy in the car behind me, who rolls his eyes and shrugs his shoulders impatiently. Good heavens, mate, it is not a second out of your life; how important can your next appointment be. But the niceties that make driving a little pleasanter: those of giving way to another, slowing down just fractionally to allow another to access the traffic flow or even the use of indicators are not observed here.

The closer Almaty comes, the tighter the traffic pushes together. Unnoticed, the two-lane road has been converted into three lanes, then four, until the cars are jammed so tight that opening a car door is no longer possible; neither is moving forward or back. A traffic light is faulty. In Almaty the concept of the intersection reverting to a four-way stop is advanced thinking way beyond the mental reach of people who seem to have stepped directly from a horse's saddle into the driver's seat of very expensive luxury vehicles, which came with driver's license attached as an optional extra. From all sides, the drivers of Almaty pile into the intersection, until every available space has been filled with car. And then – all together now – they lean on their car horns, and attempt to create enough noise to blow all other cars away – leaving behind only 'they', because 'they' have superpowers that will spare them the obliteration that they wish upon everybody else.

Then a wedding cavalcade appears in my rearview mirror, and proves that 'they' have superpowers, which miraculously open a path through the tangle of traffic. The string of cars is led, not by the bridal carriage, but by a BMW cabriolet, in which stands a back-to-front cameraman filming the event. He notices the Wish Mobile, and swings the camera over to acknowledge it. The beribboned cars dodge and hoot, while the inmates smile and wave peace signs. They indicate that I should join them. Why not? There cannot be a law against wedding chasing, and it will fish me out of this traffic jam in no time. My best driving tip for Almaty: put a few ribbons and plastic roses on your car; it will give you the superpower to part the raging river of traffic.

Bed 71

Almaty seems to have had an economic explosion in recent years, and the population has gone from poor to rich in a very short time. This has lured the worst kind of Western investor here; the place is a cheap bazaar that has aspirations of Harrods. In the flush of new wealth, the party rages on, but style and value are completely missing. This is a place where that tank spawn, the 'Hummer', is considered the height of elegance and good taste. The ostentatious stupidity of the newly rich, who will spend millions on rubbish just to prove they can, has resulted in more casinos springing up than can possibly be good for the population. Exchanging foreign currency has never been so simple. In tiny alleys lined with moneychangers, there is a fierce currency competition going on; here the value of a euro or dollar changes from stall to stall. This is an easy come, easy go, money city.

Trying to find a hotel room in Almaty, where quality and price coincide, is almost impossible. To maintain my calm, I employ the help of a travel agent. Yulia is of Russian lineage, and artfully groomed from the roots of her bottle-blonde hair to the tips of her plastic fingernails. To my question of how it is possible for the hotels to be charging so much for so little, she replies proudly that her people can afford the price. Maybe so, but why would they want to.

Yulia sends me to a hotel at the Medeu Ice Skating Rink, built in a valley of the Zhailisky Ala-Tau Mountains, which tower over Almaty. At 1 700 m above sea level, it claims to be the highest ice rink in the world, but as with most of the 'in the world' claims, it chooses to see only those parts of the world that comply with what it wants to prove. Thing is, Johannesburg is 1 753m above sea level, and I distinctly remember an ice rink or two there as well. The road to the rink leads through the luxury end of town, where walls, giant gates and guards separate the rich from the poor. The road twists past autumn-tinged trees, where the view over the flat land of Kazakhstan rolls over the far horizon. If the earth were indeed flat, I could see the Alps from here.

The Medeu Ice Rink has no ice in the summer, but the canned muzac is playing at ear-aching volume. My search for the entrance to this 'hotel' already makes me doubtful about the suitability of this establishment. The whole center has an aura of stinking decay. A worker finds me wandering about, and leads me through dank passages to the caretaker's office. The ladies there look at me disbelievingly, and ask repeatedly if I want a room for four days. A room for four days I want, but the first whiff of foul air in here had already decided me that this was not a place I want to stay for four minutes, let alone four days. But I am curious to see what money will buy you in Almaty, where the people can afford to pay for any rubbish, so ask to see the room on offer.

I am led down into a dungeon of a passage that reeks of overflowing sewer. The damp walls are cancerous and green in the harsh neon light. There are now four ladies leading the way. Are they sticking together for mutual protection against any slime monsters lurking in the gloom? Or perhaps they are just curious to see what I make of the room. Right at the end of the horrible corridor, a shiny door opens onto a damp cellar, which, judging by the presence of something that looks like a shower, must be the room. I point out that the shower is collapsing, and that several fungus cultures are threatening to take over the whole cubicle. The ladies shrug. The room has only a bed and a neon light, no window, and the power point has been filled in. When I ask about this, they reply that they don't have luxury rooms. They are wrong; they don't have rooms. On the way out, I spy a group of tatty young men in a stinking 'cafeteria'. This must be the clientele they are accustomed to, but even for a backpackers' hostel this place is beyond vile. I think Yulia mistook my refusal to pay extravagant prices for inadequate rooms as not having money to pay for a room at all.

This is one of the things that hardened capitalists love about new money: it allows absolute rubbish to be flogged at massive prices purely because no one wants to be seen as not having the money to pay for a thing. We have allowed money to define us; we set our own value by the things we can afford. We have forgotten that money is just a measure, and if we keep stretching and shrinking its value, it is hardly surprising that we have not the faintest idea of what does, and what does not have real worth. But this is all too much for Yulia, and in a desperate measure to get rid of me, she finds me a room in the Chimbulak ski resort half an hour out of town.

The place is manageable, but the plebeian management and staff are in desperate need of training. Breakfast at the hotel is served ready plated and with no choice: tea, toast and porridge. Communist thinking with capitalist goals. Not being a porridge fan, I ask for an extra slice of toast instead. They bring me the toast, one cold slice on a plate, no butter, but a bill, the equivalent of 1€ for a slice of toast, and I thought a plate of porridge for a slice of toast was a generous exchange. I send for the manager, and ask him if he is not completely embarrassed at sending me a bill at all, let alone one for this price. He starts to argue, but then he consents that perhaps they were overreaching themselves. Here it is again, the fear of seeming poor that allows commerce to run amuck.

In Almaty there is an abundance of shiny shopping malls and supermarkets that all have very well stocked deli sections. I am beginning to think that here people don't cook at all; they just buy the evening meal at the deli, and I am getting quite good at this myself. The food is tasty, but very spicy, with a breathtaking amount of garlic. In the main street, fashion-conscious shoppers are a mix of Kazakh, Han Chinese, west and east European, and the odd Buddhist monks, who wear only saffron. Military fatigues, which are very popular in the whole of Kazakhstan, are pushed to their fashionable limits in Almaty. Buff young men rush about in purple camouflage; they must look absolutely smashing when driving their Hummers. Much of my time is spent in a slick shopping center with open-plan Internet café, where the young, hip and happening gather to take tea, shop in brand-name stores, and lounge about looking good, looking to be seen. But I don't have time to waste.

The shipping of the Wish Mobile to America needs to be finalized, but without the Chinese car visa this is not possible. It has been some countries since I heard from my Chinese travel agents, and am happy to finally find a letter from them in my inbox. But instead of sending me final confirmation, and at least copies of the documents that will allow my car into China, they inform me that they have helped themselves to the balance of the quoted price. Not so fast. This is totally unacceptable. I let the Chinese agent know that I have instructed my bank to stop this payment, as I still don't have car papers, and am still heading toward China with only their rather flimsy word assuring me that I will be able to continue my journey there. Payment will be finalized when I say so, and that will be when the Wish Mobile and I are safely in China. Fortunately, though, the agent has included the CVs of my guides, so I am at least a little more sure that I will be driving through China.

Leaving the coffee shop crowd to their posing, I hunt out the place where the masses shop, the Green Market. At first I thought the name derives from it being a fresh-produce market, but the market building is actually green, and here everything under the sun is for sale. In the glass-roofed main hall, beautifully arranged fresh produce is spot-lit by shafts of sunlight that turn the whole bustling scene into a romantic movie set. Narrow passages lead to a maze of tiny stores that offer goods from shoes to stationary, pots and pans, hardware, software, underwear, outerwear, silverware, Tupperware, anything from anywhere and everywhere.

From the Green Market it is a short walk to the Zenkov Cathedral, a 19th-century Russian Orthodox cathedral, which claims to be the second tallest wooden building in the world. Its curls and curves are brightly painted in yellow and white ,and its gay harlequin steeples topped by golden bulbs and the double Orthodox cross. The church is set in Panfilov Park, where the beggars lie among their discarded bottles and packets, while around them children feed a battalion of grey pigeons. I set off to find the opera house, but even walking in Almaty does not spare you from the traffic. Here the use of the car horn is considered the only measure of a good driver, and by that measure they are all experts; the noise levels are mind numbing. May all the car horns in Almaty be struck dumb. I hereby do solemnly and with some authority place the drivers of Almaty at the top of my world's worst drivers list.

I cannot wait to leave, and have Yulia arrange a home stay for me deep in the south-eastern parts of Kazakhstan. But she is not at all sure about sending me into the wilds of Kazakhstan alone.

'Usually we take people with a four wheel drive and   guide; this is very rough territory.'

'I just drove here from Munich.'

She is less than impressed. I try a different tactic.

'Have you ever been to Kazakhstan north of Aral?'

'Why would I want to?'

Her point is well made. I reply with a fairly lame

'Well, it cannot possibly be worse than that.'

Yulia is still not convinced, and only very reluctantly writes down turn-by-turn instructions that will get me to Canti [san tui], a town that does not appear on any map. I also receive a note in Kazakh for Elchibai, whom I must find in Canti, and he will take me to my accommodation, which is beyond the end of the road.

'How will I find him?'

'Oh just ask anybody.'

Now it is my turn to be skeptical. To drive out into the wild blue yonder, this I am fine with. But then to just start asking stray people where I might find Elchibai, this part I am not too sure about. Yulia on the other hand thinks that this is the least of my problems.

Heading out of Almaty towards Talgar City, the trucks start displaying Chinese symbols. China is just around the corner! Then the trees slowly disappear into the steppes, and all traces of vegetation vanish on a subtle climb onto a high dry plain; no rain falls here. Suddenly the flat plain plunges into a landscape in negative; a pitch-black canyon ridge is barely visibly against the hot grey sky. Sinister rock shapes in grey and brown with bizarre spots of sienna cut through the wine-red earth. The landscape is bleak and uninviting, forged by the ages, untouchable and austere. It is impervious to human intervention; we can do nothing here except pass through. But a road sign informs me that I have misread Yulia's Cyrillic instructions, and I should not pass through, but turn around, as I have been heading off in completely the wrong direction and am 100 km off-course, curses.

The right road turns to gravel or dust. The gravel road is such a shake, rattle and roll tire-chewing nightmare that I prefer to take my chance on the desert sands. The road on the plains is like a river, big wide yellow rapids that weave and plait into a tangle of tracks. But the sand is hard, so the going is very good. I fall into Paris-Dakar mode as I scan the multiple-choice road ahead. Which track to choose? Which will be faster, smoother, harder? This is extreme driving, none of that falling asleep behind the steering wheel highway stuff. I gear up, down, brake, accelerate, dodge potholes, bounce over ridges; driving was never this much fun. When the speedometer hits 100, I come to my senses. You are driving a delivery van, woman, slow down; driving here at this speed could cost you the trip; and a very long walk to nowhere.

A little gravel hill gives me an excuse for a driving pit-stop. On foot I climb up to see what I can see; I see that the eagles are back on the signposts, surveying the flat terrain, and a lone green tree stands guard over a gravestone. The tree is dripping with hankies and cloths of all sorts. Why? And the tree, how can it survive here? Do the people who tie cloth to its branches also bring water to nourish its roots? Far below I see that the Wish Mobile is a silver blip on the great beige flatness, while behind me in the far distance, across a field of small orange leaves, stands a homestead, dinky toy against lavender stone mountains. How do people end up living in the middle of nowhere? Where did they come from, why did they stop here and why do they stay?

Standing unprotected in the desert, the wild dry heat pours over my head, builds a ridge on my lips, and makes the corners of my eyes itch. I stretch out my arms and let the heat pool in the palms of my hands. My mind slips away from me; like a lost balloon it floats into the blue. Thoughts, ideas, questions push from all sides. From this little rise I see that we are not over-populating the planet, only the places that can sustain us. We are destroying the habitat not just of other species, but also our own. A thermal breeze picks at the hair on my head, I shiver, and walk back to the car. In the empty all-round silence there are no answers, just questions.

The desert plains turn to rolling hills; clouds pile in the sky. I think the last time I saw a cloud was in Saratov. Cows and horses chew thoughtfully on the late summer grass until the herdsman decides to show off. With the languor of a lifelong horseman, he gallops by, and quite unnecessarily chases the herd about for a bit. I wave; he tips his cap. At the roadside, purple flowers are visited by white butterflies, while golden seed heads send new flower generations out into the wind. The warm air is filled with the smell of freshly mown grass. A haystack rumbles by, then another, odd. I follow at safe distance. The haystacks stop in Zhalanash, a small town where men with pitchforks slowly reveal army green trucks under the moving piles of hay. Here the hills fall into mountains, where pine trees grow along waterfall streams, and the road collapses as I drive down to Canti around sharp bends, sharper rocks and deep potholes. The Wish Mobile will have to climb back up this road; memories of Mount Olympus are quickly pushed aside; I will worry about this in a few days time.

Bed 72

Canti is at the end of the road. The Kazakh map stops here. In the tiny village, built along a stream, I ask the first person I see for Elchibai. She turns around, waits for a moment, and when an old man walks around the corner, she points: Elchibai. Is she joking? Then I remember what century I am in, and even if they have no GSM reception here, some form of telecommunication must exist. Yulia probably alerted these good folk that I was on my way.

Elchibai is an old man with Mongol features, a round face with slit eyes, his grey hair hidden under a jaunty beret. He always wears a tailored jacket and a friendly smile. Taking both my hands in his, he introduces himself with a bow of the head.

'Elchibai.'

'Annette.'

And that is the end of that. He speaks only Kazakh, and I speak no Kazakh. In silence Elchibai leads me six kilometers closer to nowhere, along a rutted track to the house of Xharat and Elmira.

Grey split-pole fences draw a boundary around their small holding. The house is the same Kazakh grey I have seen since arriving in Kazakhstan, and is dwarfed by a haystack that hides the cowshed from the road. The slick white satellite dish is huge and out of place in a rough brown world. The air is chill and dry; it smells dusty and familiar, like winter in the Free State of South Africa. The house has no decoration; nothing superfluous clutters the space. The front door opens into an entrance hall; the kitchen with both electric and wood-fired stove straight ahead. A long communal room on the right is furnished with a simple wooden table, two long wooden benches, a fridge, a clock on the wall, a colorful rug on the wooden floor, and a small dresser, on which balance round golden loaves of flat bread, called buarsak. Glimpses of the family room show a bed and a television.

My room for the next few days is a small dormitory that should house six, but during my stay it will only be me. The curtains are pieces of old newspaper, and under the colorful quilted bedcovers I discover straw-filled mattresses. Miss Priss, whom I haven't seen in a while, immediately conjures up a straw mattress world of creeping crawling things. This calls for a bed transfer, so I impress the socks off my hosts as I whip out the air-mattress, turn on the air pump, and within seconds have a hygienic bed. For my back, I try to explain, not wanting to seem completely rude about the beds on offer. With the bed made to my satisfaction, I explore further.

There is no running water in the house. But with a scoop of a bucket, pure mountain water, from a small clear pebble-bed stream that runs a few meters below the house, is poured into a cistern behind the washbasin that is equipped with a tap and – hey presto – running water. As the washbasin is right next to the front door, early morning ablutions are a very sociable affair. I become quite accustomed to saying *dobre ootero* with a foam-filled mouth. For privacy and hygiene, the bright blue outhouse is many meters downhill from the house, and is reached by a narrow plank bridge over the stream. Here I finally encounter the dreaded hole in the ground, or rather open ditch in the ground, where every morning before I arrive, someone has spread sand and leaf litter over yesterday's offerings. So the first business of the day is conducted in quiet contemplation of the spectacular view over the valley, with only the unfamiliar cold draft making things a little uncomfortable.

Xharat and Elmira keep a small herd of cows, which provide them with food and income. Every morning they are up before dawn, and after milking the cows Xharat drives the herd to pasture, while Elmira sits on a low stool in an airy plank shed skimming the milk with a hand-operated skimmer. She makes her own cottage cheese by the sackful, which Xharat and I deliver to the shop in Canti. Her homemade butter is so good that I spread it thick and salty onto the chewy open-textured flat bread she bakes, and consider myself very well catered for. Elmira prefers to eat her bread with the sour cream called 'clici' in Kazakh. A small bowl of clici is a permanent fixture on the table; it gets thicker and yellower as the days go by; eventually it is probably a mild cheese.

The food here is simple, and we constantly seem to be eating. Breakfasts vary from intense sunshine-yellow omelettes, made from the organic eggs Elmira collects from her hens every morning, to porridge. Maintaining an English stiff upper lip I force the white gloopy stuff down my throat, reminding myself with every mouthful that I am not in a hotel now, but in someone's home, and to not eat the food presented would be downright rude. Dinner is usually bread and stew, called 'shorpo', with either potatoes or handmade noodles as a base. Scraps of mutton and soup bones are added for flavor. There is no discrimination against fat and gristle; it is all considered good and nourishing. I, being a spoilt Western brat, prefer my first-grade fillet raw with fresh basil, parmesan and virgin olive oil, direct from the family mills of Province, so I leave most of the animal protein in my plate: fat, gristle and bone. Xharat makes no comment, but gives a silent lesson on how to get a bone spotlessly clean. Wielding his dagger like a scalpel, he removes and eats every scrap of flesh from even the most canny of spinal bones. When he is done, I could string his bones on a chain, and wear them as exotic organic jewelry. I look at my plate somewhat shamefaced.

With the meals, there is always tea, made in the 'Russian' way, and it is always served by Elmira. I sense that just grabbing the pot and helping yourself is not the done thing. There is a hidden rhythm and ritual at the table, which is respectful of the animals they slaughter, and the hard work that went into the production of the simple food we are eating. Elmira and Xharat add milk with a thick skin to their tea; the skin seems to be the favorite part. No thanks, never been much of a milk fan myself, and to have great bits of skin floating about in my tea is not my idea of heaven. But the dried raisins, apricots, peanuts and boiled sweets that are always on the table for dessert are a welcome treat.

After dinner Xharat starts talking about kumis, which is a traditional slightly alcoholic drink that is produced and drunk by the Turkic tribes of Inner Mongolia. After pantomiming the fall-about effects of the drink, he decides that I must taste some. Elmira is not so sure, and with hands and feet makes it quite clear that I should drink only a small amount, as the beer will cause me a very soft stomach long before it intoxicates me, and the only stumbling about I am likely to do is to try and find the distant toilet in the dark of night.

Kumis is horse-milk beer, which is very high in lactose – equals laxative – and sugar that allows it to ferment. The fermentation also makes the lactose digestible to the people of Inner Mongolia, most of whom are lactose intolerant. Kumis looks like low-fat milk, watery with a slightly blue cast. It tastes sour, not in the sour milk sense, more in the sour fruit sense (plum skins spring to mind); but then it has a smoky meaty aftertaste, sort of like drinking your smoked duck with plum sauce. It is not gut-wrenchingly offensive, but definitely something that you have to grow into. I leave the kumis to Xharat, while I crack open a Baltika, a Russian lager that is comfortingly familiar.

Elchibai has given me instructions on what I am to see here. First on my list is Kolsai Lake, which is the full stop at the end of the Kazakh road. Just to the south is Kyrgyzstan and a few kilometers to the east, China. The lake is a blue-grey mirror in the densely forested valley. A comfortable wooden walkway leads all along the edge of the lake, where one lone fisherman tries his luck. The forest is very noisy, with an immense rustling and chucking in the pines. Once I get my eye in, I spy dozens of large burnt sienna squirrels with long tufted ears and great grey fluffy tails. They are very agitated at my presence; they glare and chuck and leap about in a little squirrel frenzy. I must have interrupted some secret squirrel ritual.

A quarter of the way around the lake the path vanishes under a shale rockslide. I had planned to walk all the way around the lake, and refuse to be stopped by a little rockslide. Gingerly placing one foot onto the small stones, I apply just a little pressure; it seems fine, so I step onto the shale; then three steps in, a subtle shift underfoot makes me bounce across the stretch of loose stone like a startled deer. The top layer of the mass slowly slides into the water many steep meters below. That was not a good idea. I look to the opposite shore of the lake; similar rock falls have pulled down trees at regular intervals. Perhaps I should have done a proper survey before starting this walk. Too late now, my impulsive sprint across the loose shale has put the rockslide between me and safety. I am not keen to cross the shale again, and decide to climb the cliff over the top of the rock slide. The rocks are as brittle as eggshells, and every movement causes more of the shale to crumble into the green water twenty meters below.

Sweaty-palmed with exertion and a touch of panic, I reassess my situation. Climbing over the top is probably more hazardous than crossing the rockslide. I put a foot onto the rock, give it a good shove and watch. Only the rocks directly beneath the pressure point start sliding down to the water. It took about ten steps to cross the first time. With a few fast long steps over the rocks, I should make it before the whole lot starts moving again; nothing to be done but to try. With a running start I bounce athletically across the rocks, and just as I hit firm ground, a low sigh behind me makes me turn to see the whole rockslide sag into the water. On and on the rocks churn the clear green water into a pale white mud. While watching the clouds of mud roll out below the water surface like a fast moving storm, I give myself a stern talking to.

Now that was spectacularly stupid. You are not in the movies here, girl. There is no 911 to the rescue, no call a friend or prince on white charger; it's your life, your responsibility. You are the only thing you can be sure of, and right now the only thing I am sure of is that that little stunt was fairly idiotic. Get a grip.

The squirrels tut-tut me from the pines, as I make my way back to the Wish Mobile. Elchibai has invited me for lunch to meet his wife, Emir. His house is in the center of the village, and consists of four buildings; one for the formal living room and bedrooms; one for the workshop; one for the livestock; and one for the kitchen. In the kitchen house the seating is traditional: on the thickly carpeted floor we sit on low stools at a round table. Two children appear, and I discover that Xharat and Elmira are parents not just to the two-month old Aslan, but also to Caram and Nazgul, a little girl with an impish grin and apple cheeks. In the West – thanks to Tolkien's 'Lord of the Rings' – a Nazgul is a half-dead thing that serves pure evil. In Kazakhstan, Nazgul is a girl's name and means delicate flower. And so easily do global misunderstandings come about through careful sifting, shifting, slanting of information.

Elchibai steps into the kitchen; he has harvested a basket of deep red tomatoes, which he slices into rough chunks. Emir brings a ball of home-made butter and loaves of freshly baked bread to the table. The tea, the dried fruit and nuts, all make their appearance. We chat with hands, drawings, mime and the pictionary. We laugh at half-understood jokes, and we all wish we could speak the same language. Language is a currency more valuable than money. If I were given a choice of a global survival tool, I would choose to be able to speak and understand every language on the planet.

For dessert Elchibai picks apples from the trees outside. This part of Kazakhstan is thought to be the ancestral home of the apple, and Elchibai's apples are possibly an ancient strain. Their appearance will not satisfy any food stylist, as they are small and lacking the perfect apple shape and color we have all come to know and love, through advertisers and on TV. These apples are small individuals, marred by hail and birds, but no thought is given to that; the flavor and texture are topmost in our minds. They are tree fresh, crisp, juicy and tart, with a sweet background note; the perfect apple. After lunch Granny Emir takes the opportunity of a lift out to Elmira to visit her grandson Aslan.

While the family visits together, I walk out into the valley. It is hemmed by gently rounded mountains, and clouds pile black and thunderous in the sky. With primitive hoes a family harvest potatoes. The timeless image is dated and catalogued by a shiny red motorbike standing at the far end of the field. At my feet a tiny adder slides by. Innocently I point it out to the nearest potato digger, who immediately wants to set his hoe to it. With a stream of meaningful *njets* I buy the poor creature some time, while trying to shoo it into the grass with my foot. The man smiles and nods, and as soon as I leave, calls his son over, who proceeds to kill that poor little snake pulp dead with the grunting mindless violence that only young boys seem to posses. I am so sorry, snake.

Horses graze on the yellow grass; they are unconcerned as I walk between them; but it is a fly-filled space, so I quickly move on to fly-free distance. Two cows trot by; they disturb an enormous flock of pigeons that circle above with a silk-gown rustle of wings before they settle again on the far side of the field. The cows are heading straight for the Xharat homestead. It reminds me that tonight is banja night, and Xharat has been preparing the bathhouse for this occasion.

Armed with brush, shampoo, soap and towels, I make my way across the stream through the grassland to the banja. In the sauna-type room I take a second to look around and see how this all works. The banja is built of wood split poles and is snug and warm. In the outer changing room, a long bench with hooks above invites me to whip my clothes off and get to it. But slowly now, once naked, what then? A raw wood door leads to the bathing room, which is about the size of a single bedroom. In the wet room there is a metal drum of water, heated by a coal stove set underneath it, and by the metal chimney that runs directly through the water. Milk cans full of icy river water stand next to the stove. There is a painted bench and a low wide shelf, which holds a big plastic bowl and a large rusty enamel mug. I test the system by dipping the mug into the cauldron, but the water is much too hot for comfort. To test the heat of the chimney, I splash some water onto it; the water turns instantly to steam and the room's temperature shifts up a notch. A eureka moment.

I push up the heat of the wet room to sauna temperature; and only then get undressed to start my banja. The plastic bowl is used to mix water from the cauldron and the milk cans until the correct water temperature is achieved. This water is then poured over oneself with the help of the big rusty mug. I soon have my banja technique down pat. Two rusty mugs over me, one rusty mug over the chimney pipe, and so the room temperature remains nice and toasty as I wash and scrub. This is all going swimmingly until the hot water disturbs the little grey frogs that reside in the outflow. They all start hopping about my feet, causing me to hop about as well. I speed the bath process up a touch, while I adjust the water temp down a touch. Living frogs I can cope with, but I don't want to be responsible for boiling them alive. I already have a snake on my conscience today.

Squeaky clean and content with the world, I meet Xharat smoking a cigarette on the rickety bridge over the bubbling stream. He points to the moon.

Eye, says he.

Aye, say I.

In Kazakh the moon is called eye, a big eye in the evening sky.

It is time to wish the family farewell and move on. Elchibai and Xharat have been thinking about their wishes, and while they write on the Wish Mobile, I receive bread and butter from Elmira and apples from Emir. I give Aslan the small world globe I have been carting around with me. In exchange I receive a carved talisman, and with a *desvedanje* I head out of another group of lives. Looking back over the last few days, I lacked for nothing, but by Western standards these people are poor. Yet they served delicious organic food at every meal; they are very healthy; their active daily routine discounts the need for a gym. Both the younger and the older couple laugh into each other's eyes, and they all love and care for the children. Friends drop by for long discussions around the dinner table. Theirs is a rich life, after all. But with the arrival of satellite TV, they will soon find out what they should be missing, wanting, needing.

Bed 73

I want to spend the next few days camping in the wilds of Kazakhstan. For someone who not long ago was a sworn non- camper, I have become quite the convert. My aim is to find the Charyn Canyon; here they claim it to be the little brother of the Grand Canyon. But first the Wish Mobile must heave us out of the Canti valley. The worst roads are the ones you cannot do slowly or carefully. Like this one: it is an axle-breaking combination of potholes, loose rocks, deep gullies and impossibly steep turns. But pussy-footing is not an option, as the Wish Mobile will not have enough power to get up the mountain without a touch of speed. I rev up the engine, grip the steering wheel, and let fate do the rest. Without mishap – the Wish Mobile and I are becoming quite the team – we heave ourselves out of the valley, and straight into the furnace heat of the desert.

The heat has pulled the horizon forward into a grey mirage that dissolves the road into the pink and yellow sand. In the distance my eyes fix on small shimmering bumps; slowly tombs find solid form. In magnificent isolation I step from the air-conditioned cool into a heat that takes my breath away. I feel an 'Indiana Jones' moment coming on, as I convince myself that I am surely the first European woman to set foot in this place.

The tombs, like giant four-minute eggs, have lost their heads; cracked and empty, they are slowly disintegrating back into the desert sand. The plaster has fallen off the outer walls, exposing the hand-formed mud bricks underneath. Entering the structures through a narrow arched doorway, the floor shows evidence that the tombs are now used as stables for goats. A goat has lost a horn, a souvenir that will add dimension to a painting one day. The mud bricks and rough adobe walls of the exterior have in the round doomed interior been finished with a fine layer of smooth mud plaster that has been decorated with carved stamps, creating a deeply embossed effect. The organic, intricately decorated walls make beautiful graphic photographs; only the camera shutter breaks the silence.

Stopping in the in-between places, stepping into moments like these is what life it is all about.

But unless I want to set up camp in the dark, I had better make an effort to find the Charyn Canyon. Then the canyon finds me; as the road winds through black rock cuttings that crowd out the light, they dramatically fall away as the mountain turns to canyon. The heat rises out of the dark rock canyon like a translucent curtain, behind which the landscape trembles and shifts. Far below, a cream soda river winds its way through pink and yellow sand.

By now the sun is making a dive for the horizon, the light paints the sand shades of purple, pink and gold, very pretty and all, but I really need to find a place to camp. Sharp left onto the first dirt road I see, I bounce along next to the river until a little road takes me onto a rise with a splendid view of the canyon. An excellent camping spot, and within minutes the rice is boiling, the bed made, GPS reading taken and the day's photographs downloaded. While the sun vanishes over the western horizon, I set up my tripod, and photograph the full moon as it rises over the eastern canyon wall. All around me, night creatures make small holes in the silence.

I am a homeless, far-away person, not forgotten, not forlorn.

In the clear morning sky, the sun take the moon's encore, and my tea creates a very small cloud that floats in the rising heat. All is well in my world, until a big truck in army camouflage stops right in my view. How rude. Out of the truck oozes a great slob of a man.

'Neht fotographia.'

Is this Soviet brainwash serious?

Whipping out my Kazakh tourist map I point out that Charyn Canyon is one of Kazakhstan's major tourist attractions, and if he had not noticed, tourism and photography are pretty synonymous nowadays.

He is not swayed. He indicates that I should move along, as in his opinion tourists are destroying the canyon. To make his point, he then starts inspecting my campsite. Too bad for him that I am pretty Boy Scout when it comes to camping, and other than the footprints, no trace of me is to be found. But I am horrified to notice that he walks directly to my – now closed – hole in the ground. Has he been watching me? Last night's little sponge bath comes to mind. I have become fairly back-to-nature about my camping activities and now with the suspicion that this fat slob was watching me, the whole joyful earth goddess thing gets swaddled in a grey cloak of suspicion.

The thought that this big slob of a man or more of his ilk might be following me about in the canyon changes my plans from finding a camping spot to finding a hotel, and it becomes a dawdle here, dawdle there kind of day. The main road leads through the width of the canyon, which is guarded at one end by a white painted statue of a ram, and at the other by a black painted statue of an eagle. The jagged canyon fades into the haze north and south. East and west the canyon edge stands in stark relief to the cloudless sky. It is a big empty world, where the silence is only broken by the occasional car. Here in the outback, cars are luxuries that are nursed along with whatever means possible, and are used to transport whatever will fit. On the side of the road an old couple are pouring cooking oil into their bright yellow car, while four sheep look placidly out of the backseat windows, as if four sheep taking a drive on the back seat of a Trabant is quite the most natural thing in the world.

A little desert critter charges across the sand with a great green lettuce-looking thing in its mouth. I play bushman and sneak up behind him. One of his clan spots me, and with high-pitched shrieks sends little beasties shooting across the sand from all directions to dive into their little holes. The guardian critter is a brave chap. He does not hide, but stands fearlessly on his hind legs, sending little squeaky alarms to his mates. Choosing a likely-looking hole, I get into a standing meditation position and wait; time for some game photography meditation. It is very pleasant out in the cool desert morning. Soon there is movement, as the wee beasties adapt to my presence. But my chosen hole remains empty. No matter I have time, I can wait.

The sun is warm, the breeze cool and fragrant. I sink into the silence of my mind, allowing calm slow somersaults of thought to rise to the surface. Our caged minds make us violent, sad and bored. Our minds are like tigers in a zoo, fat and flabby, but it suits our keepers that it should be so, a little touch of fear, a control of the food supply, all these things reduce us to puppets. I realize that I am exploring not just the world, but also forgotten or never imagined canyons in my mind, and am discovering that it is here that true freedom exists. Around me, the beasties gather dry twigs and then, pop, the hole becomes a vole, snap gotcha! The desert beastie and I inspect each other; he is the size of a big hamster with round black eyes, a little white collar, and otherwise is the color of sand. He twitches his nose, I press the shutter, and the vole becomes a hole.

There are only four towns between me and China, but still three empty days before my official entry. Finding a hotel is proving difficult; the town of Charyn is a dead loss. They don't even have a decent store, let alone a hotel. Koktal is a better bet, but still no cigar. Zharkent is an oasis town with flowing rivers and green trees; the shade is a luxury in which I indulge myself with a siesta, as I have no pressing engagements. Cornfields stretch in every direction. It is harvest time, and donkeys stand knee-deep in the husks of the corn that men sweep into huge yellow circles on every flat surface, to allow it to dry in the autumn sun. Children in school uniforms skip at the road side; black suits and ties for boys; and tartan or black skirts with white shirts for the girls. The hair fashion for little girls is hair tied into ponytails with outrageous big white ribbons like enormous pom-poms on either side of their heads. But still no hotel.

In the dusty main street of Ajdarlih, a donkey with a huge erection stares at me intently; down, boy, wrong species. Brightly colored handmade quilts are draped over a long stretch of wire fence that runs along the road, which leads into the desert, past elaborate tombs in a small graveyard. Ruins behind dead trees that have been chopped to jagged stumps lure me out into the heat. Between the fallen walls, the bleached and cracked bones of a cow paint a phantom image of a slow strangled death in a coil of barbed wire. The ruins, the silence, and the splintering bones give the world an overstayed-your-welcome feel. Rolling the cow bones into my carpetbag, I move along.

The last stop before China is Korgass; hopefully I will find a hotel there. In the distance there are snow-capped mountains; this is exciting as the world has been disappointingly flat for weeks now. I had expected great Himalayan-type things, but obviously my geographic knowledge of this area leaves much to be desired. A traffic jam, of trucks, busses and the usual rag-tag assortment of Kazak cars, at a huge military fence brings me to a halt. Military officials with big guns demand to see my passport. Getting a bad feeling about this, I pull to the side of the road to consult my maps. According to both the Kazak and Russian maps, Korgass is safely inside Kazakhstan, but the Chinese map is a bit ambiguous about whether Korgass is on the Kazakh or Chinese side of the border. To try and clarify this, I start asking the truck and taxi drivers who are crowding around the Wish Mobile pointing, laughing and generally behaving like gawkers at the town fair freak show. This is starting to get a touch tedious.

'Korgass ve Kazakhstan?'

Much head nodding and pointing straight ahead

Yes, I know Korgass is straight ahead; what I want to know is, which country is it in.

'Korgass ve China.'

Much head nodding and pointing straight ahead. This is not helpful, but there are no hotels back from where I came, and the joy has gone out of camping. I will try my luck in the great unknown ahead of me.

Two kilometers later I know that things have just gone pear shaped. This is most definitely a border and on the other side of the border is China, and I am three days early. But in the hands of the border officials I get swept forward and feel helpless to resist. I obey all orders, hand over my passport, follow fellow to office one, follow fellow to office two, drive my car over a chassis check. The customs man riffles through the car, then rolls open the carpetbag and, like an African sangoma, he quite unexpectedly throws the bones, great big cow bones. Souvenirs, shrug I, with sheepish grin. He looks at me silently, then rolls the whole lot up again. I can see the movie turning in his head; a woman alone in a delivery van with writing all over it carrying cow bones from Kazakhstan to China? Let the Chinese deal with this. With a final stamp, a steel gate swings open, and I am swept into China on a wave of misunderstanding and incomprehension, three days early with no car papers and no re-entry visa. The steel gates clang shut behind me.

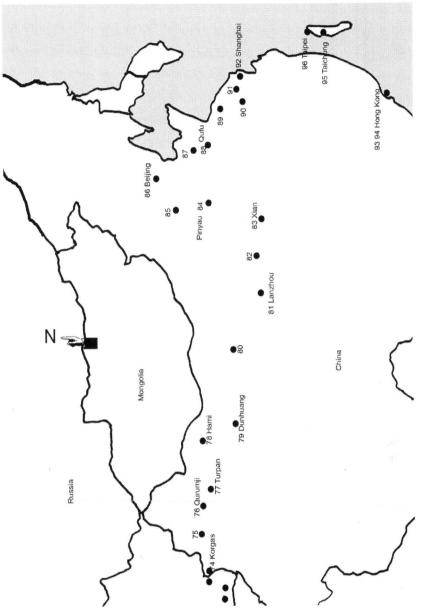

Map 5 : China - Taiwan

The Wish Mobile in Pinyau , China

China

Korgass–Dunhuang

Bed 74

I am swept forward at such speed that my headlights are two hours ahead of my taillights. My hands are in teatime, while my stomach is just digesting lunch. Times stretches … when it snaps back I have lost two hours of my life, and, like Alice falling through a time zone, find myself in Chinaland. There is no no-man's-land between China and Kazakhstan, just a steel time-gate. In Kazakhstan, it is 14h24, while in China it is 16h24.

In Kazakhstan, border guards slob about in faded fatigues. In China, border guards wear full dress uniform: black, white and red. Stiff, smooth-shaven little men salute smartly from small round podiums. The generals of Chinese border crossings march at me, four abreast, in uniforms a-jingle with multicolored medals; they take their borders very seriously here. With a single stamp of well-boned shoe, the generals create a human barrier in front of the Wish Mobile. Regal white-gloved hands make it quite clear that I am to stop. Not to pass begin, not to collect two hundred dollars, not to enter the Middle Kingdom, but to go straight back to Kazakhstan.

'No can do, mate, I have no re-entry visa into Kazakhstan.

Perhaps we can phone my Chinese travel agent?'

Mr Wong is not exactly pleased to hear from me.

'You are three days early. What are you doing in China?'

'Well, it was like this, you see. I have this Russian map   that is quite convinced that Korgass is in Kazakhstan. Also, I had a little misunderstanding with all the people that I asked for help along the way, and, well … I think we must accept that it was preordained months ago that these three empty days would be unavoidable.'

I hand the invisible Mr Wong to the top-dog general, and after a long string of ting tong ying yang yo, it is agreed that I may enter China, but the Wish Mobile may not, at least until the papers arrive in three days' time, at which point my status will be reassessed.

Walking across the bare slab of concrete with my computer and camera bag slung over my shoulder, my entry into China is – as with most things too much anticipated – just a little disappointing.

As I step into China proper, the silence in my mind is shattered and shaken by small people, shouting pushing pushing shouting waving hands shouting *qian qian qian*. What in blue blazes do they all want? Money notes flap in my face, *qian qian*. The moneychangers shout and scream *qian qian qian*. I have no idea what the exchange rate is, but I do need money for the taxi, and I want these people to disintegrate, so exchange 10€ for some Chinese-whatever, probably get totally ripped off, but with the transaction done, the men miraculously vanish.

Standing alone, laden with bags, I take in the bare concrete slab, the wide road and dirty functional buildings that vanish into the arrow-straight distance. I want my little Wish Mobile; I feel like a hermit crab without a shell. A taxi stops in my view. I heave myself inside with one word, hotel.

The driver understands, and within minutes drops me at a three-star hotel, which is a revelation. The foyer is air-conditioned, slick, modern, the staff efficient, and strangely excited to see my passport. My substitute all-purpose language of charades helps me to discover that they have a reservation for me in three days' time. So, with much smiley head bobbing, I rent the same room, three days in advance. The room is the most luxurious I have seen in months, and the sight of the gleaming porcelain in the bathroom releases a sigh that stops me in my tracks. I gently stroke the smooth surfaces until I catch my blissful silly grin reflection in the mirror – time out!

'Annette, old thing, you are becoming very strange. Let's at least try to make a stab at normal.'

As it is teatime in China, a cup of tea would be comfortingly normal, but staring at the little squiggles that inform – those fully literate in Mandarin – what is on the room service menu, I realise that once again the all-powerful borderline has stripped me of my hard-won knowledge. Russian and Cyrillic are meaningless here. There are only two signs I can read in the room. One tells me to lick the door. Lick the door? Cannot be, the reflection is playing tricks on me. The sign really wants me to luck the door. Ever obedient I bow solemnly, and bestow a blessing on the door; strange security systems in China. The other sign solves the mystery of the border time trick and advises me that;

'Hotel has Beijing time; all China time Beijing time.'

This means the perfectly respectable breakfast hours from seven to nine become the most uncivilized breakfast hours from five to seven.

In the dewy morning hour, I stroll across the green manicured lawn, which separates the dining hall from the hotel, and slowly come to a stop. In South Africa, green lawns and swimming pools are as common as discarded plastic grocery bags, and I have never given a lawn a second glance, let alone a thought. But I now realize that the last time I saw a green lawn was in Switzerland, halfway around the planet. For the first time in my life I recognize what a huge luxury it is to have the spare ground to plant grass that is nothing but decorative, and also to have the spare cash and time to tend it.

I mull this over, while practicing my early morning chopstick routine on the piles of crunchy greens that make up a Northwestern Chinese breakfast. I am quietly in my head until I bite into a red chili with an evil temper, and that things bites right back, nearly killing me in a horrible fiery death. My sinuses start squirting; my nose turns into a waterfall; my throat contracts; I lose my breath; my eyes started streaming; my inner ears start tingling; my tongue goes numb; and it takes all my willpower to keep from coughing. Experience has taught me that once you start a chili-cough, it is very difficult to stop, as the cough action just aggravates the problem. I quickly discover why the rice soup and steamed buns are so bland; their dull white morass smothers the fire of the chili. The Chinese men all around stare at me in silent fascination. What a fabulous way to start the 5h30 day.

Stepping into the street, my aim now is to find an Internet café, but I have reached a new level of incomprehension. Before, I was still able to decipher the Internet cafe signs; now, nothing. The streets are jam-packed with tiny stores that fill basements and alleyways. Shops are reached through other shops, and advertising billboards turn every shop front into a brightly colored, incomprehensible graphic. Without actually going into every store, I have no idea what's what. It would take two lifetimes to find what I need by this means: a change of tactic is required. Returning to the hotel, I get the reception staff to write down all the shops I need in Mandarin. Back in the street, I hail the first three-wheeler tuk-tuk taxi, hand him my destination requests, and so quickly find the Internet café

… where I discover that my bank has paid out the remaining money to the travel agent, despite the letters of objection I wrote them in Greece and Kazakhstan, and I believed that my money was under my control. Another delusion shattered. But, water under the bridge, I am in China, they can keep the money, and hopefully I will never have to deal with them again.

After my transglobal communications have been dealt with, I tackle the food issue, and am confronted with a new set of challenges. The dairy problem that has been plaguing me since reaching Bulgaria now vanishes altogether. Instead, I am faced with produce that is so unfamiliar that highly specialized food questions such as is it meat or vegetable, fish or fowl, sweet or spicy, raw or cooked can no longer be addressed, as I am not even sure whether the things in the packets are food. Based purely on a visual assessment, they could be pot scourers or dried pork rinds, fifty-fifty chance. Wandering aimlessly up and down the aisles, I pick up packets, look them over hopelessly, before putting them down again. I can find no starting point to help me decipher what the packages contain, until I find chocolate biscuits: they look the same the world over. Triumphantly I carry my small purchase to the till where I discover, that while chocolate biscuits might look the same the world over, numbers don't. I have no expectation of understanding the cashier, but the by-now-familiar trick of peering at the till display to find out what the goods cost shows me that even this small measure of comprehension has been removed. Having no way of telling what my biscuits cost, I simply hand the woman a note of unfamiliar money, and hope she gives me the right change.

Back in the sunshine, I stare at the small packet of biscuits and the unfamiliar coins in my hand, and realize that this trip is teaching me the most unexpected things. In my youth, I watched in fascination while illiterate farmhands in Africa did their shopping at small rural stores. They would choose an item and take it to the cashier, where they would hold out their handful of money, from which the cashier took the amount owing. When this transaction was finalized, the farmhands would assess the money they had left, then return to the shop to fetch the next item on their small lists. This continued until they had completed the list or their money ran out. Usually the latter came first. Today I have much in common with those workers, a bit more money perhaps, but probably a lot less comprehension. Even if I had a shopping list, I would not be able to find the produce I wanted in any shop.

Just as I make peace with the fact that I will have to survive on breakfast and chocolate biscuits, at least until my guide arrives, I spy a tiny eating-house. Peering through a doorway protected by a pink plastic-bead fly-curtain, I see a dark kitchen with a large wok and no hygiene. Fortunately, I lost my puritan need for clean some countries ago, so this is less of a concern than the clientele. The place is almost full, so whatever they are cooking in the kitchen, it is not being stored for long, and that suits me just fine. I take a seat on a three-legged stool at a small table, covered with a bright blue and pink plastic tablecloth. Instead of a carton of paper-wrapped straws, a carton of paper-wrapped disposable chopsticks stands on the table, next to a dirty ashtray – unfortunately, in China you can smoke wherever you like – and a bowl of raw unpeeled garlic cloves.

As snack, I am meant to chew a raw garlic clove? This will never become a hit in polite society.

There is no menu, but with the help of my pictionary, the cook and I decide on a big vegetable stir-fry. The greens arrive, perfectly balanced with reds. One bean, one chili is the basic stir-fry recipe here. With some dexterous chopstick chili sorting, I crunch my way through the mountain of greens, returning the mountain of reds to the ear-to-ear grin of the waitress. The fresh and crunchy meal costs me three yuan, about 30€ cents. So I become a restaurant regular, and the cook stops asking what I want. As I step through the pink bead curtain, all eyes turn toward me, smiley heads are bobbed, the cook ducks into his tiny kitchen, and within minutes my food arrives: stir-fry vegetables with chili on the side, a huge bowl of rice, and liters of tea, which is brewed in huge aluminum kettles with the whole green tea leaf. Great big soggy leaves float about in my tea glass, which I blow to the opposite shore before I sip, but before long they once again dock against my upper lip.

After three days of adjusting to my new circumstances, a soft knock on the door announces the guide's arrival. I have been spending time with my Mandarin course, and greet her with a cheerful

'Ni hao.'

The guide is more keen to practice her English:

'Good morning, pleased to meet you.'

She is a tiny member of the Uyghur ethnical minority group. Uyghur is a collective name for the ancient tribes that have lived in this area since 300 BCE. China gave this ancient claim a small nod by making this part of China the Xingjian autonomous area of Northwestern China. The Uyghurs look very similar to the Turkic tribes further west, with whom they share a sweeping history, many traditions, and the Islamic faith. Their script and language are similar to Arabic. They are not limited in their population growth by the one-child law, and apparently get preferential treatment in such fields as tertiary education.

My guide is very proud of her Uyghur heritage, and does not have any concept that she might also be Chinese, nor does she look in the least Chinese. With her pop eyes and tremendously long red-brown hair – with which she fiddles constantly. However, she is equipped with the Wish Mobile's release papers, a Chinese driver's license, a travel permit, and Chinese number plates, which will be the most expensive souvenirs I will get on this trip.

We immediately set out to rescue the Wish Mobile, and I have visions of driving it into China within the hour. But I soon discover that my little helper is a rather ignorant, primitive sort, who is completely out of her depth. Unfortunately she is also someone who, despite, or perhaps because of, her immense ignorance, refuses to listen to or take advice from anybody. In the foyer, she starts bossing the staff about, and the happy smiley bobbing heads become still and sullen. She commandeers a tuk-tuk, gets in, and curtly informs the driver where she wants to go. Should I go along or will she just take things from here? The tuk-tuk stops at a building some kilometers from the border post.

'Zerrin, my car is at the border post. If I was only arriving today as planned, we would be meeting at the border post. Don't you think it would be a better idea to go there directly?'

She disagrees, steps out of the tuk-tuk, informs me I owe the man 3 yuan, and marches into the building, where she immediately starts a verbal sparring match with the woman behind the counter.

I try to get a word in edgeways.

'Zerrin, I am sure we are not meant to be doing this here.'

She does not feel this comment is worth acknowledging, and continues her sparring match with the woman behind the counter, who, in the blizzard of short sharp words, loses her patience, snatches up my very expensive envelope, and calmly breaks the customs seal, which is only to be opened by some high authority. I stare in disbelief as she scans the document, realizes she has perhaps over-reached herself, staples the envelope closed again, and sends us to the border post.

The border official looks at the no-longer-sealed envelope with deep suspicion. He is not impressed. After reading through the papers, he starts going on and on about Shanghai. For some reason he does not like the papers; something seems to be missing. Zerrin refuses to translate the proceedings, so I am reduced to coat-stand status, while with a startling degree of insolence and rudeness, Zerrin takes control of my life. The customs officials match her insolence with their own. Strong racial tensions exist between the Han Chinese and the Uyghur, and the release of the Wish Mobile seems to be stuck in the middle of a racial game of tit-for-tat, in which I, who have driven all the way to China and around whom all this is meant to be revolving, play no part, and am completely ignored. My ego gets into one enormous huff.

To rub salt in the wound, the Wish Mobile gets in on the act, and refuses to reveal where it hides its engine number. After half an hour's fruitless search, the customs official wants to start dismantling the engine. At this point, I make my point vehemently clear. No one is touching any part of the Wish Mobile engine unless he or she is a qualified mechanic, and that is that. Stalemate, but at least I get everybody's attention, and my ego is appeased for the moment. The customs people take revenge by giving the wench and me the run-around. We bounce from customs house to customs house, from border to town; we stand in queues; ask questions; get sent from pillar to post. As I still have no clue what the problem might be, and Zerrin is not doing any explaining, I am starting to build a head of steam that is getting dangerously close to exploding. I try relaxing – a bit of meditation – but what I really, *really* want to do is rip someone's head off. Preferably the wee wench's, but then she would be so short, she would probably be mistaken for a chihuahua.

We have been at this for nearly ten hours, and closing time is drawing near. Then, with the relentless time slide of the electronic clock, at precisely 19h00 the customs house closes shop for the day. The Wish Mobile will remain in custody for another night. In stony silence, Zerrin and I return to our hotel room.

I am not a billionaire or millionaire. Heck, I don't even qualify for the hundredthousandaire stakes, and China has already gobbled up more than its fair share of my budget. To economize, I now find myself in a situation where my life is controlled by – and I am sharing a room with – an unbelievably primitive being, who has possibly never seen indoor plumbing in her life.

Swanning into the bathroom first, she leaves behind a swamp: dirty soap-scum water in the basin, more water on the floor than could possibly be used in a single shower session, damp towels draped over the toilet and floor, and a disgusting abundance of that very long hair floating about everywhere. Only the truly brain dead can be this rude. I check my diary. How long do I have to live with this individual. Twelve days ... no-o-o, I don't think I can cope. However, in light of this, it is far too early to be throwing my toys out of the cot. I steel myself, I have come this far, I can do this. Time to set some rules. Rule one, I use the bathroom first from now on. Rule two, I will not get involved with the Chinese bureaucracy, and the next morning I send her on her way to sort out the car, while I practice my Mandarin.

By 11h00 the paperwork is cleared, and all that remains is for the Wish Mobile to get scanned. China likes things super-sized; nothing as mundane as manual car searching here. The Wish Mobile is sent through a huge x-ray machine built for cargo trucks; it hums its way across the car's surface and – green light – all clear. Just one quick stop to attach the Chinese number plates, stick various official-looking papers onto the windscreen, and China here I come.

Bed 75 & 76

China is a busy, busy place. The small towns we pass through are all concerned with the corn harvest, which is spread out onto every available flat spot, including the road. The road is the road, is the pedestrian zone, the corn-drying zone. The road is the market place, the parking place. The road in China is the place. My driving skills quickly include street-spread-corn-avoidance, and suddenly-stopping tuk-tuk dodging.

Despite my fascination at my surroundings, and the mental stimulation of the intense hustle after the long silences of Kazakhstan, Zerrin is a disturbing presence. A brooding dissatisfaction hangs around her that blurs my focus to the outside world, as I try to create a harmonious atmosphere in the car. She cramps my Dictaphone style, and makes me almost apologetic when I stop the car – yet again – to take pictures of something she has probably driven past, but never seen, a thousand times.

When we hit the first bit of the Chinese expressway, this problem is resolved for me. The road is too good; the barriers and fences make it impossible to stop; and I am completely isolated from the landscape. The Chinese road builders have designed turquoise crash barriers that are exactly at eye level, reducing the view down to a strip of tar that is vacuumed to hourly perfection. The only distractions are the tollgates. They follow hard and fast, and soon I have my first Chinese phrase down pat. At each tollgate I enquire with a distorted

'Do shau qian?'

The reply is usually 10 yuan.

The road to Urumqi leads through flat grey desert, where little people, their mouths and noses protected by bright pink rags, shovel red chilies from giant bags. The hot peppers spread like a bloodstain over the grey sand, where they slowly darken and dry under the desert sun. More and more photo opportunities flash by behind green metal railings. I hunt for off-ramps, but there are none, and there is no place to stop. Irritated, I demand that Zerrin navigate us off the expressway, but according to her, this is the only road through the desert. The map I have of this area confirms this, but at a scale of 1 : 500,000, it is hardly an accurate representation of the facts. Although Zerrin knew that she would be in charge of navigation, she did not think that bringing a detailed map was important.

This oversight backfires as we hit Urumqi, which is her hometown, and, with a population of 2.6 million, a big city serviced by many highways. Following Zerrin's detailed instructions, we drive backward, forward, left, right, snake up and down on and off ramps, and end up in a grim industrial zone, which I am sure I was never meant to see. Exasperated I pull onto a greasy potholed pavement, next to a row of oily workshops, and demand that she make a call to get directions.

When we manage to find our way to the centre of the city, I realize I have still not quite arrived in China. Urumqi has the Chinese writing, and the odd Chinese-looking person, but it is very much like the central Asian states I have just been through. In common with them, this area has a bloody and conflict-ridden history. During the Qing dynasty an estimated one million Dzungars were exterminated here in an ethnic genocide. Urumqi means 'beautiful pasture' in the language of the Dzungars, but, like the Dzungars, the pastures have been obliterated, and up to now, all I have seen is grey desert and concrete.

Regardless, I am excited to be in a big city, and want to get out to get the feel and flavor of it. I want to see the city, the markets, the people. Zerrin, however, has other ideas. On a rattling square blue bus, with wooden slatted seats, we travel not to the market, but to a flashy pseudo Bukhara-style restaurant. From the plush interior of the restaurant I look onto the street below, where I see Uyghur women who are covered in cloth and rags from head to toe; they even wear gloves. Zerrin is dismissive of them, saying that they are just con artists pretending to be destitute widows. The begging bundles of rags probably rented the small children they have with them for show and added sympathy factor.

Then, without asking about my preferences, Zerrin orders pilov, which she informs me is the Uyghur national dish. So I chew my way through yet another pile of rice, while opposite me she makes no secret of the fact that she would rather be somewhere else. As would I. This is a complete waste of time. I have only one day in Urumqi, and I do not want to spend it sitting in some tourist-trap restaurant, eating bad pilov at big prices, so I pull my inner cow onto centre stage.

> 'Zerrin, I did not drive all the way to China to sit about in a touristified restaurant eating a pile of rice, and no, I don't want seconds, I don't want dessert and I don't want tea or coffee, I want out of here. I want to see the locals in action.'

When paying, I see the reason I have been dragged here, the wee guide quite unashamedly gets her palm greased. It is not the inner cow, but the *Milch Kuh* that is on centre-stage here. This guide thing is going to take some getting used to.

We stroll across to an inner-city market, where Zerrin could not be less interested. She makes it known by steaming ahead, while I peer into ingenious bread ovens. A small fire is built on the floor of clay ovens that look like giant terracotta pots. The oven is allowed to get hot, and then bun-sized pieces of dough are thrown onto the walls of the oven, where they stick like moth eggs to a leaf. When the buns are crisp and golden, they are removed with long handled tongs. This is a bit of an art, as one slip up would make the lost bun coals for the next batch.

Under the blue glass gleam of modern high-rises, shashlik grills are constructed right next to shashlik stands. Welding sparks fly as fans blow the delicious smoke of grilling shashlik through the narrow streets. As I take my eyes from the camera viewfinder, I catch the wee guide with her hands on her hips, rolling her eyes. Will she go as far as tapping her foot? This guide thing is going sour very fast. Back at the hotel she mentions she would like to see her family.

> 'Oh yes, absolutely, you must. I wouldn't dream of stopping you.'

I reply with some relief.

> 'Is it all right if we meet up again tomorrow?'

> 'Absolutely no problem. Run along. Take your time.'

As she leaves, I heave an involuntary sigh, which turns to a barely contained gag, as a well-dressed woman audibly and visibly spits the contents of her sinuses into the foyer ashtray while we are waiting for the elevator in the hotel. In Urumqi the art of spitting is very well developed. I shudder with disgust every few meters as someone feels the need to expectorate.

In my room, thinking that, as it has been a long and stressful day, a small nap would be in order, I surrender myself to gravity, flop down onto the bed, come to a bone-jarring stop, and nearly bite off my tongue. Recovering from the shock, I rip the sheets off the very comfortable-looking dark-wood bed, and discover that the mattress consists of little more than a yoga mat. There should be a large warning sign:

'Beware: do not fall onto the bed; it could kill you.'

The air mattress in the car would be useful at this point, but the Wish Mobile is in a parking lot several city blocks away. Visualizing the awkwardness of dragging the fully inflated mattress from the car, through the mass of humanity that crowd the streets, into the foyer, and squashing it into the elevator, I cast about for a less tiresome solution to the bed problem. Discovering several spare eiderdowns and blankets in the cupboards, I manage to fashion a comfortable little nest, which I immediately put to the twenty-minute nap test.

In the early evening, the sparkle lights come on, and the people come out to play 'shop-till-you-drop' in the night markets and streets of Urumqi. The hawkers, high-rises, slick boutiques and general slovenliness all remind me of the First-World–Third-World combo I am used to seeing in South African cities. Reflected in glass and chrome, men with wooden push carts sell pomegranate juice squeezed by a machine right out of the Spanish Inquisition; people crowd around, more to see the machine in action than to buy the juice. Vendors roast chestnuts in beds of hot stone under electronic advertising billboards that promote global brands, which are for sale in big halls where hundreds of small electronic stores all share floor space. The result is overwhelming noise and mind-numbing choice.

In a dark side street, I stroll through my first Chinese fresh-produce market. It is crowded with people who push and poke at me, at one another, and at the produce: living ducks, chickens, pigeons, and some other small birds that are kept in makeshift cages. Small women expertly check under wings and poke at breasts; freshness is taken for granted; but the health of the animal must be ensured. With the chicken now in limp resignation of its fate, the deal is struck, and the living bird trussed and stuffed into a shopping basket, then transported home.

Alternatively, there is a fast food variety, where the animal is lopped, peeled and chopped in front of the watchful eyes of the customer.

The cold efficiency with which the living bird is reduced to food makes me faintly nauseous: to take a living chicken, chop its head off, rip its feathers out, gut it, roast it, and then eat as Sunday lunch is unthinkable to me. But, give me a nicely packaged supermarket chicken, squeaky clean and wrapped in glossy cling wrap, well, then I am capable of rustling up a large variety of delicious chicken dishes, and eating them with relish. With my Western cellophane-wrapped hypocrisy, I can get away with being a squeamish bunny hugger and eat chicken whose health and living conditions I never think about, and have no way of judging. The scraggily Western battery hen would be quite safe from the butcher's block in China. Here no one would dream of eating such a sickly looking animal. The health test performed by the clientele must have some advantage for the animals, as it ensures that the animal's living conditions are kept to an acceptable standard. There is a brutal honesty to this system: the Chinese still know that an animal must die for it to be eaten, and if you cannot cope with the killing bit, you don't eat meat.

But not eating meat is no problem in China, as fresh crunchy vegetables are in abundance, even at breakfast. Every morning a grand buffet of vegetables greets me in the hotel dining rooms and, as the vegetables are usually accompanied by very hot chili, I have become a big fan of steamed buns. Chili as a pick-me-up in the morning beats coffee hands down. The rice soup I can do without: it tastes like the smell of boiled cotton. This morning, while I am still slurfing my tea through the usual floating foliage, the wee guide appears in a very agitated state, and falls right with the thing topmost on her mind.

'Have you seen the envelope?'

'Which envelope?'

'The envelope with all the car papers in it.'

'Oh, the big brown envelope that you just left lying about yesterday before waltzing off to see your family?'

She looks at me indignantly.

'Yes, have you seen it?'

'Certainly, you left it lying about in the car, so I have put it into safekeeping with the rest of my very important papers.'

Zerrin's face is an odd mix of haughty relief.

> 'No! That is not possible! I must have the papers; they are my responsibility.'

> 'Sweetie, I think that at the end of the day, the car and the trip are my responsibility, and I assure you the papers are quite safe.'

Zerrin is turning an interesting shade of red, and she is starting to get very loud. Will she burst into tears?

> 'No, I must have the papers! I must keep them with me   at all times!'

Her voice starts cracking, and tears well in her eyes. Tears I don't need, so give her the envelope, which she stuffs into her little cloth handbag. I will have to keep an eye on that little bag, as the wee one's concept of safekeeping does not inspire confidence.

Bed 77

Our destination today is Turpan, and while Zerrin has now acquired a map book from her boss, she admits that she has never had to read a map before. I stare at her in a long moment of mystified silence: what is she doing here then? I try deciphering the map, but I meet my match. In Xingjian Province street signs are in two languages: Uyger, which looks like a bunch of curvy flowing squiggles; and Chinese, which looks like a bunch of square squiggles. But the map does show me that the wee one was right; there is only one road that skirts the edge of the northern rim of the Taklamakan desert, and it is simply a join-the-dots line from oasis town to oasis town, so getting lost is highly improbable.

We soon leave the suburbs of Urumqi behind, and drive deep into the Taklamakan, where the horizon slices the world into two even parts: top half brilliant blue sky; bottom half glaring white sand. Hours later a vast wind-farm that stretches to every horizon tacks movement to the clean graphic. The wind-eaters tear and claw at the cold wind; they digest the movement; and expel energy. As the wind-eaters sink into the horizon behind us, the blue sky turns to dull steel, and the desert to windswept grey gravel. In the distance, the red 'O' of a diesel station rises from the shimmering shifting horizon and shines like a brilliant beacon in the monotone grey. Looking for any opportunity to stop, I slow down to take the off-ramp. This jolts Zerrin out of her coma, and she is not happy.

'We shouldn't get off the highway. It is not safe; Turpan is not far.'

I am beginning to see the light; Chinese guides are the perfect little teacher's pets. In China, only the fully indoctrinated may become tour guides. The little red book of propaganda posing as my guide has already informed me how great Mao was, and how everybody still loves him, because he did such great things for China. If things are so great, why not show off a little, but her job is quite clearly to prevent me from seeing any part of China that is not on the official tourist route. But, what can she do, it's my car, and as long as I am driving, we stop when I say so. I have a little Napoleon moment.

I am in charge; this is my car, my trip, mine, mine, all mine. HAH, so there.

Leaving the highway, I discover another side of China, one that huddles hidden from view in the grey shadow of the elevated expressway of technology, and China's latest great leap forward. The diesel station is a tiny building with two pumps: one petrol, one diesel. A small thin man, dressed in a patched jacket that is not keeping him warm, comes out to serve us. Zerrin offers to go inside to pay. I am sure she is just trying to be helpful, but I want to see everything I can possibly see.

The tiny concrete building has a front door, protected by a thick steel gate, and the windows are decorated with heavy steel bars. Inside the space is perhaps 20 meters square, and divided into two rooms: the reception room where I now find myself, and from where I can see a small kitchen; and a sleeping platform, behind a sheet of bulletproof glass. The couple and their little dog live in a tiny world of diesel, wind and grey gravel, from which they can escape only through the flickering television bolted to the wall. The silence underlying the gusts of howling wind, the rare customer, and the babble of the television must be deafening.

The small road leading past the fueling station is heading our way, so despite the wee one's protests, we remain off the highway, dodging potholes, and small rocks, and occasionally passing through villages that are no more than two strips of ugly, small square buildings plonked straight into the desert. There is no pavement, no tree or blade of grass, just grey gravel, cutting wind, blinding sun and hard blue sky. This is a part of China where climate and ideology have blasted away every soft corner and every unnecessary detail, a side of China that tourists never see.

Hour after hour, the northwestern Taklamakan desert is table-top flat, then, without warning, the Tien Shan Mountains soar out of a vivid green pasture. The pasture is a tiny fleck of life, quickly past, as we plunge into the dark mountains that are the same color as the tar. Triangular signs, warning of falling rocks, leap out like yellow exclamation marks. Here nature's palette is so subdued that at first glance all looks grey. Then my eyes adjust and I notice tiny tufts of grass, then shades of raw umber, burnt sienna, touches of green, and tiny flecks of crimson. A rockslide reveals the raw sienna belly of the mountain; it leaps out like brilliant flame in this burnt charcoal world. Then, just as abruptly as the mountains rose out of the desert, they sink back into a wasteland of grey gravel. Here there is nothing, no bird, no roadkill, no people, just the new merchants of the Silk Road: giant trucks, their roar lost in the howling wind that sweeps across the silent fields of stone.

Turpan is an oasis of startling green vineyards that fill every available space, and trellised vines that create shaded walkways past houses of mud adobe decorated with delicate filigree work. But Turpan city is not on our sightseeing list; the ancient city of Jiao he is.

Jiao-he was already an important city on the Silk Road in 108 BCE, and remained so until Genghis Kahn destroyed it in the 13th century. The city was built from adobe on a small island in the middle of a river, where yellow loess cliffs provide natural protection and a view over the far flat horizon. The river still runs on one side of the ruins, and from the high sand cliffs, I see a man driving his donkey cart along a dusty track in the narrow canyon, where every small patch of soil is planted with crops. In the ruined city, tiled walkways lead past mysterious mud-brick walls and cave-like buildings, where the imprint of long-dead builders' hands can still be seen in the dull yellow plaster. Square openings in the high crumbling walls frame the deep blue sky, and small round holes reveal where wooden floors once lay.

Jiao-he is the wee wench's tour guiding specialty, but after having conducted tours through here a hundred times before, she is understandably bored with the whole business. She marches ahead, her long pigtail bouncing on her pert little butt. I wonder if it ever gets stuck between her bum cheeks like dresses sometimes do, and my wayward mind spins off to matters unrelated to ancient cities.

'One should always remember to pull one's clothing straight when one gets up, because the dress or trouser stuck

in the butt is very disturbing for onlookers. I never know which is more polite: to ignore the unfortunate clothing configuration and hope it works its way out, or to politely inform the affected person. But how does one politely say, excuse me, but your dress is stuck up your butt? I am quite sure, though, that giving hands-on assistance would not be the way to go.'

Down brain: I really should take the head to obedience lessons.

With Zerrin more interested in finding a patch of shade than being a guide, I allow my imagination free rein, and make up my own story of Jiao-he. From the high vantage of the city, I imagine a huge dust cloud on the horizon as the caravan slowly approaches...

'The news spreads quickly through the narrow alleys, cool in the searing midday heat. The people have been waiting for this sign for days as a scout on fast camel had alerted the city elders that guests were on their way. The farmers and artisans hurry their produce to the market; the trade will soon be good there. Stable hands send boys for water and hay. Hours later, the first dusty travelers enter the massive carved wooden gates. They wash their hands and feet before climbing down steep flights of stairs into cool courtyards. The men are offered tea and dried fruit, and while resting against pillows and carpets, share news of faraway Beijing. Later roast goat is served with nan and vegetables, highly spiced with chili and cumin. To end the evening, the men enjoy a water pipe, while the Sodgina girls of Turpan – who had a certain reputation, which stretched as far as Astana in Kazakhstan – provide entertainment. Throughout the city the eating-houses, markets and water wells are centers of information; after months of solitude there is suddenly much to talk about. Then, before heading west, across the vast gravel wasteland to Urumqi, the caravan chiefs make offerings at the temple built of sand.'

Today, the temple is enclosed by scaffolding, and two men in white overalls and facemasks spray the adobe wall with silicone glue, as the Chinese government tries to keep it together for another couple of hundred years.

The camel trains along the silk route that connected the faraway here and there must have traveled through many dust storms that would have made worthwhile the facemasks that the tourists who today frequent this place all wear. In the course of my journey I have become an expert tourist spotter, and can determine the origin of the tourists by their tourist suits. The Europeans, especially the Germans, all look as if they are going on safari in the deepest darkest wilderness.

With their hiking boots, khaki all-weather gear, and the wristwatch that does everything, including tell the time. The English favor revealing clothing in pastels, while the Koreans dress as if they are going into a quarantine zone. They are covered head to foot against the elements; masks, gloves, hats and long tunics ensure that nothing is to be seen of them at all. Do they believe that this strange outfit will protect them against the unknown?

During my long slow travel, I have learnt something that cannot be discovered when flying from comfort zone to comfort zone. It is in exploring the nowhere places between the scenic spots, in setting aside the comfort zones, that you conquer your fear of the unknown and broaden the horizons of your mind. My thinking has become quite simplistic; if there are humans living there, it follows that I can survive there.

Not a sentiment shared by Zerrin. While exploring the markets of Turpan, I realize how vast the empire of the Turkic/Mongol people once was. From Turkey to Turpan, traces of the same culture are found. There are strong similarities between the crafts and dress of the far-ranging Turkic tribes. The doppilar and pointed slippers are identical to those I saw in Bukhara. The architecture, with its intricate tiles and turquoise mosaics, reminds of Istanbul, Samarqand or Cantui. In Turpan, they make pure wool carpets. The patterns are in harsh bright colors that bite the eye, and remind me of the green and white abomination the carpet dealer in Bukhara tried to force on me. Shashlik is still the takeout of choice, although here they use chili and coriander to spice the meat. The Chinese influence is apparent in the use of the wok and the traditional Chinese medicines, dried herbs, lizards and various ground insects that are for sale, although these remind me more of the 'muti' used by African natural healers than anything I saw in Central Asia.

I am pulled from my mental spin around the world by the wee Zerrin, who, quite unexpectedly, throws a tantrum and bursts into hysterical tears. I am flummoxed.

'What is the problem?'

'It is 1h30 and I will get deceases if I do not eat regularly.'

'Deceases?'

'I had a kidney replaced last year and I have blood sugar problems!'

Whoo, that sounds serious. Trying to find a quick solution to her blood sugar problem, I look around at the market. We are surrounded by stalls: there is fruit; there are nuts; there are meat dishes; and sticky sweet things for her plummeting blood sugar levels. I am at a loss.

'There is food everywhere. Why don't you just buy yourself something to eat?'

'Because I am a Muslim, and my faith demands that my food must be properly prepared.'

'But Turpan is the centre of your culture; surely you can safely eat the food here.'

'I only eat in certain restaurants.'

'So you want me to stop what I am doing, so that you can eat in one of these particular restaurants?'

There is no logic here, but the tiny hysterical mouse thing is gnashing her little chompers, and creating such a scene that I relent, and while I am taking her to the restaurant of her choice, I have an epiphany: a man moment. In trying to stop her totally irrational behavior, I meekly did what she wanted me to do, while what I really wanted to do is to give her a 'snotklap' right there in the market place, but instinctively knew that that sort of thing is only possible in the movies. Slapping one's Uyghur guide in real life would probably see me in the Chinese clink. From my reaction to her irrational behavior I come to the conclusion that while the average male reaction to the female 'weep and wail' might seem chivalrous, in reality he probably thinks she is being a hysterical twit, and wishes she, or he, were somewhere else.

While Zerrin eats in her chosen restaurant, I have another epiphany: she is a shareholder in the greasy-palm chain of restaurants, and I remain forever the *Milch Kuh*. But something puzzles me about her, and I wonder aloud what she will do tomorrow when we leave Uyghur territory behind and enter China proper, as I have discovered she will not even drink tea in a Han restaurant. She informs me in a huff that her mommy has given her food for the road. Fascinating – I now move on to wondering where in the Wish Mobile she has stashed ten days worth of food – if I catch one whiff, the wee mousey thing is mince.

But I do realize that it must be difficult to be thrown into a situation where you are suddenly expected to set aside your carefully cultivated social status and eat in a market, when you are quite convinced that only a fancy restaurant is good enough for you. It has been some time since I have had the social maps to know who is meant to be superior to whom, and I have never known which restaurant is cool and which is not. While I am aware that many people live their lives by these society-defined route markers, I am quite happy with my reduced arsenal of measuring tools for people and places. Everybody I meet is a potential ally and not a prejudged enemy. I may be being a bit hard on the wee one, but the last thing I need now is to start judging people and situations based on someone else's prejudices, and she does seem to have quite a few of those.

Unfortunately, even well fed, the silly girl seems unable to control her sulky mood, and drags that thing around with her all afternoon. On the sightseeing to-do list is the ancient city of Gao Chang, built from the red sand that defines the northern rim of the Tarim basin. The city is a vast ramshackle repetition of Jiao-he. As the sun is setting fast, we opt for a quick donkey-cart trot through the ruins, but no matter how fast the donkey trots, the young boys controlling the speed are not satisfied, so they beat the poor beast with unbridled enthusiasm. With no language connection, I have no way of asking them politely to stop this behavior, and Zerrin, having sunk into a silent funk, refuses to speak, or perhaps she is blind to all but her own little problems. To try to solve the donkey's problems without becoming physical, I hunt about in my head for an appropriate word from my vast Mandarin vocabulary.

Bu – the mandarin for no – seems a good choice.

So I bu up and I bu down, I bu flat and I bu sharp, but no matter how I pronounce that two-letter word it has no effect other than to bring a smirk to Zerrin's lips. This midget is pushing all the wrong buttons.

On our way back to Turpan I silently make my wish for the world: one universal language. I think the whole Tower of Babel thing teaches us only one lesson: never act when you are caught in a jealous rage, even if you are an all-powerful being. To take from humans the one tool that could make them understand each other is no way to create a peaceful society. The multitude of languages we speak might be an individual source of pride, but on a global scale, they form invisible barriers between us that give power to the unscrupulous, and will always see us beating each other over the head in sheer frustration and misunderstanding.

The sun sets suddenly in the desert, and on a completely dark road, with no markings or barriers, I nearly collide with a tuk-tuk that is dragging a small trailer full of children. The vehicle has no lights, no reflectors, and I see him only at the last minute. My involuntary;

'That man is crazy'

brings an icy

'How you dare call my people crazy.'

from Zerrin.

'I beg your pardon? I was not making a general judgment about your people, but about the driver of that tuk-tuk who with his lack of lights and totally un-roadworthy vehicle   and trailer is endangering everybody on the road, including you.'

'You think you can come here and insult my people!'

I am floored; this is one very touchy little person. Why anyone thought that she would be the best person to guide me through China is beyond my understanding.

The next morning, the Wish Mobile is surrounded by interested tourists. This is the perfect time to get the first Chinese wish, but the wee Zerrin is nowhere to be found. Eventually she arrives. Are we going somewhere special today? The disgustingly long hair is loose and floating all over the place. The pink lipstick, combined with bright blue eye-shadow, is a rather unfortunate addition to the face. I catch myself staring, then manually pull up my jaw, before asking her to explain to the crowd what the Wish Mobile artwork is all about; perhaps one of the men might like to add his wish. She tells me with dismissive air that she does not think that there is anything to explain about the car, gets in, and waits for me to chauffeur her to her next port of call. I conclude that she is laboring under a misconception. It is time we clarified something.

'Zerrin, the only reason that you are getting a private all-expenses paid trip through China is because your government will not allow me to drive through China alone. If I had any choice in this matter, you would most definitely not be here. For some reason you were chosen to accompany me, although I have yet to discover any particular strengths, abilities or endearing qualities in you that would explain why. But, as you are now here, can I kindly request that you try to be at least the tiniest bit professional about your role, and when next I ask you to translate something for me, I do not expect you to refuse, but to remember quite clearly that by asking you I am   merely   being polite.'

She bursts into a flood of tears … again. They could put her to good use greening the desert. Then she starts yammering on and on about her human rights, that she is a human being, and she has rights.

> 'Sweetie, human rights are not this easy to abuse. It is repulsive to me that you are making light of something abominable in order to disguise your own incompetence. This is not an abuse of your human rights, but a short sharp criticism of your lack of professionalism, and if you have any backbone at all, you will learn   something from it, and   not whine about your human rights.'

She moves into hysteria mode and, as I drive off, opens the car door. Is she truly going to leap from the moving vehicle? This girl has a problem beyond a missing kidney. Plummeting blood sugar levels cannot be the cause of her bizarre behavior, as she's just stuffed her face with breakfast. I decide to blame all this on false expectations. She has probably been looking forward to living the highlife while traveling through China, and then she met me. What a disappointment I must be for her.

Bed 78

This morning the sky is white, hot, and the air thick with pollution, and the desert wind a blessing. The industry out here in the faraway Taklamakan is oil and petrochemicals, with a massive production of toxic fumes as a by-product. The first place I want to explore this morning is Goa Chang Flame Mountain, which the hazy light turns into Ember Mountain. Zerrin sullenly informs me that it is not interesting and not worth the drive. This makes me quite sure that I will find the whole thing very interesting, and at this point simply stop listening to one thing she has to say. So the silly little thing sulks and rolls her eyes; she sighs so mournfully and frequently that soon the air in the Wish Mobile is full to overflowing with a deep blue funk. I should have let her jump ship when I had the chance.

With long slow curves, the black tar leads into an alien world, where red sand flows down the slopes of mountain-high dunes. In gentle swells and ripples, the sand dams against red ridges, creating red rivers that pour over red sandstone rocks in transparent red sand falls.

In a valley, a water river creates a startling display of green reality against the backdrop of the surreal red mountains.

The road stops at the 77 grottoes of Bezeklik Thousand Buddha Caves, which are carved into the red sandstone. In each grotto, the arched ceiling is covered with an army of blind Buddhas, 1,000 per grotto. For centuries, the Uyghurs and other local tribes were Buddhists. They went to a lot of effort to dig the 77 grottoes and paint these thousands of Buddhas. Then the same tribes changed their mind about their religion, and after converting to Islam, went to an equal amount of trouble to put out the eyes of every little Buddha. Interesting that the paintings did not simply lose their spiritual significance, but still had enough hold on the converts that they had to be vandalized. I don't get this. If a god and a religion are all powerful, why aren't they?

Back on Route 312 we head east, direction Hami. Raisin houses form small raisin cities between the road and the sand dunes. The buildings are square airy lattice works of mud bricks in which the golden grapes of the region hang from wooden poles and get dry and wrinkly together. By the side of the road, a small grape stall is a delicate symphony of colour: pale yellow and blush of rose and the small spark of green against the backdrop of pale rose sand mountains. The grapes are huge, alluring, and, were this Germany, I would be happy to help myself and leave the money, as there is no one attending the stall. But this might not be the way things work in China, and, as the wee one feels no need to get involved, I get no grapes today.

The oasis of Turpan vanishes as the Wish Mobile, a small silver blip in a dusty beige world, transports us deep into the desert, the road a grey arrow splitting the red sand. On the left, mustard, green and purple mountains slowly rise and dive into the red sand like ridge-backed dragons. They follow us for hours, until they freeze into cool blue and crimson mountains that reach, black-capped, to the white-hot sky. A ridge of pure black basalt splits the desert floor, opening a portal through the mountain, where a wave of blood-red sand breaks against the earth's grey crust. Wide mineral ores of green, yellow and red zigzag through the black rocks like bright graffiti.

In a valley between the fierce black mountains, a field of deep green gravel draws me out. Gung ho, I stride into the heat, failing to notice that the bare bits of ground are covered with small, almost invisible plants. Their existence is a daily struggle, and I have just obliterated a whole lot of them, without a second thought. Very carefully, I tiptoe back to the car. Even leaving footprints is sometimes too much. The brilliant mountain dragon dives back into the red sand, which changes to green, to yellow, to grey as the kilometers fly by.

Soon we reach Hami, where, to avoid getting lost again, Zerrin has arranged that her uncle will meet us on the national road outside town. The whole day she has not managed to pull herself out of her own ass, and when she gets out of the car to join her uncle, she takes with her an atmosphere so thick that in my relief I spontaneously burst into song. As we are in Hami for two nights, I suggest that she go with her uncle for lunch and sightseeing. Maybe they will invite her to stay for the night ... no such luck, but I am shot of her for the afternoon.

The following day the wee one's uncle accompanies us on a tour of Hami. He turns out to be a salt-of-the-earth fellow, which lightens the atmosphere, but to impress him, Zerrin suddenly goes into tour guide mode, and is determined to drag me to every historical site in town. After the first tomb I pull rank; I have been in Samarqand and Bukhara, and the tombs of Hami are not in the same class; and enough with the dead people already. From now on, we will do as I please.

On driving into Hami yesterday, I spied a cotton-weighing station. This seems to me a good place for some local-flavor photography. Also, I have never seen a cotton plant, flower or raw cotton, for that matter. The cotton is picked by foreign labor from South East Asia, mainly women with an unhealthy helping of little girls, who fill bags bigger than they are with cotton bolls, each boll carefully picked by hand from the hard curved brown membranes. A small tractor drags the cotton to the weighing station, where giant fluffy mountains dwarf men and women, their mouths and noses covered by rags to prevent them breathing in the cotton fiber. While wrestling the soft stuff into giant bales, they grin for the camera, tiny sun-brown faces in clouds of white.

Hami is famous for its pottery, although today there is none to be found. But there are plenty of melons, and, as the people of Hami claim their Hamigua melon to be the sweetest, juiciest melon in the world, I need to put this claim to the test. At the friendliest-looking stand I ask to try the famous Hamigua, I am not a melon fan, having always thought melons were much ado about nothing. But with my first bite into the sun-sweet flesh of the Hamigua that melts like cool ice in my mouth, I am sold. The Hami melon moves to the top of the World Melon pops.

The food market is under a huge roof over a stamped earth floor. On long benches at narrow tables, people bend their heads to their food. Shashlik stands line the walkways between the tables, where men deftly flick-fold dozens of shashlik across the coals onto endlessly waiting plates. Stopping to watch a man who is artistically folding some white fleshy stuff into interesting curls and spirals, before threading the whole lot onto a skewer and grilling it, I ask Zerrin what it is. Instead of answering my question, she informs that it is only for Chinese people, and that I wouldn't be interested. I stare down at her in amazement, and it crosses my mind that with a well-aimed pelvic thrust I could punch her in the nose.

As the day draws to a close, I invite Uncle Hami for late lunch, early dinner. He takes us to the – in his opinion – best restaurant in town. Like all the other restaurants I have seen so far, it has the shashlik burner right on the edge of the very wide pavement, allowing it to be as visible and smellable as possible. Then several wonky tables and chairs stand al fresco in front of a very small restaurant that is taken up mainly by the noodle kitchen, where anyone insisting on Western hygiene standards would be very disappointed. Uncle Hami orders the beef noodles for which this restaurant is famous. Beef noodle is just that: one-meter-long handmade noodles in a broth of beef with small bits of beef for decoration, and the dish is eaten with chopsticks. Broth, one-meter-long noodles and chopsticks – there is no polite way of eating this meal, so I make like the locals, hold the bowl to my mouth, and scoop-slurp up those noodles, biting them off, and allowing the remains to fall back into the bowl when my mouth is full. It is the quickest, if not the most civilized way, to get the noodles from my plate to my mouth.

After dinner the burly uncle takes out a packet of bright blue cigarettes; this I have to try. I need to be able to say: I once smoked a bright blue cigarette with a Uyghur man in China. To accompany the blue cigarettes I order us a couple of green Tsingtaos – which is a very good German-style pilsner, with spirulina added for your continued good health – much to Uncle Hamis's joy and Zerrin's displeasure. In amiable silence, Uncle Hami and I smoke blue cigarettes and drink green beer, while my sniffy little guide displays her true character for all to admire.

Life often throws us unexpected tests of character, usually not in terribly heroic circumstance; for her this is one. By translating, she could turn this little gathering into a happy information exchange, but she chooses to translate nothing, preferring to sit in silent superiority.

She has fortunately spent some of her time doing something useful. Tomorrow in Dunhuang, I am to get a new guide, and so as I blow a thin stream of smoke into the cooling afternoon air, the wee wench slips out of my regard.

Dunhuang to Xian
Bed 79

In the fancy hotel foyer in Dunhuang I start to feel very much like the top-secret briefcase in a spy thriller. I am introduced to my new guide; and am then carefully set aside, while mysterious envelopes and papers are passed between them; I am becoming a spectator to my own life. Suddenly Zerrin turns to me, and bluntly informs me that I will now be going to view thousands of Buddhas at Mogao Grottoes, just outside Dunhuang. My appointment is at three sharp, and if I am late, I will miss the tour, but will have to pay anyway, so we should be leaving now. Was I asked? Consulted? No chance. I am just a piece of luggage that needs to be quickly and efficiently transported through China. This information sharing on a need-to-know basis is getting on my nerves, but it seems that visiting Dunhuang without visiting Mogao Grottoes is just not done.

Mogao Grottoes are the Chinese equivalent of Neu Schwanstein, a high-tech tourist production line. Tour operators are in radio contact with each other to ensure an unhindered flow of thousands of people in and out of the grottoes that honeycomb the high sandstone cliffs. In 366 CE a Buddhist monk – working under divine instruction – started to dig grottoes here. Others soon followed his example, turning each new grotto into a small temple. These were used by monks and travelers as places of refuge, instruction and contemplation. To aid in this, the pilgrims painted the interiors with scenes from Buddhist teachings. Wealthy families started to build grottoes as private temples, and took to decorating them with elaborate sculptures of Buddha. Over the years, the number of temples grew to more than 1,000, until at some point after the 11th century, the grottoes were used as depositories for old parchments and scrolls, which were walled in, and then slowly vanished from living memory. The grottoes, and the ancient documents they contained, were rediscovered in the early 1900s. Today 492 grottoes have been excavated; 30 are open to the public; and all this is what I have been brought here to see.

Shashlik vendor, Hami, China

The grottoes house sleeping Buddha, sitting Buddha, tiny Buddha, single Buddha, massed Buddha, a thousand different, but always smiling serenely Buddha. The giant Buddha of Mogao Grottoes is forever captive in his narrow space. The grotto is tiny, the Buddha massive – at least thirty meters high – and this automatically puts one in the position of humble worshipper, whether one likes it or not.

It is never possible to see the whole Buddha at once, or to look him straight in the eyes. Onlookers are forced to stare up at him in wonderment and awe. But no matter the size or body position of the Buddha, at the foot of every one, Buddhists gather. They bow deeply; listen intently to their guide; and then do Buddhist ritualistic stuff. This includes making offerings of money, which is stuffed into transparent collection boxes, so everybody can see how much is given – no slipping in the loose change here.

There is something puzzling about this. Buddha, being Buddha, has reached Nirvana, and is therefore beyond desire. Logically he doesn't even desire for others to become Buddhists or to strive for Nirvana – in the state of Nirvana nothing is everything. So how does the logic follow that to make offerings of whatever kind to Buddha will help you reach Nirvana? He doesn't care, is unaware, somewhere out there. The worshippers must know this. They must also know that to reach Nirvana requires the loss of desire; but a human in a crowd always desires to be seen to be doing the right thing by the crowd. In this case doing the right thing seems to be to stuff big wads of money as visibly as possible into the transparent moneyboxes.

E M Forster once wrote, 'the old, old trouble that eats the heart out of every civilization: snobbery, the desire for possessions, creditable appendages; and it is to escape this rather than the lusts of the flesh that saints retreated into the Himalayas' (EM Forster 1934, *A passage to India*. London: Routledge).

Pity then that the desire for the Western money-fuelled lifestyle has now reached even the Himalayas.

But in the name of a greater ideal, humans once again surpass themselves in their craft. I have seen more houses of worship in these last few months than I have in my entire life, and they all have one thing in common. In the belief that we are addressing something greater than ourselves, something we believe has everlasting value, we surpass ourselves in our creativity and craft. Here in the Kumtag Desert oasis there is nothing but sand, water and straw, and from these basic ingredients all the elaborate figures in the grottoes have been constructed. The freestanding larger-than-life guardians that accompany every Buddha, with their flowing garments, finely detailed muscles and terrifying facial expressions, are a mastery of these basic construction materials. Unfortunately those who recently renovated the figures felt it necessary to paint them with brilliant gloss enamel, in garish colors that are completely out of context of the region and totally unbelievable.

In contrast to the statues, the murals that cover the walls and ceilings of the grottoes are simplistic in the way of ancient oriental art, and the use of color restricted by the earth shades and natural pigments that were available to the artists in ancient times: lapis lazuli, malachite, red oxide, yellow ochre, and lead white. The lead white was used mainly for the whites of the eyes, but over the years the lead has turned black, so all the grottoes sport little blank, black-eyed Buddha. While the scenes from the teachings of Buddha are faded and flaking, it is still possible to see that the use of perspective was well advanced here, hundreds of years before the Italian Renaissance perfected its use in the West.

Back at the hotel, I have the room to myself, and I am beginning to see the most unlikely things as pure luxury. So I am making use of the privacy to give myself a little pampering session, while watching a Chinese film awards program on TV. Now it really hits me just how separate this world is from the one I know. The awards format is the same as in Hollywood, but there are no Hollywood stars here. This is China, and it is self-supporting in all ways. A Chinese boy-band, cute in the girly-boy kind of way that appeals to sixteen-year-old girls, rap in English, and do bad Michael Jackson dance impersonations. The fans go wild – very quietly – the audience is massive, but completely silent. To show their appreciation they all have orange glow-in-the-dark sticks, which they wave about madly. The master of ceremonies is the usual 'hyper' type that motor-mouths his way through announcements and jokes, occasionally throwing in an English word to seem cool. A female winner – in the smallest actress category, I think – stalks onto the stage; her shoes are like stilts, yet the podium is still too high for her. I am riveted by the show. What normal Chinese person goes to the scenic spots that tourists are trotted to like sheep? Not one. They stay home and watch shows like these. I am going to tell the tour guide to stick her scenic spots in her pipe and smoke 'em, I am watching Chinese TV from now on to get a grip on modern Chinese culture.

However, I soon discover that my new guide, Genji, is a no-nonsense type who has other ideas. She telephones to say that I have a pre-dawn rendezvous with a mountain of sand and a camel. I had better get some sleep then. At 05h00 sharp, my phone rings again. Genji is in the lobby. It is pitch black out; is this really necessary? But we are in a hurry, it seems. Park the car; secure the keys in a well-zipped pocket; you can hear nothing fall in the sand, says Genji. A brisk walk down a dark and deserted street, down some unseen steps and then I feel sand underfoot. In shifting lamplight, moving camel shadows are waiting for a small group of sunrise enthusiasts. The camels rise as camels do, with their hind legs first. The uninitiated screech and cling to camel necks to prevent flying nose first into the sand.

Slowly the dawn picks out forms from the dark. On the slope of an enormous sand dune, I am at the tail end of a train of camels, making its way to the lookout. The sky turns nursery shades of pink and blue. In the still air, a low cloud of dust hangs at the camels' feet. I close my eyes to the gentle swaying of the camel, listen to the bell jingle and quiet squash-squeaking of sand under soft camel foot. The air is lightly chilled; it smells musty dull brown. I am on the Silk Road to Persia, bearing news of faraway places, and brilliantly colored digital images.

On top of the sand dune, the guides shoo the tourists to the best viewpoint for photographs. The group meekly set up their cameras as told, and wait for the sun to rise. I hang back to photograph the camels, but the guides are nervous.

'Hully hully sunlise.'

To keep them calm, I walk up to the top of the dune. The guides smile and nod in knowing relief – until I walk right over the crest and down the other side, pointing my camera not at the rising sun, but at the tourists waiting for it. The guide feels it his duty to come and advise me of my error.

'Sunlise sunlise.'

He says earnestly, while pointing over my right shoulder. He looks on with concern as I fall about laughing, but poses obligingly as I photograph him instead. Once the rising of the sun has been duly documented, we are all summoned back to our camels. I decide to walk down, and give up my camel to a very grateful, if incredulous, Chinese man. I have paid for the ride, why not take it? I suppose, had I been consulted, I would not have paid, knowing that taking photographs from the top of a camel is almost impossible; and taking photographs is the thing to do in the early morning light, an opinion that the sunrise enthusiasts do not seem to share.

With their cameras packed away, they get cameled back down the dune, which slides in long buttery curls across the deep blue lake of morning sky. The clarity of light and saturation of color is slowly smudged by yellow dust, kicked up by the camel trains that trudge hundreds of tourists up and down the dune. Every tourist is dutifully decked out in the hat, dust mask, and bright orange sand socks that they are supplied with at the bottom of the dune. I have a fine time swapping *'ni haos'* with the locals as they sway by. Each one corrects my pronunciation to suit his or her particular dialect. Soon I am so confused I just say, hi.

At the bottom of the dune, organized chaos rules. Giant tour groups, bound together in brief brotherhood by same color cap, follow same color flags, floating in the breeze, to camels that sit lie roll bellow fart, while tourists giggle squeak squeal. Camel-men smoke and spit; dust floats and hangs and catches in my throat. I wonder what else is making its way into my throat via the dust, and beat a prudent retreat to the Crescent Lake oasis. I hear my name. Odd to hear one's name being called after such a long time; whom do I know here; who knows me? I turn to see Genji jogging awkwardly across the soft sand. While I quite forgot about her, it is clear she didn't forget about me, and is on the verge of a nervous breakdown.

'Where were you? Why you were not on the camel?'

'I decided to walk down to take photographs.'

'Yes, but you must do as I tell you!'

'I must?'

'China is dangerous!'

What is it with the Chinese and danger? I come from Africa. I have no fear. Besides, I just drove all the way to China without anyone's help. I am sure I can walk down a sand dune without mishap. But I sense that Genji doesn't care how I got to China. Now that I am here, I am her responsibility. I am back in the spy-v-spy movie, and realize that she must have firm instructions not let me out of her sight, and her main duty is to control my movements.

Standing high on a crescent-moon sand dune, overlooking the temple and lake in the sand valley below, a reality of the lives of the Chinese becomes real for me too. Life in China is absolutely regimented and controlled, even while on holiday. With my Western insistence on doing what I like, when I like, I am like the ball in a pinball machine. By bouncing around trying to break out of the tourist gristmill, I keep hitting barriers that light up and sound alarms. Soon the game may tilt, and in the end I will still be in China, and will only have succeeded in making life difficult for Genji. With that, I resolve to try to be a bit more compliant, but I refuse point-blank to take pictures from the government-selected spots. Dotted all about the scenic spots of China are little signs:

'Position for the good photograph.'

This is far too much control for my taste.

But the

'sleaze do not climb'

sign on the ridge of the crescent dune, I must obey. I have a pinched nerve, and have had shooting pains up and down my legs for days, not something the camel ride helped in curing. I have visions of deep vein thrombosis from all the sitting in the car. I think I might be a closet hypochondriac, but Genji has a ready answer. She has a friend who is a blind, fully qualified masseur. A Chinese massage by a blind masseur. This sounds good. Genji is on the phone immediately, and, while waiting for the connection, tells me that certain trades or crafts are reserved for those with disabilities, as in the blind masseur.

The blind are given first choice for places in learning institutions if they wish to study in these fields. As her friend has studied the art of massage for six years, this is sure to be my most expert massage ever. The masseur arrives; at six foot he is the biggest person I have seen in months. He, his wife and Genji all bundle into the hotel room. When I enquire how he would like me to present myself for my massage – naked or clothed –they giggle in embarrassed fashion. Through her giggles and blushes, Genji explains that phony blind massage and sex for sale have unfortunately become synonymous in China. My question was therefore seen in quite the wrong light.

But the question must be asked. One never does know whether one is to take everything off, just the top half or keep everything on. It is best to clarify this point at the outset to avoid later embarrassment. After some discussion, we all decide that light loose clothing would be most suitable. As Genji and the wife settle down in the comfortable armchairs, creating a small spectator ring, the masseur warms his hands, and I settle on the bed. Then without any gentle introduction, the masseur proceeds to attack my back with such enthusiasm that I seriously doubt his qualifications. But only a minute or two later, I can feel him grabbing hold of my lower spinal cord, and shifting it about. The pain vanishes, just like that, but he is just warming up. He does some quick measures with his fingers and, wham, pokes them right into various acupuncture points. The pain returns, shooting into my heart and brain, I yelp, my audience and masseur giggle. I am pummeled, squeezed, rubbed and turned from side to side. He throws in a bit of chiropraxy, a bit of reflexology, and more pain. He finds more acupuncture points, more yelping on my part, more laughing on theirs. This is starting to sound highly suspicious; I hope the guests in the neighboring rooms are still out sightseeing. Each of my fingers gets massaged, each toe pulled. My legs – thank goodness for the clothing, this would have been very embarrassing naked – are lifted right over my head, folded down, then given a resounding yank. As a grand finale, he puts his arm around my throat and cradling my chin in the crook of his elbow, picks me up by my neck, I go limp with shock and – crack – my spinal cord is as straight as it has never been. By now, my audience is limp with mirth. This is the most entertaining massage I have ever had, and, if laughter really is the best medicine, it did my audience just as much good as it did me. Alone again in my room I stare at my back in the mirror and try to grab hold of my spine; it is impossible, how he did it is a mystery. No matter, I am pain free, and fall into a coma-deep sleep.

Bed 80

Waking to a morning sky that is a dull grey pink and far too close for comfort, the air smells like hot iron, and the door handle shocks; there is violence in the wind. Genji arrives, equipped with maps. Our destination today is Zhanye, and yesterday she spent time in the library, reading up on our route, and poring over maps. However, a map can unfortunately not prepare anyone for a road that cannot be seen. With every kilometer that we drive deeper into the Gobi, the wind builds in strength, until it is Herculean, lifting every part of the desert that is not nailed down, and hurling it across the road. Visibility is clear gone clear gone. The sand hisses across the Wish Mobile, while Genji and I stare pop-eyed through the windscreen, willing our eyes to see through the billows of dull orange sand. The national road turns into the expressway, but our relief is short-lived – the expressway is still under construction. Our self-congratulating smiles turn into frowns of disbelief as the expressway ends with a row of enormous bollards, far too heavy to move, even if we did dare to step out into the sand storm. On the other side of the bollards, the missing traffic we were wondering about is making its way from a dusty detour onto a new stretch of expressway.

We have no choice but to turn back. Somewhere in the wind and sand, we missed a sign or perhaps the sign is missing. We drive up and down several unfinished off-ramps and service ramps. We drive on the left, then on the right of the expressway. Trucks appear like magic out of clouds of dust, vanishing again before I have time to get a firm grip on their position. My eyes are burning with the effort to turn into x-ray vision. I give up and adopt the 'that car looks like he knows what he is doing' navigational technique, and start following the only other car on the expressway. I have tried this technique before, and it has yet to work, but perhaps this time. In the sand blizzard we lose sight of the car we are following; we lose sight of the road; we lose sight of the Wish Mobile, as every window shows only sand, which pushes and retreats, swirls and rolls along the glass. I edge forward slowly. Chinese trucks stop for nothing, and to stop could be more dangerous than to keep moving.

Suddenly the wind drops, and in an instant, the world around us is flat orange sand, clear blue sky, and huge army tanks. Where did they come from? Genji looks up at the soldiers in shock; they look down in disbelief.

'Drive drive ... drive!'

'Where am I going?'

'Just go!'

'Where to?'

'There there there the road.'

Sure enough, just across a small stretch of desert is the detour we have been hunting for, but how to get there? I have by now caught up with Genji's mindset: military roads in China are definite no-go zones, even more so when you are driving a foreign vehicle through China. I can sense that the last thing Genji wants is for one of the soldiers to get quizzy. But I have also had my experiences with driving gung-ho across fine desert sand; it's not advisable for a quick getaway. Then a track, not much, but enough, allows us to bounce across the Gobi, just as the wind heaves itself out of the sand, and resumes its game of 'hide-the-world'.

We fall into the slow-moving queue of trucks and tuk-tuks, and an hour after our enforced u-turn at the bollards we make it back to the same point again. The pace is slow, but steady, and the desert turns to grey gravel. In a cold fury, the wind howls and shrieks across the barren wasteland, but can find nothing to throw about. It cleaned up here centuries ago. A vast field of wind turbines is unmoved by the wind. Its rage would tear them apart, so the wind wastes its energy on shaking trucks, and torturing tuk-tuk drivers.

The traffic builds and slows and slows and builds, until a small red light commands us to stop at a one-way roadblock. Our turn to move will come soon. Unfortunately, owing to the total lack of warning signs, only the cars that can see the little red light know what is going on. The cars and busses coming from behind believe that the stationary cars are just having a little picnic to take the bracing desert air, and they start filling the oncoming traffic lane. Once the oncoming lane has been filled, the tuk-tuks get in on the act, and fill the space between the lanes, until the vehicles are jammed as tight as battery hens. By now, we might as well chuck the picnic idea, and break out the camping gear. An hour later, when trucks and front-end loaders threaten to bulldoze lesser vehicles into the desert, and car horns compete for airspace with the howling wind, one of the road crew realizes there might be a problem. He looks down the road, first left, then right, shrugs his shoulders, then saunters, Italian style, toward the end of our side of the traffic jam, which is now kilometers to the rear and growing. Hours go by before the traffic loosens sufficiently to make headway. The Chinese are climbing up the 'worst drivers in the world' scale pretty fast.

Stressed and exhausted, we reach Zhanje just in time for dinner in a crowded food market, where flames heat woks, heat steaming stir-fries that fill the air with flavor. Bowls are filled with layers of noodles, vegetables, lots of chilies, and finally a few slices of meat. At last, I feel I am in China proper. The high cheekbones and narrow faces of the Turkic tribes have been replaced by the round faces, button noses, and almond eyes of the Han Chinese, who are very small people. I am a Gulliver among the Lilliputians. People stare and ask to have their picture taken with me. While I play at being a tourist attraction, Genji orders the specialty of these parts: the short fat noodle that we combine with chilies and crisp stir-fry vegetables. We share a plastic covered table with two locals, who wait for me to start eating in silent suspense, but my chopstick skills are pretty good, so they soon lose interest in watching me eat.

At yet another cloned tourist hotel we park the Wish Mobile next to the by-now-familiar luxury tour busses, and drag our bags into yet another cloned hotel room, where a short passage with built-in wardrobe leads past a spotless bathroom, equipped with all the bits and bobs one requires in that small room, into a huge room with twin beds in matt neutral shades and a view of a grey inner city. All rooms are equipped with desk, Internet connection, TV, bar fridge and kettle for tea. I cannot complain from a comfort point of view, but from a learning and adventure point of view, this succession of Western-style tourist hotels is as bland as porridge. Although, I am pleased to discover that not only is Genji funny, down to earth, and a good navigator, but she knows her bathroom etiquette, and I am no longer confronted with the horrible specter of strange hair all over the sanitary ware.

Another advantage of this unexpected guide change is that Genji has not had the time to be fully trained in what I may and may not do, so she is quite happy to avoid the expressway, allowing us to amble along country roads, where the late summer harvest is in full swing. Women stand chest high in fields of bright orange chrysanthemums that contrast sharply with their screaming pink headscarves. The corn harvest is complete, and the farmers stake their claim on the road with empty water bottles, before spreading their corn out to dry on the conveniently flat, dry and hot surface. Everybody meekly drives around these fragile barricades; even the kamikaze busses and trucks slow to a crawl, so to not disturb the farmers' drying corn. While the corn is drying, the corn stalks are also neatly cut, tied in bundles, and stacked to be stored as fodder for the cows. Everything gets used in China, every part of the plant; every piece of ground is under till, right up against every electrical pole, and under every pylon. Freshly shorn sheep graze between gravestones and on the narrow grassland at the road's edge. People go about their business on tractors and tuk-tuks. Grandfather drives his grandson to school on the crossbar of his bicycle. Private cars are hardly to be seen.

Abruptly the Zhanye oasis ends, and we are back in the desert. With their dense green fields, small dams and canals it is easy to forget that these isolated towns are surrounded by desert for hundreds of kilometers. A family gravesite makes a graphic black and red statement against the pale sand and the distant Longshou Shan Mountains. Genji explains that the elaborate little building with curling luck dragons on the roof that stands at the center of the gravesite is the spirit house for the ancestors, and the headstones fanning out on either side are arranged according to generations. The oldest generation is closest to the spirit house, with younger generations moving progressively away. The empty spaces in the formal arrangement are reserved for the granny or grandpa, who is still in the land of the living. There is a reassuring order about this: one day when your spirit floats into the ancestors' house, your body will be placed in its correct family position. And so all are arranged according to their station and your spirit is cosseted in the bosom of the family ... one hopes.

With expert navigation, Genji manages to keep us off the expressway. I like her more and more by the minute. Our road skims cities, where red trucks, pink busses and red tuk-tuks paint the air blue with carbon and diesel. The instant cities are Soviet ugly, function without form. In tiny dusty villages, where foreigners never come, I negotiate the Wish Mobile along roads that have deteriorated to potholed dust. People, still wearing the dark blue uniform of the Mao years, stop and stare; they call to friends, who appear from behind bright pink doors that lead into the dark interiors of small square shops with white tiled facades. A carved wooden arch, its delicate flowers and leaves now cracked and dry, seems extravagantly beautiful in the midst of the mundane. It is the imposing entrance to a collapsing mud-brick house, which will soon become another faceless white tiled square. In tiny side streets, houses hide behind high walls the pink doors surrounded by red tiles and Chinese blessings.

Running alongside the tiny road is a broken wall of mud.

'What's that?'

'The Great Wall of China,' is Genji's laconic reply.

'The great wall itself? Where are the watch towers, battlements, flying flags?'

Out here in the faraway desert, the Great Wall was constructed of mud, and only built high enough to hinder horses; it is not exactly a breathtaking sight. But in honor of the moment I stand up close, and put both hands on the 600-year-old wall; it is warm and rough. While I contemplate the age of the structure and the giant vision behind it, a slick silver-blue train hisses by. For brief moments I stand between the two faces of China. The train quickly vanishes over the far horizon as the wall slowly vanishes into the desert floor, and the tiny road stutters and jolts along the side of the expressway.

High above, cars and trucks roar by, ignoring the small villages for which the national road must once have been a source of income.

Today filling stations and stores stand abandoned, as the expressway makes no allowance for such small enterprise. Finally, the country road gets so bad that I reluctantly decide to get back on the expressway. The baffled tollgate keeper demands to see my papers, all my papers, and so my Chinese driver's license comes into play for the first time. But the gatekeeper refuses to believe their authenticity; she turns them over and over, holds them up to the light; will she actually call the police? But cool as a cucumber, Genji floors her with a lengthy yin yang yo, followed by a short stabbing ting tung to, until the gatekeeper admits defeat, and we are allowed back onto the expressway, which is the new Great Wall of China that separates the haves from the have-nots, the may from the may-not, most efficiently.

Bed 81,82

Route 312 turns south towards Lanzhou and, leaving the desert behind, the landscape gets gentler. The mountains turn from jagged dragon rock to round rolling loess. In a wide valley, a river sparkles through delicate green and yellow pastures. Bundles of grass, neatly stacked in cones, await their place in the enormous beehive-shaped haystacks that men with straw hats and women with bright pink headscarves work side by side in building. The late afternoon sun slides behind a veil of cloud, gilding the rural scene. The sand mountains are sparsely vegetated, and under a delicate lace of pale green, the deep rose-colored earth shines through, creating a surreal landscape that I would like to photograph, but there is still nowhere to stop on this over-sanitized road. 'Sanitized' is no exaggeration: the expressway is dotted with straw-hatted figures wielding giant twig brooms, their sole occupation being to sweep the road.

The loess mountains close in around Lanzhou. Their sensuous golden rose curves are accentuated by the pale sunlight, and by evenly spaced lines running horizontally across the mountains; it looks like the sky printer is running out of ink. On closer inspection, I see the mountains are terraced from top to bottom, and volunteers are planting baby trees as part of China's massive reforestation project. Kilometer after kilometer the mountains continue; kilometer after kilometer, tiny people move about on the high terraces, planting thousands and thousands of trees. The size of the project is frightening; the Chinese know how to think big.

In Lanzhou Genji informs me that the dish for which the city is famous, is beef noodle, but, as we had that for lunch in Wuwei, and life is too short to eat beef noodle twice a day, this evening we will eat pork belly. Yes, ma'am. I have learnt that Genji knows her food stuff, so am happy to go with the flow. In a small restaurant, the hostess leads us upstairs into a private room. Many restaurants in China have a public room and one or two private rooms. Those who believe they are very important – or those who do not want to be seen – eat in private rooms. The rabble eat in the public room. This evening Genji and I pretend we are very important people, and sit staring at each other in our bright yellow private room. Daft really, I would rather be checking out the masses in the public room. But when it comes to food, Genji is in charge. Soon the dishes arrive: a huge bowl of rice, various vegetables, steamed buns, tea, and just as I believe we will need a bigger table, if not room, the grand moment, braised pork belly. The air fills with the smell of cinnamon. Our bowls are set on small burners. Bite-sized squares of deep brown pork belly bubble in a caramelized sauce of sugar, soya, chilies, cinnamon and star aniseed. The pork is meltingly soft and so full of flavor I manage to forget that it is also full of saturated fats. Anybody with a cholesterol problem should not try this meal, although, when sinking my teeth into the richly flavored fat, it is so deeply satisfying that I change my mind, and decide that perhaps everybody should eat Mao Zedong's favorite dish at least once in their lives.

In Lanzhou, not just the food but the air is saturated and unhealthy. Lanzhou has played an important role in Chinese history for more than 2,000 years, and must once have been a small city in a beautiful fertile valley, surrounded by distant mountains. Today the city crowds right up to the edges of the unstable loess mountains. Looking out of the hotel window in the early morning, the city is only half there. The city's size, position, and the huge petro-chemical industries that surround it, have combined with actual low-lying clouds to pull the visibility horizon down to the 13th floor. Never get a hotel room too high up in a Chinese hotel; you seldom see anything other than yellow green smog. Genji is not impressed; a desert flower needs her daily dose of sunshine and brilliant blue sky.

In the breakfast room, we have the chance to eat the famous stretched noodles of Lanzhou after all. Two chefs conjure noodles out of lumps of dough, twisting stretching folding swinging, stretching folding twisting swinging. The resulting thin strands of noodle are dumped into boiling pots of beef broth, and when they float, are scooped into deep bowls. We slurp them up for breakfast, along with fiery chili vegetables. Well fed, we leave Lanzhou, which soon vanishes into its own pall of smog.

In deep rural Gansu Province, life is a struggle of man against mountain. The bare loess mountains are so unstable that they crack and calve like glaciers, dragging the valuable topsoil into useless rubble.

The farmers, desperate for arable land, cultivate every tiny plateau that still possesses its topsoil. Tracks wind up down around tortured sand cliffs, and through canyon mazes to high tiny fields that are florescent green islands on top of a grey-beige world. Everywhere there are signs warning the locals against the danger of this practice, but the need to earn a living drives them on. On a small hard-stamped clearing, a group of straw-hatted farmers winnow their crop of linseed. With beautiful wooden spades, two men throw the seeds high into the wind, releasing yellow clouds of chaff that rain small brown seeds. Women, wielding twig brooms, sweep the seeds into piles, before sifting them through hand-plaited reed scoops into large round baskets.

I have a little moment of inspiration, and decide to photograph the men through the flying chaff of the linseeds. The chaff gets in my eyes and onto the lens, and for all my trouble, I don't get a shot. But the crazy white woman, totally covered in linseed chaff, is too much for the small group; they lean on their spades and brooms, surrendering to their laughter.

The road climbs right to the top of the mountain and winds along the ridge. From here, the view is down onto a familiar picture-book China. Terraces are built in stacked curving patterns up and down the slopes of the loess mountains, creating sinuous graphics of muted browns, greens and yellows in the misty light. In the distance, farmers plough their terraced fields with oxen and wooden ploughs. But beasts of burden are rare; mainly their duties are assumed by people who drag their tiny carts, almost hidden under their harvest, along the incredibly busy roads.

Trucks and public busses race by within a hair's breadth of the people-powered trolleys. Here the speed of the German, the unbridled aggression of the Ukrainian, the unpredictability of the Transkei taxi driver, and the complete inability to drive of the Romanian, combined with a particularly Chinese disregard for any rule of the road, convince me that there is no worse driver in the world than the Chinese. The vehicles seem to be steered by kamikaze dropouts. The traffic is unspeakable: trucks; busses, three-wheelers, scooters, bicycles, hand-drawn carts and people, anything and everything goes. There is no animal road-kill on Chinese roads; here the road-kill is people. Hit-and-run accidents that leave dead and bleeding bodies lying in the road seem quite common, and the traffic just moves on by. Trucks and busses fall into ditches and over cliffs; cars collides with trees, pedestrians and bicycles.

The driving gets more and more abominable, as does the road. Finally, it collapses into a succession of muddy puddles, where dogs, chained to posts outside muddy hovels, bark and howl at the Wish Mobile. Open-pit coalmines create black rivers on the roadside, and send black trucks into the traffic. They burst onto the national road from narrow private roads without the smallest hesitation. There is a very bizarre and dangerous take on right turns in China. If a car is coming from the right, regardless of whether it is an intersection, a t-junction, a yield or a traffic light, the man turning right into the traffic flow believes he has complete right of way, and will complete his right turn without so much as a glance at the on-coming cars, or any thought of slowing down.

Nothing on China's roads can be taken for granted, other than the tollgate. The tollgates in China are as regular as the bell tolls, and they are taking an enormous toll on my budget. But while I am usually tolerant of these things, the tollgate of China is intolerable. Relentlessly they drag the money from my wallet; what it is used for is a mystery; it is not for maintaining the roads, that is certain. At every tollgate, the traffic piles into a dense, throbbing monster with greasy black breath and evil temper, while the red tuk-tuks slide through the busses and trucks like mosquitoes searching for a victim. The trucks howl their anger; their blaring horns fill the valleys and canyons, echoing off damp slate mountains. After each tollgate everybody wants to be first; at rage-filled speed the trucks and busses crunch gears and burn tires for position, the tuk-tuks dodge and dive, bicycle riders balance on the knife edge of destruction, but nobody gives an inch. They would rather die a squashed, blood-squirting, bone-splintering death than let anybody past. The Chinese have an unwavering faith in the little red rags they all tie onto their cars for luck. I don't believe in the red rags for an instant, and go into total avoidance mode. As far as I am concerned, the whole world can pass me by; we are not heading towards the same goals, anyway. I pull off, wait for the road to clear, then proceed in peace.

After a high mountain tunnel, the road winds down into a valley, where we cut through a tiny piece of Ningxhia Province. The ethic majority here are the Hui, who are very similar to the Uyghur. Hui women with pink headscarves sell red chilies next to magenta hollyhocks that grow wild by the roadside. On the high plateaus, perfect blushing pink apples are for sale. They are cold, crisp and juicy, with just the right combination of tang and sweet. In small ugly villages, huge piles of apples, fodder for the pigs, lie in the muddy streets, while on the trees, apples for export are nearly ready for harvest. Each apple has been wrapped in red paper as protection against the birds and elements. Cheap labor makes anything possible.

Pagodas and pavilions with curling red rooftops make fragile statements in the muted misty landscape. The buildings are now mainly of fired brick with only the occasional mud wall. All the rooftops are finished with intricately placed tiles set into a bed of mud and straw. At each end of the roof, a luck dragon guards over families that live in family compounds. These consist of a central house, to which smaller houses are added as the family grows, eventually creating a small private courtyard, which is entered through a beautifully carved door, decorated with blessings written on red cloth, and topped by an intricate multilayered, tiled and luck-dragon-decorated rooflet. There is so much to see and photograph that we are making hardly any headway. Then Genji joins in on the image hunt, and at this point we may as well bring out the camping gear. Physically we are getting nowhere, but my mind is expanding like a hot-air balloon.

Genji points out cave-like houses in the sandstone cliffs, called *yaodong*. These caves are one of China's oldest and most basic forms of shelter. Poor families dig an arched grotto out of the cliff, then build up the front wall to support a door and window. The cave is furnished with a raised platform, built of loess adobe, called a *kang*. The kang is used as a sleeping platform during the night, and as living space during the day. The slab of adobe is heated by a flue system that directs the heat from the cooking fire under the bed, heating the thick adobe platform, which retains its heat all night, resulting in an ancient – the first primitive kangs were used in the Neolithic age – form of under-floor heating. As the family's material wealth increases, they build rooms out from the original shelter. While different levels of wealth are already clearly to be seen in rural China, there are several things all the houses have in common. Because in the soggy highlands, the road is no longer a good place to dry corn, every rooftop, entrance arch and tree is festooned with bushels of drying corn and chilies, and every house has a huge pile of raw unwashed, unrefined coal in the courtyard. The individual pieces of coal are massive, and must probably be beaten to size with a sledgehammer before they can be used for heating and cooking. Looking at the mountains of coal in front of every house, the extreme level of pollution, even out in deep rural China, is hardly surprising.

I am a giant ! Food market; Zhanje

Xian – Shanghai

Bed 83

In Xian Yang City we stop at Great Buddhist Temple. In the courtyard, at a grey stone altar, decorated with luck dragons, red ribbons and bells, a father and son are burning wads and wads of yellow 'hell notes'. They light a multitude of pink joss sticks, and say long and earnest prayers. In China, money and Buddhism have a strong connection. They believe that if they burn hell bank notes or joss money in this world, their ancestors will receive the real thing in the afterworld. The question is: why do we insist on believing that the gods find valuable what we find valuable, and why, if we are progressing to a higher plane after death, do we need something as banal as money. Perhaps they do it because the exchange rate is so good. In this world, a few yuan buy huge wads of hell money, which, once it is converted into the real thing on the other side, must be worth a small fortune. They say you cannot take it with you, but perhaps, in your next lifetime, you can bring it back.

The centre of Xian is cowering under a blanket of smog, which is constantly reinforced by the crush of afternoon traffic, which pushes from all sides, but we are not stressed. In the last few days we have become a team. Genji is as cool as cucumber, and navigates with ease, as I slide the Wish Mobile through the traffic to the bell tower. Here six, seven or eight lanes of traffic roar, where there should be four, and the scooters make a couple more. Nobody indicates, everybody honks his or her horn, and no one is giving an inch. No problem. You can do anything on Chinese roads; just do not show fear. Without a moment's hesitation, I power into the flow, claim my rightful position, and pop out at our exit, first time round. It is going to take some doing to rattle me in traffic again.

At night, Xian hides its heavy cloak of smog, and puts on its party dress in a dazzling show of fairy lights that reflect in the wet streets. The warm drizzle is no restraint on the movement of the people that flow around the bell tower in a solid moving mass. For the first time I sense the huge population of China. In the walled city, people push and jostle to buy groceries and souvenirs, tiny restaurants line narrow alleys, and everyone is doing a brisk trade. I spy a very tall blond man with a Chinese girlfriend; she complains that people are staring at them. It is true; the Chinese stare, and they stare hard. In

China, the separation of Chinese and foreigners is very clear; a mix of the two is odd. Even my paring with Genji attracts stares, which she comments on, and finds uncomfortable. I am getting used to being stared at, as a tall white woman driving her own car in China. I am so out of place that I become a novelty attraction wherever I go.

Fortunately, in China the tourists will never outnumber the locals, so the concept of a tourist restaurant being different from a local one is rare. In the local dumpling house, Genji goes off to get the dumplings from the self-service counter, while I slide onto an open space on a long metal bench at a paper-covered table. The huge, brightly lit hall is pale yellow with steam, light and sound. Across the table, two young men in black, with black hair and eyes, stare at me curiously. To my left, two older men, in shirtsleeves and relaxed after-hour-ties, delicately lift soft dumplings from hard wicker baskets. A waitress arrives at my side, takes one look at me, and starts giggling uncontrollably. This sort of thing is very bad for one's self esteem. The older men speak English, and get the waitress to calm down by asking if I need help. How nice, but before I can reply, Genji arrives back and takes matters in hand.

I continue to have mixed feelings about this. On the one hand, having a guide makes life very easy; on the other, you don't push yourself. My Chinese has not progressed, and I just sit like a lump waiting for Genji to do her thing. In previous countries, where I was forced to make an effort, I was very quickly able to communicate with the locals. Although I have been doing Chinese lessons for about an hour a day, and my Chinese vocabulary has increased to include *ni hao* (hello) *duo shao qian* (how much), I want that one this one / that one *(Wo yoa zhege/ nage)* no *(bu)* thank you *(xiexei ah)*, *Wo bu dong* (I don't understand) and *Ni dong ma* (Do you understand) is about as much as I can manage. However, as my pronunciation is so abominable, no one understands me, and Genji is always at hand to sort out my queries before I have the time to correct what I am trying to say. So in this little comfort zone I don't really try as hard as necessity would force me to.

While this is running through my head, the young men across the table are sneaking pictures of me on their mobile phones. This is really getting out of hand. Now I know how the tribes of Africa must feel when overbearing European tourists photograph them like objects of interest and curiosity. I am now in the same situation, and I don't like it. Our dumplings arrive in stacked bamboo baskets. They are soft steaming little mounds of white dough that contain unknown fillings.

With the whole table watching, I attempt to eat my first dumpling with chopsticks. I am too fast, too rough; the dumpling sticks to the basket; it tears; I try to rescue the situation, but the slippery little thing sinks into a soggy ragged heap, bleeding sauce and strange filling into the weave of the basket. The men across the table stare in fascination, while I stare at the dumpling contents; what is that exactly? Genji is a tad embarrassed, and issues a curt command. Two waiters leap to my aid, one with a spoon, the other with knife and fork. But I have face to save; not just mine, but also Genji's. Learning from my previous error, I grasp the next dumpling so that no chopstick point can pierce the skin and gently loosen the delicate dough from the bamboo basket, then ever so elegantly place the whole thing in my mouth – thereby searing my tongue with the boiling hot filling, but with the men across the table still sneaking photographs, I will not lose face again. Turning an increasingly crimson shade of pink, I gently ease that blob of white lava down my throat. By dumpling number three I have my dumpling eating under control, and the masses get back to their own dumpling eating. Being under constant scrutiny is an exhausting business.

That was my last supper with Genji. This evening she hands me over to Ling, who will escort me all the way to Shanghai. As my guides have official business to attend to, I accept an invitation for drinks with the Chinese travel agent – Mr Wong – in the hotel foyer. Mr Wong is a smart young man who sets great store by his outward appearance. Leaning back on the plush sofa, he exhales a thin plume of cigarette smoke.

'Can I offer you a drink?'

'A Tsingtao. Thank you.'

After a few polite asides, the conversation quickly turns to my car and my plans in Shanghai. I briefly sketch my arrangements to store the car with the shipping company, and then to explore more of China before visiting Japan, and then, when I am ready, to ship the car to America.

After listening politely, he bluntly tells me that my travel plans will have to change, as my car must be off Chinese soil on 11 October. During my stunned silence, he takes the opportunity to light another cigarette.

'I was told that I may not drive my car in China after the 11th of October; no mention was made that it had to be off Chinese soil.'

'That is the situation.'

'But according to the travel schedule you arranged for   me,
I will only arrive in Shanghai on the afternoon of 11
October. Did you imagine I would have a cargo ship
waiting in the harbor for me to just drive onboard?'

He shrugs nonchalantly.

'That is not my problem.'

He is probably right, but conveniently forgets that he created the
problem, which my mind now spins around. After further questioning, I
discover that he has yet to send the shipping company the papers
needed to finalize the shipping of the vehicle into America. I imagine
that had he done so, someone would have noticed this problematic
detail. As it is, I will arrive in Shanghai in two weeks, and before the
shipping company receives the correct documents, no reservation for a
shipping container can be made.

'When will you send the papers to the shipping company
in Shanghai?'

'Your guide has them; she will deliver them by hand.'

What planet does this man come from? In his mind, I will arrive in
Shanghai in the late afternoon, process the shipping paper work in five
seconds, then drive directly onto a container ship just as it is pulling in
its last anchor lines. The Chinese have supreme confidence in their
efficiency; I on the other hand have my doubts.

'Mr Wong what will happen if my car is not off Chinese soil
on 11 October?'

'The car will be confiscated.'

'And then?'

'Scrapped.'

To prevent myself from flying across the table, and roughing up his
slick exterior, I take an unladylike swig of my drink, help myself to one
of his cigarettes, and after a long mind-numbing drag, calm down
sufficiently to use my voice.

'Mr Wong I am sure you will understand that your
arrangements are optimistic in the extreme and have placed
me in a very awkward position. I kindly request that you do
everything in your power to extend the vehicle visa to allow
my car to remain in storage in China for at least another
month. This would give me time to arrange for the

shipment of the car and to complete at least part of my travel plans.'

He shrugs, and I think to myself, if Mr Wong gives on more shrug, I will rip his shoulders right out of their sockets, but I smile and nod gratefully at his

'Ms Jahnel, I will do my best.'

I have absolutely no faith in that promise, and a wave of frustrated anger starts in my gut, threatening to drown my last shreds of calm. The Chinese seem to have a compulsion to withhold vital information.

To distract myself I wish Mr Wong good day, and go shopping for shoes. What kind of Pavlovian response is this? I don't have a thing for shoes, and I don't like shopping. But I have heard so often that shoe shopping makes people happy, that I am happy to try it too. There are hundreds of brightly lit shoe stores, their flashy advertising signs reflecting in the wet street. I scan the thousands of pairs on offer aimlessly, until out of sheer boredom, I choose a pair of sandals.

'*Wo yao zhege, sishiyi.*'

The assistant starts giggling; as this is a fairly normal reaction to my Mandarin, I wait until she gets a hold of herself. But she then repeats my question to her fellow assistants, and they start giggling. A severely styled lady – no bigger than Thumbelina – comes over to apologize for her employee's behavior, but regrets to tell me that the largest shoe size they know of is a size 38. They were not laughing at my Mandarin, but at my big Western feet. Now I feel like Coco the flipping clown. Shopping is a very stupid therapy. All it has managed to do is to give me a big foot complex.

In my hotel room, I attempt to let my frustration slide away as I slowly move through a Tai Chi exercise, but a knock on the door breaks the silence. If it is Genji, I know she is so polite, she will wait for me to reply, but the door bursts open, and a tall young woman enters with a purposeful stride. Whoa, who the hell are you, and who said you could enter the room? She invades my space, sticks out her hand, and gushes all over me.

'I am Ling. I have been so looking forward to meeting you. I am sure we will have a wonderful time together.'

Okay, I am glad you got that off your chest, now back away. But she hangs onto my hand, smiling sincerely. Looking over her shoulder, I catch Genji rolling her eyes, a tiny smile around her lips.

'Crikey, not another one.'

How did they select these girls: 'Guides needed for free trip through China; only the most sycophantic pro-government bossy women need apply.'

Then, without any preamble or long goodbyes, Genji takes her bag, saying she has a train to catch. No, no, stay stay, don't leave me alone with this woman, but just as suddenly as she appeared in my life, she vanishes, leaving behind a few days of memories. All the while Ling continues to hang onto my hand, while giving me tomorrow's schedule. We are off to see a pottery army, Xian's pride and joy. That's fine, whatever you say; just give me my hand back and leave.

The morning arrives cloaked in yellow grey fog or is it smog? I cannot quite decide. In a fuming traffic jam, I conclude that while there might be a small pinch of fog in the gassy stew, mainly what we are breathing this morning is smog. We are off to the eastern suburbs of Xian, where in 264 BCE a 13-year-old boy declared himself the first emperor of China, and decided to play war games. Keeping to the Chinese habit of thinking on a grand scale, he roped in the labor of 700,000 men, and built himself a life-size battlefield, with an estimated 8000 terracotta warriors, 130 chariots and 670 horses. Over the centuries, time played havoc with the emperor's game, and now the Chinese government is trying to put all the king's horses and all the king's men back together again. They have managed to rebuild 2,000 warriors from the ancient tomb, which was rediscovered by seven unfortunate peasants, whose reward was a few yuan, the destruction of their fields, and forcible removable of the inhabitants from the ancient Yang village.

The government moved in, built a hangar over the site, landscaped the surrounding countryside, ensured there was sufficient parking and an electronically activated pay gate, and with that, they had themselves a little tourist money-spinner. The locals get to partake in the money-making machine only as far as forging signatures in the official 'how it all came about' book, telling of the finding of the vast cultural treasure. Ling earnestly assures me that I am very lucky to see one of the actual seven men who found the first terracotta warrior. Apparently he is only here today because they are expecting a VIP group. Wrinkled and bad-tempered, Yang Zhifa sits on a raised chair in the crowded souvenir hall, signing books for hordes of tourists. When he sees a camera, he taps his desk impatiently: photography forbidden. Ling says he is a very wealthy man now. My dark and cynical side comes out in full force. I think he probably gets a pitiful salary to sit there, and the government takes the cream.

Later in my hotel room, I do a little surfing, and discover that I was right: the old chap sitting there earns less than the cashier. He signs books nine hours a day, every day, but as the government has bulldozed his village, robbed the villagers of their traditional homes, their fields and livelihood, the tourists better keep buying those books, as it now his only form of income.

The terracotta warrior complex is the kind of sightseeing I can do without; everything is laid out, spoon-fed, and regimented. Walk here, look for five minutes, move along, shoot your picture trophies, get on the bus, and leave. As I walk through the aircraft hangar of a hall, dodging masses of people, I get more and more irritated. Every scrap of history or soul there might have been has been swept away. I try to get some background information from Ling. This is her tour-guiding stomping ground, but she can offer no insights that are not printed on the official brochure. After half an hour of I don't knows, and having to endure the idiot's guide to touring, during which Ling shares such information gems as

'That is a terracotta horse that has not yet been repaired,'

while pointing into a hole in the ground, containing a pottery horse head, and various other bits of horse anatomy, my irritation levels get out of hand.

'Ling, we are leaving.'

'But there is still much to see.'

'Tough, I'll catch it on TV.'

In the parking lot, a man leaps in front of the Wish Mobile. His tour was obviously as bad as mine, but why does he feel the need to commit hari-kari in front of my car? Perhaps he can sense that in my current state it would give me immense satisfaction to mow him down, but calm, calm, ohmmmm … I tweak the steering to the left. He jumps to the left as well; either he really wants to die or he really wants me to stop. I opt for the latter explanation, and discover he is a German tourist who is blown away by seeing a car with a German number plate in China. All his friends share his amazement, and the chat-laugh-point gathering around the Wish Mobile attracts other tourists of various nationalities. To make use of all the available men, I start handing out black marker pens, and so a great writing of world wishes ensues. Tourists smile shake hands bow nod smile, and the Wish Mobile racks up another brownie point for tolerance and global understanding. Totally not what I am feeling, so Ling takes the safe route of staying with her family for the night, her dream of a glamorous road trip through China well and truly popped. I spend the evening giving myself a stern talking to:

Annette, you are being a right brat; behave already.

I blame it all on the weather.   Somewhere out there the sun is probably shining in a clear blue sky, but down here in central China, the smog pushes at me from all sides. The dead air is hot, still, and smells like I don't really want it in my lungs. I turn the air conditioner on full blast, and pretend it is a giant air filter, but know that in reality I am just breathing well-chilled smog. The national road makes its battered, honking, kamikaze way through charmless villages, where coal-streaked hovels crowd the oily mud pavements. Smoking chimneystacks spew rolling clouds of yellow, brown and black into the potent brew that passes for air in these parts. For the entire 626 km from Xian to Pingyao, China remains hidden behind a wall of smog. There is nothing to be seen, nothing to be photographed, and nothing to be learnt, except that Ling has a weak bladder, and requests that I stop at every second village.

Over the months my bladder has been well trained, and normally only requires my attention twice a day. As I have nothing better to do, I investigate the local ablutions. In highway rest stops, rows and rows of squat toilets are set on steel grid floors, so even if you overshoot the mark, the floor stays relatively clean. This is helped by the flushing system, which flushes not just the bowl, but also the floor underneath the grid. After familiarizing myself with the foot-pedal flush system, I look around, and without any effort, observe the goings-on in the cubicles beside me. The dividing walls are only built Chinese-lady high, and make no allowance for six foot tall women. The need for total privacy when on the toilet seems to be a very Western thing. This is confirmed at the next rest stop in a tiny village; here the ablutions have been reduced to a wall shielding an open-fronted concrete structure, with a brutally functional floor. A slab of concrete, with two large round holes, floats above two enormous piles of sunlit shit. One look sends me into hasty retreat; I will wait for the next rest stop. But with the shock of it all my bladder shrinks, and now I have no choice, I need to go. Under different circumstances, I would have opted for a roadside squatting session, but in this part of China this is difficult, as there are people lurking behind every bush, tree and tuft of grass.

While I pluck up the courage to re-enter the stinky grey cell, I run through ways of reducing the time I will need to spend in there. Loosening my belt and zip before entering will shave off a few seconds, but that is about all I can think of doing. Taking a deep breath and holding my nose, I step into the smell, my eyes fixed on the walls, the ceiling, anything but the holey floor. With my free hand, I yank at my jeans. Quick quick shuffle over the hole, which is far too big for comfort; if I lose my balance, it will be very, very unpleasant. Then my bladder takes revenge on all the steely control I have subjected it to over these past few months, and opts for the slow vent option. As my bladder dribbles through its function, the warm wind of moldering feces blows through my hair; my lungs are bursting; my thighs are burning and starting to shake; soon I won't have the strength to straighten up. I will not breathe, I will not breathe … if I don't breathe soon, I will faint, and fall bum first into a pile of pooh. When this little thought reaches my bladder, it decides it has made its point, empties in one quick flush, and, jeans around my knees, I hop to the shielding wall, stick my head into the outside air, and gratefully suck huge quantities of yellow smog into my lungs.

While this is not the most pleasant toilet experience I have ever had, it highlights the difference in attitude to a perfectly natural substance that we all – if we are lucky – have to deal with once a day. In rural areas the human waste is seen as a valuable and constantly renewable source of manure, and the people are part of the natural cycle, while in the West with our wasteful flush toilets, human waste is an unspeakable subject to be flushed away to never-never land as quickly as possible.

Bed 84

After a long day of potty training we arrive in Pingyao, as the ill light of day oozes into the never-dark night. The walled city of Pingyao is a slice of old China, dating from the Qing and Ming dynasties. Although normally only residents may drive their cars into the walled city, the Wish Mobile is granted special entry. As we drive under the arch of the Lower Western Gate, modern China slips into a hazy memory. Warm light spills onto pale flagstones from ornate wood-screened windows. Red lanterns make splashes of brilliant color against ancient walls, stained black by centuries of coal soot. The Wish Mobile finds a resting spot in a shabby, 600-year-old courtyard. We walk past small restaurants and mysterious Siheyuan, hidden behind ancient carved doors. Our hotel for the night is a Hui Yuan folk custom guesthouse with traditional rooms decorated with dark wood carved furniture. In a corner niche, a brick kang covered in tamtami and multiple red satin pillows is supplied with an intricately carved short-legged table where, cross-legged, I take tea served in delicate blue and white porcelain.

In anticipation of beautiful subject matter for photography, I am out at dawn. Already the smog pulls a soft focus filter over long dark alleys that end in small courtyards, where bicycles rest against coal-black walls. Snarling stone door-gods guard heavy wooden doors, pasted with red and gold blessings. A bent old lady sweeps her courtyard with a twig broom, while a man gingerly steers his bright yellow earthmoving machine through the narrow grey streets. An early morning baker is hard at work producing small round flat breads. His bakery is against a blackened alley wall, his worktable a slab of concrete resting on a pile of bricks. Here he rolls out small balls of dough; the rounds of dough are pressed onto a wooden mould that imprints a symbolic blessing into the soft bread. The breads are baked on an iron griddle resting on an oven that looks like an oversized champagne cork. An empty 50-gallon drum with a fire in the bottom has a bulbous mud top, which spreads and retains the heat. Once the flat breads are golden brown, they are beautifully arranged in his hand-drawn trolley. With the trolley full, he joins the growing stream of early morning hawkers, leaving the baking station to the next vendor. An egg-seller shouts her wares; restaurant and guesthouse owners step out to buy fresh eggs for breakfast.

On street corners. impromptu markets form: squawking chickens are fished out of deep wicker baskets; yams and onions tumbled onto woven reed mats. Nothing is bought or sold without loud haggling and finger wagging; prices fly up and down, until everybody is satisfied, and the yam is sold. On the sidewalk, a shop owner displays her wares on a grey cement slab. Maize is poured into a large pewter dish, forming a yellow pyramid pile. A white sack has its neck rolled back to show off green dried beans. A tin dish is filled with a tumble of small brown ceramic bowls. Eggs and flour fill cast-iron pots. Bicycle bells warn me to step out of the way of commuters rushing to work. Restaurants set out menus promising full English breakfasts. The thought of buttered toast and tea with milk and sugar lures exhausted tourists longing for the small comforts of home. Every morning during hotel breakfasts, English tourists complain about the lack of sugar, milk, butter and toast, while German tourists complain about the lack of coffee, decent crispy buns, butter, and wouldn't it be nice to have a slice of cheese.

As the sun struggles to cast shadows through the smog, dust-kicking children in bright neon sweaters and sneakers dawdle to school under the Yamen Street *paifang*. The paifang is an enormous five-pillared arch, with double sweeping yellow and turquoise ceramic tiled roofs that balance on thick red cross-beams, which swarm with carved deer, bats and tortoise, while brilliantly painted water lilies, peonies and lotus flowers curl around blessings stamped in gold. In Southern Main Street, hundreds of souvenir shops open their doors, and, under a vanishing perspective of sweeping grey tiled rooftops and dangling red lanterns, set out jade, silver and copper Buddhas. Ivory chopsticks and ancient calligraphy pens jut from carved wooden vessels. Large green crickets chirp in very small ornate cages. Boxes of jade hold pornographic mahjong sets. Bows and arrows hang across tiger skins. And right here my credulity runs dry: the skins have to be fake. Actually, I don't believe any of it. Everything looks like it comes from the Ming dynasty, but as the bulk of China's cultural heritage was taken to Taiwan to save it from the clean sweep of the Cultural Revolution, who knows where all these artifacts are coming from. Judging by the price and the fact that the Chinese are excellent forgers, I am sure that not one thing here is older than last season. No matter, they look the part, so I haggle for three 'ancient' calligraphy brushes.

By eleven, the tourist industry of China shows its muscle. Italy is small potatoes compared to this. The Chinese do not like traveling alone, or without guidance. Enormous cap-wearing groups, led by tour guides that spew information over loud portable public announcement systems, squash into tiny courtyards. In one courtyard, three groups converge; no tour guide gives an inch. Chinese is a sharp language, which the tinny public announcement systems hone to samurai blades. The guides demand to be heard. With the barbs and stabs of a thousand small words, they slice and slash at the silence. It floats away like silver confetti. I flee the noise to the street, where I become an expert tour-group spotter, and time my entrances into old courtyards just as one tour group leaves, and before the next group arrives.

In empty black-walled courtyards, white doves with silence in their wings flutter down to admire their reflections in water-filled ceramic pots. Windows covered with paper screens allow soft light to fill the small rooms furnished with delicately carved chairs, inlaid with flowers made of mother of pearl and jade. The brick and mortar kangs in every room are heated by the cooking stove built next to them, and have space enough to hold a large wardrobe with a special drawer, where the tamtami is stored in the morning. Technically one need never move from the comfort of the kang.

I imagine a cross-legged old man with wispy beard writing poems in flowing calligraphy at the low table, which is placed by the window during the day. Respectful granddaughter enters on small feet to pour tea that is heated by the kang stove. When grandfather complains that the room is cold, she bends, and adds another piece of coal to the fire. Outside, verandas lit by red lanterns, lead around the courtyard to stone stairs, carved with dragons and godheads, which lead to the top floors from where the roofscape of Pingyao is a curling sea of grey tiles, in which floats one bright yellow roof of an imperial residence. Three colors dominate in Pingyao: red for luck, gold for prosperity, and black, which is said to encourage the gods to descend to earth.

Against the grey-black walls, even the red fire spades and red sand buckets make perfect camera fodder. Just like me. For the Chinese I seem to be a tourist attraction on the move. I discover that I can tell – even from a distance – when I am being photographed. This confirms my theory that to take someone's picture without permission is an invasion of privacy, no matter if the person is in a public space. To take revenge, I slip into tit-for-tat mode, and start pointing my camera at all and sundry. Climbing onto the city wall at the South Gate, I make my way westwards, peering into the private backyards as I pass. Seeing a woman sitting on a small chair watching her rhubarb grow, I snap away merrily, until she leans forward, picks up a stone, and hurls it at me. Serves me right. Then a tall good-looking young Chinese man walks over, and introduces himself with a hesitant.

'I enjoy you; may we have photo together?'

Put that way, I cannot resist, and smile nicely for the camera.

Bed 85

Waking to another day of smog, I remember reading that there is a saying in China that

'when a man smells pollution he smells money,'

but they don't want to face the horrible truth that in China pollution is fast replacing the oxygen, and without oxygen, money is of no use at all, so the weather forecasters call the smog 'fog'. A hot fog Sunday pulls a grey veil over ugly chimneystack town after ugly chimneystack town, and all the countryside in between. I now understand why those folk on top of the sand dune in Dunhuang were so keen to see the rising sun. It might have been the first time in their lives that they saw the sun so clearly, and the sky so blue. The Chinese skipped the fun part of capitalism, and went straight from suppression to depression. China's rush to play catch-up with the West has left their air stronger than a cheap cigar, and a large percentage of the water so polluted, even the factories can't use it.

Capitalism may have lifted millions of Chinese out of poverty, but has left a billion more behind, and has robbed them of clean air and water. Scientists estimate that if by 2025 China hasn't made an ecological u-turn, 350 million Chinese will become ecological refugees. Where will they flee to? Perhaps this is why the Chinese are already preparing Africa with new infrastructure and roads; it's for the expected millions who will have to flee their ruined ecology. While the concept of ecological refugees is a very modern one, it is not the only reason China is looking to Africa. One of the cornerstones of capitalism is the need to exploit the labor of others. To get the millions of Chinese that are still Africa-poor out of poverty, the capitalist system demands that the Chinese find a source of labor cheaper than their own. Considering that the Chinese thirst for money has catapulted their homeland into an Armageddon future, where people must pay to see the sunrise, I wonder what they will do to a country to which they feel no bond.

As we make our way north to Beijing, we stop in Yinxian to view the pagoda of the Fugong Temple. Built in the early 10th century, it is the largest, oldest wooden pagoda in China, and therefore, I would imagine, in the world. But first I need to get hold of Mr Wong to see what has been done about extending the car visa. Trawling the dusty streets for an Internet café, I have the chance to try out my Mandarin on the unsuspecting locals. I politely ask a man on a street corner.

'Ni hao, wam ba zai nar?'

The man glances at me, then moves away quickly.

The intonation of these small words is very important. Just by going up, instead of down on the vowels I might well have been saying that his mother is a cat.

I try several variations of pronunciation on the people I pass.

'Wam Ba zAi nar.'

Blank stare.

'WAm ba zai nAr.'

Silly giggles.

'Wam bA zAI nar.'

Silent suspicion.

This is like trying to crack a safe.

In a modern jewelry store, I finally manage to get my pronunciation to such a point that I literally see the lights go on in the woman's eyes. She immediately changes from suspicious to friendly – the tiniest language connection will do that – and instructs her shop assistant to guide me down a dark alley and up some smelly stairs to the nearest Internet joint. Once inside, the filth of the place hits like a sledgehammer: the air is blue, and the floor covered in ash, cigarette butts and spit. I would preferably be wearing surgical gloves to touch the keyboards and Skyping with those headphones, unthinkable. However, there is no email from Mr Wong, so I will have to brave the telephone after all. Digging out some paper hankies, I cover the phone as best I can. A quick conversation tells me everything I don't want to hear. Mr Wong's solution to my timing problem has been to shorten my trip by two days. He has informed Ling about this, and she was to inform me in due course. I succumb to a great wave of rage, which I surf back to the pagoda to confront my inscrutably smiling guide.

'Oh, yes. Mr Wong spoke to me yesterday, but I did not want to upset you.'

To work off some steam, I rage up and down the famous pagoda, Ling keeps a safe distance as I stomp here, storm there, and generally behave like a bull in a China pagoda. Tall buildings in China – where architecture emphasizes width rather than height – are rare, and the Fugong Pagoda with its fancy joinery that uses no nails or glue is apparently a woodworking wonder. Pity then that I am just not feeling very handyman right now, and refuse to be impressed, although the quaint English signs always manage to cheer me up. Here a sign warns,

'No Smoking. A small match may destroy a thousand-year-old Pagoda.'

This is so much more effective than the common – no smoking, fire hazard – warning. The Chinese have taken the rather abrupt command – do not litter – to an elevated realm

> 'We salute the tourist who continuously safeguards the public hygiene.'

There is grandeur about this – 'we salute' implies reward, while 'safeguard the public hygiene' implies heroic deed. By not littering, you are rewarded by salute for your heroic deed. The poetic

> 'the civilized and tidy circumstance is a kind of enjoyment',

as opposed to a fairly banal 'no spitting', makes me want learn to speak Chinese. Do they always speak in little poems? Although when expressway signs warn that;

> 'It is forbid to chuck jetsam.'

I wonder why the Chinese bureaucracy does not have their signs written by a native English speaker.

Despite all the signs warning not to spit, smoke and litter, litter is not the problem in China. Everything that can be recycled is collected and sold, not for any ecological reason, but because any way of making money is quickly adopted here. Someone urgently needs to devise a profitable way to extract the chemicals from the air and rivers of China, then China will be as clean as a German Wurst factory in a quick slurp of a beef noodle.

But until that day comes, there seems to be absolutely no restriction on air pollution, and the smog is persistent. I have seen nothing of the countryside for days, and am getting more and more irritable and edgy by the hour. This is not helped by Ling's refusal to negotiate off the expressway. If I am going to see any part of China that has not been decided for me, I will have to take matters into my own hands, and so start leaving the expressway at random off-ramps. Ling frantically scrabbles around for her map to find out just where we are, before SMSing our position to her HQ. There is not much more she can do; she is not about to karate chop me while we are traveling at 80 km/h in the middle of nowhere. On my map I notice that the Great Wall of China runs through the city of Zhangjiakou , and that's where I am heading; Ling will just have to tag along.

The country road takes us up out of the smog planes and into the sunshine. Giant willows, their roadside branches crew-cut, line the country road. For kilometers we drive through a rippling pale-green tunnel, where dried willow leaves float around the car like exotic snowflakes. The road passes small villages, where the houses are made of adobe like those in Northwestern China, but here donkeys, not people, do the donkeywork. The late summer harvest is being brought in; dried corn, beaten from the cob, is spread onto a circle of sun-baked soil, then ground with a human-powered grinding stone, which looks like a wheelbarrow constructed of three sturdy branches with an enormous round stone as the wheel.

Just outside Zangjiakou, we cross an invisible time zone, and drive into the 21st century. Zangjiakou is a bright modern city where glass high-rises reflect the river that runs through the city. Our road takes us into the backstreets of the old town, where we drive back into the 19th century; China is a place of many ages. The road leads under an arch of the Great Wall, which marches through towns, over hills and through dales on its steadfast way east and west. It is big wide brown-brick high, but what was once a formidable barrier cannot keep the Chinese 'safe' from the 'enemy' today. Today the wall that keeps China 'safe' from the world is an invisible wall that floats in virtual reality.

While keeping the Chinese 'safe' from the information age is topmost on the government's agenda, safety is not a concept that is taught in Chinese driving school. Judging by the way Chinese drive, they observe only three rules of the road:

1. He who is first is right.
2. Don't hit anything.
3. Don't let anything hit you.

Once you have memorized these, go to the nearest shop, buy a little red ribbon, tie it to your car, and that's it; you go drive, boy. This lack of driving training is reflected on the expressway to Beijing. Here the driving has become so aggressive and recklessly dangerous that it is a supreme test of concentration and intuition. My world shrinks to my windscreen; I switch over to virtual reality mode, and treat the expressway like a high-speed video game. Cars dodge and weave, no one indicates, no one slows down, no one cares if they live or die. Ever adaptable, I join right in … from a distance I judge the spaces separating the trucks, I guess their speed, and, hoping they will stay in the lanes that they currently occupy, check the cars coming up from behind, try to divine their next move, gear down, hit the gas, and zigzag my way past a blue truck carrying pink pigs, and dodge a fuel truck, as it swerves to avoid the BMW that shoots into the traffic from the emergency lane, I zip left through an opening, past a truck carrying cows (do they even bother with slaughter houses here or do they just give the animals collective heart failure on the highway). I try to overtake a chicken truck on the right, but a faster car has squeezed between the truck and the barricade on the left, and fills the gap I was aiming for. Brakes. Drat. Stuck. I sneak a glance at Ling. She is an interesting shade of green. I had better slow down; getting the smell of upchuck out of anything is almost impossible.

While wondering about Ling's stomach contents, I do not notice that the traffic composition has changed, until a man leaps into the road; the Chinese are amazingly harry-casual about their lives. He waves me down. Have I broken some traffic law? Probably, but why stop me, when there are hundreds of other cars on the road? Then I notice that there are no cars on the expressway; there are hundreds of trucks, but no cars. I stop reluctantly. Ling heaves a sigh of relief, takes a moment to gather herself, before she and the suicide wannabe have a little natter on the roadside. Getting back into the car, she informs me we must turn around.

'We are on the expressway, Ling; common sense dictates that one does not just turn around and drive into the oncoming traffic.'

'The man says we must turn around.'

This is like pulling teeth.

'Ling, I will not drive into the oncoming traffic without a very good reason. Why must we turn?'

'The highway is closed ahead.'

'But there are still trucks driving by'

'Only trucks drive here as they must be weighed before entering Beijing. We should have gone into the slipway about five kilometers back.'

And then I see it, another lane of traffic behind a high barricade, which is where all the cars have gone, and that is where we need to be. The only way to do this is to turn around. This is going to be fun. With its hazards flashing, I head the Wish Mobile upstream and play chicken with the oncoming trucks. Fortunately, when everybody drives without any regard to the rules of the road, everybody expects the worst, so everybody is on full alert and fully focused. The trucks are not at all fazed by my approach, and without a hoot or a touch of the brakes just flow around me. By the time we reach the start of the slipstream, where traffic officials prefer to sit about smoking, as opposed to directing the traffic, I am as green as Ling. But, turning was a good call. The trucks are in a twenty-kilometer queue. Had we landed in that, we would not have reached Beijing for days.

Bed 86

As it is, we hit Beijing in the rush hour and Ling once again, despite my insistence, begging, nagging, pleading, did not bother to get turn-by-turn directions to the hotel. We are guessing our way into a city of 12 million inhabitants. I must say Ling is very self-assured. I just wish she would go and be self-assured somewhere else. One hour of chaotic traffic later, and Ling is still not admitting she has no idea where we are. I consider punching her in the nose, but drive into a car that is parked in the middle of the road instead. The driver leaps out of his vehicle, looking about to have heart failure, so I stop to assess the damage. The tiniest bit of my black bumper plastic has rubbed off on his black bumper plastic. It is not an exact match, and he starts insisting I must pay for the damage. What damage? Don't mess with me, little man. I lost my sense of humor at the wrong highway exit an hour ago, so you can ying yang yo, chin chong cha at super-volume as long as you like. I am not impressed, I don't understand a word, and Ling is not getting involved; chicken.

Well, in that case I'll just have to get this off my chest in English.

> 'Listen, mate. If you had not chosen to turn this lane of traffic into your very own parking spot, the accident would never have happened, but if you feel truly wronged, here's the card of my insurance agent in Germany. Why don't you just give them a call. They are sure to sort you out. Now if you will excuse me, I have a hotel to find.'

Two hours later, daylight turns to flashing neon light in inner-city Beijing, where twelve lanes of traffic are all full to capacity, but moving at top speed. Anywhere else on the planet, this would have been logjam, but the Chinese disregard for any little civility, and their absolute focus on being first seems to work in rush-hour traffic. In Beijing, rush-hour traffic is not a misnomer; the crush of traffic is in a hell of a hurry. But I have had it with fighting with the traffic; it's been hours; it is time to force Ling to admit she has no idea where we are. I kick her out of the car, and tell her to get a taxi to take us to the hotel. In the raging traffic, trying to get a taxi is not as easy as it might seem. After twenty minutes she manages to pull up a cab. She gets in; he roars off. Hey, wait up! I am meant to be following you.

In this pandemonium, following anything, let alone a green taxi that is weaving at top speed through a thousand green taxi clones, is no simple matter. Cars and taxis weave and plait across the road. I drive right up my taxi's butt. Leaving even the smallest gap is an open invitation for someone to muscle in. There is always a faster lane, a little gap, and no opportunity to get ahead is left untested. My concentration slips, a different green taxi bulldozes into a split-second gap. I push-push for speed, blend to the left, ease to the right, dodging the traffic from all sides to keep the right taxi in my sights. I have memorized his number plates, but if I lose him now, I will never find Ling again ... hmmm, there's a thought. After another hour of intense concentration I collapse, grinning, onto my tourist clone hotel bed; what a rush.

Before big events, Beijing spring-cleans the sky by seeding the clouds to ensure rain and clear blue skies for half a day or so. As China is preparing for this weekend's National Day festivities, a blue sky is obligatory, in order to induce feelings of wellbeing and patriotism in the flag-waving masses. The big blue sky does the trick for me; my mood brightens; and the thick smog soup of the past week is instantly forgotten. It is time to see the 'no-longer-Forbidden-to-anyone-who-can-pay City'. Our route leads us through narrow twisting streets under untidy electrical poles, where hundreds of cables loop from shabby building to shabby building. Washing hangs in every available space, while children play in grey alleyways, and parents sit on pavements, chatting over a morning cigarette. Bead curtains shield mysterious shops and tiny eating-houses. The neighborhood road joins a large pedestrian walkway, where steamed dumplings are sold by one-man operations, small family-run eateries or highly stylized establishments. Depending on where you eat your dumpling, the price ranges from ridiculously cheap to ridiculously expensive.

An elaborate doorway draws my attention. Thinking it might be a temple, I peer inside. Behind the traditional façade is a gleaming, air-conditioned temple to health. The high priests here are white-coated consultants who are expert in diagnostics and the prescription and preparation of the correct remedy for any ailment. The four-storey department store stocks every exotic natural medicine in the ancient art of Chinese healing. The shelves are packed with swallows' nests in beautiful boxes. There are shark fins and turtle bits, various insects, a variety of pupae and worms. There are whole snakes in bottles and powdered ones in pills. Dried lizard, ground lizard, frogs' feet and

1,000-year-old eggs. Plant materials are displayed like sweets in glass-fronted shelves. There are seeds and flower oils, leaves and bits of bark and at the top of the medicinal pile must be the wrinkly ginseng root in a red velvet box at 280,000 RMB for a fair sized root and 28,000 RMB for a small one. Will we pay anything, do anything, to stop the wasting of our flesh?

Past the Beijing Metro Station, we approach Tian'anmen Square. The square is a vast empty space that one has to cross to get to the Forbidden City. We are swept along by the holiday happy crowd, vanish into the subway under Dongchang'an road, and pop out the other side just under the great wall of the Forbidden City. The city is red and yellow, turquoise and blue, with lashings of gold leaf and flowers, dancing dragons, ferocious lions, and thousands of evil eyes to ward off the bad spirits. The deep yellow rooftops stretch themselves luxuriously over 9,999.5 rooms; one half a room short of the mythological 10,000 rooms of heaven. The monumental palace complex swallows the crowds into its multitude squares and courtyards, which range from immense ten thousand people size to small private spaces, where once the 'back palace three thousand' amused themselves under deep shade verandas, watching koi roll and curl in clear ponds, while waiting for the duty call from their imperial master. I am guessing the call never came for most of them: to pleasure all those concubines, the emperors of the Qing dynasty would have done little more than have sex all day, every day. An exhausting business, I would think. Even just walking through the vast pavilions of the Forbidden City is exhausting. I manage about 20 rooms, then decide it is time for tea.

This is a good thing, as I have a tea date this afternoon with 5W Françoise, whom, of course, I have never met, but I am looking forward to chatting to someone other than my delightful Chinese guard. Françoise owns a coffee shop in the diplomatic quarter of Beijing, and getting there involves taking the metro. The Beijing metro line is circular and very easy to negotiate, but then I need to take a bus, and busses are always a bit more complicated. I cannot recognize the names of the bus stops, so the bus driver and all the surrounding passengers get involved. It turns into a public debate, but in the end, the kind folk manage to get me off at the right point.

The diplomatic quarter is the side of China that the Chinese government loves to show off. Sleek boutiques, modern coffee shops, and elegant restaurants line neat pavements dotted with potted trees. Stylish men and women, displaying designer bags and perfect hairstyles, hurry to their next appointment or dawdle over cocktails, while sleek new sedans purr quietly in the traffic jam. On a leafy pavement at a traditional Parisian café table, Françoise and I pretend we are old mates, and chat about this and that over a cup of Earl Grey tea and a hip-sticking slice of carrot cake, with actual sugary creamy icing. Refined sugar is a rare commodity in China; sweet things are most often made from sweet vegetables, which is a very good thing, but even this advantage the Chinese are throwing to the four winds in their great rush to be just like us. As I munch my way through the delicious sugary – pretending to be healthy – treat, I learn that Françoise came to Beijing on a language scholarship, met the man of her dreams, and never left. They travel to Inner Mongolia for their annual vacations, where they enjoy the vast prairie, the sand dunes and the sunsets.

The sun is also setting over Beijing, and if I am ever to find my way back to my hotel, I had better leave before all the buildings turn on their night-lights, and Beijing performs the Asian Cinderella trick that every city here seems to have mastered. The strings of tiny lights that outline every significant building make magic of even the dreariest of daytime streets. They also unfortunately make nonsense of all the landmarks that I have memorized. I lose my way in the Qianshi Hutong, which lies between the metro and my hotel. It is the only hutong in Beijing that twists and turns, and trying my luck with the narrow twisting streets in the dark would not be wise, so I retrace my steps to the main flow of pedestrians. I will just walk straight ahead; at some point, I will have to make a direction decision, but for now I enjoy the spectacle of the citizens of Beijing out in the streets, eating, eating, eating. China is all about food. The pedestrian road ends at a t-junction; shall I run left or right? Best to ask. I wave my hotel card in front of several people, but in a city the size of Beijing, many people live their whole lives only in their own neighborhoods, and are of no help. I consider hailing a taxi, but am aware it could become a very expensive involuntary trip through outer Beijing. I will first try again in a music store. Musicians are international folk, and perhaps I will find help here, and I do. In perfect English, a charming young man directs me to my hotel.

Morning comes, bringing with it a dense layer of smog. But no time to complain and no official tourist sights, today I want to see the unofficial side of Beijing. North of the Forbidden City, on the sidewalk of a busy street we come across Saturday morning mahjong players. The low tables take up the whole sidewalk, and stretch into the distance, interrupted every now and then by small stalls offering sidewalk haircuts, shaves or foot massage. In front of a temple, young men show off their kite-flying techniques, while under us the traffic roars through inner-city highways, lined by formal rose gardens.

I point at a road on the map; that's the one we will walk down. It turns out to be a building site on the remains of one of Beijing's old hutong neighborhoods. Here families lived for generations, until they were forced to make way for more Dutch- and Australian-designed skyscrapers. Like everywhere else in the world, the poor are pushed about, but where should they go? So the people live in the rubble and ruins of their homes. On the banks of an evil-looking river, shirtless men play mahjong on tatty boards; upside-down drums act as tables to backless chairs. Children hang onto mothers' hips, their little bottoms hanging out of the split-back trousers all children of potty training age wear in China. Very practical: mommy, mommy, I need to make a number one. Split the pants and away you go, no fiddle, no fuss. On the narrow sidewalk women wash their hair, clothes and dishes in tiny plastic bowls. A mother and her two children live and work in a sidewalk space that is no wider than a passage behind a roller door. She sells bags of flour during the day; at night the bags of flour are the family bed. Nobody hits me for change; Ling says it is illegal to beg in China. A man with a pedal-powered trolley sells punched circles of pressed coal that fit the small coal braziers, which are used to prepare lunch, heat water, steam dumplings, and fry bread sticks. All living here is done on the street; the exhaust fumes are eye watering, but life goes on in its fashion in this dying corner of Beijing.

On the expressway, trucks and cars rule, but here anything goes, in an unbroken fuming torrent; cars, busses, green taxis, three-wheeler taxis, pedal taxis, manpowered carts, bicycles and scooters roar past. The side road empties its traffic load into Di'anmen Xidajie, where the traffic makes no allowance for pedestrians. Giving pedestrians the right of way seems to be a criminal offense in China; it might slow down the economy; can't have that. Amid the teeming traffic, the fumes, the noise, and the clamor, a man in a black suit and well-polished shoes squats in front of large sheets of white paper spread on the pavement. He is a calligrapher, and as his clients look on, he, with gracious flowing strokes, slowly paints the requested message in deep black ink on snow-white paper.

Through a circular moon gate, we step out of the grey stinking traffic into a gentle green world. In the enormous Beihai Park, willows sway gently to the sound of soft calming music, piped through speakers along the walkway around a manmade lake. Immense paifang span ponds, where a mother and daughter throw breadcrumbs to the swirling koi, creating a living kaleidoscope that draws golden orange patterns through the deep green water. A stone arch through a red wall frames a tango lesson where, to dramatic rhythm, women dance with the morning breeze. Further along, practitioners of Tai Chi move in slow motion, waving hands in clouds, and grasping tigers by the tail, while a martial arts teacher shows high kicks to his admiring students. In the distance, a merry twirl of dancers spin and skip under the willows to a rollicking polka beat. With an oversized brush, an old man with wispy beard writes Chinese poems with water on the grey slate paving. As the characters evaporate, he writes again, ever-changing, ever-vanishing, incomprehensible, beautiful words.

A slow boat take us to White Pagoda Island, from where we make our way through the East Gate and onto a pedestrian shopping street. All the brands are here: KFC, McD, the Fabianis and Guccis have all staked their claim in this booming city. I could be anywhere in the world, were it not for the Chinese writing, and the mini Chinese flags that everybody is carrying to commemorate tomorrow's Chinese National Day.

Bed 87

Unfortunately, my splendid travel agent felt that I should not partake in the National Day festivities of Beijing, but should instead drive to Jinan on a day obliterated by smog. But then there are so many hidden rules and restrictions for foreigners, perhaps my waving a flag on Tian'amen Square is against the rules. Who knows, I might just ask some irritating little questions about students, soldiers and suspected slaughter. From the highway I can just make out the scenery; there is a lot of water, I think. Then for some reason Ling navigates us right into the centre of Tiayan City. Although it is the Chinese National Day and a public holiday, there are traffic jams lying in ambush behind heavy curtains of smog. At a chaotic intersection, we ask a traffic official for directions, and to write a wish on the car. While he thinks about his wish, he asks if this is the first time we have been in Tiayuan. He suggests we never come again as it is a horrible place, and then inspiration strikes. He writes his wish, and commands Ling to translate for me,

'A clean world and clean air for everyone.'

He then rattles off some directions, which Ling refuses to translate, so I have no way of judging if they are adequate. Our relationship is getting decidedly icy. This is not helped by the fact that because she does not know how to drive, she forgets that I cannot simply go up a one-way, or reverse on a speedway, or make a u-turn at the most convenient-looking spot. But then again, I have knowingly driven against the traffic on an expressway, which probably gives me license to do just about anything I please, and, whoopa, I add another illegal maneuver to my already impressive record.

Around Jinan, the capital of Shandong Province, the houses look rather prosperous. They have actual stables, and the stables here look better than the houses I saw in Northwestern China. The double-storey brick houses have businesses on the ground floor and living quarters on the first floor. Although the houses push close together, every bit of open land is still farmed.

Under the light of the green full moon rising in a purple and orange sky, we find our way through empty streets to the local night market. Ling chooses a pavement restaurant that serves only a choice of little shashlik; beef, chicken, lamb, seafood, and grilled buns on a skewer. The shashlik are cooked on the same type of shashlik grill I recognize from Uzbekistan. Waiters carry dozens of ready grilled shashlik to the low tables, where we sit on little chairs just inches from the grimy pavement. We select our choice of shashlik from the waiters as they pass our table , and at the end of the meal they count the skewers on our plates , and so we pay. A very pared down operation, they even cover the plates with plastic bags. But the shashlik are delicious, and despite the complete lack of hygiene, my stomach is quite happy. I have still not had a single upset, and considering some of the places I have eaten at, this is a miracle. If Western hygiene fanatics are to be believed, I should to all intents and purposes be stone dead.

Ling does not care for shashlik, preferring to eat mitten crabs, which are currently in season. She trots to a restaurant on the opposite corner, buys her meal, and comes to eat it with me. Would I have liked a mitten crab? I don't know. But now I have a plate full of shashlik, and must be content, although maintaining my calm while eating opposite Ling is testing my politeness levels to the extreme. She hoovers down her food, and when she comes across a bone or any small obstacle in her meal, the offending object gets nibbled at with her front teeth, gradually working its way out of her mouth to dribble onto her plate, lap or the table. Watching her eat the crab is more than my stomach can master, so I concentrate on the people around me, all the while acutely aware that I am being stared at with vacant eyes, as they mechanically chew their way through mountains of food.

Chinese table manners require certain adjustments, especially at breakfast. In China, it is quite normal for several unrelated parties to sit at one big round breakfast table. In the far northern parts of China, this was not a problem, other than trying to find a table that was not a mess of leftover bits of noodle, vegetable, and whatever else the locals were trying to get into their mouths. I would have thought that after centuries of eating with little sticks, they would have mastered the art, but apparently not. When we hit the tourist centre of China, fried eggs were suddenly added to the breakfast menu, and while the Chinese have developed a great liking for sunny-side-up eggs, they have not worked out a way to eat them with any finesse. Admittedly, this is difficult even with a knife, fork, and a handy piece of toast to soak up the yolk. In lacking all these items, the best idea the Chinese have come up with to solve this slippery little problem is to pick up the whole egg with their chopsticks, and systematically shove it into their mouths, simply ignoring the yolk, which slowly drips back onto the plate, as the egg is chewed with wide-open mouth. To be confronted by a whole table of this type of eating first thing in the morning is nauseating, so I quickly learn to keep my eyes firmly glued to my plate. Fortunately Jinan is not a foreign tourist trap, so this morning, breakfast consists of finely cut vegetables, raw peanuts with cucumber, celery with beef, tiny green beans, and steamed buns with a variety of fillings, ranging from sweet taro root to fiery chili vegetables, but, thankfully, no fried eggs.

Bed 88

By midday, we drive under the city wall of Qufu into the hometown of Confucius, but it is hard to place one of the world's greatest philosophers in what is today a dirty little tourist trap. Here everybody professes to be a descendant of the great man, and are all trying to make a mint out of a tenuous 2,500-year-old connection.

Confucius popped off this mortal coil in 497 BCE. Those were the golden years of humanity, it seems, as Buddha lived at the same time, dying just a few years earlier. Confucius, like Buddha, concerned himself with the behavior of Homo sapiens. His teachings and philosophy centered on increasing our knowledge to achieve the four pillars of humanity – honesty, kindness, respect and self-control – when alone, as well as in the presence of others. In 213 BCE, Qin Shi Huang, who was not so keen on honesty, self-control or kindness, ordered that the belief system of Confucius be destroyed, except the 'I Ching' (Book of Changes), a book about the art of telling the future: even evil despots, it seems, would like to know when they should 'duck'. By 191

BCE Confucianism had been all but exterminated, and was only actively revived during the T'ang dynasty around 620 CE.

Considering all this, what are the odds of any physical thing that relates to Confucius still being around? But apparently one can view his house, his temple and his gravesite in Qufu. I send Ling out on a scouting expedition. She returns with the news that the courtyards are the same as all the others we have seen before, and the volume of the tour guides PA-systems are head splitting. I decide I will survive without visiting this particular scenic spot, as once again the areas designated for tourists have a distinct 'made to order' feel about them.

I set out to find the real world, which doesn't take long. Just outside the ancient city wall, the beautifully paved roads, well-tended gardens, and up-market restaurants are replaced by squalid streets, crisscrossed with electrical cables that form an untidy grid across the sky, where an orange midday sun hovers in the pink smog. A man on a bicycle picks his way through the potholes and the mud. To let off steam, he lets fly a kick, and yells at a small dog that is rummaging through a pile of garbage growing against the non-tourist side of the city wall. Scooters transporting whole families wobble by. Dad is the driver, mom sits behind him, squeezing baby in between, and big brother brings up the rear. Helmetless they race off into the smog, dodging the usual assortment of unruly Chinese road users. Turning a corner, the road spreads out into a food market, where next to muddy puddles, food vendors set up stands, selling bowls of beef noodle, and the Chinese version of a hotdog, which involves a pita-type bread, a chemical red Vienna and a squirt of sauce. In cast-iron pots that are sticky soft with ages of congealed grease, breads fry in deep fat. Noodles are shaved into boiling vats, and all around locals are head down, slurping up their food.

The activity on the market square gets more and more hectic as the day fades. Today is the Mid Autumn Festival, and tonight is a very important night. According to a 3,000-year-old belief that stems from the days of Chinese moon worship, the sun – the male Yang – has his annual date with his wife, the moon – the female Ying – tonight. The Chinese believe that this full moon is the most beautiful full moon of the lunar year. Tonight the beauty is enhanced by pollution special effects: the moon hangs blood orange in a strange purple sky; beautiful in a very 'tripping' kind of way. Inflatable red arches with green and yellow dragons crawling over the top span the roads, creating long tunnels under which the locals gather around spot-lit stages, where superstar wannabes are enticed to show the crowd what they've got.

Slowly the daytime fast-food market is joined by the fresh-produce market, and now things start getting interesting. So close to the East China Sea, the piles of fish, crabs and prawns are not surprising, but the spiny sea urchins, and things that look like giant lice, piles of strange wormy-looking creatures and enormous pupae that flinch when touched, send shivers down my spine. I opt for a harmless vegetable stir-fry with smoked tofu, and live to drive another day.

Bed 89

As we near our goal of Shanghai, Ling finally succumbs to the temptation of the unknown, throws caution to the wind, and navigates us direction Huai'an on tiny back roads, or perhaps she is just totally lost. I am not complaining either way, but do check the compass every now and then just to be sure we are heading more or less in the right direction. Then the road stops, without prior warning, at a great mound of rubble where a billboard map indicates the detour, no problem, and off we go. But the map was it; there are no further signs to indicate which of the multitude of back roads we should take. We try a small dirt road that bounces us through a baby forest. China has vast tracts of baby and teenage trees, but very few fully grown ones. After massive floods and mudslides due to deforestation, a countrywide tree-planting drive was implemented in 1998. The millions of young trees planted since then have made China the only Asian country that is increasing its forest cover – not hard, if first you decrease the tree cover to catastrophic levels.

Crossing a river, I carefully dodge women, children and piles of washing, because the low bridge, which is just centimeters above the water, is really the local Laundromat, where cars are not generally expected. Neither are cars really expected on a road that is no more than a freshly ploughed field, where the potholes are stuffed with straw, which is not a terribly effective solution. In the field, a man carefully runs seeds into the furrows, while a woman and her daughter shuffle-step behind him, to cover the seeds and stamp down the soil with their feet. They lift their heads, and silently watch as I bounce the Wish Mobile across their field. Embarrassed, Ling looks stoically at her lap. With a small avalanche of soil, the field becomes a potholed dirt road, which leads through a time gate into a pre-modern China.

Men guide oxen that pull wooden ploughs across fields only thirty oxen steps long. People with giant wooden forks build mountains of hay on human-powered carts. Stone cottages line the village dam, where willows sweep the reflections of the old men strolling by into abstract lines of light. At the market, ducks and chickens placidly await their doom. It must have something do with the fact that their feet are trussed, and many of them are hanging upside down. Housewives, moving in the shade of giant straw hats, check under wings, pinch and poke until the deal is made, and yuan swapped for fowl. Then the chickens are snapped into metal bicycle carriers, where they are in for a very uncomfortable ride to the pot. By the time the chickens get to wherever they are being carried, they will be so stressed, battered and bruised that all the prodding and poking that went on before buying them seems totally ridiculous. It reminds me of old ladies who firmly squeeze every tomato in the supermarket, and then complain afterwards that the tomatoes are all bruised.

A traffic jam builds around a butcher who is skinning a goat; freshly slaughtered, it hangs bleeding by the roadside. A living goat falls off a bicycle, and then the bicycle falls in front of the Wish Mobile. As the owner straps the goat back onto the crossbar, two motorbikes wobble by. Each bike is carrying four living sheep, two trussed across the fuel tank and handlebars, and two tied together, then strapped onto the passenger part of the saddle. While waiting for the traffic to move, I suddenly have a Chinese face directly in front of my face. This guy just thought he would stick his head into the Wish Mobile window and have a little look around.

That's it! The staring, the spitting, the shouting, the filth, the appalling table manners, the short-changing, the hooting, the ripping off, the noise, the general aggression, the surreptitious picture taking, and the inane giggling all suddenly get to me. While Genji had the finesse to step into the fray to control her fellow countrymen in their rude excesses, Ling just sits there staring at her lap, so I have a little sense of humor melt-down, and yell at the smiling yellow teeth just centimeters from my eyes.

'Hey, get your face out of my face!'

The yellow teeth vanish, but the face remains.

'Get your head out of my car!'

The man looks at me blankly.

Ling, sensing trouble, makes the face vanish with some curt orders, and with some surprisingly astute navigating, she manages to direct us through the squeeze of the bicycle traffic jam, under a low bridge up a small steep road until, most unexpectedly, we are overlooking the Hongze Hui.

A potholed dirt track runs all along the top of the massive dike that contains the waters of the Hongze Dam. I stop, turn off the engine, and step into a warm humid world, where, as my ears tune into the silence, I become aware of bird song, then the quacking of ducks, and the gentle slop-slop of water against the boats of the boat-people, who make their living off and on the water. On a grey houseboat hung with washing, a woman tends to her pots under a small lean-to. Her stovetop is supported by thick wooden beams constructed over a fire built in an enormous terracotta pot, which is fitted with rusting chimney pipes that draw the smoke to the outer deck. Here two small dogs laze in the sun, while their master tends to his shimmering nylon fishing nets. In the shallows, the nets are strung into neat squares with a boat road in between. A young boy lifts a crab trap from the murky grey water; the movement swirls the floating acid green algae into ever-growing patterns. The houseboat ducks, alerted by this activity, swim from shore to the boat to see if perhaps lunch is served.

The quiet watery scene is such a relief from the chaos of the main roads of China that I quickly regain my sense of humor. As we bounce along, my shoulders relax, and a tiny smile builds in the pit of my stomach. However, as soon as we reach the smooth asphalt of the main dam wall, and we once again join the expressway south, the time-gate closes, and the rural and agricultural activities of this morning are a thing of the past. The cities of China are oases of the 21st century, surrounded by a country still in the 18th century.

Bed 90

China's prosperity grows as we drive closer to Nanjing, where the highway junctions swoop over and around beautifully tended Zen gardens that are the traffic islands. The city has enough money to employ toll-takers for every tollgate, and whereas paying toll has sometimes taken longer than an hour, here we drive onto 1.5 km Yangtze River Bridge with only the smallest delay. The river is a steel-grey water highway, where container ships, coal barges, and boats wait for docking space in China's largest inland port. The far shore is a faint smudge, where industries smoke and fume, and their smog veils everything in misery. Nanjing was once the capital of China, and the Chinese economic miracle is very apparent here. New apartments crowd the road in a variety of European styles, Neoclassical, Tudor and

'New World Little Town', which could have been airlifted straight out of Amsterdam. We drive past a high-tech glass building that manages to be impressive, even next to its slick neighbors; it is the 'United Chinese English School'. This follows a pattern I have noticed before. In every centre, the best-looking, best-maintained building is sure to be the local school. For centuries, Chinese society recognized only two classes: the educated and the uneducated. In China scholarship was, and is still revered.

In the Nanjing CBD, we walk down the pedestrian zone of Commerce Talking Street. Here the usual comers, KFC and McD, have giant food emporiums next to Italian restaurants, noodle restaurants, and traditional teahouses. In front of a multilevel shopping complex, shiny electric scooters in sweetshop colors are parked so tight that finding your scooter again must be a miracle, and getting it out of the parked masses, impossible. In Hutan Road a wedding fair is taking place. On the sidewalk, tiny platforms have been constructed and extravagantly decorated in traditional wedding flounce or city sleeker chic. Couples browse through large portfolios before choosing a wedding planner. On comfortable couches, perfectly groomed salesladies walk their prospective clients through the virtual wedding of their dreams, with computer simulations and fabric samples. Traditional Western-style white weddings are very much in demand; the princess dress the bride gets to wear always wins the vote. But the ceremony ends up being no more than a themed party which, had the couple chosen differently, might well have been a hippie wedding for all the significance the symbolism has here.

Back at our hotel, a white wedding is just starting; the bride and groom, along with their pages and flower girls, wait outside the balloon-filled restaurant, while inside the master of ceremonies describes their many virtues to the guests. We freshen up for dinner, and as we leave the hotel, the bride and groom are marching left right left right into the restaurant to the strains of *Here comes the bride*. After dinner – with Ling this never takes long – we return to the hotel, where the wedding is over, and the hotel staff are cleaning the restaurant. I cannot believe my eyes. All that time, effort, and money, and the whole thing could not have taken more than two hours from beginning to end. There is no time to party in China; once the official photographs have been taken, it's back to work, folks.

Bed 91

Leaving Nanjing, our route turns east into densely packed urban areas, but every open bit of land between apartments and factories is still farmed. The road is lined by carefully tended topiary trees and green grass; the Chinese government is definitely trying to impress someone. But then a frail old lady, dressed in Mao blue with a straw hat on her head, walks by dragging an enormous cart filled with recyclables. She belies the shiny image China wishes to show the world. In every town and village of China that I have passed through, the old people – small, frail and fragile as twigs – weave through the tourists and youthful masses, pulling their enormous loads of produce or scrap, or whatever else they cart around to make money.

These old people have lived in the worst of times and the worst of times. They lived through the Japanese invasion that marked the beginning of the Second World War in these parts; then the uprising against Chiang Kai-shek; then the Mao Zedong years; the Cultural Revolution; the Great Leap Forward, and finally a harsh communist regime. Those were long years of need and want, in which they were denied the opportunity to build up a nest egg for their future, and then, with the arrival of the Chinese form of capitalism, the iron rice bowl that kept them from starving was ripped away.

In ancient China, ancestor worship was the basic belief, and spirituality revolved around the family. Old equaled wise, and old people were revered and cared for by loving families or society. However, China has discovered that the free market needs a few things to function, one of which is a target market that is easily influenced, easily bored, and easily enthralled by the latest greatest gadget. Over the last few decades, marketing has become more and more focused on the youth, until today the aged have become sidelined, and the youth have become the group that steers the global economy, and therefore society, even in China.

While the youth may be our future, adults and the aged are the present, on which the future will be built. If we do not place the youth of today in the right context, and as long as the old with their learned wisdom and self-control are denied their rightful place to balance society, we will never break out of the downward spiral of values and morals. If we continue to allow commerce to guide our choices, our children will live in a future that will be nothing more than a futile search for happiness in shoe shops.

We make a little detour through Wuxi. It is one of China's most prosperous cities, beautifully set in wooded hills, where I 'China-stare' at recreational cyclists with helmets and neon fitness outfits. Having seen the conditions under which most Chinese live, the aerodynamically designed bicycles and their riders look as if they are from a different planet. We drive through parks and manicured green recreational areas, surrounded by Western-style double-storey houses in a whole variety of flavors. Tudor, Georgian and Victorian, you name it, they've built it. I spy a mosque-style house, an 'Arc de Triomphe' replica, a 'Cinderella' castle, then another mosque. From the fronds of luxurious palms that reach above the high walls surrounding the properties, I am guessing that there are no crops growing in the hidden gardens, and that the business that occupies the owners of these villas has moved from the ground floor of the house to the top floor of a glass skyscraper.

By early evening we reach Suzhou, a city of rivers, canals, and contrasts. As we make our way to the city centre, we pass ordinary Western-style houses, long rows of modern condos, and high-rise buildings. These give way to tatty pollution-stained Soviet-style apartments that surround the modern glass skyscrapers that crowd the business district, while the remnants of Chinese culture, and the ancient gardens that made the city famous are scattered about the city.

In 'The Lingering Gardens', pagodas with rooftops that curl skyward, to keep the evil spirits away, overlook koi ponds with tranquil views over bamboo groves and scholar rocks. 'Scholar rocks' are intricately weathered stones used as a visual stimulation aimed at inducing profound contemplation. The scholar rocks blend into the scenery, where their grotesque forms turn into stone clouds that reveal new shapes from every angle. Small clear notes penetrate the thick bamboo stand. Following them through a round moon gate to an isolated pagoda, I see a beautiful young woman, in flowing sky-blue kimono, with white roses in her jet-black hair, playing an ancient string instrument. She is lost in thought, her reflection in the koi pond trembles as the notes fall like raindrops from delicate, almost translucent fingers, each one with a thick skin-colored plaster around it, a painful business plucking string instruments nine hours a day, every day.

The bonsai garden, with its ancient forest of tiny gnarled trees set in beautiful landscapes of mini scholar rocks and moss, conjures images of bewhiskered men in red and black kimonos that gently coax trees into miniature shapes, a slow and patient art. The harsh commands of the tour guides tear at my delicate illusion. The slow art of bonsai is an art which the modern tourist is allowed no time to appreciate, as the tourist crowds are herded quickly to a more immediately impressive scenic spot.

The Chinese tour guides are a national horror that double as a censorship board, which operates the Chinese tourist production line to bland perfection. The guides are quite clear on where you should look, go, from which vantage point you should take your photograph, and they give you minutely detailed information about nothing. I watch as a Chinese guide describes in perfect detail a room in which the tourist group is standing. The ceiling is so high; the floor space so big; the walls are blue with pink spots. If one did not know better, one would be led to believe that the tourists were all blind. One by one the tourists' eyes glaze over as they sink into a bored stupor. Soon the Chinese government has the tourists exactly where they want them: so overwhelmed by useless information that they have no energy to do some real exploring, to look behind the scenes, where they would discover that a universe could fit comfortably into the gap between the China they are allowed to see and the China the Chinese live in.

The next stop on our official agenda is the Humble Administrator's Garden, which is located on the far side of town. Ling is thinking, we will take the car; I'm thinking, with her navigating we might never get there. We will take the bus, and unexpectedly take part in an unofficial Guinness Book of Records attempt at how many people can squeeze into a bus. The official bus boarding system in China is that you get in at the front door, pay the driver, and then move through the bus to the back door, from which you disembark. This system, like any system designed to control human behavior, looks good on paper, but in reality is a disaster.

We get in the bus, and are immediately jammed right against the driver's seat by the impatient and unruly crowd wanting to board the bus after us. Within seconds, moving in any direction is not possible, and getting to the exit at the back of the buss would require a level of violence that I am not prepared to get involved in. The locals have no such reservations, as although the bus is full to capacity, the driver must stop at the bus stops to let people out. However, before anyone can get off the bus, people desperate to get on the bus start entering at the exit as well as the entrance door. Now no one is getting off; no one is paying; and more and more people push into the already sweating squash of people. The bus driver starts yelling and hooting. He edges the bus forward, trying to stop the oncoming masses, but the masses who want to get off start protesting. There is a great pushing and shoving at both doors. A tsunami wave of frustration and anger rolls through the bus, bashing me into the driver's seat. He yells at me, I yell at him, we yell at the bus in general, but he is trapped, I am trapped, people trying to get off are pushed back on, people trying to get on are pushed back off.

Ling raises a told-you-so eyebrow at me. So you were right, we should have taken the car, but now that we are here, we had better start thinking of a disembarkation strategy. Then the driver has an epiphany; he stops twenty meters before the next bus stop. Passengers fighting to get off catch on quick; they leap overboard, and before the passenger wannabes storming the bus can reach us, we are off. Only in China does a bus driver actively try to avoid taking on passengers. The system works, and by the time we get to Dong Bei Street, order has returned to the interior of the bus, and we are able to disembark with only the smallest of scrums.

The Humble Administrator's Garden is a misnomer: the gardens are grandiose, but as tour guides are banned, they are mercifully silent. The cloud-studded peak rock rises above a sea of yellow and white chrysanthemums. Small wooden bathtub boats float under giant water lily leaves, while koi push the green algae into arrow waves. Bridges zigzag over small waterways, and the grey tiles of the swooping pavilions are decorated with a fall of red maple leaves. In Chinese architecture, the striving is towards formal symmetry and simplicity, while Chinese gardens try to emulate the unruly harmony of nature. The garden gives the impression of walking through a perfectly maintained wilderness, by formal pathways that invite pause at scenic spots described by little poems.

> '*Hidden from view by algae*
>
> *fish are swimming*
>
> *against green ripples*'

The sun dips low as we arrive at Shan Tang Street, where a museum house hints at a 'once upon a time' life of music and conversation, of the gentle arts of bonsai and calligraphy, of good food, and of lazy boats rides along lamp-lit canals, where ladies in silk hid their faces flirtatiously behind painted fans, while men conducted business over bottomless cups of tea, and only after hours of agreeable conversation would come to a mutually acceptable agreement. Tonight as we wander down the dim alley on the non-tourist end of the Shan Tang canal, we discover a 'new world China', one where privacy is not high on the priority list, curtains are non-existent, and the inhabitants act out their lives on the small stages of their tiny homes. A counter onto the street indicates a shop where cigarettes and a small selection of groceries are for sale. Behind the one-shelf-shop the family lives its life.

The front room is the only room, and at this time of day the table is the kitchen, which consists of a gas burner and a wok. After the wok is cleared away, the table serves as dining room, where the family gather to slurp up the rice and vegetable of the evening. With the dishes cleared, the table becomes the schoolroom, where children do their homework, while dad has thirty winks in front of the television. Indoor plumbing is sporadic, and women wash dishes and clothes in bowls in the street. Dim streetlights pool around a small fresh-produce market, where men play mahjong, while children chase each other through the alleyways. As we move closer to the CBD, Shan Tang canal slowly dresses for dinner with red lanterns, old-style barges, fancy bars and restaurants, where the Chinese who are part of the economic miracle sip expensive drinks, and throw peanuts to the fish.

Bed 92

Up with the smog this morning I carry my bags to the Wish Mobile for the last time in China. Ahead of me is a quick 150 km hop from Suzhou to Shanghai. Soon I will have completed the journey across the Eurasian continent that so many people said couldn't be done. After plonking my bags into their familiar position, I turn the ignition key, and steer the Wish Mobile south. My thoughts are not in the moment, but are revolving around the next stage of my trip – crossing America. With the demand of the Chinese government that the Wish Mobile is off Chinese soil in two days, America is coming at me like a freight train. I have still not decided where to next. I have no car insurance, no transport out of China, and no place to stay after the next two nights. Despite this, I am filled with a happy calm as Ling and I part ways in Shanghai, and the thought of being on my own again is blissful.

In my blissed-out state, I allow Ling to navigate us up, down, around, in, out, on highways, skyways, on-ramps, and off-ramps. She sends me into dead-ends and down wrong-way streets. I have long since given up on trying to get her to phone for turn-by-turn directions to our hotels, and, as my hotel destinations are only given to me on a strictly need-to-know basis, I zone out, and just do as am told. However, as we do seem to orienting ourselves by the Pearl Tower, which occasionally appears on the horizon, I start anticipating Ling's last minute instructions by the position of the tower, and by some small miracle we find our way to Liyang Road. From my room I have a view over the Huangpu River and the Pearl Tower, while at the feet of the hotel the rusting rooftops of one of Shanghai's few remaining old towns create a haphazard mosaic in dull shades of brown.

It is time to drink a toast to celebrate my journey. After a long indulgent shower, I slowly work my way through the unfamiliar routine of hair and make-up, fish out some clothing that does not look too wrinkled, and then, looking more or less the part of a global citizen, step out into the humid streets of Shanghai. Crossing the Waibai Du Bridge, I stroll onto the walkway between the Bund and Huangpu River, sit at a small table with a view, and order myself a beer. Sipping slowly while looking over to where the sun starts gilding the Pearl Tower, I cannot help but think that there are times in life that having a friend nearby would be good. As a stopgap measure, I simply tell the German tourists sitting at the next table of this auspicious occasion. They are suitably impressed, and toast my health before turning back to their conversation. The sun sets slowly over the Bund; the Pearl Tower gleams pink and silver on the far shore; and the air fills with the sound of camera shutters as another hoard of photographers capture this same image, this night, and every other night of the year.

Morning comes too soon. I am up at 5h00, because today presents one of those now-or-never moments. The Wish Mobile is going into a shipping container, but before that happens I need proof that we were here, and only the Shanghai Bund as a backdrop will do. During yesterday's impromptu Shanghai tour, I spotted the perfect location right on the apex of a flyover. While stopping on an expressway in Shanghai is not recommended for the sane of mind, after six months of having to adapt to some of the world's most exotic driving styles, I am quite beyond caring about such small details. I have masterminded a fiendishly clever plan that involves my being out and about at 05h00, to get to the chosen spot before the rest of Shanghai's traffic makes stopping anywhere impossible, let alone in the middle of an elevated highway. However, I soon discover a fatal flaw in my plan. With no map I cannot find my way back onto the flyover that I scouted out yesterday. In the still dark and empty streets of Shanghai I drive up and down the wrong-ramps, time is creeping, the sun is rising, the traffic is building, and soon this little 'once in a life time' adventure will not be possible. I am getting just a touch hysterical when, with some relief, I find the correct on-ramp and to loud protests from passing drivers get the Wish Mobile into position. The protest turns to near hysterical hooting when I stand right in the middle of the road to get the shot. The people of Shanghai really need to get out more.

Next stop is to meet Andy and Bruce from the shipping company. We have been mailing since July, and I must admit to a certain curiosity. They are very friendly, but all business. The Chinese government must be obeyed. They have only two days to get the Wish Mobile off Chinese soil, and this does not give them much time to wade through the mountain of paperwork that is involved with intercontinental transportation of cars. After Ling adds her official envelope to the pile, she vanishes out of my life, while I get escorted to the loading bay; but first the Wish Mobile needs a very thorough wash, as America does not like foreign soil on its soil. This is a prime example of human idiot thinking. In our insane drive to control everything, we refuse to see how puny our attempts are; perhaps if we did, we would all just go into collective depression. The winds of Earth transport in the region of 3 billion tons of sand, soil, bacteria and seeds around the planet, and most Asian wind-borne dust lands in the heart of America so I hardly think the few grains of soil stuck to the undercarriage of my car are going to make a difference.

But you know how it goes, give Stupidman power, and chaos is the result. We spend millions in trying to predict tsunamis, earthquakes, volcanoes, and then, when we inevitably get it wrong, have a happy old time of pointing fingers and shouting: Why didn't you tell us, why was there was no warning? Wrong question. The question is not why we cannot predict nature, but why we are incapable of recognizing that the earth will shake, volcanoes will erupt, and rivers will flood, and rather adapt our behavior accordingly. The starting point, as Confucius already knew thousands of years ago, is self-control. The only thing you can control is yourself, but while the answer is simple, the application is difficult. Who wants to control themselves when there are 6 billion people and at least two dozen deities we can blame when something goes wrong?

After driving the spotlessly clean Wish Mobile into the steel container, where it will live for a month, it gets strapped down, has airbags fitted, I take my final photographs, and with a slightly tearful:

'Goodbye, Wish Mobile, see you in the US of A.'

I watch as the steel doors slam shut, are sealed, and a big front-end loader lifts the Wish Mobile container in the air, and trundles it off into the anonymity of thousands of containers just like it. Will I ever see my little travel companion again?

Mr Wu chauffeurs me back to my hotel, where the doorman suddenly becomes much more attentive. Arriving in a long black, chauffeur-driven luxury vehicle obviously impresses those with little brain. In my hotel room all plans to explore Shanghai are set aside in favor of collapsing on my bed. With the Wish Mobile gone, my brain and all vital functions go into free fall, and I spend the rest of the day in a coma sleep. When I wake, night has fallen over Shanghai. In the distance the 468 m Pearl Tower is a bulbous beacon of light. I have been in Shanghai for 48 hours, and have seen nothing more of it other than through various car windows, and still Shanghai will have to wait; I have things to do.

While the good folk of Shanghai are settling down in front of the telly after a long day in the office, the day is just starting in America, and there are still a few work hours left in Africa and Europe. Feeling like a global executive in my corner office with a view, I soon have e-mails flying to all continents of the planet. Car insurance is required for America, and money must be transferred from Africa to Asia for the car shipment. Without a car I must be more structured in my sleeping arrangements. What shall I do for November? I surf about in Japan, but my heart is not in it. I need a holiday from all the traveling. The idea of staying put in one spot is very appealing, so I mail a friend in Taiwan.

'One wayward wanderer seeks accommodation for a week or two or three.'

Vincent's reply is short and sweet.

'You're welcome anytime.'

Life without friends would be a sad thing.

So that part of November is sorted out. Now how to get to Taiwan from China? It is not far as the crow flies, but the Taiwanese and Chinese have bigger neighbor issues than the Greeks and Turks. There are no direct flights to Taiwan from Shanghai, but there are flights from Hong Kong. Hong Kong has never been on my got-to-see-list, but, hey, when opportunity knocks ... so I surf out of the virtual world of Japan and boogie-board across to Hong Kong. But something is going on in Hong Kong; there is not a hotel room to be found. My 5W list comes in handy. I find two members; Sandy is out of town; and Elaine suggests we meet at the Oktoberfest. An Oktoberfest in Hong Kong? This should be good. I'm in. But first a room, a room, my kingdom for a room, but as I have no kingdom, and very little else of any value to trade, the lack of room is not surprising. I lower my search requirements until I hit on Mirador Mansions in Nathan Street. Browsing their website, I convince myself that while the price seems a bit steep, the rooms don't look too bad. I decide to risk it. Now for the flights. Shanghai – Hong Kong – Taipei 'clickedy click barbar trick'. How did we live without Internet? My flight to America I will deal with in Taiwan.

Emails start coming back; insurance quotes, money transfer confirmation; 5W members and assorted friends send greetings from America, Africa, Canada and England. My orgy of administration ends just as the sun starts its daily slugging match with the pollution. Bed would be nice, but no time. After a quick shower and small breakfast Mr Wu picks me up, as I need to sign official documents, swear oaths at a notary's, and do whatever it is the Chinese and Americans require of me to get my wee car safely over the Pacific. As I swoop over the high-rise highways of Shanghai, I figure that this must be the way most celebrities travel; their travel experience reduced to the view through the tinted backseat window of a chauffeur-driven car. *Ag shame, man*, the poor things, how fantastically boring. I jokingly thank Mr Wu for showing me so much of Shanghai; he takes me seriously, and heads off on a citywide joy ride. But after a sleepless night and a long day of backwards and forwards, in and out of a variety of offices, signatures and stamps I fall asleep, and as Shanghai flashes by, I slumber in air-conditioned comfort. At the hotel, I have only one thought – food. I have a faint memory of eating breakfast, but it might have yesterday's.

In the hotel restaurant the strange ritual, of showing off while ordering food, is taking place at the table next to mine. The host is making a big fuss over his choice of wine, which comes in a fancy wooden box. With exaggerated attention to ritual, he sniffs the cork, inspects it minutely, carefully pours a drop of wine into his glass, swings it about, checks the color against the green glow of the neon lights, sniffs, slurfs, and finally declares the wine drinkable. Then he proceeds to share out the wine, each glass is filled, bit by bit, until all the glasses are meniscus tension full, and the bottle is empty. The guests have done this before, it seems. They lean forward and take delicate sips without moving their glasses. Then, so much food starts arriving, it makes me think that the Chinese are not yet over the famine of 1960, caused by Mao's Great Leap Forward, in which at least 14 million people starved to death in China. Either that, or they think the excessive consumption of the West is the only way to behave for those who wish to be seen as hip, rich and happening.

There are only four guests, but the host has ordered food for a battalion of people; platter after platter gets piled on the table. An adjoining table is pulled up as the diners start vanishing behind the piles of food. The Chinese do not do things on a small scale; if there is to be waste, let there be mountains of it. The guests don't seem to be very hungry; they take a bite here, taste there; and the only thing that will not be wasted is the wine. Considering the poverty I have seen in inland China, this is revolting, but not uncommon. After all, what is the point of being rich if nobody knows about it?

Excessive food consumption is the entry-level public bragging device of the newly rich, which is soon joined by fancy shoes, expensive women, fur coats, jewels and luxury cars, until finally, when all other options have been exhausted, the bragging returns to the food table. Only, at the top end of food bragging pile it is not quantity, but rather scarcity, and paying more for a single plate of food than many people earn in a year, that proves your wealth, good taste and superiority over your fellow human being. Already in 497 BCE Socrates voiced his option on the excesses of the flesh, saying to Glaucon;

> *Like cattle with their eyes always looking down and their heads stooping to the earth, that is the dining table, they fatten and feed and breed, and in their excessive love of these delights, they kick and butt at one another with horns and hoof which are made of iron; and they kill one another by reason of their insatiable lust. For they fill themselves with that which is not substantial, and the part of themselves which they fill is also unsubstantial and incontinent.* Plato, *The Republic.*

It seems that we are stuck in a vicious circle of our own creation, where money has become not the measure of value, but the measure of greed, and as the greedy get more money, they don't change their gluttonous habits, they just make them more expensive. Pity really that the acquisition of money is not linked to the acquisition of wisdom. Wouldn't the world be a happy place if the wealthy were also wise in equal measure, with a dash of humble modesty thrown in. That this is just wishful thinking is confirmed as I stroll through Shanghai in the early morning smog. Following a thin old man with a tiny pick-up, who is collecting the drums of wasted food that stand outside each of Shanghai's thousands of restaurants, I conclude that the pigs of Shanghai eat better than most of the people in China.

Leaving the old guy to his slop business, I walk through one of Shanghai's old-becoming-new neighborhoods, where blue glass skyscrapers grow from the dull brown of the low metal-and-wood buildings that line one-car narrow streets. The sidewalks are places where no one walks, because pavement eateries, random armchairs, and fresh produce, crowd every square centimeter. Over the entrance to a tiny eating-house, ten headless ducks are hanging on a wire, while white steam pours from black iron cauldrons, filling the restaurant interior with misty light. Dragon gates deny strangers access to small alley neighborhoods, where half-dressed children play, and shirtless men smoke. Drops of unwelcome water bombard me from washing hung on long bamboo poles that jut over the street from second-floor balconies. Above the washing, a crisscross tangle of electrical cables creates a technological boundary between these small busy streets and the futuristic towers that hide their full height in the pollution.

In China, one lives above or below the pollution line, which is added to in no small measure by the belching scooters. There might be 'nine million bicycles in Beijing', but there are possibly ten million scooters in Shanghai, which the Shanghai municipality, to its credit, is trying to tame. On every street corner a traffic warden controls the flow of scooters by taking his life into his own hands each time the light changes to red, and he steps into the road to halt the marauding mass with only his little orange baton as protection. The scooters snarl and shift uneasily, while watching the traffic light with intense concentration, as does the traffic warden. The instant it changes to green, he leaps to the relative safety of the sidewalk as in a cloud of blue smoke the scooterlami of Shanghai starts again. As a pedestrian, do not be lulled into believing that you have the right of way when the little green man says walk. I hop skip skedaddle across the road, and have the distinct feeling that whereas in Rome the scooters tried to avoid me, in Shanghai the scooter drivers would kill me, given half a chance.

To avoid the scooters, I stroll along the shores of Suzhou Creek, where the homeless sleep in untidy bundles on the green manicured lawn, their bicycle pickups tethered to the river railing like a herd of steel horses. In the shade of immaculately pruned trees old folk do Tai Chi; their slow moving arms mirror the cranes that swing building material in wide arches across the river. The steel grid of the cranes contrasts with the bamboo scaffolding and reed matting that cover each of hundreds of building sites. Bamboo scaffolding has been used in construction since ancient times in China, and even today, steel scaffolding is hardly seen. People believe that bamboo has good feng shui properties, and can be a bringer of good luck and calming energy. This must a great comfort to the builders working twenty storeys high on a platform of gently swaying bamboo.

In Xinzha Road, the Shanghai Metro opens a portal through which I descend under the smog into a cool clean air-conditioned world, lit by neon advertising light. The Shanghai metro is modern, simple and cheap – if you watch your change – the Chinese will try their luck every time; the constant pilfering is wearing on my nerves. Only on my insistence does the surly chap behind his bulletproof glass reluctantly hand over the money he owes me.

I hop on board the next train south, and soon emerge into the sunny smog of 'The People's Square', where twisted metal sculptures frame the soaring glass needles of glitzy hotels. From here, the distant Pearl Tower is a faint smudge in the sky, and after three days of being in Shanghai, I feel that I should really make an effort to see the famous view close up. Turning east, I stroll down Nanjin Road: a pedestrian shopping street where South African diamonds, South East Asian pearls, Chinese plastic and American KFC all jostle for attention on a street where anyone who can pay the rent is welcome. The crowds are as colorful as the billboards. Tourists in shorts and sneakers, locals in rip-off designer wear, old ladies in Mao blue, and executives in sharp black suits with gleaming pointy shoes all do the sidewalk samba so popular in the cities of the east. Exhausted, I escape again into the cool of the metro, and pop out in the cloying heat on the Pudong side of the Huangpu River.

Being slightly too close to the Pearl Tower, I nearly put a crick in my neck in trying to see the top of it, but it vanishes into the smog only halfway up, so going onto any of its 15 observation decks seems a spectacularly stupid idea. A babbling stream of brilliant color attracts my attention. I follow the group of preschoolers at a safe distance until they vanish into the Shanghai aquarium. Underground is the way to go today. I slowly slide underwater via an escalator in a plastic tunnel, past the frenetically paddling feet of black swans, while giant fish watch with boggle eyes as I sink into the depths of the aquarium. There I am deposited onto a rolling walkway that trundles me past watery ecosystem after watery ecosystem. Fish watch me from all sides, until I feel like a piece of merchandise on a conveyor belt. It's all very nice, but the aquarium at the V&A Waterfront in Cape Town is better. Another escalator heaves me back into the smog ... no-o-o, it's hot, stifling and muggy up here. Quick, back underground or underwater, as the case may be. I take a psychedelic trip back to the Bund via the 646.7-meter pedestrian tunnel that runs under the river.

The Bund is a stretch of historical buildings along the western shore of the river, whose eclectic mix of building styles from all ages and places is probably the source of inspiration for the newly rich homeowners of China. The Bund was once the financial heart of Shanghai, but today it is tourist central. People of all nations crowd the boulevard, posing against the famous view of the Pearl Tower and International Convention Centre across the grey water of the Huangpu, where the throbbing of a hundred ship engines competes with the beating of a thousand drums from a women's drumming competition that shakes the smog like lemon jelly. Multi-colored flags and balloons compete for attention with the drummer ladies. Each troop has its own Mardi Gras outfit; those in tangerine with gold sparkles and bright green shoes, turn their backs on those in green and silver with scarlet trim and roses in their hair. Ladies in scarlet and pink with bright orange trim sit, stand, tap, and chat, as they wait their turn in front of the panel of judges.

The whapa whapa of the drums fades as I head back to my hotel, crossing the Suzhou Creek via the Waibai Du steel bridge, where the roar of overhead traffic drowns out the drums and boats. Wedding photographers shout instructions to their newlywed clients to coax them into flattering poses against the famous view, while assistants carefully arrange the lacy, graying hems of white princess dresses artistically on the filthy sidewalk.

To wash the sensory overload of Shanghai out of my hair, I take a shamefully long shower, haul out my red dress, strap on my high heels and touch up my nose. Tonight I have a sort of date, dinner with Andy, hopefully in a decent restaurant. Primped and preened. I swan into the foyer. The doorman leaps to his post. Andy's chauffeur helps me into the luxurious beast of a car that will transport us to the swish end of Shanghai. On the back seat of the fat black luxury vehicle, Andy and I look down on lesser mortals as we fill the air with a flurry of words and jokes. I have lots to say; it's been months since I spoke to a native English speaker. I am thrilled to discover that Andy has a wicked sense of humor, an eye for a classy restaurant, knows his way around a wine menu, and likes to end the evening with a fine cigar and cognac. Oh happy day. Eating on pavements is all very interesting, but I am a bit of a madam, and beautiful surroundings with well-trained waiters, a good bottle of wine, and intelligent company do it for me. I have a fabulous evening shooting the breeze, but forget that for months I have been doing some seriously clean living, the cognac and cigar assault my sparkly clean liver with a toxic dose of overindulgence. I wake up with a ripping hangover.

Groaning, I drag myself about the hotel room, in and out of the bathroom, and my bags downstairs, where Mr Wu awaits to chauffeur – okay, okay, despite my socialist complaining, this chauffeur business is very very easy to get used too – me to the Maglev Train Station. The Maglev Train is the most efficient and normally painless way to get to Pudong Airport. But this morning the three hundred plus kilometers per hour and steeply inclined curves do not sit well with my hangover. Seven long minutes later, I, the hardened rollercoaster rider, arrive at the airport wearing a very worrying shade of puce. I must learn to time my excesses more carefully.

Mercifully the security checks at Pudong Airport, compared with what I have experienced in the West, are almost nonexistent; 9/11 has not left its neurotic legacy here. I slip out of Shanghai without any fuss, land in Hong Kong, board another fast train, cross various very long sea bridges, hop on an air-conditioned bus, and only when I get off the bus, about an hour and a half after landing, do I sniff the un-air-conditioned air of deep city Hong Kong. The name 'Hong Kong' is a phonetic approximation of spoken Cantonese, and means 'fragrant harbor', which it still is, but not, I am sure, in the way the Cantonese intended it. The air is thick with moisture and suspect aromas that vary in pungency, depending on the proximity of the sewers, my head, my heart, my heaving gut. Life is difficult sometimes.

Bed 93

Dragging my suitcase down Nathan Street I quickly become aware that Hong Kong is like no place I have been before, Shanghai is dozy compared to this. This place is pumping; there must be a representative of every country on the planet here; and everybody is busy. Man, are these people busy. Energy bounces off the pavements, zigzags up the glass buildings, ricochets off the damp cloud ceiling to bounce back off the pavements again. This is the city that never sleeps. The inhabitants cram their way along the sidewalks. Everybody is trying to sell everybody else something: watches, computers, silks, cigarettes, shoes, massage, anything and everything is for sale, and the sellers are insistent! No thank you, no thank you, not today, thank you. I am going to be wearing my manners pretty thin around here.

With a small twinge of apprehension, I make my way to the hotel entrance through the teeming ground-floor market in Mirador Mansions, which is like a set from a sci-fi film that paints the future grey, crowded, poor and bleak. Dripping washing hangs in the grimy central courtyard of the 15-storey tenement building that has 'hotels' on every floor. A 'hotel' can consist of only three or four rooms, which are small, very, very small. The tiny over-full lift slowly pulls me to the top floor where I pick my through squalid passages and past heavily barred doors into a small reception area that is overflowing with cleaning aids, ladders, dishes and half-finished bottles of water. My mind is desperately casting about for a way to not have to stay here, but I know from my Internet search in Shanghai that every decent hotel is booked solid and, with no Wish Mobile to fall back on, I am trapped. The hotel owner shows me my room, and warns me to ensure that the bed is tightly pushed against the back wall or else the door will not open. This is not the case now, and as he opens the door, I guffaw with shock: the room is literally the size of a bed. The fully tiled walls push at the bed from three sides. There are no widows. It is as if they have turned a small bathroom into a hotel room. The room is so small that the suitcase fills the only floor area that is not filled by bed. In order to open the door, I must heave my suitcase onto the bed. To get into bed, I squash against the wall to close the door, then heave the suitcase onto the floor. Now in order to get to the bathroom, I must climb over the suitcase. There is a showerhead mounted above the toilet; another one of those showers where I wonder if it is worth getting undressed for. I decide not. Hong Kong is so whiffy; nobody is going notice the pathetic amount of body odor that I am able to produce.

When 5W Elaine comes up to collect me, she is very curious to see the room, and is suitably flabbergasted. While I have by now found some humor in the stark contrast of my luxurious, chauffeur-driven stay in Shanghai and this room, which would not be out of place in an insane asylum, Elaine is not to be convinced, and is very keen to get back onto the street. An action that requires patience as there are only three small totally over-worked lifts, and the fire escape is barred. The jam-packed lift bounces to a stomach-lurching halt on floor 13. Here there is a whole nest of tiny 'hotels' from which emerge Norwegian blonds, North African blue-blacks, Middle Eastern gold, Central European pinks, and of course the tan Australian. Young people, old people, these termite hotels cater for everybody who booked through the Internet, which is the only world in which these 'hotels' manage to look and sound like 'hotels'; in the real world they are very expensive prison cells. If a fire should break out here, we will all be toast, unless of course the lift cable breaks first, in which case we will be international pâté.

Reaching the German restaurant that is putting on the mini Oktoberfest requires that we take a walk down Nathan Street direction water. At the Sheraton Hotel we cross Salisbury Road, make our way across the public space of the Hong Kong Space Theater, Museum of Art, and arrive at the Avenue of Stars, just as the nightly laser shows start on Hong Kong Island. Across the black water of Victoria Harbor, the closely packed cathedrals honoring the great money god, soar into the green blue sky. They glitter, flash, and send rays of golden laser light into the heavens in a nightly thanksgiving to the global markets; long may they rule.

The Oktoberfest menu is small: Wurst, Eisbein and Bier. A Bavarian touring group, dolled up in lederhosen and dirndl, manage, with slap dancing, twirling and very enthusiastic singing to the oompapa sounds of a brass quartet, to wrest a very small Oktoberfest feeling out of the Hong Kongers; a very reserved bunch to whom clapping, singing and schaukeling don't come naturally. But they do surprisingly well in the beer-drinking competition. The little Chinese men beat the bulky Germans and the strapping Aussies every time. During the course of the evening Elaine must have been weighing me up, and having come to the conclusion that I am harmless, invites me to come and stay in her home; I am touched and relieved. The windowless shoebox room is not my idea of heaven.

Bed 94

Elaine's home is in North Point, which is a crowded part of an already crowded city. Hong Kong is the world's most densely populated city in which everybody, other than the super-duper wealthy, lives in huge high-rise apartments that are squashed together so tight, you can have a quite comfortable conversation from one building to another. More people live and work above the 14th floor here, than anywhere else on the planet, making Hong Kong the world's most vertical city, and also one of the world's leading financial centers, where time is money, and taking time out to cook the family meal is a luxury the domestic time bank cannot afford. The huge residential complex that Elaine lives in is like a walled city of old, a self-contained fortress with restaurants on the ground floor that cater specifically for the residents.

Because Elaine has early morning online business to deal with, her Pilipino maid escorts younger brother to his school, while older sister shows me how the restaurant works. There is a choice of a self-service section or menu; payment is made with coupons. Over eggs and toast, the frantic lifestyle of Hong Kong comes into focus. In older sister's bag I spy a time management manual. She is only twelve. Who needs to time-manage their lives at twelve years old? I need to get to the bottom of this.

'What do you do over the weekends? Do your friends come over or do you meet them at the movies?'

Older sister is unimpressed by my silly assumptions, and replies with a haughty

'My friends and I are far too busy to meet socially; we only see each other at school.'

With that, she grabs her school bag, says a polite goodbye, and heads for the bus stop. I finish my tea thoughtfully. In China, education takes top priority because, in a country of 1.6 billion, it takes fanatic dedication to the cause to stand out from the crowd. The bulk of Elaine's budget goes to educating her children, as in China teachers are traditionally figures of prestige and respect, and – in Hong Kong – very well paid. The best teachers have long waiting lists of pupils, who have to apply for selection to be tutored. The intense competition has pushed the price of education so high that the days of getting a place at a good school by academic merit alone are long over, preventing many able students from attaining school places.

The overhead clock catches my eye. I gulp down the tea in one go, grab my things, and find Elaine waiting for me at the building entrance, a tiny frown creasing her normally placid brow. I will need to brush up on my time-management skills pronto, as not only has Elaine made space for me in her small family apartment, but she has also managed to carve a slice of time out of her hectic schedule to go sightseeing with me, and I, who have nothing to do but shoot the breeze, am late. I administer myself fifty virtual lashes with a wet noodle.

We hop on a bus, and are soon in the queue that will allow us to head up to the Peak in the historical funicular train. However, the weather is not in a happy mood, and pulls a sulky grey veil over greater Hong Kong; all we can see are the tops of the highest buildings that penetrate the thick soup of fog-smog below. The Peak is covered in dense subtropical jungle, which produces thick musky air that I suck gratefully into my lungs. This is the best tasting and most expensive air that I have had in a month. Below the smog line, a dense concrete jungle supports a teeming mass of humanity; up here, luxurious villas can be spotted, half hidden by the dense jungle forest. Only the super-wealthy of Hong Kong can live in this rarified air (relatively speaking). Our five minutes are soon up, and we must head back down into smog city. Elaine has to get back to her precisely planned schedule, so she hands me a map with her details, and a big cross, indicating her apartment building, then leaves me to find my way back to North Point from the CBD.

Pointing my camera skywards to capture the steel graphics against the steel grey sky, a raindrop falls, splat, into the middle of my lens. Although the lens is in desperate need of a cleaning, and still smells faintly of diesel, water is not the answer. The raindrop is quickly followed by millions more. I am not too keen on having a lukewarm shower, and make a mad dash for the comfort of the elevated walkway that crosses at Cavanaugh Road. The elevated walkway is an extensive pedestrian link between the buildings in the CBD. From here, Hong Kong looks as if an international architect's competition took place, with the specifications that the only building materials to be used would be glass and metal. The buildings are packed so tight that the sky is reduced to a small square straight overhead, but the glass and metal buildings bounce this small light from window to widow until hundreds of thousands of windows are all segmented sky. The rain stops as I reach the Standard Charter house, where, in a small Western-style bakery, I buy an enormous chocolate chip muffin. In the nearest park, on a bench surrounded by round rocks and trees, to the sound of waterfalls and bird song, I indulge myself with my first chocolate anything in months. The sponge is dark, almost black, moist with a dark heart of smooth molten chocolate. A little espresso round about now would make this experience sublime, and then, instead, the grey clouds vanish, and sun pours golden heat into the top of my head.

As I follow Hennessy Road towards North Point it changes its identity, in name, sight and sound. The Yee Wo Street pavements become more and more crowded with tiny shops and restaurants. The clean lines and manicured parks of the CBD are left behind as I enter Hong Kong's urban zone. The pavement is a weave of people so tight that with my kindergarten sidewalk skills I am pulled along with the flow, unable to resist or choose my course. A small alcove provides a safe harbor from the current of humanity. Here I stop to give myself a moment, and watch a young man who has set up a tabletop, and is wrapping mitten crabs. With a rubber-gloved hand he reaches into a crawling, creeping basket of crabs, extracts one, then with a deft move, folds all the legs in, and, with a quick crisscross of a length of reed, wraps that crab into a neat square bundle. That crab ain't going nowhere but the pot. We share a smile. I thank him for the little demonstration, and stepping out of the alcove, am swept away by the river of people.

Sunday dawns bright and early in the Elaine household. We are up at 06h00 to go to Victoria Park to take the air, and get some exercise. Why this is necessary, considering the speed at which people live here, is beyond me. But I soon see that all is not as I imagine it should be. In a beautiful calm landscaped setting that opens onto a trim lawn, several groups are doing Tai Chi; here exercise is not for the body, but to calm the mind. But, as with all things in Hong Kong, this must be done quickly, and soon we are stepping lightly across stone pavements that with intricately laid out river stones massage our tired feet right through our shoes. A do-it-yourself foot massage while you walk is something that only a nation with no time on their hands could dream up. Minds and feet revived, we arrive at the bus stop just in time to hop onboard. Elaine knows the fare and the timetable of every bus and metro to, from and in North Point. She knows how many minutes it takes from point A to B, and has worked out which bus we must take in order to be on time for the rest of the day's appointments. This is all part and parcel of a properly time-managed day.

When we reach the apartment, the children have already taken themselves down to the restaurant, where they have had breakfast; no breakfast for adults, we will have lunch. As we hit the street, Elaine and the children pick up speed. We must catch the next metro under Victoria Bay, otherwise they will be late for their two-hour rehearsal with Hong Kong's children's orchestra. They are merely walking fast, while I am in a semi-trot to keep up. We leave the kids to their violins at the Hong Kong Cultural Center, and head out to view the highest residential buildings in Hong Kong. This is not really my thing, but Elaine oohs and ahhs at the splendor of it all. Time moves at speed in Hong Kong, and soon we dash back to fetch the kids. Now older sister has another violin lesson to attend, so we escort her part-way, before she vanishes confidently into the crowd. Was that girl ever a child? We are off to one of the Hong Kongers' favorite dim sum restaurants, where older sister will join us later. Elaine and little brother discuss the menu, and soon the table is groaning under beautifully presented little things: some steamed dumplings, broiled pork belly, a bit of seafood, mini spring rolls, smoked tofu, a good soup, rice, and tea.

By the time we get 'home', I am exhausted, but after a brief half an hour breather, older sister has to go off to another lesson, then a student comes to Elaine for German lessons. At 15h00 Elaine and I hop on the No 10 bus, and take it all the way to the end of the line to Sai Wan, opposite Green Island. She has always wanted to do this, but has never found the time. Watching the small fishing boats heave and sway over ocean liner wakes, I think that there is something very sad about a life that is so busy that no time can be found to take a twenty-minute bus ride just for the fun of it. We walk back toward North Point with no particular plan; I sense that this is foreign to Elaine, like a tiny holiday from the top-speed life she leads. Dawdling up a flight of mossy steps under a flower-laden tree, we step into a little village street where single-storey houses, with flower boxes and cats in the windows, line the cobbled street. In a city of tightly packed high-rises, this place has something of 'Alice in Wonderland' about it. Elaine looks about silently; she has been swooning over every little balcony she has seen. Her greatest wish is to have a private balcony, a little space, where she can stand outdoors, that belongs to her, where she does not need to move, dodge-step lightly, where she can just stand still, and watch the world go by.

But time, as always, is topmost on her mind. We have still a way to go, and as she would like to walk, we step lightly, dodge and duck through the crowds. Elaine picks up the pace. She is about half my height, and I must skip-trot-walk to keep up with her, mainly because I am always getting in someone's way. I have heard about the rude elbow society of China's cities, but watching Elaine glide effortlessly through the closely packed pedestrians, I conclude that only the tourists get the elbow. Walking the pavements in Hong Kong is like driving on the roads of Shanghai: it takes a level of skill that cannot be mastered in a day. We rush through a backstreet meat market, where butchers cut and carve the streets to an interesting, slippery mess. Turning a corner, the market is replaced by a long row of tightly packed restaurants. We arrive at the favorite family restaurant in time to order a meal, which arrives just before the children do after their 18–19h00 badminton lesson. Did I mention that today is Sunday?

Waiting for sleep to take me, I mull over how hard people here have to work, to get so little in return. I think about the children on whom the pressure to perform is relentless. I am not sure what the result of this will be. While the day-and-night quest for pre-packaged knowledge and information will produce highly qualified people who know how to follow every instruction, will it also produce original brilliant thinkers or only drones, who will not question the system or rock the boat. Learning and thinking are not the same thing. In a society where failure is not acceptable in any form, imagination must get lost, as imagination needs the freedom to make mistakes. Original thought does not necessarily spring from more learning; it might even be hindered by it. As our progress comes only in brilliant leaps of the imagination, what progress we will make once the imagination has been stilled.

Taichung Taiwan

Taiwan

Bed 95

With military precision, Elaine gets the children off to school, then deposits me at the correct bus stop, before weaving her way through the crowds, her small frame soon swallowed by the masses. The bus arrives precisely on time. Instantly I am caught up in the modern commute, from air-conditioned bus to air-conditioned airport to air-conditioned airplane, and soon I am flying across the Taiwan Strait. From my position high above Taiwan, I look down onto how the future might look if we don't change our polluting ways.

Taiwan is covered by a bell glass of deep yellow carbon dioxide, in which white cumulus clouds bob about like ice-cream in a coke float. Slowly the plane descends through the murk, and as the sky changes from blue to yellow, it hits me: I will be breathing this stuff for a month. Vincent has assured me that Taichung has the best climate and least pollution in Taiwan, but looking at the dense layer of smog that now engulfs the airplane, I think more or less pollution down there is a moot point. On ground level, the strange-smelling air is a motionless yellow haze that pulls a soft focus filter over the few trees and many buildings.

The carbon dioxide-laden air dulls my senses, and for the first week of my stay in Taichung, I sleep almost non-stop. It is as if all the plugs have been pulled. Even when awake, I walk around in a grey fug, punctuated by the slow whoop whoop of my pounding head, which starts every morning as the ice-cream truck carillon of the garbage collectors wakes me. In Taiwan, the garbage collection is a fairly do-it-yourself affair. On hearing the truck bells, the locals gather their garbage together, and toss it into the truck themselves, making quite sure that it has been well sorted beforehand. The Taiwanese are great recyclers, even separating leftover food, which goes into the pig slop bin. After a cup of hot water and lemon juice, I sit down and stare at my computer, trying to penetrate the dull thud in my mind in an attempt to produce thoughts that do not direct me straight back to bed.

Vincent is somewhat disappointed in my less than scintillating company, and leaves me to my own devices. My retreat into mental silence seems to be relentless, and I really have to concentrate on communicating. I know that Vincent finds this frustrating, as I sense in him the same yearning to know, to share, to also see the world beyond the horizon, to get away from it all, that I have detected in people all along my journey.

I have learnt that you cannot get away from it all; it is impossible; you are it all; you are your whole life. I think that one of the reasons we all yearn to travel is the realization that while our high-speed day-to-day existence might make us more money, it makes less of us. Commerce and governments force us to sit still, as markets are best developed in a controlled environment, and yet we long for the far-off shore, the greener pastures. I think that in our primal minds we are still nomads. We slowly colonized the earth, not because we ran out of space, but because there were always those among us with an insatiable curiosity for the unknown, the view from the next hill, the taste of the water from higher up the mountain stream. We yearn to travel as we hope that by breaking out of the deadening routine of daily life, we will once again feel alive and hope that elsewhere we will find the truth. We forget, though, that we always are wherever we go, and the world is always just the way we choose to see it.

Commerce has tapped into this yearning, and, to ensure that we always get what we think we want, has turned the art of travel into a precooked, plastic-wrapped convenience, turning the grand adventure into a totally predictable and immediately forgettable TV-dinner. Travel should be like a slow cooked meal, which in its eating brings a sense of deep satisfaction, but also the wistful knowledge that this meal will never be quite the same again, making the flavor and slow enjoyment of every mouthful so much more intense.

A low growl from my stomach tells me that I should eat at some point. Getting up from my desk, I wander into the kitchen, and looking into the empty fridge, realize that unless I want to starve, I will have to get dressed, and step outside.

The grey huddle of six-storey buildings that I currently call home has a tiled inner courtyard, which is the gathering place for women, who gossip over a cigarette, while their children scoot about on various wheeled toys. In the small, well-maintained park opposite, the old women of the neighborhood do their morning exercise. A little later, young mothers bring out their toddlers to play on the jungle gym. After work, men walk determinedly round and round or practice their golf swings, while older children play Frisbee with their dogs.

As night falls, a buzzing silence descends on the small neighborhood, which is a maze of corners in which every taxi driver I employ gets completely lost. I make my way past the foot massage parlor, and the stir-fry restaurant, then step into one of the teeming main roads of Taichung. In this sleepless world of noise and neon light, the scooter is king. They zip through traffic gaps, and over pavements; they fume impatiently at traffic lights; and they spew their stinking breath over everything. Walking in a city where everybody scoots is a difficult thing, as all the pavements have been invaded by take-out restaurants that cater to the scooting citizens of Taichung, who get off their steel steeds only if absolutely necessary. Thousands of impromptu pavement kitchens wash their waste into the storm water drains, creating very pungent sewers and turning the small rivers that are channeled through the city to greasy dishwater.

Walking along the smelly canal leads me to Hua Mei Nightfall Market, where I buy freshly squeezed orange juice from the store that first won my vote by returning my money when I misunderstood the price, and paid far too much. In China, this would never have happened. After two nights, the stall keeper and I are on friendly smile and *ni hao* terms. From her stall, where the smell of orange peel hangs like a bright yellow cloud, I move deeper into the market. Dodging scooters, people and prams. I pass stalls where small women in bright aprons behead blue chickens with giant silver cleavers. A young girl paints black nail varnish on pink pork trotters before putting them on display. Skinny purple eggplants are a safe haven for one lost green chili, and periwinkles and mussels lie in piles of crushed ice. At a fruit stall I select a scarlet dragon fruit, add a bright orange papaya, two white guavas, and a hand of deep yellow bananas to my purchase. They will turn into a huge fruit salad, which the juice of the dragon fruit will stain bright pink. The smell of roast duck wafts across the walkway, and my nose decides that dinner will be roast duck, stir-fry vegetables and steamed dumplings.

The route home leads past a small bakery; here I get myself into a tangle with exotic pastries, which I think are sweet when they are meat. What I assume is grilled cheese turns out to be shaved pork. I select a yellow 'custard' tart, and discover it is taro root paste, and what I believe to be chocolate chips in the muffins are actually red beans. After a few culinary surprises I quickly adjust, and am just as happy with a taro root pastry as with a custard one. Pottering about in the kitchen, I conclude that being able to nurture yourself by preparing exactly the kind of food your body needs is good, not just for the body, but also for the soul. Of all the things I have given up for this year, cooking for myself is the thing I miss most.

As the days pass, I fall into a small routine. After a hearty homemade breakfast that makes my life seem almost normal, I spend a few brief hours sightseeing, before taking my seat at my computer under the steel-barred window of my room, where the thudding of army helicopters, which patrol the shoreline of Taiwan, interrupts my thoughts. From the window, I look down on the dead concrete jungle, where everything we need to live must be brought in from outside. Life in a city, concentrated on the acquisition of money, breaks the connection between the planet and ourselves. When we move into cities, we become disconnected from nature, and no longer have any concept that we need the diversity of the planet to survive. In a city it is easy to believe that as long as there is a supermarket around the corner, and a petrol station within driving distance, all will be well.

It has been months since I could read or understand anything, and without the constant haranguing of the media to buy, buy, buy, I have lost the need for acquisition. In a few weeks I will be in America, where I will understand every word and every sound. Staring at my computer screen, I wonder how I will cope with that. It is a strange and slightly frightening thought, soon to be walking straight into an overwhelming wave of consumer-driven information. As the helicopter blades mince the yellow air beyond the steel bars of my bedroom window, I have a sudden longing for the silence of the Karakum, where starlight cast my shadow on the desert floor.

Vincent indulges my antisocial behavior for a week, then declares that all this slothing about simply will not do, and drags me out into the countryside, which would be on the west side of the island. Taiwan is split in two on its north-south axis. On the east side of Taiwan, the gentle sloping plains have been built up into one uninterrupted city from Taipei in the north to Kaoshiung in the south, while on the rugged mountainous west side, the island is still the little paradise that earned it the name Formosa – 'Beautiful Island' – from the first Portuguese explorers.

Our goal is Sun Moon Lake, the largest natural lake in Taiwan, which lies high in the mountains of central Taiwan. We leave in the early morning haze; it softens the hard square lines of the ugly buildings that line the road, and swaddles the scenery in a muffled coat of yellow grey. Only the rice paddies that are cultivated on every bit of open ground put up a fight against the muddy light, and are a green slap in the face. The narrow road takes us high into the mountains, where the unruly chaos of the indigenous mist forest is slowly being replaced by the regimented rows of betel nut palms that march up and down the mist-filled valleys. The nuts are sold by 'betel nut beauties' who stand in small glass-fronted stalls at the roadside, advertising their wares with green flashing neon lights and revealing clothing. While the 'betel nut beauties' are endemic to Taiwan, the betel nut is chewed and spat throughout East Asia and the Pacific islands. The juice of the betel nut stains the teeth and mouth of the user deep brown-red, resulting in a ghastly grin, which I find revolting, although in Taiwan poems have been written about the beauty of young women whose mouths are delicately stained by betel juice. Whatever turns you on, I suppose. Which is exactly why people chew the nut; it is a highly addictive stimulant and to satisfy this need, the indigenous trees must make way for the betel nut palm.

On the top of a steep rise, Sun Moon Lake slices through the trees, opening a hole to the sky that reflects its watery clouds on the still water. From the roadside, the lake stretches into the blue haze, its edges fringed by exotic white flowers. The lake laps the feet of strange carbuncled mountains; their jumbled shapes are testament to the complex geography of Taiwan, resting as it does on the battleground of the Philippine Sea Plate and the Eurasian Plate. In 1999, a clash of these two global super- powers caused one of the worst earthquakes in Taiwanese history (921 quake). Its epicenter was just a few kilometers from Sun Moon Lake. Today yachts bob about in the shadow of huge utilitarian apartment blocks that poke malicious fun at the beautiful scenery. These buildings were destroyed by the '921' earthquake, but instead of taking the opportunity to improve the design, the locals are rebuilding them in exactly the same way.

This small excursion to Sun Moon Lake whets my appetite for further exploration in Taichung. Unfortunately, I cannot expand my mind to embrace a greater understanding of the Chinese symbols on the street signs, which in China was easy, with their simplified symbols. But the Taiwanese are traditionalists; more Chinese than the Chinese; and here the symbols are still in their ancient form. There are Pidgin English street names, but the Taiwanese have not standardized their translations or spelling. So the reality of my map and the world it attempts to chart are so far apart that I leave the map in the apartment, opting rather to take Vincent's address card with me, so that I can always summon a taxi to deposit me back 'home'.

In the cloying sunless heat, I sweat my way along a busy Saturday street, where brilliant billboards create canyons of graphic color, under which the traffic torrent roars. The roads fork and twist.

Soon I am lost among stores that spill electronic goods and plastic. From the sharp angles of modern buildings and billboards, a Taoist temple, its rooftop teeming with bright green dragons, snarling warriors, flowers and brilliant phoenixes, makes an elaborate sweeping bow to ancient China. In parks and public squares, people dance to the sound of hip hop or tango that blares from small ghetto blasters. On the plaza of the Museum of Modern Art, large groups move slowly through their Tai Chi exercise, while under shady trees, in small pagodas men huddle around mahjong tables. In Changdun Park young lovers row out into the center of the small turgid lake, where they float in imagined privacy, listening to birds that compete vigorously, but lose hopelessly against the roar of traffic.

As I step into the gardens of the Taichung Confucius temple, the noise is suddenly stilled. Ancient trees, beautifully pruned to graceful umbrellas, create deep pools of shade and silence. The yellow curved roof of the temple rests low and heavy on short red lacquer pillars that run all along the courtyard, where women bang rhythms on small drums, while old men use the covered veranda as an exercise track. In spartan classrooms, children are instructed in the art of respecting one's elders and self-control, while outside the traffic rages. Staring at the ceiling of the Ta Chen Palace, the foreignness overwhelms me. Not having the familiar hidey-hole of the Wish Mobile has exposed me to the full onslaught of this strange world. Commandeering a taxi, I return to the comfortingly familiar surroundings of Vincent's apartment.

Vincent is having none of it. We have a lunch reservation in 'The Teahouse' in an up-market part of Taichung, where koi glide under the tables, and waterfalls cascade over fern-fronded rocks. Sitting at a small table, silence hangs between Vincent and I. I can find no words to fill the spaces designed for conversation, and realize the silence that I enjoyed has slowly slipped into isolation; I am not here and not there, the goal of China reached, the American adventure ahead, and Taiwan but a small pitstop to recharge the batteries. Despite my sense of alienation, this holiday from experiencing new things every second of every day has allowed me to pull myself together again, and tonight I leave Taichung for Taipei.

Bed 96

Taipei is set in the triangle of land between three rivers: the Keelung, the Danshuei and the Xindian. Night has fallen by the time my bus reaches the inner city, where futuristic neon lights roll, float and flash, up and down high-tech buildings. Green, orange, purple, red, pink and yellow lines glide over the sleek contours of luxury vehicles that are stuck in a slow hurry to somewhere.

Once in my hotel, I contact David, whom I met briefly in Taichung. He has offered to show me around. First stop a cash machine situated in a 7-Eleven store. Here Taipei shows off its international flavor. In the short queue at the cash machine, a blonde backpacker couple in baggy shorts and sneakers queue behind a group of porcelain-doll Taiwanese girls, dressed in the latest girly fashion. Behind them towers a huge man, his ebony skin contrasting sharply with his orange kaftan, while at the rear a group of German businessmen, in smart suits and neat haircuts, line up to use the money machine. While I wait for David, I browse the shelves, where familiar Western brands are in abundance. I feel America creeping closer.

David leads me through the crowds, the smells, and the steam to the sensory overload that is the Shilin Night Market. It is the biggest night market in Taiwan, the food hall has more than 500 food stalls, each one doing a roaring trade. There is such flavor in the air you could sip it with a straw. At a teppanyaki bar, we sit at the last two chairs to watch as the chefs wield their metal spatulas, preparing dishes with lighting speed. A zing of metal warns that the show is about to begin. A handful of diced chicken hisses onto the hot surface, the spatulas flash, sprouts and tofu fall, receive a splash of soya, releasing a sweet salty aroma; the chef adds ginger, and thinly sliced cabbage; and the aroma receives a warm sharp note, as he lifts and folds. With a flourish, the finished meal is elegantly slip-lift-dropped on my plate, crunchy fresh, deeply flavored and delicious.

Sated, we plunge into the flow of energy that is an Asian city at night, and at last I experience the thick of things, the human traffic jam, the solid moving mass of people, which I have been expecting since arriving in Chinese-speaking territory. The alleys of the market are narrow, the official stalls crowd both sides, and illegal stalls take up the center. The crowds are enormous, personal space reduced to millimeters, but everybody is respectful of those around them, and we fall into the gently dodging dance that one learns very quickly in these crowded alleys. The temptation to buy is overwhelming; for shopaholics this place could be deadly. The choices are enormous: hundreds of boots, thousands of sneakers, watches, phones, hats, vibratility condoms, and jumpy eggs. One long alley is a costume jewelry blaze of sparkling, glittering diamante and paste. Then there is a whole street of stores selling only gloves, hats and scarves. There are alleys that specialize in boots, pots, pans, handbags and designer ware. Unfortunately, the designers cater only to the locals, and as the women in Taiwan are all the size of a small Western twelve-year-old, there is not much that fits me.

Eating while you browse the night market is quite the done thing, and the food vendors have adapted to the needs of the 'eating on the move' crowd. Here all food comes on a stick, so as you shop, you can slowly eat your way through a five-course meal, from slices of melon and snow-white guavas to roasted squid and duck. I watch as a man breaks tiny quail eggs into a mini waffle tray; he flavors the egg with minute fish; and once the eggs are cooked, threads six little eggs onto a stick, presenting me with a fishy egg lollipop … no thanks. At the next stall I watch a contender for the 'messiest ice-cream in the world' record, prepare his ice-cream pancakes. He scoops two balls of homemade sorbet onto a thin pancake, adds a sprinkle of peanut brittle, folds the ice-cream-laden pancake into a neat square parcel, and hands it to the client on a paper napkin. In the humid heat of Taipei, the race is now on for the client to eat this odd confection before it turns into a sticky soggy pulp. The client takes the folded dessert delicately in two fingers, tips his head back, and for one brief moment becomes a boa constrictor, as he appears to unhinge his jaw, and slides the whole confection down his throat.

The mass of people sweep us along, past hundreds of tiny dogs with enormous pedigrees and young women who have acrylic nails, with three-D mini worlds of flowers and fairies attached to their fingers. We fight our way out of the river of people, and attach ourselves to a long queue. David insists that I sample the local drink, the specialty of Taiwan: pearl milk tea. With the first scoop of pearls – white slimy things that look like frog's eggs – I start to have misgivings. The vendor scoops crushed ice onto the gloopy things, and then tops up the whole lot with brownish liquid, which I am guessing is tea. I suck dubiously at the drink with a very fat straw, which allows a whole string of the slimy little 'pearls' to shoot up, and float about in my mouth. With a small shudder of revulsion, I tentatively try chewing them. The texture is gross, but I discover that the little blobs have a faintly malty taste. With my next sip, I try ignoring the slimy intruders, swallowing as quickly as possible. This results in a gag action, which is very gross. My final solution is the best: I give my drink to David; he really seems to like the stuff. He is also looking at his watch, as it is long past the witching hour, and the stalls are slowly starting to pack away their wares; time for some shut-eye.

In the morning, I cast an appraising eye over the dull yellow light filtering through the hotel window, then, with a small grin, snuggle down, and enjoy a few more hours of sleep. In Taipei I feel no guilt at my daily sleep-ins; waking early is pointless in a polluted city, where the light remains a constant dull haze all day. The lack of oxygen also dulls my brain, and I feel a strange, empty melancholy settle over me, as I set out to discover the capital city of Taiwan. I have become completely isolated, and seem to be drifting in a private bubble of silence that is intensified by the hot eerie atmosphere. The smog covers everything in a pale yellow haze, so dense that buildings on the opposite side of the street swim in and out of focus. The sun heats the yellow air, until it becomes a tangible presence that tears at my eyes and sinuses.

To find relief, I duck into the Jianguo Flower Market, past Buddhists with begging bowls, and young girls selling fluffy puppies. In the market, massed orchids compete with chrysanthemums and bougainvillea for the attention of the hordes of locals, who carefully inspect every bloom before making their purchases. In the dense concrete maze of Taipei, plants spill over every balcony, fill every foyer, and line the neighborhood streets, in an effort to make what is undeniably ugly, beautiful.

My destination for the day is the Taipei 101, which is the first building in the world to top the half-kilometer in height mark. It towers over all the buildings, and by keeping it in my sights, I negotiate my way through downtown Taipei. Despite its colossal size the 101 vanishes and reappears in the yellow haze, leading me on a merry chase through small side streets, where families go about their business on fuming scooters. I walk past shops selling ugly furniture, international hotels that roll out the red carpet for every comer, and cross giant streets chocked with traffic, which adds its fuming smog to the already potent chemical mix. By sunset I reach my goal, and entering another 'once upon a time' highest-in-the-world building, I consider that I am setting some sort of world record for going to the top of high buildings. Fortunately I am spared the need to climb the stairs, as using the high-speed elevator is part of the 101 experience. At 17m/s or about 61km/h, it is one of the swiftest lifts in the world, and it delivers me to the top of the 508 m tower in 30 seconds flat, with not a popping eardrum to be found, thanks to the pressure equalizers in the elevator. Climbing the last few stairs to the open-air lookout, I look down into disappointment, as only the brightest of city lights manage to penetrate the dense smog.

Sunday arrives with a slight breeze, which keeps the pollution at bay, and the sky is blue above Taiwan for the first time in a month. The Taipeians are quick to take advantage of the weather, and are out and about in Daan Park, across the road from my hotel. Families gather on the lawn, and photograph each other in front of floral arrangements that represent Western themes, such as white weddings and Valentine's Day. As a foreigner, I feel very welcome here. People smile, say hello, and try to help; and even though they are so busy, there is a cheerful energy here that Mainland China does not have. The energy in Kong Hong is intense, but diffuse; there are too many nationalities, with too many agendas. In Taipei, there is a very strong sense of being Taiwanese, a one for all and all for one sense of belonging. I get the sense that this is the energy that the Chinese culture was built on, and not the desperate grubbing for material gain that seems to currently be the only driving force in Mainland China.

At the Chiang Kai-shek memorial, I count my way up the white steps – each step symbolizing one year of Chiang Kai-shek's life – to the giant white pagoda. Reaching step number 89, I step into a marble hall, where a statue of Chiang Kai-shek stares into the distance, dwarfing the sarcophagus, the tourists and the motionless guards, who stand as still as mannequins, while their comrades dust imagined lint from their shoulders, wipe the sweat from their brow, and provide them with drinks from a straw. In the giant plaza in front of the memorial, groups of young people rehearse their dance movements in a synchronized hip-hop display, while the more spry young men flick-flack across the cobbles. As the day draws to a close, I stroll slowly back to my hotel, past beautiful boutiques and ice-cream parlors, where long queues form to buy the exotic ice cream: Pig's Feet Beer, Drunken Beef, Sesame Chicken, Gaoliang (Taiwanese vodka), Wasabi. Compared with these flavors, my choice of Red Bean ice-cream is decidedly boring.

My time in the East has ended, but as the bus takes me to the airport, I am aware that I am still traveling east. Where does the Far East stop or start? To the people of the 'East', the Americas are east, and Europe the Far East. It's all relative to your position. Some very clever philosopher once proclaimed that

'What is, is, and what is not, is not'.

The sentence is flawed, because what is to me, is not necessarily to you, and what is to me, is most definitely not to a dog, and vice versa. What is, is determined by what I am, or you are. The 'is' depends on the 'are' or, in this case, 'where' you are, and where I am, is a tiny flying world, in which the stewards are the masters of all they survey. After boarding, they plunge us into a time zone all of their own making. Just on midnight, they serve dinner. Then lights out, and they remain out until one hour before landing, at which point local USA time is 20h00, and supper would be a welcome meal, but we are served breakfast. While eating, we should all be thinking of bed, yet are all wide-awake and ready for the day, which is in fact yesterday. I wonder again at the strange thing that is man-made time, which allows us to land in Los Angeles 12 hours after, yet at the exactly the same time and date that we departed in Taipei, time-warp on an airplane.

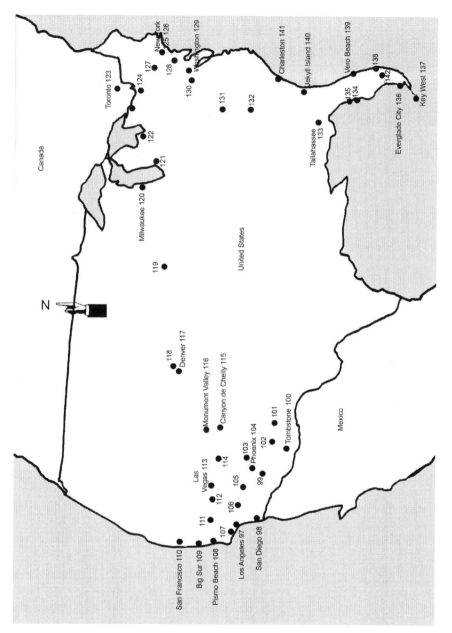

Map 6 : United States of America

United States of America
California
Bed 97

In America, I hit the ground running. I can read every sign, comprehend every sound. Ground stewards give directions left, right, forward, back. We are advised where to walk, when to stop. Signs tell us how to use the elevator and the escalator. We are advised when to start lifting our luggage, and when to put it down. The customs man gets chatty; the passport man gets chatty; and before I have moved through the arrivals gate, I have understood more, and have had more conversations than in the last few months. Then out of the chaos of sound, I focus on a familiar name:

"Annette."

"Annette!"

"Aaaannettte!!!"

Before I can determine the source of my name, 5W Kathy bursts from the crowd. She is big, vibrant, with Rasta dreadlocks and a huge grin. She steps up, and with a joyous ...

"Welcome to America!"

wraps me in a giant bear hug.

Whoa! I stiffen involuntarily; this is as up close and personal as I have been in months, but she is not deterred. After a hearty squeeze, she pulls away.

"Come, give me your bags. Let's go. Astro is in the car. I hope you don't mind dogs. I am so excited to meet you I have so many questions. I hope you will be comfortable; my home is not large; but ..."

I squeeze 'yes', 'no', 'I'm sure it ...' in where I can fit them, and soon we are on one of Los Angeles many highways. The traffic is civilized, but I am not comfortable at being driven, and the thought that tomorrow I will be reunited with the Wish Mobile makes me very happy. I cannot believe that I am missing a hunk of metal. Some people form warm loving relationships with their pets. I have formed one with my car, and feel my travels can only continue properly once we have been reunited.

In a suburb on a small ridge, overlooking the flatlands of Los Angeles, I am shown upstairs to the guest room.

"It's not much."

Kathy says apologetically, while I look around at a brightly colored, beautifully decorated room, which has every convenience I could hope for. Not much in America perhaps, but more comfort than I have had for a long time.

Having just had breakfast on the plane, I decline supper, and withdraw to my room, where I spend the night waiting for morning. Come daybreak, I have only one thought: the Wish Mobile, my Wish Mobile; today I get my Wish Mobile back. In a small office in Long Beach, the shipping agent looks me over curiously.

"So you are the woman driving around the world."

Several more women come in to look at me, and after a moment, they ask the same questions I have heard from all around the world. All of these I give my knee-jerk answers to, but to the question...

"Aren't you afraid?"

I am beginning to formulate an answer to. Essentially, we are afraid of the unknown. This is a terrible thing, as it stops us from questioning, exploring, pushing boundaries, until we become captives in our lives. All the time wondering what it is that we are missing, but too afraid to go and find out.

After filling in and signing several documents, the Wish Mobile and I are reunited. With a small flurry of excitement, I get behind the wheel. The happy grin that I have been missing starts growing in my stomach as the Wish Mobile leaps to life with the first turn of the ignition, and I ease into a new country, new roads and new rules.

Immediately I discover that I am the driving barbarian now. All the residual bad habits I picked up from the Ukraine through to China come into sharp focus in 'oh so proper' America. Compared with the starting-gun concentration of China, the American drivers seem to be wallowing in boredom in their air-conditioned SUVs. But the Americans are inventive. To liven up their driving experience they multitask behind the wheel: drink coffee, talk on the phone, do their make-up, and read the paper, all this while driving down the highway. When I throw in my singular style of driving, which by now is a daredevil mix of every outrageous driving trick in the world, I soon have those sharing the road with me in apoplectic fits of rage. I quickly discover the bad driving trick of the American, a wild rude flipping of the middle finger, accompanied by some inaudible, but very visible cursing, screaming and general redness of the face ... and I didn't even make a u-turn on the highway ... the Americans should live a little.

After a quick stop to buy some small necessities at a local mall, I ease out of the parking space, and, keeping what I believe to be a civilized distance, slowly follow a man who is jiving his way down the middle of the road. At some point, I obviously get too close, and invade his personal space. He turns, takes a running leap, and lands both feet on the Wish Mobile bonnet. The Wish Mobile bounces violently in response, while I am frozen with shock.

What the ...!

From his impromptu podium, he yells at me through the windscreen, sweat and spittle flying. He spins around mid-sentence, to share his fury with the rest of Los Angeles, then, with a lurch of the Wish Mobile suspension, leaps back onto the road, and makes his arm-waving way into the night. Staring at his vanishing back in stunned silence, I realize that the American rage might just be more dangerous than the driving of the Chinese. Subdued, I very slowly, very carefully, and with due consideration of every visible American's personal space, edge into the sludge of traffic that fills the roads of Los Angeles.

After two days of finding my bearings in a new country, and getting my sleep cycle into some form of order, today is the day for the big 'cruise'. My goal is to find the HOLLYWOOD sign, as I want to get a shot of the Wish Mobile with the sign in the background. My quest takes me into Griffith Park, which is one of America's largest urban parks, situated in the Santa Monica Mountains at the northeastern edge of the city. While this area has been called the Central Park of Los Angeles, it is a wild and rugged terrain that holds memories of what the land must have looked like before the palm trees, the irrigation, and the lawns made their mark on the scenery. The road winds up through gnarled pine, and ends in a parking lot at the observatory, where a hiking trail begins.

The trail winds high along the mountain. Below me, the city sprawls towards the Pacific under a thin blanket of smog, but up here, the sun shines in a brilliant blue sky. It is only 07h30, but already the breeze is warm and sweet-sour with the scent of the low scrubland. On the trail, I meet the whole United Nations that is America: Asiatic-Americans, Latin-Americans, African-Americans and European-Americans, and I discover that I am eavesdropping. I seem to have lost the built-in filter we all have that prevents us from hearing and registering everything we can understand. After the long months of intense concentration required to understand anything at all, my brain has been trained to register everything around it in minutest detail, so I discover that the citizens of Los Angeles who take walks along this trail in the early morning say 'Oh my gawd' and 'f-ck' quite a lot, and rather loudly.

Rounding a corner, I spy the Hollywood sign towering over the houses of Hollywood Hills. This very exclusive neighborhood makes life incredibly difficult for intruders with its narrow winding roads. I am soon disoriented and completely lost. After the fourth dead-end, I decide that the Hollywood sign can probably only be approached by helicopter, and changing tactics, I apply my mind to try to find my way out of this maze. In desperation I once again try the Zen and follow-the-car-ahead-of-you method of navigation. While this has not yet worked anywhere on the planet, I remain hopeful, but no, the driver I choose to follow is as clueless as I am. My next course of action is to only turn into roads that lead downhill, and by this method of elimination, soon turn into what I discover to be Sunset Boulevard, where I enter a sort of virtual reality.

Driving in other countries, everything was new and strange, but here the names evoke virtual memories. Like…

Well, what do you know? Here I am in Sunset Boulevard

or

Oh look, it's the Chinese Theater.

or

Who would have thought I would ever be driving in Beverly Hills?

It is like finally meeting those virtual friends you chat to on the Web, and, like those friends, these familiar places have some surprises not shown in the pictures. I discover that Sunset Boulevard is very long. After winding its hairpin way past the manicured perfection of huge houses with palm trees and swimming pools, which the Americans here call average middle class, it takes me through less savory neighborhoods of Little Armenia and Thai Town, through

Hollywood proper, right to the exclusive areas of Beverly Hills and on to the Pacific.

In Beverly Hills, I stare in slack-jawed astonishment at the cars. They are eno-o-o-rmous great land cruiser things that would have served me well in Kazakhstan. Complete with shiny chrome bull bars, roll bars, handlebars and cocktail bars. Why does the American driver need so much car? The tires are huge hulking things; they rumble and they roar. The amount of fuel they use must be horrific. The argument is voiced that in case of an accident it is safer to be in a big car. This seems to me excessively paranoid, considering the granny-style driving of the American. All that car power just to transport beautifully styled blondes, with diamonds in their earlobes, and plastic at their fingertips, from swanky shop to swanky shop, on streets so perfect that, no matter how I stretch my mind, I cannot find one good reason that such rugged vehicles are required. A bragging device perhaps?

But then I discover the truth of the matter. Sound tax advice in Beverley Hills is to buy a heavy vehicle, as these vehicles are a tax dodge. The enormous SUVs that all weigh in at over 6,000 kg are classified as trucks, and therefore are an immediate and complete tax write-off. But what about the fuel consumption? No worries there either. As the SUVs are 'trucks', they are exempt from gas-guzzling laws, and don't have to comply with the same strict safety standards as normal cars. Not surprising then that manufacturers of SUVs ensure that their vehicles all top the 6 tonne mark. The Wish Mobile is but a trifle in this land of the enormous car, and attracts hardly any attention at all. Cute does not cut it in Beverly Hills.

Checking my map, I discover that if I turn into Coldwater Canyon Drive, it will take me through some very exclusive real estate and onto Mulholland Drive. The virtual reality of my situation grows as I drive deeper in the money belt of LA. The wealth on display is so immense that my mind does backbends to try to put this and the Kazakhstan world of Elmira and Xharat on the same planet. If Xharat were to walk along these manicured roads, the cleanest in America, he would not comprehend the level of wealth surrounding him, and he would not have very long to try to work it out. Beverly Hills has some peculiar laws that forbid you to walk through the villa-lined streets. If the innocently strolling Xharat were to be confronted by a local law official, and could not produce suitable identification, he would be arrested for vagrancy. Walking is not the only thing forbidden in these exalted neighborhoods. Signs at regular intervals warn,

Cruising forbidden

How easy it is to become a criminal here; just driving or walking through certain neighborhoods will do the job – all this in an attempt to protect the rich and famous from curious, ordinary people. Although organized bus tours and jogging tours are allowed. So friend Xharat would be quite safe from the long arm of the law as long as he kept running. Strange, in South Africa it's the guy running through an up-market neighborhood that is looked on with suspicion.

Stopping at a lookout at the top of Mulholland Drive, I am looked on with some suspicion by a busload of tourists. A man comes up to find out what I am all about. After reading my little blurb on the windscreen, he has only one thing to say.

"You decide to drive around the world, and then you decide to do it in a French car?"

He looks at me pityingly, mentally classifies me as totally addled, and walks away, shaking his head slowly at the irrational behavior of women.

The handsome young tour guide, who is also an 'actor', has a different take on the matter, and asks for my card. Card, what card? It never occurred to me that I should have a business card for driving around the world. Pity, says he, as he has connections in the TV industry, and he can get me a TV show, snap, just like that. Yeah, right – LA, the city of dreams – this chap is cute enough, but been out in the sun too long.

Getting into a small tussle with my directions, I end up at Paramount Pictures – excellent – if I cannot get a photograph of the Wish Mobile with the Hollywood sign, this will be a good second choice. The security guards at the gate are not as sure. They have visions of me holding up the traffic for hours, while I set up the lights and the dancing girls. I assure them that this is not a Hollywood production, and I would be but a moment. They fall about laughing, while firmly declining permission, but then relent, and tell me to come back before seven in the morning, and they would let me get the shot.

From the heights of Baldwin Hills, Kathy and I stand overlooking the precise gird of streetlights that draw long perspective lines to Beverly Hills, and, despite the mountain of food waiting to be consumed in the fridge, we decide it will be a far better idea to go out and eat Mexican.

In a cozy wood and stained glass cantina, I experience my first all-American restaurant service. The waiter stuns us with a dazzling smile, throws in a few well-chosen, niceties, informs us of his name, and tells us that it will his great pleasure to be our service provider this evening. I am so relieved that he feels this way. He then rattles off the entire menu as if we are all illiterate or blind. By the time he is done, I am so confused that I need a moment to look at the menu. We place our orders, and thinking we are done with the decision making, I try to get back to my conversation with Kathy. But the man is a selling machine, and overwhelms us with more choices:

> Would you like that fried, dunked, crisp, soft, round, square, pink, purple …

Six questions later, I start wondering whether I should not simply go to the kitchen, and prepare the meal the way I like it, thereby saving everybody all this time and trouble. What he failed to ask, though, was, would I like a meal for one or for six. As the food arrives, I have a flashback to the food bragging in China. Did we invite someone else that I was not aware of? The salsa, the chili, the guacamole and the refried beans all arrive in such quantities that I am a touch embarrassed at having ordered it. Head down, girl, and eat and eat and eat, but the quantity of food defeats me.

"Would you like a box?"

The smiley waiter enquires?

A box? What do I need a box for?

But Kathy agrees that we each need a box, and so boxes arrive at our table, at which point I discover the practicality of the enormous meal. You eat as much as you can, then pack the rest in a to-go box, so tomorrow you eat again. Groaning, I walk out of the restaurant, clutching my box, thinking of the logistical problem of finding a space for the boxes in the already overflowing fridge.

Dawn comes, and still not hungry, I skip breakfast; the food in the fridge is slowly wilting. Today is the day to take a more detailed look at Hollywood, but first that appointment with Paramount Studios. Feeling like a born-and-bred LA person, I follow La Brea all the way across the valley, turn right into Melrose Ave, and find Paramount Pictures again with no problem. With a cheery hello, the guards greet me like an old friend, but tell me to get a move on, as even this early in the morning, some VIP might arrive, and it would simply not do if they were kept waiting for even one second. Fully understanding that I am very low in the Hollywood pecking order, I get the Wish Mobile into position, take the shot, and two minutes later am off to the 'Hollywood

Walk of Fame', where the; 'I have just stepped into my own movie' feeling continues.

In front of the Chinese Theater, tourists crowd around vampires, clowns and Conan the Barbarian. The wannabe actor, tanned, toned and buff, flirts with the girls, then hits them for a big tip once the picture taking begins. My picture taking begins as I look down onto possibly the world's most famous bit of pavement. Here is where the superstars of the moment go down on their hands and knees to press their famous flesh into fresh concrete. All around the world, I have been photographing my feet on every which surface they happen to be. I have documented my feet on a Croatian beach, a Chinese sidewalk, on cobbled streets, and on soft sand dunes, and now my feet are stepping into the footsteps of Fred Astaire.

With that thrilling little moment documented, I duck into a small neighborhood street to have a look behind the scenes, and am confronted with American suburbia, up close and personal for the first time. Low bungalows and small cottages are set in the most fanatically neat gardens, or yards, as they are called here. After my long travels in places where gardens were simply an inconceivable luxury, the obsessive neatness of this scene is astounding. The grass on the curb is within a blade of perfection, the edges razor sharp, the trees clipped to military precision, and not a spent bloom in sight.

At lunchtime, a neighborhood supermarket lures me inside. The place unfolds into five aisles of fridges stuffed with fast food, a huge meat counter, endless processed foods, and at last, a fresh-produce section, where I am stopped in my tracks by the apples. These are apples that the wicked queen in 'Snow-White' would have been proud to use. They are huge, deep red, their perfection highlighted by a mirror gloss finish that is slightly worrying. Are they real? Then I spy the small sign: 'waxed apples'. Further along, slightly more normal-looking apples are stacked under the sign: 'un-waxed apples'. Decisions, decisions. I opt for un-waxed, carry my prize to the counter, say a cheery hi, the cashier tells me the price, I whip out the cash, and goodbye. This business of understanding everything is like sending my brain on a little vacation.

Stepping back into the street I take a huge bite of my perfect-looking apple, end up with soft, mealy, flavorless mulch in my mouth, and desperately start looking for a place to spit the offending mouthful. My instincts tell me that to spit on an American sidewalk would not be the done thing, so in desperation I resort to the old spit into tissue trick, while my mind spins back to the apples of Kazakhstan. Crisp and sweet-tart juicy, their flavor undiluted by selective cultivation for the sake of good looks, their irregular size and shape would never allow these ancient apples onto the modern supermarket shelf.

I remember as a food photographer picking through dozens of apples to find the perfect specimen, which would be washed, polished, lit and shaded, until that apple was the fruit equivalent of a fully primped super-model. This was then presented as the only type of apple worthy of our attention and that could safely be eaten. Is it not perhaps time that we backed off a bit from this quest for the impossible, and consider that with a little shift in our perception of perfection, we could go a long way towards preserving what is left of our natural heritage?

My sightseeing takes me direction Broadway through the central business district of Los Angeles. In the shadow of the usual soaring glass towers and futuristic banking headquarters, a man in a black business suit is showing a monk in saffron robes how to work the parking meter. On the road, giant letters spell out

PED XING

What does it mean? What am I to do? Damn, just as I thought, I understood everything, life throws me a curve ball. The words appear at every intersection

PED XING

I am at a loss. Is this some sort of Chinese invasion? Finally I work it out. I was reading the words as I would have in Chinese, but changing gears back to English, it becomes perfectly obvious what I am dealing with. I soon come to the conclusion that my brain is just not on top form today. There is a sign pointing to Perishing Square. I have to see a square that is perishing, but when I get there, I discover that the square is not perishing, but it is Pershing Square. Here the buildings go supercolorfragilistic, bright canary yellow, deep purple, and, like a room that Mary Poppins has just worked her magic on, it is super clean. There are no advertising signs cluttering the facades of the buildings; the roads and pavements look freshly scrubbed; there are no pungent smells rising from the storm water drains. Even the hobo carefully picks up all his trash, and deposits it into the litterbin. Squeaky-clean America.

The historical center of Los Angeles is slightly frayed around the edges. Film crews block the roads, setting up lights, and talking most importantly into radiophones, while they turn the beautiful, falling-into-disrepair art deco buildings of Broadway into a film set. Around this 'Hollywood bustle', the locals of the area go about their business, which includes doing stunts on bicycles on their way to work, talking to themselves on street corners, and wearing highly exotic clothing. With everybody trying so hard to be noticed, the bizarre turns into the ordinary. Those wishing to stand out from the crowd in Los Angeles should wear ordinary clothing, and act normal.

Back at Kathy's house, the discussion turns to race. My white apartheid background makes me an interesting specimen in America, where racism is rife, but carefully ignored. While Amador writes his wish on the Wish Mobile,

> *'Si le gente vieron el munod sin colures se darian cuenth de que todo samos igualas y tenemos las mismas necesiodanes'*

Kathy mentions that often African-American history in American schools is taught only from the point of the Africans arriving as slaves in America, thereby negating the fact that the slaves were normal people, going about their daily business, before being dragged from their homeland by barbarians set on profiteering from the labor of others. The more things change, the more they stay the same, except the lords of commerce have learnt a lesson. They no longer import labor; they rather export jobs. Kathy has invited her Black Consciousness leader to write a wish,

> 'One love 4 world peace'

Not exactly fire and brimstone or profound, but the global quest for peace exists, even in America. Phil from next door steps out to see what going on, and adds his wish.

> 'Understanding and compassion are the key to lasting world peace'

Optimistic man, we have to establish world peace before we can make it last.

I catch myself. Now that I can understand the wishes, I am judging them. Life is a constant learning curve. There I was thinking I had acquired tolerance on my journey, but now discover that to be non-judgmental when one understands nothing is easy; to be non-judgmental when you understand everything is a far more difficult task. This will not do. I will only provide the vehicle on which the men write, and I will not judge what they write.

Bed 98

Having re-established the ground rules, I head off south, destination San Diego. The sun is shining, I have my slipslops on, and in my mind's eye I am going to the beach. However, when I reach the Pacific Coast Highway (PCH), I drive straight into a fogbank that reduces my visibility to the fast food take-outs that line the road in endless succession; McDonald's, Starbucks, Denny's, Wendy's and Jack in the Box. The small beach communities are swallowed in a grey damp cold, all the way to Sunset Beach, where I finally emerge into sunshine, and find myself deep in the money belt of the Pacific Seaboard of America. Here the good folk live in beautiful houses, each with a parking spot for their private yachts. To add to the charm of the scene, the houses are adorned with inflatable plastic turkeys on the rooftops, bright orange plastic pumpkins on every porch, and brilliant green plastic leaves trailing in delicate tendrils around every balustrade and windowsill. Americans are big on holiday-decorating, first Halloween, then Thanksgiving, then Christmas, and the Chinese are smiling. A wisp of conversation from the last few days pops up in my mind. I had commented to someone on the clear blue sky, comparing it to the smog of China. This drew the unexpected response of

'Yes, but the problem is, the Chinese pollution is making its way across the ocean to the USA.'

This is true. Owing to the prevailing winds across the Pacific, the air pollution of China makes landfall in America. Eventually everybody's pollution will be everybody's problem, but looking at all the plastic schnick-schnack trailing off rooftops, over garden fences, and on front porches. I cannot help wondering whether the Americans make any connection between their massive consumption and the pollution in China.

At Laguna Beach, a bride steps out of a flower-bedecked stretch limousine. She is wearing the same international brand of white meringue dress I have seen from Uzbekistan to China. The bride and groom make their way to the lookout, and, with the cliffs, the golden sand and the setting sun as a backdrop, they have the happiest day of their lives immortalized in digital. The position of the sun gives me a little wake-up call. I am running out of daylight because at this time of year the sun sets at 16h30, and by 17h00 it is dark, and I have long discovered that to arrive in an unknown city in the dark is not a good idea.

To make up time, I leave the winding coastal road in favor of the San Diego Freeway, and soon find my way high into the hills north of San Diego, where in a beautiful house, overlooking the Pacific, Carolyn welcomes me. She does not know me from Eve, yet purely on the request of a friend whom I have never met either, she opens her home, and puts me up in luxurious suite of rooms, throws open the very well stocked fridge, and simply makes me part of the household. America, the land of the large, and not just cars, but hearts as well.

To repay Carolyn for her hospitality, I bombard her with words. Since arriving in America, I have become aware of a rather disturbing thing. I open my mouth, and a great deluge of words pours forth, which I seem quite unable to control. I think my brain is enjoying the pleasure of producing a well-turned phrase. So I chew poor Carolyn's ear off, but quickly discover that I am going to have to temper my more extravagant opinions. Much like elsewhere on the planet, American thinking is steered by its media, and here my descriptions of the wonderful people of the Islam faith whom I met in the course of my journey are contradicted by statements of suspicion and mistrust. I find myself ducking and diving around issues and topics that might offend.

The following morning, Carolyn has recovered sufficiently from my verbal onslaught to offer to show me about the historical spots of San Diego. Our first stop is the Cabrillo National Monument, which commemorates Juan Rodriguez Cabrillo, the first European to set foot on the western coast of the USA. To celebrate this great step forward in European world domination, a monument was erected on the bluff high above the city of San Diego, where a small plaque catches my eye.

'... the Spanish believed they had a duty and a right to conquer the 'New World'. They believed their duty was to the Catholic church to bring Christianity to the 'heathen' natives and their right was to the land's riches both real and imagined ...'

The more things change the more they stay the same. Looking down on the Sunday morning regatta, where the steady breeze unfurls the spinnakers, and the sprays of white against the sea of deep blue reveal the speed of the yachts far below. The roar of an airplane attracts my attention, as it slowly comes in to land, skimming just above the rooftops of San Diego's CBD.

San Diego airport is smack in the middle of the city's built-up area, making it one of the few airports in the world that has a curfew: no departures before 6h30 or after 23h30. Across a small stretch of water is Coronado Island, linked to the mainland by the elegant 3.5-km curved sweep of San Diego Coronado Bridge. Turning away from the view over the harbor and city, I look over the Fort Rosecrans National Cemetery, where 91,467 casualties of the ongoing quest for global domination are buried. The morning light skims across the smooth white marble, and finds no blemish; there is nothing to distract the eye from the cold brutality of the block. As I stroll past the precisely laid out rows, they blend and shift into ever-changing graphic perspectives.

Lunchtime sees us in a suburban, 'eat as much as you like' buffet-style restaurant, where I dither over twenty different salad greens, five types of tomatoes, and stand undecided in front of the sprouts. There are so many things to decide in America: should I have bean sprouts, lentil sprouts, mung bean sprouts or peanut sprouts? To add to my mental distress, the size of the clientele keeps distracting me from my very important decision making. Will I ever get this salad mixed? Surrounding the salad bar are the fattest people I have ever seen in my life. Coming from Africa, where fat is beautiful, and often still equates to wealth, I am accustomed to seeing hefty people, but the girth of these salad-eating folk is on another level altogether. While I pile up on the salad leaves, raw carrots and beans, I cannot make a connection between the fat folk and the low calorie food. But on reaching the salad-dressing department, where a huge selection of thick creamy sauces are available, with which to drown those offending leaves, a small glimmer of understanding creeps into my head – although a little creamy salad dressing does not such fat folk make. Moving along in the queue the full answer is revealed.

The salad was but the dressing; the real food starts now. Six flavors of oversized muffins, four creamy soups, a whole selection of breads, then pizza, pasta and more cooked vegetables. The innocent salads are soon drowned in cream and starches, and the mountains of food people carry away from the buffet dispel the mystery of their gargantuan size. To end the meal, a selection of frozen yoghurt is on offer, which is a hilarious bit of self-deception; after all that food, why not just go the whole hog at eat proper ice-cream. But as yoghurt is meant to be healthy, people convince themselves that if they eat frozen yoghurt, it will not be as fattening as ice-cream. Get real. Yoghurt or milk, once you have added all the sugar, flavorings, and thickening agents, there is no difference between the two.

The following day, while on a little city tour, I am again confronted with fat America. After hopping onboard a trolleybus, I watch in fascination while the tour operator prepares to help a super-size woman board the bus. It seems quite routine to him. He puts out an extra step, holds onto the bus railing with one hand, grips the lady's hand with the other, and while her husband pushes from behind, his hands vanishing in the soft folds of her ample buttocks, the tour operator pulls her up first one, then a second low step. The exertion for the three is so great, they all turn the same shade of red. Once onboard, the fat lady squeezes down the aisle, her hips straining and stretching against the seats on either side. As she passes me, I involuntarily move as close to the window as possible. She squeezes into the seat behind me, giving me the full and unedited version of her wheezing and gurgling, as she tries to catch her breath from the strain of taking the two steps from the pavement into the bus. Sneaking a quick glance at her red sweaty face, I have a pang of concern that she might die of heart failure right there.

What if she falls forward, she would break the seat. I would be smothered, crushed, flattened … death by fat lady. No-o-o-o.

My attention is drawn back to reality as the trolley tour takes us over Coronado Bridge, although thoughts of death continue. This bridge is a favorite suicide spot in San Diego. About 220 suicides have been registered here so far. Signs warning against the dangers of jumping from the bridge and emergency phones dot the highest point of the bridge. The tour winds past the famous Coronado del Hotel where *Some like it hot*, starring Marilyn Monroe, was filmed. Cameras snap dutifully.

Back in San Diego, I stroll around the inner city and yacht harbor, where I browse through small shops that sell all things nautical, and finally I visit the famous San Diego Zoo, but my heart is not in it. I am itching to leave. I am craving the solitude that I lost at the Kazakh–Chinese border. I want to see the wide-open country. I am done with cities for the moment. It seems that I have been in one continuous city since arriving in Beijing almost two months ago. I want to hit the long road, to drive into wide open spaces. I want to stand under the vault of deep blue sky, and breathe clean air, and most of all, I want to sink into my silence again. Just the thought of it starts a small happy smile in the pit of my stomach.

A grey fog hides the sun as I leave the comfort of Carolyn's home with no real idea where I am heading. I have a vague plan to head south on Route 94 toward the Mexican border, maybe just to touch it, but not to cross it, and then head east toward Yuma on Route 98. After that, I will just play it by ear.

It is a working day in America, and trucks rule the freeway. Compared with the oil-smeared, fuming trucks of China, these American primped trucks are the beauty queens of the trucking world. Passing several chromed cabbies I start thinking that I could easily swap the Wish Mobile for one of those, and immediately have a guilt attack. My little Wish Mobile has done itself proud. To make amends, I give it a reassuring pat on the dashboard as I ease into the morning traffic, with the help of an interesting American invention, the two-car traffic light. A very slow blinking light controls the inflow of traffic onto the freeway, letting only two cars through at a time. It seems to work, as, although the freeway is packed, there are no bottlenecks.

Soon the city and fog vanish to reveal rolling hills of pale yellow grass, dotted with dark green desert scrub. At Jamul, I drive through my first taste of small-town America. Whitewashed wooden houses stand in small yards surrounded by white picket fences. Horse paddocks and wind pumps dot the scenery, and the general dealer shop looks like a prop for a western movie. Stopping to photograph a modest wooden church next to three skinny cypress trees, I become aware of the air: it is like cold spring water, crisp and irresistible. The sky is clear blue, the autumn leaves golden, and suddenly the excitement of the new and unexplored wells up. At last I feel my journey is beginning again.

Route 98 winds through the Mountain Spring Pass, where the mountains are built of rocks that are as round and regular as giant dinosaurs' eggs in shades of gold and pink. From the height of 3,000 ft, I look over the Yuha desert, a dull brown, rocky landscape that stretches to the faded blue horizon. The world around El Centro is tabletop flat, and geologically desert, but with the help of giant irrigation dragons that sweep water across the flatlands, the desert has been converted from dull brown to brilliant green. Mile after mile, tiny seedlings march in precise rows to the vanishing point on the far horizon. They are completely out of place here, but represent some of the richest farmland in America, and by definition the world.

Heading toward Calexico, I smell it long before I see it: my first cattle feeding lot, where the cattle are held in heavy metal cages with forked fronts that force the bullock's head downwards, so that it may never have the thought of perhaps stopping with the eating for a moment, to look up at the sky. It is a beef factory with a brutally simple production line: huge blocks of hay are stacked in enormous towers; the bullocks turn the hay into meat and manure; the manure feeds the desert, which grows more hay to feed the bullocks to provide America with meat. To keep the bullocks from over-heating in the sun, solar-powered fans churn the air, blowing a hot pungent wind across the desert. One photograph is all I have the stomach for, before diving back into the air-conditioned comfort of the Wish Mobile, and heading closer to Calexico. Hidden under a dense yellow smog, Calexico is the end of the road, the never-thought-about, nowhere part of America, the sort of place that you cannot wait to leave, and never admit to coming from.

Skirting the American–Mexican border, Route 98 finally merges with Interstate 8 on the Algodones Dunes, just outside Yuma. The Algodones Dunes are not only the largest dune ecosystem in America, but are more famously the earthly representation of the planet 'Tatooine', the home planet of Luke Skywalker of *Star Wars* fame. In keeping with this futuristic, racing-across-the-sand-dunes theme, rich America comes here to play with its sand toys. Recreational vehicles (RVs) that are as big as public busses, drive out on the shifting sand of Algodones in such numbers that small towns form in the space of a few hours. Camping American-style entails finding a suitable parking space for the RV, then flicking a hidden switch, which magically transforms the bus into a comfortable three-bedroom home. Table and chairs are set out under an awning, the barbeque fire lit, and in the space of half an hour, an all-American suburb has sprung up on the desert sand. Once all the comforts of home are in hand, all the family leap onto their private dune buggies, and roar about over the dunes, until the blue sky vanishes behind a yellow cloud of dust. This casual display of wealth constantly triggers comparisons with the rest of the world that I have seen. The culture shock of traveling to China was nothing compared with the shock of coming to America.

Leaving the Americans to play in their oversized sandpit, I, much to my surprise, drive through the center of the world. I have been to the center of the world before. The last time it was in Delphi – that center was so declared by Zeus – but this is America, and here you can make up the rules as you go along. Felicity is a town created by one man, Jacques-André Istel, who decided that as Felicity was his town, it was the center of the world. Not only must Jacques-André be a man of great vision, but also one of great persuasive power, as he managed to convince the Imperial County of California, as well as the Institut Géographique National of France, to recognize a spot on his property as the 'Official center of the world'.

I quite like the concept of making the place where one lives the center of the world. My center of the world will be wherever I am, and in this way I will manage to be totally centered at all times.

Saguaro Cactus, Arizona

Arizona – New Mexico – Arizona

Bed 99

At Yuma, I cross the Colorado River into Arizona, where time jumps forward by one hour, as I drive from Pacific Time to Mountain Time. Yuma is situated in a huge flat depression, surrounded by mountains. Its claim to fame is that – according to the *Guinness book of world records* – it is the sunniest place on earth. Of the possible 4,456 hours of daylight each year, the sun shines in Yuma for roughly 4,050 hours, which makes it a very popular wintering spot for Americans who live further north. This becomes evident as I hit the Thanksgiving traffic, and get stuck in my first, all-American traffic jam. We creep along at no miles an hour, until finally we pass a truck in a ditch ... that's it. A truck in a ditch ... no blood guts gore, no fire and explosions, but everybody is slowing down, and taking photographs. The Americans really need to get out more. After we pass this spectacular event, the road miraculously clears. The scenery is still flat fields of bright green seedlings that stretch in strict rows to the horizon. There is nothing to distract me other than the occasional American in a car.

After months of driving in outrageously bad traffic conditions, I am still having a hard time adjusting to the American way of driving, which is very sedate, slow, and with enormous following distances, yet on this completely flat road, there is suddenly a car on my tail. There are no other cars on the road. There is a clear view all the way to Florida. Why is this car on my tail? I slow down to help the chap to overtake. The entire driving population of the Ukraine would have passed me by now, but this guy is not moving.

Get on with it already!

Finally, my irritation levels boil over.

What is your problem! Are you asleep or trying to read the wishes, what!!!

Completely freaked out, I pull over, and let the man pass. He just moseys on by, quite oblivious ... fast asleep behind the wheel.

While I wait for him to get as far away from me as possible, I consult my map, and decide that I want to visit the petroglyphs in Woolsey Peak Wilderness in the morning. I have no idea what a petroglyph is, but as they rate a mention on my map, they should be worth a small detour. To be close to my goal I will overnight in my first-ever motel, which I find in Gila Bend.

Gila Bend is a flat, one-dusty-main-road kind of town, where a selection of motels are on display: an expensive one, $82, for a motel room? Give me a break. A cheap one, $22, scraping the barrel perhaps, but it is clean, and were I in Russia, I would have been very happy with this room. But as I have a choice, I opt for the medium one, which, at $44, is still within my budget. Stepping into the lobby, I smell a very distinctive and familiar, yet surprising smell, the smell of dahnia or fresh coriander. Fresh coriander is an acquired taste. For the uninitiated the bitter-sour smell is deeply unpleasant, but once hooked, it always brings the same reaction – mouthwatering. Lost in a little culinary cloud of deep aromas in which I now recognize star aniseed, ginger, curry, and the smoky smell of basmati rice, I don't notice a man entering the lobby.

'Good evening, may I be of assistance?'

Behind the counter, a small Indian man in crisp white shirt and well-pressed trousers waits enquiringly. Beyond the half-open door behind him a beautiful woman in a deep purple sari kneels on the carpeted floor, and so I make my acquaintance with a particularly American institution, the Indian motel owner. A group of Indians (from India), many, if not most, of whom are called Patel, have slowly taken control of the motel industry in America, the Patel motel cartel, if you like. Indians now own a huge portion of the motel industry of America, and are worth billions. This has started attracting the jealous attention of those who consider themselves 'true' Americans, which would be those that arrived here by ship from Europe about 500 years ago, and not those that walked here across the Bering Strait 20,000 years earlier. But in 'the land of the free and the home of the brave', whoever cracks the American dream has got my vote, so I book into my first Indian-American motel. My stay is a great success, and I am soon an avid fan of Indian motels. Conveniently dotted about the countryside, they are easy to find, and the rooms have everything a hardened traveler could ask for: clean, comfortable, well appointed, with huge beds, modern bathroom, a fridge, coffeemaker, microwave, channel TV, a desk, usually an Internet connection, and, very important, a safe place to park the Wish Mobile, at no extra cost. Finding places to sleep will be no problem in America.

Sunrise sees me at Painted Rock, staring at petroglyphs, which are grey granite rocks piled into a hill. The surfaces of the stones are roughly carved with deer and other animals, surrounded by a whole lot of squiggles. Dating from about 900 CE, they were created by the

Hohokam culture, who founded a series of small villages along the Middle Gila River. Interesting, if scratches on rocks are your thing. I am more impressed by the sun, the sky and the silence. It surrounds me, and fills me with a deep calm that I have not felt in months.

Silence and starlight: two things that are vanishing from our lives without fanfare, but things that we need to feed our primal minds, and keep us anchored. A small breeze strokes my face as I turn towards the sun, and step up close to a saguaro cactus couple. Their thorns catch the light, creating a golden halo around them as their stubby green arms reach to the deep blue sky. These silent giants feel like kindred spirits. They remind me of the 'halfmens' (half human) succulent that grows only in the Richtersveld of South Africa. The halfmens has something in common with another inhabitant of the Yuma Desert. The top of the halfmens usually points north, giving it the nickname of 'North Pole'. Here in Yuma, the fishhook barrel cacti that hug the ground, round, rose pink and spiky, usually point south, giving them the nickname of 'compass cactus'.

I crunch across the gravel plain toward Woolsey Peak, picking my way carefully around fragile desert plants. The pale skeletons of long-dead saguaro stand like the steel girders of high-rise buildings, cutting the sunrays into equal-thick shadow slices that fall and stretch on the gray gravel. On the slopes of Woolsey Peak, the golden-green saguaro cling to deep orange rock, their iconic shapes etched against the clear pool of morning sky. While photographing this classic image of the American Wild West, virtual memories well up, and I feel I am finally meeting a friend that up to now I have known only through words and pictures.

Bed 100

While I have been out photographing, my car kettle has come to the boil, and now, sipping a cup of tea while the sun slowly heats the world, I scan my map trying to decide where to go next. By chance my eye falls on Tombstone. I didn't know this was an actual place; I thought it was the figment of some scriptwriter's imagination. But there it is on my map, so the decision is made: tonight I sleep in Tombstone.

To get some distance behind me, I stick to the interstate, roar right through Tucson, and then take a sharp right onto Route 83, where I discover that Patagonia is only 27 miles from here. I didn't realize I was quite so far south. Heading closer and closer to the Mexican border, I start attracting unwelcome attention. After emerging from a dusty side road that I couldn't resist exploring, my eyes are drawn to my rearview mirror, where a great wailing of alarms and flashing of lights convinces me that I should probably pull over. A crisp young policeman steps smartly over to the Wish Mobile, and demands my papers. I try the photocopy trick; he looks at me with steely eyes.

'Ma'am, this will not do. Please present the originals.'

'Yes, sir!'

He scrutinizes all the documents with exaggerated care, but in the end, he is really just quizzy about the car, declines my offer of pen, so that he might add his bit of wisdom, and sends me on my way with a huge grin and wishes of good luck.

By late afternoon, I drive into another scene that is familiar from the movies. The San Pedro River, with its golden cottonwoods, bright against the blue sky, stops me in my tracks. This calls for closer inspection, which is achievable only by climbing over a barbed wire fence, and picking my way through low shrubs. I put a hand into the cool water as it ripples over round stones, breaking the yellow reflection of the trees that meet overhead, my imagination conjures up cowboys on horseback, and women in long skirts fetching water. A few minutes later, I am walking through the ghost-town streets of Fairbanks, where small wooden huts have painted-on windows, and the side streets have been reclaimed by nature. The eerie silence that hangs over this tiny cluster of fall-apart houses belies the heyday of Fairbanks. It was founded in 1883 with the arrival of the railroad and the building of a station. Then it was a small, but busy town, a place through which silver and copper were transported, where men got drunk, and trains were robbed ... just like in the movies.

But it is in Tombstone that reality warps into a little virtual world of its own. After booking into the Doc Holliday room of the Tombstone Motel, I chat to a lady airing her stomach on the porch. She complains of feeling fat, and, as she is not fat at all, I enquire why.

'I hate Thanksgiving lunches; it is the day we Americans just have to prove just how abundantly well life is treating us. So we always prepare an embarrassingly large pile of food. Not to eat it would be impolite, so we all sit there and stuff our faces for hours, and now I can hardly move.'

This is a little *eureka* moment; no wonder all the roads have been deserted, and all the shops and restaurants closed.

'But today is Thursday.'

say I innocently

'I always thought Thanksgiving would be on a Sunday for some reason.'

The feeling-fat lady gives me a quick lesson in America tradition. Thanksgiving is always on the third Thursday of November, and I must be the only person in America that didn't have lunch today. My stomach immediately starts to complain, but the only place where I can find anything resembling food is the local fueling station, where I cobble together a Thanksgiving dinner of vegetable juice, which will act as a cold soup starter, followed by a salad of tuna and roast sunflower seeds with a huge tub of Ben & Jerry's choc chip cookie dough ice-cream for dessert.

Oh yeah, this is going to be a revelation.

I have heard about Ben & Jerry's ice-cream from the movies and TV, and today, on this, my first Thanksgiving day, I will see what all the fuss is about. But first, a different bit of fuss to get through.

To wash down my little spread I decide on trying another American delicacy, and would like to buy just one Miller Light Beer, but come up against a whole new problem, one I have never encountered anywhere on the planet.

'Good evening, ma'am. May I see some form of identification?'
'Why?'
'Ma'am, I cannot sell you the beer without seeing your identification.'
'Why not?'

'I may not sell alcohol to persons under the age of thirty and would need to see an identification document to confirm your age.'

By now I am convinced this guy is pulling my leg. I haven't looked under thirty in years, and not to sell beer to people under thirty seems a bit puritan. But he won't budge, and a foot-tapping queue is forming behind me, if I want to try that Miller Light, I had better do as I am told. While digging about for the passport in the Wish Mobile, I wonder if the young man might not be in serious need of glasses, although by the time I have fished out my passport, and get back into the store, I have decided to take it as the best compliment I have had all year, making this a great ending to a thoroughly satisfying day.

At Boothill Graveyard I eat my Thanksgiving dinner while sitting on the Wish Mobile roof. From my high vantage point, I watch as the sun bounces vermillion off the giant rocks that rise abruptly from the cactus plains, before it vanishes over the horizon. America is a very good-looking place, and the Ben & Jerry's choc chip cookie dough ice-cream is deadly yum. With the sunset, the world becomes instantly ice-cream cold, so I slide off the Wish Mobile roof, and bed down in the enormous Doc Holliday room of the local motel.

tung tadadadadaaa trrayiiinnng taaang tanng

Strolling into the dusty deserted morning streets of Tombstone the *High Noon* sound track spins in my mind. My shadow shoots like an arrow down the street as I strut slowly past saloons and trading stores. My silent footsteps make me wish I had spurs, so that I can jingle, just a bit. Familiar names of American folklore are printed in bold reality: the 'OK Corral' where a pinto pony is tied to a pole, 'Big Nose Kate's Saloon', 'Virgil Earp – Marshall', 'The Bird Cage Theatre', once the wildest, wickedest place in the west. I stroll slowly down the middle of the street, my trigger finger itching, then I spot it on my left, shoot, and to my right, shoot. I shoot without pause, and by the time I hit the crossroads my first chip is full. After a quick reload I round a corner, and shoot a saggy woman in an unflattering brown uniform, while she is hoisting the American flag in front of the Victorian redbrick courthouse.

A garbage truck, driven by a woman, slows to allow an old cowboy to pass. He tips his sweat-stained Stetson, and nods his grizzled head, as she yells

'Good morning, Dallas!'

He slowly swaggers across the road. His spurs jingle, and floorboards creak as he pushes open a swing door, and steps into a diner. I follow. If this establishment is good enough for an old cowboy called Dallas, then it's good enough for me. He takes a seat at a small reserved table, while I scan the room for a table with a good view of the locals. Besides a few more old cowboys enjoying a leisurely breakfast, there are three groups tucking into huge pancake piles. Other than their choice of food, they have an odd thing in common: the three couples, two with children, are all a combination of American man with Oriental wife. This brings a flashback from my day in the San Diego Zoo, where the American male preference for Oriental wives also caught my attention.

My eyes shift to the window, where the garbage lady picks up her next load. I wonder if the militant feminism of America has improved the lot of the American women. Do they really want to drive the garbage truck, while their spouses lie in bed enjoying a leisurely cup of coffee? The curse of women's lib is that it has stolen the free time and some measure of dignity from women. Fully liberated women can do it all, but at what cost? When doing everything women always used to do – child rearing, cooking, cleaning – and then adding to it the responsibility of bringing in half, if not all the household income, there is not much time left to breathe, let alone have a sensible or original thought at the end of the day. It is in thinking that people define themselves, and thinking takes time. I wonder if in this mad rush to be just like men, the American woman has not shot herself in the foot – being in gun-slinging Tombstone and all.

Another disturbing thing about radical feminism is the reverse sexism that has spread into society, and has resulted in unjustified, generalized male bashing. In light of this, it is not surprising that men prefer women of other cultures, who have a softer take on woman's liberation. Yes, absolutely, bring on the votes, the equal rights, the jobs and the career, but treat me like a lady while you are at it. So the gently liberated female treats her man like a man, he treats her like a woman, and they love in happy harmony, while the militant feminist drives the garbage truck, and an old cowboy named Dallas sips at his coffee.

A hearty

'There ya go, dearie'

brings my attention back to the table as the well-padded waitress places a huge pile of steaming pancakes with crisp bacon and lashings of maple syrup in front of me. If you cannot beat 'em, join 'em; fat America here I come. It seems to me that in the short while that I have been in America, I have eaten more sugar than in the whole of the previous year.

Stepping into the street again, I realize that all the shops in Tombstone have small signs informing the world that they will only be opening their doors again on Saturday, so I decide to roll on out of town.

Bed 101

On a dusty back road heading direction Gleeson, I spot a sign.

Rattlesnake Ranch

Excellent. Bouncing down the narrow track, I am confronted by an almost obsessive collection of Americana. Rusty carpenters' tools, blacksmithing tools, shoemakers' dyes, glass and crystal are all bundled together in a decaying array of rust and dust. In 'Memory Lane' unicorns, uniforms, cash tills, and coffee mills, horns, hoes, and blunderbusses all bleach and crumble under the glaring sun. A sign

HALT

HIER

GRENZE

Bundesgrenzschuts

brings me to a halt in front of a trailer, which announces that,

'Today is self-service day; please deposit the money for your purchases in the box.'

Bemused, I make my selection, do some math, and deposit my money in the box. Try this in South Africa, and in half a day, you would have not one thing left standing. The moneybox would go first, then the trailer and all its contents, then every bit of scrap metal would be carted off to the scrap dealer, and the bones sold to the witchdoctors. This honor system reminds me of the cultivated flower fields in Germany, where you cut yourself a bouquet of flowers, count how many stems you have, then deposit the money in the box, before leaving the knife where the next customer can find it. The day that this would be possible in South Africa, is the day the country could be said to be 'healed'.

While making my way through the tightly packed open-air shelves, past a tumble of sun-bleached skulls of animals, I spy an alien skull on a spike, and instantly conjure up a plan to drive as far as Roswell to spot myself a flying saucer or two. My chosen Route 181 takes me off the beaten track onto a road which a sign informs me is a

Seasonal, unimproved road

This road is not maintained

Use at own risk

In America there are signs for everything, right down to one mile counters, so you know exactly how far you have traveled. The whole world could take lessons from the Americans as far as road markers, route numbers and directions are concerned.

Some signs are so cryptic they have had me foxed, but now finally I get it; they indicate how far the next junction with whatever route is. One is extremely well informed on American roads, but this information glut has a downside. The effect of all the warning signs is not to make me feel safe, but fearful. Elsewhere in the world I had no idea where I was going or whether the road was maintained or not, and I never gave the matter a second thought. Here, with prior knowledge of every possible danger that might befall me, I am becoming a right old lady. I dither about should I, shouldn't I use this road; perhaps I will get stuck; maybe I should drive the long way around. Pathetic! This is America. How bad can it be? With an air of bravado, I drive onto the road less traveled

It is a bit of a shake, rattle-'n-roll up the mountain, but nothing to rival Kazakhstan. The narrow and steep road climbs up and over the Pendregosa Mountains, where it folds open a view of rocky blue hilltops and a pale sea of cactus-studded grassland that vanishes into the purple distance. The difference in temperature from the plains to the high point of the pass is measured by the trees. On the plains, the trees are all still decked in autumn orange and red, while here, they stand white skeletons against the shadow rocks, which are laced with grey lichen and the sky above is sky, sky blue. The downhill road is slowly crowded on both sides by golden cliffs and huge freestanding rocks, until I am in a deep canyon. High above, the sky becomes a narrow winding river, fringed by leaves of orange and gold. At Portal, I burst from the golden canyon into a vast landscape of silver grasslands, blue mountains, and arrow-straight roads that lead me to

New Mexico

'The land of enchantment'

My goal for the day is Silver City, as tomorrow I intend to work on improving my knowledge of the American Indian.

I admit to never thinking about the 'injuns' at all, other than as the nemesis of the cowboy, in the 'Cowboys and Indians' movies of yesteryear. They were heathen savages, and whatever else the Hollywood western fed into my childish brain. I am looking forward to enlightening myself. My first discovery is that the phrase 'American Indians' is no longer considered politically correct. The term 'native American' is now the acceptable term, but the native tribes – who have been part of this land for tens of thousands of years, long before the concept of America existed – do not like the name 'native American', as it lumps them together with every other person born and sworn into America. The indigenous tribes want to be recognized as 'being' before the political state of America existed. The only correct way to describe them, then, is as the original people of this continent, the aboriginal Americans, who are made up of many cultures, which are split into many tribes.

Up high in the Mogollon [mo-go-yon] Mountains in the Gila [hi-la] Wilderness – the first designated wilderness area in America – people of the Mogollon culture built the Gila cliff dwellings on the west fork of the Gila River. The road winds narrow and steep into the mountains, where grey mule deer leap across the road, then stand watching from the dappled shadows. On the high plateau, where the west fork of the Gila River bends and folds silently around sleeping trees, which catch wisps of steam rising from the hot springs, the road ends in a parking lot. A ranger, of the square-jawed, tall and strapping variety, bids me hail, fellow, well met, looks over the Wish Mobile, nods sagely, and writes

'God bless America.'

This is a wish for the world? But there I go again, judging. No judging; looking, learning, listening is the name of the game.

The narrow wooden bridge creaks as I walk into Cliff Dweller Canyon. Very little direct sunlight penetrates to ground level in the cold winter months, allowing frost crystals to grow on hardy leaves and tiny icicles to hang from slender branches. A subtle grey-green beauty fills the canyon, where wooden bridges lead over rushing streams, and the narrow sky is laced by high pines. The cold in this deep cleft gnaws slowly at my nose, ears and fingers. Beauty be damned, I race for the sun further up the slopes.

The Mogollon people that built these rooms in the natural caves high in the cliff certainly had an eye for a spectacular piece of real estate. The low winter sun penetrates deep into the caves; the crystal water lies just below; hot springs are not far away. Despite this, the tribe stayed here for only thirty years; their departure is a mystery, as is much of their culture. Most of the clues to the past are lost, as the caves were vandalized long before archaeologists reached this site, but the atmosphere lingers in the small fireplaces and the now roofless rooms that huddle inside the cave. Round holes in uneven stone-mud walls show where floors must once have been. But the cold remains.

As I step into the sunshine to defrost, a small round ranger comes over to chat. She, like all the other rangers here, is a volunteer.

This is my first taste of an American national park. It is extremely well run, in a low-key unobtrusive manner. Rangers are at hand to answer any questions; they are interesting, interested, and knowledgeable, not just about the site on which they work, but also suggest the most interesting things to see in the area.

Bed 102

On the advice of the ranger, I abandon my Roswell UFO spotting mission – it's apparently not the season for it, anyway – and continue my travels on the 180W, which takes me past flat shrubby grassland dotted with yuccas and cacti. Small upright fence poles march steadfastly through a prairie of white gold grass that billows like morning mist on the rolling hills. The grass looks so soft I want dive in, and swim through it, but then remember the small problem of the pesky cacti that lurk in these parts. As the road curls down into the valley, it reveals Mule Creek, a small huddle of wood and tin houses, surrounded by the delicate grey tracings of winter bare trees that make a subtle link between the ice blue sky and cool yellow grass. Mule Creek soon vanishes behind me as the road winds up onto a high mountaintop, where I cross over into the land of the Apache and Arizona. Here something happens to the time, or not; time is very confusing down here. With Pacific Time and Mountain Time, all is well, but then not all states observe Daylight Saving Time, or some Indian reserves do, while the state the Indian reserve is in does not, or perhaps it is the other way around. As I said, it's complicated.

The road plunges through a cutting, where the setting sun paints the massive rocks to deep orange and red. A wind-blown veil of cloud shatters the light, which falls over the distant view, and catches in the white grass and spiky yucca, until their haloes dazzle against the shadows. The shimmering serpentine road winds along a razor mountain top; the land falls away into deep purple shadow on either side; while horizon blue mountains frame the golden scene. I look silently at the perfection in front of me, and can understand how the ancient cultures of this land formed their belief systems around nature; there is a natural power here that I have not felt elsewhere on the planet. My smile builds from the pit of my stomach, and grows to a broad grin of excitement as I look to the far northern horizon where America is waiting. Soon I am driving along the winding serpentine road, and in the Apache world of sky, grass, and light, the Wish Mobile and I become part of the scenery. Then I pass a sign

State Prison

Do not stop for hitchhikers

and the reality of fearful America returns.

In the valley, the red earth is drawn into strict lines that have a light dusting of leftover cotton wool, which the wind blows into small drifts along the roadside. The highly mechanized cotton harvesting in America is centuries removed from what I saw in China. In China, all actions, from picking to baling the cotton, are manual hands-on processes. In the USA they wait until the plant is dry, then send a harvester-baler across the fields. This results in huge, highly efficient cubes of cotton, but a lot of waste. Were this in China, somebody would latch onto this small money-making opportunity, and not a fiber of cotton would be blowing in the breeze.

The dusk slowly gathers in the distant mountains and shrinks the fields to within reach of my headlights, as I drive into Safford, a town so nowhere that it has become somewhere. It is the setting for the film *Lost in America*. Owing to its isolated position, Mount Graham, situated just a few miles out of Safford, is an important observatory station, where the world's most advanced optical binocular telescope is being built. Finishing my daily tasks just before midnight, I turn out the lights, and step into the cold. With my head thrown back, I look up into the deeply starred sky, and in the calm, cold silence, re-establish my connection to the universe. Turning my back against the chill, I snuggle into yet another strange bed, and before I fall asleep, come to the realization that in life there is only one thing I can be sure of – that if I awake in the morning, I will be there; that is all, and that is enough.

In the frosty morning, my breath hangs on air, as I load up the Wish Mobile, and continue on my quest to learn more about the aboriginal tribes of America. Before entering the San Carlos Indian Reserve I stop to buy lunch in Geronimo, where I meet up with two fat men of the Apache tribe. One, a pastor, writes a biblical verse on the Wish Mobile, while the other asks, with some concern, if I need money or any other sort of help. The fact that I have driven halfway around the world, and that the wishes, to which they have just added, were written by men from China, Russia and Greece seems to make no impression on him. To him, I am a homeless person in need of financial assistance. I catch a glimpse of myself in the car window, taking in my cap jammed onto the back of my head, my any-which-way hair escaping any which where it can, my tatty jeans, sneakers and army parka, I realize that I have let myself slide. I am in desperate need of a bit of grooming, as is the Wish Mobile, but later. First, there is the San Carlos Apache Indian Reservation to be explored.

The R3 takes me far into the backcountry, direction Coolidge Dam, where the road, through low scrub and cactus country, deteriorates to bone jarring and pothole dodging. The air is clean, the sky a bowl of pure blue light, then, rounding a tangerine rock cutting, I arrive at Coolidge Dam, where plates of white concrete zigzag down multicolor cliffs, and eagles frozen in stone overlook the canyon. Parking the Wish Mobile in the dead center of the dam wall, I turn off the ignition, and step into the silence. It grows and pushes at me from all sides, until in self-defense I lean over the dam wall, scoop a deep breath and yell

HAAALLOO

The silence shatters and breaks as the rocks respond.

HAAallo hallo hallo hallo

Quietly, quickly, the silence flows and fills the spaces until its surface is once again ruffled only by the warm wind.

Grinning at my brief moment of glory, I swagger back to my silver steed, and make my way to the tiny town of San Carlos, where the roads are dusty and bare of trees or grass, lined with small prefab houses that are pale grey and equipped with huge satellite dishes and air-conditioning. A bunch of bright balloons draws my attention to a group of well-rounded people who are carrying plates of food to an already groaning Sunday lunch table set out in the yard. In front of the house, large shiny pick-ups and SUVs fill the dusty street. Next door, a man sprawls across the roof of his bright red pick-up, talking on the phone. On the ground around him lie a party-leftover of beer bottles, and an assortment of junk, in the universal way of poor people who hang onto stuff, thinking it might be useful one day, until their properties look like dumping sites.

Away from the southern California coast, the American car obsession had tempered somewhat, and I had been noticing a normal mix of vehicles, but here the massive contrast between the expensive cars and the shabby houses brings the American and global obsession with cars back into focus. The car is – more than any other thing we possess – our alter ego. It is an extension of our personalities, a clear symbol of our status. The car is our moving universe, in which we are the sole masters, and from where we can rage against the world. In Germany, the cars are solid and reliable, black and silver; in Italy, fast, furious, red and small; in the Ukraine, they are a highly visible class division between the haves and the have-nots; in China, they will drive anything that will get them from A to B faster than yesterday; and in America, the cars are BIG.

Looking at the big shiny cars in front of the small shabby houses, it seems that the thinking is, as long as you are looking good when you are driving around, all is well; just do not invite anybody home; and the petrol sheiks are smiling; and the world spins round and round.

Bed 103

Consulting my map while driving slowly through the small town, I decide to scoot up Route 10, so I can drive part of the scenic route through the Apache Mountains. The road is sandy and empty. In the distance, across a plain of cacti and tangerine stones, small mountains trace a blue jagged line along the horizon. A long-eared desert hare bounds in slow motion across the road, while tumbleweeds turn somersaults across the yellow sand. I am at peace with the world, and slip into a daydream, until the dirt road starts peeling off in all directions: choices, choices, unexpected choices. I choose right, wrong! The road step-tumbles down a small ridge, and after a brief jolt-slip-bump I find myself in the dry riverbed of the San Carlos River.

What just happened?

Where is the road?

I am not doing this!

Here I have a choice. In Kazakhstan it was forward or bust. In America, there are multitudes of roads to choose from, and I choose, for the first time on my trip, to forget Road Trip Rule 3 – never go back – and pick my way up the steep riverbank, turn around, and go back. Then make my way onto the Old West Highway, which winds its perfect tar surface around lazy bends, past rolling hills and craggy red rocks, over which march a silent motionless army of giant saguaro cacti to the Roosevelt Dam, a shard of sky in the burnt sienna landscape

Here, in the Tonto Apache Reserve, the Salado culture built adobe houses in the cliffside caves. The path to the caves picks its delicate way past a particularly nasty cactus, called the cholla. Signs everywhere warn to keep pets and children under control. The cactus has a nickname, the jumping cactus, as at the lightest touch it breaks and hangs tiny thorny balls onto, into its victim. The thorns have reverse hooks, so pulling them off is almost impossible and incredibly

406

painful. That this cactus is also called the teddy-bear cactus says something about the slightly strange humor of the American.

Along winding mountain roads, I drive through Payson, and on to the Mogollon Ridge, to a town called Strawberry. In Strawberry Lodge the proprietress, Ella, walks over, and with a firm handshake, and a square look in the eye, demands to know all about my car.

'Why'ya having people write on your car?'

'They are wishes for the world.'

'Why?'

'It is a global artwork, a participation piece called 'One Planet One People'. Men from all around the world have written wishes for the world on the car.'

She raises a skeptical eyebrow, serves me a fine bacon and egg sandwich, with the best fries I have had in ages, then steps outside to investigate further. The fire crackles behind me, as I watch her through the window. Slowly she makes her way around the Wish Mobile, occasionally stopping to read. She comes back inside, and with a curt

'Good on you'

returns to serving massive chocolate brownies and steaming cups of coffee to the locals, while I finish my sandwich, and then I follow the example of all the customers at the counter, and round off my meal with a chocolate brownie and a mug of coffee, which is served in actual ceramic. This meal is a small miracle in this land of fast food, Styrofoam and plastic.

Food is such a problem in this land of plenty. I find myself trawling the fridges and endless aisles of huge supermarkets, and somehow not finding real food. There are fast food outlets everywhere, where the price of food is reasonable, but where no reasonable person would eat. In restaurants where the food looks if it will not actually kill you, the prices will do in your budget in a flash. My obsession with label reading on supermarket foods has reached ridiculous proportions. A raw nut is a perfectly good wholesome food source, but in the USA they feel obliged to add 'value' to it: oil it, roast it. There are candied nuts, salted nuts, chocolate-coated nuts; the peanut rears its ugly little head everywhere. Trail mixes, which I have always considered a healthy snack food, here become a minefield of corn syrup, yoghurt balls and bits of chocolate. But finally, after discovering that a simple muffin has a list of ingredients that read like a highly complex chemical experiment, and includes no fewer than five kinds of sugar, I come to the conclusion that label reading is a basic survival tactic in America.

At first I could not make a connection between the fat Indians, their shabby houses, and the cost of food, thinking that either they earn a whack of money or spend a disproportionately large part of their income on food. But after reading the labels and ingredients of the food, it no longer surprises me that America is the land of the fat. They are totally undernourished, subsisting on fats, sugar and carbohydrates, with an assortment of indigestible chemicals thrown in for added flavor. Through intensive research, driven by hunger, I discover that it is possible to eat healthy food in America; you just have to be rich to do so. As I do not fall into that category, I opt for the raw food route: carrots, apples, and the most organic yoghurt I can find.

Wishing Ella farewell, I make my way down the mountain through a small town called Pine. The originality of the name makes me believe that the people here must be quite exceptional and worth a visit. As I park the Wish Mobile in front of the local library, a man steps up, demanding to write a wish on the Wish Mobile. Absolutely, wishes are the name of the game. Handing him a pen I step aside, and watch as he writes his wish in huge letters, and with his one wish,

'Come to Jesus Christ, the ONLY WAY TO TRUTH AND LIFE'

he simply negates the spirituality of billions of people around the world who do not believe as he does. Smiling politely over clenched teeth, I retrieve my pen. Encouraged by this, the man, starts systematically criticizing the other wishes on the car, and somehow manages to work Hitler into the conversation, me being German and all. At this point, I feel I have two choices: I punch the idiot in the nose or I leave. I leave; so much for Pine. On my way down from the cold mountain air to Phoenix, which lies in the heat of the Valley of the Sun, I debate whether to remove his wish. But censorship in art is not a thing I want to get involved in, so decide to leave the wish in place, hoping that the wishes of more tolerant men will soon drown out his offering.

Bed 104

In Phoenix, thanks to Women Welcome Women Worldwide (5W), I have a fixed destination, and no need to hunt for a bed, as 5W Donnis has offered me three days of hospitality. Phoenix was the winter home of one of America's best-known architects, Frank Lloyd Wright. He called his designs 'organic', and believed that architecture must be in harmony with its surroundings. The city planners of Phoenix have taken this advice from Frank Lloyd Wright to heart. When looking over the Valley of the Sun, it is hard to image that one of the largest cities of the USA lies there. The high-rises of Phoenix center only on the CBD, and the sand-colored houses blend like rocks into the surroundings. Even the four-storey highways, their sound walls and barriers, are all the colour of the sand, and the interchange islands are landscaped with desert plants in minimalist style. While I think this is a fine example of organic town planning, I discover that some locals find it quite boring. To make up for the year-round brown and beige, they go all out once a year, and get really flashy with the Christmas lights.

When night falls over Phoenix at Christmas time, the city transforms into a twinkle-light wonderland that beats any Chinese city hands down. Donnis and I cruise the Christmas-mad neighborhoods. In a slow-moving traffic jam, we pass extravagantly lit houses that compete for best display and greatest use of lights. The record is around 45,000 little lights; the electricity bill must be a killer. I hope Santa chips in with some change down the chimney. We stop to chat to a young girl, who is putting the finishing touches to her display. She proudly tells us that this is the first year she has been allowed to take complete charge of the family Christmas decorations. She has gone all out to show her parents that their trust has not been misplaced. The lawn has a thick coating of cottonwood snow, where a herd of white twinkle-light deer mechanically dip their heads down to a blue twinkle-light lake. Surrounding the lake are giant flashing snowflakes, and a nativity scene glows warm yellow and red against a hanging curtain of glittering blue icicles. In a more affluent area, a sweeping front entrance is blocked by a life-size twinkle-light sleigh, with a full contingent of reindeer that stand waiting for the brilliantly flashing Santa, who is dangling from the roof by a rope of light. Surrounding the house, and in all the neighboring gardens, every tree and garden feature, every coconut, cactus and rooftop is a gleaming glittering glow, in Phoenix's once-a-year Christmas light show.

Not something that Lloyd Wright would have approved of, as our tour guide points out when I visit Taliesin West, which is where Frank tested his architectural theories, and is still a school of architecture. Apparently, when the first power cables were strung across the prairie, held up by the smallest wooden poles, Frank was so offended by this intrusion on his view over the 'rim of the world' that he reportedly never looked at the view again. What he would have thought of the giant power pylons that today stride across that landscape like alien invaders is anyone's guess.

When I return 'home', I discover that Donnis has put on her publicist's hat in my absence. She informs me that I have newspaper interviews and television interviews laid on, and would I please get myself into some sort of respectable shape. Well ... this moment has been threatening for some time, so I do the hair and the make-up, then appear on the eight o'clock news, looking more or less decent. I am guessing that I have now used up my full quota of fame, as predicted by Andy Warhol, but should I ever appear on television again, I must remember to keep my hands from flapping about. I came across like a dervish caught in a swarm of flies.

The following morning, my mission to discover the aboriginal tribes of America continues in the Heard Museum, which has gained international recognition for its thorough representation of the 21 tribes that live in southwest America. Despite all the efforts of the early European settlers to destroy their culture, these are still a proud people, who continue to keep their language, crafts and traditions alive. In the museum, pottery pieces that were made hundreds of years ago stand next to pieces made in the 21st century. Many of the tribe names, when translated to English, mean 'the people', and so I discover that the aboriginal Americans are also known as 'The People of the Land', and finally I have found a name that sits well with me. While the tribes have many different beliefs and rituals, 'The People of the Land' knew that they were a part of nature, no more important than any other part.

I cannot help but wonder whether the world would not be a better place, had the early Europeans settlers in America chosen to learn something from the locals, instead of forcing the locals to learn from them. The Europeans settlers saw in 'The People of the Land' the only societies that they knew that were 'truly free'

> *Natural freedom is the only object of the policy of the* [Native Americans]; *with this freedom do nature and climate rule alone amongst them* ... [Native Americans] *maintain their freedom and find abundant nourishment* ...
> [and are] *people who live without laws, without police, without religion.* Jean Jacques Rousseau, in J H Kennedy, *Jesuit and savage in New France*, New Haven, Conn: Yale University Press, 1950, 187.

It is speculated that the American concept of democracy was inspired in part by this. Unfortunately, a free society requires steely self-control from the individual, and that lesson the European settlers never bothered to learn, preferring to create more and more laws, until today the concept of America being 'the land of the free and the home of the brave' is an illusion that is shattered with every new label and every new sign with which Americans try to protect themselves against their own laws.

Huge billboards advertising the services of lawyers who are building strange class-action suits dot the roadside in every town. My take-out coffee cup has a large label,

'Warning, the contents may be hot.'

I should hope so; I like my coffee hot. But in America, providing this simple service could put a company in the courtroom. The litigation-happy culture of America has created a counterculture in which nobody is prepared to take responsibility for his or her own actions. This in turn has put the American coffee-brewing industry in a dilemma: how to serve a good hot cup of coffee at a temperature that will not burn the customers. The Americans' worst enemy is their own legal system, followed closely by the media. Both are designed to control through fear.

The American media create this fearful mindset purposefully. The American press is not free, and those who control the press know that the easiest way to control the masses is to keep them fearful. More than half the people who die in America per year do it by their own hand, either by shoving a gun, a bottle, a cigarette or some of the stuff the Americans fondly like to call food, in their mouths. Statistics show that Americans are 12 times more likely to die from accidental suffocation in bed than from a terrorist attack, not something the comfort-loving Americans seem to have any fear of. Despite the overwhelming evidence against it, the thing the Americans fear most (other than public speaking, if Jerry Seinfeld is to be believed) is to die by the hand of a terrorist. This mindset is created solely by media manipulation of a very emotional topic. It is always good to have someone else to blame for one's woes, and even more satisfying is to have something one can get really racist, bigoted, and uppity about. After all, it's very hard to lose one's temper and sanity over a goose-down pillow.

The only things America is free of, it seems to me, are common sense and self-control.

Bed 105

After three days of easy companionship, I leave Phoenix, giving Donnis a bear-hug goodbye (I have become quite fond of the big American hug), and start the slow dawdle back to the West Coast and San Francisco, where Alexandra will arrive for the last of the three legs of my journey that she will share with me.

I have no particular plan, other than to stay off the interstate as much as possible. My route leads me north out of Phoenix onto R74 West, where hot-air balloons polka dot the sky with brilliant color above a beige desert landscape. The world rumbles by, flat and dull. By comparison, the desolate town of Salome seems an interesting place to stop. Stalls line the dusty road, selling second-hand junk, opposite shacks with broken windows and trailer homes that look well past their sell-by date. These less-privileged folk are shy, and seem a bit embarrassed. It is a strange contrast to the cheerful confidence of all the Americans I have met so far. To be poor in America carries with it the strong stigma of failure. It takes some persuading before one of the men plucks up the courage to add his wish to the car. He is semi-literate, and needs help with the spelling.

'Peace to all people'

His offering, compared with that of all the professors and educated folk, is the most generous wish I have had from an American so far.

As the road slipstreams onto the Interstate 10, I am forced to speed along with manic trucks. Let me off! I have grown to like driving at American granny pace. A quick right and I cross an invisible boundary into the Colorado River Indian Reservation, where the whole squeaky-clean America thing falls to pieces. In these small pockets of Third World in the world's first, First World country, the roads deteriorate; the street signs are shabby; and the housing is poor. The more I see of Indian reservations, with their immediate drop in living standards, and deteriorating infrastructure, the more they remind me of the old Bantustans of South Africa. Where self-determination becomes a curse, not a blessing, another small freedom myth vanishes. In America, toe the corporate line or starve is the name of the game.

Outside of Parker, I spy horsemen doing fancy tricks with ropes. This calls for closer investigation. Bouncing down a dirt track, I arrive at a small pay booth, where a lady in jeans, Stetson, and red plaid shirt looks me over,

'Where ya from?'

'South Africa.'

'What's deal with the car?'

I am getting rather tired of this, and am fast learning that there was an advantage in not being able to speak or understand everything, but once again plunge into the explanation

'I am driving around the world ...'

'Say what?'

She gives me a look that makes it quite clear that I should get professional help, then waves me through to attend my first rodeo.

Where to the enthusiastic urging of the announcer, the gates shoot open; a calf makes a wild dash for freedom; the horse and rider in hot pursuit. Dust flies, a lasso curls, catches calf head or hoof, the horse brakes, the cowboy dives, the calf rolls its eyes in terror

'What did I do, what did I do?'

and in three flicks of a tasseled wrist that poor calf is trussed like a thanksgiving turkey. The cowboy retrieves his hat, hits it twice across his chaps, releasing a small cloud of dust, before he struts back to his horse. Those cute little calves just don't stand a chance.

Braver men climb onto unwilling mustangs that bolt, stiff-legged, from the stall. The horses bounce and buck, they spin and stop. 'Injuns', dressed like 'cowboys', hang on for dear life, but when the hat goes flying, the cowboy is soon to follow. In the stalls, enormous bulls wait to take vengeance on the mistreatment of their younger kin. That should be fun to watch, but no, they will only be ridden tomorrow. What a pity, I was rather enjoying watching grown men being made to eat dirt by dumb animals.

View from Highway 1 California

California
Bed 106

After two days cloistered in a motel room in a small town called Parker – catching up on my blog and various administrative chores – I hit the road, and lose the plot completely as I drive merrily on the wrong side of the road. I am not even aware that I am doing this, even when the oncoming locals try to warn me of the error of my ways. A strange mental shift: it has been months since I drove on the left-hand side of the road. Perhaps it is the back-home feeling of the Bantustan surroundings that has suddenly transported me back to South Africa. Fortunately, the locals are very polite. At an intersection a man stops next to me, hoots gently, lifts his eyebrows, gives a small shrug, then waits patiently while I work through my left-right problems.

Back on the right side of the road, and heading in the right direction, I soon cross the Colorado River, and find myself back in California, traveling on Route 62 West, which takes me past the Big Maria Mountains, the Turtle Mountains, the Iron and the Granite Mountains. Then forking off onto Route 177, I drive towards the Chuckwalla Mountains, which leap lavender from the pale blue sky, their shapes, shadows and colors clearly defined in the crystal air. The road rolls by a burnt-out fueling station, its jagged metal skeleton casting thin shadows across gaping fridges and bleeding-stuffing sofas, a small jarring note in the sienna lavender landscape.

The day is so sunny and bright that I get out of the car to take photographs without bothering with the all-weather jacket. Five minutes later I dive shivering back into the warmth of the Wish Mobile. In that short time my body temperature plummeted to dangerous levels; one could easily freeze out here. The brilliant sunshine is deceptive; the cold creeps up on you so stealthily that you don't realize that you are freezing until your fingers start to ache. A gnarled finger of fear tears at the bunny fur around my brain, as for the first time in my life, I face the brutal truth that this planet that sustains me can just as easily kill me. I have never been in fear of the weather before, but now I realize that if the Wish Mobile dies, I could die right alongside it. In this cold I doubt whether I would last the night.

The far horizons and steely sky of the Colorado Desert roll by, hour after hour. The sometimes-subtle sometimes-dramatic shapes of the naked earth speak of eons of unwritten history, the delicate colors evidence of the chemical building blocks of the planet. As I approach the Chuckwalla Mountains, where giant rocks push directly out of the sand like yellow misshapen teeth, my thoughts spin slowly out to space. I look down on the vast amount of desert I have driven through on my journey, and wonder if the planet is mainly desert, or perhaps I just chose the desert route. What is clear from this distant vantage point is that most of the planet is not suitable for human habitation, and we should really take better care of the small parts that are. A delicate grey missile catches my eye. With a sharp thud a small bird leaves a puff of life on the windscreen. My thoughts plummet back to earth together with the fallen bird.

To the sounds of Gregorian chanting, I turn into the Joshua Tree National Park, and enter the weird forest world of Dr Seuss. The wacky and fantastical tree shapes in those quirky children's books are not an invention of a warped mind, but a direct copy of nature: a perfect example of fact being stranger than fiction. The Joshua trees twist and bend their shaggy grey limbs at logic-defying angles, each branch ending with a little spiky tuft of grey-green leaves. The trees grow in a buttery grey landscape, where time has worn enormous rocks from angular to round over 100 million years. The strange trees give a sense of the surreal, which continues as I drive over the Fried Liver Wash, and stop at a field of lemon-yellow teddy-bear cactus, which trap the sun in their thorny arms.

Climbing to the summit of Ryan Mountain through forests of green-gold-grey plants, surrounded by rocks in shades of tangerine green, the view slowly expands across a sun-dappled plain, where rocky outcrops pierce the lavender earth and silver grass folds around the spiky yuccas, the spiky cholla and the spiky Joshua tree. In the distance, mountains decorate the rim of the blue bowl of sky. On the summit of Ryan Mountain, a warm thermal spirals the low sweet smell of sun-baked grass over my arms, into my hair, and up in the air, where eagles drift on invisible skyways. Some bend, backs aching, to build a rocky shrine, a balance of time, a blend of endless patience and the impossible, to make rocks stand on end; defying gravity, they sway gently in the autumn breeze.

In the distance I see the Wish Mobile has attracted attention to itself again. People gather round to read and wonder. Someone is putting something under the windscreen wiper. At every stop, I meet up with Americans road-tripping through their country. These traveling folk are friendly, curious and frankly critical of their government. Chris approaches; he has something to say. Taking a pen, he bends down and writes.

'BUCK FUSH'

He returns the pen with a wicked grin.

'So what do you think of the Americans?'

The question catches me off-guard. What do I think of the Americans? What an odd way of phrasing the normal 'So what do you think of America?' Judging by his quizzical expression, I decide he is baiting me, and reply with a very diplomatic.

'I haven't met many Americans yet, but those that I have met have been very nice.'

He bursts out laughing.

'You have a good trip now.'

He gets in his SUV, and drives off, still laughing. How odd.

This day of subtle colors ends in the small town of Twentynine Palms. As a full moon rises in an airbrushed sky of brilliant pink and blue, pigeons come home to roost on the still sagging telephone wire. In a cloud of blue smoke, a man emerges from a red rusty truck. He scrawls on the Wish Mobile

'If we could all live together in peace, those with money and those without.'

He drives off, only to return a minute later, desperately hunting for his wallet. No matter how you feel about it, in America, you need money; it defines you in every way.

The debt-management advertising on the radio and on the roadside billboards, promising to get folk out of their credit-card debt, makes me think that the wealth of the Americans is an illusion. Debt is king in America; it is a growth industry and keeps the American dream humming along. On the one hand, debt-consolidating companies are advertising to step in, and help solve people's debt problem, at a price. On the other hand, the credit card companies are making it easier and easier to pay for everything with plastic; even the Internal Revenue Service can be paid on credit. Next to every billboard promising to get you out of your debt, there is one promising that the fulfillment of the American dream is just one more credit-card purchase away.

Bed 106 & 107

On my global quest to find the road less traveled, I turn onto R247 in a roundabout direction to Los Angeles. Here the fastidious American road builders took a day off, and just went with the heave and dip of the landscape. The road undulates and flows. It suddenly falls … my stomach lurches into my mouth, the negative Gs lift me off my seat as I rollercoast past small shabby ranch houses, rusting wire fences and fall-apart postboxes. Closing in on the foothills of the Saint Bernardino Mountains, shabby is slowly replaced by neat picket fences and small horse ranches. The closer I get to Los Angeles, the grander the houses and ranches become. This is where the American dream resides, just east of Los Angeles, complete with glossy horses.

In the greater Los Angeles area, my road choices are reduced to the interstate and the afternoon rush hour. Despite all the fuss the Los Angelos make about their traffic, it really is not bad. The drivers behave, and the roads are wide enough to keep the traffic moving, and now, having adjusted my driving style to suit the locals, the flipping middle finger is nowhere to be seen. But the sun is sliding over the western horizon, and it occurs to me that I have no idea where my next bed will be. In the back country I never give where I will be sleeping a second thought, but here in a city, a bed is all I can think of. In a heightened state of neurosis, I head direction Malibu on the Pacific Coast Highway (PCH) north. This is rich America's stomping ground, yet the PCH is surprisingly polluted right here. This is difficult to miss, as with the 'adopt a highway scheme', the roads in America are very clean, and the discarded rubbish that is a feature of roads around the world has been almost totally absent. But here, where the rich folk live, the roads are filthy. The rich do not pick up litter, it seems. Just before I drive through a built-up zone, a sign declares the start of '27 miles of spectacular scenery'. Yeah sure, if the working end of the beach cottages is what rocks your boat, then this stretch is for you.

After booking into a Malibu motel, which, judging by its decor, seems to cater exclusively for clandestine afternoon trysts, rather than guests who intend to stay for the night, I find an opening to the beach between the tightly wedged cottages, where the electric wires are strung in the spider-web style of a South African squatter camp. The setting sun bounces off the skyscrapers of Beverly Hills far across the bay as I step onto the famous white sand of Malibu Beach. I have strolled along some stunning beaches in my travels, and this one does not rate. It is just a stretch of sand with houses right on it. The movie hype has blown the beauty of the place out of all proportion. Then again, the beach is empty; perhaps it is the people one comes to see, and not the beach.

My road for the next few days will be the famous 'Highway 1' heading due north to San Francisco. The road hugs the contour of the American

418

west coast, where grey-green pines cling with gnarled roots to golden rocks that plunge into the white foam of the deep blue ocean. The scenery is so familiar that for a moment I am transported back to South Africa. I could be driving from Cape Town to Hout Bay, and on to Chapman's Peak. In the distance, a grey fogbank swallows the horizon; soon the sparkling weather will be over.

'Highway 1' soon leaves the coast, taking me across the Oxnard Plain where, in some of the world's most fertile soil, a whole mixed salad of vegetables are cultivated on a scale that stretches further than the eye can see. The area is famous mainly for its strawberries, and, as it is the beginning of December, I have caught the first harvest, and see menial laborers working the fields for the first time since arriving in America. Looking over the bent backs of the workers to the oversized pick-ups they drive, I realize it is better to be a beggar at a rich man's table than at a poor man's. That is the essential difference between poor people in America and those elsewhere. There is such abundance in America that the poor man lives fairly well here, compared to the poor man of China or India, where very few scraps fall from the table.

Bed 108

Rumbling through Santa Barbara, I notice that the Wish Mobile urgently needs fuel, but I get a weird block in my brain. I need fuel; I should stop and fill up right now, but I don't; why not? I have no idea. Perhaps I am hoping the fuel will get cheaper. Perhaps I am trying to see how far I get before running out. Perhaps I really do want to stand at the side of the highway thumbing a ride.

Get fuel already!

Then, just as the fuel tank is almost dry, I discover that not every fueling station has diesel in these expensive parts of America. Creeping along the highway I seriously question my sanity; what kind of idiotic behavior is this? Then with a sudden release of tension I spot the sign I have been hunting for,

DIESEL AVAILABLE HERE

At massive cost, I must add, but when you have left yourself no choice, you cannot argue.

Over a cup of warmish coffee in the rest stop, I scan my map: what to do, where to go, should I have a destination at all? Then my eye falls on a small notice on the display of tourist attractions of the area. One of the planet's little miracles is currently playing out at Pismo Beach. I shall stop over to have a look.

Because monarch butterflies cannot survive frosty winters, they migrate for thousands of miles every winter to warmer climates, and always to the same locations, among which is the grove of eucalyptus trees in Pismo Beach. The butterflies cluster in the very tops of the trees, where they slowly fan the sunshine with their wings. The rays of sun create occasional shafts of light that reach to the ground, enticing the fluttery beasties to tumble-fall through the light, in a dazzling wingspread of orange and black, only to float up and away again as the light shifts. The migratory butterflies have a miraculous trick up their folded front legs. Not only does this generation of butterflies live several times as long as the non-migratory generations, but they also find their way back to the same trees every year, although the last migration took place four butterfly generations before. As the butterflies float by on silence and sunshine, I stand with my head thrown back in awe of the grand miracle of their tiny lives.

Just north of Pismo Beach, the houses at Shell Beach look over the Pacific, which shoots white foam through craggy holes in giant rocks that stand like guardians just off-shore, breaking the force of the sea. Each rock is crowned with a colony of brown pelicans, which slowly ice the rocks with digested crustaceans and fish. A fogbank rolls across the sun, scattering the brilliant light into a million small prisms that sparkle and fade. In the gentle breeze, faint rainbows float by on gossamer fog, while the blue-eyed pelicans spread their enormous wings, then fall forward to let the air currents lift them, just before they plunge into the water. The wind turns; my stomach churns. Those houses on the cliff might have a good view, but there are certain drawbacks to being so close to a colony of very large birds that favor fish for dinner.

As the road winds further north, the low gnarled trees grow taller, until the mountains are clad in a thicket of trees and vines that thrive in the coastal mist. The long pier at San Simeon lures me out of the Wish Mobile. The pier shakes and heaves like the deck of a ship, as the huge storm-driven waves roll in low and fast, their energy exploding against the wooden structure. Exhilarating, but a clear warning to enjoy the sunshine while it lasts. Down by the old San Simeon post office, I fall into an impromptu conversation with a woman who is out airing her grandchild. She has been reading the Wish Mobile, and is keen that I see everything the area can offer. Her best bit of advice is about the elephant seals, which swim in from the far corners of the oceans to mate on the beaches right here. For once, my timing is perfect, as December is when the mating season begins.

But the seals seem to be all mated out for the moment, and while the enormous blubbery things are having a collective snooze on the pale sand, the smell surrounding them is alive and kicking, so I maneuver to an up-wind position to observe the beasts outside of the stink. A bull is lifted ashore by a giant wave. He undulates, blubber shaking, up the beach, taking a rest after every three or four heaves of his 4,000-pound body. Incredibly, elephant seals can undulate at up to 8 km/h, although I do wonder whether an elephant seal has ever traveled a full kilometer on solid ground. While their ungainly bodies limit their terra-firma activities, once under water these creatures are able to dive up to 5,000 feet, and for most of the year travel immense distances to feed.

Then in December, they always return to this beach, where the underwater acrobats turn into mating machines. The giant bull bellows through his long flop nose, and homes in on a seemly, but unwilling female. He is a take-charge kind of guy, and snorts at the pup, which is still mewling for milk. The pup might be young, but knows when he is not wanted, and makes like a caterpillar to a safer part of the beach. The buxom female shouts her rage, but the bull is having none of it. He grabs her by the neck with his enormous canines, and lets her have it. Whatever happened to foreplay? But then, if you have harem of up to 50 wenches to service in one short mating season, and have the unwelcome attention of several other males to deal with, you don't, I suppose, have time or energy for lengthy fondling sessions. The big fellow concludes his business, then flops down, into a blissful stupor, scratching his belly with flippers that look like human hands in tight-fitting flipper gloves. While the alpha bull snoozes, an immature male decides to sneak a little necking, a little come-hither nibble of the female neck. The female is having none of it, and starts bellowing her disapproval. The alpha male is on instant full alert, and undulates to the rescue at surprising speed. The young Casanova makes a prudent retreat into the ocean.

Leaving the seals to their carnal bliss, I return to Highway 1, and soon find myself driving between a rock and a wavy place. The Santa Lucia Mountains crowd the road, until they rise steep from the Pacific Ocean, and the switchback turns become so sharp that vehicle length is limited, and the road is for use only during the day. At Ragged Point, as the Beethoven-Liszt Fourth Movement I have playing at full volume reaches its crescendo, the storm hits land where giant redwoods march to the ocean, their crowns slicing through the fog. The wind chases the rain and clouds across the steel surface of the sky, creating sweeping spotlights of glittering light on the slate grey sea. At a high lookout, I turn down the music to hear the roar of the ocean, as it crashes white froth onto black rocks.

Staring onto the sunspot sea, I become aware that the truth of the ocean is hidden behind a liquid shimmering mantle, which forms a boundary. We look at the waves and the reflected light, forgetting that beyond that boundary, there is a far greater world than ours, where deep ocean currents sweep water, each drop containing a million living particles, around the planet. Why do we look into the cold depths of space with so much more fascination that down into the teeming density of life of the oceans? Darwin says we all evolved from the sea. Why then do we prefer to look to the stars for guidance? Why do our gods come from the stars? Why do we read our stars every day? Why does everybody want to be a star, and nobody want to be a starfish? Do we look to the stars because they are easier to see? Is the sea too close to see, a case of not seeing the wood for the trees?

Why are we so uninterested in the sea that we use it as a dumping ground, sewer and general garbage disposal unit, if this is where our ancient origins lie? We will never walk at the bottom of the ocean, as we do on the moon. We will probably end up walking on Mars, and swim backstroke through the rings of Saturn, but we will never walk on the deep ocean floor. Why do we not have the same fascination for the oceans as we do for the starry sky? Is Darwin right or wrong?

So many questions. How is it possible that dolphins, elephant seals, penguins, even butterflies, can instinctively travel the unseen energy highways and byways of this planet, and unfailingly know where they are going? Yet we humans, who consider ourselves the most advanced of all species, with all our maps, compasses and GPSs, have not a clue where we are going, or where we are from?

Bed 109

The rain lashes down, forcing me back into the Wish Mobile. I slowly curve my way along the streaming cliff, stopping at an art gallery just outside Big Sur, where the Wish Mobile opens the door to a conversation with the owner. She strongly suggests I stay at Deetjen's

Big Sur Inn, a historical wagon stop since the 1930s. It is a place of whimsy, crackling fireplaces, and ye olde worlde rooms, built from scavenged redwood. The room is quaintly charming, but completely inadequate for my needs. At a very small table, perched on a little bentwood chair, I try to complete my daily chores, but the wind breaks open the clouds to allow a lightning bolt to trip the power, plunging the cliffside hotel into darkness. I give up on the writing, leap into the redwood bed, and with my crocheted and quilted bedcovers pulled up to my nose, listen to the wind tear at the giant trees as the thunder rattles at the windows.

The morning is silent and serene, the beautiful coastline lost in a landed cloud. I find a public phone.

'Hi, Maureen, Annette here. The weather has gone pear shaped. Mind if I arrive a day early?

'You are welcome. We won't be here, but I will put the key under the mat.'

The cliff and giant redwoods play hide and seek behind the slow moving cloud, which rolls like a waterfall down to the sea. A bakery materializes out of the fog; it is a Big Sur early morning watering hole. Locals with heavy duffels, big beards, and funny hats sip great seaming mugs of coffee. The smell of baking flavors the air, and I stock up on enormous homemade muffins; by now any foodstuff that does not come out of an American supermarket is fine by me. While I munch at the bran muffin, a man asks to write on my car, so we get to chatting. John is an arty poetic type, and he goes on about the wonderful positive energy around the Wish Mobile. Although I am not normally given to entertaining such thoughts, I must agree. The Wish Mobile is growing into something that I never really imagined. Now covered in wishes from around the world, it is no longer just a glorified delivery van, but a global ambassador of goodwill. The poet gets down on his knees, and adds his bit of positive energy.

'May all people everywhere realize that we are one, one god, one life, one love, expressed in an endless variety of ways. Seek how we are the same, not how we are different. Give instead of take, love instead of hate'

Thank you, Mr Poetryman, and suddenly all is well with the world; the maple leaves are brilliant orange; the grass is green; the wind is howling; and I am freezing. San Francisco, here I come.

Bed 110

In the neat suburbia of middle-class America, I rummage under a welcome mat, find a key, unlock a door, and, standing on the threshold of the home of a total stranger, am not too sure how to proceed. A beautifully decorated Christmas tree glows in the dark, and a small dog looks at me enquiringly from the sofa. Cautiously I sit down next to him, wondering what to do next, but then nature makes the decision for me, forcing me to venture deeper into the house, where a bright painting catches my eye. The colors are arresting for a moment, but forgotten before I get to the toilet. Passing the painting again on my way back, the childlike signature catches my eye. I laugh at myself for being fooled by the paint splashings of a child.

Sitting down gently so as not to disturb the sleeping dog, I wait, and while I wait, I wonder what are we doing, meaning, and thinking when it comes to fine art? What value is there in it when the daubing of a child or a chimpanzee can be mistaken for, or considered art? What point has art if those that view it, scornfully say, 'I could have done that' and when the only reply the artist has 'yes, but you did not, and I did', implying that the actions of a self-declared artist are enough to make the things they create art. This panders directly to the malaise of the personality cult. The reduction of art to personality is the destruction of the meaning of art. True art is something that anybody can stand in front of and know that this is something that they could never aspire to, but that it inspires them to do their best at whatever they do aspire to.

Artists are those people who have the ability to make new and unique connections between apparently unrelated things, people who can step outside of their own field of experience, and are able to describe the experience of the whole. These are singular gifts, and it is an unforgivable thing that these gifts have in the last few decades been channeled into avenues that satisfy only the ego of the creator and the cash till. Fine art should be a sublime communication that allows those not gifted in this way to say, not that 'I could have done that', but rather 'oh, that's how it is; I knew that instinctively, but could never express it.' The viewers should walk away from the piece, not filled with the artist's vision, but filled with a vision of their own.

My thoughts are interrupted as the little dog bolts off the couch, seconds before I hear the key turning in the lock. The scoundrel! From his behavior it is clear that sleeping on the couch is forbidden. He give me a conspiratorial look as he waits innocently by the door. As

Maureen steps into her house, the dog and I welcome her home. A bizarre, funny moment, so we laugh at the strangeness of being strangers, and are soon strangers no more. We are actually sort of family, about six hundred times removed, and on this small foundation we proceed to build a small friendship.

I wake to a damp grey dawn, and not wanting to interrupt the frantic early morning household routine I can hear through the door, I watch the neighborhood cat chasing a squirrel up and down the garden wall. The squirrel mocks the cat as he runs, stops, runs, stops, and then leaps nimbly into a tree, where the cat is reluctant to follow. I watch the game of cat and squirrel until the house is silent, before walking to the kitchen. Maureen has family affairs to attend to, so I am left with her instruction to just help myself. Opening the fridge, I stare at the contents aimlessly, and close it again without touching anything. Turning on the kettle, I hunt about for the coffee, the cups, and the teaspoons while the water comes to a boil, and, finally, with my cup of coffee, sit in front of the computer.

With Alexandra flying across the ocean to arrive in San Francisco tomorrow at noon, I will be stressed until she is once again safely on the ground. To keep my mind off Alexandra, I attend to my administration, and then do something I haven't done in months. I put on my German Hausfrau hat, and spend the afternoon cleaning the Wish Mobile. Things are looking rather trashy in there, and my inner Miss Priss is getting more and more embarrassed, especially now that the language barrier is no longer a problem. The Wish Mobile attracts attention wherever it goes. The 'One Planet One People' artwork has gained in momentum, and I am mortified when men have to first dig through layers of grime to create a clean spot on which to write a wish. After several hours of vacuuming and polishing, I can once again hold my head high in public.

At the airport, I feel a soppy advertising moment come over me as Alexandra appears in the arrivals hall. We stand toe-to-toe, eye-to-eye in silent, fully connected greeting. Arm in arm we step out into the fog, Alexandra has been breathing recycled air for thirty hours, so some oxygen-rich air will do her the world of good. Our goal for the day is Muir Wood, just north of San Francisco, which means we get to drive across the Golden Gate Bridge, but the fog is so dense that we might as well be driving across a desert for all that we see of the bridge. The famous orange towers do not even show their first crossbeam, and the roadway floats on a billow of cloud.

A narrow mountain road winds along unseen precipices past the misty shapes of ancient trees into Redwood Canyon. This canyon, once in danger of being flooded by the damming of the Redwood Creek, was saved only through the quick thinking of Congressman William Kent in 1907. He donated the land to the federal government, after which Roosevelt declared the area a national monument, and named it after the naturalist John Muir, who helped establish the national parks system in America.

Today the giant redwoods (sequoia) lose their full height in the sodden clouds. As we reach out to touch Earth's biggest trees, we touch time and ancient light. Sequoias can live up to 3,500 years.

Do behold the King Sequoia! Behold! Behold! seems all I can say. Some time ago I left all for Sequoia and have been and am at his feet, fasting and praying for light, for is he not the greatest light in the woods, in the world? Where are such columns of sunshine, tangible, accessible, terrestrialized?

John Muir [From a letter to Mrs J Carr]

We step into the world of giants where, with our heads thrown back, we feel very small. Alexandra leans against a tree, and becomes smaller still. Her little arms give the rough red bark a tiny squeeze. A hush falls over us as we pull the rich tasty air – a brew of musty earth, mushrooms and crisp fog – deep into our lungs. The cold brings a flush to our cheeks, while small dewdrops form in our hair. We gently run our hands across red, rutted bark, peer at tiny mushroom forests, golden slippery smooth, growing from carpets of moss, and we look up, and look up, and look up and, like the silent fog settling in the ancient treetops, a deep primal calm settles into our minds.

The cold and damp gives us an enormous appetite, so we put our heads down, and head off to San Francisco's Chinatown, where I realize just how flexible I have become in my eating habits. Stockton Street in Chinatown is quite authentic. It looks almost like Hong Kong, with the same tiny restaurants, the iffy chopping blocks, the vegetable buffets, and the steamed buns. I introduce Alexandra to steamed buns, and at the same time order some chopped duck – in Chinese – much to the chef's surprise, but the duck I ask for turns out to be pork, got that pesky intonation wrong again. But no matter, Alexandra is not having any.

'Mom, did you see that chopping block! I am not eating that.'

I don't push the subject, some things you have to ease into slowly.

Bed 111 & 112

A quiet evening in front of the television acquaints us with the American weather channel, which is soon to become our best friend. Tonight it shows us that we are in for some weather trouble, as huge snowstorms are sweeping across the plains and mountains of North America. Our master plan to visit the Yosemite National Park, and cross the Sierra Nevada on Route 120 is scuppered. A morning of Web surfing and phoning weather stations tells us that all routes north have been blocked by snow. We will have to try to cross the Sierra Nevada much further south, as the closest crossing that is still open is Route 155. A huge detour, but if we want to get across the Sierra Nevada at all this winter, it is our only option. Alexandra takes over navigation control, and while I negotiate the notorious San Francisco fog – now there's a place I have been, but never seen – reroutes us south on the 99 to Delano, before we head east again on the 155.

The world remains hidden in the fog until we reach the 'Garlic Capital of the World', Gilroy, and are able to get off the interstate, into Cottonwood Creek Wildlife Area, where brown Longhorn cows graze on the pale grass between 'live oaks' that are strange, gnarled, dull grey and green. The sun breaks through the fog; the world changes instantly from grey to a brilliant blaze of color. A stand of bright yellow cottonwoods, knee-deep in a sky blue lake, makes me scramble for the camera, but a small breeze shifts the fog, and the scene fades to everyday.

Route 99 is a grey truckers' alley that we are desperate to get off, but our choices are limited. It is forward or bust, as that storm on our tail might close our only escape route over the Sierra Nevada by nightfall. In Fresno, 'the Turkey Capital of the World', the road is lined with fast-food joints that sell not turkey, but chicken or beef. As it is lunchtime, we tick off number one on Alexandra's to-do-in-America list: eat an American fast-food hamburger.

A warning bell tells me that this is the point where living dangerously moves into the realm of living stupidly, but I will try anything once. The images above the service counter look mouthwatering: juicy thick burger patties, crisp green salad, firm tomatoes, and melting cheese on plump golden buns. Reassured, we each order a cheeseburger, a portion of fries, and a chocolate milkshake. The food arrives in plastic, on plastic, covered with plastic. We then select the required pieces of plastic that aid in the consumption of this American delicacy, a plastic knife and fork, wrapped in plastic, salt, pepper, ketchup, all in their own little plastic wrappers, and a serviette in a plastic bag. Laden with plastic, we sit at a small plastic table, inspect our meal, and conclude that here there is a strong case to be made for false advertising. The hamburgers are small soggy facsimiles of the backlit image above the service counter. We hesitantly take a bite, and ask ourselves; how bad can a hamburger be before it becomes a criminal offense to sell it? We sip the milkshake, and burst out laughing at the disgusting sugary sweetness of it. After binning the food, we agree that the only good thing about this experience is that we will never have to do it again.

In Delano we meet working-class America. The graffiti-covered buildings give us flashbacks to Brezeg in Poland. Here the same air of hopeless exhaustion hangs over everything. Huge square vineyards stretch to the horizon in every direction. All the plants grow in precise measured rows, with not a root out of place. This is not a vineyard, but a grape factory. Out of this tabletop landscape rise the last outcrops of the Sierra Nevada, and hopefully our passage to Death Valley.

As we climb deep into the mountains, the day fades into a strange monochrome. The road winds through half-seen trees in soft shades of grey as the mountains vanish in a cold fog. Somewhere up there, hiding in the clouds, is a high mountain peak called Greenhorn Summit. The switchback road takes us slowly higher and higher, and the world vanishes in clouds of white that trail swirling water vapor around the Wish Mobile. Breaking through the clouds, into a blinding world of snow, sky, sunshine and clouds that lie at our feet, we scrabble for sunglasses. To honor the moment we build a very small snowman, while the wind chews at our ears, noses and fingers.

An hour later, we are stripping off the winter gear and turning up the air-conditioner as we descend into Death Valley National Park, the hottest driest place in the USA, which easily kicks the Gobi desert off first spot for weird landscapes of the world.

The valley stretches into a shimmering mirage north to south. Black ravens circle above green cliffs, shot through with brilliant orange. The road into the valley hugs towering rock walls that count down the eons of the planet in multicolor layers: grey, green, raw umber and purple. Red Cathedral cliffs dwarf us with their size, and awe us with their color. Sandwich-cake layers of red oxide, yellow ochre and cream stop abruptly above a confection composite of lavender white and lemon yellow. On the valley floor, Alexandra, giving herself over to the austere grandeur of the moment, walks gently across the jigsaw puzzle mud of the ghost of Panamint lake, sits down cross-legged and becomes one with the shimmering heat, the bitter smell of dry earth, and the cawing of the raven overhead.

In Mustard Canyon, the world is one color only: bright mustard yellow. It is a place of coarse textures, hot dry wind, and eerie creaks and pings as the canyon cools from the midday heat. At Golden Canyon, where narrow walkways lead between soaring rocks of golden yellow and red, we realize that we have not left enough time for exploring Death Valley properly. The fast-setting sun and the many kilometers between us and anything resembling a bed put wings on our feet as we quickstep through the canyon.

At Artist's Palette, nature has a moment of complete abandon. Giant chemical mounds of peppermint choc swirl, tangerine dream, and raspberry ripple, heap like mounds of Italian ice-cream on the roadside. Prickly pale desert holly stands in green camouflage against a delicate jade-green rock, which is set in sunset-orange sand against purple mountains with pink stripes that butt against gold mountains, veined with oxblood red. Mother Nature is an artist favoring fauvism, it seems. The road is a narrow ribbon of sober grey weaving through the giddy landscape, which glows in Technicolor splendor with the setting sun.

The dusk paints Badwater Salt Pools pale blue as we walk out to the lowest point in the USA. In the mountain shadow, the salt lies like snow in the valley. It crunches gently underfoot, and sticks to the soles of our shoes, until we both grow a couple of centimeters taller. Looking back to the road, we see the sea level marker high on the cliff; we are 85.5 meters below sea level, and should the sea decide to come rushing in, in a whole lot of trouble.

Today started at 6,000 ft above sea level in the cold and snow, and ends at 200 ft below sea level in the salty heat of Badwater. A day of extremes, which is not quite over. The light dissolves into deep blue-black, and in perfect solitude we drive through the land of the Shoshone, where the ancient tribes lived in harmony with the sparse land, and felt themselves wealthy in their self-sufficiency – until the Europeans came with their hunger for material wealth and rampant deceases, destroying a once-harmonious relationship between man and the land on which they lived. With the imposition of the values of the Europeans, the proud tribes lost nothing, but became impoverished.

Nevada

Bed 113

In the morning silence geese run across the sky, leaving ring-round distortions in the mirror lake. Their long low calls pierce the air, and fade into the softness of blue-grey-blue mountains that frame the world of the ancients. Slowly the desert gives way to small houses, set in strict grid patterns that stretch for miles in every direction. The houses are painted in all the colors of the Artist's Palette, but in this high-density development, where only dark alleyways separate the houses, and hundreds of signboards advertise properties for sale, the brilliant colors somehow manage to look plastic and fake.

Soon the desert and reality vanish under concrete. As we drive down 'the strip', the casino center of Las Vegas, we enter an alternative universe, where all the world is clustered on the roadside. The 'Sphinx' reflects in a glass pyramid, which overwhelms the surrounding buildings with its size and design. Further along, the 'Statue of Liberty' stands in a small puddle of water, and the 'New York' skyline is surrounded by a massive rollercoaster. Then, just before we reach 'The Eiffel Tower', which pierces the roof of a Parisian café, we find our bed for the night, and are welcomed into the room with the sound of sex in the afternoon, which comes screaming through the plank-thin walls.

yes yES! YES!

The thumping on the wall settles into an urgent rhythm.

We freeze, look at each other, burst into fits of laughter, dump our bags, and leave. Slamming the door behind us to notify the couple engaged in the sex scream-fest next door that they have been heard, and could they perhaps turn the volume down a touch.

With the dancing fountains of the Bellagio just across the road, we go into 'Ocean's Eleven' mode, to try to find the glamour and excitement in the world of casinos. What we find instead is that it is somewhat disorienting to step from daylight into the never-ending night of the casinos. Trailing aimlessly through fake worlds of stale air and empty promises, past hundreds of one-armed bandits and gaming tables that create the whirr ching, ting ting ting background music common to all casinos, we discover that for the ordinary person there is no glamour in casinos, just a faint air of desperation. Semi-dressed women intent on showing off as much of their flesh as is legally possible are plentiful, but beautifully dressed women are hard to find. The only men wearing sharp suits are the casino staff, who are quick to guide us away from the gambling machines. Alexandra is underage, and may not even step from the straight and narrow tiled walkway onto the carpet. This is no fun, so with determination, and no small amount of luck, we find our way out of the gambling labyrinths, and back in the grey daylight street.

Our goal is the New York-New York Roller Coaster. The roller coaster is a beast; at 62 m high, and with a top speed of 108 km/h things get fairly hair-raising and painful. This is not a smooth ride, but one that jolts and bumps its top-speed upside down round and round, way up, over and through the New York- New York casino. Alexandra fortunately keeps her eyes firmly shut for the duration of the ride, providing a perfectly good excuse to do it all again. Monster roller coaster defeated, we make our way with jelly knees back onto the strip, where men on street corners hand out flyers advertising clubs, shows, strip joints and a variety of other amusements that can be advertised with photographs of suggestively posing, semi-naked women. They flutter to the pavement like confetti, where the bare breasts and pouting lips are mangled by the feet of the uninterested crowd.

Slowly neon lights replace sunlight, and ordinary cars are replaced by black stretch limousines, as the big spenders roll into town. Under brilliantly lit hotel canopies, they step from the mysterious depths of the limousines into VIP lounges, where the fabulous glamour of the gambling world must reside, while back on the street the dancing fountains of the Bellagio Hotel shoot and flow-flood their way through *Fly me to the moon*, for the enjoyment of the crowds that carry their beer in plastic mugs, pushing and shoving to get a better view. The women, in honor of the night, have stripped off yet more of their clothing. But then, like a trumpet blast, the storm that has been on our tail for days sweeps into Las Vegas on an ice-laden wind. Instantly the temperature plummets, and when sleet starts pelting down, I feel real pity for the underdressed girlies.

To get out of the freezing rain and away from the boom and bust of the casino world, we skip from brilliant hotel foyer, through extravagantly themed casinos, back to our hotel, which is not as peaceful a haven as we would have liked. The relationship of our neighbors has deteriorated from the thump thump sex-fest into a hysterical screaming match.

Female soprano:

'You don't love me! How can you treat me this way?'

sob sob wail, underscored by sheepish, murmured embarrassments in male baritone.

'Don't cry. Why are you crying? I don't understand.'

Alexandra and I roll our eyes, turn up the telly, and hope the silly wench gets over herself or him, or something, and soon. Our prayers are answered by a huffy bang of the door. In the ensuing silence we look at each other; an unspoken question fills the space between us. What are we doing here?

Las Vegas is that kind of place. You come because it seems to be the thing to do. When you are there, you do what you think you should be doing – throw money into the already bloated coffers of casinos, drink, watch shows that feature breasts, biceps, and bums in the starring role. Pretend that this is the best time you have had in your life, then wake up with a hangover, and wonder, what was that all about?

We seem to have forgotten what it is that makes us happy. The ancient Shoshone tribes of Death Valley had, and needed very little, yet were happy, and considered themselves wealthy. Today we are bombarded with new things that advertisers assure us will bring eternal happiness, which we rush out to buy, only to discover with every new purchase that things cannot make us happy. What makes most people happy is companionship, to be needed and loved, to trust and be trusted, and to find recognition in the circle in which they move. All people would like to be respected, and have their small eccentricities tolerated. But this is contrary to what makes the world economy go round. Our modern lifestyle depends on division and strife, loneliness and chronic competition. It is important that we remain forever dissatisfied, as only then will we continue to hunt for happiness in shops.

Arizona

Bed 114

Sunday dawns crystal clear; last night's storm swept the sky, and dusted the mountains surrounding the city with snow. The street sweepers of the city have also been busy; there is no evidence of last night's revelry. Although Las Vegas has the reputation of being America's sin city, it is still squeaky clean and ever so neat. The Americans are very hygienically sinful. On deserted and silent streets –

Las Vegas is not an early morning kind of place – we pass a long train of wedding chapels. It seems all you need is an old house, onto which you plonk a spire, add a big advertising sign saying something like 'I do wedding drive through', add a motel consisting only of honeymoon suites, and you are in the wedding business. To create a full service business, all you would need to add is the quickie divorce court out back.

Our destination today is the Grand Canyon, via Route 66, that legendary stretch of road, which has largely been replaced by the soulless interstate. An interstate, autobahn, autostrada, express-way, call it what you will, but if you insist on driving on one of those immense slabs of tar you might as well fly to your destination for all the adventure, excitement and new experiences it offers. However, sometimes they are unavoidable, and to get to our destination we roar on bland tar past the sprawling suburbs of Las Vegas, where each house sits in an oasis of lush green grass and waving palms, while all around the natural world of semi-desert and low grey scrub belies this apparent abundance of water.

The Hoover Dam is a huge block of concrete wedged into the Black Canyon on the border of Arizona and Nevada. It is not a wide dam, but a very high one, and considered one of the engineering wonders of the world. So much concrete was used to construct the dam wall that it could have paved a two-lane highway from San Francisco to New York. With all this information buzzing around in our heads, we dutifully walk across the dam wall, oohing and aahing at the height and wonder of it all. But we are really more astounded that nobody is panicking at the disturbingly low water level, which leaves meters of exposed lime-coated rock like a white bath ring all around Lake Mead. All those palms trees, golf courses and water fountains are making their mark here.

In the middle of the dam-wall we have a moment of divine power as on the state-line of Nevada and Arizona, we walk forwards back in time, and backwards forward in time. Then by hopping from leg to leg over the state line, we theoretically make time stand still. Soon bored with our stab at the impossible, we move onto Kingman, where we find the first bit of the old Route 66. The small towns that grew prosperous in the heyday of Route 66 are looking rather desperate today; the building of the interstate has wreaked havoc with their economies. The road giveth, and the road taketh away. The roadside signs are fun, though.

Don't overtake on a slope …

Unless …

you have a periscope.

A pink Cadillac with 'Elvis' reclining on the fender, and a New York taxi cab parked in the street draw our attention. We stop at the roadside store that promises 'neato 50s stuff' and a small whiff of the Route 66 that once was, but the inside of the store is pure 'made in China' commerce and disappointment. The road from Las Vegas direction Flagstaff is unremitting semi-desert, low round shrubs and rolling hills, until near Williams, we find Devil Dog Road, which takes us up rocky mountain slopes bearded with conifer to a flat plateau at 6,000 ft, where the road levels out, straightens out, and takes us the 36 miles to the edge of the world, where one lone peak bumps up the horizon.

The Grand Canyon hides and hides until the last minute. As we catch our first glimpse through gnarled trees, Alexandra responds with a casual

"Oh, that's pretty cool."

Then the trees vanish, the clouds part, and sunlight slices across the earth, which drops away into the full grandeur of the pink, purple and orange crevice that splits the planet's crust. Alexandra stares out over the layers of ancient time that roll in jagged ridges, crests, and peaks out to the purple horizon, and her appreciation turns into a deep-throated

"Wooaah! That is so amazing!"

And it is.

We walk on a soft carpet of fresh snow to the edge of the canyon, which tells of a two-billion-year-old history of earth, when the 'where' we are standing on now did not exist. To climb down into the depths of the canyon to where the Colorado flows, a slim line of shining sky through the deep shadows, would be to climb past rocks that lay exposed in a time when oxygen was still being formed. Past a time when the first simple organisms started to colonize the planet. Past a time when shallow seas ebbed and flowed, leaving their sediment behind in tiny layers of color and texture. Ice ages came and went, each leaving behind its mark on the planet. Then, 1.2 million years ago, the Colorado River set its course, and slowly dug its way back into time to reveal the earth's layers again.

The sun catches on the frosting of snow, which adds dimension to the sea of ridges and buttresses in shades of blue, purple, rust and cream. Small gnarled trees cling to catches of soil in narrow clefts, and far below the Colorado River now rarely reaches the ocean. Humans, with their unchecked need for water, are bringing to an end the slow creation of this spectacle, for the moment at least.

A sound draws our attention. Turning we discover we are being watched by a small group of grey mule deer. The setting sun reflects in their black eyes, and pushes the saturation level of the canyon to the maximum. A few lonely peaks catch the last light, flaring bright orange against the deep purple shadows, then night falls, and with it, the temperature. We hurry to the hotel dining room, where we eat huge bowls of creamy potato and leek soup with homemade bread.

Bed 115

Fresh snow comes with the morning. It swirls towards the windscreen, and snakes across the road. The landscape is flat, with small grey bushes dotting the red soil. Bright pink and gold rocks glow in sudden brilliant color, as rare shafts of sunlight penetrate the clouds on this grey day. We leave the spectacle of the Grand Canyon behind, as we enter the Hopi Indian Reserve. Here Mother Nature favors a more minimalist approach to landscaping. In the distance, a white stone canyon, with a single brilliant red line of ore running along the middle, reminds us of the pink bath ring in the Dr Seuss *Cat in the hat* books. In every nook and cranny, and under every tuft of grass, snow hides from the pale sun, while it waits for reinforcements, which are not long in coming.

The Hopi live in shabby little bundles on the vast open plains. From the roadside we see small shacks with rusting cars that paint a picture of startling contrast between mainstream America and 'The People of the Land'. In South Africa these Third World conditions are almost expected, but here, in this great First World superpower, this sharp distinction in wealth between 'The People of the Land' and the people to whom the land now belongs pokes us in the eye. The road runs through bleak and barren countryside, where occasional small fields tell of a hand-to-mouth existence. There seems to be no living to be made, other than out of tourists. Signs everywhere try their best to get travelers to stop and shop.

Chief Yellow Nose loves you

Oops, you missed us

Stop! Nice Indians behind you

and finally

Old chief says turn back now

So we do, to shop at the Brian McGee craft center and supermarket. Stepping inside, I step right back into the apartheid-created homelands of South Africa, complete with the bare concrete floor, the odd assortment of goods, the inadequate refrigeration, the smell of faint decay, and the undeniable poverty. However, on speaking to the owner, I discover that I was wrong in my assumptions. The Hopi do not consider their situation 'Third World', but rather 'Fourth World', which is their term for that condition to which they believe all the world will revert to, one of humble, but sustainable living in harmony with nature.

With our arrival at Canyon de Chelly, the blue-black cloud mass breaks, and allows misty sunlight to flood over the canyon of smooth yellow stone, which concentrates the sunlight until the whole canyon glows, throwing golden light back into the sky, turning the lazy snowflakes into floating scraps of light. The snow settles gently on every tiny surface, until every crack, every ledge, every branch of every tree, and every blade of grass is picked out in crystal white lines. The colossal stone blocks dwarf the tiny roads, tiny houses and tiny fields far below, but despite its grandeur, Canyon de Chelly is a place where the ancient mysteries of the Navajo are still tangible. It is a place of square adobe ruins, reduced to ant size by the sheer rock faces to which they cling, of tire tracks in the fresh snow that reveal that somewhere in the corners and crannies of this ancient canyon, the Navajo still continue their traditional lifestyle.

We meet traditional Navajo artists Antonio and Darren at the roadside. They are selling stone art from a blanket on the ground, and are happy to continue their artistry on the Wish Mobile. As Darren draws, Antonio seems to go into a trance, while he relates in singsong voice the meaning of the symbols that are slowly appearing on the Wish Mobile. A healing hand combined with a Navajo spiral represents the journey to the four corners of the earth through vision, dreamtime, spirit and doctor journeys. A few feathers represent the creative force of life, and an eagle, the symbol of wisdom, which enables us to see that changes need to be made in our lives, and gives us the courage so that we can move forward, and make those changes.

He tells us about the Thunderbird, also known as Waykinyan, who is the keeper of truth, and has been known to kill liars by shooting lightning bolts from his eyes and beak. Darren adds the medicine arrows that represent; in the north, wisdom; in the south, innocence; in the east, the ability to see the future; and in the west, dreams and introspection. Finally a small man called U'ki'ut'l is sketched out on the silver metal of the Wish Mobile. U'ki'ut'l is connected to the cycles of life, and the endless choices we make on life's path – a journey that, if the choices are made correctly, will lead us to harmony. But how can we know if our choices are correct until harmony is reached? When do we know we are on the wrong road? In Turkey there is a saying that no matter how far you have walked down a road, if it is the wrong one, turn back. But again, when does one know?

I do know, however, that our road forward will be hair-raising, and getting to Milwaukee by Christmas will be like threading a needle in a storm. By now, I am on first-name terms with the weather channel, and they are playing out like a horror movie. Two storms are moving in on the central plains of the USA. Our escape route via Kansas has already been cut off, and a huge powerhouse of snow and ice is moving rapidly over the Sierra Nevada towards the Rockies and Denver. This is our only other choice north, and we will need to speed ahead of the storm if we want to make any progress at all. Come morning, we step outside into a pea-soup fog. It snowed overnight, not too much here, but according to my friends on the weather channel, much more elsewhere along our route.

What to do?

I enquire at the reception,

> "Is it safe to drive?"

> "Oh no, you cannot go; the schools have closed, and it will not be safe on the roads."

I phone the police station,

> "Madam, I advise that you stay put; they have cleared the roads, but it is still dangerous to drive."

I start buying into 'Fear Factor America', and consider staying another night. Alexandra rolls her eyes in exasperation, forcing me to pull myself towards myself. I have single-handedly braved the world, crossed the Karakum, gone where no European woman has gone before – or so I fondly like to believe – get a grip, woman!

So I do, and firmly gripping a piece of luggage in each hand, I march resolutely out of the door. The fog lasts exactly 500 m before we emerge into a perfectly clear day and clear roads. Just goes to show; moderation in all things. Too much information will make you fearful and doubtful of your own judgment.

Soon great monoliths of stone rise out of white snowfields, the gateway to Monument Valley. According to geologists, the great towers of rock were formed by eons of sediment build-up, which, after millions of year of slow sculpting by nature, was washed away, leaving only the stone pillars that stand unblemished by plant or man. According to the Navajo, however, the 'Changing Woman' formed Monument Valley. In Navajo mythology this beautiful woman represents the seasons, and together with her twin children, used the magic they learnt from the 'Spiderwoman' to turn the terrible monsters that used to walk the earth into the red stone pillars.

A muddy track leads into the park. Uncertainty wells up in my stomach. Turning to Alexandra, I start voicing my doubts.

"That looks rough and muddy. I think we will get stuck. Perhaps we should give it a miss."

Alexandra gives me a very fierce glance, and I catch myself. I am at it again. Doubt, fear, uncertainty, is this what happens in an over-regulated society? Not to me; we are going on that road.

The road is a bit muddy, but nothing the Wish Mobile and I cannot handle. The scenery is outrageous; the red rocks soar to the clear blue sky. Alexandra is reduced to a matchstick as she climbs up to hug a 25-m-high rock colossus. We look over the plains, from which the stone pillars rise, white snow adding definition to brilliant orange landscape, and are in awe.

Colorado

Bed 116

Hunkering down in a motel in Mexican Hat, I make phone calls to the family in Milwaukee, and to 5W Nancy in Denver while keeping a horrified eye on the weather channel. Two massive snowstorms are sweeping across America from east and west, closing roads and airports in their wake. The American Christmas traffic, both land and air, is slowly sinking into chaos. The storms are destined to collide tomorrow night over Denver, which is where we are heading. Denver is 750 km away, not really that far, but considering the weather, our chances of reaching Milwaukee by Christmas are looking grim. I make an executive decision: we leave at 4 am tomorrow morning. Driving in the dark will prevent us from seeing the remainder of Monument Valley, but it will up our chances of reaching Denver before the storm collision.

From our warm room we step into a cold so bitter that I warn Alexandra not to put bare flesh to metal. The Wish Mobile leaps to life, and in the headlights I see that Mother Nature is going to make things as difficult as she possibly can this morning. The beams stop short and spread in the thick fog that leans heavily against the windows. I try driving with only the fog lights. This works for all of five minutes, before Mother Nature plays her next card, and throws a swirling shifting fall of snow into the mix. The snow materializes out of the fog like static on a television screen, sweeping across the windscreen; the tiny spots create a billowing vortex of snow and fog. My sense of direction vanishes; the Wish Mobile gives a stomach-sinking lurch across a drift of snow; I yank the steering to get us back on the road; and slow down, and slow down, and slow down, until at a snail's pace we creep into Bluff.

We need diesel urgently.

Cruising past all the pumps we discover that once again the diesel pump is nowhere to be found. In America the diesel pump is always tucked away in some hidden corner. Fuel discrimination exists. In the station the assistant turns from her phone call, and to my question about the location of the diesel pump, informs me:

"You don't want diesel, honey; you want petrol; and the pump is right there next to your vehicle."

She waves an airy hand at the snowy courtyard behind me.

I stare at her in bemusement.

"My vehicle takes diesel. Do you have a diesel pump?"

"Are you sure, honey?"

Is she kidding me?

Finger Rock , Monument Valley, Arizona

'I have just driven here all the way from Germany via China, and in all that time I have been using diesel, so, yes, I am fairly sure.'

'What kind of car do you drive?'

Astounding, she actually does not believe me.

'A Kangoo.'

'Never heard of it.'

With that, she dismisses my funny car and me outright. She points vaguely towards the dark snowdrifts, before turning back to her phone call.

'It's over there.'

Stepping back into the cold I peer into the dark, and in the distance make out a solitary fuel pump, barely visible above the snowdrifts that surround it. This could be problematic. Inching the Wish Mobile through the powdery snow is not difficult, but getting stuck could be equally easy, and being stuck in a fuelling station in Bluff is not part of the master plan, so I cautiously maneuver just close enough for the nozzle to reach. But then discover that the nozzle is ice-welded to the pump. My puny yanking and pulling make no impression; that thing is frozen solid. But I have a plan. Stomping through the snow to the back of the car I fumble about for Olga, and, with a sharp thwack of spade on pump, release the nozzle from its icy prison. A half-hour after pulling into the fuelling station I finally get to the point where I can fill up.

All the while Alexandra sleeps … until we burst from the fog onto a high prairie and brilliant blue sunlight falls across her eyes. Yawning, she looks over the passing world. Fog fills the valleys; it bounces the sunlight back to the glittering ice-filled clouds. Rainbow haloes shimmer around the sun, which etches a line of light around every snow-fringed branch and blade of frozen grass. Alexandra watches the scenery flash by for a few minutes, then turns to me with one word.

'Food!'

Good call! Pulling into the parking of a roadside diner on the outskirts of Moab, we are reassured by the lack of parking space: the food served will be palatable. Sliding into a fifties-style plastic booth, we make a snap decision. This frozen morning is the perfect morning for an all-American breakfast of piles of thick pancakes, crisp bacon, and lashings of maple syrup, washed down by two bottomless cups of coffee. While we eat, the overhead television spills out bad news: the storm has arrived. Only Interstate 76 to Denver is still open, but there is doubt that the Vail and Loveland passes will remain open for long. With that, we gulp down the coffee, and get ourselves onto the interstate heading east. If there is to be any closing of passes, it is to be after we have passed.

But Mother Nature is just not playing nice this morning; the break in the weather at Moab was just a brief intermission between acts. Act 2 begins as Mother Nature opens the heavenly gates, and within minutes, dumps tons of snow on Earth, completely obliterating the road, the sky, the sun, and the planet in general. She then increases the windspeed a touch, turning the snow into a solid billowing curtain. The only points of reference in the whiteout are the taillights of the car in front of me.

Slowly all cars move into a single file in the center of the interstate, held together only by the small faith that the driver in front of each of us knows where he is heading. I have visions of lemming-like nosedives off a cliff as we slowly make our way up Vail Pass. At an elevation of 10,000 ft, orange emergency signs flash out of the white. They command trucks to apply road chains. On the barely visible roadside, truckers labor around and under their great vehicles, heaving heavy chains into place. I think of the little snow chains under my seat, and wonder whether I should put them on too. I have never driven in snow, and have no way of judging when a car might require a snow chain.

The long upward slope of Loveland Pass makes the decision for me. At 11,992 ft the incline is too steep, the snow too deep. The Wish Mobile meets its match, loses its grip on the situation, as we slide and snake across the road. This is starting to rival Kazakhstan for insane driving conditions. Time for snow chains. I step into the blizzard, and, sinking onto my knees in the snow, scrabble about under the car, clutching the instruction manual in one hand, while trying to place the chains with the other.

> *Curses, a little practice run in less hazardous conditions would probably have been a good idea.*

The wind blows snow into my eyes. Cars and trucks skim by with inches to spare. The cold chews at my fingers, until the pain of my slowly freezing hands warns me that perhaps I should have worn gloves. By the time I manage to get the snow chains in place, the snow has packed on the windscreen, the wipers are frozen, and the little windscreen water tank is a block of ice. My fingers slowly turn black, as I hack away at the snow-laden windscreen. When the pain in my fingers becomes more urgent than seeing through the windscreen, I step gratefully into the warmth of the car, closely followed by the blizzard. Alexandra, not dressed for the elements, howls her protests. These are drowned out by the silent howls of pain emanating from my fingertips as they defrost, shooting pain into my heart, and screaming their anger at the abuse they have had to endure. But the snow is building on the windscreen again. Time to move; the pain must wait.

Slowly we crest Loveland Pass, and as we descend into the valley, heave sighs of relief, believing that the worst is over, only one more small hill, and then Denver. But as the traffic spreads over three lanes, it doesn't speed up, as would be expected. Instead, each lane of traffic slowly comes to a halt. Alexandra finds the local traffic channel, and we listen with foreboding as the announcer reels off a long list of roads that are closed. Although the 76 is officially still open, we are not moving. The snow comes down in thick flurries, slowly burying the rows of cars as the day fades. Realizing that we might be here for the night, we take stock of our situation. We have spare fuel, bedding, water, a kettle, food, lots of warm clothing and blankets. Despite this, the thought of spending the night on the intestate is not appealing. With my snow chains on, I am confident that we can fall in with the large SUVs that, two lanes to the right, are making their way past the stationary trucks. I wait for my chance, then slip into the snow ruts of the larger vehicles. The snow scrapes the bottom of the Wish Mobile. If we get stuck, there are going to be some mighty angry SUV drivers stuck behind us.

Alexandra catches the mood, and starts speaking very nicely to the Wish Mobile, while I get into second gear, keep the revs up, and nurse us through the snaking parking lot that the interstate has become. On the steep hill, two trucks slid into each other, closing the highway to any further trucks, and reducing the traffic flow to one lane, which bends and twists its way around the scattered trucks and cars that were not up to the challenge of the snow-covered hill.

Two and a half hours later, we have crested the hill, and are once again making reasonable progress, but then the radio announces what we feared: the I 76 is now officially closed, and the snowplows have gone home. The sky is still dumping tons of white stuff, and the day has turned to snow-swept night. It could be a long cold night for all the people in the cars stuck in the valley behind us. But for all our headway, we are no better off. In the swirl of snow we faintly see the huge drifts of snow that obliterate every exit. We are prisoners, forever stuck in forward motion on this nightmare road. I feel panic rising as the snow packs on the windscreen. The wipers are moving at full speed, but succeed only in packing the snow into a solid ice block. With a last scrape across the icepack, the wipers stop, and so must I.

Pulling over as far as possible, I step into a white black world of horizontal snow, where my first call of action is to clear the snow packs from the taillights and hazard lights, so the Wish Mobile at least has some way of warning the few oncoming cars that we are here. Then I attack the ice pack on the windscreen, and as soon as the wipers regain some momentum, leap back into the warmth of the car. After long moments of wheel spinning, the Wish Mobile finally finds a small amount of traction, bumps over the snow tracks, slides into the deep snow grooves left by other vehicles, and relieves me of any need to use the steering wheel. The wheels are heading in one direction only, whether I like or not.

On our right, suddenly an off-ramp opens to a fuelling station and a motel. I force the wheel right at the last moment; the Wish Mobile reluctantly battles its way out of the groove it is in, grinds its way through virgin snow, locks into the off-ramp grooves, and minutes later we gratefully slide into the nearest available space in the snow bank that is the parking lot. Grabbing just the bare essentials, we wade thigh-deep in snow to the reception.

'Congratulations, you have the last one.'

'Last one?'

'The last room; we are now full.'

The man waiting behind us groans, Alexandra and I grin with relief and spare a thought for those hundreds of people still stuck on the Interstate 76. It's been 13 hours of driving hell, but we have driven through the worst blizzard to hit Denver in two decades, and have emerged triumphant. This is cause for celebration. Alexandra rustles up a feast from the food she scavenged in the car: a box of Cheerios, a packet of beef jerky, a jar of olives, trail mix, tea and one Bud Light.

Bed 117 & 118

While Alexandra splashes about her early morning ablutions, I sip a steaming cup of tea, and stare out of the motel window. The snow has reached the windowsill, and only the backs of the garden chairs penetrate the smooth white surface. The world has been reduced to its basic form; everything is white round soft, but promises hard work. In the parking lot we join the other motel guests in carefully assessing the gently undulating snowfield in front of us, each trying to remember exactly where we parked our vehicles in last night's snow-blown dark. The distinctive shape of the Wish Mobile makes finding it easy, although driving away is less so. While Alexandra works to remove the snow pack covering the car, I apply myself to road building. Between us and the narrow track created by the snowplow are many meters of thigh-deep virgin snow.

With my borrowed snow shovel, I scoop a great scoop of white stuff, then swing it from side to side, trying to decide where to dump it. Not to the left, as that would upset the man trying to free his car, and not right, for the same reason, and not in front of the car, as that would be counterproductive. My only solution is to first dig a path to the back of the car, and then to slowly build a great wall of snow between myself and the car behind me. If he thought he would benefit from my hard work, he was mistaken; every man, woman and child for themselves here. And so I discover why, in the end, even the snowplows must go home. When it is no longer possible to move the snow to where it does not create another obstruction, there is simply no point in moving it at all. While we dig and scrape, passers-by add wishes to the 'One Planet One People' project. A man wishes for world peace and then adds,

'And that my family stays together'

A strangely personal wish, which I hope, stays true.

On the road to Brighton, all guidelines have vanished under the snow. There is no middle marker, no lane marker, and no indication where the road turns to ditch, other than the half buried cars that found out the hard way. In Brighton we receive a Christmassy warm welcome from 5W Nancy, who shows me the green side of America. While we all tuck into hearty soup made from her garden vegetables – she has a firm commitment to eating food from as close to the source as possible – I learn that not all Americans are rampant consumers. Thoughtfully she explains the destruction of the American way of life through globalization, and the American corporation's obsessive focus on creating ever-larger profit margins, which is building a debt mountain that is slowly burying the values that made the American way of life the most desired way of life on the planet.

The snow stops falling, Alexandra uses this as an excuse to get away from the adult conversation. Nancy and I watch as she launches herself into the soft powdery drifts, and while she lies on her back – making her first-ever snow angel – I realize that the changes the world needs start with people like Nancy, people who commit to changing their behavior one small step at a time, slowly laying a foundation for the big changes; this is the only way we can change our values. To wait for somebody else to start will never bring any result at all.

Bed 119 & 120

The sun rises apricot-pink behind snow-laden trees into a crystal clear day. Irrigation dragons with long ice beards stand in diamond-frosted fields, where black cows punch cow-shaped holes into the blinding white landscape. The trees, coated in ice, shimmer and sparkle like upside-down chandeliers. The clear weather is well timed, as after days of dawdling, we now have a deadline: Christmas in Milwaukee; and our route is due east on the Interstate 80, the fastest, shortest way across the American Midwest.

Nebraska speeds by unnoticed. The slick-slush road surface holds my full attention, as with each passing car and truck the Wish Mobile receives another coating of mud, and soon the windscreen is a thick ooze, which the wipers spread into an opaque yellow-brown filter. Watching the clean windscreens of the passing cars, I wonder whether The Wish Mobile has a design flaw. How do those folk keep their windscreen water liquid? Do they have windscreen tank heaters? Mine has been a block of ice for days. To avoid having to stop every few minutes to clean the mud from the windscreen, I open the window, and attempt to throw water on the windscreen, while traveling at 120 km/h. This is not a very effective method of window cleaning, as most of the water flies into the great beyond, an unpleasant percentage flies back onto me, and only the smallest amount actually hits its target. The things we southern types don't know about driving in snow and ice would fill a fairly thick book.

Just past Grand Island, the snow fades, the road dries, my windscreen problem vanishes, and the earth rolls by in shades of brown and beige. Small corn silos tower like skyscrapers, and red barns are extravagant spots of color. Now there is no stopping, no photography, just drive. We chew up Interstate 80, zoom through Omaha, Des Moines, Iowa City, Davenport, and while Alexandra sleeps her way across America, my thoughts return to the question of values.

Americans are big on old-fashioned values, yet they lead the way in setting false values through the relentless advertising of pointless merchandise, aided by beautiful people – the blank canvases of society – onto which marketeers project the things they want the masses to desire. The lifestyle these beautiful people represent is unobtainable for most, and for those who do strive to achieve it, it is the most inefficient, stressful way of life imaginable. It is based on all the things we try teach our children not to be: callous, egocentric and selfish. A culture of 'I want it all, and I want it now'.

In a society in which only money measures value, the most meaningless jobs are the best paid and desirable. We have created a world in which men, whose only talent is to maneuver a ball from one end of a grassy field to the other, are paid in millions, while those who could save millions by manufacturing medicines to cure the ills of the less privileged don't, because there is no profit in saving poor children. We live in a society in which undernourished women, wearing bizarre outfits, get paid a fortune to walk past wealthy bored people, while women who walk from poor house to poor house, trying to save undernourished children, get paid nothing.

But our true enemy is our own corruptibility. We all want more than we need, convinced by the media that the more we have, the happier we will be. But worse, as the rich get richer, they start to believe they deserve even more and that their labor is worth infinitely more than that of the poor; passing snide comments during this week's third game of golf that if the poor just worked harder, they would not be struggling to make ends meet. Yet there is nothing to support this theory, other than the ego of the rich, and the desperation of the poor.

Crossing the Mississippi into Illinois, we negotiate the afternoon traffic in the densely urbanized and industrial area around Chicago, and soon cross the state line to Wisconsin and Milwaukee. Milwaukee is called the 'Cream City', owing to the creamy gold color of the many face-brick buildings. The color of the bricks results from the high lime content in these parts. Milwaukee is also a city of immigrants: German, Polish, Italian. After a few more traffic jams and a short drive through suburbia, we arrive at our 'home sweet home', for Christmas. Well... not our home, but home of family, so that will do.

Christmas for my family must at one point have had some religious significance, but over the years our particular family ritual at Christmas has become a thing of tradition and continuity, regardless of whether a member subscribes to the underlying religious messages. The ritual is what binds us, and although our family is spread across three continents, at this time of year no matter where I were to visit, the ritual of Christmas would be the same.

December 24 is spent preparing delicious food, putting the finishing touches to the Christmas tree, and wrapping those last few presents, before adding them to the growing pile under the tree. In the evening all retire to their rooms to spruce up for what really is seldom more than a family gathering, but with the ritual of primping and preening - Alexandra and I have brought along cocktail dresses for just this occasion - the family gathering is given gravitas and a symbolism that we know is being shared by other loved ones, in other time zones around the world.

All electric lights are dimmed, and in the soft candlelight the beautifully decorated tree has pride of place. If the architecture allows, the fully lit tree festooned with candles and presents would be allowed to be seen only after all the guests have been assembled. As you can imagine, arriving late, even a fashionable five minutes, is frowned upon by all concerned. For children of all ages this is always a time of great anticipation. Even adults have been known to get tears in their eyes as they first see the beautiful tree, and memories of a long-forgotten childhood suddenly, and surprisingly overwhelm them. Over glasses of champagne and all manner of tasty treats, the ritual of giving and sharing is a one-gift-at-a-time affair, so all can enjoy the surprise and pleasure of both giver and receiver. This ritual of giving is dragged out until just before midnight, and then to bed.

In the morning we wake up to a grey day with no snow. We are very disappointed. I was sure that being way up in the Great Lakes country, snow would be assured. But no, no snow, just grey, no white Christmas this year. The lack of snow is no excuse for lack of food, and we all indulge in the 'The Big Eat': turkey with all the trimmings. When evening falls, we take a drive through a working-class neighborhood, where the people have an annual charity event, which involves decorating the houses and streets as extravagantly as possible. Most of the decorations are handmade and somewhat crude, but the emotion behind them has a much firmer grasp of the spirit of Christmas than the professionally decorated houses I have seen elsewhere in America. This Christmas arts and crafts display has over the years gained a large following, and has raised thousands of dollars for the local children's hospital. As we stop at an intersection, young men and women carrying large collection tins step up to the car, and so we add our offering to the all ready impressive tally of $16,000.00

The last days of Christmas roll by doing family stuff, talking, eating our way through the Christmas leftovers, sleeping, and walking in the woods. I increase my claim to fame by appearing on local television and in the newspapers. Then we bow out of Milwaukee with a fancy reception held at my aunt and uncle's fancy country club. There I discover one new thing about myself: it seems I have quite lost my fear of public speaking. When the inevitable speech moment comes around, I am quite at my ease, not a sweaty palm or pounding pulse to be detected.

To live life without fear; if that is the only thing that I walk away with after this trip is over, it will have been worth it.

Indiana

Bed 121

My kind of town, Chicago is …

Chicago is a bold, muscular place, appropriately nicknamed 'The City of Big Shoulders', where the money walks down Michigan Avenue, and the buildings rise to the occasion. There are many buildings, all high, and all rather well designed. This carries on a long tradition of high buildings in Chicago, which is where the first skyscraper in the world was built.

The Home Insurance Building, built in 1885, had 10 storeys, and rose to the grand height of 138 feet (42 m). In its day it was an architectural wonder that had the city fathers highly concerned for the safety of those who entered it, and dared to ascend to the top floor. This is very funny when compared to today's giant, the John Hancock Center, which clocks in at 100 storeys and 1,127 feet (344 m). Chicago is a city defined by its skyscrapers, even the Quakers have one. Chicago is also defined by its history of crime, mafia, molls, and infamous bank robbers like Baby Face Nelson and John Dillinger, who once stormed through the front doors of banks, relying on the persuasive power of their Tommy guns to command those inside to lie on the floor,

Nobody moves, nobody gets hurt

and then, under threat of death, ordered the hapless bank manger to empty the safe of its contents. After the robbers had fled, the banker alerted the police, who hunted the robbers down, until the last one was brought to justice.

Things have changed a bit since the good old days. Today the robbers flaunt their wealth on the Magnificent Mile, one of the world's most exclusive shopping streets, where they adorn themselves with the world most exclusive and most expensive merchandise, Hugo Boss, Bloomingdales, Neiman Marcus, Saks Fifth Avenue, Macy's, Max Mara, Vera Wang, Jimmy Choo, George, Yves Saint Laurent, Jil Sander, Prada, Montblanc, Marc Jacobs, Ralph Lauren, Bottega Veneta, Hermès, Gucci, Louis Vuitton, Giorgio Armani – the glittering brands roll out the red carpet for these men and women with limitless credit.

Beautifully groomed, they stroll through the front doors of the world's biggest banks, glide up glass elevators to corner offices, where, with manicured fingertips they enter secret passwords that open the doors to all the world's money, and slowly the bankers have become robbers who steal the world's value away. They get away with this because the world has forgotten that money has no value; it is a measuring sick against which we measure things of real value: land, sheep or human endeavor. Money was created purely to make trade easier. By slow degrees bankers have turned this concept upside down, until today we are brainwashed into believing that the ruler that measures the land has more value than the land itself.

Crossing the Chicago River, we double back to walk up 'State Street ... that great street ...' and with the words of that old classic floating through my mind, I again have that vague sense of familiarity that I have felt since arriving in America. Chicago has been the setting for hundreds of films from the classic *The blues brothers* to *My big fat Greek wedding*. The city is a film star in its own right, but its soul is as elusive as that of a real film star. We wander up and down empty grey streets. The city feels cold and sterile. There is nothing here that can compare to the vibrant, inclusive street life and human mass of the oriental city.

But our time in Chicago is far too short to judge properly, as once again we are chasing a deadline: New Year with Tom in Toronto and more immediately a Friday night fish fry with 5W Mary in South Bend. Having left Chicago much too late, we arrive hours after dinnertime to the warm American welcome we have become accustomed to. Over cheese and wine a journalist appears, and I find myself rattling off the same old answers to the same old questions.

'Which was your favorite country?'

'Croatia.'

'How far have you traveled?'

'50,000 km; I don't know what that would be in miles.'

'How long did it take you?'

'Up to now, nine months.'

The American media is a well-oiled machine, but I don't really know why they ask the questions they ask: they are not important. The journalist ends with the question for which I have yet to work out a good answer.

'So what do you think of the Americans?'

I reply with an automatic.

'All the Americans I have met up to now have been incredibly friendly and helpful.'

The following morning the doorbell rings, and another journalist joins us for breakfast. Sitting in the sunroom, overlooking the sunrise lake that is Mary's backyard, we munch our way through a pile of home-baked blueberry muffins, hot from the oven, while I trot my way through the same old question-and-answer routine. I am begin to have a small inkling of what it must be like to be a famous person, having to do this all day, everyday … it is like your life is on constant replay. With the photographs done, Alexandra and I leap into our trusty carriage, and set off direction Rochester Hills via Amish country.

The Amish, an offshoot of an offshoot of the Reformist Church, as started by Martin Luther, determinedly manage to maintain their simple lifestyle against the onslaught of American commercialism and new technology. They still don't allow electricity in their homes, and don't have privately owned cars, although some do use tractors to plough their fields, and the children get transported to school in an old-fashioned yellow school bus, but for private transportation, the black horse-drawn buggy reigns supreme.

At the Yoder supermarket, the buggies are tied to a post on the parking lot. The horse-drawn buggy may fit in well with the Amish beliefs, it does not fit well onto the modern parking lot. While waiting for their masters to return, horses do as horses must, leaving the area around them a mess of dung and urine. A little sandy patch under a tree would surely not be too much to ask. Those horses work hard. The buggies we see on the road are all going as fast as one-horse-powered buggies can. The sight of the overworked horses shifts my opinion of the Amish down a bit. The Amish may strive to be sedate and calm, but they make those horses *schwitz*. Despite their stated beliefs, it does appear as if the drivers would rather be driving a Porsche, and take their frustration out on the horse.

In Shipshewana on the Indiana R20, Yoder rules: Yoder market, Yoder truck company, Yoder this, and Yoder that. In the Yoder craft market we admire the quaint chairs, quilts and doilies, imagining the many Amish hours that must have gone into creating each item, until a tiny label gives the game away, 'Made in India'.

Michigan

Bed 122

Our route heads north-east towards the USA–Canadian border. We are deep in the Snow Belt, and while the road-kill count on this road is enormous – badgers, raccoons and minced squirrels – there is not a flake of snow to be seen. The sky is blue, the fields neatly studded with freshly painted red barns, and the air thick and pungent as the farmers apply manure liberally over the pancake-flat earth. But there is danger at hand. We seem to have entered a war zone where the use or nay of compost is being fiercely fought. Signs, both professional and crudely hand drawn, shout protest from the road's edge.

'COMPOST STINKS'

We can vouch for that.

'SAVE OUR CHILDREN NO MORE COMPOST'

What are these children doing with the compost that it should be life threatening? Perhaps the author of that poster should add more fiber to her children's diet; keep them off the compost heap. The battle rages on the roadside for miles as farmers and rich city folk demand their right to use the land. Sadly, money wins, and daily more family farms are pushed out of business. The old farm buildings give way to the forces of commerce and nature, sagging slowly to the ground as the world loses yet more of its best farmlands to housing developments and roads. The loss of the small farms of the world puts the control of the global food supply into the hands of the few. We are already led by our noses in matters oil supply and money supply; I wonder how life will be when our food is as cynically controlled. I don't think we have long to find out.

The 12 E, also known as the Historic Heritage Route, is a stop-start of little villages. Coldwater is a village of quaint shopping streets, and large fanciful houses with turrets, frills and towers, bay window and shutters. The front porches are festooned with Victorian lacy detail in a multitude of contrasting colors. Allen is a village specializing in antiques, selling books from barns, alongside bits and bobs of every description. We drive through a village called Moscow; earlier we drove through Angola; we really are getting around today. Judging by what we see of the city of Ann Arbor, it's a city of forests, lakes, cycle tracks and splendid golf courses, really a rather pretty place, until we hit the industrial zone, but even that is clean and neat, with not a belching chimney in sight.

The Pontiac Route takes us through leafless forests, where the sun shines through winter-bare trees, creating flashing zebra stripes that fly over the car, and onto the road. Soon we find ourselves in Salem. Thinking that this must be the infamous witch-burning Salem, Alexandra works herself into a total froth, seeing boogiemen and sinister happenings behind every brightly painted door. Before Alexandra fizzes over in her imaginary witch-hunt, I remind her that the infamous Salem is in Massachusetts, and we are quite safe from persecution here. The scenery changes from roadside forest to rolling manicured lawns, around sprawling luxury houses. The houses and size of the properties are enormous, made doubly so by the American convention of no fences, so the houses appear to be set in huge parklands, through which grey deer roam freely.

A disturbing phenomenon mars the quiet semi-rural scene. The plastic inflatable Santas that adorn many front yards are all looking decidedly flat. Alexandra's imagination runs wild, again:

'A Santa slasher stalks the suburbs of America!'

Proclaims she, in headline tones.

Been watching to many schlock horror movies, thinks I.

Set in a grassy parkland is the home of 5W Josetta and hubby, Don, who are very friendly folk with artist leanings, so we hit it off immediately. But as we step into the grand house, with a view down to a wooded dale, where grey deer graze, I cannot help making global comparisons, and find myself somewhat embarrassed at the excess of the West, an excess of which I am a part. In the many conversations I have had in the past month, I have discovered that there is a general agreement that, because Americans work incredibly hard, this lifestyle is their just reward. I agree, hard work should result in a comfortable lifestyle and a peaceful retirement; if it doesn't, what is the point of working hard. But then I think of Olena in the Ukraine in her postage-stamp apartment, which could easily fit into Josetta's kitchen, and the three jobs that she juggles to ensure one pay check. I think of the frail old Chinese woman I watched dragging her huge pile of recyclables along the highway to try to earn enough for a daily meal, and I think of Elaine in Hong Kong, whose dearest wish is to be able to afford an apartment with a small balcony. They would all disagree that hard work automatically equates to wealth or a gracious lifestyle.

For most of the people on the planet, hard work often only results in enough to survive. Often in this world of upside-down values, it is those people who perform tasks most important to society, nurses for example who work all hours of the day, and still struggle financially, while those endowed only with good looks, who act as the mindless billboards of commerce, don't bother getting out of bed for less than $50,000. Value has become defined by what is easy to see, what looks good on TV.

While I have been trying to get my head around this global inequality of the value of human labor, Josetta has arranged a telephonic interview with the local newspaper.

'Which was your favorite country?'

'Croatia.'

'How far have you traveled?'

'50,000 km; I don't know what that would be in miles.'

'How long did it take you?'

'Up to now, nine months.'

'So what do you think of the Americans?'

'All the Americans I have met up to now have been incredibly friendly and helpful.'

I should write a press release; perhaps then I would get to say something new.

While Josetta cooks up an organic storm, Don takes us on a quick tour of the town. We are a bit baffled as to why we should be doing this, until we hit the main road of Rochester. Phoenix and Las Vegas, eat your hearts out. The prize for the town with the most outrageous Christmas lighting is ... Rochester Hills. Every shop façade is covered in solid sheets of tiny lights. Only the doors and windows have been spared this lighting extravaganza. Back at the house Don shows me his collection of stuff – the sort of stuff I can relate to - bits of this, pieces of that, and everything has a brilliant idea tied up in it somewhere. To the untrained eye this is just rubbish, but to the true inventive, it is a treasure horde of possibilities. Then friends and neighbors start arriving . Over glasses of wine Alexandra and I answer all the usual questions, before I sneak off to bed and leave her to it. She comes up half an hour later, not impressed.

'Don't you dare do that again!'

Toronto , Front Street

Canada

Bed 123

In the morning the Wish Mobile gets another wish from Don before we set off direction Canada.

'That we learn to live together and build a better world for all'

At Port Huron, we reach the end of the USA road: in front of us grey water and grey ships, above us grey sky, and filling all the gaps in-between, the distinctive smell of natural gas. The town is deserted, cold and windswept. On a grey steel bridge, I have to cross a border for the first time in months, and for the first time on this journey, I wish the crossing were just a little more official.

There is no border control on the American side, and on the Canadian side the customs lady doesn't even get out of her booth to search the car. She flips through our passports, gives each one a quick stamp, and with a nasal

'Welcome to Canada.'

waves us through.

I am not too happy about this.

'Before we go, don't we need to register the car, or get insurance?'

She shrugs

'No, ma'am, that's it.'

This is too easy, much too easy. I foresee problems on re-entry into the USA. But nothing is to be done today. That will be next year's problem, so on a span of arching grey tar we drive into Ontario, Canada. A 100 km/h speed limit sign tells us we are back to dealing with the metric system, which is a relief. But 100 km/h on a freeway is very slow? We soon discover that Canadian road surfaces leave much to be desired, and as such, the speed limit is quite sensible. In a thin sleet we drive past the natural stone houses of Dorchester on Thames, near London, and soon we approach Toronto via the Queen Elizabeth Way.

Some places that I have visited on this journey I didn't know existed until I arrived there, and some I did. I just never really thought about them. Toronto is such a place. It has always been just a vague concept drifting about in the nether reaches of my brain. Now, as we enter the economic capital of Canada, the vague concept takes solid form in the shape of tightly packed black and gold glass skyscrapers (on the North American continent Toronto is second only to New York in its number of skyscrapers) that have a view over Lake Ontario and Toronto harbor, where massive cargo ships lie at anchor. Alexandra and I still have a hard time thinking of these huge sheets of water, complete with 'ocean-going liners', as fresh water, and constantly have to shift our thinking from driving on a coastal highway to driving on a lakeside one.

There is only one reason that we have made this detour into Canada. I want to see my friend Tom. While this might seem a rather extravagant gesture, Tom takes it all in his stride. Pointing out that when one uses a world map to route one's road trip, a 500-mile detour is but a triviality. The weather turns to indoors, and so, huddled around an old oak table, our evening goes as evenings do when meeting up with good friends one has not seen in years – much talk, lots of laughter, and far, far too much champagne, but then we have much to celebrate. A reunion, a birthday, and a very Happy New Year. Hangover tomorrow, but sometimes they are worth it.

My hangover arrives right on cue, but, as nobody else seems to be suffering, a democratic vote is taken, and I must concede to dragging my hangover up the CN Tower, highest freestanding structure in the world. I thought the Taipei 101 was the highest building in the world. One really has to be very careful about this 'in the world' claim. It transpires that the Taipei 101 is currently only fourth highest, after the CN Tower, the Ostankino Tower, and the Sears Tower. But the normal high-alert security that going up a tall tower involves is the same the world over. Once I am declared 'safe', I drag that hangover kicking and screaming into the high-speed lift, which leaves my stomach on ground floor, my face slightly green, and my head enraged.

This is not a good idea, and it gets worse with every added meter of height. Stepping out into the Sky Pod gives a nauseating (yes, yes, 'dramatic' is probably the correct term, but I just wish the tall skinny tower would stop moving) 360-degree view of one of the most diverse cities in the world. Do I care? No, just stop this needle from moving.

'Hey, Tom, can you feel the tower swaying?'

He looks at me as if I am addled.

I can feel it moving ... I think I am getting sky sick.

'Alexandra, is the tower moving or is it my imagination?'

'Mo, it's all in your head.'

Damn right, it's all in the head, residual champagne, and a totally out of whack inner ear.

Before things get embarrassingly out of hand, I descend to the lookout level, and in my delirium, step out of the elevator and straight onto the glass floor. One look down sends my brain into topspin. I am rooted to the spot.

Where did the floor go! This is NOT good. I am going to be ill ... I will not be ill. I will not be ill. Oh, sweet mama, get me off this floor before I spew all over it!

It requires steely control to hold down my lunch, and to put one foot in front of the other to walk slowly to a piece of floor that is not see-through. My brain is not happy, but I cling firmly to the thought that things can only improve, and they do. After this ordeal, I am allowed to go 'home', and have a nap.

Good thing too, as this evening we have a rendezvous with Toronto TV, right smack in the middle of Dundas Square. I drive the Wish Mobile onto the paving, park under a globular blue Christmas tree, where the production crew proceed to shoot so much footage of the 'Wish Mobile' that I am sure to get a whole half an hour TV special all to myself. The interviewer gets so into the whole concept that Tom, Alexandra and I withdraw to the nearest coffee shop to defrost, while the TV guy plays out his directorial debut. The Wish Mobile is soon surrounded by admiring and curious onlookers, who get their ten seconds of fame by writing wishes, while the TV guy immortalizes them and the Wish Mobile in digital, and great fun is had by all.

Unfortunately, being out in the freezing night air does Alexandra in. She has been feeling a bit off-color, and wakes up with a full-blown strep' throat, and as Tom is not well either, we all trundle off to the clinic. All medical care in Canada is state-run, so not being regular or registered patients we each take a facemask, a number, and wait – for only about 15 minutes – then we get fast, efficient service, pay our very reasonable bill, and, clutching our stash of medicine, make our way back to Tom's apartment, where we spend a quiet day recouping. To fill the time, Tom and I amuse ourselves by building a Google Earth file that will allow us, and now you, to 'fly' to each location that I slept in on my trip around the world.

Our time as always is too short, but once again, we have a deadline as Alexandra flies back to South Africa soon, and we must be in New York in good time. We wish old and new friends farewell. Tom adds his wish to the 'One Planet One People' project.

'Think before you speak; speak before you act; act with respect.'

With that bit of wisdom added to the Wish Mobile, I ease out of the dark parking garage into the sunshine, and set course for America via the 'White Thunder', 'The Big Smoke Rising', 'The Place of the Dancing Rainbows' or whatever it is the ancient tribes called that great tumble of water that is Niagara Falls.

But first, provisions for the road. St Laurence Market comes highly recommended by all Torontonians. It is a cavernous hall, dedicated only to delighting the eyes and the taste buds. The food on display comes from every corner of the globe, reaffirming the Toronto claim of being one of the world's most diverse cities. But such decisions, and so early in the morning ... olives stuffed with pimentos, or with almonds, or perhaps slivers of lemon peel, or rather those stuffed with goat's milk cheese. How about the wrinkly dry and salty ones? But no, those are better with cocktails. Rather the big juicy green ones or maybe we should go with the peppers stuffed with goat's milk cheese. However, we both agree dolmades must be bought and cheese. But which one brie, camembert or that one with the cumin seeds. Oh look, a really good blue. Maybe just a cheddar, but sharp or mild, aged for how long? How about smoked cheese or cheese in balls, Swiss roll cheese, sweet cheese, cheese with ginger, cheese with ... it's all too much for an early morning stomach. A coffee would be good, and there it is, good coffee, and back into the fray. Bread rolls, baguettes, seed loaf, croissants or rye?

Do we really need so many choices? It takes up days of our lives just trying to decide what to have for one picnic lunch. Finally clasping a multitude of clear plastic tubs in which lie our gleaming, succulent choices, we stumble out past the fish market, and here, looking at the neatly stacked legs of giant spider crabs, it strikes me why I always feel a little uncomfortable about eating fish.

It is all happening out there somewhere, isn't it? Way out in the deep blue ocean with no one to really police what's what. Out there, where we humans are completely out of our element, a place to which we give very little thought. There, great fleets of fishing vessels drag their nets across deep ocean floors, weighed down by weights that bash and grind roads of destruction through reefs and corals that are thousands of years old. Out there we set free invisible nets that ensnare, trap and kill every type of sea creature that tries to pass. I stare at the neatly stacked crab legs, and wonder how it would be if two great tractors, dragging a chain between them, rampaged through the ancient forests of the world, uprooting trees, and capturing every creature, big and small, all to be milled to fine meal to satisfy the beasts that we slaughter to satisfy our hunger. Or perhaps some fellow will soon invent sky nets, which will sweep the birds from the sky. The uproar and protest from far and wide would be dreadful to behold. Yet out there, in the deep blue sea, creatures are harvested, unchecked, day and night. Our relationship with the ocean is one of extreme arrogance. It is a territory that we cannot own, will never inhabit, and do not understand, and so, in the way of our species, we treat what we cannot control with disdain.

Driving into Niagara Falls City is like driving into a Las Vegas wannabe town. Lights, casinos, motels and hotels line the main road. On the promenade along the edge of the abyss, a multitude of nations gather, all rather uncertain what to wear. There is no appropriate dress code in a climate where one moment we stand in bright sunshine, trying to spy the falls, which hide behind a veil of mist, but the next the wind blows in our direction, and has us zipping up the jackets, and pulling on the hoods: the water-wind combo is freezing. The eddying wind changes direction, and sweeps the wall of vapor aside; the horseshoe of tumbling water is revealed. Rainbows dance and bounce in the billow of earth-bound cloud. White gulls swirl and dive, visible invisible in the cauldron below. The wind shifts, our view is lost, and then regained, the wind dies, the mist hangs, and we see no falls. There is some local muttering that the erecting of all the high rises has affected the wind patterns around the falls, and now it is obscured by mist far more often than it ever was.

To get as 'up close and personal' with the great curtain of green water as possible, we brave the tunnels in a 'Journey behind the Falls'. The idea to view the falls from below and behind was first made possible in 1889, at which time heavy raincoats, thick boots, and guides with lanterns were required to ensure that guests made it through the mole holes in the rock in one piece, and preferably dry. Today things are all fully automated and brightly lit, not so adventurous any more, but still cold and wet. The wind generated by the falling water blows whirlpools of spray out of the side tunnels. I convince Alexandra to brave these horizontal showers to oblige my need for a photograph. The water that roars just meters behind her ends up looking like a sold white wall.

Back in the sunshine, Alexandra looks at the digital image

'I got soaking wet for that?'

she demands, singularly unimpressed

I shrug

'They cannot all be masterpieces.'

She is not convinced, and steals away the last pickled mushroom.

'Hey!'

After our in-car picnic, we discover there is not much else to do at Niagara Falls, unless going over it in a barrel is your cup of tea, but then be prepared to pay a hefty fine. Sailing a barrel over the lip of the falls is strictly *verboten* ...

... as is driving into the USA with a foreign car, unless all the correct documents are presented. Trying to wing it, I pull my Russia stunt, and simply hand the man controlling the tire spikes all the papers that have successfully helped me over several borders around the world. But the Americans are not so easily fooled. He knows exactly which document he wants, a customs release form, and I don't have it. For this, I blame my American shipping agent entirely. What was she thinking, giving me all sorts of documents, but not the one I should actually have. Without the required document, he has no protocol with which to continue.

As I have no idea how to proceed either, I wait politely while he works out this new and unexpected problem. His confusion is quite understandable. Cars with German number plates probably don't cross this border all that often. To pass the time, I glance into my rearview mirror, where I see the cars behind me piling up, but nobody is hooting. The Americans are so polite, or perhaps they know that if they upset this guy, they too will get the whole nine yards. In an attempt to be useful, I enquire whether I shouldn't just move out of the way, so that the traffic may continue to flow back into America. The spike controller looks me in the eye.

'No, ma'am, they will just have to wait.'

Right ho, then.

After a terse conversation on the phone, he sends us (much to the relief of all those waiting behind us) to the customs house on the far side of the parking lot. The place is packed, even standing room is scarce, as is fresh air. This is going to take a long and unpleasant while. To try to move things along, Alexandra falls into the very long queue, while I go back to the car to see if I can find some sort of paper that will appease these chaps. Wrong move. A guy with dark glasses, a blue uniform and a big gun comes at me.

'Get back inside the building, ma'am,'

he says in menacing tones.

Okey, dokey, back in the building with naughty old me; just don't shoot.

But by some miracle Alexandra has been transferred to a separate office. The chap behind the counter starts sounding off about the customs release forms, and what we should have done, and how it would have made all our lives so much easier. Yes, well, perhaps, but we didn't, and it didn't, and can we just skip the lecture and move on? Finally running out of steam, the uniform sends us on our way and, with no papers, no stamps, no finger printing, no searching of the car, no checking of chassis numbers or registration papers, we drive back into the US of A. Sometimes you just get lucky.

Colgate clock , New Jersey shore of the Hudson River

United States of America
New York State
Beds 124, 125, 126

But our luck doesn't last. The weather closes in, and from Niagara to New York we travel in a dull grey drizzle. To avoid the tedious stop-start of small villages, which remind me very much of Germany, we stay on the interstate, where the brown and gray landscape turns to mud in the incessant rain. As we near New York City, heavy industry, smokestacks and shunting yards start to dominate the scene. To add to the general dullness of the day, my health is in slow decline. Of all the viruses I could choose from in Toronto, I chose the chest cold from Tom, and a small dry cough that tickled my throat this morning has now turned into a chest-heaving bark.

Thankfully Alexandra is no longer in pain, and navigates impeccably, straight to Lincoln Tunnel, and, right on cue, the sun break through the clouds ...

'Start spreading the news ... If you can make it there you'll make it anywhere, New York, New Yo-o-o-ork', the place that is so great they named it twice, the Big Apple, the City That Never Sleeps, a big screen superstar. That's a lot of hype, and we are dying to get our share. From the depths of the Hudson River tunnel we burst into ... tara ... a city ...

A very quiet city: the familiar buildings are all there, but where is the traffic, the noise, the maelstrom of people? Perhaps everybody is having a nap. We make our way up the west side of Manhattan to 79th street and our hotel, which is perfectly positioned, two minutes from the Natural History Museum and Central Park, with metro stations all round. The doorman whips open the door; we are well pleased with our choice, until the receptionist mentions that the parking that they advertised, and which we discussed at length while I was making my booking, they actually don't have. I cannot believe my ears. Parking in New York is a major issue, one that must be carefully considered with every decision you make when staying in New York. As it is, I am double-parked in the street, with Alexandra keeping a wary eye out for tow-trucks, clamp-masters and other assorted traffic hazards. To park a car in a parking garage is fantastically expensive, the same price as a motel room outside of New York, and parking in the road is a very subtle art, which I don't have the time to acquire right now. Once I have recovered from my well-contained tantrum at the lack of parking, the receptionist hands me the booking sheet, and I once again clench my teeth in frustration at the 'American way'.

America has an interesting take on sales tax: it is a hidden thing, which nobody mentions until you get the bill. An all-important question all travelers to America should learn to ask immediately is: 'Does that include tax?' This is important, as it makes a big difference. For example, this establishment advertised their rates as a winter special, which, with the inclusive parking, sounded very reasonable, but with all the state tax, occupation tax, bed tax, city tax, toilet tax, tissue tax (okay I am making some of these up, but regardless) the actual room price is 20% more than the advertised rate. That's a fairly hefty amount of tax that is not disclosed, and adding the extra parking I will have to pay, the room is now almost 50% more than anticipated. My tantrum container runneth over:

'Madame, do I have a choice in paying these taxes?'

'No, Ma'am.'

'I cannot decide not to pay the tax.'

'No, Ma'am.'

'In which case the tax is a fixed part of the total bill, am I right?'

'Yes, Ma'am.'

'In that case your room price to me is not the amount as advertised, but the full amount including tax.'

'Yes ma'am, but we don't profit from the tax portion.'

The receptionist rattles this off in the way of those who have repeated the same thing many times before. I am not surprised, as there is something a tad dishonest about the whole system, which must cause the blood pressure to rise in every new guest.

'In that case why don't you just advertise only the profit portion of the room price; that should get you some serious custom ...'

and right in the middle of my well-contained tirade, a tickle in my throat builds up. It becomes irresistible, until, caught in an uncontained cough convulsion, I bark my germs all over the hapless woman. She backs off, but is stuck in her tiny receptionist space. Sweet revenge, serves her right, but of course, the whole situation is entirely not her fault. We small guys always beat up on each other, leaving the real culprit to doze peacefully on some palm-fringed beach in the Caribbean.

But I am as great a victim of the need for instant gratification as the next guy, so feeling much better in my silly belief that my loss of temper made any difference at all, I heave myself back into the Wish Mobile. The plan is to take a slow cruise around Manhattan, to get a feel for the place, and to check out the lie of the land. The traffic is mild to say the least, and, other than the occasional hoot from an impatient cab driver, the driving is ever so polite. The occasional outrageous maneuver is hugely exaggerated by the fact that outrageous maneuvers are completely unexpected.

We drive down Broadway, through the heart of Manhattan, all the way to the Financial District. The huge billboards and flashing lights of Times Square in the Theatre District demand a night-time visit; every show under the sun seems to be running simultaneously here. We cruise through the Garment District, slice through a bit of Chelsea, then into Gramercy, where young men slouch over parking meters, and congregate in huddles on street corners. In Greenwich Village we take the fork into Lafayette Street, which should take us all the way to Ground Zero, but things don't quite work out as planned.

In the Financial District the marriage between map and road lands in the divorce court. On this tiny spit of land, think of a small ... very small ... Italian village, where the inmates went berserk and built huge skyscrapers along its narrow streets, creating a giant glass and steel maze, which has not fully recovered from 9/11. The one-car narrow roads are chaotic; detours, closures, building sites, great machines parked willy- nilly, sirens and police cars. Then suddenly an accident. How is it possible to have an accident at zero miles/hour? This just about proves my theory that because everybody drives so correctly in the States, everybody is fast asleep behind the wheel. One more detour, and now our orientation is completely 'out the window', but after three haphazard passes, we slowly start to recognize landmarks, and, piecing together our route, we escape into the sunlight, right by Brooklyn Bridge. So we hop on, drive over, make an illegal 'China-turn', and drive back; been there, done that.

Heading back north through a thoroughly New Yorkified Chinatown, a bland, square-looking Little Italy, we find ourselves in Park Avenue. Cue song: 'Did you see the well-to-do up and down Park Avenue?' Nope, no well-to-do, but I suppose they must be here somewhere, as the real estate is very dear, I am told. This is a world of swish boutique hotels in old brownstones, guarded by doormen in top hats and tails, bellhops in redcoats, with chauffeurs idling in black limousines.

From this genteel side-street world, we step into Fifth Ave, right opposite the Metropolitan Museum of Art, and find the noise we were waiting for. The street is ablaze with yellow cabs and red busses. The steps of the museum are a happy gathering of faces turned to the sun. Locals or tourists? Hard to tell, it is a very intercontinental mix, but not really enough cameras for them to be tourists, so I assume the locals like to hang out on the steps of the Metropolitan, and it is a glorious day for it.

In Central Park the trees are in bloom, the grass is green, but out of bounds. Winter is its time for rest, even if it happens to be an Indian spring. One belligerent man simply cannot, will not, refuses to understand that the weather is due for a severe correction, and has a blazing argument with one of the park caretakers about his right, as a tax-paying New Yorker, to use the grass. The caretaker tries to explain the tender grass shoots would normally be protected by a blanket of snow at this time of year, and to open the lawn now would be to spoil it for the summer. The man insists that for him an exception must be made, and cannot understand that if he gets on the grass, everybody else will demand the same. The caretaker has heard it all before, and shoos him away with an irritated flap of the hand. The belligerent fellow nearly pops a blood vessel.

We cannot stay to watch the outcome of this battle of wills, as we must deal with the parking problem. Cruising the streets around the hotel, we discover that not only is parking more difficult to find than a hotel room, the parking system in New York is designed to discourage anybody from bringing their cars into the city. The parking garages do not charge by the hour; minimum fees apply; and in some garages a full daily rate applies, regardless of how long you park. Great if you want to park for a day; terrible if you want to park for an hour or two. Fortunately we have a couple of days' stay. Unfortunately the parking will cost almost as much as a motel room, but for the moment there is nothing to be done, but move on.

Back at the hotel, the doorman, who was so helpful earlier, does not open the door or say hello. Odd. As we reach our room, it hits me; he expects me to tip him every single time he opens that door for me. There I was thinking that a tip is something you give for service above and beyond the call of duty. Had the chap found me a parking spot, he would certainly have deserved that tip. I have traveled in countries where tips are refused, as the people believe they did not need to be tipped for doing their job. Not here. Here you are expected to pay the guy to do the job he is already being paid to do; otherwise he just doesn't do his job at all. I refuse to support this way of thinking, and will just put in the extra effort it requires to open that door myself. In fact I will share door-opening duties with Alexandra, and somehow we should muddle through. With that little wrinkle ironed out, I have a fine night's rest, and wake up to a very full tourist stuff agenda.

I feel strongly that we must go on a boat. Alexandra feels strongly that we must go shopping. As I am firmly in charge of matters financial, I pull rank, and we go on a boat. The density of living space on this little island reveals itself as we float past thousands and thousands of windows, layered, jammed and jostling against each other. A sudden gap of blue sky changes the guide's tone from chirpy to funereal, as he relates the deadly facts and figures of the fall of the World Trade Center, but for us the bombing of these buildings was all happening on TV. To try to find any emotional response that is not totally contrived is difficult.

On her private island, Lady Liberty is green and stern in her resolve to hold that golden flame up high. She never gets a moment to relax that arm, the poor old dear, as she is constantly watched by the thousands of windows that fill the airspace on the shores of Manhattan. As we drift past, the guide quotes some fairly cosmic property prices for those determined to have a view of said lady. At Hell Gate our boat makes a u-turn, and, having seen, having marveled, and having taken many photographs, the whole boat catches forty winks. As my chest cold has now become a very unpleasant sounding gurgling cough, it has cleared the deck for meters all around, so Alexandra and I have plenty of space to stretch out in the sunshine.

Although my health is going downhill at reckless speed, sights must be seen; the lot of a traveler is not a happy one. In trying to put brakes on my rapid decline, I start flinging Vitamin C, cough medicine, and throat lozenges into my system at an alarming rate. To conserve my strength, we choose the least taxing item on our must-see list, the MoMA (Museum of Modern Art). Here I am issued with a headset, and once it is securely clamped on my head, I instantly go into a tourist glazed-eyed trance. The disembodied voice drones on about a series of flat gray paintings, which are defined by a small edge of imperfection at the bottom. To my brain, which is by now reclining soulfully in a pink puddle of cough medicine ... or maybe my brain is the pink puddle ... even the grey painting are taking on a slightly pink hue. The paintings all look identical. According to THE VOICE, the artist believes painting is all about the surface ... there should be no breaking through the surface ... this seems to me a very practical approach to applying paint to canvas ... how this makes him a super-duper artist worthy of wall space in the MoMA is not so clear.

Staring intently at the smooth grey surfaces, I conclude that the artist must have an orgasmic time rolling pale grey paint onto the walls of his house; no chance of him breaking through the surface there, no matter how hard he pushes ... I must admit the man has an eye for grey ... and he does some pretty sexy stuff with beeswax polish. Apparently the buyers and sellers of fine art simply love this chap. Quite understandably ... you can never make the wrong decision when buying one of his paintings, and the galleries can take advance orders for years to come, knowing that the buyer cannot be disappointed, as every painting is exactly the same.

But what do I know ... and besides ... I am not well. Unable to correlate the voice in the headset with anything sensible on the walls, I drag myself to the nearest available bench, which happens to face a collection of Jackson Pollack works. Staring in halfhearted fashion at the drippiness I see before me, I start feeling a certain warmth and kinship to the squiggly painting ... I feel as if I am actually getting it ... I am definitely taking too much cough medicine.

Once Alexandra has absorbed her fill of modern art, she drags me away from my Pollack ... noo ... I like it here; it is warm ... and ... confusing ... is there no escape from the traveler's lot? I hack and cough my way past Times Square, whine and moan my way to the Empire State Building, cough loudly at the security guard, zoom up to the top of another high building ... which also seems to be swinging about. What it is with high buildings: can they not be built to stand still? We look over another city of glass, concrete and steel; watch another pollution-red sunset. I want my bed, where, with a final swig, I finish the bottle of cough medicine, and collapse in a furry pink haze, much to Alexandra's disgust.

On waking, I notice two things. It is another brilliant blue crystal day, and the sheets are hurting me. Slowly and painfully I retract my hands from under the covers. Things have gone from bad to worse overnight. The pink cough medicine has left my brain, and has settled in every joint of my hands, causing bright red shiny welts that are incredibly itchy, but too painful to touch. As my feet hit the floor I realize that putting on shoes will be excruciating today. A quick glance in the mirror shows me that even my face is afflicted. The lot of the traveler is not an easy one. I gingerly pull on the four layers of clothing that the New York cold demands of me, gently ease on my shoes. Alexandra shakes her head impatiently at my small moans and whimpers; am I to get no sympathy at all? Finally with only my nose poking out, I allow Alexandra to open the door for me, and hobble into the cold.

Today we have a plan, a to-do-list that has been prioritized according to convenience of public transportation. But all that must wait. I now have only one priority: a chemist. I need more medicine, but am prepared to take professional advice on it this time. The chemist listens to my tale of woe, her eyebrows slowly rising behind her fringe, as I run through my self-medication regime of the past few days. Without a word, she hands me a huge bottle of antacid and a smaller dose of antihistamine. She throws in a complimentary glass of water, to ensure I take the medication immediately. The effect is almost instant. In my zeal not to become ill, I succeeded in giving my system a toxic shock, and evoked an allergic reaction. Feeling, but not looking, a whole lot better, I am ready to follow Alexandra down into the grungiest subway system in the world. Post-apocalyptic, spare, cold and draughty, the subways in New York are purely functional. I rather like them; to me they are the most 'typically' New York thing I have seen so far.

Just as we board the train, a morbidly obese young man enters the compartment, carrying a large basket of chocolates and candies. In a high wheezy voice he informs us that he is selling candy to make money to further his education. Is this a joke, does he not see the irony? He is the worst possible advertisement for his wares. Nobody dares look at this kid as he waddles by, forcing his girth through the doors to the next compartment. This has to be the worst marketing plan I have ever seen.

At the World Trade Center – Ground Zero – we try to feel the moment, but it is difficult to feel anything about a construction site. Standing here only reminds me of the conspiracy theories surrounding this event, one of which claims that the BBC announced on live television the collapse of Building 7 *half-an-hour* before it actually did, because the authorities released the 'news' too early. I wonder again at the value of any of our 'news' reports. It has been said that while the news might not change what we think, it is very good at changing what we think about.

We make our way along the gray and glass canyons of the Financial District, where determined people dressed in black step impatiently around us, as we look up the vanishing perspective of a thousand windows, to the small rectangle of sky far above. In these buildings reside the Federal Reserve Bank, the New York Stock Exchange, and several of the world's largest banks. The fate of the world is decided in these buildings, which catch the blue sky in every window and have the ability to channel the cold wind; it snipes at us from a new direction around every corner.

It's warmer underground, so we make our way to Grand Central Station via the metro. While the New York Metro is built on the principle of form follows function, Grand Central Station was built when train travel was still considered the height of glamour. From the green-tinged grunge of the underground we emerge into the soft warm light of the high vaulted building, where brass and wood trim soften all the edges. To provide as much comfort as possible to the thousands of daily commuters, there are bars, restaurants and take-outs of all kinds. Seating is provided in the form of faux wingback chairs, made out of rock-hard fiberglass, not comfortable, but they give this teeming space the feel of a temporary living room or private club, which is how many people seem to be treating it. Relaxing, reading the paper, having a cup of coffee. New Yorkers must be the best-read bunch of commuters on the planet. One out of two New Yorkers reads on the subway, I counted. Not just any old thing, hefty hardcover books, manuscripts and serious technical-looking stuff are being read on the subways of New York.

Standing at the station entrance, we fumble about with our map trying to work out which way Central Park would be, when we discover that under their grim exterior, the New Yorkers are a friendly bunch in their own 'no frills' manner. They overhear us trying to figure out where we are, or where we are going, and with a quick tip set us right, no long conversations or lengthy intros needed. We discover that if we mumble the magic words

Where are we?

loudly enough, a quick response is sure to come from the sidelines to set us right. Rather like the prompter back stage, helpful, but not intrusive, odd, but rather nice.

With the help of these small pointers, our path takes us past ice skaters at the Rockefeller Center, where monks in saffron robes remind me that out there somewhere, the wind is warm, and people wear colors other than black, white and grey. In the jewelry district we pop into Tiffany's to see if they have anything we like. We look at people and into shops, rummage around in vintage stores, and poke at the entrails of a knifing victim in a 'mask and costume' store that specializes in the ghoulish. Halloween must get pretty scary in this part of NY. We try on bloody hands, count the teeth of a variety of skulls, and put on the odd wig.

At Central Park, we weave our way through the horse-drawn carriages, waving off the advances of the drivers, as we have discovered that we are both overcome with guilt when being dragged about in a carriage by a beast of burden. Adding to our negative feeling towards the horse-drawn carriage is the New York by-law that states that no horse shall poop freely in the city streets. So all the carriages have 'nappy' bags that catch the poop as it falls. Now the passengers have the delightful prospect of having the smell of fresh poop up their noses for the entire trip, and not just for the moment that the bowel movement occurs. We'll walk, thank you.

In Central Park, we pass a hotdog stand, opposite the Sheep Meadow. Hotdogs seem a fine plan, so we order two, with all the trimmings, including sauerkraut. It is the best fast food we have had in the US of A. The path takes us between Strawberry Fields, a memorial to John Lennon, The Lake, and finally into the Museum of Natural History. In the giant dome of the planetarium, unimagined worlds unfold, giant planets collide, their fragmented remains spiraling into space. We are so inspired we both immediately want to become astrophysicists. The museum is huge, and the displays super-realistic, in an old-fashioned kind of way. As we walk past a family of life-size elephants, we remember that *Night at the Museum* is playing on Times Square, and that it was filmed right here. This evening's entertainment is decided then and there, and later, to the irritation of all around us in the movie house, we have a right silly time of it saying 'been there, saw that', and so on.

Waking up on Alexandra's last day in New York, the first thing that pops into my head is that I feel sorry for the New Yorkers. They look a very sad, grey, exhausted and thin bunch to me. The cost of living here is so incredibly high that for many, I am sure, it is just an endless struggle for survival. They have the satisfaction of living in the most hyped city in the world, but it must be quite a burden living with the reputation of being the world's hustlers, the world's go-getters, the biggest, the best, you make it there, you make it anywhere ... and if you don't make it there? Or perhaps I am just sad because Alexandra must fly away today.

JFK Airport is not far as kilometers go, but as some twit decides to double-park just before the entrance onto the Queensboro Bridge, this throws a cookie in the milk jug, and the traffic grinds to a noisy, messy halt. When we finally get past the jerk, I take great satisfaction in leaning full tilt on my car horn to show him just how upset I am, and feel so much better for it. The simple pleasures of life. Now all is smooth sailing. Fortunately we left in very good time, so all is not lost, except a good seat for Alexandra on the plane. She walks through the security gates, and vanishes from view. Alone again ...

My trip back into Manhattan goes without a hitch, as the drivers in New York are not half as daring as they think they are. That reckless disregard for private property that is displayed in the east has been lawyered right out of the drivers here. They are the most flamboyant of all the American drivers so far, but still pussycats compared with most places I have driven. But then, right in front of my hotel, I spy my quarry. I am almost certain that I am right. A man slows, fumbles in his pocket, and, bingo, takes out his car keys. I pounce, hovering protectively over my prize as he eases out, then, before the big sedan that is trying to muscle in on my turf has even the smallest chance to maneuver, I do a smooth flawless reverse park. Sitting back, I savor the moment; I found a convenient parking spot in Manhattan! This is a feat that I will list in my memoirs as one of my proudest moments.

Pennsylvania
Bed 127, 128

My time in New York is over for the moment, and it is time to head south, to the sun, YES! But first there is one last thing I need to do before leaving the Big Apple. I need to get a New Yorker to write on the car. The New York reaction to the 'One Planet One People' project has been very strange. The Wish Mobile is almost totally covered in wishes, and although it is very hard to ignore, the New Yorkers are giving it their best shot. Whenever I catch them sneaking sidelong glances, I attempt to engage them with a grin, but their eyes go blank and slide away. I am astounded that the bolshiest smart alecs in the world are so reluctant to acknowledge my car; it's like they are waiting for some guru of cool to sanction it before they will admit that it is cool. I am determined that the Wish Mobile will have a New York wish, and wait in ambush for the first eligible male that walks past.

'Hi.'

He tries to ignore me.

'Can I ask you a favor?'

His mouth compresses in displeasure

'I have just driven here from Germany.'

I catch a glimmer of interest

'Via China.'

He stops, and actually looks at me.

'I have been asking men to write a wish for the world on my car.'

I point over his shoulder to the Wish Mobile. He takes this as an invitation to have a proper look.

'I really want a wish from someone in New York. Will you write on the car for me?'

Before he has a chance to consider, I walk into his space, hand him the black marker, and continue to close in on him. He moves backwards to avoid me, until he reluctantly turns , quickly scribbles

'Bring our soldiers home safely'

and hands me the pen, before briskly walking away.

While he probably was thinking only of the American soldier, his offering does have universal appeal. Satisfied with my New York wish, I head the Wish Mobile south.

I have decided to drive all the way down to Key West, but first make a small detour through Damascus, to visit friends Trix and Phil. The narrow winding road takes me deep into the rural backwoods of Pennsylvania, and to the outskirts of the tiny town of Damascus. Here, in the middle of Baptist Country, I find Trix. She lived for many years in New York, before trading it in for her own piece of rural paradise.

We fall into a comfortable when-we and-now-we conversation, as we roam through her frozen forest, where the expanding ice splits open the earth to reveal miniature caves of icy stalactites and mites. We leap over small waterfalls; frozen leaves crack and shatter underfoot as we land. Trix describes how the flying squirrels and birds vie for best pickings off the many feeders outside the kitchen window, and how, in the summer, black bears come sniffing at the door, after roaming through her vegetable garden. The bears are given free rein, but the fox families must be kept at arms' length, as these clever creatures know when they are onto a good thing. Possums and raccoons are also regular visitors, and all the birds and beasts of the forest are subjects of the fanciful oil paintings Trix (http://www.willowrivergallery.com) produces, combining bird, beast and bloom in a slightly surreal, aloof reality.

Ponds and wetlands surround her home, where beavers build dams, and bare trees reflect in the half-frozen water. I pick my solitary way through bogs, and around hidden pools into a dark and silent forest, where a thick carpet of moss glows brilliant green in its dull surrounds. It muffles my footsteps as I slowly move closer to a deer supping on moss and mushrooms. But when I lift my camera, the light catches the lens, the deer leaps, twists, and vanishes into the shadows. In the fading light, I make my way back to the house, past red berry bushes and silver seedpods. The angular glass and cold steel of New York seems a lifetime ago.

Where is the American dream, here or in New York City? Here, I think, but without the close proximity of the city, this lifestyle would not be possible; it is funded by the money machine of NYC. That's what cities are in the end, money-making factories in which millions of drones labor ceaselessly to create the money to fund the lifestyle of those who are truly living the American dream.

After three days of intense conversation about the myth that is 'American dream', I find myself wishing for my own company, to sink into my thoughts, to allow them to percolate and filter down. With my bags neatly stashed in their Wish Mobile spot, well stocked with popcorn tea, chocolates, and instant noodles, and in possession of all the insider's knowledge I need to get down south on the most scenic route possible, I wave Trix and Phil goodbye, and in a swirl of snowflakes follow the Delaware River south, destination Key West and sunshine.

The cliffs on the side of the road are covered in a sheet of ice; small waterfalls have frozen into long pale blue icicles; but all around the scenery is brown, grey and gloomy. I sink into my thoughts, which turn out to be grey and gloomy as well. What is the American dream? Is the American dream, which the American media exports around the globe, wrapped in soap opera and sitcom, based in any reality? Although America has mainly worked itself free from the day-to-day grind of simply staying alive, it has not evolved into a grander thing.

The American dream has become an ongoing rerun of throw away and buy new. Stuck in this repetitive cycle of constant acquisition, this society, like so many successful societies throughout history, just goes round and round, measuring its success in units of stuff, monetary wealth and power (over other humans). True and lasting success, the kind that cannot be stolen, repossessed or controlled by others, is measured in personal growth, self-control and the acquisition of wisdom. To attain this level of success requires that we take an evolutionary step in our minds. Unfortunately, the general disregard for exercising our brains is a failing of humankind. Brain gyms is what we need, so we can all be a bit more in control of the grey matter sloshing about in our craniums, to train our minds to think deeply and profoundly, then it will become clear to us what the real ideals are that we should be striving for. Unfortunately the system in which we live does not encourage us to think. It seems to me it attempts in every way possible, to prevent us from thinking about anything other than our next shopping excursion.

Small towns dot the winding river road: Barrydale, Pond Eddy, Port Jarvis, Deer Park City, Sparrow Bush; and by the time I reach Milford, I need some early morning sustenance. Stopping at a small diner, which seems very popular with the locals, I indulge myself with a hot chocolate and cheesecake; the first bite of sweetness of the cheesecake is barely manageable; but the pre-sweetened hot chocolate defeats me. My mouth contracts, and I shudder involuntarily at the sweet blast it delivers, fondly remembering the taro root cake of Taiwan. Here in America, with its excess sugar, dairy, and suspect oils, I fear far more for my health than I ever did at any one of the dirty pavement eateries in China. Although the kitchens in China looked as if the food they produced would kill me instantly, it was as healthily as I have ever eaten. Here I leave my order virtually untouched. I pay my bill and leave. No one enquires why. They probably wouldn't understand anyway. America, oh America, you will die young from all the sugar.

Route 209 heads through the Delaware Water Gap. Because a water gap is a geological formation, where a river cuts through a mountain range, this is a place of woodlands and waterfalls. Tiny winding roads take me deep into the forest, where, all alone, I pick my way down slippery pathways to the white cascades of Raymondskill Falls. At only four feet lower than Niagara Falls, they qualify as the highest falls in Pennsylvania. As I climb down into the Pocono ravine, the ancient hemlock trees shut out the sky, and not one person on the planet knows where I am. These alone moments are moments of intimate awareness of self and of surroundings. The inner silence that I discovered in Kazakhstan is becoming easier and easier to summon. When my mind moves into this meditative space, I experience a deep sensual calm, and a heightened awareness of my surroundings: the smell of rotting wood, of mushrooms, of the organic spray of water from the falls, and the sound of the wind that hushes through the trees. Mushrooms are golden slippery wet on the moss, brilliant green against the red bark of fallen trees. A deep content fills my head. For long minutes, I lean against an old tree, watching the water fall, crash and foam against the rocks, before gathering itself to flow dark and silent down the mountain to the next rock, where again it breaks and roars only to regain its calm ... looks a lot like life to me.

As I climb back up to where the Wish Mobile waits, I recognize once again that life is fully lived in these moments of mindfulness of self and universe.

Steering the Wish Mobile direction Washington DC, small chocolate-box towns called Bethlehem and Nazareth flash by. Here small-town America is a place of extreme privilege. The wooden houses are beautifully looked after, and delightful in their detail, painted in grayed-down shades of green, blue and yellow, with curly wooden window boxes and shutters in dull red and purple. There is such pride of place here that each porch, garden and house seems perpetually ready to be photographed for *Garden and Home*. The pretty American houses are not going to win any architectural awards, but they certainly look good enough to live in, happy homes that snuggle into the countryside.

But the American obsession with decorating for every occasion spoils the image somewhat, as the inflatable plastic Santas on the perfect grass verges have been replaced by giant inflatable football players that stand under American flags, in front of very big houses with signs proclaiming,

'We support our troops'

I am sure the troops will be relieved to know this. There is a great concern among the Americans for their troops, but perhaps this business of them being shot and killed should have been thought through before America entered into yet another dubious war. One of the unfortunate side effects of our technology and media glut is that we are losing the ability to see the full picture. We no longer think about the information that swirls around us. We merely grasp at a few sound bites, and base our decision and actions on that, before the next wave of information hit us. These never-ending waves of information, which we are constantly trying to process, are drowning out reasoned, logical and critical thought, and this lack of thought, about what we are doing exactly, is what is destroying the value system that once formed the basis of the American dream. The American dream has become a money-making product to be bought and sold to the highest bidder,

As I close in on Chesapeake Bay, America starts to remind me very much of Germany, jam-packed with people, similar architecture, and lots of highways. Very genteel living up here though, between the water and the forest, gorgeous old houses, golf clubs, yacht clubs and water, lots of water. I decide to turn onto the R213, which will take me to Tilghman Island, in Chesapeake Bay on Maryland's eastern shore. This is as far as I will have time for today, and am hoping for some spectacular scenery.

The small islands and coves are stitched together by bridges, long and short. Trees crowd the few bits of high ground, and on a tiny green field, turkey buzzards feast on the corpse of a deer. The amount of traffic on these little spits of land tells me that in among the pine trees, maples and bare oaks, a rather large number of people have hidden their homes.

I have still not come to grips with the short winter days of the north, and long before I manage to reach Tilghman Island the light is fading. St Michaels, which dates back to the mid 1600s, when it was a trading post for tobacco farmers and trappers, is as far as I get. Here the houses and little village center are so utterly charming that I cannot get over myself. It looks so perfect, as if a set builder has just completed it for the ultimate all-American movie. The buildings are all sparkly lights and candy-cane windows, where shops entice with mouth-watering window displays; it is the prettiest pretty. The preservation of the historical houses is thanks in large to the first successful 'blackout' staged here during the 1812 war, in which the wily residents hung lanterns in the trees above the houses, so that the British warships overshot the village, all except for one house, which to this day is called Cannonball House. The land ends at a pier of wooden poles, where fishing boats and private yachts float in deep blue, mirror-calm water, but somehow there is not much to photograph; it's all rather flat.

By now the sun is touching the horizon, and as Washington DC is still at least two hours away, I reroute to cross to Washington DC via the Bay Bridge, a huge span of steel that soars above the water of

Chesapeake Bay and the setting sun. A truck roars by. The driver is not watching where he is going, as he is photographing me. To take my mind off the potential danger of this situation, I photograph him right back. He blows his horn, and I answer. I am getting very good at the American style of driving, where multitasking is the name of the game. Because of this, I discover that I can take some rather interesting photographs by balancing the camera on the dashboard; this is, of course, a spectacularly bad idea, nearly as bad as reading the map while driving

Washington DC, The Capitol

Washington DC
Bed 129

In the gathering dark, I join the solid flow of light on the Capital Beltway. Everybody is in a hurry to get home. But it is not to be. All the traffic on the four lanes of the I495 come to a grinding halt. What a drag, probably a tiny bumper bashing up front and total chaos behind, as the peculiar overkill reaction of the traffic police sets in. Police cars box in the accident site; ambulances and tow trucks appear by default. While all these emergency cars turn the road into a parking lot, the remaining traffic must wait. By the time we are all allowed to move again, it is pitch black, and there is still nothing like trying to find your way in a new city in the dark. I finally make it to Cousin Mark's apartment, hours later than our restaurant table reservation had allowed for. But these are big city folk, and time means nothing, so we go out anyway, eat piles of mini hamburgers, drink beer, and discus the next day's schedule. Mark has arranged for an honest-to-goodness American general to add a wish to my project, and so that the general is not too inconvenienced, a special inner-city parking has been arranged for the Wish Mobile by tapping into the deepest secret intelligence available in Washington DC.

The following morning I slide into my VIP parking spot on Pennsylvania Ave, just a block away from the White House. The general arrives, gets on his knees in front of the Wish Mobile. I am liking this project more and more. Hey, how often have you made a full general get down on his knees? He writes.

'It would be good if people could learn to get along despite their differences. To agree to disagree.'

While this is going on, and photographs are being taken by public relations people, I dream up a scheme. This is the true center of the world, is it not? The place where highly educated and deep thinking individuals make decisions that ultimately affect not just Americans, but every citizen on planet earth? With this in mind, I decide I will try an experiment with the 'One Planet One People' project. I am assuming that the men of Washington DC will not need to be told how the project works. Besides, there are so many wishes that even if they cannot read the blurb on the windscreen, they should get the general idea just by reading the car. I put out a small notice

If you are male and above 35 years old, please feel free to participate leave two pens tucked under the windscreen wipers, and set off to see the sights of Washington DC.

The White House is surprisingly small for all the symbolic weight it carries. It is set apart from the world on a stretch of road not used by any other than the president and his men. Surrounding it are manicured lawns, on which is pitched one little tent, in it a single protestor. What he is protesting I do not know, but the futile idealism of this action is depressing. I imagine that at the beginning of this protest, the individual truly believed he would make a difference. But now, however long into this course of action, the tent is but a piece of furniture that might even be viewed by those who make policy as a convenient sign that freedom and democracy exists. The guy in the tent has a problem, though. His effort is futile, and the only way to get out of the tent and back into a comfortable home is to admit defeat, and nobody likes doing that. We will have to think of more creative ways to protest before we can hope to make a difference to a system that has made us instantly replaceable worker ants in the chain of supply and demand.

To get to the United States Capitol on the far end of 'The Mall' I duck into the nearest metro station, and am dumbstruck. This has got to be the most luxurious subway 'in the world'. The huge station has a high arched roof, soft mood lighting, and not a squiggle of graffiti to be seen. Stepping onto the train, I look down in astonishment: the floor is carpeted, and the plush seats are arranged in first-class rows. No hard plastic benches meanly squashed along the length of the train, so the bulk of passengers must stand. Not in Washington DC. Here commuters do it in soft style.

Leaving this place of comfort, I emerge on The Mall, where Washington has arranged all its museums, galleries monuments and memorials. This is a brilliant plan, as it eliminates the need to rush frantically about a strange city, battered map in hand, to try to find the various sights. Here it is a straight walk up one side, u-turn at the Capitol, and then down the other, and you're done fast, efficient, but somewhat lacking in adventure. The Washington Monument, slim and pointy, is the tallest stone structure and tallest obelisk in the world. The Capitol is a big classical pile, white and imposing, but I have done my share of looking at pompous buildings, and simply cannot work up any enthusiasm for America's most favorite building. The machine-gun-toting marines in black outfits don't help much to bolster my enthusiasm either. I do an about-turn, and make my way back to the White House end of the Mall. As I walk I conclude that 'The Mall' is a bit considered, a bit too matter of fact. It is as if a committee decided that as Washington DC is the capital of a great nation, monuments to things are needed, and to make life easier for all the tourists, who would be sure to come and look at them, they should all be placed together in a neat row for easy viewing.

When I arrive back at the car, I discover that quite a few men took up the wish challenge today. But how disappointing, the day's catch of wishes are sad, banal and shallow, and this from highly educated world leaders, or leaders to be. With all information and power at their fingertips, they couldn't think of anything better to say than

'Don't sweat the small stuff'

and in reply

'Sweat the small stuff'

or

'Follow the $$$$'

Is this a wish or a global command?

'Rock and roll'

This is an interesting take on a wish. There are a couple of tags, a smiley face. One man turned the Wish Mobile into his own private advertising medium, and then the rather plaintive

'Don't be so hard on America (we are the good guys)'

That would depend, I suppose, on which end of a cruise missile you happen to be standing. And then it hits me ... what do I think of the Americas?

There is an endearing innocence about most of the Americans I have met. They meet your eyes with an open innocent sort of gaze, as if nobody in the world could possibly do them harm, and they don't harm anybody. They are just protecting the innocent and the American dream, after all. From the shocked and 'How dare you!' responses I have had to any questioning of the American system or values, I believe Americans are not inclined to really investigate the facts or to find out the truth about themselves.

A democracy is taken as the greatest form of governance, as it attempts to give everyone equal rights and freedoms, but what people often forget is that with these rights come responsibilities and shared blame. If the government wages unjustified war against a sovereign nation, and the people say nothing, then every person who draws advantage from the democracy is as complicit in the act of violence as the trained marine who pulls the trigger. The old saw that 'evil grows when good men do nothing' finds very fertile soil in a democracy, where the people choose to enjoy only its advantages, and refuse to shoulder any of the responsibilities.

Result of wish experiment, failure.

A new day dawns bright and sunny but cold. A dry icy wind slices through every bit of exposed flesh, as I take myself off to Arlington National Cemetery, where I expect to see thousands of white crosses in neat rows stretching to the horizon. The truth is somewhat different. Not a white cross to be seen (according to a caretaker that is just a Hollywood myth, all the white crosses are in France). But with perfect timing I arrive at the memorial to the Unknown Soldier, where the super-slow motion of the changing of the guard is taking place. While this is going on (very very slowly) a group of boy scouts gather at the top of the steps. They have brought wreaths, which they will lay at the memorial. A soldier gives the serious-faced youngsters a full and detailed set of instructions: three steps up, then left, then backward, then stop, then trumpet, then salute, then step forward, lay wreath, step back, about turn, three steps forward, right turn ... huh? The boys are blank, and not just blank, but blue. Blank and blue with cold, as the laying of the wreath is done in just their shirt sleeves, no jackets allowed. I can see them going from pink to blue, their noses start running, while the guard, dressed in a thick woolen coat with gloves, hat and scarf, goes through his slow motion explanation. He has no awareness that the children in front of him are soon to suffer from hypothermia; he is warm, so where is the problem?

My time in Washington has come to an end, but before I head south again, I want a photograph of the Wish Mobile in front of the Capitol building. To achieve this, I am up before dawn. The temperature has plummeted overnight, and the Reflecting Pool, where yesterday the gulls floated, this morning they walk. Cold cold cold. Quick, get the shot, back in the warmth of the car, and off to find the Blue Ridge Parkway.

Virginia–North Carolina
Bed 130, 131

It starts to snow as soon as I leave Washington. Soon it is snowing so hard that I miss my turn-off onto the scenic route, and the road is icing up. For reason unclear, the car in front of me decides to slam on anchors. I follow suit, but a loud rumble informs me my brakes have packed with ice. They shudder and groan. I yank the hand brake. It sort of works, but not enough to prevent me from heading towards the stationary car in front of me with alarming speed. If all else fails, there is always the snow bank on the roadside, but getting stuck in snow is not a happy thought. The car in front of me slides closer and closer as I frantically pump the brake.

Clear, dammit!

With inches to spare, the brakes grip, the Wish Mobile slides to a reluctant halt, and I make a snap decision. No, nope, I am not doing this all day. In Woodstock I spy a motel through the white spotted air, and by 12h00 I am snug in a room. With nothing better to do, I fling myself on the bed, and watch an all-American sitcom. It feels like a holiday.

I awake to a world reduced to soft shades of white and raw umber, touched with hints of deep green. Swiss rolls of hay lie in the fields where everything is lightly iced with snow. In the Shenandoah Valley, the frosted hills are dotted with grey farmhouses and red barns, which play hide and seek behind clouds of fog. As the sun climbs above the fog, it bounces off the snow and valley-bound fog, creating a blinding sparkling kind of day. I set off south without a care in the world, until a pile of snow flies off the top of a truck, and lands on my windscreen, scaring the sunshine right out of me, and completely blocking my view. My windscreen wipers are overwhelmed. I frantically try to clear the windscreen with my hand, but end up having to stick my head into the freezing wind to see how to negotiate my way to the emergency lane. Just as you believe you know everything there is to know about a thing, a new thing hits you in the face. I discover the hard way why cars keep a very long following distance between themselves and trucks in snowy weather. There must be a law against this. This is America, for Pete's sake. They have laws against hot coffee, but none against the potentially far more lethal flying icepack? That just cannot be.

Keeping a wary eye out for any more marauding snow-slinging trucks, I continue on my quest to find a way onto the Blue Ridge

Parkway, which is a 469-mile-long (755 km) scenic route, running from the Shenandoah National Park in Virginia to the boundary between Great Smoky Mountains National Park and the Cherokee Indian Reservation in North Carolina, but alas, it is closed due to snow. The northern winter is so inconvenient.

I am doomed to travel the interstate, where the only thing to see is churches: The Bible Church, The Church of the Nazarene, The Victory Church, The Baptist churches, the Lutherans, United Methodist Church, Christ Reformed Fellowship, Presbyterian Pentecost, Grace Bible church, Seventh- Day Adventist – there is a fierce competition for believers in this neck of the woods – First Church, Church of God. All these different takes on the bible seem to me to be self-defeating. If the bible is the truth, the whole truth, and nothing but the truth, why are there so many different churches? But I am behind in my thinking. 'The People of the Land' saw the problem centuries ago.

> Brother, you say there is but one way to worship and serve the Great Spirit. If there is but one religion, why do you white people differ so much about it? Why not all agree, as you can all read the Book? *Sogoyewapha, 'Red Jacket' – Senaca*

The churches look across the road to a string of Burger Kings, Pizza Huts, McDonalds, Wendy's and Waffle Houses... I have got to get off this road.

In desperation I swing sharp left at the first available road to Natural Bridge, and within minutes am in a rural world of farmhouses and frozen forests that gleam and glitter like crystal in the sunshine. As I step out of the car to take a photograph, the noise takes me by surprise. The defrosting forest clicks, pings, cracks, and jangles like a teaspoon rattling around in the crystal cupboard. A strange and unexpected experience. Stranger still is a huge construction that looks vaguely familiar. Up on a small hill, it casts long shadows on the frozen grass. Crunching across the snow to a small wooden gate, I discover that I am looking at 'Foam Henge' a scale replica of Stonehenge, created out of Styrofoam. I love the playful insanity of the Americans when it results in wonderfully wacky off-the-wall stuff like this.

But the short loop road to Natural Bridge soon deposits me back on the nowhere land of the interstate, where I rumble along hour after hour, sinking into a truck- and tar-induced trance. Wake up, wake up, the world is roaring by unnoticed. At the next off-ramp I turn into Wytheville, and into the muddy parking lot of a store selling homemade jams, cakes, cider and steaming mugs of tea. As I am chatting to the owner, getting advice on more scenic routes south, his wife phones the local newspaper. They come rushing over in true newshound fashion. Strange how you get used to something. I hardly notice how my car looks, but it is obviously very striking to others. So standing in the café with my tea and carrot cake, I am interviewed by a youthful journalist who, after asking all the usual questions, blurts out.

'It's my birthday tomorrow!'

Though somewhat bemused by this, I do the polite thing.

'Congratulations, how old will you be?'

'Twenty one.'

'Well, double congratulations to that; what will you be doing to celebrate?'

'I am going to get totally off my face.'

He replies with a huge grin.

'Why?'

'Because I will be legally allowed to drink.'

It seems that America is not a law-abiding, but rather a law-fearing country. It is a country in which the citizens are held hostage by their own laws. Or it could be said that a government that tries to rule its citizens with infinite petty laws is much the same as a dictatorship, as it takes away the people's responsibility to think for themselves. If everything is governed by law, it follows that if there is no law against it, it is not a crime. The obsessive lawyering here has taken personal moral responsibility away from the people, and this is a very bad thing.

As I leave, the owners present me with a huge flagon of cider and a jar of honey. How kind. I really do enjoy these impromptu encounters with people, but they tend to take great chunks out of the day. Before I can drive off, the young journalist summons us for a photo call with the Wish Mobile. Just then a huge truck delivering Coke stops in my way. The driver, called Jim, hops out, slouches over, and I have relate the whole story again. Without a word, he puts out his hand, I give him the pen, and he writes

'Pray for freedom and dignity for all.'

By the time I am finally back on the road, the old barns and farms start disappearing into the gloomy dusk, and it might snow again. Please, just not now, not while I am out in the deep backcountry of Virginia, with no place to stay, no place to call home, no home to call, oh, woe is me. But this is America, and a motel, with twin beds, bathroom, kitchenette, and parking for the Wish Mobile is never too far away.

Waking to a bright sunshine day, I switch on the computer, drift over to the kitchenette to make a cup of hot coffee, but on sitting down to attend to my emails, discover that I cannot electronically connect to anything. Leaping to the conspiracy conclusion, I go into full panic mode: cyber terrorists have blown up cyberspace! My cards are frozen; I have no cash; no phones work; no email can be sent for help, I have no way to contact anyone who knows me; I am stuck in Glade Springs forever ... arrrgh.

Pull yourself towards yourself, woman!

I peer out of the window, where life seems to be going ahead as normal. Then a 'ting' from my computer tells me a connection has been made. I instantly relax; my alienation from the world, and dependence on my Internet connection is getting out of hand. Without it, I have no idea what is happening, other than what happens right in front of me.

As what has been happening right in front of me has been terribly tedious for the last few days, I inspect my maps with great care to try to find a way south that will also allow me to see more than just the interstate. It is time to cross the Appalachians, and head toward Tallahassee. The R23 is just the road for the job, and to add a bit more country flavor, I loop onto the 19W. Deep rural North Carolina is a world of swing bridges, wooden churches, neat farmyards and rusting cars. It is also apple country: apples are advertised for sale everywhere, but they are not in season, so the wooden stalls stand deserted. The 19W spits me out just before Ashville, but soon another little loop road takes me to Chimney Rock and Hickory Nut Falls, where Daniel Day Lewis did battle in the film *Last of the Mohicans*. Not having seen the film, I have no idea what to expect, and quite unexpectedly find another mad American moment.

At some point the owners of this land decided that the big old chimney rock was too difficult to climb, but the view was too good not to share, so they blasted, and dug away in the adjoining cliff face until they had the space to install the second highest elevator in Virginia. This was some time ago, so this statistic is probably outdated, but it must still be the wackiest lift in all of America. I walk through a dank rock passage, hit the up button set in stone, and 'true as bananas' a lift arrives. This is like something out of an Enid Blyton children's adventure story. Up I go, and at the top make my way through the obligatory gift shop that is standard in every single one of the planet's tourist attractions. A wooden walkway, suspended high in space, leads to the summit of Chimney Rock, on which hangs the American flag at half-mast. The Americans are fundamental patriots, and now, with the death of Gerald Ford, the excuse to fly that flag, even if it is only half-mast, is taken up with great enthusiasm by every flag-flying citizen of America.

The view from this 500-million-year-old rock is spectacular: along Hickory Nut Gorge to Lake Lure, clear across to Kings Mountain beyond the Blue Ridge Mountains, or just straight down into the valley, 1,200 vertical feet below. The way back down those 1,200 feet is via a series of inventive wooden stairs, which cling to the nooks and cracks of the rock wall, snake through deep crevices, and plunge down cracks into moon-shiners caves, finally ending on the trail to Nut Bush Falls, which are very disappointing – perhaps there was more water on the day of the famous Daniel Day Lewis battle. In the fading day, I find my way along wooded winding roads back onto the bland and boring interstate.

There are two definite worlds in America, one on and one off the interstate. Driving on the interstate, McDonald's, Burger King, Subway, Days Inn, Comfort Inn, Waffle House, Wendy's, Holiday Inn, Motel 8, Motel 6, Budget Inn are repeated endlessly. If one never ventured onto the back roads, one could easily believe that this is all there is to America. The national chains are rivaled only by the huge selection of churches; one house, one church seems to be the way of it, with crosses to spare. 'Jesus died for you' proclaims a giant neon sign. Right royal waste that was. I stop over in the aptly named Travelers Rest, where a semi-literate man allows his daughter to spell out his wish, as he laboriously writes it on the car

'Trust in Jesus'

I might have known ... and there it is again, judgment day. I have fallen into a self-righteous frame of mind that I cannot seem to shake. I must really make an effort, as my own presumption is coloring my appreciation of America, although as I travel further south, I am starting to feel much better about life in general. With the lengthening days and the increasing heat, I am slowly climbing out of the deep winter funk I have been in for a while.

Georgia

Bed 132

The road leads through woodlands, lakes and gently rolling countryside before crossing the Savannah River into Georgia, where the fortunes of the Americans suddenly take a turn for the worse.

I have become so accustomed to the well-maintained, almost obsessively neat houses and yards that the crummy-looking trailer parks that hide out in the woods come as quite a shock. In the shabby yards, magnolia trees and camellias are blooming; their bright reds and pinks are the most brilliant color I have seen since the bright lights of Las Vegas. I lie ... the bright lights of Rochester Hills. But the porches of the houses tell me that I have reached Deep South poverty, and to go with it, trash now lines the road, and fills the yards. The American dream is not for all Americans.

Small businesses have set up stalls on the roadside, every one selling hot boiled peanuts. As I near Florida, pecan nut sales start competing with the boiled peanuts. While I am not a peanut fan, I am rather partial to pecans, so stop at a table set under a pecan nut tree, on the side of a beautiful green meadow. I step into humid, sweet smelling air. For the first time in months my winter jacket is far too warm. Munching at my pecans, which, combined with raw carrots, make a delicious snack, I drive through a most unlikely looking Cairo. Vines hang off bearded trees that stand with their roots in dark water. There is something close and sinister about the scenery that makes me not want to be here after dark.

Florida

Bed 133

Crossing into Florida, the fortunes of the Americans change again. Huge Georgian mansions, elaborate gates, lush manicured gardens, complete with fake lakes and fountains, epitomize gracious southern living. It's all quite lovely, but I don't know where I am. The map is not helpful, so I step into a conveniently placed police station where my

'Excuse me, could you tell me where I am?'

brings a somewhat bemused reaction.

'Where are you wanting to be, ma'am?'

Smart Alec

'I am not wanting to be anywhere. I am wanting to know where I currently am.'

This is not a difficult question, surely.

'Tallahassee, Florida, ma'am.'

This reply delivered with a faint air of disbelief.

Well, how was I to know? It's been a long day on the 'everywhere-the-same-view' interstate, from South Carolina right through Georgia into Florida, where the street signs are positively Russian in their abundance. I have negotiated several interstate off-ramps and subsequent T-junctions, with no signs whatsoever to point me in the right direction. The highway exits are identified just before the turn-off, so I keep missing my exits. The exits do not follow numerically either: they are in numerical order, but they skip a couple of numbers, that is, Exit 33 comes after Exit 25, so I really have no idea what's going on

... except that the poverty levels are rising as I get further south. Following the instructions of the police officer I make my way into the back end of Tallahassee, where they sell wigs, lots and lots of wigs ... odd.

The motel recommended by the police officer has an incredible luxury feature: a breakfast room, with table and chairs, where they serve a real-food breakfast, served on an actual plate, with metal knives and forks, and, by George, a linen napkin. Incredible. A bit of the gracious southern lifestyle is still hanging on in this land of polystyrene and plastic. But even here the 'always-on' television is always on. It informs me that I should be truly thankful for being way down south. I have been running just ahead of a massive cold front that has put the north into deep freeze. It has been dumping so much snow that motorists have been trapped on highways and byways for up to three days. Just as I am congratulating myself on the decision to travel to the warm south, the motel receptionist walks in complaining bitterly of the cold. Everything is relative.

I have obviously become somewhat hardened against the cold, but I am definitely feeling much better being down south again. The cold of the north had me hunching my shoulders, jamming my hands deep into my pockets, screwing up my eyes, and turning down the corners of my mouth in a deep grimace. It is really not possible to be completely happy when you are constantly freezing, and your face looks as if you have just chewed a lemon.

On the outskirts of Tallahassee, roadside stalls sell guava jelly, and shabby restaurants advertise turkey melt and sweet tater fries. Trash lies around ramshackle houses that display the patched-togetherness of poor people. I drive past the closest thing to a squatter camp that I reckon I will see in America. Here I spy my first evacuation route signs. This brings home the fact that this is hurricane country, and if you know that the chances of your house being blown away is pretty high, it makes sense to build flat, low and cheap.

At Crystal Springs I get the distinct feeling I am moving into the Florida money belt. Glider planes, light aircraft and big recreational trucks replace the junk-filled yards. A sign pointing to a place called Homosassa catches my eye. As my life would not be complete without having visited a place called Homosassa, I turn sharp right. Immediately the swamp forest swallows me up into a world of green light, where trees grow from blue-sky water. The dirt road deposits me at Homosassa harbor, where shrimps are for sale, and pizzas are delivered free to your boat. There are some pretty strange-looking people down here; it looks as if there is something wrong with their faces. One such person steps up to the Wish Mobile. I can smell him before I turn to see him. Travis the crab fisherman has been at the local pub all morning, and now wants to know all about me and the Wish Mobile.

He is a big, red-haired, blue-eyed, but misshapen, and ill-spoken man. His hands are dirt ingrained, thickly calloused, and scarred from the crab knife. His nails are so cracked and dirty that the cigarette he holds between his fingers looks positively virginal in its pure unlit whiteness. I gingerly hand him the pen. Miss Priss has sent out a clear message: those hands are not to touch me under any circumstances. With no hesitation, Travis the crab fisherman adds his thought to the Wish Mobile.

'Slow down; look at life.'

Straightening he hands me the pen with a

'Do ya wanna see the harbor?'

I look around at the harbor we are standing in; how drunk is he?

'We are in the harbor.'

'This ain't the harbor; this is a tourist hangout.'

His attitude is so well meaning, I feel it would be churlish to refuse, but as he gets into the car, I realize just how pungent he is, and make no excuses for opening all the windows. Miss Priss starts chewing my ear off; of all the men in the world you could have given a lift, you decide to choose *him*? This sentiment seems to be shared by all the locals. As we drive off, I can feel their eyes on me. Our arrival at the working harbor brings the working to a standstill. Travis obviously does not often get driven around by a woman; it is not hard to guess why. I am relieved when he steps into the great wide world, leaving only his aroma behind. I leave the Wish Mobile running, doors and windows open, fan on full blast. Hopefully by the time I get back the air will have cleared.

After showing off the crab boat he works on, Travis explains the catching method for the stone crabs, which are in season from October to May. They remove only one claw, then fling the beastie back to re-grow his claw, so it can be caught again another day. It is all very interesting, but my close proximity to the smell of Travis is working Miss Priss into a gut-wrenching frenzy. I manage to beat her down long enough to photograph the hands of Travis, I have never seen such hard working hands. Leaving him to enjoy his beer and cigarette, I set off to find the jetty he mentioned, and proceed to get totally lost in Homosassa; it is a tiny, but very wobbly place. After a few curves and false starts, I meet up with Phil, who looks after the airboats for hire. He wishes to save the trees, but, despite my determined efforts, refuses to write on the Wish Mobile. The penny only drops later that he is probably illiterate, that I am a twit, and had I been more sensitive, I could have offered to write the wish for him. It certainly has more value than the offering of George and son, who arrive on an airboat, and have no problem immortalizing their wishes.

'God bless America'

And the rest of us? The inward-looking mindset of Americans is really starting to get to me. How does 'God bless America' in any way qualify as a global wish?

Bed 134, 135

The road south is lined by national franchises. CVS pharmacy, Walgreens, Kmart, 7-Eleven, Burger King, McDonald's over and over. Trying to find a scenic route is impossible. The islands of sand that are right at the frontline when a hurricane strikes are completely built up with condos and motels, through which I cannot even get a glimpse of the ocean. Not the wisest of places to build a house, on a spit of sand in the teeth of a hurricane. But one of these islands is St Pete's beach, where 5W Josette lives, and this is where I am heading, happy in the knowledge that this is not hurricane season.

Josette is a kindred spirit, who restores my faith in the Americans, and brings into focus the confusion I have felt about the kindly friendly Americans and their government.

In seems that the 1970s America essentially legalized bribery and corruption, by allowing 'special interest groups' to fund election campaigns for political candidates. Over the years, 'special interest groups' have found more and more loopholes in this law, which allow them to pledge very large contributions to a candidate's election campaign. In exchange for this 'special interest group' funding, candidates are, by unspoken agreement, expected to sign their votes away according to the wishes of the interest group. As electioneering has become a massively expensive pastime in America, the candidate is in a catch-22 situation. In order to have any chance of gaining entry into Congress, to represent the people of America, he or she must campaign. This costs piles of money, which is overwhelmingly supplied by 'special interest groups'. By the time the idealistic politician reaches the giddy heights of Congress, he or she has essentially sold his or her soul to some or other 'special interest group', and the one vote American people get to play with every four years is valueless.

But all rant and no rave makes us dull girls, so we put on our swinging skirts, fling ourselves into Josette's red convertible sports car, and, with the warm wind off the Gulf of Mexico blowing through our hair, take ourselves off to the St Pete's annual contra dancing ball. Contra dancing is a form of line dancing, which I have delusions of simply watching. No chance. There seems to be a rule in contra dancing that no woman shall be a wallflower. I get whipped into the first dance, and 'swing your partner round and round' by an endless line of dancers, who do the occasional docey-do, before all the spinning starts again. I get spun until the world spins. Why did no one tell me that the business of staring your partner directly and intensely in the eye was not a come on, but a safety device, so you don't end up flat on your face from sheer giddiness. With two contra dances done, I feel it is time to leave before I lose my lunch, and, as Josette must show her face again tomorrow, we go while the going is good.

Three days follow of girly-style bonding, strolling along beaches, learning to play shuffle board (a misnomer as nothing is shuffled, and there is no board), eating delicious very healthy vegetarian meals in the company of well-traveled friends, who thankfully spare me the need to relate my whole travel history, as they have very interesting stories of their own to tell. My favorite is that of a lady in her late sixties, who recently followed her man, an ex-Russian spy who was banished from American soil, to Russia, where he was unfortunately not very welcome either. And lives with him in 'outer Siberia'. While listening to this wildly romantic story, I silently hope that true love lasts in this case.

As the conversation around the table drifts to topics shared between old friends, my mind drifts to the various conversations I have had about love since arriving in America. The search for love is a huge theme in America. Everybody wants to find love, but somehow there are always unrealistic expectations and personal demands, which require compromise from both parties, but which neither party is prepared to make. I wonder if, when people start on their search for love, they want to find someone who will love them, or whether they are looking for someone with whom they can build a bond of love. I think for the most part people want to be loved for what they are, without compromise. This is possibly the main reason that love so often fails. Both parties want to be loved, and no party is prepared to give love. Perhaps this fear of losing a small part of our perceived identity prevents us from building towards a love that will make our lives infinity better.

Fear, trust, and love are linked. Are we so fearful to be vulnerable that we don't confess to love? But if we don't confess to love, how can the beloved know that he or she is truly loved? To love and to be loved is first and foremost trust, and in an environment of trust, fear vanishes. This makes me think that until we trust and love ourselves completely, we will not have the means to love and trust another completely. We cannot give love until we have love, and we cannot have a constant supply of love until we have found it in ourselves. To do this, we have to love ourselves, so it comes back to self-control, as in order to love ourselves, we must strive to be that person we would want to love.

When we love ourselves, we stop searching for love, and by drawing from the wellspring of love that is inside us, we are able to give love freely, without fear of losing any part of ourselves. Then we can grow in love until we can each independently dive deeply into the possibilities of life, knowing without a glimmer of doubt that we are loved, and while we might fail sometimes, it is a small matter in the light of the supporting ocean of love and trust that surrounds us, which we helped build.

It is time to pack my bags yet again. Not far to go today, just an hour north to Tarpon Springs, where I spy my first Florida golf course. It is green, manicured, fountainous, and inhabited by men in loud checkered shorts. Meeting me in front of her brand-new house, 5W Charlene looks a tad nervous, I am her first-ever 5W guest, and all her friends have been questioning her sanity in allowing a total stranger into her home. But she soon discovers it is not all bad, so the next two days roll by amicably, with everybody dealing with his or her own set of chores: builders for Charlene, storage for Kirk, her son, whose visit coincides with mine, and travel arrangements for me.

My most pressing task is to finalize shipment for the Wish Mobile to England. As ever, everything is available online in America, so finding a shipping agent who deals with roll-on-roll-off vehicle transportation is no problem, but getting my details across to the young lady who has been assigned to my case is. Is it possible that the constant connection of portable phone and Internet has made us incapable of planning forward by more than one minute? The young lady calls, asks me one question, hangs up, calls back five minutes later, asks another question, hangs up, calls back a few minutes later, asks another question, and before she can hang up, I insert a quick question of my own.

'Is there any more information that you need from me?'

'No, that is all for the moment.'

'For the moment' is right. Five minutes later she calls to ask another question, and finally, after countless phone calls, we have managed to fill in my booking sheet, and there is debate whether the Internet is making us dumber or smarter?

For our farewell dinner, we tootle off to the local Greek at the Sponge docks, where Kirk spontaneously offers me the use of his yacht while in the Keys. The yacht or, as Kirk insists, sailing boat, is on dry land just at present, which is fine by me. I accept, and just like that, accommodation in Key West is dealt with. Isn't life a grand old thing?

Bed 136

After the past few days of homey comforts generously provided by my new 5W friends, I am once again itching for the long road and new horizons. The road obliges when, just after St Petersburg, it lifts off onto the Sunshine Skyway Bridge, which soars high above the murky grey water of Tampa Bay, expanding the horizon to show small islands all round. I feel adventure coming on strong. At Port Charlotte, the clouds break to spotlight a red fishing boat drifting on brilliant turquoise water. The fisherman draws up his net, but the odds are against him getting any of the catch, as birds swoop and dive, swamping the boat.

At Naples, the land slowly gives way to mirror-still water, which perfectly reflects a falcon swaying gently on a palm, and white egrets that are arranged like Christmas decorations on a giant leafless tree. Enormous flocks of pink birds wade in the swamp grasses, roost on mangroves, or hang effortlessly in the warm air currents. Floating in slow motion, they skim the tops of the swamp reeds and grasses, sometimes misjudging their road crossings, where they are squashed, interesting for those birders wanting a more scientific view of their quarry.

A road sign informs me that the way to explore the swamps more intimately is go an airboat ride. This sounds like a plan, but as soon as we set off, at neck-wrenching speed, I start having serious doubts about this mode of transportation. It appears the airboat driver is fully convinced that we would all like to speed about the swamps, making an eardrum-popping amount of noise, while scaring the bejesus out of every living creature for miles around. He knows exactly where the alligators lurk, taking us right up against a nest of tiny alligators. They scatter, and hide in terror. Should we really be getting so close that we disturb the nest? What are the conservation rules here? Our skipper seems totally unconcerned that we might be giving the baby alligators future psychiatric problems, and proceeds to inform us that, owing to global warming, the alligators are breeding too early. In making this sweeping statement, he seems to forget that the alligators and their kin are prehistoric beasties who have survived virtually unchanged since the dinosaurs left their footprints in the mud of the planet. I would imagine that if mama alligator feels she can squeeze in two clutches of eggs during these long hot days, then she is breeding right on time to do so.

What an arrogant bunch we are, laying down judgment on the long run of nature, armed only with our two seconds' worth of half knowledge. My concerns about the concept of global warming are the size of it, and the time scale we measure it by. We judge the change of the planetary conditions by our lifespan, and by that small part of it that we have recorded. We hold a ruler to the sky, and by that measure make weather proclamations that suit our own particular agenda. Perhaps the globe is warming, but perhaps in the slightly longer term we are heading towards an ice age, or perhaps all this is just a perfectly normal changing of the seasons on a planetary timescale.

My head returns to the present, just as the testosterone-laden skipper throws a plastic bottletop into the water to attract an alligator, which is lurking in the shadow of the mangroves. I am gobsmacked, and even more so when he pokes the alligator on the nose with a paddle, causing the alligator to rear up, mouth agape, all teeth on show, giving all and sundry a great photo opportunity. I unfortunately missed the moment, being as I was in a state of indignant shock. What the heck is this, his own private circus show?

Alligators done, we request to have a moment to look at the abundant bird life. But the captain of the ship has the non-birder's take on the situation. If the bird is not an enormous bird of prey or a gaudy parrot, it is simply not worth looking at. He takes us to a tree where bright pink roseate spoonbills are settling down for the night, gives us two seconds of silence, and then roars off over the swamp, scaring every bird that had just tucked its wee head under its wing for the night into full and confused flight. He is obviously firmly of the opinion that we are not getting our money's worth unless we make as much noise, and scare as many birds as is humanly possible. So we broadside and wheelie our way around the swamp, shattering the mirror calm of this once-was-silent place. I am embarrassed to be a part of this; next time I will opt for a self-propelled canoe trip.

My misguided boat trip has convinced me, though, that the Everglades deserve to be seen in decent light, and at a more leisurely pace, so I bed down in Everglade City. It is a really functional place, where trailer homes are jammed together, interspersed by the occasional very good-looking house on stilts. But for the main part it is not terribly exciting, just a rag-tag of broken boats, cars and rubbish, and an overpriced motel with a bathroom that has Miss Priss in a full huff. I go to bed dirty, thinking of the banja in Kazakhstan that the prissy one seemed to have no problem with. She has been thoroughly spoilt by the consistently high hygiene standards of the US of A.

The next morning, my first stop is in Otopee, where a huddle of people live among the alligators, the mosquitoes, and the hundreds of birds, but, because there is no actual wildlife deep in the Everglades, they have pink plastic flamingos decorating their yards ... or perhaps those are decoys. I step into a small store to buy some provisions, and discover that there are completely different brands in the shops down in southern Florida. It really is starting to feel like a different country. But I do spy a brand I know from TV, an O'Henry bar, and now I will finally find out exactly what an O'Henry bar is. Sinking my teeth into the sticky bar of peanut buttery chocolate, I discover it is so sweet it stings, and makes my eyes spin. OK, been there, done that. One bite is enough to convince me that to continue eating this would not be a good idea The sugar load in American food is mind boggling. While Americans love their sugar, they don't do fat. Everything must be 'fat free'. Nobody is telling them that a fat-free diet is bad for your brain. If they did, the Americans would work out that to promote a sugar-free diet is not profitable, while promoting a fat-free diet is. Fat-free milk for example is a wonderful creation. It works to the producer's total advantage. They are skimming all the cream, selling the watery result for lots of money, and are still in possession of the most valuable part of the milk. Devilish clever that, almost the perfect analogy of capitalism American-style.

After a sign warning me of 'Panthers crossing' – wouldn't that be exciting? – I turn onto the 94 loop road, a dirt road that leads deep into the swamp. On a bridge, where bizarre trees touch overhead, casting green light, shadows, and perfect reflections into a smooth black pool, I forget about the possible appearance of panthers, turn off the car engine, step into the warm embrace of the humid air, and put to practice a lesson learnt from a friend long ago in the African bushveldt. Standing silently, I allow all my senses to tune into what surrounds me. As my eyes find focus in this magic mirror world of brilliant reflections, where everything is right side up and upside down, birds magically appear on seemingly empty branches. The wind of silent wings brushes my neck, as a grey bird, red of foot, skims my head. The illusion of silence is ripped and torn by bird shrieks, squawks and squeaks. In the black water, an alligator rises and sinks according to his will, while overhead the buzzards circle. In deep shadows brilliant flashes of white draw my eye. Heron, spoonbills, egrets and scared ibis, birds with yellow feet, with bright red heads, and with shimmering feathers, dive and spear at the water teeming with fish.

Quietly I drink it all in, and then spy another alligator in the shining shadows. My alligator count notches up to four that I have found by myself today. This is much more exciting than the dished-up lot from yesterday. I start believing I might even see a panther. The chances are slim, but the thought is a happy one. As I drive off, a bird escort lifts to the air; they fly overhead, behind, and with slow stately beats of giant wings, ahead of me, until I am stopped by a flock of buzzards in the road. They look at me with beady black eyes set in wrinkled grey faces, as they completely ignore my attempts to shoo them off the road, I take a moment to make a buzzard portrait session out of it. But they are camera shy, flapping off to land on a dead-looking tree, where air plants are in bloom, making red, pink and purple trumpets of color against the dull grey bark.

The road alternates between deep mangrove jungle, with all the accompanying squawks, and open swamp grassland, dotted with the odd leafless tree and bushy stands of palm, until the loop road joins up with the tar of Route 41, and my wilderness safari comes to an abrupt end. The swamp gives way to head-high corn, banana and tomato plantation. Huge nurseries, selling a massive variety of palms and exotic flowers, line the road. By now it is so hot I turn on the air conditioner for the first time since north-west China. At Key Largo the road starts heading across open water, and from the dense green of tangled jungle, I enter a clean blue world, where the brilliant turquoise of the Atlantic stretches to the blue horizon on my left, mirrored by the Gulf of Mexico to my right.

Bed 137

Houses with yachts parked in their watery driveways hide from the road behind sways of palms. At a palm-roofed bar, where yachts and dinghies jostle for position, a giant yellow conch shell is the pink-lipped centerpiece to cascading fountains, surrounded by plastic pink flamingoes. The pink flamingoes compete for attention with white fiberglass manatee and giant grouper (a big fish), with postboxes shoved most decoratively into their wide-open mouths.

Signs every few miles indicating the nearest hurricane shelter and excavation routes make the hurricane threat very real. The Seven Mile Bridge skips from key to key, some so narrow that the houses on both sides of the road front onto the ocean. This must be really hair-raising during a hurricane. I am sure these small keys of ancient limestone must simply vanish under the sea. People walk along Seven

Mile Bridge, and although this is the most exotic road I have ever driven on, I cannot imagine a more boring walk, just tar, ocean and sun.

On arriving in Stock Island, I discover that Kirk has just beaten me here. After his lengthy absence of two days, a great gathering of the yachting tribe has been called, each member bringing an offering of a case of Bud Lights, which get consumed while all stand in a circle around the paint-covered workbench under Kirk's boat. This merry band of sailors on Stock Island dry docks show me a completely different side of America, although I am not sure if Key West is part of America at all. The conversation revolves around far-off shores, and great sailing adventures, delayed only by the eternal task of repairing, fixing, and maintaining the sailing boat. The talk is of sails and spinnakers, inlets and outlets, gizmos and grommets. Night surrounds us and several beers closer to total inebriation, someone remembers an engine that must be collected from a vessel anchored way out on the deep blue sea. This cannot wait until the sober morning hours, but must be done immediately, and I, as guest of honor, must come along ...

Like pirates we take to the tiny boarding vessel, navigate in the dark, through treacherous channels and sandbanks, further out to sea than I feel totally comfortable with. In the heaving bopping waves the engine is transferred from boat to boat, and when successfully landed, another celebration is begun. We gather at the yachts just down the jetty that have long lost their wanderlust. This part of Stock Island marina is like suburbia. The yachts even have little gardens onshore, in which we congregate, while other members of this clan bring more beer and other diverse refreshments and relaxants. But commerce is threatening this floating neighborhood of once-were-sailors. Stock island is due for a major facelift, so all current tenants must go. We drink to the passing of an area. As the beer intake climbs, more and more reasons for celebration are discovered. The merry band of drinkers move hither and thither, eventually coming to rest again under the keel of Kirk's boat. This seems like the ideal time for me to bail out. I am in danger of drowning in Bud Lights.

Upstairs in the master cabin, with earplugs inserted against the profound discussion below (never travel without industrial-strength earplugs, and a basin plug), the conversation slowly dies as one by one the sailors drift off to their beached yachts. But sleep will not come, held at bay by the noise of some piece of windblown metal clanging against something. Arrg!! In a state of deep irritation I clamber out of the front hatch to tie down the riggings or whatever they are. Straightening I turn to take in the full moon, become fully aware of the warm salt air on my skin, and imagine myself sailing to Cuba. Call me sailor woman. Diving back through the hatch I drift off into a sea adventure-filled sleep, until the sun stabs me in the eyeballs.

Stumbling into the middle part of the yacht, whatever the correct term for that may be, I find my gracious host still asleep in a shaft of sunshine. His beautifully toned torso decorated with half a dragon tattoo? I stare at it as he slowly wakes; he looks at me with enquiry in his grey-green eyes ... oops, tempting, but no. Instead I convince him to pose for a photograph, which I will, at a later stage, have fun in converting to a painting. There is a reason that the masters of old liked painting nudes. While they might have contended it was all for the sake of art, the truth of the matter is – and here's a little secret that some of you might have picked up on in the film *Titanic* – it is a very sensual thing to paint a nude, especially if the subject is standing right in front of you. You might as well be stroking the real thing, and not the canvas, and while I will be deprived of that pleasure, I do look forward to my painting session some time in the future, during which time I will complete the tattoo. Kirk pulls on his shirt, while telling me of the fate of the tattoo artist, and the reason for the half-finished tattoo. The artist was strapping something to his bicycle, with those elastic bicycle ties with hooks on either end, when one jumped out of his control, spun back, and hooked out his eye, ouch!

Over breakfast I learn that sometime during the night Kirk organized my day, and has assumed the dual role of private skipper and tour guide, and intends to show me around Key West from the water. We set off to board our means of transportation for the day, one of those cigarette boats (a small version of the cigar boats as favored by oil sheiks) where there is just enough boat to keep afloat, and more than enough engine to make that boat plane across the surface of the water at lip-distorting speed. Unfortunately the weather is not playing along for such high-speed adventure; the water is so choppy that the boat bangs about alarmingly; and the resulting spray instantly drenches us. Okay, we will take things at more restful pace.

As we round Stock Island into the Gulf of Mexico, a single mountain, affectionately known as Mount Trashmore, draws my attention. This mountain is the garbage dump of Key West. It is the highest point in the keys, and has a perpetual crown of buzzards drifting on the updrafts that are generated by the decaying trash. Mount Trashmore is an ecosystem unto itself; it has been seen to glow purple in patches in the dark of night; and is covered in strange green vines. To prevent the mountain of trash from blowing its top like some mad

Frankenstein volcano, pipes penetrate deep into its rotting core that release noxious vapors, and occasionally spew flames. Surrounded only by ocean, it is hard to hide the tons of garbage this tiny community creates. This puts into perspective the piles of garbage the rest of the world must produce.

We cruise into the Key West yacht marina, tie up the surfboard with giant outboard motor alongside luxury yachts that loom far above, and saunter to a waterside restaurant for lunch. Does this all not sound just too fabulous? Are you all not green with envy? During lunch we are serenaded by a hilarious, if somewhat sexist blues singer. Several very big, actually let's call a spade a spade, very fat men, smoking fat Cuban cigars, hog the bar, their big bums hanging over the bar chairs, and images of boobacious babes emblazoned on their t-shirts, fall about laughing at the lyrics. For some reason they worry me. What is such a large posse of very large men doing here? Is this a stag weekend, a very fat man convention, a fat man support group ... why do I care?

With the setting sun I set out for a night of exploring the infamous Duval Street, where legends are born, reputations built and destroyed, although tonight things seem quiet, but it is still early. Snake charmers with lovey parrots slide up to say hello. Drag queens grace the street corners, and lure reluctant, giggling tourist into dark clubs. I get lured, by a very enthusiastic Englishman, to view an exhibition opening. The exhibit includes very powerful sculptures of human forms, which surge from their pedestals. They are made from, of all things, silver teaspoons. Sounds daft, but it works. I get to chatting to curator Pat, who invites the 'One Planet One People' project over to join the fun. So in the great spectacle that is Duval Street, the Wish Mobile makes a spectacle of itself, and a great wish making ensues.

'Make haste slowly.'

'Be and let be.'

'Just get on with it; we have no choice.'

'Live in the now.'

'Give God his job back.'

'You can't fix yesterday, you're not promised tomorrow, so BE right NOW.

'Be true to yourself and be kind to others.'

All the exhibiting artists sign the car, so now my artwork is signed by other artists, a strange upside-downess to that. Boban, of the teaspoon people, assures me that my artwork is now worth at least $10,000 more. Wouldn't that be nice?

After stopping off to buy a couple of Buds – the only time you cannot buy alcohol in Key West is from 05h00 to 07h00 – I get back to the yacht just before midnight, at which point Kirk and I decide that this would be a good time to order pizza, a plan sure to cause indigestion, but somehow with the help of a few Buds, and a long slow conversation, we manage to devour our midnight feast.

Despite this, I am up before dawn, as I want a photograph of the Wish Mobile by the southernmost blimp. As these photographs usually involve some illegal maneuvering, it is best to get them done before the whole world is up and about. Not possible in Key West. Early birds live way down south, so I draw more attention than I need. The two old hippies on a bicycle are fine, but a traffic warden? For heaven's sake! What is she doing up at this hour? This is truly the American town that never sleeps. She looks me over, looks at the car, and remaining surprisingly nonchalant, comments that,

'We have had lots of people parking on the road to get the shot, but never one on the actual pavement.'

Well, there is a first for everything, and, as this is the first Kangoo to drive around the planet, there is no reason that it should not be first to end up on a pavement at the southernmost point of North America. But she is quizzy, and hangs about waiting to see if I will get the Wish Mobile off the pavement again. I am not all together sure about this myself, and was hoping for an audience-free moment. Fortunately the wee car rises to the occasion, and without so much as a scrape of paint against bollard, away we go. Not far, as the next stop is to photograph the Southernmost House of North America, a Victorian fantasy in tropical pastels, which is the favorite resting spot for American presidents and honeymooning couples.

But before I leave Key West, I must mention the chickens. They are protected here, and much like the cows of India, wander the streets without fear of man or beast. Their presence is the cause of a long-standing chicken war, which, like most modern wars, will probably never be resolved. But in trying, the residents have come up with some interesting, but as yet unworkable plans to reduce the chicken population. One being to set loose a bunch of bobcats in Key West to catch the chickens. Personally I would prefer to take my chances with a chicken. Then it was suggested that foxes, with their reputation for fishing chickens out of henhouses being well known, be set on the chickens. But some serious deductive thought brought the good citizens of Key West to the realization that the chickens here are not in henhouses, but free range, and therefore the foxes would need to be free range as well. Back to the drawing board, which then threw up the idea of banishing the entire chicken population to Mount Trashmore, but unfortunately the Key West chickens, much like their local human counterparts, are an active bunch, and can fly very well indeed. To fence them in would have cost millions. So, with no better idea yet forthcoming, the chickens rule the roost in Key West.

Bed 138

Now it is my reluctant duty to head north again, as my, and indeed the visa of the Wish Mobile is running out, and the Americans are as sticky as the Chinese about folk, and their vehicles, overstaying their welcome. But the heat is so beguiling, it has been a wonderful lift of the spirits, and after a few days in the heat and company of the laidback 'almost sailors' of Stock Island, I am feeling much better about life in general. Up north it promises to get cold again. The cold, dark and damp of London is not a happy thought, and right now I just want to stay, but it is not to be. With another haul of wishes, I wave my new friends farewell before setting off across Seven Mile Bridge, where blues and greens merge and meld, in a hazy marriage of sky and sea. A pelican paces me. With no visible effort, it glides perfectly parallel to the bridge, a virtuoso performance that is abruptly interrupted by a fish far below. The pelican folds its wings and plunges towards its lunch.

Before long I am in Miami, and any thought of laid-back flies right out of the window. Miami seems to be in a state of siege, or perhaps the folk of Miami are just a whole lot more gung-ho in their driving style than the rest of America. It is aggressive, fast, and using indicators is against the law, or so it seems. By virtue of a few unexpected turns, and the lack of a decent map I find myself heading toward the Bay of Biscayne on yet another huge bridge. The traffic is a tangled mess, but moving at a clipping pace nonetheless. In the middle of all this, I take my in-car multitasking to a whole new level. A chap winds down his window, and at 35 m/h we start a car-to-car conversation; this is probably not the cleverest of plans.

'Hey, where are you from?'

'South Africa.'

'WHEre?'

'SOUTH AFRICA.'

I sneak a quick look at the road to adjust my lane positioning while he yells

'NeAT, WHERE ARE YOU HEADING?'

Hmmm ... to be, or not to be a smart Alec? To be, definitely.

'England.'

'Say what.'

He swerves to avoid a slow moving vehicle; soon he is alongside me again

'You're going where?'

'I AM DRIVING AROUND THE WORLD.'

He takes a brief moment to concentrate on the traffic streaming around us, then yells.

'FOLLOW ME.'

'OKAY.'

What the heck, why not.

Ralph has decided that he needs to take me to the chamber of commerce. Thanks, Ralph, that was very kind of you. Here I discover that I have arrived just in time for the American NFL Super Bowl Sunday. The lady at the desk informs that this is like the World Cup, where only America is involved, isn't that just saying something? Owing to this momentous occasion, Miami is indeed under siege by hordes of football fans. The lady supplies me with a map, marks the location of the tourist information center with a fat red cross, and says with rueful assurance.

'You won't find anything. Miami has been booked up for months.'

But there is nothing to be done but try.

South Beach is closed to traffic, and getting close to it at all is impossible. The perfect plastic Ken and Barbies that I had hoped to see rollerblading along the promenade are engulfed by hordes of super-sized football enthusiasts, and suddenly the fat man convention in Key West makes a whole lot of sense. The place is packed; just how many people fit into a stadium? In the Friday afternoon rush hour my attention wanders, and I accidentally land up right in a downtown logjam, great! Road works, building sites, masses of traffic, and a speed limit of one mile an hour have my nerves churning. At least I am providing a public service, as the Wish Mobile provides reading material for the cars that surround me. I, however, feel like a flipping fish in a bowl. The light is fading, and my chances of getting a room are fading right along with it. Finally I find the tourist information center. The chap behind the counter looks at me in bemusement. What planet are you from? says his expression. Yeah, yeah, we can't all be football enthusiasts. Heaven help humanity if that were the case. He can offer me only two options: a room for $500 a night in a motel that normally costs $89, or I can camp in a parking lot for $10 a night. No and no. I don't mind camping in a desert in the Kazakh outback, but on a parking lot in Miami, no way.

I keep heading north, past cruise liners that float on the right, and on the left, fancy houses with their own marinas line the road on which stretch limousines rule. Too rich for my wallet, I am out of here, through a canyon of luxurious condos and hotels that completely obscure the beach. The traffic is not letting up, and I am beginning to wonder whether that parking lot is not a good idea after all. In order to be prepared for any eventuality, I stop off at a supermarket, and push my way through throngs of fat people to try to find some provisions that are halfway edible ... bananas and the least chemically enhanced yogurt, I can find. Standing in the sweaty crush of the till queue I am just plain pissed off. In moments like these, road trips are just no fun. Plunging back into the traffic chaos, I spend three and half hours of my life looking at Miami from a traffic jam; aesthetically it is not a bad looking place. But to hell with Miami. Consulting the map, I head out to Hollywood City, where I figure I will have more luck in finding a room. A room is available, at $199. That's capitalism for you; these rooms are usually $69, and then already overpriced, but it is 22h00, and I need to sleep somewhere.

Bed 139

I consider my moves for the day over the motel breakfast, which has not one bit of real food in it, (I lie, there are bananas and apples, but everything else is plastic packaged in plastic). In America you have to be in a pretty swanky place before you get close to real crockery and cutlery. Considering how many millions of Americans frequent fast-food places every day, where food is served in plastic, on plastic, with plastic knife and fork, all of which gets dumped after one use, the waste and pollution generated must be horrific.

The waste is not just in what we throw away, but in the energy we use to create what we throw away. Over 7 billion pounds of PVC are thrown away in the US each year, of which only about one quarter of 1 per cent is recycled. Just the chlorine production for PVC uses almost as much energy as the annual output of eight medium-sized nuclear power plants each year, and then one should still factor in the energy used to collect and store all that waste. The amazing thing is this is all started in the name of hygiene. I think if we all stepped back from our hygiene obsession, the environment would thank us for it. But not just that, our immune system would too, as there is a direct correlation between the increase in extreme allergies and the obsession with hygiene in the West.

Looking around the foyer, which is heaving with fat football fans, I make peace with the fact that I will not be getting a true Miami experience this weekend. Also, judging from all the tags that have materialized on the Wish Mobile overnight the 'One Planet One People' project is in danger of being swamped by the unthinking and somewhat inebriated.

It is time to head north again, but on the interstate the drivers are more aggressive than I have a mind to deal with today. At Palm Beach I slipstream onto the coastal road, and, oh, the moneyedness of it all. This must be where America's insanely wealthy live. It is painfully neat; the grass verge is perfect; the road looks washed; the palms sway in precise unity; and dogs bark only in key. The houses look like boutique hotels, and the clubhouse looks like the Ritz. The seafront houses have a tiny plot of the beach to themselves, on which the owners have built fancy pagodas with all the luxuries one would expect in a well-appointed lounge, nothing more than one requires to enjoy a day on the beach.

Driving down the luxurious hodge-podge of Royal Palm Way, where every bank in America is represented in as ostentatious a building as they can manage, I am surprised at the lack of people. Palm Beach is deserted at 15h30 on this Saturday afternoon; there is not a soul to be seen. Perhaps really rich people don't walk in public. Taking a walk through the 'The Church of Bethesda by the Sea', I discover that the people are here, or at least some of them. They sing hymns in the beautiful gothic courtyards, and hold mass behind closed wooden doors.

In this super-money zone, privacy is king, and the hedge is brought to a high art form. In Palm Beach there are truly spectacular hedges. It seems that street inhabitants have hedge meetings to decide just how high, how wide, and in which shape the topiaries shall be cut in order to achieve the most pleasing and opulent result. In Palm Beach, hedge trimmers must rival hairdressers in social status and desirability. Leaving the hedges behind, I reach the Haitian part of Palm Beach, where the affluence level tumbles a couple of notches, although life could still be a lot worse. But the fortunes tumble still more, until the neighborhood is decidedly shabby. What a contrast. This is probably where the cleaners and gardeners live, not the hedge trimmers though; they must be higher up on the social totem pole of Palm Beach. The fortunes of the residents of Palm Beach slowly rise again, until the obsession with the hedge returns. Edward Scissorhands would feel right at home.

At Juno Beach the ocean is emerald, and manicured picnic areas with tables set on sweeping lawns, under wide shade trees, create the ideal beach setting. While I stop to take in the scene, a huge shiny black SUV (the kind that most men can only dream of) stops behind me. Out steps a man-boy of no more than 18; this cannot possibly be his car! I console myself with the thought that he is driving daddy's or mummy's car, but judging by the wealth on display here, I just cannot be sure. The opulence moderates as I head further north, until on the beachfront of Fort Pierce, modest beach houses stand half hidden behind a wild tangle of sea breeze-loving plants.

My goal is Vero Beach, one of a string of narrow islands just off the coast of Florida, where a flat succession of gated communities is the neighborhood of choice. Here I am staying with a friend of a friend. Kathy has invited me into her home purely on the recommendation of Trix. I am constantly amazed at the hospitality, friendliness, and openness of the Americans. Our time together is spent working. After Kathy leaves for the office, I spend the day getting the Wish Mobile ready for shipping. In the evening we do what every other American is doing at this moment. We watch the NFL playoff. It is pouring with rain in Miami; the game is a soggy mess, which is all the same to me, as I have absolutely no understanding of the rules of American football. But I do 'get' Prince (or whatever his name currently is), the eternal professional. At half time he stands encased in a suit of purple sequins, embracing the rain, in danger of being electrocuted, as he belts out 'Purple Rain' for all he is worth. A grand moment.

Daytona Beach, Florida

Georgia

Bed 140

My journey north takes a little detour today. Going to Disneyland has been on my to-do list since I can remember, and now with Orlando just a hop, skip and jump away, it is time to draw a line through that wish. But life does not always work out as imagined. After paying a huge amount just to get into the parking area of Disneyland, I suddenly feel that this would be a very sad thing to do alone. Also the weather is not playing along. Wet, cold, windy, it is not a good day for roller coasters. As I stand about in the almost empty parking lot, dithering whether to put on a brave face, and do the solo roller coaster thing, a family pulls up. They are so excited; they passed me on the interstate; and they are thrilled that dad and hubby will be able to add his wish. He goes down on his knees and writes.

'Happy wife happy life.'

In exchange for this his wife gives me five dollars. I am nonplussed and, feeling like a bellhop, refuse. But she says she just wants to contribute something, and flings the note onto the passenger seat. So there it is, a five-dollar bill on the passenger seat: money and the Americans, an unbreakable union; the one defines the other. This incident makes me feel even more isolated. For some things in life you need a partner, and riding on roller coasters is one of those things. I leave Orlando behind and head back to the coast. At Daytona Beach I discover that the thing to do is to drive on the beach. Driving on beaches is not really something I consider altogether necessary, but as it is what one does in Daytona, I take a right, and find myself at the beach road tollgate. The $5 on the passenger seat is just enough to get me on the beach, where one is allowed to drive only on the very top clearly demarcated bit. Not the willy-nilly drive as you please, as I had feared. So I drive and drive. It's a fairly boring thing, driving on a beach, but the Wish Mobile seems to be enjoying its first beach outing. Perhaps it is remembering the wild freedom of Kazakhstan. And then we get stuck. No problem. Haul out the yoga mat. It works like a charm, but two feet later, stuck again. After a brief reconnaissance of the surrounding beach, I discover that the sand has a thin deceiving crust, and each forward movement just gets the Wish Mobile stuck again. There is nothing to be done, but to look helpless and forlorn, and soon a great truckload of friendly folk leap to my aid, pull me out of the sand, and put me back onto the road north.

I have decided to overnight on Jekyll Island, about which I know nothing, other than it looks like a fun little jutting out bit of land on the map. Jekyll Island is a national historic landmark. In my hotel room I surf about to find out why, and discover that this little island, which I have randomly chosen to visit, is steeped in history that has changed and shaped America, and consequently the world. With the completion of the Jekyll Island Club in 1888, Jekyll Island (owned at the time by JP Morgan) became a gathering place for the world's wealthiest families, some of whom built mansion-sized 'cottages', which still stand as testimony to the inequality of the world. But possibly the most pivotal event of modern history took place here in complete secrecy.

To understand this, it is necessary to recap my ongoing rant about money, and the value thereof. Money itself has no value: it was created as a measure of value in order to facilitate trade. It is merely our faith in the value of money that makes it valuable. If religion and faith are the same, then money is probably the world's only global religion. We all believe it has value, but actually ... it doesn't. It may once have had, when it was still made of, or measured against something like gold, but since the abolishment of the gold standard, the value of money is a free agent, able to warp and shift its worth as those who control it see fit. This makes things that money was meant to measure the value of, mainly human labor, essentially without value. That is the thing that makes America, and indeed the world, what it is today, and it all started here on this idyllic little island off the coast of Georgia

In the Jekyll Island Club on 22 November 1910, seven men, representing one quarter of the world's wealth, gathered here under such secrecy that even the regular servants were replaced with strangers, and only first names were used.

Forbes magazine founder Bertie Charles Forbes wrote several years later:

> Picture a party of the nation's greatest bankers stealing out of New York on a private railroad car under cover of darkness, stealthily riding hundreds of miles South, embarking on a mysterious launch, sneaking onto an island deserted by all but a few servants, living there a full week under such rigid secrecy that the name of not one of them was once mentioned, lest the servants learn the identity and disclose to the world this strangest, most secret expedition in the history of American finance. I am not romancing; I am giving to the world, for the first time, the real story of how the famous Aldrich currency

report, the foundation of our new currency system, was written ... The utmost secrecy was enjoined upon all. The public must not glean a hint of what was to be done. Senator Aldrich notified each one to go quietly into a private car, which the railroad had received orders to draw up on an unfrequented platform. Off the party set. New York's ubiquitous reporters had been foiled ... Nelson (Aldrich) had confided to Henry, Frank, Paul and Piatt that he was to keep them locked up at Jekyll Island, out of the rest of the world, until they had evolved and compiled a scientific currency system for the United States, the real birth of the present Federal Reserve System ...

The upshot of all of this was the creation of a banking system in which the printing of currency (creation of money) was taken out of the hands of the American people, and their chosen government, and placed in the hands of these very wealthy men. Nice, what? The right to print money or not, as and when it is most advantageous for the few, and usually to the detriment of the many, now that is where true power lies. The early presidents of America resisted and abhorred this system, knowing full well that the people of America would suffer under it. But the politicians of today ... well, they could be said to be just ill-paid employees of the bank, and the reality is that the American people no longer get to choose their government.

It is not surprising that Americans, and increasingly everybody else on the planet, are constantly in debt. Debt equals profit to the bankers, and it is therefore imperative that debt levels are maintained. Debt makes the world go round, or your hamster wheel, depending on how personally you wish to take this simple fact of life.

Compared to this, all else that happened on Jekyll Island, such as the 1700 battle here against the Spanish, called Battle of Bloody Marsh, pales into insignificance, although the name Bloody Marsh is very descriptive when, in the light of the setting sun the hidden water of the marsh turns red. But today the only drama here is played out on the manicured golf courses, where battles are fought with a very small white ball.

After five hours of staring at the computer screen, downloading the day's photographs, taking a GPS reading, transcribing the day's musings from Dictaphone to computer, blogging, answering mail, printing postcards, and writing postcards, my contact lenses are sticking to my eyeballs. It is time to shower and bed.

At breakfast (an actual food breakfast with waffles, eggs and bacon *and* crockery, hallelujah) a hail and hearty golfer lady, dressed in pink cap, bright yellow, boldly branded sport shirt and violently checkered pink and yellow half-mast trousers (Why?) comes to say hello. She has to know all about the Wish Mobile, and then, somewhere in the conversation, the inevitable question; What do you think of the Americans? Not, do you like America, are you having a good time here, but what do you think of the Americans – asked in the same cringing way that I have been asked this strange question many times before. Again I answer.

'All the Americans I have met so far have been very kind and helpful.'

But actually ...

Americans remind me of highly pedigreed well-groomed golden labradors: beautiful to look at, extremely friendly and helpful, but in their unbridled eagerness to please, totally unaware that their happily wagging tails are wiping all the best china off the coffee table, and in their well-meaning innocence, they have no idea who is holding their leash.

South Carolina
Bed 141

Charleston is my goal for the day, as tomorrow the Wish Mobile must be handed over to the port authorities, and I still have much administration to finalize. The day's journey is on Interstate 95, so by default there is not much to see, mainly pine trees. Turning onto R17, I drive over a shimmer of water, shaded by giant pond-cypress, bearded with Spanish moss. A sign points to a wild animal viewing area. Sounds good; any distraction will do at this point; so I turn onto a narrow track that leads directly into the swamp.

The land is slowly replaced by glassy black water, the trees crowd closer, and long strands of moss sway slowly in the heat. It has been raining here as well, and the track turns into two thin ridges surrounded by black water. A small tingle registers danger, bad idea, turn back, in my primal mind. One tiny little problem, I cannot turn, to the left of me, and to the right is mud and spooky black water. A shiver runs down my spine, I am not going in there, no way, no how, not now, not ever. Stopping is not a plan either, as the two ridges the car is balancing on immediately start to melt. Only one thing to do, reverse. This is going to be tricky. There is no room for error – one slip left or right, and I will be up to my axles in bog. I re-adjust the rearview mirrors directly onto the track behind me, and inch, by snail's pace inch, work the Wish Mobile tail first out of the swamp. When will I learn that when you are alone, the smallest slip of judgment could mean disaster.

But my memory is short, and soon I find myself on another track, which ends at a ghost house under massive trees, which spread their branches high above, like the arched span of a cathedral roof. Long strands of Spanish moss hang from above like deadman's tinsel. The house broods in its cloak of peeling paint and vine-covered walls. As I wander about in the humid silence, I can feel it watching me ... an insane urge to yell

'Scooby DOOOooo, where AAare you?'

overwhelms me. A swamp is a weird place; I don't like it much; and actually, I am done now. Time to get to Charleston, finalize this leg of the trip, and just chill.

Another unknown city, and yet again, no map. I drive up and down just being in the moment, and the moment delivers a tourist information center, brilliant. Here I book a motel room for $59, get a complimentary map, and now that I have a destination, set forth with zeal and determination to find it. While waiting my turn at the motel reception, something odd happens. A man walks in off the street, requests a room price, is quoted $109, which he negotiates down to $99. A man watching this, who had made an advance booking, and was charged $129 for the same type of room, is understandably somewhat upset. I don't mention that I paid only $59 for exactly the same room. Wouldn't want to spoil the pleasure of guy one, or upset guy two even more. Besides the rather odd shifting of room prices, the strangest thing about this is that, had guy two, of the advance booking, found the room for $59 on the Internet, he would not have booked it, believing that it was too cheap, and therefore below his standard.

Finally I know what defines the price of a hotel room. It is fear. The evening pitstop is what gives travelers the most concern. As we lower our drawers at the end of a long day, we are confronted by a basic fear of lowering our material standards, which we believe define us, which induces us to pay more for something than it is really worth. This is probably why companies that feed on fear make such a killing. Insurance companies, banks, and even the fashion industry thrive on fear. Fear is a wonderful motivator and manipulator, and this fear is actively promoted, as fearless people, whose sense of worth is grounded in meaningful values, would just tell everyone to take a very large hike.

Late afternoon I take a quick hike about the lovely streets of Charleston, at last a city with flavor, or maybe I just like the sense of history that is contained in the buildings and old cobbled streets. But I am too preoccupied with the shipment of the Wish Mobile to really enjoy the sights of Charleston, and make my way back to the motel, where I complete the last few packing chores, strap everything down, screw on the box tops, and fill in a slew of documentation.

In the morning I have three tasks: first, the shipping agent for the final bill, and while I am at it, I drag him out to write his wish. Next the bank, where I hand over the shipping invoice and my credit card, and wait and wait and wait. Finally the clerk returns, holding my card as if it has suddenly turned into a very large and slimy worm.

What's her problem?

'Madame, your card was rejected.'

A hush falls over the bank. A rejected credit card, no-o-o-o fate worse than death. I am not fazed. I checked my balances yesterday, and there are ample funds.

'I am sure it is just a technical problem. Please try the card again.'

The hush in the bank deepens.

'Madame, that will not be possible.'

The clerk replies, holding the offending card way out in front of her, as if it is the carrier of a contagious decease.

'Why is it not possible. There are sufficient funds. I need to pay this account, and I am requesting that you please attempt the card again.'

The clerk refuses, and places the offending card gingerly on the counter, as if she is afraid that it might infect the whole bank. By now I am getting my back up. I am being treated like a criminal on the basis of some piece of plastic that is not doing its credit card duty.

'Please call your manager.'

Her eyes light up. This is the best idea she has heard all day. The manager duly arrives, and I repeat my request that they try the card again, as I know there is no problem with the available funds. The manager replies in the patronizing tone of those who believe they know everything.

'Madame, your card has been rejected, and it is the policy of this bank not to further entertain a rejected card.'

The poor little card, shame, man, how cruel.

He goes on.

'I advise you to contact your bankers to see what the problem might be.'

'My bankers are in South Africa.'

'I see ... '

He is stumped for a reply, but I suddenly have an epiphany.

'Perhaps the daily limit of the card has been reached, I am trying to pay a rather large amount after all.'

The clerk and manager look at me dubiously. I warm to my subject, and perkily suggest we split the bill in half, put one half on one card, and one half on the other. The manager goes into the whole 'we cannot entertain a rejected card' explanation. So I strike a deal.

'How about you try this card first?'

I say, as I whip out a fresh card with a flourish.

'Put half the amount on this card, and if that works, well, perhaps we could try that card.'

Say I, while pointing at the forlorn little reject card, which seems to be trying to hide the shame of its credit malfunction under the plastic fern. The manager and clerk consult and, realizing that I 'ain't going nowhere' until the shipping bill has been paid, agree.

And what do you know, card one works, and then card two, buoyed by this success, works as well, and the whole bank and its clientele, who have been watching my little show in fascinated silence, can go back to their money exchange business, while I drive out to the port

... where I discover that the Wish Mobile has to wait for a week before it is shipped. I am not happy about this, but there is nothing much I can do. I do, however, get the men at the port to write wishes on the Wish Mobile, figuring that once that they are personally invested, perhaps they will keep a little eye out for the wellbeing of my traveling companion. But the crew on the ship ... well, let's hope all the good wishes have a positive influence on them too.

Once I am car-less, my energy levels plummet. I am done with America for the moment, and simply couldn't be bothered with sightseeing, so withdraw to my rooms, where I lie on the bed watching TV for hours. While mindlessly surfing the channels, it slowly dawns on me that Anne somebody or other, fat blonde ex-porn star, once married to a millionaire, died. This is huge news, all over all the news and talk shows. It seems she was very fond of drugs and drink, which may have been the cause of her death. Prime time news in America – 'drunken drug-soaked blonde bimbo dies'. Her one distinction, which gets her top news rating: she was really really rich.

While I stuff a quart of Ben & Jerry choc chip cookie dough ice-cream down my throat, I watch an editorial on diabetes. They predict that 5,000 Americans are diagnosed with diabetes per day; that is a frightening statistic. The USA Center of Disease Control figures that in one year, one million more Americans will have diabetes, because of all the sugar Americans consume, and more especially, all the corn syrup they consume. Obesity and diabetes are becoming the biggest killers in America, and the greatest strain on the medical aid system. As I watch this, a gob of cookie dough ice-cream slides down my throat, and my waistline, which is swelling like well-leavened bread, slowly bulges, white, dimpled and flabby over the top of my jeans. AAARGGG, I am being sucked into the American sugar vortex, get me out of here!!

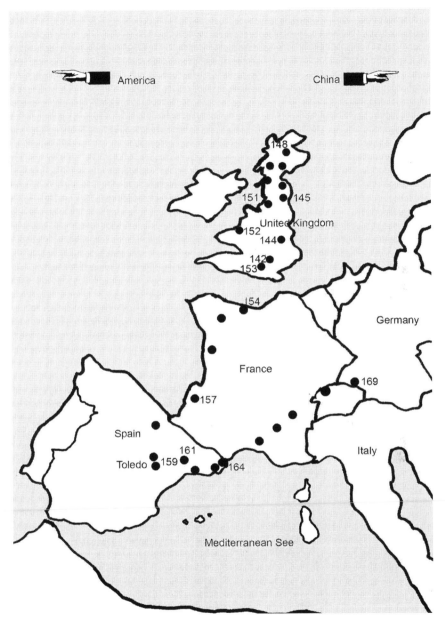

Map 7: England to Germany

United Kingdom
England
Bed 142, 143

The day of the big commute to London starts at 05h00. In the neon-lit dark, I fling my bags into the taxi, and we make our way in silence to the airport. Stepping into the bright shadowless interior of Charleston airport, I am confronted with American-style airport security for the first time in my life.

Before even getting close to the check-in counter, our baggage and person are subjected to the scrutiny of security guards. These guys do not look like the normal half-baked airport security one is accustomed to at airports, but like fully trained marines. I watch in dismay as the elderly, twin-set and pearls lady in front of me goes through the search station. Nothing so mundane as baggage x-ray here; she is required to open her suitcase, and allow the security guard to rummage through her delicates at will. And rummage he does, putting onto full public view flesh-colored D-cup brassieres, enormous bloomers, those stretchy body suits that hold your fat together, stockings, toiletries and shoes; everything is up for display. Throughout this, the little lady stares stoically straight ahead, then, when the man is done, calmly repacks her suitcase in as dignified a manner as possible.

I compare myself to the lady in front of me. I have on a leather bomber jacket, super-baggy hip-hop trousers, sneakers; my hair is shoved in a cap; and my bag is an American army haversack. Considering what the neat little lady had to go through, I could be in for a full body search. I mentally rummage through my knickers to see just how embarrassing this security check could get ... very. But the security guard just waves a magic wand thing over my baggage and over me, and that is that. I must be the most innocent-looking sort on the planet, or the army haversack won him over.

The sun rises as my first flight leaves at 07h20. Then, just after breakfast, I disembark back in Miami, where I sit quietly in a meditative trance, occasionally interspersed with a bit of writing, until 19h00, when it is time to board my flight to London. The day has passed calmly, without problems, without frustrations, without the need to DO anything.

Somewhere on my journey, I acquired the ability to simply sit, to allow my thoughts to make lazy somersaults through the midnight-blue recesses of my mind, leaving streams of glowing phosphorescent trails that fade and shift, making strange connections, and filling me with a contented silence. The most wonderful thing I have learned on this journey is the ability to still my racing mind, and I have discovered that life should be lived on a deeply intellectual level, where thinking becomes a conscious act. To think deeply, to push the boundaries, to open the mind to new possibilities, is to bring a deep sensual satisfaction to the act of thinking. It feels like a mind massage.

After a long day of massaging my mind, I am totally relaxed, chilled, in the moment, and fully Zen, as I step aboard the flight to London. It is almost empty; there are only 174 passengers in a double-decker jumbo jet. The result is that each of us has a row of seats to ourselves, so we sleep our way most comfortably across the Atlantic.

Stepping into Heathrow airport, I experience several minutes of total confusion. Where are the signs, the instructions to tell me where to walk, which direction, when, how, what to do? Then I realize that in England it is assumed that we are big boys and girls, and that we actually know what we are doing. There are no instructions here, so I reluctantly haul out my fully relaxed mind, give it a quick polish, find the on-switch, and discover that life is not so confusing after all. But squeaky-clean America is a thing of the past. Heathrow looks decidedly shabby, compared to the airports I have seen in America. It is also completely multicultural, multiracial and multilingual. I immediately feel at home in this mix of nations, and then from the babble, my ear picks out Afrikaans. Now there is a language I have not heard in a while. Before I have time to source the origin of the Afrikaans, I hear the distinctive plummy tones of dear friend Sharon.

Annette ! Welcome!

We hug; she looks me over

You haven't changed a bit!

Oh?

Back in her kitchen in Kingston upon Thames, we sit about, sipping wine, and yakkedy, yakkedy, yak, while Ralph cooks up a storm. A complete foody, and enthusiastic cook of real food, he fusses over the steaming pots, while Sharon opens another bottle, and I unleash a torrent of information. I simply cannot stop talking, and have a very disturbing image of myself with a blue-black flood of words shooting out of my wide-open mouth.

The worst part of all of this is that some time back I felt the sadness of ignorance lost – not that I am any more enlightened. It is more a case of knowing the deep unshakable truth that I am completely ignorant. What it is, is a loss of ignorance of my ignorance ... if you get my drift. I am painfully aware that every time I say something, I am probably spouting forth complete rot. That blissful ignorance of being able to juddah juddah, without giving a thought to the validity of my utterings, is irrevocably gone. Yet I cannot seem to stop talking. Fortunately Sharon and Ralph are indulgent friends, and only now and then nudge me back onto the straight and narrow. For this, I am grateful. I feel I am turning into an insufferable bore. I really need some downtime to digest all this information I have banging about in my head.

Fortunately, there will be plenty of time for that soon, as the friends are off to Cape Town, and I will have their house to myself for a month, while the Wish Mobile makes its way across the Atlantic. But first, England is experiencing a very early spring, and the English know well to make use of every bit of sunshine. Sights must be seen, and on the agenda is a walk in the park.

In this country of kings and queens, it is not just any old park, but Richmond Park, a park that has been recognized as such since the early 12th century, and has been a royal hunting ground since the 15th century. Today it is an area of special interest, both for its nature and its history, and it is still home to great herds of red and fallow deer, as well as masses of waterfowl and the odd parakeet. Apparently the parakeets are the descendants of the feathered extras that were used in the making of the film *African Queen*, and escaped, or were set free, no one knows for sure, but now sightings of bright green parakeets are quite common in Richmond Park.

A trip to Oxford is next on the must-see list. It is about an hour's drive away, so I offer to pay for the fuel, and am shocked at the price of it: 99 p/l sounds like a deal? Do the conversion: it explains why the English like to walk, and why vehicles of the American gas-guzzling sort are extremely rare beasts here. Economical fuel consumption must be top of the priority list when deciding to buy a car in England. I give silent thanks that the Wish Mobile falls squarely into that category, and that the British Isles are small. The fuel bill here promises to be rather steep.

'Pleb' that I am, I have never actually given Oxford any thought at all. I have a dim awareness that it is a seat of ancient learning, where the privileged young English gentlemen and ladies go to obtain their degrees. What I discover is that the city of Oxford is a dense drop of English history and superlatives. Some form of education was undertaken here as far back as the 11th century. It is the oldest university in the English-speaking world, and the second oldest in the world. It is one of the world's 'golden' brands. It has produced 26 British prime ministers, 12 saints, 20 bishops of Canterbury, and countless authors, actors, actresses, and diverse other famous persons. It has been the setting for several well-known books, from as far back as 1400, including Chaucer's *Canterbury tales*, and most recently, the dining hall of Christchurch College was the setting of the dining room, as seen in all the Harry Potter films. This is the great tourist attraction of the moment, so we too wander through the hallowed halls of Harry Potter – another completely unexpected moment, to walk where Dumbledore walked, such exalted stuff.

I am just a touch jealous of those who have the opportunity to study here, and cannot imagine anybody failing to get straight As. Studying in a place like this, it must simply inspire one to greatness. But then the English, being constantly surrounded by all this grand history, are understandably rather ho-hum about it all.

The week draws to a close, and for the first time in a long time I am the one to stay behind, as my friends leap aboard an airplane and wing their way south. Alone again ... bliss.

But not really. I am very unsettled, my sleep disturbed by nightmares every night. To nip this unfortunate development in the bud, I put myself on a strict detox diet, and slowly wean myself off sugar, to which I seem to have become quite addicted. I sleep late, sleep at midday, go to bed early. What is this? Just no enthusiasm. Get a grip, girl. After three days of fresh vegetables and lots of water, I feel my energy building, and then, one bright morning, I wake up with the clear knowledge that all is well again with the body of Annette. But not with my future plans.

An email informs me that the Wish Mobile will only make landfall around 8 March. This is two weeks later than anticipated, and puts a bit of a stop to my immediate plans. It also forces me to rethink my plans to travel as far south as Lisbon. France is huge, so is Spain, and it's a heck of a detour. Perhaps I should just do the Low Countries and be satisfied with that.

A 'clip-clop' draws my attention. Through the rain-streaked window, I watch a black horse with white plumes, pulling a hearse to the graveyard just across the way. The driver, with top hat, whip and spats, guides the glass carriage with mahogany coffin through the gate to its final destination. One black stretch limousine follows, while black crows watch from the moss-covered gravestones a black cat brings death to the squirrels' game of catch. A break in the clouds releases a rainbow, and the graveyard glows golden green. Rain or shine seems to be the choice I need to make ... sunshine, and Spain it is. Back to the computer, and the paperwork, work, work. The last few weeks of my journey are falling into place.

After a week of total solitude, it is really time that I stepped out. The fridge is bare, my brain is fried, and my hermitic tendencies are starting to get worrying. As my administration is up to date, it is time to venture to London. The day is dreary and wet, but in England, that is no excuse for staying indoors.

In the grey streets of London, the people are a great mass of unbridled self-expression and rainbow hues. Every nation on the planet must be represented in London, and not just in the form of a diplomat gliding about in government-sponsored comfort, but by ordinary people just living their lives. They are a so totally mixed bunch that the bus timetable booklet is printed in 12 languages. The razorblade massacre of hairdos that I thought was a particularly Asian fad is all the rage here as well. The aim is to hack into the hair to create lots of sticking-out-all-over-the-place hair on the top of your head and down to your ears, then long thinning strands down your back. It is a great good fortune that hair grows back – although judging by a bright pink Mohican on an aging punk, some folk just never change their style. Muslim girls make their headscarves look trendy, but combined with tight jeans and skinny tops, all claims to modesty must be set aside. These headscarves are now but a symbol of belonging in a multifaceted society, no more endowed with religious significance that the Mohican of the aging punk, and she who claims otherwise is a bit of a hypocrite.

The weather catches my mood. The clouds part in a small scattering of rainbows, and become great white sailing boats scudding across a crystal blue sky. Big Ben gleams freshly polished in the sunshine. Westminster Bridge is having its face lifted, and so shrouding bandages block out the view of the Houses of Parliament, but frame shabby protesters, who do their cause no justice. To try to convince that aggression is wrong by using aggression, even in speech, will not convince. The passing crowds jeer and mock, not those who kill in an unjust war, but those who protest it. Such is the way of the world.

Westminster Abbey is the church of kings, queens and a proud tradition. The dearly departed of heroic England crowd the abbeys and galleries of this great space, and are remembered by heroic marbles and flowery eulogies.

> He combined the finest mental endeavor with the best contrivance of the heart. Amongst his talents, too many to be counted here, a great orator, a defender of small children and sexy women …

and so forth and so on. In unassuming brown stone boxes lie the remains of King Edward and Henry I. In great decorative private mausoleums lie some of the less famous queens. Henry VIII lies in fabulous isolated splendor in a hall with spanned roof and a multitude of flags. A nifty little mirrored table in the centre of this highly decorated space enables one to look down in order to look up, and suddenly I remember the water wells in Moldova. What odd connections the mind makes. Elizabeth I lies under a marble rendition of her dead self, still attended by her chambermaids. Hopefully, these were allowed to live out their lives before being interred here. Their families must still be proud of this grand distinction. Oh, yes, my Great-, Great-, Great-, Great-Aunt Mildred lies at the foot of Elizabeth, don't you know.

After a few hours of tombstone reading, and surreptitious photo sneaking, for which I get sternly reprimanded, I walk into the light, and into the bustle of Victoria Street. To the palace, to the palace. I have urgent business with the queen, as do throngs of others. Buckingham Place is really not much to look at from the outside, and staring at motionless guards with funny hats is not my idea of a good time. Onward, onward, through St James Park and into Mayfair, where the Savile Row suits and high-end haircuts live. I have been having a bad-hair-year, and here it becomes embarrassingly obvious. I am under-dressed and under-groomed, and that just for walking down the street. When I decide to step into a gallery with only Chagall originals on display, the gallerist asks if I am all right, in a tone that hints I need serious help in the styling department. Too true, but not today, André. The doorman looks down his nose at me, so I look him square in the eye, and burst out laughing at his snooty expression. In my opinion, judging a book by its cover gives serious doubt to your literacy levels.

I plough my way through the slick and stylish, past Bentley and Rolls Royce dealerships, past chauffeur-driven cars that idle at chic restaurants, full of the beautiful people pushing their beautiful food about. Turning a corner, I am at Oxford Circus, and what a circus it is. Gone are the well-to-do, the silent hush, the slick hairdo. Here all the world is a stage, and all the actors are relishing their moment in the sun.

The street fashion is inspirational. Guys, girls, young and old, everybody is strutting their stuff. Miniskirts, lots of leg and boots is the name of the game. I pass a young Indian couple, from India, or so I presume, having a little lovers' spat. As I close in, I expect to hear English or some Hindi dialect, but, no, they are having it out in fluent German. Globalization at street level. The energy radiating from every angle vibrates in the air. I think I see the future here, or a pretty good version of it; the languages, the faces, the hues and shades of us all are invigorating and exciting.

But I am in pain, no walking in America for months, and now six hours' solid. My knees doth protest. I arrive back at Waterloo Station in time for the rush hour. In this great hall of light, tourists with backpacks stare at the spinning numbers on giant overhead display boards that indicate which one of the many platforms will take them to their destinations. The daily commuters weave through the stationary mass, to make their trains with split-second timing, coffee in hand, and newspaper under arm.

I too have a newspaper, and spend my time on the train reading about the world news, and very depressing it is too. Far more interesting is a tiny advertisement for volunteers to lay hedges. British Environment Trust is involved in all sorts of practical environmental protection and enhancement projects: in this case, maintaining hedges in an urban environment, as the hedges provide flight paths for birds, and habitat for the local small game. Volunteers muck in by providing the muscle to make the projects a reality. In exchange, they get fresh air, good exercise, camaraderie, a sense of achievement, a cup of tea, and a rather nice biscuit or two. To partake, I should be at House Park at 08h00 tomorrow morning. Right ho, then; time to discover how one goes about laying a hedge.

To get to House Park, I must travel from one side of Kingston to the other, as it is some distance, and because I am a touch late, I decide to do so by bicycle – a mode of transportation with which I am as unfamiliar, as I am with the streets of Kingston, so find myself wobbling up, down, under, through, around and about this ancient settlement, in complete confusion, but do finally get to see the local sights.

Kingston upon Thames was once occupied by the Romans, and there is a record of a council held there in 838, at which Egbert of Wessex, the first king of All-England was present. It is a lovely little place, built at the first crossing point of the Thames, upstream from London Bridge, and you can still cross a bridge, Kingston Bridge, at the same point today. From those early days, the town was the farmstead for the kings, and with the building of Hampton Court Palace, and the subsequent take-over of it by Henry VIII, it remained that for many a year. Today a market still exists on the market square, but it is given fierce competition by Marks and Spencer's and Sainsbury's, which now also call this borough home, along with the whole united nations of locals.

I finally make it across Kingston Bridge, turn left into the gates of House Park, just in time to join the merry band of volunteers, pulling on gumboots, and sloshing through a muddy meadow to the hedge that must be laid. While an overly friendly carthorse sniffs at my hair, I learn about the ancient art of hedge laying.

What we have in front of us are two rows of closely planted young hawthorns, with great big thorns. They are all growing upright, as trees should, but that is not the way of a hedge; these trees must be made to lie down. What this involves is first getting rid of all unnecessary branches, which is the reason the horses are so friendly. In this unseasonably warm weather, the highest branches are covered in buds and blossom, which normally the horses couldn't reach, but now we are laying them at their feet. Once the trees have been trimmed, the fun part starts. The base of the tree needs to be thinned on one side, until the tree bends over naturally, and lies down. But one must be careful to maintain enough bark on the thinned trunk, so that the tree does not die, yet has plenty of 'open wound', from which new risers will shoot, thereby creating a dense hedge. This thinning is done with a vicious-looking instrument called a billhook, and if the tree is skinny, an easy enough task. But this hedge should have been laid ages ago, so the trees are a bit large, and the task soul destroying. While your soul is being destroyed, your hands are feeling the pain, and the trees, I am sure, are not too happy either. To make the pain more bearable, we get tea from a billycan, and a couple of very nice biscuits. Billhook? Billycan? Billygoat ... Who on earth was Bill? I contemplate the mysterious Bill, while laying into another few trees, but overdo the hedge laying totally, and have to pop painkillers in the middle of the night to still aching hands, as sleep will not come.

My plans to paint a mural, as part of my house-sitting chores, are thwarted, owing to my enthusiastic hacking at hedges. My hands are stiff, sore and covered in blisters, the *pain*. But after my New York experience, I know what to do when not feeling too well – go look at modern art; it is always good for a laugh. So off to Tate Modern, as I am enticed by the thought of sliding around on some art. Given my take on art, this touchy-feeling participation appeals. But I admit to some disappointment. The silver and Perspex slides are very high, this is sure, but they are direct rip-offs of the slides that I saw in every up-market playground in Northern Germany. Perhaps the 'artist' designs playground slides for a living, and this Tate gig is his big breakthrough into the art world. One never can tell.

Perhaps the actual slide construction is not the artwork, but the 'experience' of sliding is. If this is the case, I decide I shall film my 'experience' going down this silver tunnel.

'Not so fast,'

says the chap on the stool, who is employed to ensure that we all do the slide thing correctly.

'No photography.'

He refuses to allow me my 'experience' until the camera is stowed. I think that if the art part of the work is my personal experience, then surely I have the right to film this experience, as it is mine. But I can tell that to have this esoteric discussion with a chap on a stool, while I am sitting in a silver tube with my legs wrapped in a giant tea towel, will bring nothing of value. So I push myself into the tube, and zoom down to ground floor in a very small spiral. It's a fast, round and round, bumpy experience ... a roller coaster is better.

Wandering through the rest of the gallery, the Gilbert & George Exhibition appeals, merely because of the irreverent and playfulness of the authors. But the Martin Creed, creed of 'I want to make the statement, but I don't' leaves me cold. This guy has serious issues with making decisions. I watch the faces of the public, stepping out of the 'light on and off' room. They are blank masks. No word is spoken. Is this a sign of silent reverie in the presence of greatness? Or simply one of complete incomprehension, and the fear of seeming stupid if an opinion expressed might stand in opposition to the great reputation of this artist, and the fact that this piece won for him the Turner prize. I think Turner would turn in his grave if he knew what his name now represented in the world of art.

Art without purpose is like a human without purpose. It sinks into slow degradation. Picasso with his statement that his art needed to make no sense in a senseless world opened a Pandora's Box that allowed art to become meaningless. Contemporary art leads the public on a merry chase of the said and unsaid, by using mangled philosophies – expressed in words with far too many syllables – to describe meaning that is not there. But in order to try and understand, I step into the undecided room, and open my mind to the experience. I meditate quietly, as the light goes off, then comes on, and goes off, and comes on. I employ all my senses to try to find some sense of achievement in this piece, but the magic eludes me. All the while, I have in the back of my mind the knowledge that the public has been proven wrong in rejecting a host of artists that presented a new way of seeing in the past, and I could be missing something quite fundamental. But then I console myself that we – Mr and Mrs Joe Public – have also made vast advancements in our way of seeing the world, with the endless stream of visual stimulation that we are accustomed to processing every day, so I am quite happy to say I don't get it, and feel no further need to try.

I am amused by a giant shiny copper box, which is protected by the usual

'Do not touch'

signs, which are directly protested by the green fingerprints that decorate the rim of this thing. The thing I like most about Tate Modern is the space. Great white stretches of wall are flooded by soft light. It seems a shame to have to hang 'art' onto them.

To get a more contemporary view of London, I decide to visit Camden Markets. Camden Town Main Street is the closest thing to Asian street energy I have found since leaving Taiwan, enhanced here with a quirky eccentric sense of personal expression. With young girls, black leggings, miniskirts of the 'isn't that actually meant to be a sweater' variety, or hot pants with shiny belts, boots and short coats are all the rage. Punks in tartan tights, topped by yellow Mohicans, try to control their hangovers by hiding in a telephone booth. Goths, all in black, with deathly pale faces, float serenely through the crowd. The S&M followers, joined by their lip-piercing, need no umbrella; their clothing is slick, waterproof black. The facades of the shops that cater to these folk are an eclectic display of fiberglass art, with spiders, boots, ghouls and ghosts, bugs, whips, chains and all things fetish.

Those of Asian origin fit right in. This is just like home. They dominate the food stalls, where pretty young things entice customers to try their wares. In the open-air market, hundreds of independent designers flog their creations. This is shopping heaven for the cutting-edge fashionista, and we all bop along to the heavy thumping backbeat that emanates from every shop and stall, making Camden Town so very festive that I get so caught up in the energetic spectacle of the place that I quite forget the time.

Daytime is nearly over by the time I make it back onto the very efficient London public transport. The tube is a good reflection of the area you are in. The commuters in Camden Town station are a mix of young backpackers and locals, dressed in every nuance of fashion. Opposite me sits a girl-woman, just at the clubbing sell-by date, but still hanging in there. Her chinless-wonder boyfriend wears a porkpie hat, too short skinny check trousers, a preppy blazer, and great clunking shoes. She has jet-black hair, Goth pale face, and wears a green mini dress and fishnets. Not the black, heavy, stripper variety, her stockings are delicate nude fishnets, more fish-scale stocking, in a golden shade. But she finds the metro seating uncomfortable, heaves her legs up onto the seat, thereby giving me a full view of her pasty inner thigh, which bulges out of a great ragged tear in the delicate stocking, shocking sight, fortunately obscured every now and again by the young men passing cans of beer back and forth down the aisle. This loud group of men perfume the air with beery sweat. They are not bad-looking fellows, just a tad pissed. They are accompanied by a lovely lass of the blonde English rose variety, who is unfortunately not altogether sober either, and insists in sticking out a very furry tongue to make known her displeasure at the world. Just then, a host of angels come to herald my stop. I prepare to follow them up into the light, but they blow their cover, when they step onto the escalator, instead of simply unfolding their wings to fly away. I knew it was too good to be true.

The train that takes me out to the suburbs is inhabited by large families, blue-rinse ladies, groups of girls, and single young men. The scowling young men, who probably wish they were on the Camden line, come and go in sullen silence. The girls shriek, giggle and whisper, the old ladies look worried and sad, and the families sit in silence. Because of inattention, I miss my station, and in the dark must now disembark in the middle of Kingston upon Thames. The rain is pouring down. I have no umbrella. I have never been here before, and I have no map to show me my way 'home'. I wander aimlessly through the dark and empty streets, hoping for a little miracle. It comes in the form of a familiar street corner, and with aching knees, I make my way 'home' in the wind and the rain. Life is tough sometimes, but there is always a silver lining.

I wake up to the happy news that the Wish Mobile has been granted entry into England. Hurray! Time to be reunited with my little car. I am so excited! Some people get emotionally attached to their dogs; I am emotionally attached to my car, my little mechanical traveling companion. Far more useful than a dog – can't drive a dog around the world.

It's a long commute by train from Kingston to Southampton, with much changing of trains, and hanging about at stations. But with my laptop at hand I feel quite the working girl, typing away as the scenery rushes by outside.

At Southampton it is a matter of handing over a wad of cash to the shipping agent. In exchange, he gives me a release form, and tells me to walk across the road, and just pick up the car, nothing to it. I stride confidently into Southampton harbor, and I stride and stride and sweat and stride. The place is huge; it is the largest car-handling port in Britain. I stride past trucks, past tractors, past sedans, and past SUVs, but there is no Wish Mobile to be seen. Slowly panic starts rising. I have been trawling the harbor for ages. There is no office and no one to ask. This cannot be the way of it. What is the system here? A reliance on chivalry, it seems. A knight in a pick-up sees my distress, pulls up his rusty steed, and after establishing that we have an African connection – he is from Zimbabwe – my hero feels it is his absolute duty to reunite me with the Wish Mobile. But even with an insider's help, this is not an easy task. We drive here, ask directions there, and make u-turns everywhere. We drive up, down, in and out of several gated areas, and everywhere, cars, cars and more cars. I am getting just a touch concerned; this is like finding a needle in a haystack. Fortunately, my needle is very conspicuous, and a call to the loading centre brings the answer,

'Oh, yes, the car with the writing is in bay F14.'

Sure enough, I am finally reunited with my now somewhat hairy, car. It seems the ship's cat felt that my car was the most comfy spot on the ship, and left half its fur behind as a thank-you present. Hairy car starts immediately, and we are off!

With one slight adjustment to make, I am now driving on the left of the road, with a right-hand-drive vehicle. To prevent any unnecessary mishaps with the oncoming traffic, I drive through Southampton, chanting loudly to myself, keep left, pass right, keep left, pass right. Unfortunately with the steering being on the 'wrong' side, I cannot see past the trucks to overtake, so this is sure to be a test of patience on the narrow country roads that take me past houses of red brick, with steeply sloping roofs. It suddenly strikes me that this architecture is the real thing: no faux Georgian, Victorian or Tudor.

These houses were actually built at the time that these styles were fashionable. The houses give way to green fields, where a crooked sign points to 'No man's land' and 'The hidden pond': it all sounds very mysterious. Then my keep-left, pass-right chant gets in a muddle, and I am keeping right, passing left. The oncoming cars find this very upsetting, and blow their horns with loud indignation.

My immediate destination is Stonehenge, which sits in the middle of a rounded flattish elevation called Salisbury Plain. While the English like to call this a great plain, I feel it is giving the space too much credit, although in the confines of the English landscape, it is a fairly large, flattish space, in the centre of which the famous stones demand attention. But years of unruly tourists have limited the access to the henge to a distance of ten to twenty meters all round. Standing in the magic circle is forbidden. The crows now have the best seats in the house. I do the obligatory circuit around the stones, with the audio guide chatting away amiably in my ear. Despite the best efforts of the audio guide, it cannot conceal the fact that really no one has a clue why this circle of stone was constructed, or how it was done.

All agree, though, that this site has had many centuries of cultural significance, as the stones are 'henge version three', the first henge, constructed around 5,000 years ago, being but a ditch, and the second henge a blue stone construct. Astronomers have given the current stone construction an interplanetary significance, as the sun, moon and stars line up with various stones at various times of the year (seems inevitable). What is disappointing is that the silence that must once have been part of the allure and mystery of this spot is completely obliterated by the incredibly busy roads that hem it in all sides. Circuit completed, the setting sun sends me 'home' to Kingston, past dairy-bell cows and black-faced sheep that graze in the fields surrounding the henge.

But enough with the walking. My knees are not in top form, and I am looking forward to road tripping once again.

England East

Bed 144

Waking early to miss the rush hour, I stumble bleary eyed and in my birthday suit to the bathroom. Watching me with great mournful eyes is an owl. I close the bathroom door behind me...? Wake up … let's play that again. Opening the bathroom door, I look out, and indeed there it is, a white and tan barn owl, looking at me with black eyes that reflect all the sorrows of the world. I realize that I am without a stitch of clothing, and that this could well be the cause of the poor owl's distress. Sneaking to the bedroom, I drag on some clothes, and present myself to the owl again. The owl has nodded off, but sensing my presence, glares accusingly from hooded eyes. I am overwhelmed by guilt at disturbing its sleep. Good grief, it is too early in the morning to feel guilty, and that by an owl who has decided that the best resting spot for the day is the window ledge, just at the staircase landing, past which I have no choice but to go, unless I fling myself headfirst over the balustrade. We engage in a small battle of wills. The owl out-stares me. Defeated, I leopard-crawl past the window, silently sliding all my gear downstairs, while the owl keeps a very close hooded watch on me. Finally it is done, the owl sleeps, and I head direction Scotland via Cambridge.

The price of fuel in England is shocking. It costs me £38 to fill up my tank. The fuel here is three times as much as the USA, China or South Africa. Thank goodness this island is small, and my time here limited. I imagine England is the only place on earth where the question of how many miles per liter makes sense. They really cannot decide which side of the metric fence they are on. The M25, the orbital road around London, is very busy, and moves at speed. The English driver is far more aggressive than the American, or perhaps I am just not quite comfortable with driving on the left yet. Also, I am not yet sure how wide awake the English are behind the wheel, but they do keep left most beautifully, though, at times there are no cars at all in the middle and fast lanes, but then the English are known for their love of the queue.

The Owl

My bed for the evening is the home of Vicky from 5W, who does research at the University of Cambridge. This university was first established around 1209, so once again the history of the place is overwhelming. Vicky is a very political animal, and the conversation moves to the international arms trade. I imagine this is a very need-to-know topic, and rather depressing. She does let fall the tantalizing tidbit that should the queen or other high-ranking royal be seen visiting some far-flung forgotten corner of the planet, it is usually a sure sign that England has just flogged a huge arms pile to that hapless nation. The world of arms deals would make the blackest comedy ever. We sell arms to you, then pick a fight with you, go to war against you, allowing the weapons we manufactured to be used to kill our soldiers. This generates more business, so we sell you more weapons, and just to make sure the profits keep ticking over, we send a couple more of our soldiers along to keep the war going for just a little longer.

This is a perfect example of the perversion that the Hegelian dialect 'to play both sides against the middle' has become. Conspiracy author Texe Marrs once said that if one understood this simple fact, one would understand all of history. It certainly makes me understand why, despite that, nearly every wish on the Wish Mobile asks for peace, love, tolerance and no war ... we just do not seem to ever get to that much-wished-for state.

In 1967 Dial Press printed the 'Report from Iron Mountain'. The report was the result of a study of the 'problems' of long-term peace. The conclusion of the report was that war is necessary and desirable to control human society, and has been used successfully as such for centuries. To quote just two justifications the report set out for the necessity of war:

> War has served as the last great safeguard against the elimination of necessary social classes.

> War provides means to deal with the antisocial elements of society through the selective service system.

The report states that if war as a system of control were removed, an alternative system would need to be found to replace the 'functions of war'. While war is an excellent means of controlling us through fear and doubt, it is also the most profitable enterprise that we ever invented. To get to the happy state of world peace, love and tolerance, it seems to me, we really need to work on making peace profitable, and on our own self-control

Before the conversation gets too depressing, we start sharing travel stories, discover that the world is still a wonderful and inspiring place, and my final thought for the day takes me back to the owl on the windowsill. An owl might have a very small brain, but perhaps it is better to have a small but fully functional brain, where all faculties work together with elegance of purpose, than a big brain, of which only an owl-size portion is used, and the rest is clutter.

Bed 145

Early morning traffic in Cambridge is a mix of the ruddy-faced youth of England with the not-so-ruddy faces of the rest of the world, a whole United Nations on bicycles. They cycle to their colleges through lanes of trees, dressed in soft spring leaves, and past green meadows lined by daffodils. I turn into the back entrance of King's College, over a small bridge, and through beautiful wrought-iron gates, where I wouldn't be surprised to see a nobleman's carriage drive by. King's College is set in a park on the River Cam, which is where the name Cam-bridge comes from. I leave these privileged students behind, as I head north on the A14, past trees and hedges covered in blossoms. The petals float down like snow, covering the pavements in pink and white. My destination this morning, Sherwood Forest.

This area has been forested since the last Ice Age, and a silent walk through still-bare trees brings me to the granddaddy of this forest, the Major Oak. At between 800 and 1,000 years old, this is said to be the actual tree where that hero, or bandit, depending on your point of view, gathered his merry men to plan the raids on the carriages that passed through here. That was a time of crippling taxes, and unfair wealth distribution. Some things have not changed in merry old England. We forget that change does not equal progress, and as long as we just change for the sake of change, without progressive goals, we are doomed to live in constant cycles. The biggest hindrance against permanent change for the better is that each of us must change first, before we can expect 'them' or 'it' to change, and to change ourselves is very difficult.

The wind whispers through the trees; the sun slants over the daffodils in pale green glades. Caught in silent contemplation, I walk past burnt-out tree trunks, and under the skeleton shadows of ancient trees. Their gnarled and twisted limbs tease the imagination. They could be friend or foe. At night, this place must be spooky, and the mythical fear that Sherwood Forest evoked in its heyday well earned.

After gaining some distance on the A1, I turn off toward Thirsk, to take a drive through the North York Moors National Park. From flat meadows, the road climbs at an impossible gradient, revealing the gently rolling landscape of central England, clad in a medley of soft greens. In England, a national park is a historical preservation area, in which people continue to live, but which they may not develop. I notice for the first time that the electrical pylons that mar the scenery almost everywhere on the planet are missing here. The rural scene is virtually unblemished, and the small villages beautifully preserved. At Helmsley, a ruined castle looms on the hill. An imposing church tower dominates the quaint skyline, above tightly packed red-roofed houses, built from the local golden stone. In a small brook, ducks float tail up looking for lunch, while I look for lunch in the market square, where farmers' stalls sell full country flavor.

Each new village is a charming and delightful arrangement of cottages, houses, church spires, and tiny shops, fronting onto cobbled streets. I get the feeling that the village planners of old were in a competition to outdo their neighboring villages in creating quaint English charm, ensuring that their villages would be picture perfect from every angle. Pity about the pheasants: these birds do not seem very bright, as they are dead and squashed everywhere on the roads of England.

Golden light floods the valley of Durham and Tyne as I approach Lanchester, where I will be staying with 5W Janet and her five cats. Here I reflect on the difference in reception that I have received in England from that in America. In America it was immediately a big bear hug; hail, fellow, well met. In England, my welcomes have been enthusiastic and friendly, but restrained. No hugs, not even a handshake, no touchy-feely here, although the Friday night fish fry seems to be a common thread, and a good excuse to have some greasy battered fish, with a pile of really good chips. Over dinner we discuss our past travel adventures and tomorrow's plans. Janet has organized a private tour through Durham Cathedral.

The cathedral, which today is a world heritage site, and 'one of Britain's favorite buildings', started off in 995 as a shrine to St Cuthbert. St Cuthbert's claim to fame was that, according to legend, his corpse never rotted. This is a very fortunate thing indeed, as his corpse was dragged from pillar to post for around 300 years, before the monks finally decided that he should be laid to rest (never was the term more appropriate) right here in the loop of the River Wear in Durham. They built a little chapel, 'the white church', which remained until 1026, then the Normans got in on the act. They built this giant stone cathedral, which is the greatest Norman building in all England, and possibly all of Europe. They also built the adjoining castle, which now houses the University of Durham.

In the village of Lanchester, I stock up on provisions, bananas, carrots, and McVities biscuits, having developed a rather unhealthy fondness for this particular chocolate-covered digestive. In my absence, the Wish Mobile has attracted the attention of a group of bored young lads. They lean and drape themselves over a backyard dry-stone wall, with fags hanging out of rosebud mouths, and skullcaps pulled low over porcelain brows. They are excited about the car in an understated, cool kind of way. Brilliant idea, say they, the youth of England's north. I am inordinately chuffed that they should think so.

Bed 146

My destination is Hadrian's Wall, via the R689, through the Pennines, an area that has been officially declared to be of outstanding natural beauty, and it is. Black clouds crowd the hilltops; the sun sends silver light shavings just under the dark mass; the light catches on the rough edges of the dry-stone walls, which parcel out the gently rolling land. Sheep graze on pale green grass, dotted with daffodils that shimmer electric yellow against rough grey stone, and people with ginger red hair say hello. Their children peer at me with wide sky-blue eyes above rosy cheeks, set in pale fair skins.

The weather, however beautiful the light, is in a very precarious frame of mind. High in the Pennines, the sun loses its battle with the blue grey clouds. The pale yellow grass of the moors of Alston fades to grey in the rolling mist that slowly covers the mountains. At 300 m above sea level, Alston is one of the highest towns in England, and by definition, England is fairly flat. I stop for a walkabout in this ancient settlement, where the first evidence of human activity is dated to 2000 BCE.

The stone houses are so well settled in the landscape that deep green moss and pale green lichens vie for position on their grey walls. Bright red doors bring cheerful relief from the leaden sky and stone in these gloomy parts of England. I am decidedly gloomy each time I need to fill up with fuel. It comes as a cruel blow to my now completely disabled budget. It's on a life support system at the moment, and only the barest essentials are being afforded.

Somewhere near Acomb, I take a wrong turn, and drive right off my map into deep rural England, where the roads are narrow and tightly contained by dry-stone walls. Hemmed in by the rough stone walls, I cannot see my way forward, I don't want to go back, and am not sure if I want to turn either left or right. To get an overview of my situation, I clamber onto the Wish Mobile roof. Through the rain and fog, glimpses of far vistas are visible. There are narrow lanes crisscrossing the landscape, but this is not the moment to get too adventurous. These English lanes are a nightmare of twists and turns, and as the map is of no help, I carefully reverse my route, until once again the map and road are in agreement.

The rain paints the world dark grey. In the distance, the red cape of a Roman legionary is a brilliant beacon in the dull light. Then two more legionaries appear. They cycle slowly by, their red capes flapping in the wind ... mystifying. In the gloom, the Twice Brewed Inn is a welcome sight. The interior is an English cozy of dark wood, floral prints, and squashy cushions, around a crackling fire. The young girl behind the bar counter quotes me £48 per night, double room, no bathroom. I am amazed at the price, and when I see the room, burst out laughing. All the most basic America motel standards fly out of the window. The room is tiny; the bed is tiny. Two people in that? Let's hope they are still on honeymoon. The décor is a sad, pale floral affair. There is no desk, no wifi, no TV, and the shared bathroom? It won't be used. Well, let's see what breakfast brings.

Breakfast is a full English revelation: bacon, sausages eggs, tomatoes, hash browns, cereal, toast, jam, tea. I eat enough to keep me going all day, pig, but I feel obliged to get value for my money, considering the price of the room. But in the end the room charge comes to only £28. Perhaps they had a rethink after my incredulous mirth of the night before. So I got my money's worth, and then some. I should try laughing loudly at outrageous prices more often.

This morning the rain and fog have been replaced by a wind that tears at my clothing, and rips the Wish Mobile door from my grip. The clouds scud fearsome fast across the blue-grey sky. I had better walk Hadrian's Wall pretty smartly, as the weather looks about to make a turn for the worse. At Steel Rigg, which is part of the National Trust trails, I park the Wish Mobile as far away from the trees as possible: this is a tree-felling wind. Consulting the public map, I decide on my route, and set off over moorland and stile. Great flagstones keep my feet dry as I cross watery grassland, then heave my aching knees up steep uneven steps, hewn out of solid rock, as the wind howls and tears across the stubby grass. I mentally put weights on my feet to prevent the wind from tripping me up as I climb down the precarious cliff. Leaning forward against the gale at a 45-degree angle, it occurs to me that if the wind stopped now, I would tumble to my doom.

Built under order of Roman Emperor Hadrian, back in 122 CE, as a border to demarcate the northern-most border of the Roman Empire, Hadrian's Wall spans the narrow waist of England from the Irish to the North Sea. At between 1.8 and 3 meters wide, and with a once-upon-a-time height of 5–6 meters (now only about 1.8 m) it is still a very impressive and very neat construction. With its bread-loaf-shaped stones, it is completely unlike the random construction of the dry-stone walls of the surrounding farmlands. I follow the wall onto a cliff, high above a disused quarry, which is now a watery refuge for swans and a multitude of ducks. On a distant field, the spotlight sun etches a farmer, ploughing his land on a bright red tractor, against the black sky. Gulls wheel white against the clouds, diving to feed on the plough's harvest of worms.

Long-haired black-faced sheep and black birds share the brilliant green unploughed fields. It is lambing time in Hadrian's Wall country. The lambs dropped just yesterday, judging by their size, brilliant white coats, and still wobbly walk. Happy little sheep live in England, all seeming to roam about more or less as they please; green juicy grass to chew on wherever they look; and just to make sure they should never feel the rumble of hunger, farmers put out hay feeds as well. The wall leads up onto a high grassy hill, where the wind punches at my back, trips up my ankles, and generally behaves in a most unruly fashion. This is ridiculous. I had intended to walk to Housesteads Fort, the best preserved of the many forts that mark the wall at one-Roman-mile intervals. But with the wind in such an uncouth mood that it forces older walkers to slide down the steep stairs on their bottoms, to avoid being swept across the faraway land, and where walking along the cliff has become a matter of living stupidly, it is time to call it a day. Hip, hip, hurray, cry my aching knees. I have been determinedly ignoring their cries of mercy and pain, as they slowly lost the battle against the wind. It is time to rest the knees, and put the Wish Mobile back to work.

A hiker comes over. He has something to say, and in the howling wind, the 'One Planet One People' project grows by one more piece of wisdom, as Peter writes.

'Live simply so that others may simply live.'
Gandhi

Scotland

Bed 147

The sky is low and leaden, the scudding clouds now a solid mass, grey stone walls hem me in, sheep and sheep, on and on; the road rises and falls to the will of the land; and the rain sets in. Then a sign declares that this area is the emptiest, most uninhabited, wildest place in England. While it is empty, to my eyes it is just a tame pastoral scene. Nothing wild here. But it is incredible that after all these centuries, all the millions of people, all the comings and goings, there are still places like this in little old England –where there are just walls, sheep, moors, and not another car to be seen.

I drive through Border forest, and I am in Scotland. No great song and dance, just a little sign. On my left is a field of daffodils, bright sunshine yellow, as far as the eye can see. The dry-stone walls are replaced by hedgerows, and the world seems a lot more rugged here than the gently pastoral England. My arrival in Edinburgh is perfectly timed to coincide with the Six Nations Scotland–Ireland rugby playoff, and the city is packed. For someone who does not care a jot about ball games, I am certainly timing my arrivals with imperfect precision. I trawl the streets for a bed. Fortunately, the Scots have a good system: one road is completely given over to B&Bs. Shoulder to shoulder they stand, all fully booked, simply brilliant. Finally, after a making my way from one side of the city to the other, I approach a man on the driveway to his bed-and-breakfast mansion.

'Do you have a bed to spare?'

'Spare beds are rare tonight in Edinburgh, but you are in luck.'

Says John with the red hair.

'It will cost you £45.'

'What!?'

Say I.

'45 quid!

'Yes, but it does include enough breakfast to stop a horse.'

'I don't have a horse I want to stop. What? Are the sheets made of gold?'

Scotland: Urquhart Castle

He confesses, no, not quite gold, but gold satin. so I get five quid discount, oh joy. The room is a cheap honeymoon fantasy of golden frills on a four-poster bed. I would have preferred less on the frill side, and more on the practical wifi and desk side actually. But no matter, after trawling the sodden streets – does it ever stop raining here? – for a bite to eat. I return to my room and by George, if that frou-frou golden bed will not take issue with me. It looks at me disapprovingly, as if to say, are you actually going to sleep in me alone? What is the matter with you, you wrinkled old prune. I am a bed of golden magnificence, and only romantic couples are to sleep in me. I look that shiny, slippery bed right in the eye. Don't give me grief. I am alone. I will sleep here alone and you ... you are just an overdressed bed that is going to lie still and enjoy it.

And I am surely losing my mind ... talking to a bed ... whatever next.

Next, I would like to address all usurpers of the term 'bed and breakfast'. Come to the United Kingdom to see what bed and breakfast really is all about. You get a bed, and then you get breakfast, a real breakfast with real food. It starts with a buffet laden with jams, yoghurts, stewed fruit, creamy milk, and a selection of cereals. This is followed by a choice of hot breakfasts, presented on real china, and served at your table with a smile, and as much tea and toast as you can still find room for. I find my inner horse and tuck right in. There should be some statute of limitations on the term 'bed and breakfast', like they have on the term 'boerewors'; in order to use the name certain standards must be met.

At the neighboring table, a beautiful young couple are gazing soulfully into each other's eyes. I guess their bed had nothing to complain about last night. Red-hair John fawns around them, insisting on speaking French, although they repeatedly ask him to speak English. Is John deaf? Finally, the man states in very loud exasperated voice.

'We don't speak French. Please speak English!'

John awakes from his Frenchified daze.

'But I thought you were speaking French.'

'No, we are speaking Fazi.'

Careful John, just because you believe a thing to be so, does not make it so. Before I drive off, I invite him to write on the Wish Mobile. He has obviously been thinking about it, as there is no hesitation as he takes up the pen and writes

'Better education for all will cure the world's ills'

I wish something would cure the ills of my knees, as after that huge breakfast, I would really like to do the tourist thing, and walk about Edinburgh, but my knees are on strike. After my three hours' traipse along Hadrian's Wall, the pain is so bad that walking is no longer possible; I can barely manage to drive. But if I am to see any part of Edinburgh, drive I must. Edinburgh is a very imposing city, with a really odd smell. When I first noticed it, I thought someone was cooking porridge, lots and lots of porridge. Perhaps this is the smell of whisky in the making. While Edinburgh is second only to London in the British Isles, the wide roads remind me of Munich. It feels the same: neat, tidy and bombastic. Edinburgh did go through a Germanic phase, at which point the name received the Germanic suffix 'burgh'. This small Germanic flavor is a leftover from those days.

Edinburgh is a city where Gregorian chants do not sound out of place, so with monks chanting loudly from the depths of my sound system, I find myself in a medieval inner-city village, where the roads are narrow cobbled lanes. Rumbling out on the other side, medieval is replaced by 'evil', in a nightclub district where The Dungeon, Jekyll and Hyde Bar, and a variety of other ghoulish establishments are shuttered against the bright sun. After a long morning doing sightseeing from the car, while stuck in traffic jams, I decide that to pass the time, I might as well take photographs from the car as well. Just as I take out the camera, the traffic clears, and I get a completely traffic-free drive, with all traffic lights on green, right out of the city. Go figure.

On the outskirts of Edinburgh, fairly decent-sized freestanding houses, with high-pitched black slate roofs, and very small gardens, line the road. As I drive over the huge bridge that spans the Firth of Forth, I consider that I shall have to return to Edinburgh one day. I need to spend more time here than the five minutes than I happen to have today. In Dunfermline, I have a choice: highway or byway, no-brainer; and on the byway I head into deepest Scotland, past flowers and blossoms that herald spring, and intense velvet green meadows that give the impression of wellbeing. But then, considering that it rains here every two minutes, the green is a given. They probably have to beat the grass back with a big stick. It is not surprising that golf and the concept of greens comes from Scotland: the country is one huge natural golf course. The ground cover is either wildly green or sponge yellow moss, which contrasts sharply with the dark umber branches of the low shrubs, while the lichen on the oaks is so abundant that the trees look like abominable treemen.

The road goes through towns called Powmill, Gleneagles and Crieff. It crosses rivers called Devon, Earn, Almond and Braan, and it skims the shores of Loch Tummel, Rannoch and Tay. A lone mountain peak gleams snow-capped white against the dark clouds, which soon obscure it, and the rain falls. The rain stops; the sun comes out; rain sun rain sun rain. Describing the Scottish weather in one word is easy; changeable. I rather like it.

The on-off rain makes me happy every time the sun comes out to play with the raindrops. Together they create rainbow bridges over the road. The rain shifts, the rainbow follows, now ending between the road and the hedgerow, now just ahead, now in the road, and now on the mountaintop. No matter how fast I drive, I never can catch it. Then *phhpt* the sun vanishes, the rainbow too; in its place a flock of pink sheep. ANCHORS!! Pink sheep? Sure enough, a flock of fat pink sheep dash across the road onto an emerald green field. The rainbow returns to dips its tail into a river of indigo blue. Is this El Dorado, but where are those ingots of gold? The clouds shift, the sun vanishes, the sheep too ... just how many cups of coffee has it been today ... but no, it's been tea ... what blend, I wonder?

Ever north, the road passes mountains called Grampians and Monadhliath, onwards to Inverness, where in stop-start-stop-start traffic, I drive over the River Ness, where I find the B&B street of Inverness, but I am not ready to stop just yet. In an ink-black expanse of water, tipped with silver wavelets, a monster waits to be discovered. Loch Ness runs on a geological fault called the Great Glen. This, with the help of the Caledonian Canal, links the Moray Firth in the North Sea to the Firth of Lorn in the Atlantic. Loch Ness is a very deep (230 m) cold, dark and murky body of water, containing more fresh water than all that in England and Wales combined, so who knows ... there is certainly enough room for a monster or two.

Today fishing boats float serenely on glassy water, but the occasional wreck attests to some pretty fierce weather on these lochs, which are narrow and steeply contained by high cliffs and mountains on both sides. The wind that roars through here at times is so strong that it shifts the water level, making the water level on one side of the loch higher than the other. This is not physically sustainable, so at regular intervals the water flows back to an even water table, creating strange waves and ripples, which some say gave rise to the monster rumor in the first place. All around the loch there are light-filled open forests, where the moss glows electric green. This is a land of water. It squelches out of the ground with every footstep; it rushes down the mountains and under the roads, keeping the many lochs in the fresh water business.

Bed 148

As the daylight fades, I find myself in the town square of Drumnadrochit, just a few kilometers from Urquhart Castle, the place from which most Loch Ness Monster sightings are recorded. This is the ideal spot from which to launch my own monster-spotting expedition. In a small white-washed cottage, I find my room for the night, and, after a good night's rest, am ready to start the day with yet another monster breakfast. I am quite enamored of the bed and breakfast establishments of the United Kingdom. After such a huge breakfast, I have no further need for sustenance the entire day, other than tea and McVities biscuits.

Setting off to find myself that monster, I hang about overlooking Urquhart Castle for a half a hour, and then decide that life is short, and should the monster ever be found, I will be sure to catch it on TV. As I follow the steep shores of lochs Ness, Lochy and Ell, it starts raining ... again. Through the misty rain, I spy the high snowy peaks of Ben Nevis. The clouds part to allow narrow sunbeams through gossamer veils of rain. Rainbows are revealed and concealed, as I drive the tiny winding road into Glen Nevis. Here black Angus cattle graze on rolling green meadows, and the mountains crowd out the sun. The road climbs into a cloud, where the water hangs in the still air, making its way to the waterfalls by way of the branches and leaves.

Small wooden bridges creak over fast-flowing rivers. Umbrella in hand, I step into the mist to photograph the tumbling water, when suddenly, unexpectedly, irritatingly, I am up to my thigh in mud as my foot goes straight through the earth. A blast of wind blows my umbrella down the mountainside. The suspended water yields to gravity and rain buckets down. Trapped, I desperately turn my foot this way and that, trying to protect my camera from the mud and rain. Just brilliant, up to my thigh in a sink hole with one leg and knee deep in mud with the other. One hand trying to protect the camera from harm, and only one hand left to haul me out of this messy situation. The rain is now pelting down so hard that my camera and I are in danger of drowning, when finally, with an almighty yank, my foot is free.

I crawl, mud-covered and soaked to the skin, back to the warmth of the Wish Mobile. Muttering and cursing as I check over my camera, I jump at a tap on the window. Ghostly walkers surround the car with great rain ponchos and sturdy sticks; they make for a scary sight. Reluctantly I roll down the widow. The women in the group are mightily impressed by the 'One Planet' project; the men walk stoically on by. Another reason that men have been requested to write on the car: they really have a problem seeing things.

When the walkers have passed, I roll down the blinds, dig out dry clothes, and turn the Wish Mobile into a mobile changing booth. Once again warm and comfortable, I make my way out of Nevis Glen back into the sun, and to the shores of Loch Linnhe. All the surfaces are rain wet and gleaming in golden light. Stone churches, grey and mossy with age, overlook the huge stretch of water that is contained by snow-capped mountains, spanned by rainbows, which vibrate against the purple grey clouds.

I turn left into Glencoe, which is said to mean the 'glen of weeping', and drive into a world of mountains and water, where the names themselves roll in my mind like magic spells: Buachaille Etive Mor, 'the great herdsman of Etive', Buachaille Etive Beag, and Bidean nam Bian. These peaks are the remnants of a super-volcano, which blew itself to kingdom come some 420 million years ago. Today volcano-shaped peaks shoot short rainbows from the summit of the Black Mount on Rannoch Moor. The light shifts, the rainbows vanish. All around, water swells from the sponge yellow moss, meandering slowly across the moors, where highland deer nibble on neon-green lichen. The waters form small tumbling streams, gathering strength and speed, turning into white waterfalls as I descend into the valley. Here the river flows smooth. No longer the crash and tumble of Ben Nevis, it now flows stately and sure, to mingle with the waters of Loch Lomond, and again I think, isn't that just like life.

Like a mountain stream that at its source bubbles pure cold and clear from the earth, at birth our future is bright and filled with possibility. As we grow into childhood, the flow of our lives is easily diverted by every contour of the land. The course of our flow is not of our own making, but determined by outside forces. As we gain speed and strength, we cascade in waterfalls, strong and powerful. Our life-force surges forward through deep ravines, and we plummet fearlessly over high cliffs, throwing rainbows to the breeze. On our banks wild flowers grow. When we emerge from the tumble of our youth, into the hills and valleys of young adult life, our flow is steadier, the course set. We merge with other rivers, and on our banks a future is planted. Tall trees grow on our shore. The land flattens, and the flow, deep and steady, is uneventful, as now the river carries many loads. Its strength is harnessed for the greater good; dams are built to control its force. At first the water spreads out into a still clear lake, but soon the shores are built up, and your energy abused, your life-force forgotten, polluted by neglect. You sense a need, an unfulfilled longing, but you are spread so far and so wide that you can no longer see the dam wall holding you back, can no longer feel the strong current of life that brought you this far.

Sometimes, if you are lucky, events conspire to work together to shatter that dam wall. You hurtle forward into the unknown, forging new paths, surging through uncharted territory, taking with you only the most important things. You are now in unknown lands, but driving you forward is the power of your experience, you sense the deep waters of the ocean, a future beyond your wildest imaginings. There is no turning back; there is just the knowledge that what was achieved is in the past; and the future lies ahead.

I emerge into lowlands and rolling green hills. Glasgow, here I come. There is always a sense of loss when leaving the tiny roads less traveled, and merging once again with the 'same all over the world' flow of highway traffic. I hit peak-hour traffic, and discover that Glasgow is a city in serious need of a ring road. All the traffic goes through the city centre, and chaos ensues. Glasgow looks like a hardworking place, where Ballentine's is made. The roadsigns in the UK are very definite about the direction in which one travels. Three days ago, I was heading to 'The North'; now I head to 'The South'. The Brits are very clear about this. After struggling with the traffic for longer than entirely necessary, just north of Carlisle I cross back into England.

England West
Beds 149, 150

... where I seem to have hit the working-class end of Carlisle. Young girls push prams past pawnshops, second-hand shops, and hairdressers. Why are there always a million hairdressers in poor areas? As I am setting a record for consecutive bad-hair-days, there seems to be no reason to stop in Carlisle, so I head off towards the Lake District, where I dawdle along country lanes, where chickens make more chickens, and heart-melting lambs stumble about on wonky legs. The flatland drops away, and I am on a very small elevation, which allows me to see the snowy peaks of the Cambrian Mountains, and daffodils daffodils daffodils, and black birds above blue lakes, big and small. It is here that William Wordsworth wandered lonely as a cloud.

> I wandered lonely as a cloud
> That floats on high o'er vales and hills,
> When all at once I saw a crowd,
> A host of golden daffodils;
> Beside the lake, beneath the trees,
> Fluttering and dancing in the breeze.
>
> Continuous as the stars that shine
> and twinkle on the Milky Way,
> They stretched in never-ending line
> along the margin of a bay:
> Ten thousand saw I at a glance,
> tossing their heads in sprightly dance.

To wander lonely as a cloud is a strange analogy in a country where the clouds run only in huge packs. Perhaps Wordsworth was a very sociable fellow who felt the pang of loneliness easily. But the stars that twinkle on the Milky Way are being lost from view, behind the lights of cities that even here wash the night sky with an orange haze. There are societies to save the dolphins, save the panda, and the tiger. But no societies to save starlight, silence and dark nights. Through our driving need for more time, we light up the night, and unwittingly lose things that nourish our inner core. When we look up at the stars, we sense a deep connection to the universe; when we sink into our silence, we experience a deep connection to ourselves. When we lose them, we deprive ourselves of the fuel we need to be fully alive.

On this very dreary day I head towards Cockermouth, birthplace of Wordsworth and a chap called Fearon Fallows, who was the royal astronomer in Cape Town way back in the late 1700s. He discovered more than 300 stars in his lifetime – a bit of useless information that I felt the urge to share, but a feat no longer possible today.

Cockermouth is situated on the confluence of the Cocker and Derwent rivers: a rather unfortunate position, which is prone to regular flooding, as the sandbags and water gates at every front door testify. After my small walkabout, I am fortunate to arrive back at the Wish Mobile just in time to stop a traffic warden from giving me a ticket. My tactic is one of diversion, in trying to convince him to write on the Wish Mobile. He says he cannot spell. I say surely he can spell 'peace' or something to that effect. No, says he, he doesn't believe in peace. Now why ever not, say I. He was a soldier, and firmly believes that someone must dominate for there to be control and order. Instead of peace, he decides to write

'love love'

... a bit of a contradiction to love love, but not peace, then again perhaps not.

On my way to Buttermere, the rolling gently green English scenery is virtually unblemished. There are no great power pylons or garish billboards. The English, and apparently the foresight of Beatrice Potter, need to be applauded for keeping those modern horrors at bay. Buttermere is a tiny village of dry-stone walls, stone gables, farm gates, pink and blue sheep, and old people hiking in the rain with bright anoraks, sturdy sticks and shoes. In England they walk in any weather; then again, if they didn't, they would never walk.

The B5289 between Cockermouth and Keswick leads over Honister Pass – a road so narrow that only by pulling onto the occasional passing bulge, can oncoming cars avoid head-on collisions. An ice-cold wind drives grey sheets of rain across massive black rocks, strewn like the ruins of ancient pillars on the green mountain slopes. I drive past 'How Country House'. This brings to mind all the English pub names that make the most bizarre connections: 'The Lemon and Leek', 'The Spider and Pumpkin'. Making these arbitrary connections is a vital part of the postmodern art movement, where the search for truth was replaced with play, or as the band Talking Heads said, 'Stop making sense'. Very advanced thinkers are the pub owners of England;

they have been making postmodern 'Hedgehog and Hoe'-type connections for centuries.

I drive through tiny villages, where every building is a delightful collaboration of grey slate, hand-painted signs, lacy window dressings, flower-filled pots, and fresh produce that glows against the dark wet stone. For beauty and general appeal, this area is on a par with Lake Como. In fact, it might even be nicer than Lake Como, except for the weather. But with global warming, that should soon change. The food here is definitely better. The English are quite the gastronomes: another myth blown out of the water. The English can cook, and they do it with fantastic organic fresh 'fair trade' products. I think it is the English who are making Italian cooking famous.

Bed 151

Approaching Blackpool, the building material of grey slate and stone of the Lake District changes to the red and yellow rocks of the seashore, which suddenly glow deep orange against a purple sky as the sun breaks from under the clouds for the first time today. The roads are congested, the scenery utilitarian, the skyline blemished by power lines, factories and streetlights, yet the sheep still graze on whatever grass they can find..

To make full use of the weather, I decide to take a walk by the seashore, which in this part of Blackpool is not a terribly romantic endeavor. There must be some serious wave action along this coastline, as there is a very high seawall, which consists of man-made bits, wedged between natural cliffs, all of which have been hosed down with a thick coating of concrete. It appears as if they decided to build a swimming pool around the Atlantic Ocean. This charming construction is supplemented by a steeply sloped wave break, and a concrete lagoon. As I said, not a very romantic seaside walk. My choice of a B&B for the night is in a creaky old Victorian mansion, one road back from the sea. My room is a red and white floral concoction, with a bay window, and a cheap four-poster bed, all frilled up with nylon netting. While the English might have upped their cooking skills, I am not too sure about their decorating: frills, flounces and flowers rule.

In the morning I invite the fat little owner to write a wish on the car. He refuses, saying it won't come true anyway. Perhaps, but what a bleak way to live life. He then proceeds to tell me that he knows that in South Africa everybody must walk around with guns cocked and loaded, ready to shoot the marauding masses, and that in the depths of Blackpool the Indians are all drinking and drunk. I am suddenly very pleased that he refused to write on my little car.

Leaving Bispham – the better end of Blackpool, or so the little fat man tells me – early in the morning, I soon reach Preston, a stinky place of oil refineries and little squat houses. Then I hit the M6. It is a bit of shocker, after days of country lanes and ancient farmlands. I had quite forgotten that this world, of measured time, speeding trucks and cars, is the reality of the greater part of England.

On my sightseeing agenda today is Chester. Its claim to fame is the perfectly preserved Roman wall, and a whole spectrum of other Roman ruins, including a hypocaust. 'Hypocaust' literally means 'fire beneath', and was the under-floor heating system of Roman villas and public baths, centuries ago. It worked more or less along the same principle as the Chinese kang, except, due to the double floor construction, it was able to heat far greater areas.

Chester is overrun by little midget Romans, with flowing cloaks, helmets, and plastic swords: the English certainly make school outings as entertaining as possible. The guides, in full Roman gear, haul little wannabe Romans into the gladiators' ring to indulge in a bit of mock slaying of adversaries.

But Chester's main tourist attraction is to walk on the Roman Wall, which gives a bird's eye view of both the inner and outer cities. The beautifully restored black and white Victorian buildings that line the streets of Chester give a glimpse back into the days of Dickens, while the walk along the wall provides glimpses into churchyards, across bridges, and into the private gardens of the houses across Chester Canal. I stop at the Chester clock, dutifully take a picture of this second most photographed clock (after Big Ben) in England, before making my way back to the Wish Mobile and Wales.

Wales

Beds 152 & 153

... and then I am in Wales and confronted by Welsh, which is out on its own little language limb. I have no idea what to make of it.

But it has the distinction of being one of 55 languages chosen to represent earth in the Voyager Global Records, Earth's outreach program to the universe, although the greeting

Iechyd da i chwi yn awr ac yn oesoedd

('Good health to you now and forever') is one that I will not be attempting. Just trying to read the roadsigns is impossible, but fortunately the really important ones, such as stop or slow, are in both English and Welsh.

Tonight I have been invited into the home of 5W Anne and Jim, who live in a delightful little hamlet called Penryn Bay. Anne and Jim give me time to settle in. The last few days have been a blur of sights and sounds, and the discovery that the United Kingdom is great road-tripping country. The back roads through empty countryside, the craggy peaks of Scotland, and now the rugged coastline of Wales, dotted with hulking Norman castles, have all managed to retain a small wildness and air of adventure, despite their long history and habitation by humankind. But my time for reflection is short. Anne has arranged for an interview with one of the local papers, and I prepare to answer all the usual questions. The interview goes as expected, until the young lady asks,

'Did you find love?'

My instant reaction is a sarcastic

'Yes, I just scooped up the men from the side of the road as I drove by.'

What is she thinking? Of course I did not find love. Love takes time. But then later, in that semi-dream state just before one drifts into sleep, I have a revelation. I did fall in love. Not with another person, but with myself. This thought pulls me back from sleep, when I realize that this is a far more profound thing. In the course of my long journey, through the enforced stripping away of my preconceived notions of what I should be, I have discovered what I am. I have had the time to think about the baggage that I carry around, and realize now that the notion

Wales; Bodnant Garden Pump House

of letting these things go in order to forget about them is the wrong way of thinking about them. Our memories define us; they are as much part of us as our arms and our legs; and we cannot let them go. The thing is to accept them, to realize they make us what we are, and to build on that. When this acceptance becomes a reality, this has the happy effect of dispelling doubt, fear and loneliness. Without being conscious of it, I have become more open, less protective of myself, as I unconsciously was aware that there was nothing that people could take from me that I couldn't replace. Sleep takes me again, and just before the velvet night fills my head, I realize that, by accepting myself, falling in love with myself, I have stepped into the centre of my life, and no longer have to search for, or try to find love. I have become the wellspring of love and joy in my life, and am able to give love unconditionally, without fear of losing any part of myself.

The following morning arrives bright and clear, and I discover that my revelation from last night has put a small smile on my face that I cannot seem to shake. Looking in the mirror, I decide it looks good, and can stay, even though the plans for the day need a small adjustment. Anne and I were to visit Bodnant Garden, but Anne has woken up feeling very ill, so I will explore the garden alone.

Topiary hedges frame the garden, and lead through narrow green passages into a wonderland of delicate pinks and whites, as magnolias, camellias, and azaleas spread their blossoms against the blue-grey sky, and fallen petals float like snowflakes to the ground. Fields of yellow daffodils huddle under giant redwoods, as the rain sweeps drops of sunlight across the distant Carneddau Mountains. Shimmering pools reflect the elegant Bodnant House. The rain moves in and shatters the mirror ponds, sending us all dashing for cover.

Well before dawn, I tiptoe out of Anne's life, as I have a date with a boat, and France. In the half-light I find my way past, under and around dark and brooding Conwy Castle. Finally, in all my travels, I have found a castle worthy of the name. Its mighty walls and towers have imprisoned its long history, which broods over the modern houses of Conwy, groveling at the feet of this rough-hewn monster.

I am soon back in England, and stuck in a Monday-morning traffic jam. This give me a chance to observe the English cars. They are mainly modest small cars, and little hatchbacks or vans. The occasional big SUV stands out like a sore thumb. The very expensive fuel is probably the main reason for the small cars, but the English seem to be very environmentally conscious, and do try to walk their talk.

Just as I pass the towns of Puddle and Piddle (no joke), I spy in front of me, as bright as a mirror, the English Channel. My destination is Weymouth, and the ferry to France. I leave England, watching, in the far distance, the white cliffs of Dover leap forward in the last rays of sun. The ferry spews black smoke over the ocean; the filthy cloud keeps pace with the ship in the raging wind. Finding the sunset side of the boat, with my face turned to the sun, I fill my head with light. There is a feeling of homecoming in this crossing. It seems so long ago that I started my journey east, and yet I am still heading east.

France

Beds 154, 156,156

Hours later, lightning splits the night to show France, a dark line against the sky. Driving the Wish Mobile onto the European continent again, I am immediately confronted with the fact that my mind, which I thought was so open and accepting, has closed again in these last few months. The strange language on the roadsigns, and the need to drive on the opposite side of the road again have me in a small tizz. I don't know where I am, or where I am going. The lightning shows sheets of rain, as I drive aimlessly in dark suburban streets. I will never find a place to sleep here, and the thought of sleeping in the Wish Mobile is once again as foreign as it was at the beginning of my journey. Is one doomed to live forever in circles, always somehow getting back to where one started from? I cannot believe that; it seems such a waste of energy. No, that cannot be. I simply refuse to believe that nothing was achieved in all this time on the road.

> *Pull yourself together, woman; drag out that brain and   put this past year's learning to good use.*

First off, finding a hotel room in deepest darkest suburbia is not going to work. I need to head towards the bright lights, the city centre, or preferably back to the coast, where my chances of finding a bed for the night will be much enhanced. In the 'Place de la Republique', I find the Napoleon Hotel, and feeling suitably French patriotic, book myself a room. From my hotel window, I look down onto the square, and spy across the way – something that looks like an open restaurant. The rain and driving wind obscure all but the most basic outlines of the world outside, but as I have not eaten in some time, I will risk it. Stepping into the restaurant, I enquire, in perfect English, whether the kitchen is still open. I am ignored.

Ah, the French, got to love 'em. Time to twist my tongue around a foreign tongue again. Now that is an interesting thought, being in the land of the French kiss and all. Did they really invent French kissing or are they just, as is the way of the French, laying claim to yet another of life's small pleasures. There is no clear answer to this slippery question, but with the French reputation of passion and romance, they seem as good a contender as any, to have started the practice of *baiser avec la langue.*

Marans; France

Madame?

The waiter is looking at me enquiringly. Ah yes, food ...

Pardon, monsieur. Mon Francais et tres mavais. Cest votre cuisine overt?

Mais oui, bien sûr.

comes the offhand reply.

But of course? It is ten at night, and it seems to me not so very of course that the kitchen will be open. And then I remember I am back on the continent, and unlike England or America, here the folk only start thinking about dinner at ten. The restaurant is empty, not because the patrons have gone home, but because they haven't yet arrived.

Now that a small language bridge has been constructed between myself and the waiter, he couldn't be more chivalrous. This is a little secret about dealing with those rude French folk. They are actually not so rude, just rather proud of their language. So the best way to break the ice is to be prepared to speak their language, no matter how badly. This small attempt will show the French that you do care. It will prove to them how superior they are, as they can speak French beautifully, and you cannot – at which point they will pity you, and thereafter all will go swimmingly. They will afford you every courtesy, shower you with small compliments, which you will not understand, but all that is now expected of you is that you be charming, and utterly grateful. This is the duty of any foreigner when these small French niceties, and slightly reluctant services, are bestowed upon them. Whoever said the French were rude just didn't understand the rules of the game.

On the recommendation of the waiter, I order a flagon of wine and a bucket of mussels, then look around as the restaurant slowly fills. The thought pops into my head that I am happy, content, and seem to have no need for anything other than just to sit here, slowly eat my way through the bucket of mussels, and spend a delightful two hours watching excitable French people smoke, drink wine, and discuss the issues of the world, while the waiter smiles, and fawns about me.

The quiet contentment is still with me, as I wake to a crystal day, but I soon realize that my head is not yet fully awake. After four months of English, I have slid back into snooze zone: horrifying how quickly it happens. I like it better when things are not quite so comfortable, then my senses go on full alert, and I experience life more sharply. When everything is understood, it is like slipping into a coma.

That keen edge of discomfort brings with it many hidden advantages that make me feel just a little more alive.

Chanting 'keep right, pass left, keep right, pass left', and listening to my French language CDs, I make my way to Mont Saint-Michel, a monastery set in the tidal plain of the Couesnon river mouth. Currently the tide is out, revealing kilometers of wet sand, dotted by very small people, who explore this strange suck-foot landscape. It is speculated that there are more gumboots lost in this soggy bottom sand than are manufactured in all the cities of China. (I am making this up of course, but the sand is apparently very fond of boots.) Signs warn that if you do not have a designated parking space, you must be off this sometimes-island by four, as by this evening, this will all be water once more.

Legend has it that the Monastery of Mont Saint-Michel was named after the Archangel Michael, who instructed St Aubert to build a monastery here. St Aubert did not feel inclined to listen, so the angel gave him three chances to improve his hearing, before stepping in and burning a hole in the poor saint's skull with his finger. That of course got the old guy's attention, and today we see the result of the subsequent building spurt, which was dedicated on 16 October 709. I should remember this trick when next I attempt to do any building renovations.

Today Mont Saint-Michel is still the most imposing structure on the Normandy coastline: a great monastic pile of turrets, arches, small windows, slate-shingle rooftops, and wood-shingle walls. Small madonnas peer from high stone niches, and bright red and blue windows give colorful relief from the stone and grey. Relief from the tourists is more difficult to find. They arrive in busload convoys, descend on the quaint shops that line what would be the CBD of this monastery, where they proceed to shop for stuff that, until this very moment, they never knew they needed. Then upwards, upwards. They talk past beautiful views. They talk in silent alleys. They talk on steep stone staircases, and through long dark passages. They talk under imposing stone arches, and around mysterious corners, until finally in the church, which is the pinnacle of this building effort, they talk the somber atmosphere into the day-to-day. Why come all this way, is what I want to say. Why not just stay at home, and talk about your everyday?

In the sanctuary of the Wish Mobile, I head south. I want to escape the cold of Normandy. I skirt around the edges of cities with names that all ring familiar bells: Rennes, Nantes, La Rochelle and Bordeaux. The history in France is so dense that to do justice to it all would take another year. I opt to stop instead in small villages such as Châteaubriant and Cognac. With every new country comes a new rhythm, and I have always been unsettled until I have found that rhythm. Here in France it seems to be best to work early in the morning, sightsee for an hour or two, then drive to the next destination. Each day I find the market, buy the best baguettes in the world. Nobody knows how to make a baguette or a croissant like the French. Combined with an organic homemade camembert and sun-red tomatoes, this simple meal tastes like heaven. The bread has that particular slightly bitter crust that goes oh so well with the cheese, and the sweet tart tomatoes cut through the richness. I could crack open that dinky of Bordeaux I have lurking in the food box, but as it is only 10h00, I won't. I will save some bread and cheese for lunch.

In Châteaubriant, crows wheel and caw above ruined castle turrets. The castle, after which the town of Châteaubriant is called, was built as a strategic battle station, because this area and town were subjected to numerous battles and invasions during the Middle Ages. Today the castle is elegantly crumbling, the slate pillars peeling, the walls green with age, and the stone benches mottled with lichen and moss.

Here I discover for the first time a particularly French way of renovating and building. Instead of trying to replace missing pieces of old buildings with pretending-to-be-old stone, they rebuild the missing pieces with glass and aluminum, creating a marriage between modern and ancient that is so pleasing and harmonious that it goes right to the top of my best-in-the-world architecture list. In the *centre ville* of Châteaubriant this delightful marriage is taken one step further. The Teatre de Verre (theatre of glass), a perfect cube of glass, is built right next to the old town hall, but in its pure translucence does not distract from the old building, adding instead light to the somber stone.

Cognac is on a high hill, from where vineyards and small villages roll into the far distance, ending only when they meet the big sky, decorated today with white puffy clouds. Beautiful châteaux take their color cue from the sky, with white plastered walls and pale blue shutters. I would like to inherit just such a château from a forgotten lover (aunt or uncle is so boring). Chances are very slim, but it would be nice. In the town of Cognac, the color scheme is muted. The shutters are in clear neutral shades that almost, but don't quite, blend into the pale stone walls. The subtle harmony of shades is reflected in the pale blossoms of a single peach tree. The streets are silent. I still have not worked out exactly when the French siesta takes place, and with every new day am happy to have had the foresight to buy lunch at breakfast time.

Just outside Cognac, I find a field of daisies and marigolds on a small rise. From this small elevation, I experience a little out-of-body moment (or it could be the unaccustomed wine at lunchtime) as my mind's eye sees across the Eurasian continent, over mountains, lakes and inland seas, past ancient cities, and through naked earth deserts. The thin pink line of my journey wobbles around the curvature of the earth. I have seen so much, experienced new things every minute of the day. This year has been the longest of my life, and yet my knowledge? That is still only as broad as the road on which I traveled. A few meters to the left or right, knowledge once again sinks into the desert sand.

How innocent were the men of the Renaissance to believe they could know everything there is to know. To learn is not to get closer to fulfilled knowledge, but further and further away. It is like flying straight up into the air, allowing the horizon of knowledge to expand and expand, until today's point of view simply vanishes in the great unknown. I am not sure if this thought is exhilarating or immensely depressing. What we believe today to be the truth, the whole truth, and nothing but the truth, could be nothing but mist before the sun.

Not only does knowledge never stop, but it is like the view from high in space, a multidimensional thing, which continually expands into new directions, new dimensions, leading to new knowledge. We control which knowledge is revealed to us by the questions we ask. The unfortunate thing about this is that we continue to ask questions about things we know. We believe that what we know, is the only knowledge that can be known, and all new knowledge must lead from that.

The only question to ask is, are we asking the right questions? Or worse, do we even possess the right knowledge to start asking the right questions.

Bed 157

It's 15h00: time I hit the toll road direction Spain; enough mucking about; time to get some distance on the clock. The highway cuts through vineyard after vineyard, past pale stone houses with red tile roofs, and green green grass. As I go further south, the car heating gets turned down and down. The French toll roads are super-expensive. I think they even beat the Chinese. After a couple of toll stops, I decide my budget needs a break, and I head off into the hinterland, where châteaux recline gracefully in vineyards under bare plane trees. The road winds through quiet woodlands, and past fields of canola yellow. The day is fading. I peer at my map. I look again, and then decide it is time to stop.

My position on the planet is a mystery. I cannot find the road that I am on, on my map. Where did I go wrong, drat and dammit? My compass shows I am still heading SE, so not too far off the mark, but where am I? Yes, of course, I am right here, in the rural hinterland, in a pine tree plantation. The question is rather, in which direction should I be heading in order to get away from here ... ok, any direction, but I would prefer the most convenient one. That question is answered by the trucks that roar by. They are all going in one direction, and that is sure to be towards some form of highroad, or a good truck stop. Either one is fine with me. Heading in the truck direction, I drive through tiny villages, where people live in modest yet beautiful houses, some of wood, but mainly of dusky grey stone, with dull green shutters. The houses are packed together like a small crowd, overlooking a river where white ducks float. Brown chickens and fluffy white sheep congregate in the shade of a stubby little church, which glows beautifully pink in the late afternoon sun.

I make it as far as St Sever, where in a small motel I go through my evening routine, with which you are quite familiar by now, so I will not bore you with repetition.

Waking early, my goal for the day is to cross the Pyrenees into Spain. It is a dreary day to be crossing a mountain range: the clouds are low, and it will soon rain. Heading south, the world becomes tangled broadleaf forest, overgrown with vines, broken only by an occasional field. The houses are changing. They are lower; the angle of the roofs is not as steep; and the subtly austere coloring of the north is vanishing with the addition of blue, lime-green and yellow. Trucks rumble through narrow village roads, which is very unfortunate for the people living here. Rain rain rain, soggy sheep, and Frenchmen with black berets. In Orthez, I actually see people working in France for the first time. They are building, fetching and carrying bricks and cement.

Crossing the A634, I start up the mountains. The French are a nation of drivers. They like their cars, and their road trips. This is proven by the little roadside picnic sites, which are very user friendly, with great views and good tables. Not every country has these. In fact, I think America, the land of the road trip, is severely lacking in the roadside picnic spot with view. Before I tackle the mountain pass, I pull over, and while the rain shields the world from me, and me from the world, I sit quietly reading the paper, and eat an in-car breakfast of croissants, cheese and blood oranges. Just another day getting ready for the office. The newspaper has a flip little quote

'Time exists so that things don't happen all at once and space exists so they don't all happen to you.' John Orr

... and I sit alone in the rain on a French hillside.

Spain

Bed 158

A break in the clouds reveals a snow-capped peak. I hope the snow is not so low as to be a problem ... and then I am in Navarra, Spain. Just a big sign, not a border control to be seen. The Pyrenees are extremely steep, and the mountain pass is a switchback of tight curves, which soon carry me high beyond the snowline, where the world is reduced to white and grey, with thick fogbanks blocking out the view, the road, and, on occasion, the front of the Wish Mobile. I keep a very careful eye out for the string of hikers who are making their soggy way across the Pyrenees. Walking over the mountains seems to be the thing to do in these parts. I would rather be driving, and so I am. Right at the top of the pass is a tiny snow-covered village, Oreaga, which I am sure the hikers will be very pleased to reach. Here the icicles still hang long and deadly from gutters, and the snow lies knee-deep in the gardens of shuttered houses. But then it is all downhill, and soon the snow is no longer a part of my life, but certainly still a very real part of the lives of the hikers.

Driving into Pamplona where, in my misspent youth, I misspent some time, I cannot see the city with fresh eyes: my memories overwhelm me. Then it was young, hot and sunny, now it is cold, wet and windy, but some things don't change, and without trying, I find all the memory spots of that time so long ago. I don't like the feeling: it is an out-of-time, out-of-place experience that brings nothing of value to either the past or the present. Living in the past is such a waste of time: it shackles and chains the future, and you never properly enjoy the present, constantly comparing it to a rose-tinted past. I decide to leave my memories undisturbed and hit the road direction Tudela.

Where I discover, that in my absence, Spain has become big on alternative energy sources. Wind turbines grace every high ridge to catch the smallest breeze, and huge solar fields, with their grey shiny surfaces facing the sun, fill valleys and flat plains. The villages on the hillside are all covered with an icing-sugar sprinkling of snow. It is 17h00, as always, the quest for a hotel occupies my mind at this time of day. Finding a hotel is a little difficult in Spain. Unless you are in a super-tourist area, the hotels are very hidden, and it is a bit of a business finding them.

Toledo, Spain

The new siesta hours are also putting a crimp in my style. In Spain they last from 13h00 to 17h00, I think, so I must seriously shift my routine. But luck is on my side today and I arrive in Tudela in time for the daily reawakening, and, spotting a giant Jesus on a hill, I remember having a picnic up there once, a very long time ago. I can suddenly taste the bitter salty olives, and the hard chewy bread. Perhaps I shall try a memory replay, and find the town market, but it is a pale modern version of my memory. The only bread on sale is a horrible spongy version of the French loaf, and the olives may not be tasted first. That is so disappointing. The free tastings were one of my favorite things about the Spanish markets, that, and the snails that slithered slowly from huge hessian bags, sliding over table and till, in a slow-motion attempt at escape, before the snail seller languidly lifted them back into the bag, from where they were scooped into paper bags, weighed, and carried off to a Spanish kitchen – where, through some form of magic, they were transformed into the best snail stew I ever did eat. I look at my horrible bread, and wonder at the value of memories. Where will I find such snail stew here? But snails are not my pressing concern, a map is.

I have become just a touch too casual about this whole driving thing. I am driving about in Spain without any sort of map. I have the world map, but that is really not the most accurate way of getting around. Four bookshops later, I realize that maps are not very important to the Spanish either. It must be said, though, that I have become a map connoisseur, and am very fussy about my roadmap requirements. The scale, the information, the key, the fold, and the paper, all are to be considered, and the maps on offer here are just not adequate. But once I have trawled through each bookstore in Tudela, I realize that sometimes you have no choice but to lower your standards, in order to get ahead.

This little shopping expedition has allowed my brain to switch from my non-existent French to my non-existent Spanish. This morning I looked at my Spanish phrase book in complete bafflement; now I am quite happily enquiring about rooms, directions, etc. Good old brain, obviously still some form of action up there. But I still get my *bonjour, buon giorno* and *buenos dias* confused, and keep asking baffled Spaniards if they *habla Espanol*, which of course they do, instead of *habla Engles*, which most don't. My *si, que, gracias* and *mercis* are also in a bit of a muddle, but I slap a big old grin on my face to let everybody know I am an idiot, and well aware of it, which makes everybody feel very sorry for me, and things work out just fine.

With my semi-adequate map, I am able to set a course for the next few days. I will skirt around Madrid – it is just too much city for my overworked brain – and head for Toledo instead. In the distance, against the blue-white mountains, the golden stone spire of a church, lit by a ray of sun, stabs at the heavy grey clouds. The road south drives me through vineyards, and into springtime. The forests are washed by the tiniest haze of green, and the almond trees are dressed in their spring pink tutus. A man in a purple anorak, his weathered face a cactus of grey, is accompanied by a donkey and a dog. He slows the traffic with his huge herd of slightly orange sheep, which cross the road in a tight ball. They are heading towards a small orange village, its plaster and stones the color of the soil; a tangerine dream village set in a field of brilliant green.

On my left, I spy a stone chapel on a small hill. That shall be my luncheon spot. At the top of a rutted track, the chapel is a crumbling ruin that leans against the raging wind. A stone cross, lichen scoured, dominates the view, and far below the purple anorak and ball of orange sheep vanish into the tangerine village. The wind howls and tugs at the Wish Mobile, while I munch away at my not-so-nice bread, rather odd olives, and the last of the French tomatoes. Then just off the side of the dirt track, I spot three huge sandy vultures. They lurk protectively over their lunch, while glaring at me in irritated fashion.

'Sorry, boys, didn't see you there. Don't let me disturb   you. I really don't want any of what you are having.'

They seem appeased, and return to ripping the flesh off something that once was an animal.

Below me, blue mountains climb out of rolling fields of green and startling orange soil. But up here the arid climate and grey sandy soil supports only low shrubs, stunted pine forests, and low-growing cypresses, shaped like perfect miniature Christmas trees. An old man walks by, bent under his load of wood. The fat bugs that splat against the windscreen herald summer.

Ninety kilometers outside of Madrid, I hit a three-lane highway, a muddle of architecture, and semi-detached high-density housing developments going up by the dozen. Madrid sprawls over a vast plain, and my little thought of visiting, just for a few hours, loses all appeal. I am not doing this; I am going straight to Toledo. Following a convenient sign, I drive onto the ring road, and all hell breaks loose. The serenity of my long days of bumbling along country lanes, sneaking slowly through tiny villages, often wondering if the road will remain wide enough to accommodate the Wish Mobile, is instantly blown to smithereens.

The traffic on the ring road is wild, and then gets wilder still, as the whole highway plunges underground: the off-ramps, on-ramps, spaghetti junctions, all underground. There is something very disconcerting about this: it is like landing in a video game, where you are provided only tunnel vision ... and while the tunnels are certainly a feat of engineering, there is no warning of the on-ramps and off-ramps that flash by around curves and corners. Cars push and shove from all sides. I think I am doing ok, until I miss the Toledo turn-off, and it vanishes into the gloomy distance. These are not moments when you want an argumentative partner in the car, so I am very pleased to be quite alone, while I attempt to plan my next move – although when I miss the next Toledo turn-off, I do wonder whether it might not have something to do with the fact that while the traffic is raging all around, I am attempting to read my inadequate map in the tunnel half light. Perhaps having a navigator would not be such a bad plan after all.

But the drivers of Madrid could fit in well in Beijing. They seem to expect the worst, and make plenty of allowances for that. Well, if that is what it takes ... I delve into my driving memory, haul out all the tricks of China, and, by Jove, if those Spaniards don't just instinctively know when not to mess with someone. Miraculously the traffic opens, I ease into my chosen lane, shoot up an off-ramp, and back in the sun, not 1 km short of another turn-off to Toledo, which takes me onto a completely empty toll road. On entry they hit me with a toll of 0.75€c. This is very cheap; I smell rat. There are no cars at all for the whole 70 km to Toledo. I have four lanes of perfect tar to myself. When I get to the exit gate, the toll-taker demands another €5.15. No wonder there are no cars this road. This toll road is now officially the most expensive toll road I have been on.

Bed 159 & 160

Toledo is one of the world's most beautiful small cities. It reclines in ravishing fashion on a hilltop, surrounded by the blue waters of the Tagus River. Toledo has since antiquity been a melting pot of cultures, and has been blessed with wise rulers, with the happy result that, when one culture conquered another, they did not immediately resort to burning books, making Toledo a place from which much knowledge was sent into the world. With the departure of the Spanish court to Madrid, the importance of Toledo waned, but its economic decline was to the world's cultural and historical advantage. Toledo escaped the rampant modernization that has wiped the history from many of the world's ancient cities, and is today a world heritage site, in which the architectural influences of three of the world's major religions combine to create the street scenes that make Toledo unique.

Because of all this, Toledo is one of Spain's biggest tourist attractions. Daily convoys of tour busses deliver their passengers to the Puerta de Bisagra, from where everybody follows the pink signs to the views, and tourist must-see sites. As I am in a bit of a hurry, the sun is setting, and once again, I have no place to sleep, I throw caution to the four winds, and drive right into the heart of the old city. Ancient cities are a bit daunting to drive in. There is always the small doubt floating in my head as to whether I am still driving on a road, or have somehow managed to mistake pedestrian walkways for the very narrow roads. There is also always the small fear that the streets, tightly contained by three-storey buildings, will become so narrow that forward motion will no longer be possible.

To overcome all these small niggles and doubts, I continue to use the Zen 'if in doubt, follow the car in front of you' method of navigation. It still has not had any really positive results, but I rather like the random adventures it throws at me. The car in front of me zips, left right left right, zigzagging up and up, until we both emerge out of the orange and yellow shadows of the lower town into the last rays of sun at the top of Toledo – right to where all the 'hostals' (which is what B&Bs are called in Spain) are located. What do you know? The Zen method finally pays off. But only up to a point: while there are streets and streets of hostals they are *completo completo completo*. All full, and by the way the hostal owners look at me, I can tell that they are convinced I am insane. This is Toledo; it is Saturday evening; and I am only now trawling for a room? They just don't understand: there is always a room, and I find it.

Toledo is a city that inspires early morning photographic sessions, so at dawn I am standing on the shore of the Tagus River, where men catch fish in the reflections of Alcazar Fort, which captures the sunshine in its stone yellow walls. Crossing Alcantara Bridge, I enter the old town through a wooden gate, shiny smooth with age, into narrow alleys that twist around faded red walls that push closer and closer together, squeezing the alleys into narrow twisting corners. Up and up, around, and down the stairs and alleys, twist and turn. People appear from hidden doorways, making their way with assured step to cafés that have just opened their doors to allow the first coffee and cigarette of the day – to be enjoyed in the company of friends that only ever meet here, before each one moves off to fill his or her day with the chores that will pay the rent. I prefer the sunshine to the smoke-filled interior, and, sitting under an almond tree, drink tea, and eat a small cheese-filled pie. Across the way, a carved stone arch reminds of the Byzantine arches of Dubrovnik, while the tiled walls on either side bring back memories of Bukhara and Samarqand.

The thin wistful sound of a single violin draws me into the narrow streets again. At the entrance to the cathedral, a red-haired beauty, dressed in flowing white, with a bright scarf thrown around her shoulders against the early morning chill, sits on a small stool. Lost in her melody, she fills the small square with crying sound, ignored by the tourists that sweep by – their only concern is to see the interior of the Cathedral of Saint Mary of Toledo before it closes its doors for the Sunday mass.

There are many must-sees in Toledo, but I have still not acquired the taste for chasing after fixed goals, preferring to allow myself to be drawn by this sound or that stairwell, to follow a stylish young couple pushing a pram to a corner café, where another cup of tea seems a good idea. My this-way, that-way path takes me across Zocodover Square, famous for its Corpus Christi celebration, and view over Toledo. Here older locals fill the sunshine café chairs, and youngsters lounge on stairs, over walls, and over each other. Proud mothers watch their toddlers take their first wobbly steps towards doves that flap, always just out of reach of small grasping hands. A small wooden door draws my attention. Cautiously I peer inside, to a beautiful courtyard, cooled by the spray from a small fountain. It is the entrance to a convent. A sign tells me that entry is welcomed, as the nuns carry on one of the traditions for which Toledo is famous, Toledo marzipan. A small flight of stairs ends at a wall. On the right of a small arched window, a small display cabinet shows the produce on offer. Boxes decorated with Madonna of the Bleeding Heart are filled with marzipan in various styles and quantities. On the right, a bell pull chimes the bell faintly behind the shuttered window. When it opens, the light from the hidden world beyond the wall frames a nun in full wimpled regalia.

'*Buenos dias*'

'*Buenos dias*'

She listens patiently as I mangle her language with my marzipan request, walks to the long marble table behind her, selects the marzipan I think I asked for, arranges it beautifully in the blue Madonna box, and taking my money, wishes me goodbye, with the closing of the small wooden widow the mysterious world of nuns, vanishes once more. Stepping back into the sunshine street, the Spanish siesta has cast its Sleeping Beauty spell over Toledo. I have still not found the Spanish rhythm, and making my solitary way back to my hostal, experience once again a feeling of being out of time, out of place.

Working quietly at my computer, a small rumbling draws my attention. The rumble grows, until I notice the articles on the bed shaking. Staring at the bed with some concern, the thought comes to mind: earthquake? But a very very isolated one, as just the bed is shaking. After careful and meticulous elimination of movement source, I come to the conclusion that the laundry room is right below my room, and my bed is the conduit to all vibrations from there. I assure myself that there will be no washing done at night, so this strange phenomenon need not concern me. But scarcely am I back at my computer when the rumbling starts again, but this time from a different source, and with a different and increasingly urgent rhythm. When my desk start moving rhythmically in sympathy with the wall, I realize I am in a whole new territory. The thumping becomes a thunderous drumming, and then ends with the inevitable shrieks.

Hallelujah, thank goodness these things are mostly mercifully brief. But while in Spain sex might be brief, it is contagious. It seems I was not the only one to overhear this brief bout of afternoon passion, and this has infected the rooms around me. Soon my room is filled with a cacophony of bumps, squeaks, groans, and of course, the appreciative feminine shrieks that always end these little forays into passion. My out-of-time out-of-space feeling grows with every bump and grind. The odds of me ever getting into the Spanish rhythm are very slim.

What is interesting from a purely sociological point of view is how very quickly the sex act is over and done with, and, in light of this, how incredibly appreciatively the ladies do shriek. Are they really having such a good time, or just trying to speed things along? Either way, it does prove to me that we women are not a terribly clever bunch. When the sex is not fun or worth shouting about, why is it always the women making all the noise. Perhaps it is because the men are too busy feeling good to think about anything else, while the women are so busy pretending to feel good, they almost forget that they are not feeling good. But their shrieks and groans make the guy think he is doing a fabulous job, so he continues to do what he is doing. The woman eventually decides this is all just too boring, and so the sex slows and dies, and the guy just cannot understand why. Wasn't he doing everything right? Didn't she shout her approval? Hilarious and so sad.

Beds 161, 162, 163

I leave Toledo on a cold and cloudy Monday morning. My road is north through huge industrial zones, heavy with industry, that spew foul-smelling smoke into the grey and gas-smelly air. Trash lines the roads, and great trucks form an impatient queue on the one-lane narrow road. The world around Ocana is flat, with low squat buildings. Here people live in soviet-style apartments that stand row after endless ugly row. For entertainment, there is a bullring in among the piles of concrete blocks, and cranes stand in fields of purple flowers. The trash and poverty make for a very non-tourist view of central Spain. I suppose the world cannot be beautiful everywhere; all the stuff we consume has to come from somewhere.

Nearing Teruel, the villages are far more picturesque, the scenery rural, with rivers and mountains, where the willow leaves have burst their buds in a splash of spring green. Libros is built into a mountainside that reminds of the Painted Desert in Death Valley. The green and red mountains peel off to expose pale green cliffs. In a cutting, the exposed earth lets it all hang out, in lavender, yellow, pink, blue and pale green layers. It's very surprising, like catching a glimpse of the frilly, brightly colored undies of a stern headmistress.

I stop over in Teruel, where the morning brings a surprise, as I experience for the first time that childish delight in finding the world transformed while I slept. I had tuned my head into spring and summer, but now stand in a frosty white world. I love this pared-down monochrome landscape, where every tree, every branch, and every blade of grass receives its own little moment of glory. But the rain sets in, and it turns into a grim old day, so I hop on the nearest highway, and belt down towards Barcelona. But not for long. Roadworks reduce the road to a single lane, full of trucks. It's going to be a long haul on this rainy rainy day.

I arrive in Barcelona just in time to catch the afternoon rush hour. The traffic grinds to a complete halt, but I am so relaxed that all this is no problem. I have no idea where I am going anyway, so the stationary traffic gives me a moment to sort myself out. Unfortunately, as my splendid Spanish map proves to be of no use, I shall just have to guess my way around the city. Off-ramps, on-ramps, highways, flyways, cars and trucks, and all is stop start stop start, and into a tunnel. How long will it last? Is this a replay of Madrid? But not too bad, and up we go, and I have no idea ... ah ... there ... the Sagrada Familia. I shall head in that direction. There are sure to be hostals over there. But the signs to the Sagrada Familia vanish, leaving me driving aimlessly in the inner city of Barcelona. This is all too much for my brain. Finding my way back onto the highway south, I then vanish into my head, returning to reality only when I reach the heartland of the Costa Brava, and an endless succession of tourist hotels and busses.

I am suffering from a severe case of indecision today: where to stop, where to stay, should I just barrel ahead? But the day is done; it is the Easter weekend; and to be driving aimlessly about the darkening countryside seems like a very poor plan. Then on top of a hill, just outside Tossa de Mar, a friendly sign makes the decision for me. There are seaside apartments for rent. They are not yet open for the season, but are happy to accommodate me anyway. Soon the Wish Mobile is happily resting in a private garage, and I am pottering around in an apartment overlooking the Mediterranean, with staircase access to the beach. It almost feels like home. The quaint village of Tossa de Mar is just down the hill, and on Palm Sunday I will go there to watch the Easter procession into the old town.

A tiny chapel perches on the top of the cliff that protects the entrance to the bay of Tossa de Mar. Fishing boats are pulled high onto the deserted beach; the church bells chime the half hour; and slowly all the inhabitants of the tiny village make their way up the steep footpath to the chapel, from where the procession will begin. Each generation is defined by their choice of clothing. The older generations are all dressed in black. The middle generation are in their finest designer wear; and the children skip around the adult legs, dressed in their Sunday frills. They have one thing in common: they are all carrying yellow palm fronds, those of the children plaited into elaborate designs, studded with confections, sweets and small cakes.

The narrow winding path up to the top of the cliff builds to a moving mass of waving palm fronds that grow to a small forest on the small plateau, as we all await the bishop. He appears miraculously under a giant golden cross, embellished with carvings and sparkling stones. When he lifts his arms, his red velvet cloak falls back to expose the heavy gold chains hanging on his chest. The crowd falls to a hush; chests are crossed; and children shushed. In rolling Spanish, the red-clad bishop sends out his blessing to the crowd and across the

Mediterranean, and the crowd murmur their responses in the way of Catholics all around the world. The bishop mingles with the crowd, and, led by a brass band, the congregation slowly wind their way down the hill, and vanish into the cathedral to properly commune with their god.

I go for a walk on the beach, and commune with nature instead. The sunny day darkens, lightning touches the horizon, thunder rolls across the sea, and just as I get back to my apartment, the rain comes pouring down. As the thunder rolls, and the rain pelts the windows, I rustle up a small meal of olives, jamon, and ciabata, and a great sense of contentment fills my mind. All I need is right here – except maybe the security code to that wireless connection my computer keeps picking up, and having Alexandra sprawled on the couch, making silly small talk – but other than that, life is good.

That would be me.

Back to the start

Bed 164,165,166

The Easter holidays pass in a slow motion of writing, reading, walking on the beach and not much else. Then my road takes me north once again, and soon I cross from Spain back into France, where trucks of all flavors fill the road: French, German, Spanish, Swedish. Why I should get so excited about this, I don't know. In Europe, it is hardly surprising that there are trucks from all nations traveling backwards and forwards across the land. The drivers on the highway all behave perfectly, and there are times when there are no cars in the fast lane, with everybody traveling at 90 km/h in the slow lane. If I think about a similar situation in China, it is incomparable.

I don't think the French and the Chinese would be able to drive on the same road. They would just drive into one another. The French driver believes that, because the rule of the road states that when traveling on the highway, the cars entering the highway from the right must yield to the traffic already on it, no attempt should be made to facilitate their entry onto the highway. Even though there may be open lanes and they could make way, they will not budge from the slow lane, thereby forcing the incoming traffic to come to a complete stop while waiting for a gap. The Chinese, however, believe that if they are entering the traffic flow from the right, they have complete right of way, and don't even look left for oncoming traffic: they just go. Combining these two on one road would be catastrophic.

Forty kilometers outside Arles, the world is flat, covered in vineyards and huge factories making dog food: it smells like dog food in Vincent's old stomping ground. Vincent will also be shocked to know that there is now a McDonald's in his sunflower fields. The white horses in a green field set a more acceptable tone, as do the dog roses that drape long arms of delicate blooms down to the mirror of a small man-made pond, where people are fishing. How odd. It's like fishing in a swimming pool.

Red poppies sway under purple wisteria, Vincent trees line the road, and white horses nibble at green grass in all the fields. Why so many white horses? Then a road sign points to the Camargue, another completely unexpected moment. Following the signs, I loop off the main road, and find myself in the heartland of this mythical place, where white horses once thundered across the salt flats. Today the slightly mysterious air of white horses roaming among the reeds is carefully maintained, even if they never get beyond a mild clip-clop, as they carry tourists through the marsh. The road goes along a dyke, with ducks paddling in the small streams that run between the reeds on either side.

In the distance I spy a small animal crossing the road and slow down to let it pass, but it is not moving. Leaving the Wish Mobile on a grassy verge, I walk over and make my first acquaintance with a mouse beaver. I look at the animal helplessly as it slowly dies. The little critter looks like a beaver, has webbed hind feet like an otter or duck, and a long tail like a rat, bright orange incisors, and lives in burrows, just above water level. They are very good at navigating land and water, but unfortunately, they are not so good at navigating tar.

This creature was introduced into Europe by fur ranchers wanting to make their fortune from the fur of this creature. When the fur trade died the value of this creature died along side it and it is now considered a major pest.

Then the small country road unexpectedly spits me out into civilization, and I find myself heading towards Avignon. Checking my map I decide this is a perfectly good direction and allow myself to be pulled along in the slipstream of the truck ahead of me. Until I discover that it also pulls the insects out of the yellow flowers on the roadside, and sends them swirling to their death against my windscreen. What a mess, I increase my following distance out of bug slinging range. In a few kilometers, I travel from low salt flats, through lucerne fields, into white stone country, where, since the beginning of our history, men have created in harmony with nature. The evidence lies in the villages, which are as much part of the landscape as the ancient trees.

It is not hard to see why the northerners flee down here at every opportune moment. Some places on earth are blessed in ways that we all instinctively recognize, and all want to share this quiet glory, even if just for a moment. Provence, in southern France, is such a place, where the wind strokes your skin more gently than elsewhere; where the light has the ability to make the most mundane objects beautiful, even at midday.

The D94 winds through small villages, where stylish visitors and rough locals gather at sunlit cafés, sipping the rosé wine for which this part of France is famous. Stone walls are offset by blue wooden doors that speak of years of welcome. Window boxes are filled with red geraniums, and roses and lavender fill the small gardens. The road winds through long lanes of trees, past still-bare vineyards, where a solitary old man slowly walks along the vines, stopping occasionally to inspect their progress, then to puff on his cigarette, while thoughtfully looking up at the mountain peaks and sky.

Despite the beauty that surrounds me, my thoughts turn more and more inward. My journey now has the feeling of home-coming about it. I am in a soft gentle sad place. I pass graffiti on a peeling plaster wall.

'Have you made a list of all the things you haven't done.'

The list would be longer than life. You can do only so much. The problem lies in the choices we make, and how often our choices are informed by fear that springs from ignorance. We distrust what we don't understand, and instead of trying to understand it, we try to change it, force it to our will. I have discovered that we need to take a evolutionary step into the mind, to sit still, and realize that, in the end, our eyes see only so much. It is by looking with the mind that the world is properly revealed. It is important to continually push the mind to new horizons, to constantly question preconceived notions and ideas that color our choices.

My eye catches on the clock. I must stop in the next village, otherwise the siesta will deprive me of lunch. The countryside around Nyons has rolling winter-bare vineyards and huge ochre plastered villas that speak of comfortable tradition. Nyons is famous, though, for its olive oil, and finding a parking, I set out to find the oil. But my path is blocked by a semi-naked man. Memories of Los Angeles flash through my mind. He is coming at me, talking loudly and aggressively, I think. He is speaking French, so I don't understand a word. He might just be excited about the wonderful weather, and telling me that this is why he chose not to put on all his clothing today. I stand quite still, while I try to work out what he wants from me, or from life in general, but before any sensible conclusion can be reached, three gendarmes appear from nowhere, surround him, and somehow, without touching him, hustle him away. I look around. All the townsfolk have fallen silent. They all stare after the strange man, look at one another, shake their heads, start talking about this extraordinary event, and so everything goes back to 'normal'. I find my olive oil, find some lunch, and soon am back on the road, which leads higher and higher into the mountains, slowly leaving springtime behind, as a cold fog rolls through the trees.

Small grey stone villages, with roofs that look like Dutch hats with a little flip at the bottom, cluster in valleys next to small rivers. The square church towers are topped by rounded domes, with a spike on top. The little villages have one church only. What is lacking in these French villages, and in France in general, is doubt. The arrogance for which the French are famous can just as well be seen as a lack of doubt. There is no doubt in their minds that they are French, and that it is good. Their culture, their food, their beliefs are all grounded in certainty. They are what they are, and this is the church that represents what they believe in, and that's that – unlike America, where there is an overabundance of doubt, there is no firm unshakable belief in anything, even though they have coined the phrase 'the age of certainty'. Perhaps the Americans are sure of nothing, because they have come to the end of the American Dream, and have discovered that the system of massive consumption, which they have perfected does not make them happy or content; it just breeds a lust for more. But the things they lust for, fulfill none of their desires.

Bed 167,168,169

The road winds over mountains, past statues of Napoleon, down to Geneva, around grey Lac Léman and into Switzerland, where there is a plump satisfaction in the deep rural life, unlike the mean survival tactics that are required in the dry rural areas of Asia. It was not so long ago, but those barren wastelands I drove through now seem so impossibly far away that I find it difficult to remember that the most of the planet is desert. It must be almost impossible for the Europeans to conceive just how dry the world is, living as they do in this saturated green land, where magnolias unfold brilliant pink against the grey stone.

The meadows draw me out of the Wish Mobile, and onto a thick carpet of green grass that rolls down the hill into a small copse of trees and out again on the other side, until the Alps push it aside, to rise snowcapped into the sky. I have completed a circle from green meadows to green meadows, and to draw a circle within circles, I stay over on the last night of my trip with Ragi and Markus in Winterthur. They look me over.

'You haven't changed.'

No?

Satisfied that all is well with the world, Markus opens a bottle of champagne, and we lift a glass to life.

The sun rises in a clear blue sky. The ferry transports me across Boden See to Germany, and by midday, I am driving back onto the meadow that I left exactly one year ago. Annette looks up from the chores she is doing about the small cottage.

'Hey, welcome back.'

We grin at each other as she looks me over.

'You haven't changed.'

Then she sees the Wish Mobile.

'Wow, but it has!'

Some things are just easier to see.

Epilogue

The only way to live a life is simply to start living. Your goals and dreams may seem huge and unattainable, but if you do not take that first step, they will never be achieved. My Year of Beds was a succession of tiny steps that took me once around the world, but they also took me deep into myself, and in the end, this journey was a rite of passage, a stripping away of the known, familiar and taken for granted. I did not set out to find anything, but unexpectedly was confronted with my self, my ignorance, and my hidden prejudices, intolerances and petty narcissism. It has been a long road to get here, to a place where the tensions of modern life have drained away to reveal a capacity of thought that is drowned in the daily rush of deadlines and the torture of constant noise.

I have discovered that with the acquisition of knowledge, there comes sadness. Knowing too much, seeing too far is a constant source of sorrow. The world is not, on the whole, a happy place. But worse than sorrow is ignorance. Ignorance is the root cause of fear, and fear allows us to be controlled. I have discovered that our economic system runs on fear, which controls our thoughts and behavior. The manipulation of our basic fears makes us constantly dissatisfied, constantly striving towards the wrong goals, and chasing after material things, for which we can find no sensible use. Through fear, we judge others, based on half truths, and become less of ourselves in the process.

The foundation on which all great philosophies – but not, unfortunately, all religions – is built, is the mastery of self. Self-control is a worthy goal.

He who cannot obey himself will be commanded by others

Nietzsche

But our goals are dictated to us by the media, whose sole purpose has become to ensure that we never achieve mastery of ourselves, but continue to buy stuff. To do this, the advertising media present us with unattainable goals and standards, set in a world in which uninterrupted moments of bliss, perfection and happy endings are guaranteed. Our reality can never match up to this, and so we remain forever dissatisfied with our own achievements, our lives, and ourselves. Today our economy depends entirely on our continued dissatisfaction. By basing our goals on those that the media feed us, we demand to be happy all the time; then we are angry at the inability of our emotions and lives to maintain the constant stream of happiness that we have come to see as our right. We forget that every life consists of moments of bliss, hemmed in by long mediocre hours, and to envy the lives of others is to be mistaken. We tend to see only what we want to see. Every life, no matter how exciting it might seem from the outside, is mired in day-to-day reality.

The goal is to learn to recognize happiness in the million small moments of every day. To pursue happiness doesn't work; you have to be open to the experience. If you are open to the possibility of happiness, it will always come to stab a little light into the dark of whatever sorrow you might be feeling, and when it does, you have a choice. You can decide to be happy for that little light, or you can decide that the light is not strong enough, bright enough, flashy enough, to drag you from your sorrow and despair. To be happy is a choice you make each time you recognize one of these small moments of joy. Happiness is a habit that you can cultivate. But, like any choice to change something fundamental in your life, it takes discipline and work. You do not become habitually happy overnight; you have to work at it. But I have discovered that if you decide to be happy, happiness grows in you, and the more it grows, the less you need to make you happy, and you achieve something greater than happiness, contentment.

In this discovery, I have corrected the philosopher René Descartes, who said;

'I think, therefore I am.'

I prefer to say

I think, therefore I become.

When you think about what makes you truly happy, then you become happy. The goal is to recognize the moments in which you are truly happy. When is it that you experience total joy and contentment? When does time no longer matter, and the outside world vanish from sight? When are you aware that you are part of a grand unfathomable whole, and although you are a tiny part of that whole, you recognize that you are as important as the whole. Those moments of deep insight into self are the moments in which you will find your truth.

It is said that the truth shall set you free. The problem with this statement is in 'the'. 'The Truth' is an indefinable concept and to seek 'The Truth' is something that you cannot control. But if you change just one word and say,

Your truth shall set you free.

The search for truth becomes something that you have full control over. But how?

This is a journey of the mind. It is to think very carefully about things that are often forgotten or overwhelmed by the barrage of information we have to process every day. To search for your truth is to join the global movement towards questioning modern values and down-scaling. This is a revolution of silence, of stepping away from the noise of every day, and stepping back into the centre of your life.

Your truth is something you can strive for, and have total control in finding and living, but there has to be a willingness to delve into yourself, to clear the decks, to allow that truth to emerge. By taking mastery of yourself, you achieve the ability to break down false boundaries and barriers in your mind that separate you from them, you from the world and the universe – barriers that society placed there in order to control you. When you break down these barriers, you are able to judge the true value of your thoughts, your desire for things, and the goals you set for yourself.

In this revolution of thought, your truth will allow you to stop hunting for happiness in shops, because you will discover it in yourself. You will stop chasing fashions, and the latest gadgets, as you will discover that all the change you need is your growing joy. While we are conditioned to be in constant competition with one another, and we want to be seen to be different, in the end when it comes to truth, there will be a recognition that our truth is shared by everyone. We all want peace, harmony, love, security, companionship, respect, tolerance and moments of silence.

Silence and the condition of being alone are considered anathema in today's world of multimedia and constant connection, but great thought, ideas and originality do not spring from the noisy mass. It is important to embrace our silence and solitude, to hold them close and dear, as only in them will we discover the true depths of our thoughts, and the wellspring of our joy. And only in this silence can we start to create the changes that will make us fearless, happier, and more contented with our lives. We all want to change the world for the better, but often we stand on our soapboxes, and say it is they who must change. The truth is we cannot change them, or the world. The only thing we can change is ourselves, and that is hard. For many, change is an uncomfortable thing. Most people love the thought of change, the delightful daydream of living a different life, but very few choose to go through the discomfort and inner turmoil that true change requires.

Only when we are prepared to take that uncomfortable step, can we hope to bring progressive change to improve the world.

When you have found your truth, you will find a growing confidence in your instincts and emotions. You will slowly lose fear; you will lose doubt; you will inspire others; and make them confident and fearless. Through your fearless tolerance of others, they will become loving, mindful, and tolerant as well. The fearless know their minds, will trust until proven wrong, and, if so, will walk away without judgment. The fearless will step from the path, put out a helping hand, not allow themselves to be swayed by the crowd. When you are fearless, you do no harm. There is no need. The fearless spread their calm, and make others fearless too. Without fear, there is no need for violence. Without fear, there is no jealousy; the fearless do not fear loss or betrayal; without fear, there is no loneliness; the fearless stand in the middle of their lives, and embrace their silence and solitude; and open the possibilities of this vast calm universe to all who come into contact with them.

A word of thanks

For all the small acts of kindness bestowed on me by strangers.

To all the women of Women Welcome Women World Wide(5W) who not only accommodated me, but sent hints and tips, maps and encouragement from all corners of the world.

To friends and family who lived the journey with me, via my blog, and sent 'you go girl!' messages when they were most needed.

To Annette and Andreas for being there at the beginning and the end,

and finally to Michael who was my one man back up team, who never said no to any request. From helping to find the right vehicle, to corresponding with insurance companies, banks and travel agents when my own cup of politeness ran dry.

Annette is a writer, photographer, inspirational speaker and world traveler. She is a new age nomad, a pusher of boundaries, a catalyst, a peaceful anarchist and a questioner of everything. She would like to live in a world where borders and boundaries were only figments of the imagination, and language was a universal think-tank, a world where the mind advanced faster than the computer, and the only thing that governed us was our own self-control.

To see more of Annette's work visit www.ajahnel.com

Made in the USA
Charleston, SC
16 July 2014